Early Settlers of Indiana's "Gore"

ILLINOIS TERRI-TORY

1803 to 1820

(CLARK CO)

DEARBORN COUNTY

(KNOX & HARRISON COUNTIES)

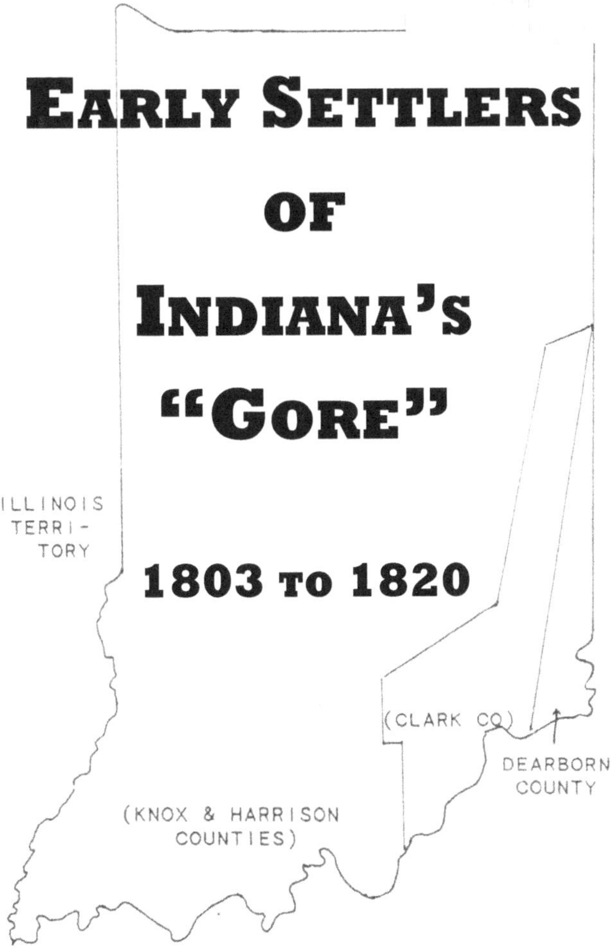

Compiled and Edited by

Shirley Keller Mikesell

HERITAGE BOOKS
2008

HERITAGE BOOKS
AN IMPRINT OF HERITAGE BOOKS, INC.

Books, CDs, and more—Worldwide

For our listing of thousands of titles see our website
at
www.HeritageBooks.com

Published 2008 by
HERITAGE BOOKS, INC.
Publishing Division
100 Railroad Ave. #104
Westminster, Maryland 21157

Copyright © 1995 Shirley Keller Mikesell

Other books by the author:

Butler County, Ohio Land Records
Volume 1: 1803-1816
Volume 2: 1816-1823 and Miami University Land Leases, 1810-1823

Early Settlers of Indiana's Gore, 1803-1820

Early Settlers of Montgomery County, Ohio
Volume I: Genealogical Abstracts from Land Records, Tax Lists, and Biographical Sketches
Volume II: Genealogical Abstracts from Common Pleas Court Records, Civil and Probate
Volume III: Genealogical Abstracts from Marriage and Divorce Records, 1803-1827; Early Deeds Recorded Late; Election Abstracts; Obituary of an Early Settler

All rights reserved. No part of this book may be reproduced or transmitted in any form or by any means, electronic or mechanical, including photocopying, recording or by any information storage and retrieval system without written permission from the author, except for the inclusion of brief quotations in a review.

International Standard Book Numbers
Paperbound: 978-0-7884-0254-8
Clothbound: 978-0-7884-7464-4

Dedicated to the memory of A. RAY KELLER
and his ancestors who settled in the Gore,
TABITHA DRAKE WHITE, JAMES WHITE,
JANE BOSWELL WHITE and BARNABUS BOSWELL

TABLE OF CONTENTS

Page

Introduction:
using entry tracts and land records   vii

Territorial Records 1

Muster Rolls of the War of 1812 7

Dearborn County............................... 15

Franklin County............................... 30

Randolph County...............................172

Switzerland County............................181

Union County..................................223

Wayne County..................................231

Index...349
    using the index
    local courthouse and library information..405

USING THE ORIGINAL ENTRY TRACTS AND LAND RECORDS

Both the Tract Books and the Deed Books are available in the specific County Recorder's office. The Tract Books were prepared by the Auditor of the State in the mid-1840's and are transcriptions of the records of the Cincinnati land office. Tracts are given as within county boundaries of the mid-1840's; some have been changed since that time. All land originally within the Gore in 1803 will be found in the Tract Books, in Ranges 1, 2 or 3W. Entries are given in Section, Township and Range, not chronological order.

Entries in a section listed first the northeast quarter, the northwest quarter, the southeast quarter and last, southwest quarter. Only those land entries to and including 1820 are given in this book. If just one name appears in a quarter, this does not necessarily means that person bought the entire quarter. The rest of the quarter may have been purchased after 1820. For a complete record of all Indiana land entries, see published works by Margaret Walters or by Berry & Berry. Please read the ENTIRE PAGE INDICATED for the person in whom you are interested. More than one land entry was often recorded for individuals. By stopping with the first mention, you may miss a much earlier purchase.

Several terms have been used in the land records which are probably not legally correct, but are an attempt to give information to the researcher. "Quitclaim" or "quitclaim deed" shows that the seller had an interest in the property, often through inheritance. That interest was transferred to the buyer. "Partition" shows that property was purchased or inherited jointly; the land was divided into smaller parcels with separate ownership. "Mortgage deeds" should be read in reverse: the apparent seller is really the purchaser. As in a land contract, failure to pay the debt returned full title to the original owner. Conveyance of title as recorded in these deeds was voided by paying the debt, an arrangement which offered all protection to the seller.

Residence identifications on the land records:
    none or township only -- person resided in the
        Indiana county being discussed
    county only -- person resided in another county
        of Indiana
    county and state -- as given

Indiana land is partitioned under the range and township system. This method was adopted for the surveying and sale of land under the jurisdiction of Congress. Measurements are exact and unchanging, unlike the old "metes-and-bounds" systems of the early colonies. When the river meandered or the sugar maple died, the boundary marker was lost.

Range numbers 1, 2 and 3 W or West indicate that the tract was in the original "Gore" area, measured in a westerly direction from the prime meridian which forms the boundary line between Indiana and Ohio. All of the rest of Indiana's Ranges are measured in an easterly direction from a meridian lying in Illinois and so have the designation E or East.

Townships measure direction north and south from a base line. Since all townships in the Gore are counted north from a base, the North designation was rarely included. Unfortunately, the base line was changed from the Ohio survey to the Illinois survey. Township numbers are not equivalent between East and West ranges. The following illustration exaggerates present day Union County range and section lines. The same situation is found in other Gore counties.

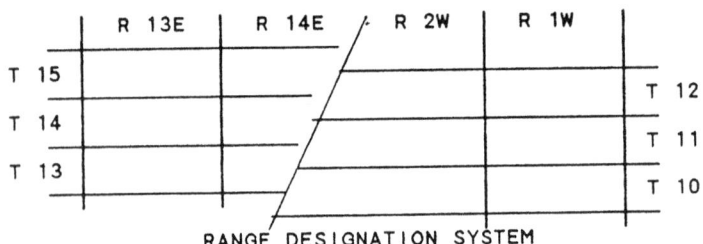

RANGE DESIGNATION SYSTEM

6	5	4	3	2	1
7	8	9	10	11	12
18	17	16	15	14	13
19	20	21	22	23	24
30	29	28	27	26	25
31	32	33	34	35	36

SECTION NUMBERING SYSTEM

THE INDIANA GORE

The Indiana Territory was formed in 1800 upon the division of the old Northwest Territory and with separation from the new state of Ohio. The Gore area remained part of Ohio's Hamilton County; its western boundary was defined by the Greenville Treaty Line of 1795. The "Gore" was named Dearborn County when it became part of Indiana in 1803. Counties covered in this book will have their earliest records divided between Dearborn and Clark counties.

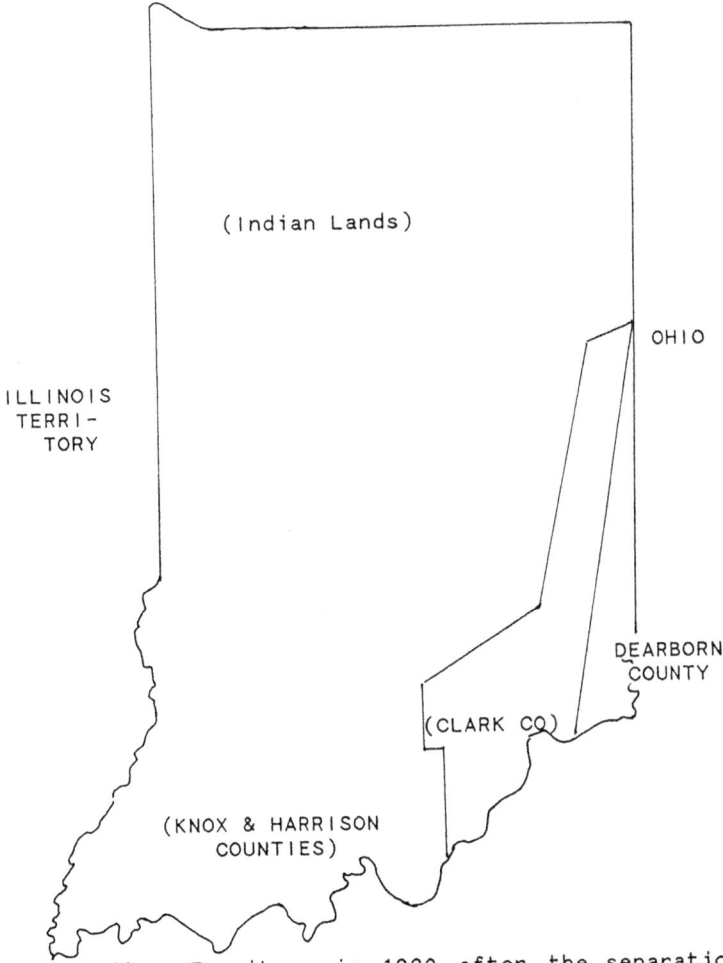

Indiana Territory in 1809 after the separation of Illinois. A ten-mile high strip was later added to the northern border in 1816, taken from Michigan.

THE INDIANA GORE

From 1803 until 1811, when the state was formed and new counties partitioned, the Dearborn County seat was at Lawrenceburg. Most records identifying the early settlers of the Gore were held at this one location. Unfortunately, the County Courthouse burned in 1826, destroying the documents vital to this book - land transactions, etc.

In order to identify the earliest settlers of the Gore and Dearborn County residents from 1811 until 1820, a variety of documents were abstracted. Most of these were letters, petitions and additional militia muster rolls. There are no voter or tax records until long after the time in which we are interested. The WPA Inventory of Public Records made in the 1930's indicate that both an INDEX TO DEEDS and an INDEX TO MORTGAGES, dating from 1802, existed in Dearborn County at that time. The present county recorder is attempting to lacate the books, probably mislaid over the last sixty years or lost in moving to a new Courthouse.

The following abstracts of early Dearborn, Franklin and Wayne counties were taken from papers held in the Indiana State Archives of the Commission on Public Records, State Library and Historical Building, Indiana Government Center at Indianapolis. The Territorial Database Records give general information concerning each entry -- area, names, etc --to assist in locating pertinent records.

Using the records is strictly a "white glove. pencils only" situation. Access is controlled: return a folder in order to receive the next folder. To protect the delicate papers and inks, photocopying is not allowed. While the system may be time-consuming, it works for the benefit of all researchers. Nothing disappears, everything is protected. References following the abstractions identify where the desired record may be found: location, box & folder.

****

A brief note to OHIO County researchers: Ohio County was not formed until quite a late date and was taken entirely from the southern part of Dearborn. All records pertaining to Ohio County are included with Dearborn in this book. In addition, Ohio County has no "Tract Book of Original Purchasers" since the books were prepared from the Land Office records before Ohio County was organized.

THE INDIANA GORE

Letter dated 1803 to Governor; return address "Ohio Bank". Signed:

JOHN BROWNSON, major	JAMES HAMILTON, lt.
WILLIAM HALL, capt.	WM. ALLENSWORTH, lt.
SAMUEL FULTON, capt.	GERSHAM LEE, ensign
DANIEL LINN, capt.	THOMAS FULTON, ensign
BARRENT HULICK, capt.	MICK'L. FLICK, ensign
JEREMIAH JOHNSTON, capt.	WILLIAM THOMPSON, ensign
ISRAEL STANDIFORD, lt.	JAMES BUCHANON, ensign
WILLIAM SPENCER, lt.	B. CHAMBERS, colonel
WILLIAM CHEEK, lt.	WM. McCLAIN, carrier

location UV 93 -- box 001 -- folder 002

Petition dated 1805 for ferry, to be operated by SAMUEL C. VANCE, location not noted. Signed:

THOM O'BRIEN	CALEB HAYES	SAMUEL ELLIOT
W. WILSON	FRANCIS F. GAINES	JABEZ PERCIVAL
STEPHEN STILES	ORIN HORNY/HONEY	JACOB HORNER
WILLIAM CALDWELL	JOHN GORDON	NICHOLAS LINDSEY
JOSEPH HAYES	JESSE B. THOMAS	HUGH CARSON
JAMES HAMILTON	JUSTICE GILECOS	C. GRAY MOORE

location UV 89 -- box 005 -- folder 305

Petition dated 1811 to name MOSES WILEY as Dearborn County Justice of Peace. Signed:

GEORGE ADAIR	JAMES ADAIR	JOHN ADAIR
JOSEPH ADAIR	WM. ALLENSWORTH	BAYLISS ASHBY
J.W. BAILEY	JORGE BALLANGER	GEORGE W. BRACKENRIDGE
HUGH BRISON SR	HUGH BRISON JR	EDWARD BOX
JAMES BRISON	WILLIAM BRISON	JOEL DICKEN
JAMES CLOUD	ABNER CONNER	JOHN ELMORE
JAMES DRIFFEE	BYARD ELLMORE	ISAAC HACKLEMAN
MICHAEL FARAND	MICKEL FARRAR	THOMAS HACKLEMAN
JACOB HACKLEMAN	MICHAEL HACKLEMAN	EDWARD JOHNSON
JAMES HARTPENCE	JOHN JACKSON SR	JOSHUA PARVIS
LUIS JOHNSON	WILLIAM MAJER	JOHN QUICK
AARON PRICHARD SR	WILLIAM PURSEL	PETER SCHROEDER
MOSES RICHARDSON	BASIL ROBERTS	THOMAS B. SMITH
THOMAS SKINNER	ENOCH SMITH	ELI SOTTEN or SOTTER
WM. SMITH SR	WILLIAM D. SMITH	THOMAS TRUSLER
MOSES TEBBS	WARRAN TEBBS	ALEX'D. WHITE
WILLOUGHBY TEBBS	WILLIAM TORRENCE	
JOHN WATTS	FORREST WEBB	
WILLIAM WHITE	JEREMIAH WILLIAMS	

location UV 89 -- box 003 -- folder 171

THE INDIANA GORE

Dearborn Co/ 1810/ 3d Reg't: election of officers.
    Captains DANIEL LYNN   &   JOHN LIVINGSTON.
Candidates:
    for captain: JAMES McGUIRE & GRIFFIN TIPSWORDS
    for lieutenant: JAMES ALLEN
    for ensign: AYMOS BRUCE & JOHN PAYNE
members voting:
CLEBURN ALLAN   JAMES BRIDGES   AMOS BRUCE
HENERY BRUCE   JAMES BRUCE   JOHIEL BUFFINGTON
JONATHAN BUFFINGTON WILLIAM CARTER   ELIAS CHAFFEN
JAMES CHEEKE   ROBERT CONNAWAY   DANIEL COX
MECHLE FLEAKE   WILLIAM FLEAKE   DAVID FREAKES
NETHEN FREAKES   DAVID GILL   ELIAS HEADY
JAMES McGUIRE   DANIEL MILLER   HENERI MIERS
SAMUEL J. PAIN   BENJAMIN PURCEL   JOHN PURCEL
THOMAS PURCEL   JAMES REED   JOHN ROSS
ROBERT ROSS   THOMAS SPENCER   GRIFFIN TIPSWORDS
WM. WEATHERS   JOHN WEATHERS   BENJAMIN WILSON
    location UV 90 -- MC 2 -- folder 158

Dearborn Co/ 1811/ Reg't not given: election of
officers. Company of (Capt) THOMAS DAWSON.
Candidates:
ENOCH BLAZEDELL, Lt.   CHARLES STEVENS, Ensign
members voting:
OBADIAH STEPHENS   JOHN MALAT   ELLET JACKSON
PETER CARBERRY   JAMES DAWSON   JAMES CHISM
THOMAS DART   JOHN DAWSON   JACOB CLARK
ENOCH JACKSON   JONATHAN BLAISDEL   DAVID NOBLE
EPHRAIM MORRISON   EZEKIEL JACKSON   JOHN PERRINE
CALOB HAYS SR   GEORGE DIGGS   PRICHARD
ELIJAH DAWSON   LEVI MILLER   LEMASTERS

Company of CAPT. LEWIS:
    REYNOLD FIELDER replaced JAMES LINDLEY as Ensign
Company of CAPT. BUTLER:
    ISAAC MEEK replaced H. BAILY as Lieutenant
    location UV 90 -- MC 2 -- folder 151

3d Reg't, Lawrenceburg, 1812: election of officers.
JAMES DILL -- Col.   ENOCH SMITH -- Lt. Col.
SAMUEL FULTON -- Lt. Col.   DECKER CROZIER -- Major
JOHN PURSLEY -- Major
    location UV 89 -- MC 1 -- folder 064

Dearborn Co/ 1814/ 3d Reg't: election of officers.
CHARLES B. CANNON, Capt.   JAMES McGUIRE, Capt
THOMAS BURKE, Lt.   JAMES CONAWAY, Lt
DAVID McKITRICK, Ensign   WM. WEATHERS, Ensign
WILLIAM WHITE, Capt.
    location UV 90 --- MC 2 --- folder 157

4

THE INDIANA GORE

Dearborn Co/ 1814/ 3d Reg't, 2d Battn.
JOHN JACKSON, Col.   DECKER CROZIER. Major
Lt. ABRAHAM GARRISON   Lt. DAVID P. SHOOK
Lt. ELIJA DAWSON   Lt. JEHUE GOODWIN
    location UV 90 -- MC 3 --- folder 017

*****

Franklin Co/ 1811/ 7th Regiment:
    JOHN WINCHELL replaced WM. P. LEVENT as 2d Lt.
    ARTEMAS D. WOODS replaced WINCHELL as Cornett.
    location UV 90 --- MC 2 --- folder 151

Franklin Co/ 1814/ 1st Reg't, 2d Battalion
    JOHN SHANK, Major
    NIXON OLIVER, Capt. (resigned)
    THOMAS CENK nominated to replace Oliver
    location UV 90 --- MC 3 --- folder 042

*****

Wayne Co/ 1813/ 8th Reg't. Staff
G. HUNT, Col.   WM. SCARCE. Lt. Col.
SMITH HUNT, Major   JAMES BROWN, Major
JOHN WALKER, Capt.   JOHN HART, Lt
JAMES WARM, Ensign
    location UV 90 --- MC 2 --- folder 094

Wayne Co/ 1813/ Letter to Gov. Posey protesting plundering by Indians. Signed by:
G. HUNT, Col.   WM. SCARCE, Lt. Col.
S. HUNT, Major   J. BROWN, Major
WM. WHITEHEAD, Capt.   RICHARD LEWIS, Capt.
ENOS BUTLER, Capt.   JOHN IRELAND, Capt.
JOHN FARLOW, Capt.   WILLIAM HOLEMAN, Capt.
JOHN WALKER, Capt.   WM. HUNT, Lt
WM. PRICE, Lt.   ROBERT GALBRAITH. Lt.
JOHN HART, Lt.   HUGH BAILEY, Lt.
JAMES WARRAM, Ensign   ABSALOM HARVEY. Ensign
JAMES LINDLEY, Ensign   JOHN TURNER, Adjutant
and following nominated military officers:
JOHN PATTERSON, Capt.   JOSEPH LEWIS, Lt.
DAVID CANADAY, Sgt.   JOSEPH SPENCER, Ensign
JOEL FERGUSON, Ensign   RUNNELS FIELDER. Ensign
    location UV 90 --- MC 2 --- folder 120

Wayne Co/ 1814/ 8th Reg't: election of officers
WM. SCARCE replaces G. HUNT as Col.
2d Batt'n: SAMUEL FLEMING, Lt.
            PLEASANT HARRIS, Ensign
            THOMAS WISEHART, Ensign
    location UV 90 --- MC 3 --- 023

THE INDIANA GORE

Due to the scarcity of Dearborn County records, the following list of Soldiers of the War of 1812 was taken from the History of Dearborn and Ohio Counties, page 201. Names which could be verified in muster rolls were omitted. Most of the following are recognized as Dearborn residents, but actual military service cannot be guaranteed. The text mentions Maj. SHATTER's brigade with blockhouses at Brookville commanded by Lt. BRECKINRIDGE, at Tanner's Creek commanded by Capt. BLASDELL and at Laughery "where Capt. McGUIRE afterward lived".

Allee, Jonathan	Annis, Thomas	Ashby, Bayliss
Bonham, Israel	Boyd, James	Brackinridge, J
Burk, John	Burroughs, T.	Calaway, Jesse
Canfield, Noyes	Chafin, Elial	Clements, Chas.
Clements, Edward	Cloud, James	Cloud, Ira
Cornelius, James	Covington, Thos.	Cross, Aquilla
Crozier, Decker	Decker, Abijah	Dill, James
Durham, John	Eads, James	Eads, Elijah
Ehler, Thomas	Ewan, Samuel	Fielding, Jacob
Frazier, Samuel	Garrison, Levi	Green, Stephen
Greenfield, John	Greer, George	Gullet, Robert
Hall, John	Hayes, Job	Holmes, James
Hollister, Ephraim	Huston, Joseph	Isgrig, Maston
Johnson, Caleb	Johnson, Casper	Johnson, Thomas
Johnson, Jeremiah**	Johnson, Jerry	Johnson, Samuel
Judd, Finley	Judd, Job	Judd, Joseph
King, James	King, William	Kimble, Timothy
Kyle, Thomas	Lake, William	Lambdon, Matthew
Laurence, Valentine	Lewis, George	Lewis, John**
Lewis, Jonathan	Lewis, Nathan	Lilly, John
Majors, John	Majors, William	Martin, Samuel
Maserve, William	Mason, Daniel	Mason, George
Mason, John	Mason, Nicholas	Mason, Philip
Miller, Col. Henry	Morgan, Joseph	Ofield, James
Perry, Samuel	Pippin, Richard	Plummer, Joseph
Plummer, Luther	Porter, Thomas	Powell, James
Priest, Obediah	Randall, Isaac	Randall, Wm
Roberts, Samuel	Roseberry, Alex	Roseberry, Caleb
Rudisal, George	Rudisal, Jacob	Rudisal, Michael
Sacket, Jesse	Salmon, Daniel	Salmon, James
Staples, Joshua	Stevens, Charles*	Swallow, Garret
Tanner, John	Taylor, Isaac	Thorn, Stephen
Thornton, Samuel	Tucker, Nathaniel	Turner, Ferdinand
Vance, Samuel	Voshell, Obediah	
Watts, Johnson	Weaver, James	Weaver, John
White, John	Withrow, James	Wood, Stephen*
Yerkees, Joshua		

identified as   **Major   *Captain

THE INDIANA GORE: War of 1812 muster rolls

The muster rolls are taken from "PHOTOSTATIC COPIES of MUSTER, PAY and RECEIPT ROLLS of INDIANA VOLUNTEERS or MILITIA of the PERIOD of the WAR of 1812." The Leet Brothers produced the four volume work in 1926, found at the Indiana State Library in Indianapolis. Due to the delicate condition of the volumes, photocopying is not allowed.

Copies of original paybooks in the US Adjutant General's office are arranged loosely into regiments, indexed in the first volume. Each company had several paybooks, covering different enlistment terms. To record the soldiers who served, all paybooks for that company must be checked. Rank is given only for officers; all others are Private in grade.

Dearborn County/ Company of Infantry of the Indiana Militia: Captain JAMES McGUIRE's Company.

ROBERT BRECKENRIDGE, Lt
THOMAS DAWSON, Ens
JUSTUS SARTWELL, Sgt
SPENCER WILEY, Sgt
THOMAS BRECKENRIDGE, Sgt
LEVI JOB, Sgt
WILLIAM FLAKE, Cpl
SAMUEL LEWIS, Cpl
JOHN CONNER, Cpl
JONATHAN BLASDEL, Cpl
WILLIAM ASHBY
DAVID AIKEN
JOHN ALEXANDER
ROBERT BARNES
HENRY BRUCE
AARON R. BONOM
JOHIEL BUFFINGTON
BARTHOLOMEW CARROLL
CHARLES CAMPBELL
JOHN CARROLL
ABRAHAM CARRYBAUGH
BAYLES CLOUD
WILLIAM CLOUD
JACOB CLARK
JAMES CALAHAN
THOMAS D. DART
JAMES DART
WILLIAM DART
JOHN DAWSON
BAYARD ELMORE
MICHAEL FARRAN
JAMES FULSOM
GEORGE GROVE
ADAM GOSNEL
MICHAEL HACKLEMAN
THOMAS HACKLEMAN
JEREMIAH JOHNSTON
ELLIOTT JACKSON
DAVID LANGLY
GEORGE W. MILLES
EDDY MAJOR
ROBERT MAJOR
THOMAS MUIR
WILLIAM NORTON
JAMES O. CANE
JOHN OSBORN
AARON PAINE
JOSEPH PARKS
HENRY PATE/PATT
EZEKIEL PETTY
ROBERT REED
JOHN ROWLAND
ARTHUR SHANE
WILLIAM SHANE
GEORGE SHANK
JOSEPH SUMMERS
WILLOUGHBY TIBBS
WARRAM TIBBS
WM. B. TORRENCE*
JOHN TRUELOCK
FOREST WEBB
JESSE WEBB
LEWIS WEBB
WILLIAM WEBB
GEORGE WILYARD
CALOB WRIGHT

*died Feb, 1813: JOHN S. TORRENCE, administrator

Dearborn Co/ Third Regt: Capt. CHARLES CAMPBELL's Co.
ENOCH BLAZDEL, Lt
THOMAS DAVIS, Lt
JOHN PAIN, Ens
JAMES POWELL, Sgt JOHN LANGLEY, Sgt
ADAM D. LEVINGSTON, Sgt HENRY BRUCE, Sgt
JAMES MOORE, Sgt

THE INDIANA GORE: War of 1812 muster rolls

Dearborn/3d Regt: Capt. CHARLES CAMPBELL's Co, contd.
DANIEL WHITAKER, Sgt ABRAHAM RICKETTS, Sgt
JOSEPH AVEY   JEREMIAH BARKSHIRE   CHARLES A.
SAMUEL BRIDGES   AMOS BROWN   BEAMER
JACOB CARRYBAUGH   JAMES CONAWAY   JARRED COX
JOSEPH DAVIS   JOHN DRAKE   JAMES D.
JOHN DOUGHERTY   JOHN EASTON   DOUGHERTY
TETRACH FOHL   JOSEPH FRAKES   JOHN HAWES
JOHN HUMES   JAMES HUBARD   JOHN HUBARD
ZELL HAMILTON   THOMAS LINSEY   VACHEL LINSEY
VINSON LINSEY   JAMES LINSEY   ROSS LINSEY
ENOCH McCARTY   JOHN MORTON   JOHN MOORE
EDWARD McGUFFY   NATHAN MILLER   SAMUEL McGARY
WILLIAM McFALLS   PROVIDENCE MOUNCE   RICHARD NORRIS
GEORGE NICHOLS   SIMON PETERS   JOHN PERCIL
THOMAS PERCIL   SAMUEL PERCELL   BENJAMIN PERCIL
SAMUEL PHILLIPS   THOMAS ROSEBERRY   ROBERT ROSS
JOHN ROSS   NATHAN RICKETTS   WILLIAM SHANE
JOHN STEWART   SAMUEL SCOTT   MORGAN SAGE
JAMES WILSON   JESSE WEATHERS   SAMUEL WILSON
GEORGE ZANES

Dearborn/ Third Regt, Capt. JUSTUS SARTWELL's Company
WILLIAM CALDWELL, Lt   SPENCER WILEY, Ens
OBADIAH STEPHENS, Sgt   THOMAS McCAHAN, Sgt
SAMUEL JOHNSTON, Sgt   JOHN DURHAM, Sgt
NOAH SMITH, Cpl   JOHN ADAIR
HENRY BAILEY, sub for   JOSEPH BANTA
    JOHN TORRENCE   WILLIAM BROWN
LEVI BANTA   JAMES BRUCE, sub for
JOHN COX   JAMES CHECK
JOHN COLLINS   DANIEL CRIST, sub for
JAMES CALDWELL   BENJAMIN McGARY
JOHN CALDWELL   THOMAS COOKSEY
WILLIAM CRIST, sub for   PAUL DAVIS, not joined
    AMOS WAY   JOSEPH DANIEL
THOMAS DART   JOHN DAWSON
JAMES DAWSON   JOHN DEFORD
RANDOLPH EZZELL   MATTHEW FERRAND
MICHAEL FARRAND   GEORGE FRENCH
WILLIAM GREEN   WILLIAM GRUBBS
FREEBURN HALL, sub for   WILLIAM HARMON, sub for
    SOLOMON DICKERSON   MOSES LYON
JOHN HARMON   JOSIAH HAYS
JAMES JOHNSTON   WILLIAM JOHNSTON
ROBERT JOHNSTON, sub for   JOHN LEPER
    JOSH HAYS   RICHARD LEMASTER
WILLIAM McBRIDE   LARKIN MONDAY AARON MINER
LAMBKIN McKINIE, sub for   JOSEPH McKINNIE, sub for
JOHN HOWARD
    JOHN FIELDS   JOHN McCONNELL

THE INDIANA GORE: War of 1812 muster rolls

Dearborn/ 3d Regt, Capt. JUSTUS SARTWELL's Co, cont'd
DAVID McKAIN   LEWIS OFFIELD
ISAAC PARKE   JEREMIAH PATE, sub for
ELIJAH PILE   JOHN FLORNOR PETER
PROBUS   ENOCH PUGH   WILLIAM PROBUS
DAVID PORTER, sub for
JOHN PRINE   EZRA GARD
JOHN RAMY   SIMON RAZOR
PETER SCHRADER   WILLIAM D. SMITH, excused
JOHN SHOOK   JOHN SIMMONS
JAMES TOWNSEND   THOMAS TRULOCK
CHARLES VANCAMP, never   JOHN WALDEN
   joined   JAMES WEAVER
WILLIAM WILSON, never   JAMES WAY, excused
   joined

Switzerland*/ 6th Regt, Capt. JACOB RHOADS' Co.
JOHN SIEBENTHAL, Lt   JOHN FIELDS, Ensign
WILLIAM BRAMWELL, Sgt   ABRAHAM MILLER, Sgt
WILLIAM WHITESIDES, Sgt EDWARD MAXWELL, Cpl
BENJAMIN COMBS, Cpl   MATTHEW HILLIS, Cpl
DAWSON BLACKMORE JOHN BROOK   JAMES CHAMBERS
RALPH COTTON   E. R. COX   JOSHUA CRANE
JESSE FUGET   RICHARD GUTHRIE JOHN HENDERSON
THOMAS JAMISON   JOHN JENKINS   SAMUEL LEDGERWOOD
ALEXANDER LEWIS   WILLIAM MAXWELL PHELIX MONROE
ZAEL PASSWATER   DANIEL ROBINS   DANIEL SEARLES
JOHN SMITH   HENRY ST. CLAIR JAMES STEPHENS
ELIAS THOMAS
     *then Jefferson Co.

7th Regt: Col. WILLIAM McFARLAND, Commander
JAMES NOBLE, Col   ROBERT M. EVANS, Col
ENOCH SMITH, Lt. Col   THOMAS SCOTT, Lt. Col
JOHN VAWTER, Major   WILLIAM LAGOW, Major
WILLIAM HELM, Adj   JOHN TURNER, Adj
NATHANIEL CLAYPOOL, Lt Adj   HENRY MILLS, Lt of Adj
HENRY HURST, Sgt Major   WILLIAM HANEY, Quartermstr
JOHN TIPTON, Sgt Major   JOHN TIPTON, Sgt Major
DANIEL SULLIVAN, Adj

Franklin Co/ Seventh Regt: Capt. SAMUEL LEE's Co.
JOHN WINCHELL, Lt   WILLIAM MORGAN, Ens
GEORGE HANSELL, Sgt   WILLIAM SINGHOUSE, Sgt
JAMES ROBERTSON, Sgt   JOHN HACKLEMAN, Sgt
WILLIAM HANNOR, Cpl   JEREMIAH DURHAM, Cpl
JOSEPH SIRES, Cpl   ELIJAH HERRAL, Cpl
JOSEPH ADAMS   HENRY ANTHONY   JACOB BAKE
SAMUEL BROWN   BENJAMIN BROWN   MATTHEW COY

THE INDIANA GORE: War of 1812 muster rolls

Franklin Co/ 7th Regt: Capt. SAMUEL LEE's Co. cont'd

JAMES CUMBEY	JOHN COLLINS	NICHOLAS CARTER
ABIEL DAIR	JESSE DAWSON	ELI DAWSON
ZACHARIAH DEVEE	TRAVIS DAVIS	JOHN M. DORSEY
DAVID FLETCHER	AARON FRAKE	MARTIN FRUIT
JOHN FREEL	JAMES FRAZER	JOHN GAVIN
JOHN GAMBLE	JOHN GOSSET	BENJAMIN GEORGE
WILLIAM GILLAM	JOHN HOWEL	JOHN HAMMON
JOHN HATFIELD	WESLEY HERNDON	WILLIAM HIGGS
ALEXANDER HIGGINS	JOHN JACKS	WILLIAM JACKMAN
WILLIS JOHNSON	GEORGE LEWIS	PHILLIP LINCH
SAMUEL MERCHANT	EDWARD MAGNER	ANDREW McKINNEY
JAMES McCARTY	ALBERT MURPHY	MICHAEL PELKEY
JOHN PRICE	TOBIAS RAMSEY	AQUILLA RAMSEY
DOWDLE ROLAND	GEORGE ROWLAND	ISAAC RICHARDSON
MICHAEL SALOR	JOHN SEWARD	JAMES SNODGRASS
POWELL SCOTT	ANDREW SHIRK	DANIEL SHAVER
WILLIAM SHANNON	ALEXANDER SIRES	HENRY STANSBURY
HARMON TYLOR	WILLIAM THOMAS	TUBAL WILD
JOHN WHIDENGER	MICHAEL WILKINS	JAMES WILEY
PETER YOUNGBLOOD		

Franklin Co/ Seventh Regt: Capt. WILLIAM HUFF's Co.

JAMES BRISON, Lt.		JAMES WILSON, Ens
DANIEL McNEAL, Sgt		THOMAS THOMAS, Sgt
JAMES NICKEL, Sgt		THOMAS TRUSLER, Sgt
GNASH GLIDEWELL, Cpl		STEPHEN SIMS, Cpl
SAMUEL HUNLEY, Cpl		JOHN LOGAN, Cpl
GEORGE ADAMS	ROBERT ABERNATHY	WILLIAM AGINS
PETER ALLEY	CORNELIUS BRISON	HUGH BRISON
ISAAC BROWN	ROBERT BURBAGE	JAMES BAILEY
JAMES CANTWELL	JAMES CARWILE	JOHN CLINTON
DAVID EWING	SAMEUL ELY	ANDREW ENSLEY
DAVID GILLIAM	WILLIAM GEORGE 2d	JONATHAN GILLIAM
ARCHIBALD GUTHREY	JAMES GOSNEY	JOSEPH HANNA
WILLIAM HARREL	JAMES HARPER	WILLIAM HOBBS
WILLIAM HARVEY	ABRAHAM	JESSE HOLDER
WILLIAM JULIAN	HOLLINGSWORTH	JOHN JULIAN
FIELDING LACY	HENRY MAPES	EDWARD MANLEY
STEPHEN MAYPLE	THOMAS MILLER	RICHARD MINOR
HEZEKIAH MOUNTS	ABRAHAM NEIGHBOURS	THOMAS NEAL
JAMES NOBLE	ISAAC ODLE	SIMON ODLE
WASHINGTON ORR	BARRAT PARRISH	CHARLES RONEY
JOHN RUSSELL	WILLIS RIGHT	JOHN STEPHENS SR
JOHN STEPHENS JR	JOSEPH STEPHENS	ROBERT STEPHENS
JAMES TANNER	JOHN THARP	JOHN VARDAMAN
WILLIAM WILLIAMS	ALEXANDER WILLIAMS	RICHARD WILLIAMS
JOHN WILSON	BENJAMIN WILSON	ALBERT WALKER

THE INDIANA GORE: War of 1812 muster rolls

Franklin Co/ Indiana Militia: Capt. FREDERICK SHULTS'
Co, succeeded by Capt. JOSEPH D. CLEMENTS
ARCHIBALD SMITH, Lt   WILLIAM MORGAN, Ens
JOHN WINCHEL, Sgt   EDWARD WHITE, Sgt
REUBIN R. PENNWELL, Sgt   WILLIAM STANSBERRY, Sgt
CHARLES WILDRIDGE, Cpl   THOMAS HALBERSTADT, Cpl
DANIEL SKINNER, Cpl   JAMES TRUSLER, Cpl
JAMES CASE   WILLIAM CROSS   JOHN F. DAVIES
PHILLIP FRAKES   JOHN FREEL   JAMES FRAZER
ALEXANDER FULTON   JOHN FRED   MOSES GRAY
RHODES GARDNER   RUSSEL GARDNER   JOHN GILLEM
ROBERT GREEN   WILLIAM GRACE/GROSS ADAM HAMILTON
NATHANIEL HERNDON   JESSE JONES   JOHN JACKS
HENRY KELLY   SAMUEL LEE   NATHAN LEWIS
JOHN LEWIS   GREENBERRY LYON   THOMAS LOLLER
EDWARD MAGNER   ALBERT MURPHY   MOSES MAXWELL
JAMES McCAW   JAMES D. MORRISON   JOSEPH MOORE
BENJAMIN McQUEEN   JOSEPH W. MORRISON WILLIAM
JAMES PATTY   JACOB PETERS   MULHOLLAND
WILEY POWELL   JOHN ROCKEFELLAR   AQUILLA RAMSEY
JAMES ROSS   WILLIAM ROSS   JAMES ROBERTS
JOSEPH RASH   WILLIAM RASH   JOHN SHANK
CHARLES SHANNON   ROBERT SHIELDS   SAMUEL SHIRK
WILLIAM TANNER   RUGLAS WINCHEL   JAMES WINCHEL
NICHOLAS WEBBER   DAVID WRIGHT   SAMUEL WARD
JOHN WELCH   JOHN WAKEFIELD
PETER MASCO hired as pack-horse driver

Franklin Co/ 7th Regt: Capt. ELLIOTT HERNDON's Co.
THOMAS CARTER, Lt   LEWIS JOHNSTON, Ens
EBENEZER SPRIGGS, Sgt   JOHN ALLEN, Sgt
THOMAS COOKSEY, Sgt   JOHN RICHARDSON, Cpl
HENRY LIONS, Cpl   JAMES PUTNAM, Cpl
ABSOLOM HASTY, Cpl
ROBERT ADKINSON   THOMAS ARNETT   JOHN ADAMS
NIMROD BRACKNEY   REMEMBER BLACKMAN   JOHN BROWN
THOMAS BELL   JOHN BARLOW   RICHARD CULP
JEREMIAH CORY   ZACHARIAH COOKSEY   ELI DAVIS
WILLIAM DAVIS   ELIAS DAVIS   SAMUEL ENDSLEY
WILLIAM FLOOD   WILLIAM FREELS   WILLIAM GIBBS
GEORGE GREGG   JOHN GAMBLE   JOHN GAVIN
MARTIN HIGGINS   AARON LIONS   THOMAS
SAMUEL NEWHOUSE   JAMES NEWHOUSE   MILHOLLAND
ARCHIBALD PARKER   JOSHUA PORTER   CHARLES ROONAN
JAMES STUCKY   DAVID SHIRK   ELIAS STEVENS
JOHN TYNER   SOLOMON TYNER   HARIS TYNER
JAMES TYNER   DAVID TAYLOR   JESSE TURNER
DAVID WEBB   ABEL WEBB   GEORGE WILLIAMS
PETER YOUNGBLOOD

THE INDIANA GORE: War of 1812 muster rolls

Franklin Co/ 7th Regt: Capt. JOHN BRISON's Company

JACOB HACKLEMAN, Lt
JOHN WILLEY, Sgt
BENJAMIN McCARTY, Sgt
RICHARD JACKMAN, Cpl
AMOS EDWARDS, Cpl
JOSIAH ALLEN
NICHOLAS ANTHONY
JAMES ALLEY
ELISHA BURBAGE
JOHN CASE
ZOPHAR COLEMAN
ELI DAWSON
DANIEL EGGANS
GEORGE FERRIS
WILLIAM GORDON
CHRISTIAN KINGRY
ABRAHAM MAYERS
and MYERS
JOHN McQUIN
WILLIAM PALMER
JOHN RUSSEL
MICAJAH SIMMONS
WILLIAM SIRES
THOMAS SMITH
MICHAEL VANBLARICUM

JAMES McGINNIS, Ens
THOMAS CRAVEN, Sgt
JOHN ARNOLD, Sgt
ABRAHAM HACKLEMAN, Cpl
JOHN CHRYST, Cpl
ELI ALLEN
WILLIAM ABERNATH
CORNELIUS BRISON
DAVID BONNER
JOHN CREEK
WILLIAMSON COLLETT
JACOB DUBOIS
JOHN S. ELLIOTT
ZACHARIAH GLOVER
SAMUEL HANNAH
ISAAC LOLLER
JACOB MILLER
WILLIAM NORRIS JR
JOSEPH NICKLES
MOSES RICHARDSON
EZEKIEL STEVENS
THOMAS SNODGRASS
WILLIAM SIMMONS
DAVID TAYLOR
JOSEPH WARD
THOMAS WHITACKER

WILLIAM ANTHONY
JONATHAN ALLEY
WILLIAM BRISON
ZACHARIAH CHANCE
NICHOLAS CHRYST
ELI DAVIS
WILLIAM DICKSON
JOHN FOREMAN
JOHN GRIFFITH
JOHN HENDERSON
SAMUEL LOGAN
JOSEPH MURPHY
WILLIAM NORRIS
JOHN NORRIS
ENOCH RUSSEL
SAMUEL STEVENS
THOMAS SHANKS
REUBEN SCARLOCK
ANDREW THARP
JOSEPH WILLIAMS
JOHN WILLIS

Wayne Co/ Eighth Regt, Col. GEORGE HUNT

Wayne Co/ 8th Regt: Capt. ENOS BUTLER's Co.

HUGH BAILY, Lt
JOHN GOUGH, Sgt
PLEASANT HARRIS, Sgt
ISAAC JULIAN, Cpl
THOMAS McCOY, Cpl
WILLIAM BEASLEY
ISAAC BEALES
JOHN CONNER
JOSEPH CAIN
ARNETT DRURY
REYNOLD FIELDER
STEPHEN GRIFFITH
JOHN FOX
CHARLES GORDAN
JOSEPH HUNT
JOHN HARVEY
WILLIAM HOPSON
GEORGE ISH
JOSEPH LEWIS

ABSOLUM HARVEY, Ens
PETER DUMONT, Sgt
WILLIAM OWENS, Sgt
ISAIAH DRURY, Cpl
JOSEPH FLINT, Cpl
ROBERT BENNETT
ELIJAH BROCK
WILLIAM CONNER
EDWARD DREWRY
SAMUEL DREWERY
VALENTINE FRUHEARTY
JOHN FARLOW
WILLIAM GILBREATH
HENDERSON HARVEY
WILLIAM HOLTZCLAW
ELIACHIM HARDING
JAMES JACKSON
JACOB LYBROOK

JESSE BUSON/BUZAN
JAMES CLENDANNON
JAMES CILWELL
JOHN DUER
HUGH ENDSLEY
GEORGE GRIMES
BENJAMIN FISHER
WILLIAM GRIMES
JONATHAN GILBERT
JAMES HARRIS
MICHAEL HARVEY
THOMAS HARDING
JAMES JONES
PETER MILLER

12

THE INDIANA GORE: War of 1812 muster rolls

Wayne Co/ 8th Regt: Capt. ENOS BUTLER's Co. cont'd
JOHN MONTGOMERY	ALEXANDER McCOMBS	WM. MONTGOMERY
MICHAEL MILLER	JAMES MONTGOMERY	PLATT MONTGOMERY
ROBERT MONTGOMERY	JOHN NYPE/KNIPE	JOHN OLIVER
JOHN PARSONS	JOHN PATTERSON	ABSOLUM RAMBO
WILLIAM G. REYNOLDS	JOHN SIMMONS	DANIEL SHELLY
	JAMES STARRET	JOHN TIBBS
HARMAN WARRAM	ROBERT WILSON	JOHN WHITEMAN
JACOB WEYMYER	HENRY WHITEMAN	LEVI WILLETS
JOSEPH WYATT		

Wayne Co/ Indiana Militia: Capt. WM. WHITEHEAD's Co.
PETER WEAVER, Lt		JOHN COLLINS, Ens
JOSEPH RIPPEY, Sgt		JAMES DRAKE, Sgt
WILLIAM RAPER, Sgt		JAMES WARRAN, Sgt
HENRY FENDER, Cpl		SAMUEL HOWARD, Cpl
JOSEPH BURY, Cpl		JOHN HOWARD, Cpl
THOMAS BRADBURY	LEVI BUTLER	HUGH BAILY
JOHN BAILY	THOMAS BLAIR	ENOCH CHAMBERS
CURTIS CLENNY	WILLIAM DURHAM	SAMUEL FLEMING
ANDERSON GORDEN	JONAS GARR	JOHN HART
DAVID HERMAN	GEORGE IMEL	ANDREW JONES
GEORGE JULIAN	RENNY JULIAN	ABRAHAM LITTLE
SAMUEL MARTIN	PETER MELLANDER	JOHN MARKS
JOHN MAYERS/MYERS	DAVID ODEM	SAMUEL R. PATTERSON
NATHANIEL ROWEND	WILLIAM STEPHENS	
NATHAN SMITH	JOHN WALKER	JOHN WATKINS
WILLIAM WATSON	WILLIAM WILLIAMS	

Wayne Co/ Indiana Militia: Capt. WM. HOLEMAN's Co.
WILLIAM BRICE, Capt		JOHN HEART, Ens
WILLIAM HUSTON, Sgt		ELIJAH HOLLAND, Sgt
ARMSTRONG GRIMES, Sgt		JOHN BOILES, Sgt
SAMUEL HOWARD, Cpl		JACOB GALYAN, Cpl
THOMAS CLARK, Cpl		DAVID COX, Cpl
FARIS ADCOCK	WILLIAM ALEXANDER	JOHN ALEXANDER
ADAM BANKS	JOSEPH BERRY	ANDREW BLOUNT
ISAAC CONLEY	JOSEPH COX	JAMES COX
THOMAS CRANER	NATHANIEL DRAKE	JOHN DRAKE
WILLIAM DUNN	JOSEPH DWIGGINS	THOMAS ENDSLEY
REUBEN FARLOW	ALEXANDER GRIMES	JOHN GARRETT
JOSEPH HOLEMAN	MATTHEW HOLCUM	AMANUEL HODGE
OBADIAH HARRIS	ABRAHAM HENSLEY	GEORGE HOPSON
JESSE JULEN	GEORGE JULEN	JOHN McCOMBS
JACOB McCONTOSH	JAMES MARTINDILL	ELI RUNNELS
EDWARD J. SWANSON	JOHN TURNER	WILLIAM WADE
JAMES WALKER	WILLIAM WALKER	JACOB WILSON
ISAAC WILSON	GRIMES WILSON	JOSHUA WILSON

THE INDIANA GORE: War of 1812 muster rolls

Wayne Co/ 8th Regt: Capt. JOHN FARLOW's Company
JOHN MONTGOMERY, Lt   JONATHAN GILBERT, Ens
RICHARD G. PARRIS, Sgt   JAMES WHITE, Sgt
JOHN PORT, Sgt   ALEXANDER GRIMES, Sgt
GEORGE ISH, Cpl   JACOB MILLER, Cpl
WILLIAM RAPER, Cpl   WILLIAM HUSTON, Cpl
ADAM ALLEN   JOSEPH BEARY   REUBIN BRATTIN
THOMAS BLAIR   JOHN BUNTON   ISAAC BEASON
DAVID CARSON   JOSEPH CARPENTER   DAVID CANNADA
DAVID COX   JAMES COLDWELL   FRANCIS COLDWELL
JOSEPH COX   MATHIAS DAWSON   ELISHA DENNIS
WILLIAM DY   PETER ENDSLEY   WILLIAM FARLOW
GEORGE FALL   FIELDING GARR   JACOB GALYAN
JAMES GORDIN   SAMUEL GUNWELL   ARMSTRONG GRIMES
ROBERT HARVEY   JAMES HOLEMAN   JOEL HILL
FRANCIS HARVEY   JOHN JACKSON   EBENEZER JACKSON
WILLIAM JURDIN   PHILLIP LYBROOK   JOHN MARTIN
THOMAS MOFFET   JAMES McDADE   SAMUEL McGEORGE
PETER MILLER   ELLET McCOMBS   JOEL MORE
JOHN PHILLIPS   WILLIAM PHILLIPS   JOHN RAPER
JACOB ROOP   MICHAEL SNIDER   JOHN SEANY
JOHN SMITH   JOHN SHAW   JAMES SHAW
WILLIAM SHAW   ISAAC SHELBY   FREDERICK SUMNEY
SAMUEL STOVER   MICHAEL SPENCER   JOHN THARP
THOMAS WALLACE   JACOB WHITMAN   WILLIAM WALKER
JAMES WADDLE   ELI RIGHT

Wayne Co/ 8th Regt: Capt. RICHARD LEWIS' Company
HUGH BAILY, Lt   WILLIAM ASKREM, Ens
JONATHAN SHAW, Sgt   REUBEN JAY, Sgt
THOMAS RAY, Sgt   ABSOLOM HARVEY, Sgt
DILMON BAILY, Cpl   JACOB DICKARD, Cpl
WILLIAM GELBRAITH, Cpl   THOMAS TAYLOR, Cpl
JOHN WOODKIRK, Cpl
SAMUEL ALEXANDER   ABRAHAM ASHBY   LEVI BUTLER
JESSE BUSAN   WILLIAM BARWELL   WILLIAM BURK
SAMUEL BOYD   THOMAS BARLEY   WILLIAM COX
THOMAS CRAWFORD   ABIJAH CAIN   THOMAS COX
JOSHUA CRANER   JOHN CAIN   ARIEL COY
JESSE DOLLARHIDE   WILLIAM DUNNMAN   JESSE HODGES
ISAAC HARVEY   SAMUEL HOWARD   ABEL JANEY
GEORGE JULIAN   JESSE JULIAN   JACOB JULIAN
SAMUEL JONES   STEPHEN JOHNSON   JOHN JACKSON
ROBERT LEVEL   ZACHARIAH LEWALLEN JOSEPH LEWIS
WILLIAM MEEK   NATHANIEL McCLURE   JOSEPH RIPPEY
SETH WAY   JOHN WATKINS   JOHN WARRAM
MATTHEW WALL

DEARBORN COUNTY

The boundary line which defined the western border of the Gore was only a suggestion to the Indians. This period was the time of Tecumseh and his efforts to unite his people and win back their land. The Whitewater River which meanders through present-day Union and Franklin counties was a favorite encampment spot. Indian resistance ended with the Battle of Tippecanoe in 1811; sporadic raids occurred for a few more years.

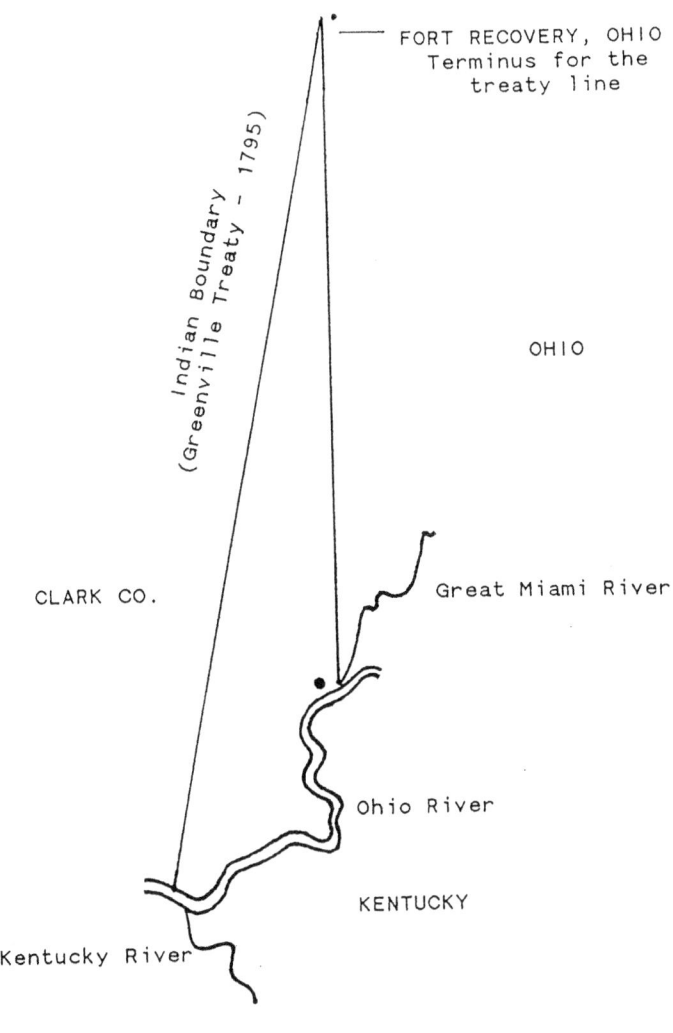

DEARBORN COUNTY

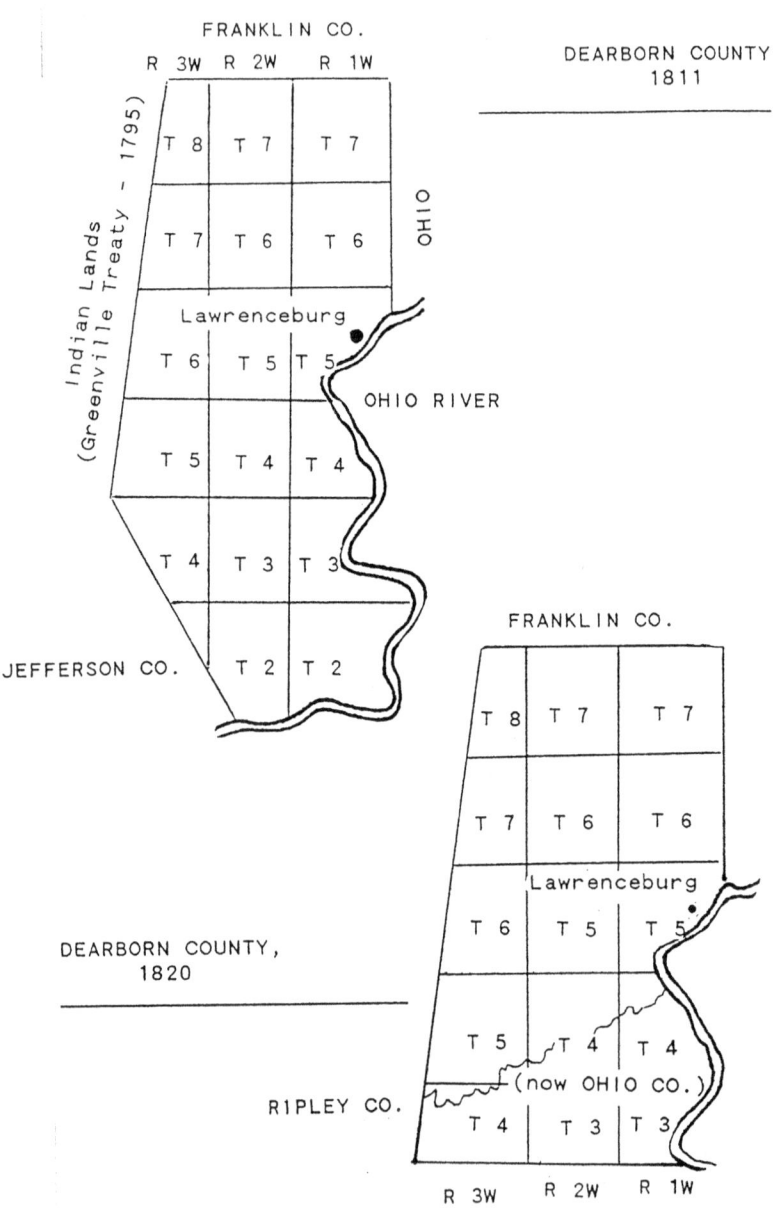

DEARBORN COUNTY: Original Land Entries Tract Book
FORMAT: Section - Purchaser - year - page;

Tract books are part of the County Recorder's responsibility, and are found in that office at the Courthouse. Most of the names listed here did become residents. Others were land speculators, hoping for a quick return on their money.

Lawrenceberg, the county seat, profited by its location on the banks of the Ohio River. It became a major stopping-over point for travelers, and was the center of Dearborn County's growth. A number of picturesque old buildings remain in the original section of the town, testifying to its heritage.

Township 3, Range 1W

1, 2 & 3 - LEWIS DAVIS & BENJ. CHAMBERS - 1801 - 1; 4 DAVID B. CLOSE - 1812 - 1; 4 - JOHN JAMES - 1814 - 1; 4 - DAVID CLOSE - 1814 - 1; 5 - JOHN PAYNE - 1814 1; 5 - MARTIN STEWART - 1814 - 1; 5 - WILLIAM HOWLETT 1813 - 1; 5 - JOHN DIXON - 1815 - 1; 6 - PETER WHITE 1815 - 1; 6 - HUGH BEATTY - 1815 - 1; 6 - JOHN MOUNTS 1815 - 1; 6 - JOHN BARRICKLOW & ROBERT ESPY - 1815 1; 7 - JOHN BARRICKLOW - 1815 - 1; 7 - HUGH ESPY 1815 - 1; 7 & 17 - HUGH ESPY - 1814 - 1; 8 - JAMES DUCRET - 1814 - 1; 8 - ROBERT DRAKE - 1814 - 1; 8 HUGH MOORE - 1817 - 1; 8 - HUGH ESPY - 1816 - 1; 9, 10 & 11 - DENNY CADBURY - 1802 - 1; 15 - P.S. SYMMES assigned to JOHN JAMES - 1814 - 1; 17 - ROBERT RICKETTS - 1804 - 1; 17 - STEPHEN STEWART - 1814 - 1; 17 ROBERT RICKETTS - 1813 - 1; 18 - SAM'L. SCOTT & RUFUS GORDON - 1816 - 1; 18 - JOHN DIXON - 1815 - 1; 18 WILLIAM ROSS - 1816 - 1; 15 - DILLARD DRAKE - 1816 1; 19 - NATHAN RICKETTS - 1816 - 1; 19 - RICHARD J. HALL - 1815 - 1; 19 - WILLIS BATES - 1816 - 1; 19 JACOB GOODNER - 1816 - 1; 20 - SILAS HOWE - 1816 - 2; 20 - WILLIAM ROSS - 1816 - 2; 20 - DAVID REMER - 1815 2; 21 & 22 - LOT NORTH - 1813 - 2.

Township 4, Range 1W

4 - DANIEL CONNER (resold to G.R. TERENCE in 1810) 1804 - 2; 5 - JESSE L. HOLEMAN - 1810 - 2; 5 - JOSEPH W. WINKLEY - 1813 - 2; 5 - GEORGE SHINKLE - 1814 - 2; 5 - JOHN WALSH - 1815 - 2; 6 - ISAAC CONNER - 1815 2; 6 - RICHARD NORRIS - 1813- 2; 6 - VALENTINE BARTON 1813 - 2; 6 - JAMES RUMBLEY - 1812 - 2; 7 - ELI GREEN 7 & 18 - SQUIRE POTEET - 1813 - 2; 7 - HENRY GROVE 1812 - 2; 7 - GEORGE GROVE - 1813 - 2; 8, 9, & 10 DANIEL CONNER (resold to O. ORMSBY in 1806) - 1801 2; 16 - JOSEPH WILKINSON (resold to JESSE HUNT in 1806) - 1801 - 2; 17 - HENRY MILLER - 1814 - 2; 17

DEARBORN COUNTY: Original Land Entries Tract Book
FORMAT: Section - Purchaser - year - page;

Township 4, Range 1W continued

BENJAMIN MILLER - 1813 - 2; 17 - R. TAYLOR & THOMAS BURNS - 1818 - 2; 18 - MICHAEL & WILLIAM FLAKE - 1813 2; 18 - JACOB SMITH & JOHN CONNER - 1815 - 2; 18 RICHARD BAILEY - 1814 - 2; 19 - JOHN HUNT - 1816 - 2; 19 - FARRINGTON BARRICKLOW - 1816 - 2; 19 - JAMES BURKE - 1813 - 2; 19 - JNO. & FARRINGTON BARRICKLOW 1813 - 2; 20 - JAMES WARNOCK - 1816 - 2; 20 - THOMAS STEWART - 1814 - 2; 20 - ABIJAH GOODRICH - 1816 - 2; 21 - HUGH MOORE - 1816- 2; 21 - JOHN BARRICKLOW -1815 2; 21 - illeg. & JOHN D. MILLER - 1817 - 2; 21 - CORNELIUS, WM. L. & JOS. D. MILLER - 1814 - 3; 22 & 23 PEYTON SHORT - 1807- 3; 26 - ISAAC SORING - 1801 -3; 27 - JONATHAN PARKS - 1816 - 3; 27 - ALEXANDER ABERCROMBIE - 1816 - 3; 27 - WILLIAM BILLS - 1816 - 3; 27 - ABM. DUBOIS & ROBERT DUCE - 1816- 3; 28 - ROBERT ESPY - 1815 - 3; 28 - JNO. W. McCOLLOUGH - 1814 - 3; 28 - JAMES STEWART - 1815 - 3; 28 - CHARLES ENGLISH 1815 - 3; 29 - EPHRAIM GARD - 1816 - 3; 29 - SAMUEL STEEL - 1816 - 3; 29 - JAMES HINDE - 1816 - 3; 30 JOHN & FARRINGTON BARRICKLOW - 1813 - 3; 30 - ISAAC DEXTER - 1814 - 3; 31 - PETER LOUSTELLER - 1814 - 3; 31 - P.S. SYMMES & LEVI WHITEMAN - 1815 - 3; 31 - ASA HAMILTON & JAMES BUCHANON - 1814 - 3; 31 - JAMES GIBSON - 1814 - 3; 32 - JONATHAN HUNTINGDON - 1815 3; 32 - FREDERICK WALDO - 1814 - 3; 32 - NOAH BABBS & JAMES STEWART - 1814 - 3; 32 - JOHN ENGLISH - 1815 3; 33 - ROBERT ELLIOT - 1817 - 3; 33 - ISAAC WILCOT 1815 - 3; 33 - CLABOURN ALLEN - 1813 - 3; 34 - DAVID B. CLOSE - 1809 - 3; 34 - ELI NATHAN KEMPER - 1804 3; 34 - SAM'L. M. JELLY - 1815 - 3; 35 & 36 - JAMES FINDLAY - 1801 - 3.

Township 5, Range 1W

1 - JOSEPH HAYS - 1801 - 4; 2 - GEORGE CHRIST & H. HARDING - 1801 - 4; 3 - BARNET HULICK - 1802 - 4; 4 TIMOTHY DAVIS - 1815 - 4; 4 - JOHN HOWARD - 1812 - 4; 4 - WILLIAM CALDWELL - 1812 - 4; 4 - SAMUEL BOND 1809 - 4; 5 - JOHN FERRIS - 1814 - 4; 5 - SAMUEL BOND 1808 - 4; 5 - AMOS WAY & ISAAC LEMASTER - 1815 - 4; 6 DAVID REES - 1815 - 4; 6 - LEONARD CHASE - 1815 - 4; 6 - JACOB BRASHER - 1815 - 4; 7 - P.S. SYMMES & LEWIS WHITEMAN - 1815 - 4; 7 - CHARLES DANSON - 1816 - 4; 7 - DAVID HOGAN - 1814- 4; 7 - ENOCH JAMES - 1814- 4; 8 - CALEB PUGH - 1811 - 4; 8 - ENOCH PUGH - 1815 - 4; 8 - JESSE LAIRD - 1817 - 4; 8 - DAVID REES - 1815- 4; 9 -ZEBULON PIKE - 1816 - 4; 9 - DELE ELDER - 1811- 4; 9 -SAM'L. BOND - 1808 - 4; 10, 11 & 12 - ZEBULON PIKE (reentered by JESSE HUNT, assignee JNO. BROWN) 1806 - 4; 13, 14 & 15 - SAM'L. C. VANCE - 1801 - 4;

DEARBORN COUNTY: Original Land Entries Tract Book
FORMAT: Section - Purchaser - year - page;

Township 5, Range 1W continued

17 - JOHN DEMOS - 1814 - 4; 17 - GEORGE WEAVER - 1814 4; 17 - DAVID DUTTON - 1810 - 4; 17 - ADAM PATE -1812 4; 18 - JAMES ROBISON - 1814 - 4; 18 - ENOCH JAMES JR 1814 - 4; 18 - JAHIEL BUFFINGTON & AMES BRUCE - 1814 4; 18 - ENOCH JAMES- 1814 - 4; 19 - DAVID REES - 1806 4; 19 - SAMUEL PERRY - 1816 - 5; 19 - FRANCIS CHECK 1812 - 5; 19 - SAMUEL BOND - 1808- 5; 20 - PAGE CHECK 1811 - 5; 20 - NATHAN C. FINDLY - 1806 - 5; 20 -DAVID REES - 1806 - 5; 21, 22 & 23 - CHARLES WILKINS - 1801 5; 27, 28 & 29 - JAMES CONN - 1801 - 5; 30 - ISAAC REYNOLDS - 1811 - 5; 30 - ELI GREEN - 1811 - 5; 30 - JOHN BUFFINGTON - 1811 - 5; 30 - CONRAD HUFFMAN -1811 5; 31 - MARTIN COZINE - 1815 5; 31 - ABRAHAM CARBAUGH 1812 - 5; 31 - RICHARD NORRIS - 1812 - 5; 32 & 33 - CHARLES NATTIER - 1804 - 5.

Township 6, Range 1W

1 - ISAAC HILLS - 1818 - 5; 1 - ENOCH JACKSON - 1817 5; 1 - JOHN GARRISON - 1811 - 5; 1 - MICHAEL SHANKS 1809 - 5; 2 - JOHN HARPER - 1814 - 5; 2 - ELIJAH GARRISON - 1814 - 5; 2 - JACOB R. COMPTON - 1806 - 5; 2 JOSEPH HARPER - 1815 - 5; 3 - GEORGE FARMER - 1815 5; 3 - JOHN GIBSON - 1816 - 5; 3 - JOHN M. CONNELL 1814 - 5; 3 - JAMES WHITE - 1814 - 5; 4 - JOSEPH RAMSBURGH RAMSBURGH - 1817 - 5; 4 - DAVID BOWLES - 1817 - 5; 4 ABNER GRAHAM - 1818 - 5; 5 - R. WEAVER - 1817 - 6; 6 WILLIAM BARR - 1818 - 6; 7 - JOHN BURKE - 1818 - 6; 7 ROBERT HUNT - 1815 - 6; 7 - EBENEZER ROGERS - 1815 - 6; 7 - JOHN SMITH - 1818 - 6; 8 - RULIFF BOGERT -1817 1817 - 6; 8 - SAMUEL HUTCHINSON - 1815 - 6; 8 - JOHN DAWSON - 1813 - 6; 9 - LEVI & THOMAS BRACKEN - 1816 6; 9 - JOSEPH WHITE - 1817 - 6; 9 - RUBEN SUTTON 1815 1815 - 6; 10 - JERRY MURPHY - 1815 - 6; 10 - AARON R. BONHAM - 1817 - 6; 10 - JOSEPH STROUD - 1815 - 6; 11 ISAAC HENDERSON - 1811 - 6; 11 - JOHN WHITE - 1816 6; 11 - NOBLE BUTLER - 1804 - 6; 11 - JOHN SHEARED 1812 - 6; 12 - SAMUEL McHENRY - 1817 - 6; 12 - MICHL. SHANKS - 1809 - 6; 12 - JAMES FULLER - 1815 - 6; 12 JOHN BARKALOO - 1814 - 6; 13 - JOHN & SARAH FULLER 1812 - 6; 13 - JAMES WHITE - 1813 - 6; 13 - WILLIAM TORRENCE & THOS. FULLER - 1818- 6; 13 - THOMAS MILLER 1818 - 7; 14 - ROBERT McCONNELL - 1804- 7; 14 - JACOB PARKE - 1817 - 7; 15 - SILAS GARRISON 1814 - 7; 17 THOMAS PRICE - 1817- 7; 17 & 18 - JOHN EUBANKS - 1811 7; 18 - PETER HIGDON - 1816 - 7; 18 - ROBERT PERRET 1817 - 7; 19 & 20 - NATHANIEL TUCKER - 1814 - 7; 19 JOSEPH HALL - 1817 - 7; 19 - MICHAEL DUNN - 1814 - 7; 19 - SAMUEL H. DOWDEN - 1813 - 7; 20 - JOHN DAWSON & JOHN EUBANK - 1817 - 7; 20 - JOHN DAWSON - 1814 - 7;

DEARBORN COUNTY: Original Land Entries Tract Book
FORMAT: Section - Purchaser - year - page;

Township 6, Range 1W continued

21 - MICHAEL SHANKS - 1814 - 7; 22 - ABRAHAM GARRISON 1811- 7; 22 - EZEKIEL JACKSON - 1815 - 7; 22 - ABIJAH HAYS - 1806 - 7; 23 - JOSEPH HAYS - 1811 - 8; 23 JAMES GOODWIN - 1812 - 8; 23 - JAMES BENNETT - 1811 8; 23 & 26 - CHARLES DAWSON - 1804 - 8; 24 - THOMAS HUNT - 1812 - 8; 24 - LEVI MILLER - 1811 - 8; 24 MICAJAH PARKE - 1812 - 8; 24 - DAVID GUARD - 1808 8; 25 - DANIEL PERRINE - 1815- 8; 27 - THADDEUS COOLLY - 1804 - 8; 27 - 1806 - HENRY C. SMITH - 1806 8; 28 - JACOB BLASDELL & ARCHIBALD STARK - 1804 - 8; 29 - JACOB BLASDELL - 1804 - 8; 29 - EPHRAIM KNEELAND 1818 - 8; 29 - JOHN DAWSON - 1814 - 8; 29 - DENCE TRUSTEE - 1817 - 8; 30 - JACOB BLASDELL - 1817 - 8; 30 - THOMAS DARLING - 1816 - 8; 30 - WM. P. MARSHALL 1815 - 8; 31 - AARON BURROUGHS - 1817 - 8; 31 - JAMES CONNER - 1817 - 8; 31 - CHARLES OSGOOD - 1816 - 8; 32 JOHN FRAZER - 1814 - 8; 32 - JOHN FOSTER - 1816 - 8; 32 - JAMES McCLESTER - 1814 - 8; 32 - JOSHUA STROUD 1815 - 8; 33 - STEPHEN LUDLOW - 1814 - 8; 33 - ELIJAH WALDON - 1811 - 8; 33 - WALTER ARMSTRONG - 1814 - 8; 33 - ENOCH PUGH - 1811 - 8; 34 - JACOB FROMAN - 1806 8; 34 - STEPHEN LUDLOW - 1814 - 8; 34 - ISAAC LAMASTERS - 1806 - 8; 34 - SAMUEL EVANS - 1813 - 8; 35 ROBERT PRATT/PIATT - 1811 - 8; 35 - JAMES HAYES -1811 8; 35 - THOMAS MILLER - 1804 - 9; 35 - JOB MILLER & HY HARDIN - 1811 - 9; 36 - JOSEPH HAYES - 1801 - 9.

Township 7, Range 1W

1 - STEPHEN FALKINGTON - 1814- 9; 1 - SAMUEL C. VANCE 1818 - 9; 1 - HUGH MOORE - 1816 - 9; 1 - OBADIAH FORD 1811 - 9; 2 - GEORGE LARRISON - 1815 - 9; 2 - JAMES REMY - 1812 - 9; 2 - JAMES BLACKHOUSE - 1811 - 9; 2 MOSES WILEY - 1818 - 9; 3 - JAMES JONES SR - 1816- 9; 4 - JAMES ADAIR SR - 1803 - 9; 4 - JAMES JONES - 1811 9; 4 - ENOCH SMITH - 1809 - 9; 5 - WM. SMITH & HUGH BRIAN - 1808 - 9; 5 - JOHN BARBER - 1816 - 9; 5 JAMES PARIS - 1818 - 9; 6 - JOHN CLIFTON - 1818 - 9; 6 - JOHN & BENJAMIN CLIFTON - 1819 - 9; 6 - CORNELIUS RINERSON - 1818 - 9; 6 - JOHN PETERSON - 1820 - 9; 8 JOHN BARKALOO - 1818 - 10; 8 - PHINEAS & ORREN JUDD 1818 - 10; 8 - SAM B. LOOKER & CARLTON CLARK - 1815 10; 8 - WM. SMITH & WM. S. WHITE - 1813- 10; 9 - JOHN BROWN - 1811 - 10; 9 - JOHN PURSEL - 1812 - 10; 9 JOHN HINKSON - 1814 - 10; 10 - JOHN HACKLEMAN - 1803 10; 10 - RICHARD MANNERING - 1801 - 10; 11 - JOHN BROWN - 1801 - 10; 11 - LEWIS DEWEESE - 1801 - 10; 12 JAMES HARSPENCE - 1815 - 10; 12 - ALEXANDER DEARMAND 1804 - 10; 12 - WILLIAM MAJORS - 1802 - 10; 13 - CAVE JOHNSON - 1801 - 10; 13 - WM. ALLENSWORTH & WM. RAMEY

DEARBORN COUNTY: Original Land Entries Tract Book
FORMAT: Section - Purchaser - year - page:

Township 7, Range 1W continued

1801 - 10; 14 - JAMES McCOY - 1804 - 10; 14 - JAMES CLOUD - 1816 - 10; 14 - BAYLESS ASBY - 1801 - 10; 15 THOMAS SKINNER - 1806- 10; 15 - WM. MAJOR - 1813 -10; 17 - WM. & SAM'L. HOLLOWELL - 1819 - 10; 17 - WM. HORNEY - 1818 - 10; 18 - WM. ROWLAND - 1818 - 10; 18 JOHN McMAHAN - 1818 - 10; 18 - WM. SAIGHMAN - 1816 10; 19 - JOHN LAMBDIN - 1814 - 11; 19 - P.S. SYMMES & HUGH MOORE - 1816 - 11; 19 - WM. CLOUD - 1814 - 11; 20 - FARRAN & HOBBS - 1816- 10; 20 - EMRY HOBS - 1817 11; 20 - GEORGE P. TERRENCE - 1814 - 11; 20 - JAMES McCLURE - 1814 - 11; 21 - DENNIS CLARK - 1814 - 11; 23 - A. WHITE - 1818 - 11; 23 - WM. PURCEL & THOS. BRACKENRIDGE - 1818 - 11; 23 - JACOB DEMARRIS - 1818 11; 23 - JOHN BROWN - 1801- 11; 24 - WM. PURSEL -1811 11; 25 - JOHN ALLEN - 1805 - 11; 25 - JONAS CRANE 1805 - 11; 26 - DAVID LATHROP - 1818 - 12; 26 - ENOCH MORGAN - 1818- 11; 26 - ABRAHAM CORNELIUS - 1817- 12; 27 - JOSHUA PARIS - 1814 - 12; 27 - WILLOUGHBY TIBBS 1810 - 12; 27 - JAMES JONES - 1814 - 12; 27 - JAMES CLOUD - 1812 - 12; 28 - BAYLISS CLOUD - 1811 - 12: 28 MATTHEW & SAM'L LAMBDIN - 1814 - 12; 28 - ELIJAH GARRISON - 1814 - 12; 28 - JOSEPH WOOLY - 1814 - 12; 29 JOEL DICKEN - 1814 - 12; 29 - JOHN GIBSON - 1816 -12; 29 - ROBERT MYERS & THOMAS WALLS - 1814 - 12; 30 JOHN L. WATKINS - 1815 - 12; 30 - ZEDEKIAH BONHAM & JONATHAN LEWIS - 1815 - 12; 30 - AQUILLA CROSS - 1814 12; 30 - HENRY MILLER - 1818 - 12; 30 - ISRAEL BONHAM 1819 - 12; 31 - WM. WEBB - 1814 - 12; 31 & 32- AQUILLA CROSS - 1818 - 12; 31 - STEPHEN WOOD - 1818 - 12; 31 - EZEKIEL JACKSON - 1817 - 12; 32 - CASPER JOHNSON 1817- 12; 33 - AARON R. BONHAM - 1814 - 12; 33 -JAMES COLE - 1815 - 12; 33 - J. BUFFUN & HENRY DIFFENDEFFER 1818 - 12; 33 - SACKER NELSON - 1815 - 12; 34 - BENJAMIN REILY - 1814- 12; 34 - JAMES CLOUD - 1817 - 12; 34 - JOSEPH A. LOYD - 1815 - 12; 34 - ALEXANDER WHITE 1815 - 12; 35 - JOHN GIBSON - 1817 - 13; 36 - REUBEN LEWIS - 1816 - 13.

Township 3, Range 2W

1 - JAMES A. WALTON - 1814 - 13; 1 - ROBERT ELLIOTT 1817 - 13; 2 - JAMES CURRY & JESSE DRAKE - 1810 - 13; 2 - JAMES CRANE - 1814 - 13; 2 - LUTHER MEAD - 1815 13; 3 - PAYTON S. SYMMES - 1814 - 13; 3 - JOSHUA SCRANTON & SAM'L. BECKWORTH - 1816 - 13; 3 - JOHN SMITH - 1815 - 13; 4 - JAMES CONLY - 1817 - 13; 4 JOSEPH RICHARDSON - 1817 - 13; 5 - JAMES DONNSY JR 1818 - 13; 5 - AMOS DONNER - 1818 - 13; 5 - DANIEL McLASKEY - 1818- 13; 5 - SAMUEL RECCORDS - 1818 - 13; 6 - HUBBARD JONES - 1815- 14; 6 - ROBERT LYONS - 1816

DEARBORN COUNTY: Original Land Entries Tract Book
FORMAT: Section - Purchaser - year - page;

Township 3, Range 2W continued

7 - ABRAHAM JOHNSON - 1817- 14: 8 - JOHN DOWNEY -1818 8 - RICHARD DOWNEY - 1818- 14; 9 - JOHN HAMILTON-1818 14; 9 - JOHN McKANE - 1816 - 14; 10 - MOSES. DANIEL & PHILIP P. TAPLEY - 1815 - 14; 10 - EZRA LAMBKIN 1816 - 14; 10 - ELIJAH THATCHER - 1816 - 14: 11 - WM. FISK - 1817- 14; 11 - MARTIN SCRANTON - 1817 - 14: 11 EZRA WEBB - 1817 - 14; 12 & 13 - JOHN EMBREE & E. HEPBURN - 1818 - 15; 12 - JAMES WOODS - 1816 - 15: 13 GEORGE NEWTON - 1814 - 15; 13 - PRINCE ATHERN - 1814 15; 13 - BENJAMIN DUBOIS - 1816 - 15; 14 - JOHN KEMP 1817 - 15; 14 - JULIUS JAMES - 1817 - 15; 17 - L. WELLER - 1818- 16; 17 - JAMES M. HILL - 1818 - 16; 18 - ETHAN A. BROWN - 1818 - 16; 19 - JACOB DENNIS 1817 - 16; 19 - CORNELIUS CULP - 1817 - 16: 19 & 20 JOHN GIBBS - 1817 - 16; 20 - CATHERINE HEDGER - 1818 16; 20 - N. LONGWORTH & MOSES BROOKS - 1818 - 16; 21 WM. BRINDLE & JAS. MURRY - 1817 - 16; 21 - CYRUS CUTTER & S. STEWART - 1817 - 16; 21 - ROBERT GILLESPIE 1819 - 16; 22 - JOSEPH ROSS - 1818 - 16; 22 - JOSEPH GULICK - 1817 - 16; 22 - ROBERT BOVARD - 1817- 16; 22 JACOB MYERS - 1816- 16; 23 - JOHN THOMPSON - 1815- 17 23 - GARRET LAREW - 1815 - 17; 23 - BENJAMIN LAREW 1815 - 17; 24 - JOHN DEWITT - 1814 - 17; 24 - JACOB LIGHT - 1815 - 17; 24 - ROBERT RICKETTS - 1813 - 17.

Township 4, Range 2W

1 - IRY WRIGHT - 1812 - 17; 1 - DANIEL HUFFMAN - 1813 17; 1 - JOSEPH E. MILBURN - 1813- 17; 1 - JACOB MOORE 1813 - 17; 2 - JAMES LINDSEY - 1812- 17; 2 - STEPHEN PETERS - 1811 - 17; 2 - JAMES WALKER - 1811 - 17: 2 JAMES BUFFINGTON - 1811 - 17; 3 - JAHIEL BUFFINGTON 1815 - 17; 3 - GEORGE ROSS LINDSAY - 1813 - 17: 3 VINCENT LINDLY & HENRY PETERS - 1813 - 17; 3 - JOHN WHEELER - 1817 - 17; 4 - CLABORNE & IRA ALLEN - 1817 17; 4 - JOHN BUFFINGTON - 1813 - 17; 4 - JOHN LEWIS 1815 - 17; 5 - SAMUEL WHEELER - 1817 - 17; 5 - JOHN WHEELER - 1816- 17; 6 - HENRY VAN MIDDLESWORTH - 1820 17; 7 - JOHN & DUNHAM DAVIS - 1818 - 18; 7 - JAMES B. JONES - 1817 - 18; 7 - SAMUEL N. ENT - 1818 - 18; 8 DAVID McKETTRICK - 1813 - 18; 8 - JAMES HUBBART 1818 - 18; 8 - GARRET SWALLOW - 1817 - 18; 9 - JAHIEL BUFFINGTON - 1814 - 18; 9 - JOHN WALKER - 1813 - 18; 9 - JAMES PRITCHARD - 1813 - 18; 9 - CALEB MULFORD 1815 - 18; 10 - JOHN LIVINGSTON - 1806 - 18: 10 JOHN WALKER - 1815 - 18; 10 - JOHN HUBBART SR - 1811 18; 10 - RALPH SMITH - 1812 - 18; 11 - HENRY CLOUD 1803 - 18; 11 - MICHAEL HOMER- 1805 - 18; 11 - ROBERT McKITTRICK - 1813- 18; 12- GEORGE GROVE - 1815-18; 12 - ABRAHAM CARBAUGH - 1813 - 18; 12 - DANIEL CONAWAY

DEARBORN COUNTY: Original Land Entries Tract Book
FORMAT: Section - Purchaser - year - page;

Township 4, Range 2W continued

- 1815 - 18; 12 - ROBERT McKITTRICK - 1815 - 18; 13 - PETER ALLEN - 1811 - 18; 13 - JOHN BROWNSON 1803- 18; 14 - DANIEL CONAWAY - 1812 - 18; 14 -GEORGE NICHALS - 1814 - 18; 15 - DAVID BOWERS - 1815 - 18; 15 - SAMUEL C. VANCE, assignee of ROMULUS RIGGS, as'ee of MOSES JEWITT, as'ee of GEORGE HIATTA, private in Canadien Volunteers - 1817 - 18; 15 - DANIEL LYNN - 1813 - 18; 15 - DANIEL CRUME - 1818 - 18; 17 GARRET SWALLOW - 1817 - 19; 17 - EZEKIEL PRITCHARD 1818 - 19; 18 - WM. ABBOTT - 1817 - 19; 18 - SAM'L. FRAZIER - 1817 - 19; 18 - JESSE VANDOLAR - 1818 - 19; 19 - HENRY BRITTON - 1818 - 19; 19 - JOHN W. NIXON 1818 - 19; 19 - ELIJAH THATCHER - 1818- 19; 20 - DANIEL CRUME - 1817 - 19; 20 - GUILFORD & TODD - 1819 19; 21 - BENJAMIN WILSON - 1819 - 19; 21 - TETRICK FALL - 1812 - 19; 21 - DANIEL CRUME - 1810 - 19; 22 HENRY CLOUD - 1812 - 19; 22 - WM. SPERRY or SPENCER 1812 - 19; 22 - WM. BLUE - 1811 - 20; 22 - JOHN JAMES 1818- 20; 23 - BENJAMIN WILSON - 1804 - 20; 23 - JOHN WALKER - 1811 - 20; 23 - JOHN BROWNSON - 1803 - 20; 24 - ISAAC CARLTON - 1814 - 20; 24 - JOHN & JAMES WALKER - 1811 - 20; 24 - JAMES ALLEN - 1816 - 20; 24 HENRY ANDERSON - 1814- 20; 25 - JOSEPH OGLEIVE - 1815 25 & 28 - JOHN WALKER - 1815 - 20; 25 - JOHN DAVIS 1813 - 20; 26 & 27 - JOHN WALKER - 1814 - 20; 26 THOMAS K. COLES - 1817 - 20; 26 - JOHN & JAMES WALKER 1814 -20; 27 - WM. BLUE - 1815 - 20; 27 - DAVID BLUE 1812 - 20; 28 - JOSEPH H. COBURN - 1819 - 20; 28 JOHN JAMES - 1808 - 20; 29 - WM. WEATHERS - 1812 -20; 29 - EBENEZER HERBERT - 1815 - 20; 29 - DANIEL CRUME 29 - ROBERT CONWAY - 1811 - 20; 30 - RICHARD SMITH 1819 - 20; 30 - ELIJAH THATCHER - 1818 - 20; 30 HAMILTON & JONES - 1806 - 20; 31 - THOMAS PURCELL 1806 - 20; 31 - DICKEY BERKSHIRE - 1804 - 20; 31 JOHN CLEMENTS - 1817 - 20; 32 - ROBERT CONAWAY - 1813 21; 32 - JOSEPH FRAKES - 1815 - 21; 33 - JOHN GLASS 1818 - 21; 33 - JAMES CONAWAY - 1816 - 21; 33 - WM. BABBS - 1818 - 21; 33 - WM. GIBSON - 1818 - 21; 33 OTIS ELLIS - 1818- 21; 34 - JACOB MILLER - 1817 - 21; 34 - JOSEPH WOODS - 1816 - 21; 34 - JAMES GARDNER 1815 - 21; 34 - EBENEZER HERBERT - 1814 - 21; 35 JOHN WALKER - 1816 - 21; 35 - JAMES CRANE - 1814- 21; 35 - JOHN ESPY - 1814- 21; 35 - HUGH ESPY - 1817- 21; 36 - WM. ALEXANDER - 1814 - 21; 36 - WM. SCRANTON 1814 - 21; 36 - JOHN BARRICKLOW - 1814 - 21; 36 BENJAMIN MILES - 1814 - 21.

Township 5, Range 2W

1 - ICHABOD PALMERTON - 1814 - 22; 1 - ELIJAH PITTS

DEARBORN COUNTY: Original Land Entries Tract Book
FORMAT: Section - Purchaser - year - page;

Township 5, Range 2W continued

1812- 22; 1 - AMES BRUCE - 1813 - 22; 1 - DAVID BLANE 1809 - 22; 2 - JAMES VAUGHN - 1813 - 22; 2 - JOHN FERRIS - 1814 - 22; 2 - ROBERT McCRACKEN - 1818 - 22; 2 - RALPH HATCH - 1818- 22; 3 - JOHN STEPHENSON -1816 22; 3 - ZEBULON DICKINSON - 1817 - 22; 3 - BENJAMIN & JOHN TIBBETS - 1817- 22; 4 - DAVID TIBBETS - 1817- 22 4 -MOSES BECKFORD - 1818- 22; 5 - JOHN TIBBETTS- 1818 22; 5 - JOHN ODELL - 1818 - 22; 6 - JAMES MILLS JR 1818 - 22; 7 - JOHN DARKIELL - 1818 - 23; 8 - HUGH McMULLEN - 1818 - 23; 8 - GEORGE STEPHENSON - 1818 23; 8 - JOHN R. ARNOLD - 1818- 23; 9 - ROBERT MILBURN 1815 - 23; 9 - WATKIN R. WATKINS - 1818 - 23; 10 DAVID JOHNSTON - 1818 - 23; 10 - DANIEL PATE - 1816 23; 10 - JOHN JOHNSTON - 1814 - 23; 11 - ANDREW COOK 12815 - 23; 11 - OLIVER HEUSTIS - 1818- 23; 11- JAMES INCE & GEORGE MANTLE - 1818 - 23; 11 - THOMAS KYLE 1817 - 23; 12 - HENRY DILS - 1817 - 23; 12 - JAMES LEESON - 1818 - 23; 12 - WM. FORBES - 1817 - 23; 12 DAVID HOGAN - 1818 - 23; 13 - THOMAS LANNER - 1817 23; 13 - JAMES MORGAN - 1816 - 23; 13 - MICHAEL MOR-GAN - 1816 - 23; 14 - WM. LEWIS - 1818 - 23; 14 JOSEPH McKINNY - 1815 - 23; 14 - LAMBKIN McKINNEY 181 - 23; 14 - DAVID G. BOARDMAN - 1814 - 23; 15 SAMUEL C. VANCE, assignee of R. RIGGS, as'ee of MOSES JEWITT, as'ee of ANTHONEY BENOIT, private in Canadien Volunteers - 1819 - 24; 15 - ROBERT MILBURN - 1815 - 24; 17 - DAVID OSBORN - 1816 - 24; 17 - STEPHEN INMAN 1816 - 24; 18, 19 & 20 - CHRISTIAN HEARSHEY/ HARSHLY/ HERSHEY - 1816 - 24; 18 - JOHN H. MUSGRAVE - 1817 24; 18 - JONATHAN VAIL - 1817 - 24; 18 - RILEY TRUITT 1817 - 24; 19 - SAM'L. B. & WINSLOW J. WOOD - 1817 24; 19 - DAVID KERR - 1817 - 24; 20 - THOMAS McINTIRE 1815 - 24; 20 - MOSES MUSGRAVE - 1816 - 24; 21 - SAM-UEL C. VANCE, assignee of ROMULUS RIGGS, as'ee of BENJAMIN W. HOPKINS, as'ee of WM. MARTIN JR, private in the Canadien Volunteers - 1819 - 24; 21 - PETER HENNEGIN - 1819 - 24; 21 - SAMUEL C. VANCE, assignee of ROMULUS RIGGS, as'ee of MOSES JEWITT, as'ee of SAMUEL AUSTIN, private in the Canadien Volunteers 1819 - 24; 22 - SAMUEL TODD - 1819 - 24; 23 - THOMAS C. PORTER - 1816 - 25; 23 - BENJAMIN HUFFMAN - 1809 25; 23 - WM. RECCORD - 1812 - 25; 23 - JAMES & AMOS BRUCE - 1806 - 25; 24 - PRISCILLA HUSTON - 1816 - 25; 24 - DEMAND CROSS - 1816- 25; 24 - JAMES BRUCE - 1811 25; 24 - BENJAMIN POWELL - 1811- 25; 25 - AMOS & D.C. BOARDMAN - 1809 - 25; 26 - JEREMIAH HUNT - 1803 - 25; 27 - HENRY BRUCE - 1817 - 25; 27 - WM. SHANE - 1818 25; 27 - DANIEL ODELL - 1814 - 25; 27 - JAMES MONT-GOMERY - 1815 - 25; 28 - JOHN MONTGOMERY - 1815 - 25; 28 - JAMES REED - 1817 - 25; 28 - SYLVESTER RICHMOND

DEARBORN COUNTY: Original Land Entries Tract Book
FORMAT: Section - Purchaser - year - page;

Township 5, Range 2W continued

1817 - 25; 29 - JNO. & HIRAM KNAPP - 1817 - 25; 30 THEODORE THOMPSON - 1817 - 25; 30 - PHINEAS L. KING 1817 - 25; 31 - CLABORNE ALLEN - 1817 - 25; 31 - WM. & THOMAS ALCOTT - 1817 - 26; 32 - JAMES LINDSAY -1817 26; 32 - JOHN JONES - 1817 - 26; 33 - ISAAC ALLEN 1818 - 26; 33 - JONES JONES - 1816- 26; 34 - JEREMIAH HUNT - 1813 - 26; 35 - WM. CHAMBERLAIN - 1814 - 26; 35 - WM. STRONG & P. HILL - 1813- 26; 35 - ADAM FLACK 1805 - 26; 35 - MICHAEL & WM. FLAKE - 1811 - 26; 36 ROBERT MILBURN - 1813 - 26; 36 - MICHAEL & WM. FLAKE 1812 - 26; 36 - JOHN H. PIATT - 1811 - 26.

Township 6, Range 2W

1 - PAUL BROWNE - 1817 - 27; 1 - CALEB WILLIAMS 1816 - 27; 1 - BENJAMIN SOUTHARD - 1816 - 27; 1 JAMES SKAATS JR - 1817 - 27; 2 - H-LANDS C. VANHOUTAN 1816 - 27; 2 - JAMES ANGENINE - 1817 - 27; 2 - CONRAD ROW/HOW - 1818 - 27; 2 - JOHN DAVISON - 1817 - 27; 3 DAVID PALMER - 1817 - 27; 3 - PETER I. BONTE - 1817 27; 3 - RATLIFF BAGENT - 1815 - 27; 3 - JANE BONTE 1815 - 27; 4 - EDWARD DROYER - 1816 - 27; 4 - PATRICK DIRER - 1818 - 27; 4 - AARON POST - 1818 - 27; 4 SAMUEL McMATH - 1817 - 27; 5 - JAMES ANGERINE - 1817 27; 6 - SAMUEL C. VANCE - 1818 - 27; 6 - SAMUEL R. ALLAIRE - 1817 - 27; 6 - THOMAS SMITH - 1818 - 27; 7 CASPER MICHAEL - 1818 - 27; 7 - CHARLES DAWSON - 1817 27; 7 - BLACKLY SHOEMAKE - 1818- 27; 8 - JOHN BENNETT 1818 - 27; 8 - PHILLIP MICHAEL - 1817 - 27; 9 - JOHN H. PHILLIP -1818 - 27; 9 - HENRY LIKELY - 1817 - 27; 9 - JOHN H. PHILLIPS - 1818 - 27; 10 - DAVID PERINE 1815 - 28; 10 - JOHN COLWELL - 1816 - 28; 10 - JOHN BORET - 1815 - 28; 10 - JOHN MULHOLLEN - 1818 - 28; 11 - WM. SHARP - 1816 - 28; 11 - AARON PAYNE & R.F. JACKSON - 1815 - 28; 11 - CORNELIUS VANHORN - 1817 28; 11 - ROBERT HOW/ROW - 1817 - 28; 12 - ROBERT HUNT 1817 - 28; 12 - RULIF BOGART - 1817 - 28; 12 - SAMUEL C. VANCE - 1817 - 28; 13 - G. MANTLE & JAMES LUCE 1818 - 28; 13 - WM. HARLUT - 1818 - 28; 13 - THOMAS HALL - 1817 - 28; 14 - JACOB NORTON - 1818 - 28; 15 WM. SHEPHERD - 1818 - 28; 15 - WM. SHEPHERD & R. F. KEIGHTLY - 1818 - 28; 17 - DAVID KETCHAM - 1817 - 29; 17 - ISRAEL NOYES - 1817 - 29; 17 - DAVID KETCHAM & GILBERT PLATT - 1817- 29; 18 - SAMUEL C. VANCE - 1817 29; 18 - WM. DAWSON - 1817 - 29; 18 - GILBERT PLATT 1817 - 29; 18 - JARED EVANS - 1816 - 29; 19 - DAN'L MILLER - 1817 - 29; 19 - CHARLES DAWSON - 1816 - 29; 19 - PARS SHERER - 1817- 29; 19 - STEPHEN WOOD - 1817 29; 20 - ISRAEL NOYES - 1817- 29; 20 - DANIEL & JAMES MILLER JR - 1817 - 29; 20 - ANTHONY BRODRICK - 1816

DEARBORN COUNTY: Original Land Entries Tract Book
FORMAT: Section - Purchaser - year - page;

Township 6, Range 2W continued

29; 20 - JOHN KINSELY - 1817 - 29; 21 - ISAAC FERRIS, assignee, Canadien Volunteers - 1819 - 29; 21 PATRICK & ESTHER WALSH - 1819 - 29; 23 - ISAAC FERRIS assignee, Canadien Volunteers - 1819 - 29; 23 - JOHN DAWSON - 1817 - 29; 24 - SAMUEL CUNNINGHAM - 1814 29; 24 - CALEB WHITE & DAVID CUMMINGS - 1814 - 29; 24 SETH DUNBAR - 1818 - 30; 24 - THOMAS HANSELL - 1818 30; 25 - THOM. DARLING - 1816 - 30; 25 & 26 - ABEL TRUE - 1818 - 30; 25 - EZEKIEL HARPER - 1814 - 30; 25 STEPHEN O. BROWN - 1817 - 30; 26 - WM. SHEARIN - 1818 - 30; 26 - JAMES COX - 1818 - 30; 26 - JOSEPH HUNTER & JONATHAN BENNETT - 1817 - 30; 27 - NATHAN PETTIGREW -1818 - 30; 27 - DAVIS WOODWARD -1818 -30; 27 - JOB SYLVESTER - 1818 - 30; 28, 29 & 30 - STEPHEN WOOD- 1817 - 30; 28 - MATTHEW & ALLEN MILCHIM & JOHN CROCHER - 1817 - 30; 28 - JOHN CROCHER & WM. TIBBETT 1817 - 30; 29 - MINERVA SWIFT - 1817 - 30; 29 - PERIN G. NORTHUP - 1815 - 30; 29 -RODERICK MOWE - 1815 -30; 30 - JOHN CUNNINGHAM - 1815 - 30; 30 - JOHN FREELAND 1815 - 30; 31 - DAVID ROBERTS SR - 1818 - 30; 31 WM. BARTON - 1818 - 30; 31 - THOMAS ALLOWAY - 1818 30; 32 - JOSEPH SYLVESTER - 1818 - 30; 32 - ELIJAH RICH -1818 - 30; 33 - SARAH, MARK & ROBERT McCORMICK 1815 - 31; 33 - ABNER TIBBETS - 1814 -31; 33 - ISAIAH FERRIES - 1815 - 31; 34 - WM. B. CHAMBERLAIN - 1817 31; 34 - JAS. or JOS. PLUMMER - 1817 - 31; 34 - JOHN PALMER - 1815 - 31; 34 - ROBERT HUNT - 1815 - 31; 35 LAUREN LAZIERES - 1815 - 31; 35 - GILES BRADBURY 1814 - 31; 35 - JAMES VAUGHN - 1813 - 31; 36 - RILEY ELLIOTT - 1815 - 31; 36 - SAMUEL WRIGHT - 1816 - 31.

Township 7, Range 2W

1 - VALENTINE LAURENCE - 1818 - 31; 2 - VALENTINE LAURENCE - 1817 - 31; 4 - JOHN SHIVELY - 1818 - 32; 5 BENJAMIN BROWN - 1820 - 32; 5 - THOMAS COATES - 1820 32; 7 - ISAAC LAURENCE - 1819 - 32; 7 & 12 - DANIEL LAURENCE - 1818 - 32; 8 & 10 - ISAAC LAURENCE - 1817 32; 9 - THOMAS BOWMAN - 1816 - 32; 9 - PHILLIP MASON 1818 - 32; 9 - JAMES FOSTER - 1818 - 32; 10 - GEORGE LEWIS - 1816 - 32; 10 - WM. LAKE - 1816 - 32; 10 ROBERT DAVIDSON - 1818 - 32; 11 - DARS FREY - 1818 32; 11 - EDWARD JOHNSTON & BASIL GATHER - 1816 - 32; 11 - MARTIN BENNINGER - 1818 - 32; 11 - VALENTINE LAURENCE - 1817 - 32; 12 - WM. ASHLEY - 1819 - 32; 12 DANIEL MASON - 1819 - 32; 12 - JOHN HALL - 1819 - 32; 13 - JEREMIAH WATKINS - 1815 - 32; 13 - ROBERT McKAGG 1819 - 32; 13 - JAMES POLLOCK - 1817 - 32; 14 - ADAM LEMON - 1818 - 32; 14 - HENRY BEAMER - 1816 - 32; 14

DEARBORN COUNTY: Original Land Entries Tract Book
FORMAT: Section - Purchaser - year - page;

Township 7, Range 2W continued

JOSEPH ADAM - 1816 - 32; 14 - NATHAN BLODGET - 1818 32; 15 - SAMUEL C. VANCE, assignee, Canadien Volunteers - 1819 - 32; 15 - GEORGE MASON - 1819 33; 17 - VALENTINE LAURENCE - 1818 - 34; 17 - ISAAC LAURENCE - 1817 - 34; 17 - ISAAC LAURENCE - 1819 34; 19 - ROBERT TERRY - 1818 - 34; 20 - VALENTINE LAURENCE - 1817 - 34; 20 - JOSEPH GOTSTEIN - 1819 34; 20 - WM. LEEPES - 1817 - 34; 20 - JOHN GREENER 1818 - 34; 21 - GEORGE MASON - 1819 - 34; 23 - JAMES COLWELL - 1816 - 35; 23 - JONATHAN LEWIS - 1817 - 35; 23 - JAMES EDWELL - 1816 - 35; 24 - THOS. DANBY 1815 - 35; 24 - JOEL DECKER - 1816 - 35; 24 - JOHN GELSO - 1814 - 35; 24 - JOEL DOCKER - 1816 - 35; 25 WM. CLOUD - 1816 - 35; 25 - HENRY KINZIE - 1816 - 35; 25 - JOSEPH ADAM - 1816 - 35; 26 - CALEB JOHNSTON 1816 - 35; 26 - JONATHAN YOUNG - 1818 - 35; 26 JAMES COLWELL - 1816 - 35; 27 - ANDREW B. ALLAIRE 1818 - 35; 27 - HALLARNIES C. VANHOUTEN - 1816 - 35; 28 - ADAM MILLER - 1817 - 35; 29 - WM. McCLURE - 1817 35; 29 - JOHN U. GEISSER - 1817 - 35; 29 - JOHN McCLUR - 1817 - 35; 29 - JOHN M. ENGLE - 1817 - 35; 30 - ABRAHAM BALINGS - 1817 - 35; pages 36, 37 missing from book, may have recorded rest of township

Township 4, Range 3W

11 & 12 - JESSE EMBREE & EDWARD HEPBURN - 1818 - 38; 11 - WM. WOOLEY - 1819 - 38; 12 - HENRY L. WILMER 1819 - 38; 13 - H.L. MANGORUM & H.Y.L. WILMER - 1819 38; 13 - RICHARD FOLSOM - 1815 - 38; 14 - WM. BARR & EDWARD HEPBURN - 1818 - 38; 20 - SAMUEL ASTON - 1818 39; 20 - JOHN SHERLOCK - 1819 - 39.   pages 40, 41 missing from book; may have recorded rest of township

Township 5, Range 3W

17 & 23 - JOHN FLEMING - 1818 - 42; 20 - FELIX BRANDT 1818 - 42; 22 - JOHN RUTHOPE - 1818 - 42; 23 - JACOB SPANGLER - 1818- 42; 23 - HENRY SPANGLER - 1818 - 42; 23 - DAVID WILLIAMSON - 1818 - 42; 24 - HENRY SMITH 1818 - 43;   24 - NEMIAH MOREHOUSE - 1818 - 43; 24 ELIJAH THATCHER - 1818 - 43; 25 - GENENT & R.A. HUSTON - 1818 - 43; 25 - BENJ. PURCELL - 1813 - 43; 25 - GENENT & ROBERT HUSTON - 1818 - 43; 26 - J. EMBREE & E. HEPBURN - 1818 - 43; 27 - NATHANIEL WRIGHT 43; 27 - ABEL JOHNSON - 1818 - 43; 28 - JOHN WATTS 1818 - 43; 28 - DANIEL KELSEY & G. PATE - 1817 - 43; 28 - MARTHA LEMON - 1817 - 43; 29 - JNO. & THOMAS WATTS - 1818 - 43; 32 - ROBERT RAY - 1816 - 43; 33 JOHN & SAMUEL COLE - 1817 - 43; 33 - FELIX BRANDT

DEARBORN COUNTY: Original Land Entries Tract Book
FORMAT: Section - Purchaser - year - page;

Township 5, Range 3W continued

1818 - 44; 34 - EZRA CLAWSON/ LAWSON - 1818 - 44; 34 JACOB FROMAN & GEO. ZINN - 1816 - 44; 34 - LAURENCE PURCELL - 1817 - 44; 36 - BENJAMIN PURCELL - 1818 44; 36 - JOHN DOUGHERTY - 1815 - 44; 36 - SOLOMON STEPHENS -1812 - 44.

Township 6, Range 3W

1 & 12 - AMES BRUCE - 1817 - 45; 1 & 2 - STEPHEN WOOD 1817 - 45; 1 - BENJAMIN JOHNSON - 1817 - 45; 2 ELISHA HANCOCK - 1818 - 45; 2 - GILBERT L. GIVAN 1818 - 45; 2 - NANCY DAINS - 1818 - 45; 3 - JOHN DASHIELL - 1818 - 45; 3 - DAVID MEDSKER - 1816 - 45; 4 - JESSE B. LORD & LEMUEL MOSS - 1817 - 45; 9 EBENEZER OLMSTED - 1818 - 45; 10 - CHARLES DASHIELL 1817 - 45; 10 - JAMES KNIGHT & JOHN INMAN - 1817 45; 10 - JOHN LEGGET & MOSES MUSGRAVE - 1818 - 45; 10 JAMES ANDERSON & MARTIN JUSTUS - 1818 - 45; 11 - JOHN BRUMLLEY - 1817 - 45; 11 - RILEY TRUITT - 1817 - 45; 11 - SPENCER DAVIS - 1818 - 45; 12 - WM. HANCOCKE 1818 - 45; 12 & 13 - JONATHAN VAIL - 1817 - 45; 12 THOMAS LAMBERTON - 1817 - 45; 13 - ADAM FLAKE - 1817 45; 13 - JOSEPH CHURCHILL JR - 1817 - 45; 14 - SPENCER DAVIS - 1817 - 45; 14 - JOHN CHANCE - 1818 - 46; 15 - SAM'L B. & WINSLOW WOOD - 1817 - 46; 15 - RANNA C. STEVENS - 1818 - 46; 15 - ROBERT GLASS -1818 - 46; 21 - SAMUEL C. VANCE - 1818 - 46; 22 - JAMES S. HOGSHEARE - 1818 - 46; 22 - THOMAS LAMBERTSON - 1818 -46; 22 - ARNOLD BURTCH - 1818 -46; 23 - THOMAS LAMBERTSON 1818 - 46; 23 - JOSH McKNIGHT - 1818 - 46; 23 - ASA GLOYD - 1818 - 46; 23 - DAVID BROWN - 1818 - 46; 23 ELIAHIM JONES - 1818 - 46; 24 - JAMES SNIDER - 1818 46; 24- JAMES SNIDER - 1818 - 46; 24 - JAMES S. HOGSHEAR - 1818 - 46; 25 - LEVINUS KING - 1817 - 46; 25 STEPHEN BURNES - 1817 - 46; 25 - THEODORUS THOMPSON 1817 - 47; 25 - GEORGE HAMES - 1817 - 46; 27 - PETER HAMARCH - 1818 - 47; 26 - EBENEZER H. PIERSON - 1818 47; 26 - MARY FAULKRIDGE - 1820 - 47; 26 - ISAAC L. JOHNSTON - 1819 - 47; 27 - JOSEPH LEE - 1818 - 47; 27 - PETER NEWCOMER - 1818 - 47; 27 - JOHN SNYDER 1818 - 47; 27 - WM. TURNER - 1819 - 47; 28 - JESSE HUNT & THOMAS STILLMAN - 1818 - 47; 33 - MARK BAKER 1818 - 47; 34 - DAVID MEDSKER - 1817 - 47; 34 JAMES HAYS - 1817 - 47; 35 - SIDNEY ROBINSON - 1817 47; 35 - ADAM D. LIVINGSTON - 1817 - 47; 36 CLAIBORNE ALLEN - 1817 - 47; 36 - SAMUEL MARSHALL 1820 - 47; 36 - JOHN SUTHERLAND & JAS. RAMSEY - 1817 47.

DEARBORN COUNTY: Original Land Entries Tract Book
FORMAT: Section - Purchaser - year - page;

Township 7, Range 3W

1 - SAMUEL C. VANCE - 1818 - 48; 1 - MICHAEL EHLER 1818 - 48; 2 - JACOB MENDEL - 1816 - 48; 2 - ENOCH CONGER - 1818 - 48; 2 - ZACARIAH C. CONGER - 1816 48; 3 - JOHN WILKINSON - 1816 - 48; 10 - WM. HAMILTON 1814 - 48; 11 - JOSEPH STATELER - 1817 - 48; 11 PHINEAS HILL - 1816 - 48; 11 - JAMES BABCOCK - 1818 48; 11 - CYRUS MILLS - 1816 - 48; 12 - JARED MICHAEL 1818 - 48; 12 - EBENEZER WESTCOTT - 1818 - 48; 12 BLACKLY SHOEMAKER - 1818 - 48; 12 - AMOS MORRIS JR 1818 - 48; 13 - SAMUEL C. VANCE - 1817 - 48; 13 FREDERICK SWAIN - 1817 - 48; 13 - JOHN STEPHENSON 1818 - 48; 13 - JESSE STONE - 1816 - 48; 14 - DAVID CONGAR - 1818 - 48; 14 - JACOB STETLER - 1816 - 48; 22 - JAS. FERRIS & JNO. FREELAND - 1818 - 48; 23 BERY BEACH SR - 1819 - 48; 23 - JOHN DOTY - 1818 48; 23 - PAUL HUESTON & J. ANDREW - 1818 - 48; 23 DANIEL HATHAWAY - 1818 - 49; 24 - GEORGE STEPHENSON 1818 - 49; 24 - J. EMBREE & E. HEPBURN - 1818 - 49; 25 - STEPHEN WOOD - 1817 - 49; 25 - SOPHIA FAGELY 1818 - 49; 25 - GODFREY SNOW - 1817 - 49; 26 - MICH. MILLER & JOHN G. HORNEY - 1818 - 49; 26 - JOHN FINCH & JONATHAN FINCH - 1817 - 49; 33 & 34 - LEMUEL MOSS 1817 - 49; 35 - JOHN R. ROUND - 1819 - 49; 36 DAVID G. BOARDMAN - 1817 - 48; 36 - STEPHEN J. PAIN 1817 - 49; 36 - ROBERT McCRACKEN - 1818 - 49.

Township 8, Range 3W

23 - DAVID PETTIGREW - 1818 - 52; 24 & 25 - THOMAS ANDERSON - 1817 - 52; 26 & 27 - DAVID BROWN & GEO. P. TORRENCE - 1817 - 52; 35 - THOMAS EWART - 1817 - 52; 35 - NATHAN LAMBERT - 1817 - 52; 35 - ELI HILL - 1817 52; 36 - SAMUEL Y. ALLAIRE - 1817 - 52; 36 - THOMAS MORGAN - 1817 - 52; 36 - SAMUEL C. VANCE - 1817 - 52.

End of Dearborn Co land entries to & including 1820

FRANKLIN COUNTY

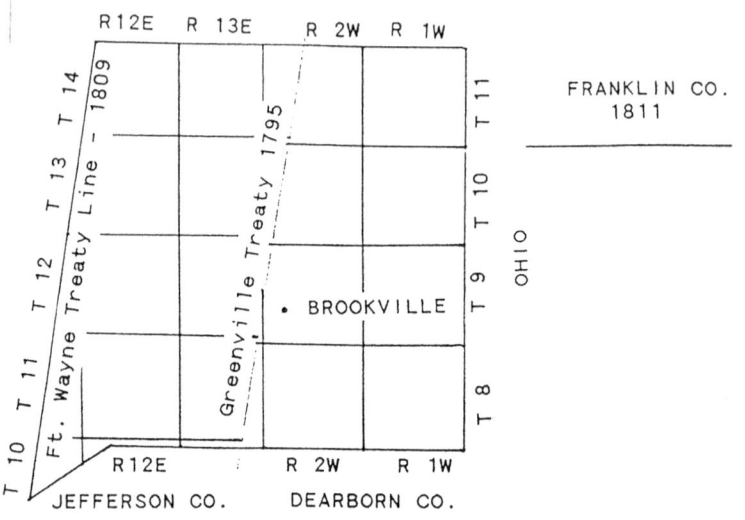

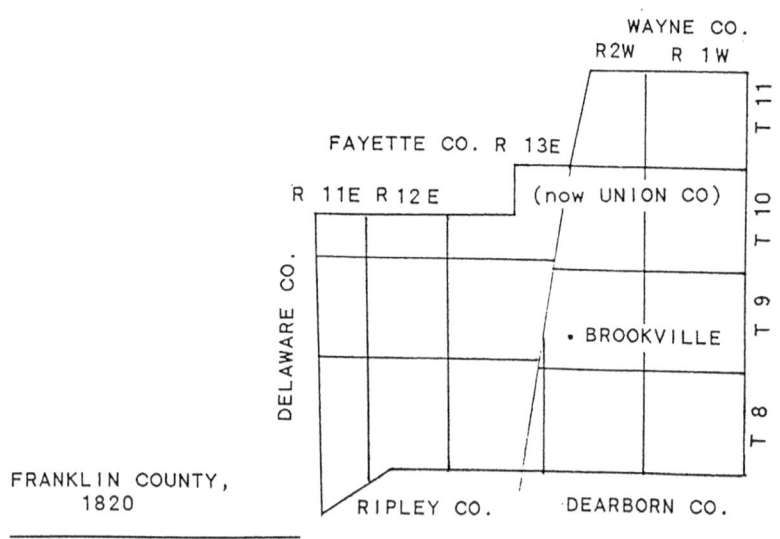

FRANKLIN COUNTY: Original Land Entries
FORMAT: Section - Purchaser - year - page;

Franklin County was one of the first separated from Dearborn. Ranges 1W & 2W mark the original Gore land; the 11E through 13E ranges were added from Indian treaty lands. Brookville, the county seat, became important because of its location on the banks of the Whitewater River and its proximity to Cincinnati, Ohio. As western lands became available for settlement, a land office was opened at Brookville.

Two tract books are available in the Franklin County Recorder's office. The following records are from the taller of the two books, simply labeled Tract Book. The other, Tract Book 1, was organized differently and was in worse condition. Random comparisons of records in the two indicated the material was the same.

Township 10N, Range 11E

3 - NICHOLAS LONGWORTH - 1818 - 1;   10 - N. LONGWORTH & M. BROOKS - 1818 - 1;   27 - JAMES JOHNSON & GEORGE L. MURDOCK - 1820 - 5.

Township 11N, Range 11E

24 - EDMUND ADAMS - 1817 - 9;   25 - THOMAS HINDMAN 1817 - 9;   36 - JOSHUA RICE - 1815 - 10.

Township 12N, Range 11E

10 - CYRUS C. TEVIS - 1820 - 11;   10 - JOHN & SIMEON BARBER - 1820 - 11;   13 - ROBERT DICKERSON - 1815- 12;   15 - ATWELL JACKMAN - 1820 - 12;   15 - WILLIAM WILSON 1820 - 12;   15 - ELIPHALET BARBER - 1820 - 12;   26 - JAMES THOMAS - 1820 - 14.

Township 10N, Range 12E

4 - WILLIAM GEORGE - 1817 - 16;   8 - N. LONGWORTH & G. TAYLOR - 1818 - 18.

Township 11N, Range 12E

4 - ISAAC STIP - 1814 - 20;   4 - WILLIAM HENDERSON 1811 - 20;   4 - ALEXANDER SPEER - 1812 - 20;   8 - JOHN CAMPBELL - 1814 - 21;   9 - ELI ALLEN - 1811 - 21;   9 - ALEXANDER SPEER - 1811 - 21;   17 - DAVID LEWIS - 1814 - 23;   17 - NATHAN LEWIS - 1814 - 23;   17 - JOHN MILLER 1815 - 23;   20 - WM. MARLIN - 1815 - 23;   20 - JACOB BURNET & A. BAILY - 1815- 24;   24 - DAVID NELSON 1814 - 24;   29 - JOHN HAWKINS - 1814 - 25;   29 - JOHN MILLER 1816 - 26;   30 - BARTHOLOMEW FITZPATRICK - 1814 - 26.

FRANKLIN COUNTY: Original Land Entries
FORMAT: Section - Purchaser - year - page;

Township 12N, Range 12E

2 - HUGH MEADE - 1818 - 28; 3 - ARCHIBALD GUTHREN 1811 - 28; 3 - SAMUEL GARRISON - 1811 - 28; 3 - WILLIAM SMITH - 1811- 28; 3 - ELIJAH LEYMPUS - 1811- 28; 4 - SAMUEL GARRISON - 1817 - 28; 4 - THOMAS WILLIAMS 1814 - 28; 5 - CAMP & KELLOGG - 1818 - 28; 5 - THOMAS WILLIAMS - 1817 - 28; 6 - WM. COX - 1817 - 28; 9 28; 9 - WILLIAM MAPLE - 1814 - 29; 9 - EDWARD TONER 1815 - 29; 9 - JAMES AGINS - 1811 - 29; 9 - ROBERT RUSSELL - 1811 - 29; 10 - HORATIO MASON - 1817 - 29; 10 - JNO. ARNOLD - 1816- 29; 10 - JAMES THOMAS - 1813 29; 10 - SPENCER & WILEY - 1814 - 29; 14 - EDWARD BRUSH - 1815 - 30; 14 - WILLIAM RUNDLE - 1815 30; 15 EDWARD BRUSH & H. LOCKWOOD - 1816 - 30; 17 - ENOCH RUSSELL - 1814 - 31; 17 - JOSHUA RICE - 1815 - 31; 19 JOSHUA RICE - 1815 - 31; 19 - ATWELL JACKMAN - 1815 31; 20 - HENRY TEAGARDEN - 1812 - 31; 20 - JAMES C. SMITH - 1813 - 31; 20 - EPHRAIM YOUNG - 1816 - 31; 21 WILLIAM VANMETRE - 1811 - 31; 21 - JAMES McCOY - 1811 31; 21 - JOHN CRIST - 1812 - 31; 21 - HUGH BRISON 1816 - 31; 22 - ALLEN SIMPSON - 1818 - 31; 22 - WILLIAM EVANS - 1816 - 31; 22 - HUGH BRISON - 1811 - 31; 24 - JAMES RUSSELL - 1811 - 32; 24 - JOHN CURRY 1817 - 32; 25 - WILLIAM GORDEN, appointee of THOMAS CURY - 1811 - 32; 25 - WILLIAM GORDEN - 1818 - 32; 26 - ARTEMA D. WOODWORTH - 1811 - 32; 26 - GEORGE WILSON - 1811 - 32; 27 - JOHN FERRIS - 1813 - 32; 27 JOHN CONNOR - 1811 - 32; 27 - JAMES W. BAILY - 1811 32; 27 - GEORGE CRIST - 1811- 32; 28 - MICHAEL MANAN 1811 - 32; 28 - JOHN BRISON - 1812- 32; 28 - STEPHEN BULLOCK - 1814 - 33; 30 - HUGH BRISON - 1817 - 33; 32 JONATHAN WEBB - 1814 - 33; 33 - JOHN FERRIS - 1814 33; 33 - ELI STRINGER - 1811- 34; 33 - JOHN C. HARLEY 1813 - 34; 34 - DAVID MOUNT - 1813 - 34; 34 - JACOB MANAN - 1811 - 34; 34 - JOHN SENOUR - 1813 - 34; 34 - MICHAEL MANAN - 1812 - 34; 35 - WM. FLOOD - 1811 34; 35 - G. ADAMS - 1811- 34; 35 - DAVID MOUNT - 1812 34; 35 - WM. ADAMS - 1814 - 34; 36 - GEO. GUILTNER 1811 - 34; 36 - JNO. REED - 1811- 34; 36 - LARKIN SIMS - 1811 - 34; 36 - DAVID MOUNT - 1811 - 34.

Township 11N, Range 13E

2 - WILLIAM SIMES - 1811 - 38; 3 - WILLIAM BRADLEY 1811 - 38; 3 - JOHN NEAL - 1811 - 38; 3 - JOHN BROWN 1811 - 38; 3 - WILLIAM WILSON - 1811- 38; 4 - HARVEY BROWN - 1811 - 38; 4 - WILLIAM ARNETT - 1811- 38; 4 SIMPSON JONES - 1811 - 38; 4 - WILLIAM WILSON - 1815 38; 5 - ISAAC WILSON - 1811 - 38; 5 - WILLIAM ARNOLD 1811 - 38; 5 - DAVID MOUNT - 1812 - 38; 5 - ELI STRINGER - 1814 - 38; 6 - ALEXANDER MILLER - 1811

FRANKLIN COUNTY: Original Land Entries
FORMAT: Section - Purchaser - year - page;

Township 11N, Range 13E continued

38; 6 - WILLIAM GEORGE - 1812 - 38; 6 - BENJ. SALOR 1812 - 38; 7 - SAMUEL ALLEY - 1812 - 38; 7 - JAMES HOBBS, JR - 1817- 38; 7 - JONATHAN OSBORN - 1813- 38; 9 - WILLIAM WILSON - 1815 - 38; 10 - JOHN STAFFORD 1811 - 39; 10 - HENRY CALFEE - 1811 - 39; 10 - JOHN WELLS - 1814 - 39; 10 - BENJ. SMITH - 1814 - 39; 11 BROWN & MARTIN - 1811 - 39; 14 - AMOS BUTLER - 1817 39; 15 - R. HALSTEAD - 1817- 39; 17 - WM. B. LAUGHLIN 1816 - 39; 18 - DAVID ALLEY - 1812 - 40; 18 - CYRUS ALLEY - 1814 - 40; 18 - JONATHAN ALLEN - 1814 - 40; 19 - JAMES ALLEY - 1812 - 40; 19 - ELISHA CROGEN 1814 - 40; 21 - AARON G. & DAN'L. GANO - 1817 - 40; 21 - ELI STRINGER - 1817 - 40; 21 - WM. C. DREW & S. TODD - 1817 - 40; 21 - J. CARLETON & DAN'L. BROOKS 1818 - 40; 28 - S. H. HUNT & WM. C. DREW - 1817 - 41; 30 - PETER ALLEN - 1814 - 41; 30 - WM. CONN - 1815 41; 30 - CALEB CRAGAN - 1819 - 42.

Township 12N, Range 13E

1 - JOHN BROWN - 1814 - 43; 2 - RICHARD DUNKIN - 1815 43; 2 - JOSEPH GLEEN - 1814 - 43; 2 - DAVID EWING 1813 - 43; 2 - TYLER McWORTEN - 1814 - 43; 3 - SAMUEL STEEL - 1815- 43; 3 - ELIZABETH TEAGARDEN - 1815- 43; 3 - MICHAEL KINGERY - 1814 - 43; 3 - SAM'L. McHENRY 1816 - 43; 4 - JOSIAH ALLEN - 1813 - 43; 4 - SOLOMON SHEPPERD - 1814 - 43; 4 - JOHN ALLEN JR. - 1813 - 43; 4 - ANN (or ARIN) DOUGHERTY - 1814 - 43; 5 - DANIEL TEAGARDEN - 1814 - 43; 5 - JOHN R. BEATTY - 1814- 43; 5 - RHODA CRUMP - 1814 - 43; 6 - SARAH JONES - 1817 43; 6 - R. CATLIN SR. & K. CATLIN JR. - 1808 - 43; 7 - NATHAN YOUNGS - 1818 - 43; 7 - JOSEPH WHITLOCK 1818 - 43; 8 - JOHN RIGGS - 1815 - 43; 8 - CALEB B. CLEMENTS - 1814 - 43; 8 - WILLIAM RICHARDSON - 1815 43; 9 - WM. JONES - 1817 - 44; 9 - JOHN RIGGS - 1815 44; 9 - JOHN FORDICE - 1815 - 44; 9 - JAMES WINDER 1815 - 44; 10 - JAMES WELL - 1814 - 44; 10 - THOMAS SHERWOOD - 1814 - 44; 10 - JOHN PRICE - 1813 - 44; 10 JAMES SHERWOOD - 1814 - 44; 11 - WM. & JAMES HARRY 1814 - 44; 11 - WM. SMITH - 1814 - 44; 11 - CHARLES HARVEY - 1815 - 44; 11 - WM. SKINNER - 1814 - 44; 12 -P. SNOWDEN & PETER DANKIN - 1815 - 44; 14 - SIMON YANDS - 1818 - 44; 14 - MALACHI SWIFT -1817 - 44; 14 EMERY SEATTEN - 1816 - 44; 14 - JOHN DELANEY - 1814 44; 15 - MATTHEW FARRAW & GEO. MILLER - 1814 - 44; 15 ALEXANDER WHITE - 1813 - 44; 15 - J. CURRY & BENJ. NORWELL - 1813- 44; 15 - CHRISTOPHER SWIFT - 1813-44; 17 - JNO. FISHER - 1819 - 45; 17 - RICHARD CLEMENTS 1814 - 45; 17 - RICHARD WILLIAMS - 1814 - 45; 19 JACOB BLACKLIDGE - 1811 - 45; 19 - RALPH WILLIAMS

FRANKLIN COUNTY: Original Land Entries
FORMAT: Section - Purchaser - year - page;

Township 12N, Range 13E continued

1811 - 45; 20 - CALVIN KINSILEY - 1817 - 45; 20 WARREN BURK - 1817 - 45; 21 - HENRY TEAGARDEN - 1813 45; 21 - CALVIN KINSLEY - 1817 - 45; 22 - WILLIAM WILLIAMS - 1816 - 46; 22 - JOS. HUGHELL, JR. - 1814 46; 22 - THOS. SLAUGHTER - 1817 - 45; 22 - WILLIAM HARPER - 1817 - 46; 23 - HENRY PRICE - 1815 - 46; 23 JACOB BLACKLIDGE - 1813 - 46; 23 - THOS. SMITH - 1814 46; 23 - THOS. SLAUGHTER - 1815 - 46; 24 - ISAAC HEWARD - 1816 - 46; 26 - SOLOMON & RICHARD MANWARRING 1812 - 46; 27 - GARRET JONES - 1820 - 46; 27 - ROBERT McKAY - 1816 - 46; 28 - HENRY HINDS - 1817 - 46; 29 SAM'L. GASTON - 1817 - 47; 30 - JONATHAN CHAPMAN 1811 - 47; 31 - JOHN KAYGER - 1812 - 47; 31 - PHILIP RICKE - 1814 - 47; 31 - DAVID MOUNT - 1811 - 47; 31 RICHARD WILLIAMS - 1811 - 47; 32 - HEZEKEAH MOUNT 1811 - 47; 33 - CHAS. COLLETT - 1817 - 47; 33 - THOS. OUSLEY - 1814 - 47; 33 - WM. WILSON - 1811 - 47; 33 DAVID STOOPS - 1811- 47; 34 - ROBERT McKOY -1816- 47; 34 - HENRY TEAGARDEN - 1816 - 47; 34 - THOS. OUSLEY 1812 - 47; 34 - CHAS. COLLETT - 1813 - 47; 35 CORBLY & MARY HENDERSON - 1815 - 47.

Township 8N, Range 1W

1 - JOHN WORLEY - 1814 - 48; 1 - BENJ. ABRAHAM - 1811 48; 1 - JOHN CALDWELL - 1808 - 48; 1 - JOHN ALLEN 1811 - 48; 2 - SILAS WORLEY - 1814 - 48; 2 - JOHN ALLEN - 1811 - 48; 2 - JAMES & JNO. CALDWELL, JR 1812 - 48; 2 - ABRAHAM BLEDSOE - 1806 - 48; 3 - WM. WELL - 1814 - 48; 3 - WILLIAM WILSON - 1813 - 48; 3 WM. BURKE - 1817 - 48; 3 - JAMES STEWART - 1815 - 48; 4 - JOSEPH SIERS - 1814 - 48; 4 - MATHEW SPARKS -1815 48; 4 - WM. LEMMAN - 1818 - 48; 5 - PETER B. MILLS-PAUGH - 1818 - 48; 5 - PRINCE JENKINS - 1814 - 48; 5 JACOB FELTER - 1818- 48; 6 - WM. McDONEL - 1811 - 48; 6 - THOS. MILHOLLAND - 1812 - 48; 6 - PRINCE JENKINS 1814 - 48; 6 - JAMES MILHOLLAND - 1813 - 48; 7 JONATHAN WINN - 1815 - 48; 7 - JOHN WELCH -1814 - 48; 9 - JOSHUA GUILE -1815 - 48; 9 -EBENEZER LEWIS - 1815 48; 9 - MOSES WILEY - 1808 - 48; 10 - MATHEW SPARKS 1814 - 48; 10 - WM. BUSTER - 1813 - 48; 10 - SAMUEL MOORE - 1806 - 48; 10 - WM. SIERS - 1814 - 48; 11 JOSEPH SIERS - 1815 - 48; 11 - WM. B. ALLEN & JOHN S. ALLEN - 1813 - 48; 11 - ALLEN SPEIRS & JNO. WILEY 1811 - 48; 11 - WILLIAM REMY - 1811 - 48; 12 - DAVID & ELI PENWELL - 1812- 48; 12 - JOSEPH WILLIAMS - 1812 48; 12 - JAS. SATER - 1812 - 48; 12 - JNO. CLOUD 1811 - 49; 13 - PHILIP HARWOOD - 1811 - 49; 13 THOMAS McQUEEN - 1811 - 49; 13 - JOHN WOOD - 1814 49; 13 - HENRY REMEY - 1806 - 49; 14 - THOMAS McQUEEN

FRANKLIN COUNTY: Original Land Entries
FORMAT: Section - Purchaser - year - page;

Township 8N, Range 1W continued

1811 - 49; 14 - JAS. & JOSIAH LOWES - 1816 - 49; 14 PETER HANN - 1812- 49; 14 - JAMES FINLEY - 1814 - 49; 15 - ISAAC S. SWEARINGEN - 1815 - 49; 15 - WILLIAM LOWES - 1818 - 49; 15 -JOHN SEELY - 1819 - 49; 17 MANUEL CHAMBERS - 1816 - 50; 17 - DAVID K. ESTE & ANDREW BAILY - 1815 - 50; 17 - GEO. RUDISILL - 1813 50; 18 - JOHN SALOR - 1807 - 50; 18 - WM. HUDSON 1815 - 50; 18 - BENJ. McCARTY & OTHERS - 1806 - 50; 19 - JONATHAN HUNT -1813 - 50; 19 - ELMORE WILLIAM & L. SAYRE - 1809 - 50; 19 - NATHAN PORTER - 1806 50; 19 - ABIJAH HAYS - 1817 -50; 20 - JOSEPH MARMON 1817 - 50; 20 - THOS. CLARK - 1816- 50; 21 - BENJAMIN GEORGE - 1817 - 50; 21 - MICHAEL RUDICEL - 1816 - 50; 22 - ISAAC SWEARINGEN - 1815- 50; 22 - RICHARD HUBBLE 1816 - 51; 23 - JOHN STANSBURY - 1812 - 51; 23 - JOHN LARISON - 1813 - 51; 23 - ISRAEL DAVIES - 1815 - 51; 24 - JAMES REMY - 1814 - 51; 24 - HENRY SATER - 1812 51; 24 - JOS. SUMMERS - 1813 - 51; 24 - WILLIAM RAMEY - 1808 - 51; 25 - MORRIS SEALY - 1814 - 51; 25 JAMES REMY - 1812 - 51; 25 - JOHN HAYS - 1814 - 51; 25 - JAMES GOLD - 1814 - 51; 26 - JAMES REMY - 1814 51; 26 - WM. SMITH & SIMON GULLYS - 1815 - 51; 26 CALEB KESLER - 1814 - 51; 26 - MICHAEL RUDISILL 1817 - 51; 27 - JNO. FOUTCH - 1813 - 51; 27 - LEMUEL SNOW - 1814 - 51; 27 - LEMUEL SNOW, JR. - 1814 - 51; 28 - SAMUEL WELER - 1813 - 51; 28 - JNO. VANBLARICUM 1814 - 51; 28 - LEMUEL SNOW - 1814 - 51; 28 - GEORGE LARISON - 1814 - 51; 29 - JNO. VANBLARICUM - 1811 51; 29 - JOHN ALLEN - 1806 - 51; 29 - ISAAC LEVY 1804 - 51; 30 - JONES & VANBLARICUM - 1810 - 51; 30 JAMES JONES - 1817 - 51; 31 - JOHN H. ROCKAFELLAR 1815- 51; 31 - THOMAS MANWARING - 1816- 52; 31 - JAS. JONES - 1816 - 52; 32 - BENJ. McCARTY - 1803 - 52; 33 - ALEXANDER ABERCROMBIE - 1817 - 52; 33 - J. & WM. WATKINS - 1815 - 52; 33 - NATHAN RICHARDSON - 1814 52; 33 - RALPH WILDRIDGE - 1815 - 52; 34 - HENRY GARNER - 1814 - 52; 34 - BENJ. LEWIS - 1818 - 52; 34 ABNER CONNER - 1814 - 52; 35 - WM. REMY - 1813 - 52; 35 - WM. VANMETRE - 1805 - 52; 35 - ISRAEL DAVIS 1813 - 52; 35 - ISRAEL DAVIS & FREDERICK SHOLTS 1813 - 52; 36 - ANDREW BAILY - 1814- 52; 36 - WILLIAM LEWIS - 1815 - 52; 36 - ROBERT M. SEELY - 1814 - 52.

Township 9N, Range 1W

1 - SAM'L. BROWN & BENJ. CROCKER - 1814 -53; 1 - EZRA L. BOUM - 1818 - 53; 1 - MATHEW SMITH JR - 1813 - 53; 1 - WM. FERGUSON - 1814 - 53; 2 - JEREMIAH ABBOTT 1814 - 53; 2 - CHARLES BUSCH - 1812 - 53; 2 - THOMAS CRASEN - 1813 - 53; 2 - ALEXANDER TELFORD - 1812- 53;

FRANKLIN COUNTY: Original Land Entries
FORMAT: Section - Purchaser - year - page;

Township 9N, Range 1W continued

3 - HENRY BUGET - 1812 - 53; 3 - JAMES TERRILL - 1811 53; 3 - STEPHEN GARDNER - 1811 - 53; 3 - JAMES McCAW 1811 - 53; 4 - LEMUEL LEMON - 1812 - 53; 4 - WILLIAM P. SWETT - 1814 - 53; 4 - DANIEL T. CURRIE - 1811 53; 4 - GIDEON WILKINSON - 1811 - 53; 5 - JNO. SMITH 1815 - 53; 5 - WM. NELSON - 1813- 53; 5 - JAMES WOOD 1813 - 53; 5 - ADAM REED - 1810 - 53; 6 - WALTER TUCKER - 1814 - 53; 6 - JOHN WANDERLICK - 1814 - 53; 6 & 7 - DANIEL REED - 1810 - 53; 7 - WILLIAM HETDRICK 1814- 53; 7 - WILLIAM & ABRAHAM HETDRICK - 1812 - 53; 7 - JOAB HOWELL - 1814- 53; 8 - JONATHAN STOUT -1813 53; 8 - ADAM MOSE - 1813 - 53; 8 - ENOCH D. JOHN 1814 - 53; 8 - THOS. OSBORN - 1812 - 53; 9 - PHILIP JONES - 1811 - 53; 9 - GIDEON WILKINSON - 1811- 53; 9 - WM. ARMSTRONG - 1812 - 53; 10 - CORNELIUS VILEY 1811 - 53; 10 - RICHARD COLIVER - 1812 - 53; 10 SAM'L. McCRAY - 1811 - 53; 10 - JOHN MILNER - 1812 53; 11 - ADAM CARSON - 1812 - 54; 11 - ALEXANDER TELFORD - 1815 - 54; 11 - BRYSON BLACKLAN -1813 - 54; 12 - CHARLES CONE - 1813 - 54; 12 - JAMES POST - 1817 54; 13 - LEWIS BOND - 1814 - 54; 13 - MARY DENNY 1814 - 54; 13 - GEORGE TODD & JAS. McNUTT - 1812- 54; 13 - ANDREW SHIRK - 1808 - 54; 14 - MOSES RARDEN 1812 - 54; 14 - THOS. SELDRIDGE - 1812 - 54; 14 MOSES REARDON - 1810 - 54; 14 - WM. ARDERY - 1811 54; 15 - ELIJAH ATHERTON - 1813 - 54; 15 - ENOCH BUCKINGHAM - 1815 - 54; 15 - PETER & ELIJAH UPDIKE 1817 - 54; 15 - SAM'L. F. & JESSE HUNT - 1817 - 54; 17 - ROBERT JOHN - 1814 -54; 17 - ANDREW SHIRK -1812 55; 17 -LEWIS BOND - 1814 - 55; 18 - RICHARD KOLB 1809 - 55; 18 - ABRAHAM TIMBERMAN - 1813 - 55; 18 WALTER TUCKER - 1812 - 55; 18 - JOHN & CHRISTOPHER STROUBE - 1813 - 55; 19 - JAMES GOUDIE - 1814 - 55; 19 - P. S. SYMMES - 1814 - 55; 19 - WILLIAM CLARK & STEPHEN GREGG - 1813 - 55; 19 - WM. McDONALD - 1811 55; 20 - RICHARD COCKEY - 1814 - 55; 20 - JOHN CARSON 1814- 55; 20 - ENOCH D. JOHN - 1814 - 55; 20 - THOMAS GREGG - 1812 - 55; 21 - GEORGE RALB (or KALB) - 1816 55; 21 - ENOCH BUCKINGHAM - 1815 - 55; 22 - ANDREW SHIRK JR - 1813 - 55; 22 -ROBERT LUSE - 1814 - 55; 22 STEPHEN CRAIG - 1817 - 55; 22 - C. SIMONSON - 1817 55; 23 - JAMES REES - 1813 - 55; 23 - WILLIAM ARDERY 1811 - 55; 23 - EDWARD WHITE - 1807 - 55; 23 - JOSEPH CILLEY - 1812 - 55; 24 - JOSIAH BEALL - 1811 - 55; 24 PHILIP WILKINS - 1809 - 55; 24 - THOS. MORGAN - 1807 55; 24 - SAM'L. HAMILTON - 1809 - 55; 25 - ISAAC WOOD 1812 - 55; 25 - JOHN McGUIRE - 1813 - 55; 25 - BENJ. BLUE - 1807 - 55; 25 - JOHN GOLDTROSS -1814 - 55; 26 ITHAMER WHITE - 1813- 55; 26 - STANHOPE RYSTER - 1812 56; 26 - ROBERT GREY - 1813 - 56; 27 - THOMAS SHAW

FRANKLIN COUNTY: Original Land Entries
FORMAT: Section - Purchaser - year - page;

Township 9N, Range 1W continued

1813 - 56; 27 - AMOS ATHERTON - 1812 - 56; 27 - JACOB FAUSSETT - 1813 - 56; 27 - JOHN RAMEY & ROBERT SCANTLAND - 1804 - 56; 28 - SAM'L. STEWART - 1816 56; 28 - ISAAC WAMELY - 1813 - 56; 28 - JOHN RAMEY 1804 - 56; 28 - JAMES HEATH - 1806 - 56; 29 - ABNER LEONARD - 1813 - 56; 29 - DENNIS DUSKY - 1807 - 56; 29 - STEPHEN DAVIS - 1815 - 56; 29 - BENJ. HINDS 1813 - 56; 30 - RICHARD KEENE - 1814- 56; 30 - JOSEPH L. CARSON - 1813 - 56; 30 - ARCHIBALD TALBOTT - 1814 56; 30 - JOHN HOLLIDAY - 1814 - 56; 31 - WM. SEAL 1813 - 56; 31 - GEORGE WALLACE - 1816 - 56; 31 - WM. CLOUD - 1806 - 56; 31 - JAMES SEAL - 1813 - 56; 32 NIXON OLIVER - 1815 - 56; 32 - JOHN CROWELL - 1807 56; 32 - HENRY R. COMPTON - 1816 - 56; 32 - BENJ. TUCKER - 1817 - 56; 33 - JOHN COULTER & WM. RAIL 1806 - 56; 33 - JOHN CLENDENNING - 1807 - 56; 34 ROBERT FASSETT - 1811 - 56; 34 - JOHN REES - 1813 56; 34 - DAVID McGAUGHEY - 1814 - 56; 34 - ARTHUR HENRIE - 1812 - 56; 35 - CHESTER HOWELL - 1811 - 56; 35 - BENJ. WOOD - 1813 - 56; 35 - ROBERT BLAIR - 1814 56; 35 - JAMES McCORD - 1813 - 56; 36 - SAM'L. DUGANS 1815 - 56; 36 - WM. SNODGRASS - 1813 - 56; 36 - JACOB HIDARGS -1813 - 57; 36 - BENJ. ABRAHAMS -1813 - 57.

Township 10N, Range 1W

19 - FLINT & GARRETT - 1811 - 58; 19 - JONATHAN COPELAND & JAMES BERRY - 1806 - 58; 19 - SAM'L. AYRES 1808 - 58; 19 - MOSES MAXWELL - 1810 - 58; 20 - JAMES DUNN JR. - 1816 - 58; 20 - JOHN FLINT SR.- 1811 - 58; 20 - THOS. REEDER - 1815 - 58; 22 - JACOB BELL - 1814 58; 22 - CHRISTIAN GIRTON - 1814 - 58; 23 - JOSEPH LEE - 1810 - 58; 23 - CHRISTOPHER SMITH - 1812 - 58; 23 - JAMES BASTER - 1809 - 58; 23 - JACOB BELL - 1813 58; 24 - JAMES CROOKS - 1806 - 58; 24- ABRAHAM MILLER 1805 - 58; 24 - DANIEL MILLER - 1805 - 58; 24 DANIEL HANSEL - 1805 - 58; 25 - CHRISTOPHER HANSEL 1805 - 58; 25 - JAMES BASTER - 1811 - 58; 25 - JOHN MOSS - 1811 - 58; 25 - JOHN HARPER - 1809 - 58; 26 THOMAS BUCK - 1806 - 58; 26 - JOSEPH KINGERY - 1815 58; 26 - JAMES BASTER - 1809 - 58; 26 - JOHN MORRIS 1813 - 58; 27 - WM. STEPHENS - 1810 - 58; 27 CHRISTOPHER & GEO. HANSEL - 1813 - 58; 27 - WILLIAM FORBS - 1815 - 58; 27 - JOSHUA HARRIS - 1814 - 59; 28 JOHN ROSS - 1816 - 59; 28 - JOHN SUNDERLAND - 1817 59; 28 - ANDREW ORR & JOHN HATFIELD - 1816 - 59; 29 ROBERT BRISBIN - 1814 - 59; 29 - JOHN CHIRINGTON 1814 - 59; 29 - JOHN FLINT SR - 1813 - 59; 29 - ABEL DARE - 1812 - 59; 30 - CHATFIELD HOWELL - 1806 - 59; 30 - CHAMNICK GELLIGAN & HYRAM CAMPION - 1806- 59; 30

FRANKLIN COUNTY: Original Land Entries
FORMAT: Section - Purchaser - year - page;

Township 10N, Range 1W continued

WILLIAM DUBOIS - 1806 - 59; 31 - ADAM NELSON - 1813 59; 31 - ROBERT PETTYCREW - 1815 - 59; 31 - BENJ. HARGEREDES - 1811 - 59; 31 - JOHN POWERS -1814 - 59; 32 - SAM'L. KAIN - 1813 - 59; 32 - JOHN HOWELL & CHATFIELD HOWELL - 1810 - 59; 32 - ZECHARIAH DAVIS 1814 - 59; 32 - ANDREW CORNELISON - 1810 - 59; 33 JAMES STEPHENS - 1815 - 59; 33 - DAVID JONES - 1815 59; 33 - SAM'L. HUSTON - 1816- 59; 34 - R. ROSS -1816 59; 34 - SAM'L. HUSTON - 1816 - 59; 34 - LEMUEL LEMMAN - 1812 - 59; 34 - WILLIAM GOFF - 1813 - 59; 35 WM. RUFFIN, assignee - 1816 - 59; 35 - LEMUEL LEMMAN 1815 - 59; 35 - EPHRAIM TUCKER - 1816- 59; 35 - ALEXANDER FURGASON - 1814 - 59; 36 - DAVID GRAY - 1810 59; 36 - CHRISTOPHER HANSEL - 1814- 59; 36 - ABRAHAM LEE - 1807 - 59; 36 - ABRAHAM JONES - 1807 - 59.

Township 8N, Range 2W

1 - THOS. MILHOLLAND - 1814 - 60; 1 - WM. H. EADS 1815 - 60 1 - BRITTON GANT - 1811 - 60; 2 - HENRY CASE - 1813 - 60; 2 - SETH GORDWINE - 1805 - 60; 2 JOHN QUICK - 1810 - 60; 3 - JOHN ADAIR - 1805 - 60; 3 - WM. WILSON - 1805- 60; 3 - JOHN MILHOLLAND - 1805 60; 3 - SAM'L. & CHAS. SCOTT - 1805 - 60; 4 - WM. HENDERSON - 1806 - 60; 4 - WM. ARNETT - 1804 - 60; 4 - JAMES McCOY - 1804 - 60; 4 - WILLIAM LYNES -1811 60; 5 - DAVID GAYMAN - 1815 - 60; 5 - THOMAS HENDERSON - 1816- 60; 5 - JOHN HALL & LEWIS DEWEESE - 1814 60; 5 - SOLOMON ALLEN (MORRISON) - 1816- 60; 6 - JOHN HOFFORD - 1813 - 60; 6 - SAMUEL C. VANCE -1817 - 60; 6 - ELLIOTT HERNDON - 1813 - 60; 7 - LYONS, McCORD & MORTEN- 1818 - 61; 7 - NATHANIEL HERNDON - 1814 - 61; 8 - SOLOMON SHEPHERD JR. - 1816 - 61; 8 - DANIEL HOSBROOK - 1816 - 61; 9 - JNO. & JACOB HACKLEMAN 1816 - 61; 9 - ADAM NELSON - 1817 - 61; 9 - JAMES & JOHN ANDREW - 1817 - 61; 9 - RYLEIGH WOODWORTH - 1815 61; 10 - ANTHONY HABERSTATT - 1806 - 61; 10 - SAMUEL CASE - 1813 - 61; 10 - JOHN LEFORGE - 1812 - 61; 10 ZACARIAH COOKSEY - 1817 - 61; 11 -JOHN SHANK - 1812 61; 11 - JOHN FUGET - 1816 - 61; 11 - JOHN CONNOR 1810 - 61; 12 - TIMOTHY & AXSELN (ACSAH? ALEXANDER?) PARKER - 1815 - 61; 12 - WILLIAM JACKMAN - 1814 - 61; 12 - MOSES CONGAR - 1813 - 61; 12 - GEO. SINGHORSE 1813 - 61; 13 - WM. HELM - 1811 61; 13 - JNO. CONNOR 1810 - 61; 13 - THOS. CLARK - 1811 - 61; 13 - JNO. WARD - 1816 - 61; 14 - JNO. CONNOR - 1810 - 62; 14 STEPHEN GOBLE - 1811 - 62; 14 - ALLEN RAMSEY - 1807 62; 17 - DAVID E. WADE - 1817- 63; 17 - JOHN STAFFORD 1818 - 63; 18 - NATHAN HERNDON - 1814 - 63; 18 PETER TRIFOGLE - 1816 - 63; 19 - GEO. W. MATHEWS

FRANKLIN COUNTY: Original Land Entries
FORMAT: Section - Purchaser - year - page;

Township 8N, Range 2W continued

1818 - 63; 20 - NICHOLAS LONGWORTH - 1818 - 63; 22 ROBERT DOUGLASS - 1818 - 64; 23 - JOHN HAYS - 1817 64; 24 - JNO. B. CHAPMAN & J. PRICE - 1817 - 64; 24 JOHN ARYRES - 1817 - 64; 24 - JOHN PAGE - 1817 - 64; 25 - ROBERTSON JONES - 1815 - 64; 25 - WM. KNOWLES 1817 - 64; 25 - CORBLY HUDSON - 1816 - 64; 26 - SION FORTNER - 1817 - 64; 26 - EDWARD CARNEY - 1814 - 64; 26 - WM. FREAD - 1815 - 65; 26 - WM. RAMSEY - 1814 65; 27 - ELI BROOKS - 1816 - 65; 27 - JOHN MERCER 1814 - 65; 27 - SAM'L. PRICE - 1817 - 65; 28 - UZZIAH KENDALL - 1818 - 65; 28 - BRADBURY COTTRELL & JOSEPH McCAFFERTY - 1818 - 65; 29 - WILLIAM STEPHENSON 1818 - 65; 29 - JOB HARRISON - 1818 - 65; 29 - JOHN DAVIS - 1818 - 65; 31 - EDWARD BLACKBURN - 1819 - 65; 32 -REUBEN CLEARWATER - 1817 - 65; 32 - WM. DAVIS 1819 - 66; 33 - NICHOLAS PUMPHREY - 1814 - 66; 34 NICHOLAS PUMPHREY - 1814 - 66; 35 - DANIEL HASTY 1814 - 66; 35 - SAMUEL PRICE & WM. MINTZ - 1817 - 66; 35 - WILLIAM MINTZ - 1817 - 66; 36 - JAMES JONES JR. 1815 - 66; 36 - CORBLY HUDSON - 1818 - 66; 36 - J. L. SPARKS - 1819 - 66.

Township 9N, Range 2W

1 - JOHN WELLS - 1814 - 67; 1 - JAMES STEVENS - 1814 67; 1 - WM. DUBOIS - 1815 - 67; 1 - EZEKIEL & WILLIAM POWERS - 1814 - 67; 2 - ELIAS BALDWIN - 1814 - 67; 2 JACOB STAN - 1814 - 67; 2 - DAVID SMITH - 1814 - 67; 2 - ENOCH BUCKINGHAM - 1815 - 67; 3 - ROBERT GLIDWELL 1813 - 67; 3 - AGNERS TAYLOR - 1806 - 67; 3 - ENOCH BUCKINGHAM - 1815 - 67; 3 - LISMUND BASYNE - 1812 67; 4 - ROBERT TEMPLETON - 1804 - 67; 5 - ROBERT TEMPLETON - 1816 - 67; 5 - PETER GERARD - 1816 - 67; 5 JOHN THARP - 1814 - 67; 5 - WM. H. EADS - 1814 - 67; 6 - ROBERT ARCHIBALD - 1816 - 67; 7 - THOMAS SKINNER 1810 - 67; 8 - LISMOND BASYNE - 1813 - 67; 8 - WM. HENDERSON - 1806 - 67; 8 - JOHN THARP - 1811 - 67; 8 DAVID BELL - 1806 - 67; 9 - JAMES TAYLOR - 1804- 67; 9 - JOHN LOGAN - 1805- 67; 9 - BLAKESLY BARNES - 1815 67; 10 - JACOB BARKMAN - 1811 - 67; 10 - JAMES LOGAN 1818 - 67; 10 - WM. MORRIS & STACY FENTER - 1814- 67; 10 - JACOB CLEARWATER - 1815 - 67; 11 - ENOCH BUCK- INGHAM - 1815- 67; 11 - RICHARD COCKEY - 1814- 67; 11 D. OLIVER - 1817 - 67; 11 - JACOB CRAIG - 1811 - 68; 12 - PETER AMBROSE - 1814- 68; 12 - WM. CROOKS - 1814 68; 12 - DANIEL HAYMOND - 1815 - 68; 13 - JOB STOUT 1815 - 68; 13 - DAVID SMITH - 1814 - 68; 13 - JAMES WALLACE - 1814 - 68; 13 - THOMAS BALDWIN - 1815 - 68; 14 - JOHN ALLEN - 1814 - 68; 14 - JNO. ALLEN & BENJ. McCARTY - 1814 - 68; 14 - ANDREW BAILY - 1814 - 68;

FRANKLIN COUNTY: Original Land Entries
FORMAT: Section - Purchaser - year - page:

Township 9N, Range 2W continued

14 - ALEXANDER CUMMING - 1816 - 68; 15 - BENJ. McCARTY & JNO. ALLEN - 1814 - 68; 15 - JONATHAN McCARTY 1814 - 68; 15 - LEWIS BISHOP - 1816 - 68; 17 - JAMES KNIGHT JR. - 1808 - 68; 17 - WM. BAN & WM. RUFFLINS 1811 - 68; 18 - FIRMAN SMITH - 1814 - 68; 19 - JOHN KENNADAY - 1808 - 68; 19 - JOHN NORRIS - 1808 - 68; 19 - THOMAS WILLIAMS - 1804 - 68; 19 - JOHN VINCENT 1806 - 68; 20 - AMOS BUTLER - 1804 - 68; 21 - WILLIAM BUTLER - 1814 - 68; 21 - BENJ. McCARTY - 1808 - 69; 21 - JOHN STOCKDALE - 1812 - 69; 21 - AMOS BUTLER 1811 - 69; 22 - DAVID WADE - 1816 - 69; 22 - JOHN KELSEY - 1814 - 69; 22 - ANTHONY HALBERSTADT - 1812 69; 23 - DANIEL G. TEMPLETON -1815 - 69; 23 - DAVID GRAHAM - 1815 - 69; 23 - DAVID BLACK - 1814 - 69; 23 CARSON & LOW - 1813- 69; 24 - DAVID HAYS - 1815 - 69; 24 - ABEL WHITE - 1815 - 69; 24 - ENOCH THOMPSON 1815 - 69; 24 - ENOCH BUCKINGHAM - 1815 - 69; 25 ARTHUR HENRIE - 1811 - 69; 25 - ANDREW REED - 1813 69; 25 - JAMES GOUDIE - 1813 - 69; 25 - AMOS BALDWIN & JOSEPH RICHEE - 1814 - 69; 26 - ARCHIBALD TALBOTT 1814 - 69; 26 - P. S. SYMMES - 1814 - 69; 26 - JOHN HEDLEY - 1814 - 69; 27 - ISAAC KINNSY - 1814 - 69; 27 SOLOMON TINER - 1807 - 69; 27 - ISAAC R. FINCH - 1814 69; 27 - DAVID PENWELL - 1811 - 69; 28 - MICAJAH PARKER - 1811 - 69; 28 - JAMES McGINNIS - 1811 - 69; 28 - RUGGLES WINCHELL - 1811 - 69; 28 - JOHN KENNADY 1811 - 69; 29 - JOHN ALLEN - 1805 - 69; 29 - AMOS BUTLER & JESSE B. THOMAS - 1805- 69; 29 - AMOS BUTLER 1806 - 69; 30 - JAMES MOORE - 1808 - 69; 30 - THOS. WILLIAMS - 1811- 69; 30 - JACOB HEDDRICK - 1814 - 69; 30 - JAMES NOBLE - 1814 - 69; 31 - ELI STRINGER 1814 - 69; 31 - THOMAS HENDERSON - 1814 - 70; 31 S.F. HUNT & WM. C. DREW - 1817- 70; 32 - SAMUEL ARNET 1805 - 70; 32 - THOS. HENDERSON - 1805 - 70; 32 JOHN RAMEY - 1804 - 70; 33 - JNO. RICHARDSON - 1811 70; 33 - SOLOMON TYNER - 1804 - 70; 33 - JOHN BROWN 1805 - 70; 33 - WM. TYNER - 1804 - 70; 34 - DAVID CLEARWATER - 1814 - 70; 34 - JNO. PENNWELL - 1808 70; 34 - JNO. COLLINS & WM. McCOY - 1811 - 70; 34 ABRAHAM HACKLEMAN - 1806 - 70; 35 - GEORGE ANTHONY 1811 - 70; 35 - DAVID BRADFORD - 1816 - 70; 35 CHARLES VANCAMP - 1813 - 70; 35 - JNO. COLLINS - 1814 70; 36 - MAY MILHOLLAND - 1814 - 70; 36 - MOSES FINCH 1814 - 70; 36 - ENOCH McCARTY - 1811 - 70.

Township 10N, Range 2W

19 - JNO. FISHER - 1816- 71; 20 - JAMES WATTERS -1814 71; 21 - THOS. OSBORN - 1808 - 71; 21 - ISAAC & BENJ. WILLSON - 1809 - 71; 21 - GEO. JOHNSTON - 1812 - 71;

FRANKLIN COUNTY: Original Land Entries
FORMAT: Section - Purchaser - year - page:

Township 10N, Range 2W continued

21 - HUGH ABERNATHY & WM. RUSING - 1809 - 71; 22 THOS. OSBORN - 1817 - 71; 23 - JOHN REILY -1815 - 71: 23 - DAVID POWERS - 1815- 71; 23 - ROBERT GREEN -1804 71; 23 - VINCENT DAVIS - 1814 - 71; 24- THOMAS WORMAN 1810 - 71; 24 - JOHN FLINT SR -1811 - 71; 24 - ROBERT WHITE - 1811 - 71; 25 - JOHN SMITH - 1812 - 71; 25 RICHARD FREEMAN - 1814 - 71; 25 - JNO. SMITH - 1812 71; 25 - DANIEL OSBORN 1814 - 71; 26 - ISAAC SELLERS 1815 - 71; 26 - JOSHUA BUTLER - 1814 - 71; 26 - ABRAM ROSE - 1814 -71; 26 - ELAM MURRAY - 1814 - 71; 27 DANIEL POWERS - 1814 - 71; 27 - JONATHAN BASSETT 1818 - 71; 27 - ARCHIBALD MORROW - 1811 - 71; 27 HENRY TODD - 1816- 71; 28 - WILLIAM LOGAN -1804 - 71; 28 - ROBERT TEMPLETON - 1804 - 71; 28 - ROBERT HANNA 1804 - 71; 28 - BENJAMIN NUGENT - 1811 - 71; 29 - WM. RUSING - 1814 - 71; 29 - JOEL BELK -1814 - 71; 29 ISAAC BULKLY - 1816 - 71; 29 - THOMAS HENRY - 1813 71; 30 - DAVID ERB - 1816 - 72; 31 - JAMES GORDON 1817 - 72; 32 - ROBERT HANNA & JNO. NUGENT - 1814 72; 32 - THOMAS POWERS - 1815 - 72; 32 - RALPH WILLI-AMS - 1811 - 72; 32 - EMERY NOLLS - 1814 - 72; 33 ROBERT HANNA - 1804 - 72; 33 - OBADIAH ESTES - 1806 72; 34 - WM. H. CHARLOTT & JNO. GILLS - 1812 - 72; 34 - JOHN DICKESON - 1813 - 72; 34 - JOHN HORNADAY 1811 - 72; 34 - ROBERT GLIDEWELL - 1806 - 72; 35 DANIEL POWERS - 1814 - 72; 35 - WM. SIMS - 1813 72; 35 - J. & C. KIGER - 1813 - 72; 35 - WM. HARVEY 1815 - 72; 36 - STEPHEN GARDNER - 1814 - 72; 36 AARON FRAKES - 1814 - 72; 36 - JOHN WATTS - 1814- 72; 36 - JAS. & JOS. STEPHENS - 1812 - 72.

Township 9N, Range 3W

1 - WM. C. DREW & ISAIAH BISBEE - 1817 - 73; 12 ISAAC FULLER - 1815 - 73; 13 - DAVID BROWN & STEPHEN C. VANCE - 1817 - 73; 13 & 24 - BENJ. McCARTY - 1807 75; 24 - BENJ. McCARTY - 1807 - 75: 34 - SAMUEL F. HUNT & WM. C. DREW - 1817 - 75; 34 - LEMUEL JETER NOT DATED - 75.

End of Franklin Co land entries to & including 1820

FRANKLIN COUNTY DEEDS: Book A

Book A is a transcribed copy of the original ledger, no longer available. Pages 1 through 4 are blank, probably indicating the corresponding pages were missing in the original Book A. The first entry on page 5 is incomplete. Throughout the volume, other pages are left blank, most likely to correspond numbering of the hand written and the typed copies.

Witness testimony, incomplete. BENJAMIN McCARTY and WILLIAM HENDERSON witnesses to deed signed by ABRAHAM HACKLEMAN and his wife, PEGGY HACKLEMAN. Note: "this deed unto the within named JACOB SAILOR"; dated 1 Sept, 1810 by ENOCH McCARTY, J.P. rec 1811. p 5

Deed dated 1810. CONRAD SAILOR of Dearborn Co to JACOB SAILOR of same. S 3, T 8, R 2W. Signed CONRAD SAILOR, CATY SAILOR. Witness: WILLIAM HENDERSON, BENJAMIN McCARTY. J. P. note: "and CATY, his wife". rec 1811. pp 5,6 (page 7 blank)

Deed of partition dated 1811. AMOS BUTLER to MICHAEL JONES & JAMES HAMILTON of Dearborn Co. S 29, T 9, R 2W purchased from USA; BUTLER selling interest in part of tract. "joining land of JOHN ALLEN". "MARY, wife of AMOS". Signed AMOS BUTLER, MARY BUTLER. Witness: none. rec 1811. pp 8, (p 9 blank), 10, 11

Deed of partition dated 1811. MICHAEL JONES & JAMES HAMILTON of Dearborn Co. to AMOS BUTLER. JONES & HAMILTON selling part of tract S 29, T 9, R 2W to BUTLER. Signed MICHAEL JONES, J. HAMILTON. Witness: none. rec 1811. pp 12, 13

Deed dated 1811. MICHAEL JONES & JAMES HAMILTON of Dearborn Co. to DAVID GOBLE. Brkv lot 47. Signed MICHAEL JONES, J. HAMILTON. Witness: none. rec 1811. p 14 (p 15 blank)

Deed dated 1811. LEWIS DEWEESE from JAMES McCOY & NANCY, his wife. S 4, T 8, R 2W. "granted (in 1809 by USA) to JACOB HACKLEMAN" transferred to McCOY. Signed JAMES (x) McCOY, NANCY (x) McCOY. Witness: ASHEL CHURCHILL. rec 1811. pp 16, (17 blank), 18

Mortgage dated 1811. ANTHONY WILLIAMS to SAMUEL WILLIAMS of Burbon Co, KY. S 1, T 11, R 1 entered by ANTHONY in 1806. ANTHONY to pay $814 to SAMUEL by 1821 to receive a full conveyance deed from SAMUEL. Signed ANTHONY WILLIAMS, SAMUEL WILLIAMS. Witness: none. rec 1811. pp 18, 19 (pp 20, 21 blank)

Deed dated 1811. BENJAMIN McCARTY of Dearborn Co to

FRANKLIN COUNTY DEEDS: Book A

CONRAD SAILERS, WILLIAM G. EADS & ABRAM HACKLEMAN of same. Two acres in S 3, T 8, R 2W to be used for Little Cedar Grove church. Signed BENJAMIN McCARTY. Witness: WILLIAM HENDERSON, JACOB (x) SAILERS. rec 1811. pp 22, 23

Deed dated 1811. JAMES HAMILTON & MICHAEL JONES to LISMUND BASYE. Brkv lot 30, "adjoining lots laid off by JOHN ALLEN SR." "MARY JONES, his wife". Signed J. HAMILTON, MICHAEL JONES, MARY JONES. Witness: none. rec 1811. pp 23, 24 (p 25 blank)

Deed dated 1811. MICHAEL JONES of Franklin Co & JAMES HAMILTON of Dearborn Co to JEREMIAH CURRY. Brkv lot 77. Signed J. HAMILTON, MICHAEL JONES, MARY JONES Witness: none. rec 1811. pp 26, (27 blank), 28

Deed dated 1811. JAMES HAMILTON & MICHAEL JONES to STEPHEN C. STEPHENS. Three Brkv town lots: 36, 37 & (no number, bounds given). Signed J. HAMILTON, MICHAEL JONES, MARY JONES. Witness: none. rec 1811. p 29 (pp 30, 31 blank)

Deed dated 1811. JAMES HAMILTON & MICHAEL JONES to JAMES WILLSON of Hamilton Co, OH. Brkv lot 17. Signed J. HAMILTON, MICHAEL JONES, MARY JONES. Witness: none. rec 1811. p 32 (p 33 blank)

Deed dated 1811. BENJAMIN McCARTY to JABES WINSHIP. S 3, T 8, R 2. Signed BENJAMIN McCARTY. Witness: JABES WINSHIP, SIMEON WESTFALL. rec 1811. p 34 (p 35 blank)

Deed dated 1811. JAMES HAMILTON & MICHAEL JONES to STEPHEN C. STEPHENS. Brkv lots 44, 45. Signed J. HAMILTON, MICHAEL JONES, MARY JONES. Witness: none. rec 1811. p 36 (pp 37, 38 blank)

Deed dated 1811. JAMES HAMILTON & MICHAEL JONES to JOHN VANBLARICUM. Brkv town lots 18, 19. Signed J. HAMILTON, MICHAEL JONES, MARY JONES. Witness: none. rec 1811. p 39 (pp 40, 41 blank)

Deed dated 1811. JAMES HAMILTON & MICHAEL JONES to SOLOMON MANWARRING. Brkv town lot 3. Signed J. HAMILTON, MICHAEL JONES, MARY JONES. Witness: none. rec 1811. p 42 (p 43 blank)

Deed dated 1811. JAMES HAMILTON & MICHAEL JONES to STEPHEN LUDLOW. Brkv town lot 43. Signed J. HAMILTON, MICHAEL JONES, MARY JONES. Witness: none. rec 1811. p 44 (pp 45, 46 blank)

FRANKLIN COUNTY DEEDS: Book A

Deed dated 1811. JAMES HAMILTON & MICHAEL JONES to DAVID BELL. Brkv town lot 48. Signed J. HAMILTON, MICHAEL JONES, MARY JONES. Witness: none. rec 1811. p 47   (pp 48, 49 blank)

Deed dated 1811. JAMES HAMILTON & MICHAEL JONES to SAMUEL SERING of Warren Co, OH. Brkv lot 42. Signed J. HAMILTON, MICHAEL JONES, MARY JONES. Witness: none. rec 1811. p 50   (p 51 blank)

Deed dated 1811. JAMES HAMILTON & MICHAEL JONES to THOMAS I. KNIGHT. Brkv lot 55. Signed J. HAMILTON, MICHAEL JONES, MARY JONES. Witness: none. rec 1811. pp 52, 53   (p 54 blank)

Deed dated 1811. JAMES HAMILTON & MICHAEL JONES to JOHN WINCHELL. Brkv lot 20. Signed J. HAMILTON, MICHAEL JONES, MARY JONES. Witness: none. rec 1811. pp 55, 56

Deed dated 1811. JOHN ALLEN & SARAH, his wife, of Dearborn Co to RALPH WILDRIDGE. S 32, T 8, R 1W. Signed JOHN ALLEN, SARAH ALLEN. Witness: none. rec 1811. p 57   (pp 58, 59 blank)

Deed dated 1811. JAMES HAMILTON to MICHAEL JONES. Brkv lot 34, 35. Signed J. HAMILTON. Witness: none. rec 1811. p 60   (p 61 blank)

Deed dated 1811. JOHN ALLEN & SARAH, his wife, to JOHN ROCAFELLER. S 32, T 8, R 1W. Signed JOHN ALLEN, SARAH ALLEN. Witness: ROBERT GREEN, ROBERT WICOFF. rec 1811. p 62   (pp 63, 64 blank)

Deed dated 1811. JOHN BROWN to DAVID GERMAN of Dauphin Co, PA. S 3, T 9, R 2W. "ANN, his wife". Signed JOHN BROWN, ANN BROWN. Witness: LANDON ROBINSON, JOHN BRADBURN. rec 1811. p 65 (p 66 blank)

Deed dated 1811. MICHAEL JONES to THOMAS STUART of Baltimore Co, MD. Brkv lot 34. Signed MICHAEL JONES, MARY JONES. Witness: JOHN JAMES, JOHN MAHARD (in OH). rec 1812. p 67 (pp 68, 69 blank)

Deed dated 1811. MICHAEL JONES of Hamilton Co, OH to ROBERT McGREW of Washington Co, PA. Brkv lot 26. Signed MICHAEL JONES, MARY JONES. Witness: JOHN MAHARD (in OH). rec 1812. p 70   (p 71 blank)

Deed dated 1811. BENJAMIN McCARTY to CONRAD SAILOR, WILLIAM G. EADS & ABRAHAM HACKELMAN. Tract in S 3, T

FRANKLIN COUNTY DEEDS: Book A

8, R 2W for use of Baptist Church on the Little Cedar Grove Creek. Signed BENJAMIN McCARTY. Witness: JAMES McCARTY, BENJAMIN McCARTY JR. rec 1812. p 72

Deed dated 1811. JAMES HAMILTON & MICHAEL JONES to CHRISTIAN KELLER & FRANCIS FORMAN, both of Baltimore Co, MD. Brkv lots 15, 16, 5, 6. Signed JAMES HAMILTON, MICHAEL JONES, MARY JONES. Witness: none. rec 1812. p 73   (pp 74, 75 blank)

Plat map of town of Brookville dated 1808. "adjoins JOHN ALLEN's quarter section". Signed S. MANWARING. Witness: none. rec 1812. p 76   (p 77 blank)

Deed dated 1812. WILLIAM G. EADS to CONRAD SAILORS. S 2, T 8, R 2W. Signed WILLIAM G. EADS. Witness: AMOS BUTLER. J. P.'s note: "EADS & REBECAH, his wife". rec 1812. p 78

Deed dated 1812. JOHN ALLEN & SARAH, his wife, of Dearborn Co to SAMUEL ROCKEFELLER. S 32, T 8, R 1W. Signed JOHN ALLEN, SARAH ALLEN. Witness: none. rec 1812. pp 79, 80   (p 81 blank)

Deed dated 1812. JOHN ALLEN of Dearborn Co to JOHN VAN BLARICUM. S 29, T 8, R 1W. Signed JOHN ALLEN, SARAH ALLEN. Witness: none. rec 1812. p 82.

Deed dated 1812. JOHN H. ROCKAFELLAR & MARY, his wife, to JAMES JONES. S 32, T 8, R 1W. Signed JOHN H. ROCKAFELLAR, MARY ROCKAFELLAR. Witness: ARCHIBALD GUTHERY, SAMUEL MARCHENT. rec 1812. pp 84, 83 (printed in reverse order). (pp 85, 86 blank)

Deed dated 1812. JOHN ALLEN SR to STEPHEN C. STEPHENS. Lots adjoining Brkv lots 26 & 49. Signed JOHN ALLEN, REBECAH ALLEN. Witness: none. rec 1812. p 87   (p 88 blank)

Deed dated 1812. JOHN ALLEN SR to JAMES KNIGHT. Brkv lots 3, 4, 10. Signed JOHN ALLEN SR, REBECAH ALLEN. Witness: none. rec 1812. p 89 (p 90 blank)

Deed dated 1812. JOSEPH SIRES to WILLIAM BUTLER. S 11, T 8, R 1W. Signed JOSEPH SIRES. Witness: JAMES WINCHELL. rec 1812. p 91 (p 92 blank), p 93

Deed dated 1812. ROBERT GREEN to PETER DAVIS GREEN of Madison Twp, Butler Co, OH. S 8, T 10, R 1W. "and ANNA, (Robert's) wife". Signed ROBERT GREEN. Witness: JOHN STOCKTON, WILLIAM (x) STOCKTON. rec 1812. pp 93, 94, 95, 96

FRANKLIN COUNTY DEEDS: Book A

Deed dated 1812. JAMES JONES & REBECAH, his wife, to JOHN H. ROCKAFELLAR. S 29, T 8, R 1W. Signed JAMES JONES, REBECAH (x) JONES. Witness: ARCH'D GUTHERY, SAMUEL MOREHART. rec 1812. pp 96, 97, 98

Deed dated 1812. JAMES HAMILTON of Dearborn Co to BENJAMIN McCARTY. Brkv lot 31. (text names MICHAEL JONES co-seller) Signed JAMES HAMILTON, MICHAEL JONES, MARY JONES. Witness: none. rec 1812. pp 99, 100

Deed dated 1811. JAMES HAMILTON of Dearborn Co to MICHAEL JONES of Hamilton Co, OH. Brkv lots 26, 27. Signed JAMES HAMILTON. Witness: none. rec 1812. pp 101, 102

Deed dated 1812. MICHAEL JONES & JAMES HAMILTON, both of Dearborn Co, to STEPHEN C. STEPHENS. Brkv lots 57, 58. Signed MICHAEL JONES, JAMES HAMILTON, MARY JONES. Witness: none. rec 1812. pp 103, 104

Deed dated 1812. JOHN ALLEN to DAVID LOWRING. Brkv lot 44. Signed JOHN ALLEN, REBECAH ALLEN. Witness: HENRY INKINSON. rec 1812. pp 105, 106

Deed dated 1812. JOHN ALLEN to EDWARD WHITE of OH. Brkv lot 29. Signed JOHN ALLEN, REBECAH ALLEN. Witness: HENRY INKINSON. rec 1812. pp 107 108

Brookville town plat map dated 1812. "line between AMOS BUTLER & JOHN ALLEN & MICHAEL JONES". Signed JOSEPH S. ALLEN. Witness: none. rec 1812. pp 109, 110

Brookville town addition plat map dated 1812. "which JOHN ALLEN laid off". Signed JOSEPH ALLEN. Witness: none. rec 1812. pp 111, 112 (p 113 blank)

Brookville town plat map dated 1812. Drawn from plan certified by SOLOMON MANWARING, dated 1808. Signed SAMUEL CHANCE. Witness: none. rec 1812. occupies 3 pages: pp 114, no #, no #.

Deed dated 1812. CHARLES SCOTT to SAMUEL SCOTT. S 3, T 8, R 2W. "ELIZABETH, his wife". Signed CHARLES SCOTT, ELIZABETH SCOTT. Witness: none. rec 1812. pp 115, 116

Deed dated 1811. JOHN ALLEN & SARAH, his wife, of Dearborn Co to THOMAS MANWARING of same. S 32, T 8, R 1W. Signed JOHN ALLEN, SARAH ALLEN. Witness: PETER RIFERNER, RICHARD MANWARING. rec 1812. pp 117, 118

FRANKLIN COUNTY DEEDS: Book A

New Washington town plat map, undated. Signed JOSEPH LEVISTON, Surveyor. THOMAS MADDEN & JOHN MALLIN, Proprietors. rec 1812. p 119

Deed dated 1812. BENJAMIN McCARTY to JAMES LOGAN. S 21, T 9, R 2. Signed BENJAMIN McCARTY. Witness: ENOCH McCARTY. rec 1812. pp 120, 121

Deed dated 1811. JOHN ALLEN SR to JAMES McKINEY. Brkv town lots 51 & 52. Signed JOHN ALLEN, REBECAH ALLEN. Witness: none. rec 1812. pp 122, 123

Deed dated 1811. JOHN ALLEN to BENJAMIN McCARTY. Brkv lots 40, 46. Signed JOHN ALLEN SR, REBECAH (x) ALLEN. Witness: none. rec 1812. pp 124, 125

Deed dated 1812. JOHN ALLEN SR to ENOCH McCARTY. Brkv lots 19, 24, 32, 33. Signed JOHN ALLEN SR, REBECAH ALLEN. Witness: none. rec 1812. pp 126, 127

Deed dated 1812. JOHN H. ROCKAFELLAR & MARY, his wife, to JACOB PETERS. S 32, T 8, R 1W. Signed JOHN H. ROCKAFELLAR, MARY ROCKAFELLAR. Witness: MATHEW SAMBDON*, NATHAN LEWIS. rec 1812. pp 128, 129, 130, 131 *transcription error? probably MATHEW LAMBDON

Deed dated 1812. DAVID GOBLE to STEPHEN C. STEPHENS. Brkv lot 47. "ALICE, his wife". Signed DAVID GOBLE, ALICE GOBLE. Witness: none. rec 1812. pp 132, 133

Deed dated 1812. LEWIS DEWEES to IABES* WINSHIP. S 4, T 8, R 2W. Signed LEWIS DEWEES. Witness: LANDON ROBERTSON. rec 1812. pp 134, 135 *transcription error - should be JABES WINSHIP

Deed dated 1812. CHARLES SCOTT & SAMUEL SCOTT to JOHN RYBOURN. S 3, T 8, R 2W. "CHARLES & ELIZABETH, his wife, & SAMUEL & SARAH, his wife". Signed CHARLES SCOTT, ELIZABETH (x) SCOTT, SAMUEL SCOTT, SARAH (x) SCOTT. Witness: none. rec 1812. pp 136, 137

Deed dated 1811. JOHN ALLEN SR to WILLIAM H. EADS. Brkv lots 27, 28. Signed JOHN ALLEN SR, REBECAH (x) ALLEN. Witness: none. rec 1812. pp 138, 139

Deed dated 1812. WILLIAM H. EADS to DAVID ATHERTON of Hamilton Co, OH. Brkv lots 27 & 28. Signed WM. H. EADS, JANE EADS. Witness: none. rec 1812. pp 139, 140, 141

Deed dated 1812. CONRAD SAILORS & CATHERINE, his wife, to ENOCH McCARTY. S 3, T 8, R 2W. Signed

FRANKLIN COUNTY DEEDS: Book A

CONRAD (x) SAILORS, CATHERINE (x) SAILORS. Witness: JOHN ALLEN. rec 1812. pp 142, 143

Deed dated 1812. JOHN McCUTCHEN & SUSANNA, his wife, of Pickway Co, OH to JAMES NICKELS. S 22, T 11, R 2W. Signed JOHN McCUTCHEN, SUSANNA McCUTCHEN at Ross Co, OH. rec 1813. pp 144, 145

Deed dated 1812. JACOB SAILERS to JABES WINSHIP. S 3, T 8, R 2. Signed JACOB (x) SAILERS. Witness: none. rec 1813. pp 145, 146

Deed dated 1813. WILLIAM H. EADS to JAMES NOBLE. Brkv lots 27 & 28. Signed WM. H. EADS, JANE EADS. Witness: none. rec 1813. pp 146, 147, 148

Deed dated 1812. ABRAHAM HACKELMAN to JABES WINSHIP. S 34, T 9, R 2. Signed A. (x) HACKLEMAN. Witness: none. rec 1813. pp 149, 150

Deed dated 1813. THOMAS HENDERSON to ELI STRINGER. S 32, T 9, R 2. Signed THOMAS HENDERSON. Witness: none. rec 1813. pp 151, 152

Deed dated 1813. STEPHEN C. STEVENS to JOHN CONNER. Brkv lots 36, 37, 3d lot/ no #. Signed STEPHEN C. STEPHENS. Witness: none. rec 1813. pp 153, 154

Deed dated 1812. AMOS BUTLER to JAMES McKINNEY. Brkv lot 55. "MARY, his wife". Signed AMOS BUTLER, MARY BUTLER. Witness: none. rec 1813. pp 155, 156

Deed dated 1813. JAMES McKINNEY to STEPHEN C. STEVENS. Brkv lot 55. "EDITH, wife of JAMES". Signed JAMES McKINNEY, EDITH (x) McKINNEY. Witness: none. rec 1813. pp 157, 158

Deed dated 1812. MICHAEL JONES of the "Illenoise" Territory & JAMES HAMILTON of Dearborn Co to JOSEPH ALLEN of PA. Brkv lots 9 & 10. Signed MICHAEL JONES, MARY JONES, JAMES HAMILTON. (JONES' signatures from Shawnee Town, Illinois Territory) rec 1813. pp 159, 160

Deed dated 1813. JOHN ALLEN SR to WILLIAM H. EADS. Brkv lots 20, 21, 22, 23, 29, 45. Signed JOHN ALLEN, REBECAH ALLEN. Witness: none. rec 1813. pp 161, 162

Deed dated 1813. STEPHEN C. STEVENS to CHARLES DAILY. Lot 26 adjoining Brkv. Signed STEPHEN C. STEVENS. Witness: none. rec 1813. pp 163, 164.

FRANKLIN COUNTY DEEDS: Book A

Deed dated 1813. STEPHEN C. STEVENS to WILLIAM H. EADS. Brkv lots 44 & 45. Signed STEPHEN C. STEVENS. Witness: JOHN CONNER. rec 1813. pp 164, 165

Deed dated 1813. JOSEPH SIERS to CHRISTOPHER LANNING of Warring (Warren) Co, OH. S 11, T 8, R 1W. Signed JOSEPH (x) SIERS. Witness: STANHOPE ROYSTER. WILLIAM BUSTER. no rec date. pp 166, 167

Deed dated 1813. DAVID BELL to ENOCH McCARTY. Brkv lot 48. Signed DAVID BELL. Witness: ARTHUR DICKSON. rec 1813. pp 167, (168 blank) 169, 170

Deed dated 1813. JOHN ALLEN SR to BENJAMIN SMITH. Brkv lots 57 & 58. Signed JOHN ALLEN, REBECAH (x) ALLEN. Witness: none. rec 1813. pp 171, 172

Deed dated 1813. DAVID ATHERTON of Hamilton Co, OH to JAMES NOBLE. Brkv lots 27 & 28. "RACHEL, wife of said DAVID". Signed DAVID ATHERTON, RACHEL ATHERTON. Witness: none. rec 1813. pp 173, 174

Deed dated 1813. JOHN SAILORS to MICHAEL SAILORS. S 18, T 8, R 1W. "on line of DAVID JOHNSON's survey". Signed JOHN (x) SAILORS. Witness: BENJAMIN SMITH. rec 1813. pp 177, 178

Deed dated 1812. WILLIAM ARNET to JOHN HALL. S 4, T 8, R 2W. Signed WILLIAM ARNET. Witness: JOHN BRADBURN, SAMUEL ARNET. rec 1813. pp 179, 180

Deed dated 1812. JAMES HAMILTON of Dearborn Co & MICHAEL JONES of Randolph Co, Illinois Territory, to BENJAMIN McCARTY, THOMAS BROWN & JOSHUA HARLAN, Judges of Common Pleas Court, Franklin Co. Two acres of land marked "Public Square" on town map for benefit of Franklin Co. Signed J. HAMILTON, MICHAEL JONES, MARY JONES. rec 1813. pp 181, 182, 183, 184

Deed dated 1812. JAMES HAMILTON & MICHAEL JONES to WILLIAM COX & JOHN HARVEY of Wayne Co. Brkv lots 32 & 32. Signed JAMES HAMILTON, MICHAEL JONES, MARY JONES. Witness: none. rec 1813. pp 185, 186

Deed dated 1812. USA to SOLOMON TYNER of Dearborn Co. T 9, R 2, S 27. rec 1813. pp 187, 188

Deed dated 1812. WILLIAM F. HUFF to TRUMAN BLACKMAN of Cincinnati, OH. S 32, T 8, R 1W. "purchased from JACOB PETERS" in 1812. Brkv lot adj JOHN R. BEATY. S 36, T 16, R 12E. "tract in Big Cedar Grove adjoining JOHN CLENDENNING's land, purchased from

FRANKLIN COUNTY DEEDS: Book A

JACOB PETERSBY".   Signed WILLIAM T. HUFF. Witness: C BURGES, JOHN MAHARD. rec 1813.   pp 188, 189, 190

Deed of partition dated 1813. JAMES PIPER of Middletown, Butler Co, OH to JOEL WILLIAMS of Cincinnati, OH. S 13, T 10, R 2. Signed JAMES PIPER. Witness: DANIEL STRUCKLAND, JOHN WARLAND (in Butler Co, OH). rec 1813. pp 191, 192

Deed of partition dated 1813. JOEL WILLIAMS as above to JAMES PIPER as above. S 13, T 10, R 2. Signed JOEL WILLIAMS. Witness: DANIEL STRUCKLAND, W. SIMILTON (in OH). rec 1813. pp 193, 194

Deed dated 1813. JOHN CONNER to ALLEN RAMSEY. T 8, S 14, R 2. "LAVINA, wife of JOHN". Signed JOHN CONNER, LAVINA CONNER. Witness: none. pp 195, 196

Deed dated 1813. JOHN CONNER to JOHN THOMPSON. S 11, T 8, R 2. Signed JOHN CONNER, LAVINA CONNER. Witness: none. rec 1813. pp 197, 198

Deed dated 1813. CHRISTOPHER LANNING of Warren Co, OH & MARGARETTA, his wife, to JOSEPH SIRES. S 11, T 8, R 1W. Signed CHRISTOPHER (x) LANNING, MARGARETTA (x) LANNING. Witness: ENOS WILLIAMS, GEORGE FOGELSONG (in Warren Co, OH). rec 1813. pp 199, 200, 201

Deed dated 1813.   LISMAND BASEY to ARTHUR DICKSON. "ELIZABETH, wife of LISMAND". Brkv lot 30. Signed LISMUND BASEY, ELIZABETH BASEY. Witness: TOBIAS SMITH, JAMES McCARTY. rec 1813. pp 201, 202

Deed dated 1813. STEPHEN C. STEVENS to ARTHUR DICKSON. Brkv lot 49. Signed STEPHEN C. STEVENS. Witness: ENOCH McCARTY. rec 1813. pp 203, 204

Deed dated 1813. JOHN ALLEN SR to ARTHUR DICKSON. Brkv lot 50. Signed JOHN ALLEN, REBECCAH (x) ALLEN. Witness: HUGH BROWNLEE. rec 1813. pp 204, 205

Deed dated 1813. NATHAN PORTER to JOHNATHAN HUNT. S 19, T 8, R 1. "corner of JOHN HAGGERMAN's land". Signed NATHAN PORTER. Witness: JOSEPH S. ALLEN. rec 1813. pp 206, 207

Deed dated 1813. WILLIAM COX & ELIZABETH, his wife, of Wayne Co to JAMES KNIGHT. Brkv lot 32. Signed WILLIAM COX, ELIZABETH (x) COX. Witness: ISAAC BLACKFORD. rec 1813. pp 208, 209

Bond dated 1813. JAMES McKINNEY to JOHN TEST. $1200

FRANKLIN COUNTY DEEDS: Book A

bond: McKINNEY to convey deed to house and Brkv lots 51 & 52 by July, 1817. Signed JAMES McKINNEY. Witness: ENOCH McCARTY, JOHN ALLEN. rec 1813. Note: McKINNEY delivered possession of premises, signed ISAAC M. JOHNSON. p 210

Deed dated 1813. JACOB PETERS & MARY, his wife, to JAMES JONES. S 32, T 8, R 1W. Signed JACOB (x) PETERS, MARY (x) PETERS. Witness: FREDERICK SHOLTS. rec 1813. pp 211, 212

Deed dated 1813. ENOCH McCARTY to JOHN WINCHELL. Brkv lots 19 & 24. "ELIZABETH, his wife". Signed ENOCH McCARTY, ELIZABETH (x) McCARTY. Witness: none. rec 1813. pp 213, 214

Deed dated 1813. JOHN ALLEN SR to JANE STEPHENS. Brkv lot 39. Signed JOHN ALLEN, REBECCAH (x) ALLEN. Witness: ANN JOHNSON. rec 1813. pp 215, 216

Deed dated 1812. JOHN MILHOLLAND to WILLIAM HENDERSON. S 3, T 8, R 2W. Signed JOHN MILHOLLAND. Witness: REBECCAH SMITH. rec 1812. pp 217, 218

Deed dated 1813. STEPHEN C. STEVENS to ENOCH McCARTY. Brkv lot 47. Signed STEPHEN C. STEVENS. Witness: none. rec 1813. pp 219, 220

Deed dated 1813. JOHN ALLEN SR to DAVID LANNING. Brkv lot 47. Signed JOHN ALLEN, REBECCAH (x) ALLEN. Witness: none. rec 1813. pp 221, 222

Mortgage signed 1812. JOHN HAGERMAN & CHRISTIAN HAGERMAN to STEPHEN LUDLOW of Lawrenceburg. No S-T-R given. "thirty-one acres on which HAGERMAN's grist and saw mills are located". Money to be paid by 1815. Signed JOHN HAGERMAN, E. HAGERMAN, STEPHEN LUDLOW. Witness: DAVID GINN. rec 1813. Note: full amount was paid, signed STEPHEN LUDLOW, dated 1825. pp 223, 224, 225

Apprenticeship agreement dated 1813. THOMAS SMITH, father of JOHN SMITH, to JOHN REED. JOHN SMITH to learn blacksmith trade, term of 14 years. Signed THOMAS (x) SMITH, JOHN REED. Witness: DAVID MOUNT, WILLIAM GASSET. rec 1813. pp 225, 226

Deed dated 1813. JOHN CONNER to JAMES NOBLE. Brkv lots 36, 37 & 3d lot, no #. Signed JOHN CONNER, LAVINA CONNER. Witness: none. rec 1813. pp 227, 228

Connersville town plat map dated 1813. Located in

FRANKLIN COUNTY DEEDS: Book A

S 25, T 14, R 12E (now Fayette Co). Signed ENOCH McCARTY. no rec date. pp 229, 230

Sheriff's sale dated 1813. ROBERT HANNA, Sheriff of Franklin Co, to JAMES KNIGHT. ELIJAH SPARKS obtained judgement for debt against MICHAEL JONES; court seized Brkv lots 6, 7, 8, 11, 12, 13 & 39, sold at auction. Title to lot 13 conveyed to KNIGHT as high bidder. Signed ROBERT HANNA, Sheriff. Witness: none. rec 1813. pp 231, 232, 233

Sheriff's sale dated 1813. ROBERT HANNA, Sheriff of Franklin Co, to JAMES KNIGHT. As sale above. Title to lot 8 conveyed to KNIGHT as high bidder. Signed ROBERT HANNA, Sheriff. Witness: none. rec 1813. pp 234, 235, 236, 237

Sheriff's sale dated 1813. ROBERT HANNA, Sheriff of Franklin Co, to JAMES KNIGHT. As sale above. Title to lot 7 conveyed to KNIGHT as high bidder. Signed ROBERT HANNA, Sheriff. Witness: none. rec 1813. pp 237, 238, 239, 240

Sheriff's sale dated 1813. ROBERT HANNA, Sheriff of Franklin Co, to JAMES KNIGHT. As sale above. Title to lot 11 conveyed to KNIGHT as high bidder. Signed ROBERT HANNA, Sheriff. Witness: none. rec 1813. pp 240, 241, 242, 243

Apprenticeship agreement dated 1813. THOMAS SMITH, father of THOMAS SMITH, to ROBERT DIXISON. Young THOMAS to learn tanning trade, term of 19 years. Signed THOMAS (x) SMITH, ROBERT DICKISON. Witness: JACOB BLACKLEDGE, JOHN REED. rec 1813. pp 243, 244

Deed dated 1813. JOHN ALLEN SR & REBKA, his wife, to DAVID RICHARDSON. Brkv lots 15, 16, 17. Signed JOHN ALLEN, Esqr., REBECA (x) ALLEN. Witness: BENJAMIN SMITH. rec 1813. pp 245, 246

Deed dated 1813. BENJAMIN McCARTY to POWELL SCOTT. S 21, T 9, R 2W. Signed BENJAMIN McCARTY. Witness: none. rec 1813. pp 247, 248

Sheriff's sale dated 1813. ROBERT HANNA, Sheriff of Franklin Co, to ISAAC BLACKFORD. ELIJAH SPARKS obtained judgement for debt against MICHAEL JONES; court attached Brkv lots 6, 7, 8, 11, 12, 13 & 39 to be sold at auction. Title to lot 6 conveyed to BLACKFORD as high bidder. Signed ROBERT HANNA, Sheriff. Witness: none. rec 1813. pp 249, 250, 251

FRANKLIN COUNTY DEEDS: Book A

Sheriff's sale dated 1813. ROBERT HANNA, Sheriff of Franklin Co, to ISAAC BLACKFORD. As sale above. Title to lot 39 conveyed high bidder BLACKFORD. Signed ROBERT HANNA, Sheriff. Witness: none. rec 1813. pp 252, 253, 254

Deed dated 1813. JOHN ALLEN of Dearborn Co to JOSEPH PARKS. S 2, T 8, R 1. Signed JOHN ALLEN, SARAH ALLEN. Witness: JAMES HARTPENCE, MICHAEL FANAN. rec 1813. pp 255, 256

Deed dated 1813. ANTHONY HALBERSTADT to JOHN CASE of Dearborn Co. Sec 10, T 8, R 2W. Signed ANTHONY HALBERSTADT, SARAH HALBERSTADT. Witness: WILLIAM MAYOR, JOHN BLADES. rec 1813. pp 257, 258

Deed dated 1813. NATHAN PORTER to JOHN HAGEMAN. S 19, T 8, R 1W. Signed NATHAN PORTER. Witness: JAMES JONSON, THOMAS CLARK, ELIOTT HERNDON. rec 1813. pp 259, 260

Deed dated 1813. JAMES WILSON of Hamilton Co, OH, to ARTHUR DIXON. Brkv lot 17. Signed JAMES WILSON. Witness: HENRY JINKINSON, CHARLES DAILY. rec 1813. pp 261, 262

Deed dated 1813. JABEZ WINSHIP to JOSEPH WINSHIP. S 13, T 8, R 2W. Signed JABEZ WINSHIP. Witness: none. rec 1813. pp 263, 264

Deed dated 1813. BENJAMIN McCARTY to ENOCH McCARTY. S 3, T 8, R 2W except land conveyed to WILLIAM FLOOD, BENJAMIN SMITH, JABEZ WINSHIP. Signed BENJAMIN McCARTY. Witness: none. rec 1813. pp 265, 266

Deed dated 1813. WILLIAM H. EADS to JAMES NOBLE. Brkv lot 29. Signed WILLIAM H. EADS, JANE EADS. Witness: JEREMIAH COREY. rec 1813. pp 267, 268

Deed dated 1813. JAMES HAMILTON & MICHAEL JONES of Dearborn Co to NATHANIEL HEMDON*. Brkv lot 33. "by land owned by JACOB & CHARLES BRAYHER+". Signed JAMES HAMILTON, MICHAEL JONES, MARY JONES. Witness: none. rec 1813. pp 270, 269: printed reverse order. *transcription error? probably NATHANIEL HERNDON. +see surname as spelled next entry & Bk A, pp321/323

Deed dated 1813. JAMES KNIGHT & MARY, his wife, to NATHANIEL HEMDON*.. Brkv 32. "land by JACOB & CHARLES BAISHURE+" "MARY, his wife". Signed JAMES KNIGHT, MARY KNIGHT. Witness: ISAAC BLACKFORD. rec 1813. pp 271, 272 *see above. + see surname as above

FRANKLIN COUNTY DEEDS: Book A

Deed dated 1813. WILLIAM G. EADS of Harrison Co, KY to CONRAD SAILOR. S 2, T 8, R 2W. "REBECAH, (Ead's) wife". Signed WILLIAM G. EADS, no wife's signature. Witness: none. rec 1813. pp 273, 274

Deed dated 1813. CONRAD SAILORS to JACOB SAILORS. S 3, T 8, R 2W. Signed CONRAD (x) SAILORS. Witness: none. rec 1813. pp 275, 276

Deed dated 1813. ISAAC SIRMAN to LOUISAR SIRMAN. "natural love and affection which (ISAAC) bears toward LOUISAR" (female). S 24, T 10, R 2W. "& BETSY SIRMAN, my wife". Signed ISAAC SIRMAN. Witness: JOHN FLINT. rec 1813. pp 277, 278

Deed dated 1814. STEPHEN STEVENS of Jefferson Co to JAMES NOBLE. Brkv lot 55. Signed STEPHEN C. STEVENS. Witness: none. rec 1814. pp 278, 279

Sheriff's sale dated 1813. ROBERT HANNA, Sheriff of Franklin Co, to JEREMIAH COREY & AMOS BUTLER. ELIJAH SPARKS given judgement of debt against MICHAEL JONES; court seized Brkv lots 6, 7, 8, 11, 12, 13 & 39, sold at auction. Lot 12 title conveyed to high bidders COREY & BUTLER. Signed ROBERT HANNA, Sheriff. Witness: none. rec 1814. pp 280, 281, 282, 283

Deed dated 1814. STEPHEN C. STEVENS to ISAAC M. JOHNSON. Brkv lot 39. Unsigned, no witness. rec 1814. pp 284, 285

Deed dated 1813. MICHAEL JONES of Randolph Co, Illinois Territory & JAMES HAMILTON of Dearborn Co to BENJAMIN DICKEY of PA. Brkv lots 21, 22. Signed MICHAEL JONES, MARY JONES, JAMES HAMILTON. Witness: none. rec 1814. pp 286, 287

Deed dated 1813. STEPHEN C. STEVENS to JAMES WILSON of Cincinnati, OH. Brkv lots 57, 58. Signed STEPHEN C. STEVENS. Witness: ENOCH McCARTY. rec 1814. pp 288, 289

Deed dated 1813. THOMAS HENDERSON to WILLIAM HENDERSON. S 33, T 9, R 2W. Signed THOMAS HENDERSON. Witness: none. rec 1814. p 290

Deed dated 1813. JAMES HAMILTON & MICHAEL JONES of Dearborn Co to JOHN JAMES of same. Brkv lots 28, 29. Signed JAMES HAMILTON, MICHAEL JONES, MARY JONES. Witness: none. rec 1814. pp 291, 292

Sheriff Sale, dated 1813. JAMES HAMILTON, Sheriff of

FRANKLIN COUNTY DEEDS: Book A

Dearborn Co, to JOHN JAMES of same. Suit for debt brought by JAMES against JAMES KNIGHT. Brkv lots 28, 29, 33 seized, sold at auction to JOHN JAMES. Signed JAMES HAMILTON, Sheriff, Dearborn Co. Witness: none. rec 1814. pp 293, 294, 295

Deed dated 1813. JOHN SAILORS to CHITESTER JOHNSON. S 18, T 8, R 1W. Signed JOHN (x) SAILORS. Witness: BENJAMIN SMITH. rec 1814. pp 295, 296, 297

Deed dated 1813. RICHARD MINER & RACHEL, his wife, to CHARLES WADDEL. S 11, T --, R 1W. Signed RICHARD MINER, RACHEL MINER. Witness: THOMAS BROWN. rec 1814. pp 297, 298

Deed dated 1814. WILLIAM H. EADS to NATHAN DAVIS. Brkv lot 45. Signed WILLIAM H. EADS, JANE EADS. Witness: none. rec 1814. p 299 (p 300 blank)

Deed dated 1814. JOHN ALLEN SR to JOHN WINCHILL. Brkv lots 37, 42. Signed JOHN ALLEN SR, RACHEL (x) ALLEN. Witness: none. rec 1814. pp 301, 302

Deed dated 1814. BENJAMIN McCARTY to ROBERT COLMERY of Washington Co, PA. Brkv lot 31. "SARAH, wife of BENJAMIN". Signed BENJAMIN McCARTY, SARAH (x) McCARTY. Witness: ARTHUR AN. rec 1814. pp 303, 304

Deed dated 1814. JOSEPH SIERS to MATHEW SPARKS. S 11, T 8, R 1W. Signed JOSEPH (x) SIERS. Witness: ENOCH McCARTY. rec 1814. pp 305, 306

Deed dated 1814. WILLIAM BUSTER & SARAH, his wife, to MATHEW SPARKS. S 11, T 8, R 1W. Signed WILLIAM BUSTER, SARAH (x) BUSTER. Witness: ENOCH McCARTY. rec 1814. pp 307, 308

Deed dated 1814. AMOS BUTLER to DAVID ATHERTON of Hamilton Co, OH. Brkv 37. Signed AMOS BUTLER, MARY BUTLER. Witness: B. SMITH. rec 1814. pp 309, 310

Deed dated 1813. ANTHONY HALBERSTADT to JOHN LEFFORGE. S 10, T 8, R 2W. Signed ANTHONY HALBERSTADT, SALLY (x) HALBERSTADT. Witness: JOHN ALLEN. JOHN DICKERSON. rec 1814. pp 310, 311, 312

Deed dated 1813. JOHN MILLER & PHEBE, his wife, to JOSEPH HARTER of Preble Co, OH. S 1, T 19, R ?. Signed JOHN MILLER, PHEBE (x) MILLER. Witness: CATHERINE (x) BAKE. rec 1814. pp 312, 313, 314

Deed dated 1814. WILLIAM H. EADS to ASA NORTHRUP.

FRANKLIN COUNTY DEEDS: Book A

Brkv lots 44, 45. Signed WILLIAM H. EADS. JANE EADS.
Witness: none. rec 1814. pp 315, 316

Deed dated 1814. DENNIS DUSKEY of Green Twp. Hamilton Co, OH to ELI JAMES. S 29, T 9, R 1W. "RACHEL, his wife". Signed DENNIS DUSKEY, RACHEL (x) DUSKEY. Witness: WM. T. CARSON (in OH). rec 1814. pp 316, 317, 318

Deed dated 1814. WILLIAM COX & JOHN HARVEY of Wayne Co to SHUBAL JULIAN of same. Brkv lot 38. Signed WILLIAM COX, JOHN HARVEY, ELIZABETH COX, JANE HARVEY. Witness: none. rec 1814. pp 319, 320

Deed dated 1814. NATHANIEL HERNDON to CALEB C. TUNIS of Hamilton Co, OH. Brkv 32, 33. "land owned by JACOB & CHARLES BROSHER*". "ELIZABETH, his wife". Signed NATHANIEL HERNDON, ELIZABETH (x) HERNDON. Witness: none. rec 1814. pp 321, 322, 323 *See Bk A, pp 269 to 272

Deed dated 1813. BENJAMIN LILLEY of Hamilton Co, OH to GEORGE FRUIT, JOHN FRUIT, JONATHAN FRUIT, DAVID FRUIT, SARAH HIDEY, MARGARET MOORE, BARBERY WEBER, CATHARINE FRUIT, heirs of GEORGE FRUIT, dec. S 23, T 9, R 1W. Signed BENJAMIN LILLEY. Witness: ETHAN STONE, S. GRESHAM (in Hamilton Co, OH) rec 1814. pp 323, 324, 325

Deed dated 1814. ALLEN WILEY & MARGARET, his wife, JAMES WILEY & ELIZABETH, his wife, to SPENCER WILEY. S 11, T 8, R 1W. Signed ALLEN WILEY, MARGARET WILEY, JAMES WILEY, ELIZABETH (x) WILEY. Witness: none. rec 1814. pp 326, 327

Brookville plat map dated 1814. AMOS BUTLER. Proprietor. rec 1814. p 328

Deed dated 1814. JOHN ALLEN JR to DAVID RICHARDSON. Brkv lot 9. JOHN ALLEN JR. Witness: BENJAMIN SMITH. rec 1814. pp 329, 330

Deed dated 1814. JOHN ALLEN SR to ENOCH McCARTY. Brkv lot 35. Signed JOHN ALLEN, REBECCAH (x) ALLEN. Witness: BENJAMIN SMITH. rec 1814. pp 331, 332

Deed dated 1814. JOHN DICKERSON & RUTH, his wife to ABRAHAM ROSE. S 11, T 10, R 2W. "land to SAMUEL DICKERSON". Signed JOHN DICKERSON, RUTH (x) DICKERSON. Witness: JEREMIAH COREY, ENOCH McCARTY. rec 1814. pp 333, 334

FRANKLIN COUNTY DEEDS: Book A

Deed dated 1814.   WILLIAM H. EADS to JOHN FLINT JR. Brkv 21, 22.   Signed WILLIAM H. EADS, JANE EADS. Witness: BENJAMIN SMITH.   rec 1814.   pp 335, 336

Deed dated 1814.   MOSES CONGER to DANIEL CONGER of Green Twp, Hamilton Co, OH.   S 12, T 8, R 2W.   Signed MOSES (x) CONGER.   Witness: J. CARSON (in OH).   rec 1814.   pp 337, 338, 339

Record of debt dated 1814.   JEREMIAH MURPHY to NATHANIEL HEMDON.   Horses, cattle, sheep, crop in ground held as security.   Debt to be paid by Jan, 1815.   Signed JEREY MURPHY, MOSES (x) MURPHY, NATHANIEL HERNDON.   Witness: ALLISON LOCKER, WILLIAM H. EADS.   rec 1814.   pp 339, 340, 341

Deed dated 1814.   SAMUEL ROCKAFELLAR to THOMAS MANWAR-ING.   S 32, T 8, R 1W.   "MARY, his wife".   Signed SAMUEL ROCKAFELLAR, MARY ROCKAFELLAR.   Witness: JAMES TRUSLER, PATTERY ROCKAFELLAR.   rec 1814.   pp 341, 342, 343

Deed dated 1814.   AMOS BUTLER to OBEDIAH WILLIVER of Butler Co, OH.   Brkv lot 56.   Signed AMOS BUTLER, MARY BUTLER.   Witness: ENOCH McCARTY.   rec 1814.   pp 343, 344

Deed dated 1814.   PHILIP LINCK to MICHAEL WELHINS*. S 24, T 9, R 1W.   "CATY, his wife".   Signed PHILIP LINCK, CATY (x) LINCK.   Witness: none.   rec 1814. pp 345, 346, 347   *MICHAEL WELKINS in body of deed

Deed dated 1813.   WILLIAM HENDERSON to ELISHA WYETH of Lazane Co, PA.   S 3, T 8, R 2W.   "MARTHA, his wife" Signed WILLIAM HENDERSON, MARTHA (x) HENDERSON.   Witness: JOHN HALL, JABEZ WINSHIP.   rec 1814.   pp 348, 349, 350

Deed dated 1809.   PETER DAVIS of Dearborn Co to ROBERT GREEN of same.   S 8, T 10, R 1W.   Signed PETER (x) DAVIS.   Witness: MICHAEL --.   rec 1814.   pp 351, 352, 353

Deed dated 1814.   ANDREW SHIRK JR & ANDREW SHIRK SR & MARTHE, his wife, to SAMUEL VANCEL.   S 13, T 9, R 1W. Signed ANDREW SHIRK JR, ANDREW SHIRK ST, MARTHA (x) SHIRK.   Witness: STANHOPE ROYSTER rec 1814.   pp 353, 354

Deed dated 1814.   JOHN THARP to JOHN MOORE & JEREMIAH COREY.   "LEAH, his wife".   S 8, T 9, R 2.   Signed JOHN (x) THARP, LEAH THARP.   Witness: BENJAMIN SMITH, LISMOND BALSEY.   rec 1814.   pp 357, 358, 359

FRANKLIN COUNTY DEEDS: Book B

Book B is available as both a transcribed copy and the original ledger. Since the original is in poor condition, page numbers used here refer to the typewritten transcribed copy. Blank pages were most likely left so that the two copies will correspond in page numbers.

Deed dated 1814. BENJAMIN McCARTY to CHARLES COLLET. S 9, T 13, R 12E. Signed BENJAMIN McCARTY, SARAH (x) McCARTY. Witness: none. rec 1814. p 1

Bond release, no date. WILLIAM LEWIS of Wayne Co to JAMES NOBLE. Signed WILLIAM LEWIS. Witness: SARAH (x) LINES, ARCHIBALD HERNDON. rec 1814. p 1

Deed of partition dated 1814. RICHARD CONNER to JAMES PRICE. S 18, T 8, R 1W. "Elizabeth, his wife" Signed RICHARD CONNER, ELIZABETH (x) CONNER. Witness: JOHN ROCKAFELLAR. rec 1814. p 2

Deed of partition dated 1814. JAMES PRICE to RICHARD CONNER. S ?, T 8, R 1W. "NANCY, his wife" Signed JAMES PRICE, NANCY (x) PRICE. Witness: JOHN ROCKA- FELLAR. rec 1814. p 3 (page 4 blank)

Deed dated 1814. WILLIAM HENRY EADS to JOHN PENWELL. Brkv lots 20, 23. Signed WILLIAM H. EADS, JANE EADS. Witn's: ELLIOT HERNDON, GEORGE L. MURDOCK rec 1814 p 5

Deed dated 1814. JOHN WINCHELL TO JAMES WINCHILL. Brkv 19, 24. "AMY, his wife". Signed JOHN WINCHILL, AMY (x) WINCHILL. Witness: none. rec 1814. p 6

Deed dated 1814. ISAAC SIRMON to WILLIAM GRAY of Butler Co, OH. S 24, T 10, R 2. "ELIZABETH, his wife". Signed ISAAC SIRMON, BETSY SIRMON. Witness: JOHN WHITWORTH, WILLIAM GIBBS. rec 1814. p 7

Deed dated 1814. JAMES PIPER of Butler Co, OH to his daughter, MARGARET WHITWORTH, wife of JOHN WHITWORTH. S 13, T 10, R 2. Signed JAMES PIPER. Witness: HENRY WEAVER, JACOB WEIDNER (Butler Co,OH) rec 1814. p 8

Deed dated 1814. ISAAC SIRMON to WILLIAM WHEAT. S 24, T 10, R 2W. Signed ISAAC SIRMON, BETSEY SIRMON. Witness: LOUISA (x) SIRMON. rec 1814. p 9

Deed dated 1812. GEORGE HARLAN to JOHN KEENY. S 9, T 11, R 2W. "land by GEORGE LEVISTON". Signed GEORGE (x) HARLAN. Witness: THOMAS GOLDEN, CHARLES McGLOTH- LIN. Note: CATHERINE HARLAN, widow of GEORGE, gave up right to dowry; THOMAS BROWN, JP. rec 1814. p 10

FRANKLIN COUNTY DEEDS: Book B

Deed dated 1814. JAMES JONES & REBECCAH, his wife, of Dearborn Co, to JAMES GOLD JR. S 35, T 8, R 1W. Signed JAMES JONES, REBECCAH (x) JONES. Witness: JAMES TRUSLER. rec 1814. p 11

Deed dated 1814. SHUBAL JULIAN of Wayne Co to WILLIAM BRADLEY. Brkv lot 38. Signed SHUBAL JULIAN. Witness: JAMES NOBLE. rec 1814. p 12

Deed dated 1814. JAMES MILHOLLAND, JOHN MILHOLLAND, & WILLIAM MILHOLLAND to JOHN ARMSTRONG of Hamilton Co, OH. S 3, T 8, R 2W. "40 acres deeded by JOHN MILHOLLAND, dec, to WILLIAM HENDERSON and 15 acres to JOHN QUICK". "JAMES, JOHN & WILLIAM MILHOLLAND, heirs of JOHN MILHOLLAND, dec." Land left by father's will to be conveyed after death of the widow. Signed JAMES MILHOLLAND, JOHN MILHOLLAND, WILLIAM MILHOLLAND. Witness: WILLIAM H. EADS, ENOCH McCARTY rec 1814 p 13

Deed dated 1814. MARY MILHOLLAND to JAMES, JOHN & WILLIAM MILHOLLAND. "MARY, wife of JOHN MILHOLLAND, dec." S 3, T 8, R 2W. "MARY having only a life estate...vested by will". Signed MARY (x) MILHOLLAND. Witness:WILLIAM H. EADS, ENOCH McCARTY. rec 1814 p 14

Deed dated 1814. JOHN WINCHILL to ARTHUR DIXON. Brkv lot 20. Signed JOHN WINCHILL, ANNA WINCHILL. Witness: none. rec 1814. p 15

Deed dated 1814. JOSEPH SIERS to MATHEW SPARKS. S 4, T 8, R 1. Signed JOSEPH SIERS. Witness: WILLIAM McDANIEL, WILLIAM BUSTER. rec 1814. pp 15, 16

Deed dated 1814. JAMES KNIGHT to CHARLES DAILY. Brkv lot 10. Signed JAMES KNIGHT, MARY KNIGHT. Witness: none. rec 1814. p 16

Deed dated 1814. WILLIAM BRADLEY to JAMES NOBLE & ENOCH D. JOHN. Brkv lot 38. "REBECCAH, his wife". Signed WILLIAM BRADLEY, REBECCAH (x) BRADLEY. Witness: JOHN TEST, ARTHUR DIXON. rec 1814. p 17

Deed dated 1814. AMOS BUTLER to JAMES McGINNIS. field "which JOSEPH RIPPY had leased." no S-T-R; bounds given. Signed AMOS BUTLER, MARY BUTLER. Witness: JOHN TEST, ROBERT McGILL. rec 1814. p 18 (p 19 blank)

Deed dated 1814. JOHN ALLEN to JAMES McGINNIS, Captain. S 29, T 9, R 2W. Signed JOHN ALLEN, REBECCAH (x) ALLEN. Witness: JOHN TEST, LYDIE TEST. rec 1814. p 20

FRANKLIN COUNTY DEEDS: Book B

Deed dated 1814. WILLIAM H. EADS to NATHAN D. GALLION. Brkv 44. Signed WILLIAM H. EADS, JANE EADS. Witness: JOHN TEST, JOHN HALL. rec 1814. p 21

Sheriff's sale dated 1814. ROBERT HANNA, Sheriff of Franklin Co to JAMES KNIGHT. Suit for debt filed by KNIGHT against MICHAEL JONES & JAMES HAMILTON. Brkv lot 66 seized, sold at auction to KNIGHT, the highest bidder. Signed ROBERT HANNA, Sheriff. Witness: none. rec 1814. pp 21, 22

Deed dated 1814. SPENCER WILEY & JAMES WILEY & ELIZABETH WILEY, his wife, to ALLEN WILEY. S 11, T 8, R 1W. Signed SPENCER WILEY, JAMES WILEY, ELIZABETH WILEY. Witness: none. rec 1814. p 23

Emancipation dated 1814. JAMES BAILEY & PATIENCE, his wife, rcvd servitude of HAZARD H. HINDSLEY, "a person of color" until he attained the age 23 yrs, as a legacy from PATIENCE HINDSLEY. Having served that period HAZARD is now released. Signed JAMES BAILEY, PATIENCE BAILEY. Witness: AARON RICHARDSON. rec 1815. p 24

Sheriff's sale dated 1814. ROBERT HANNA, Sheriff of Franklin Co to JAMES KNIGHT. Judgement against MICHAEL JONES & JAMES HAMILTON obtained by KNIGHT. Brkv lot 2 seized, sold at auction to KNIGHT, the highest bidder. Signed ROBERT HANNA, Sheriff. Witness: none. rec 1814 pp 25, 26

Sheriff's sale dated 1814. ROBERT HANNA, Sheriff of Franklin Co to JAMES KNIGHT. See case above. Brkv lot 7. Signed ROBERT HANNA, Sheriff. Witness: none rec 1814. p 27

Sheriff's Sale dated 1814. ROBERT HANNA, Sheriff to JAMES KNIGHT JR. As above. Brkv lot 25. Signed ROBERT HANNA, Sheriff. Witness: none. rec 1814. pp 28,29

Sheriff's Sale dated 1814. ROBERT HANNA, Sheriff to JAMES KNIGHT. See case above. Brkv lot 14. Signed ROBERT HANNA, Sheriff. Witness: none. rec 1814. p 30

Sheriff's Sale dated 1814. ROBERT HANNA, Sheriff to JAMES KNIGHT. See case above. Brkv lot 13. Signed Signed ROBERT HANNA, Sheriff. Witness: none. rec 1814. pp 31, 32

Sheriff's Sale dated 1814. ROBERT HANNA, Sheriff to JAMES KNIGHT. See case above. Brkv lot 1. Signed ROBERT HANNA, Sheriff. Witness: none. rec 1814. p 33

FRANKLIN COUNTY DEEDS: Book B

Sheriff's Sale dated 1814. ROBERT HANNA, Sheriff to JAMES KNIGHT. See case previous page. Brkv lot 8. Signed ROBERT HANNA, Sheriff. Witness: none. rec 1814. pp 34, 35

Sheriff' Sale dated 1814. ROBERT HANNA, Sheriff to JAMES KNIGHT. See above. Brkv lot 11. Signed ROBERT HANNA, Sheriff. Witness: none. rec 1814. p 36

Sheriff' Sale dated 1814. ROBERT HANNA, Sheriff to JAMES KNIGHT JR. See above. Brkv 56. Signed ROBERT HANNA, Sheriff. Witness: none. rec 1814. pp 37, 38

Sheriff' Sale dated 1814. ROBERT HANNA, Sheriff to JAMES KNIGHT. See above. Brkv lot 65. Signed ROBERT HANNA, Sheriff. Witness: none. rec 1814. p 39

Sheriff' Sale dated 1814. ROBERT HANNA, Sheriff to BENJAMIN SMITH. Judgement against MICHAEL JONES & JAMES HAMILTON obtained by JAMES KNIGHT. Brkv lot 75 seized, sold at auction to SMITH, the highest bidder. Signed ROBERT HANNA, Sheriff. Witness: none. rec 1814. pp 40, 41

Sheriff' Sale dated 1814. ROBERT HANNA, Sheriff to BENJAMIN SMITH. See above. Brkv lot 76. Signed ROBERT HANNA, Sheriff. Witness: none. rec 1814. p 42

Sheriff' Sale dated 1814. ROBERT HANNA, Sheriff to BENJAMIN SMITH. See above. Brkv lot 68. Signed ROBERT HANNA, Sheriff. Witness: none. rec 1814. pp 43, 44

Sheriff' Sale dated 1814. ROBERT HANNA, Sheriff to BENJAMIN SMITH. See above. Brkv lot 67. Signed ROBERT HANNA, Sheriff. Witness: none. rec 1814 pp 44, 45

Sheriff' Sale dated 1814. ROBERT HANNA, Sheriff to BENJAMIN SMITH. See above. Brkv lot 53. Signed ROBERT HANNA, Sheriff. Witness: none. rec 1814. p 46

Sheriff' Sale dated 1814. ROBERT HANNA, Sheriff to BENJAMIN SMITH. See above. Brkv 54. Signed ROBERT HANNA, Sheriff. Witness: none. rec 1814. p 47

Sheriff' Sale dated 1814. ROBERT HANNA, Sheriff to BENJAMIN SMITH. See above. Brkv 69. Signed ROBERT HANNA, Sheriff. Witness: none. rec 1814. pp 48, 49

Deed dated 1814. ARTHUR DIXON to BENJAMIN SMITH. Brkv lots 49, 50. "SARAH, his wife." Signed ARTHUR DIXON, SARAH DIXON. Witness: none. rec 1814. p 50

FRANKLIN COUNTY DEEDS: Book B

Deed dated 1815. WILLIAM H. EADS to KNOWLES SHAW JR. Brkv inlot 48. Signed WILLIAM H. EADS, JANE EADS. Witness: ELLIOT HERNDON, THOMAS HERNDON. rec 1814.* p 51 *transcription error? should be 1815

Deed dated 1815. WILLIAM H. EADS to JAMES NEWLAND & NATHAN BASCOM, both of Bracken Co, KY. Brkv lots 47 & 48. Signed WILLAIM H. EADS, JANE EADS. Witness: ELLIOTT HERNDON, CHARLES B. FINCH. rec 1815. p 52

Deed dated 1815. JOHN R. BEATY to NATHAN D. GALLION of Franklin Co, & THOMAS C. KELSEY of Butler Co, OH. Brkv lot 43. "ELIZABETH, wife of JOHN". Signed JOHN R. BEATY, ELIZABETH BEATY. Witness: none. rec 1815. p 53

Deed dated 1814. JOAB BROOKS & HANNAH, his wife, to JOHN CROMWELL. S 9, T 11, R 1W. Signed JOAB BROOKS, HANNAH (x) BROOKS. Witness: none. rec 1815. p 54

Deed dated 1815. AMOS BUTLER to ANDREW SHIRK. Brkv lot 26. Signed AMOS BUTLER, MARY BUTLER. Witness: JNO. TEST. rec 1815. p 54

Deed dated 1814. ALLEN WILEY & MARGARET, his wife, SPENCER WILEY, JAMES WILEY & ELIZABETH, his wife, to SAMUEL DUGANS. S 11, T 8, R 1. Signed ALLEN WILEY, MARGARET WILEY, SPENCER WILEY, JAMES WILEY, ELIZABETH (x) WILEY. Witness: none. rec 1815. p 55

Deed dated 1815. JOHN PENWELL to RILEY WOODWORTH. S 34, T9, R 2W. Signed JOHN PENWELL, ESTHER PENWELL. Witness: J. WINCHILL, SOPHIA SNELL. No rec date. p 56   JP's note: .."ESTHER, wife of said JOHN"

Deed dated 1815. JAMES KNIGHT to JOHN JACOBS. Brkv lot 32. Signed JAMES KNIGHT, MARY KNIGHT. Witness: none. rec 1815. p 57

Deed dated 1815. JOHN JAMES of Dearborn Co to JOHN JACOBS. Brkv lot 33. Signed JOHN JAMES. Witness: none. rec 1815. p 58

Deed dated 1814. JOHN MOORE & JEREMIAH CORY to JOHN JACOBS. S 8, T 9, R2W. Signed JEREMIAH CORY, JOHN MOORE, REBECCAH CORY. Witness: JAMES NOBLE, SOLOMON (x) TYNER. rec 1815. pp 59, 60

Deed dated 1814. WILLIAM DUBOIS to RICHARD WATERS. S 30, T 10, R 1. "HANNAH, his wife". Signed WILLIAM DUBOIS, HANNAH DUBOIS. Witness: JOHN WHITWORTH, EDMUND BILLINGS. no rec date. p 61

FRANKLIN COUNTY DEEDS: Book B

Deed dated 1815. JOHN ALLEN to DAVID MOORE. Brkv 1, 2. Signed JOHN ALLEN, REBECCAH (x) ALLEN. Witness: none. rec 1815. p 62

Deed dated 1815. CALEB C. TUNIS to JOHN JACOBS. Brkv lot 32. Signed CALEB C. TUNIS. Witness: JAMES NOBLE. rec 1815. p 62 (p 63 blank)

Sheriff's Sale dated 1814. ROBERT HANNA, Sheriff of Franklin Co to JEREMIAH CORY. Judgement against MICHAEL JONES & JAMES HAMILTON obtained by JAMES KNIGHT. Brkv lot 73 seized, sold at auction to CORY. the highest bidder. Signed ROBERT HANNA. Witness: none. rec 1815. p 64

Deed dated 1814. NATHAN PORTER & NANCY, his wife, to HUGH MAY. S 19, T 8, R 1W. Signed NATHAN PORTER, NANCY (x) PORTER. Witness: SOLOMON MANWARING, SAMUEL ROCKAFELLAR. rec 1815. p 65

Deed dated 1815. JAMES NOBLE to ENOCH DAVID JOHN. Brkv lot 38. Signed JAMES NOBLE, MARY NOBLE. Witness: none. no rec date. p 66

Deed dated 1814. STEPHEN LUDLOW of Dearborn Co to JOHN R. BEATY. Brkv lot 43. "JANE, his wife". Signed STEPHEN LUDLOW, JOHN P. LUDLOW typed, JANE written over. Witness: none. no rec date. p 67 (In original ledger - wife's signature JANE LUDLOW)

Deed dated 1815. CALDER HAYMOND to JOHN HAYMOND. S 11, T 8, R 1. "CATHERINE, his wife". Signed CALDER HAYMOND, CATHERINE (x) HAYMOND. Witness: none. rec 1815. p 68

Deed dated 1814. ENOCH LYMPUS & SARAH, his wife, to JONATHAN LYMPUS. S 34, T 13, R 12E. Signed ENOCH (x) LYMPUS, SARAH (x) LYMPUS. Witness: JAMES JOHNSON. SARAH JOHNSON (at Butler Co, OH). rec 1815. pp 68, 69

Deed dated 1814. THOMAS MADDEN to JOSEPH EVANS of Cincinnati, OH. S 17, T 11, R 1. "except 40 acres sold to EBENEZER HOWE" and New Washington town lots 6, 7, 8, 12, 13, 14, 22, 23, 24 & 26 previously sold. Signed THOMAS MADDEN, RUTH MADDEN. Witness: THOMAS PEIRCE. no rec date. p 70

Deed dated 1814. JAMES McNUTT & REBECCAH, his wife, & GEORGE TODD & MARTHY, his wife, to ANDREW SHIRD*SR. S 13, T 9, R 1W. Signed JAMES McNUTT, REBECCAH (x) McNUTT, GEORGE TODD, MARTHY (x) TODD. Witness: none. No rec date. p 71 *transcription error - SHIRK

FRANKLIN COUNTY DEEDS: Book B

Deed dated 1814. ANDREW SHIRK JR to ANDREW SHIRK SR. S 13, T 9, R 1W. Signed ANDREW SHIRK JR. Witness: none. rec 1815. p 72

Deed dated 1815. CHITESTER JOHNSON to AMOS BUTLER. S 18, T 8, R 1W. Signed CHITESTER JOHNSON, MERIAN (x) JOHNSON. Witness: J. WINCHILL, ABIGAIL (x) WINCHILL. JP's note: "MIRIAM JOHNSON, wife of CHITESTER. rec 1815. p 72

Deed dated 1814. AMOS BUTLER to JACOB HETRICK. S 29, T 9, R 2W. Signed AMOS BUTLER, MARY BUTLER. Witness: LEWIS BISHOP. no rec date. p 73

Deed dated 1815. JACOB HACKLEMAN SR of Dearborn Co to JACOB HACKLEMAN. S 4, T 8, R 2W. Signed JACOB HACKLEMAN. Witness: none. rec 1815. p 74

Deed dated 1815. JACOB HACKLEMAN SR of Dearborn Co to JOHN HACKLEMAN. S 4, T 8, R 2W. Signed JACOB HACKLEMAN. Witness: none. rec 1815. p 74

Deed dated 1815. JOHN THOMPSON to JOHN BATES of Bradford Co, PA. S 11, T 8, R 2W. "LETTICE, wife of JOHN (THOMPSON)". Signed JOHN (x) THOMPSON, LETTICE (x) THOMPSON. Witness: RUS STEVENS, ELIOHA* WYTHE. rec 1815. p 75 *transcription error? ELISHA

Deed dated 1815. JOHN QUICK to JOHN SHANK. S 2, T 8, R 2W. "POLLY, wife of JOHN (QUICK)". Signed JOHN QUICK, POLLY (x) QUICK. Witness: ENOCH McCARTY, LEONARD --. rec 1815. p 76

Deed dated 1815. JACOB HACKLEMAN SR of Dearborn Co to MICHAEL HACKLEMAN. S 24, T 14, R 12E. Signed JACOB HACKLEMAN. Witness: none. rec 1815. p 77

Deed dated 1815. GEORGE HOLLINGSWORTH to ABRAHAM HOLLINGSWORTH. S 10, T 10, R 2W. "SUSANNAH, his wife" Signed GEORGE HOLLINGSWORTH, SUSANNAH (x) HOLLINGSWORTH. Witness: JOHN HANNA, JOSEPH HANNA, THOMAS OSBORN. rec 1815. p 78

Deed dated 1814. DANIEL REED of Rockbridge Co, VA & MARGARET, his wife, to WILLIAM REED of Preble Co, OH. "Affection which (DANIEL) bears his son WILLIAM" S 7, T 9, R 1. Signed DANIEL REED, MARGARET (x) REED at Rockbridge Co, VA. ANDREW REED, Clerk of Courts, VA. rec 1815. p 78

Deed dated 1814. DANIEL REED of Rockbridge Co, VA & MARGARET, his wife, to JOHN REED. "Affection which

FRANKLIN COUNTY DEEDS: Book B

(DANIEL) bears his son JOHN". S 6, T 9, R 1. Signed DANIEL REED, MARGARET (x) REED at Rockbridge Co, VA. ANDREW REED, Clerk of Courts, VA. rec 1815. p 79

Deed dated 1815. JOHN R. BEATY to NATHAN D. GALLION. Brkv lot 43. Signed JOHN R. BEATY, ELIZABETH BEATY. Witness: none. rec 1815. p 80

Deed dated 1815. NATHAN D. GALLION to JOHN R. BEATY. Brkv 44. Signed NATHAN D. GALLION, HANNAH GALLION. Witness: none. rec 1815. p 81

Deed dated 1815. JAMES NOBLE to ROBERT McCOY. Brkv lot 29. Signed JAMES NOBLE, MARY NOBLE. Witness: none. rec 1815. p 82

POA dated 1815. RICHARD COCKEY of Baltimore Co, MD, appt'd ENOCH D. JOHN to act as att'y. Signed RICHARD COCKEY. Witness: REUBEN MONROE, J. H.-- CRAWFORD (at Franklin Co, PA). rec 1815. p 83

Deed dated 1815. ENOCH D. JOHN as att'y above to JOSHUA MURREY. S 20, T 9, R -W. Signed RICHARD COCKEY by ENOCH D. JOHN, Att'y in fact. Witness: none. no rec date. p 84 (p 85 blank)

Deed dated 1815. JAMES McGINNIS to JAMES NOBLE. S 29 T 9, R 2W. "JANE, his wife". Signed JAMES McGINNIS, JANE (x) McGINNIS. Witness: none. rec 1815. p 86

Deed dated 1815. DAVID LORING to JAMES NOBLE. Brkv lots 44, 47. "FRANCES, his wife" Signed DAVID LORING, FRANCES LORING. Witness: none. rec 1815. p 87

Deed dated 1815. JOHN HERRALD to ISAAC LIMPUS. S 28, T 13, R 12. "JOHN FRED's survey". "ABIGAIL, his wife". Signed JOHN (x) HERRALD, ABIGAIL (x) HERRALD. Witness: none. No rec date. p 88 (pp 89, 90 blank)

Deed dated 1815. PATRICK McCARTY to THOMAS POWERS. S 25, T 10, R 3W. Signed PATRICK McCARTY, REBECCAH McCARTY. Witness: none. rec 1815. p 91

Deed dated 1815. PATRICK McCARTY to JONATHAN GILEAN SR. S 25, T 10, R 3W. Signed PATRICK McCARTY, REBECCAH McCARTY. Witness: none. no rec date. p 92

Deed dated 1815. JOHN ALLEN to JAMES WINCHEL. Brkv lots 18, 13. Signed JOHN ALLEN, REBECCAH (x) ALLEN. Witness: BENJ. SMITH, JAS. McKINNEY. no rec date. (p 93 blank) p 94

FRANKLIN COUNTY DEEDS: Book B

Deed dated 1815. ARTHUR DICKSON to JAMES NOBLE. Brkv lot 20. Signed ARTHUR DICKSON, SARAH DICKSON. Witness: none. rec 1815. p 95 (p 96 blank)

Deed dated 1815. JAMES WILSON to WILLIAM KERR of Hamilton Co, OH. Brkv lots 40, 41. Signed JAMES WILSON, ELIZABETH WILSON. Witness: none. rec 1815. p 97

Deed dated 1815. ALLEN WILEY & MARGARET, his wife, to JOHN WILLIAMS. S 11, T 8, R 1W. Signed ALLEN WILEY, MARGARET WILEY. Witness: MOSES WILEY. rec 1815. (p 98 blank) p 99

Deed dated 1815. JOHN DICKERSON to WILLIAM HENRY EADS. S11, T 10, R 2W. "RUTH, his wife". Signed JOHN DICKERSON, RUTH DICKERSON. Witness: JOHN --, AARON FRAKES. rec 1815. p 100

Sheriff's Sale dated 1814. ROBERT HANNA, Sheriff of Franklin Co, to JAMES McGINNIS. Property of JONES & HAMILTON seized in lawsuit. Brkv lot 70 purchased at auction. Signed ROBERT HANNA, Sheriff. Witness: none. no rec date. p 101 (p 102 blank)

Sheriff's Sale dated 1814. ROBERT HANNA, Sheriff of Franklin Co, to JAMES McGINNIS. See case above. Brkv lot 74. Signed ROBERT HANNA, Sheriff. Witness: none. no rec date. p 103 (p 104 blank)

Sheriff's Sale dated 1814. ROBERT HANNA, Sheriff of Franklin Co, to JAMES McGINNIS. As above. Brkv lot 39. Signed ROBERT HANNA, Sheriff. Witness: none. rec 1815. p 105 (p 106 blank)

Deed dated 1815. JOHN SAILOR & MICHAEL SAILOR to NATHANIEL HERNDON. S 18, T 8, R 1W. "ELIZABETH, wife of JOHN & POLLY, wife of MICHAEL". Signed JOHN (x) SAILOR, ELIZABETH (x) SAILOR, MICHAEL (x) SAILOR, POLLY (x) SAILOR. no rec date. p 107 (p 108 blank)

Sheriff's Sale dated 1814. ROBERT HANNA, Sheriff of Franklin Co, to JEREMIAH CORY. Property of JONES & HAMILTON seized in lawsuit. Brkv lot 62 purchased at auction. Signed ROBERT HANNA, Sheriff. Witness: none. no rec date. p 109, 110

Sheriff's Sale dated 1814. ROBERT HANNA, Sheriff of Franklin Co, to JAMES WILSON. Property of JONES & HAMILTON seized in lawsuit. Brkv lot 64 purchased at auction. Signed ROBERT HANNA, Sheriff. Witness: none. no rec date. p 111, 112

FRANKLIN COUNTY DEEDS: Book B

Sheriff's Sale dated 1814. ROBERT HANNA, Sheriff of Franklin Co, to JEREMIAH CORY. See case previous page. Brkv lot 46. Signed ROBERT HANNA, Sheriff. Witness: none. rec 1815. p 112, 113 (p 114 blank)

Sheriff's Sale dated 1814. ROBERT HANNA, Sheriff of Franklin Co, to JEREMIAH CORY. As above. Brkv lot 61. Signed ROBERT HANNA, Sheriff. Witness: none. rec 1815. p 115

Sheriff's Sale dated 1814. ROBERT HANNA, Sheriff of Franklin Co, to JEREMIAH CORY. As above. Brkv lot 12. Signed ROBERT HANNA, Sheriff. Witness: none. rec 1815. p 116

Sheriff's Sale dated 1814. ROBERT HANNA, Sheriff of Franklin Co, to JOHN DICKISON. As above. Brkv lot 71 Signed ROBERT HANNA, Sheriff. Witness: none. rec 1815. p 117

Sheriff's Sale dated 1814. ROBERT HANNA, Sheriff of Franklin Co, to JOHN DICKESON. As above. Brkv lot 72 Signed ROBERT HANNA, Sheriff. Witness: none. rec 1815. p 119

Deed dated 1814. JOHN LAVISON* & ANN, his wife, to FREDERICK PLEURDOFF (OLENSDOFF written above). S 23, T 8, R 1. Signed JOHN LAVISON, ANN LAVISON. Witness: none. no rec date. p 120   *In original ledger, name appears to be JOHN LARRISON.

Brookville addition plat map dated 1815. Lots 68 to 99 by JOHN ALLEN. Witness: J. WINCHIL, JP. rec 1815. p 121

Deed dated 1815. DANIEL T. GARDEN to BARBARY CHRIST, dau of said DANIEL. S 5, T 12, R 13E. Land for sole use of BARBARY & heirs begotten of her body; land to be under her sole control. Signed DANIEL (x) T. GARDEN, ELIZABETH (x) T. GARDEN. Witness: none. no rec date. p 122 (Family name is probably TEGARDEN)

(p 123, 124, 125 blank. Original ledger has the following on pp 124, 125:
Deed dated 1814. ROBERT BROWN & RACHEL, his wife of Butler Co, OH, to JAMES BRANNAN. S 19, T 14, R 13E. Signed ROBERT BROWN, RACHEL BROWN. Witness: JOHN BAILEY, HENRY WEAVER.)

Deed dated 1814. ROBERT BROWN & RACHEL, his wife of Butler Co, OH, to PHINEHAS McCREA of the same. S 30, T 14, R 13E. Signed ROBERT BROWN, RACHEL BROWN. Wit-

FRANKLIN COUNTY DEEDS: Book B

ness: WILLIAM McCLAIN, ABRAHAM -- (appears to be TEITFORD in original ledger). rec 1815. p 126

Plat map of Mineral Springs, part of the town of Bath dated 1815. S 14, T 10, R 2W. Signed JAMES McKINNEY. rec 1815. p 128

Deed dated 1814. JOHN ALLEN of Dearborn Co to JOHN CALWELL. S 1, T 8, R 1W. Signed JOHN ALLEN, SARAH ALLEN. Witness: JOSEPH PARKS, JOHN S. ALLEN. rec 1815. p 129

Mortgage bond dated 1814. THOMAS LONGFELLOW to JOHN COLDWELL, JR. Land bought of SPENCER WILEY in S 11, T 8, R 1; LONGFELLOW to repay $138 plus interest within 5 yrs or convey good deed to COLDWELL. Signed THOMAS LONGFELLOW. Witness: MOSES WILEY, JAMES WILEY. no rec date. p 130

Deed dated 1814. SAMUEL DUGANS & REBECA, his wife, to JOHN COLDWELL. S 11, T 8, R 1W. "the said DUGANS hereunto moving". Signed SAMUEL DUGANS, REBECCA (x) DUGANS. Witness: none. rec 1815. pp 131, 132

Deed dated 1815. GEORGE GUITTNER to WILLIAM SYMONDS. S 36, T 12, R 12E. "to JOHN REED & WILLIAM GARDEN, thence south". Signed GEORGE GUILLNER, SARAH GUITTNER. Witness: JOSEPH RICHIE, DANIEL CHURCHILL. no rec date. p 133

Deed dated 1815. AMOS BUTLER to JAMES MOORE. S 29, T 9, R 2W. Signed AMOS BUTLER, MARY BUTLER. Witness: none. no rec date. pp 134, 135

Deed dated 1815. DAVID ATHERTON of Hamilton Co, OH to WILLIAM MILHOLLAND of same. Brkv lot 37. "RACHEL, his wife". Signed DAVID ATHERTON, RACHEL ATHERTON. Witness: none. rec 1815. pp 136, 137

Deed dated 1815. WILLIAM S. WHITE of Dearborn Co to JOHNSON CLARK. S 3, T 12, R 12. Signed WILLIAM S. WHITE, MARY (x) WHITE. Witness: SAMUEL ROCKAFELLAR. rec 1815. p 138

Deed dated 1814. ROBERT BROWN & RACHEL, his wife of Butler Co, OH, to JAMES BRANNAN. S 19, T 14, R 13E. Signed ROBERT BROWN, RACHEL BROWN. Witness: JOHN BAILEY, HENRY WEAVER. rec 1815. p 139

Deed dated 1815. BENJAMIN SMITH to JACOB MALSON of Hamilton Co, OH. Brkv lot 57. Signed BENJAMIN SMITH REBECCA (x) SMITH. Witness: JAMES NOBLE. no rec. p140

FRANKLIN COUNTY DEEDS: Book B

Sheriff's Sale dated 1814. ROBERT HANNA, Sheriff of Franklin Co, to JAMES WILSON. Property of JONES & HAMILTON seized in lawsuit. Brkv lot 40 purchased at auction. Signed ROBERT HANNA, Sheriff. Witness: none. no rec date. pp 141, 142

Sheriff's Sale dated 1814. ROBERT HANNA, Sheriff of Franklin Co, to JAMES WILSON. As above. Brkv lot 60. Signed ROBERT HANNA, Sheriff. Witness: none. no rec date. p 143

Sheriff's Sale dated 1814. ROBERT HANNA, Sheriff of Franklin Co, to JAMES WILSON. As above. Brkv lot 59. Unsigned. Witness: none. rec 1815. pp 144, 145

Sheriff's Sale dated 1814. ROBERT HANNA, Sheriff of Franklin Co, to JAMES WILSON. As above. Brkv lot 41. Unsigned. Witness: none. rec 1815. pp 146, 147

Deed dated 1815. AMOS BUTLER to WILLIAM HENRY EADS. Brkv lot 27. Signed AMOS BUTLER, MARY BUTLER. Witness: none. rec 1815. p 147

Deed dated 1815. WILLIAM HENRY EADS to MARY & CARBLY HUTSON. Brkv 44. Signed WILLIAM HENRY EADS, JANE EADS Witness: ARCHIBALD GUTHERY, ELLIOT HERNDON. rec 1815. p 148

Deed dated 1815. DAVID RICHARDSON to THOMAS BRADLEY. Brkv lot 9. Signed DAVID RICHARDSON. Witness: J. WINCHILL, THOMAS SIMS. rec 1815. p 149

Deed dated 1815. RUGGLES WINCHELL to STEPHEN WINCHILL. S 28, T 9, R 2. "MARTHA, wife of RUGGLES" Signed RUGGLES WINCHELL, MARTHA WINCHELL. Witness: SAMUEL RAY. rec 1815. p 150

Deed dated 1815. MARTIN JAMISON to LISMUND BASEY. Brkv lot 97. "BARBARY, his wife". Signed MARTIN JAMISON, BARBARY JAMISON. Witness: none. rec 1815. pp 151, 152

Deed dated 1815. JOHN ALLEN to ALEXANDER FULTON. Brkv lot 97. Signed JOHN ALLEN, REBECCA (x) ALLEN. Witness: BENJAMIN SMITH. no rec date. p 153

Deed dated 1815. AMOS BUTLER to LISMOND BASEY. Brkv lot 2. Signed AMOS BUTLER, MARY BUTLER. Witness: none. rec 1815. pp 153, 154

Deed dated 1814. WILLIAM NICHOLAS to JOHN DUNLAP. S 28, T 11, R 2W. "reserving to JOHN WARD JR ...6

FRANKLIN COUNTY DEEDS: Book B

acres". "ELIZABETH, his wife". Signed WILLIAM NICHOLS , ELIZABETH NICHOLS. Witness: JOHN WHITWORTH, JOHN WARD. rec 1815. p 155

Deed dated 1815. BENJAMIN SMITH to ALLISON C. LOOKER of Hamilton Co, OH. Brkv lot 49, 50. Signed BENJAMIN SMITH, REBECCA SMITH. Witness: J. WINCHILL. rec 1815 p 156

Deed dated 1815. AMOS BUTLER to RACHEL GILLEM, late wife of JOHN STOOP, dec, & exec of his estate, for use of heirs of JOHN STOOP. No S-T-R; bounds given "of JAMES MORE's section". Signed AMOS BUTLER, MARY BUTLER. Witness: none. rec 1815. pp 157, 158

Deed dated 1815. JAMES CRAIG to FREDERICK FARRIS. S 11, T 9, R 2W. "MARY, wife of JAMES". Signed JAMES CRAIG, MARY (x) CRAIG. Witness: JOHN HANNA. no rec date. p 159

Deed dated 1815. JOHN ALLEN SR to JOSEPH SEAL. Brkv lots 88, 89. Signed JOHN ALLEN, REBECCA (x) ALLEN. Witness: BENJAMIN SMITH. rec 25 Sept, no yr. p 160

Deed dated 1815. JOHN HERRALD & ABIGAIL, his wife, to JOHN FRED. S 28, T 13, R 12E. Signed JOHN HARRELL ABIGAIL (x) HARRELL. Witness: none. no rec date.p 161

Deed dated 1815. WILLIAM EADS of Harrison Co, KY to HENRY EADS. S 2, T 8, R 2W. "part of quarter sold to JONATHAN EADS. Signed WM. G. EADS, REBECCA EADS. Witness: WILLIAM HENRY EADS. rec 1815. p 162

Deed dated 1815. WILLIAM EADS of Harrison Co, KY to HENRY CASE. S 2, T 8, R 2W. Signed WM. G. EADS, REBECCA EADS. Witness: ENOCH McCARTY, JONATHAN --. rec 1815. p 163

Deed dated 1815. PHILLIP FRAKER to JOHN H. HATFIELD. S 30, T 10, R 1. Signed PHILLIP FRAKES,. PHEBE (x) FRAKES. Witness: JOHN WHITWORTH, AARON FRAKES. rec 1815. p 164

Deed dated 1815. EBENEZER HEATON of Wayne Co to DANIEL HEATON of same. S 21, T 14, R 13E. "JOANNA, his wife." Signed EBENEZER HEATON, JOANNA HEATON. Witness: CHARLES ROYSTER, EBENEZER GOBLE. no rec date. pp 165, 166

Deed dated 1815. ITHAMER WHITE & MARGARY, his wife to JACOB GATES. Sec 26, T 9, R 1W. Signed I.H. WHITE MARGERY (x) WHITE. Witness:none. rec 1815. pp 167,168

FRANKLIN COUNTY DEEDS: Book B

Deed dated 1815. ZACHERIAH DEVEE to JACOB GATES. S 29, T 9, R 1W. Signed ZACHERIAH DEVEE, JANNET (x) DEVEE. Witness: none. rec 1815. p 169

Deed dated 1815. DAVID RICHARDSON to JAMES NOBLE. Brkv lot 15, 16. Signed DAVID RICHARDSON. Witness: none. rec 1815. p 170

Deed dated 1815. ASA NORTHOP to JOHN GARRISON. Brkv 44, 45. "HANNA, his wife." Signed ASA NORTHROP, HANNAH NORTHROP. Witness: none. rec 1815. p 171

Deed dated 1815. MARTIN JAMISON to ANN COOPER. Brkv 30. Signed MARTIN JAMISON, BARBERY (x) JAMISON. Witness: WILLIAM HERNDON. no rec date. pp 172, 173

Deed dated 1815. SAMUEL LEE to ZACHARIAH DEVEE. S 23 T 9, R 1W. "PHEBE, his wife". Signed SAMUEL LEE, PHEBE LEE. Witness: none. rec 1815. p 174

Deed dated 1815. SAMUEL LEE to ROBERT LUCE. S 29, T 9, R 1W. Signed SAMUEL LEE, PHEBE LEE. Witness: none. rec 1815. pp 175, 176

Deed dated 1815. THOMAS SKINNER to RICHARD MANWARING of Dearborn Co. S 7, T 9, R 2W. Signed THOMAS SKINNER. Witness: none. rec 1815. p 177

Deed dated 1815. JOHN ALLEN to THOMAS ORANGE. Brkv 65. Signed JOHN ALLEN, REBECCA ALLEN. Witness: JAMES McKINNEY. rec 1815. p 178

Deed dated 1815. JOHN ALLEN to DAVID AGNEW. Brkv 38 Signed JOHN ALLEN, REBECCA ALLEN. Witness: none. rec 1815. pp 179, 180

Fairfield* town plat map dated 1815. S 21, T 10, R 2W "land of JAMES WILSON, THOMAS OSBORN, GEORGE JOHNSON, HUGH ABERNATHY". rec 1815. p 181 *Fairfield now lies at the bottom of Brookville Lake Reservoir.

Deed dated 1815. JOHN SAILOR to SAMUEL WEIR. S 18, T ?, R 1W. "except land sold to CHITTESTER JOHNSON, MICHAEL SAILORS, THOMAS SAILORS". Signed JOHN (x) SAILORS, ELIZABETH (x) SAILORS. Witness: ENOCH McCARTY, LEONARD SAILORS. rec 1815. pp 181, 182

Deed dated 1815. THOMAS SAILORS to SAMUEL WEIR. S 18 T 8, R 12. Signed THOMAS (x) SALIORS. Witness: ENOCH McCARTY. no rec date. p 183

Deed dated 1815. RICHARD MANWARING & ELIZABETH, his

FRANKLIN COUNTY DEEDS: Book B

wife, of Dearborn Co to SOLOMON MANWARING of same. S 26, T 12, R 13E. Signed RICHARD MANWARING, ELIZABETH MANWARING. Witness: WILLIAM SKINNER. rec 1815. p 184

Deed dated 1814. JAMES McKINNEY to JOHN TEST. Brkv lots 51, 52. "EDITH, his wife". Signed JAMES McKINNEY, EDITH (x) McKINNEY. Witness: J. WINCHILL. no rec date. p 185

Deed dated 1814. ENOCH McCARTY to WILLIAM H. EADS. Brkv 47, 48. Signed ENOCH McCARTY, ELIZABETH (x) McCARTY. Witness:JOHN TEST, ROBERT HANNA. rec 1815 p186

Sheriff's Sale dated 1814. ROBERT HANNA, Sheriff of Franklin Co, to JAMES McGINNIS. Property of JONES & HAMILTON seized in lawsuit. Brkv lot 63 purchased at auction. Signed ROBERT HANNA, Sheriff. Witness: none. rec 1815. pp 187, 188

Deed dated 1815. USA to ROBERT BARNARD, assignee of JACOB BAREKMAN. S 10, T 9, R 2W. rec 1815. p 189

Deed dated 1815. WILLIAM NICHOLS to JOHN DUNLAP. S 10, T 9, R 2W. Signed WILLIAM NICHOLS, ELIZABETH (x) NICHOLS. Witness: JOHN WARD, JOHN WHITWORTH. rec 1815. p 190

Deed dated 1815. JOHN LAVISON to BENJAMIN GULLEY. S23 T 8, R 1W. "JOHN LARISON & ANNA LARISON, his wife." Signed JOHN LAVISON, ANNA LAVISON. Witness: JOHN H. ROCKAFELLAR, SIMON GULLEY. no rec date. pp 191, 192

Deed dated 1815. MICHAEL JONES of Shawnee Town, IL Territory to ROBERT McGUIRE of Washington Co, PA. Brkv lot 34, 35. Signed MICHAEL JONES, MARY JONES. Witness: none. rec 1815. p 193

Deed dated 1815. THOMAS SKINNER to BLACKSTREE BOANIS (BARNES in text) S 7, T 9, R 2W. "ANN, his wife". Signed THOMAS SKINNER, ANN SKINNER. Witness: JAMES WINCHILL. rec 1815. p 194

Deed dated 1815. JOHN ALLEN SR to BENJAMIN SMITH. Brkv lot 34. Signed JOHN ALLEN, REBECCA ALLEN. Witness: none. rec 1815. p 195

Sheriff's Sale dated 1814. ROBERT HANNA, Sheriff of Franklin Co, to NATHANIEL WALLACE. Property of JONES & HAMILTON seized in lawsuit. Brkv lots 49 & 50 purchased at auction. Signed ROBERT HANNA, Sheriff. Witness: JOHN R. BEATY. rec 1815. p 196 (p 197 blank)

FRANKLIN COUNTY DEEDS: Book B

Deed dated 1815. NATHANIEL HERNDON to CHARLES HENDERSON. S 18, T 8, R 1W. Signed NATHANIEL HERNDON, ELIZABETH HERNDON. Witness: J. WINCHILL. rec 1815. pp 198, 199

Deed dated 1811. USA to ANDREW CORNELISON of Butler Co (no state given). S 32, T 10, R 1W. rec 1815 p 200

Deed dated 1815. WILLIAM HENRY EADS to MARY HUTSON. Brkv 27. Signed WILLIAM HENRY EADS, JANE EADS. Witness: FREDERICK FERRIS, CORBLY HUDSON rec 1815. p 201

Deed dated 1815. JOHN GAVISON to JOHN WILSON of Clearmont Co, OH. Brkv 44, 45. "SINA, his wife". Signed JOHN GARRISON, SINA GARRISON. Witness: JOHN MORRIS, BENJAMIN SMITH. no rec date. p 203

Deed dated 1815. ASA NORTHROP to NATHAN D. GALLION. Brkv 44, 45. Signed ASA NORTHROP, HANNAH NORTHROP. Witness: BENJAMIN SMITH, DAVID RICHARDSON. no rec date. p 204

Testimony dated 1815. ROBERT ADAIR, MARGARET ADAIR & JACOB SPEAR came before JP; acknowledged that slander accusing WILLIAM ARNETT JR of bugery to be false and a willful lie, that there is no ground to believe it true. Signed JOHN FUGET, JP; ROBERT ADAIR, MARGARET (x) ADAIR, JACOB (x) SPEAR. no rec date. p 205

Deed dated 1815. DAVID MOORE to JOHN JACOBS. Brkv lot 1. Signed DAVID MOORE. Witness: GEORGE L. MURDOCK. rec 1816. p 206

Deed dated 1815. MICHAEL JONES of Illinois Territory to AQUILLA LOGAN. Brkv lots 26, 27. Signed MICHAEL JONES, MARY JONES. Witness: none. rec 1816. p 207

Deed dated 1815. AQUILLA LOGAN of New Orleans, LA to JAMES KNIGHT the elder. Brkv lots 26, 27. Signed AQUILLA LOGAN. Witness: PHILIP GUISNOUR, GEORGE POLLOCK (in LA). rec 1816. p 208

Deed dated 1815. JOHN ALLEN SR to JAMES McKINNEY. Brkv 53. Signed JOHN ALLEN, REBECCA (x) ALLEN. Witness: none. no rec date. p 209

Deed dated 1815. SOLOMON MANWARING & JANE, his wife of Dearborn Co to ROBERT HANNA, SR. S 33, T 10, R 2. Signed SOLOMON MANWARING, JANE MANWARING. Witness: JOHN HANNA. rec 1816. p 210

Deed dated 1816. JAMES NOBLE to ENOCH D. JOHN. Brkv

FRANKLIN COUNTY DEEDS: Book B

lot 37. Signed JAMES NOBLE, MARY NOBLE. Witness: none. rec 1816. p 211

Deed dated 1816. JAMES NOBLE to JAMES A. PIATT. Brkv lot 38. Signed JAMES NOBLE, MARY NOBLE. Witness: none. rec 1816. p 212

Deed dated 1816. ENOCH D. JOHN to JAMES A. PIATT. Brkv lot 38. Signed ENOCH D. JOHN. Witness: none. rec 1816. p 213 (p 214 blank)

Deed dated 1815. KNOWLES SHAW JR to KNOWLES SHAW SR. Brkv 48. Signed KNOWLES SHAW JR. Witness: none. rec 1816. p 215

Deed dated 1815. JOHN JAMES of Dearborn Co to JOHN B. WHITFORD. Brkv lot 33. Signed JOHN JAMES. Witness: JNO TEST. rec 1816. pp 215, 216

Deed dated 1815. JAMES KNIGHT to JOHN B. WHITFORD. Brkv lot 32. Signed JAMES KNIGHT, MARY KNIGHT. Witness: none. rec 1816. p 217

Deed dated 1815. DANIEL HEATON to JACOB REED, HARDEN REED & ASA HARPER. all of Wayne Co. S 19, T 14, R 13E "reserving 5 acres ...conveyed to JOHN CONNE". Signed DANIEL HEATON, MARY (x) HEATON. Witness: WILLIAM HELM no rec date. p 218

Deed dated 1816. WILLIAM CUNNINGHAM to JOSEPH S. NORRIS of Scott Co, KY. S 33, T 11, R 2W. Signed WILLIAM (x) CUNNINGHAM.. Witness: GEORGE NORRIS, BENNETT OSBORN. rec 1816. p 219

Deed dated 1816. THOMAS OWSLEY to ZACHERIA OWSLEY. S 34, T 12, R 13E. "DIANNA, his wife" Signed THOMAS (x) OWSLEY, DIANNA (x) OWSLEY. Witness: JOHN TEST, JAMES RARDEN. rec 1816. pp 220, 221

Deed dated 1815. JOSEPH LEE to WILLIAM DENISTON. S 23, T 10, R 1W. "NANCY, his wife". Signed JOSEPH LEE, NANCY (x) LEE. Witness: none. rec 1816. p 222

Deed dated 1815. GEORGE L. MURDOCK to NATHANIEL FRENCH. Brkv lot 73. "ANNA, wife of GEORGE". Signed GEORGE L. MURDOCK, ANNA MURDOCK. Witness: J. WINCHILL, MOSES FINCH. no rec date. p 223

Deed dated 1816. JOHN B. WHITFORD to JOHN JACOBS. Brkv lot 33. Signed JOHN B. WHITFORD. Witness: JOHN TEST. rec 1816. p 224

FRANKLIN COUNTY DEEDS: Book B

Deed dated 1815. THADUES WHELAN to JAMES KNIGHT SR. Brkv lot 12. Signed THADDIUS WHELAN. Witness: DAVID RICHARDSON. no rec date. p 225

Deed dated 1816. JOHN SALYER to JOEL SCOTT. S 33, T 13, R 13E. "my wife ELIZABETH". Signed JOHN SALYER, ELIZABETH (x) SALYER. Witness: none. rec 1816. p 226

Lease dated 1816. STEPHEN C. STEVENS to MICHAEL C. SNELL. Term: 7 yrs, conditions specified. No S-T-R, bounds only. Signed STEPHEN C. STEVENS, MICHL C. SNELL. Witness: JOHN TEST. rec 1816. pp 227, 228

Deed dated 1815. SAMUEL SIRING of Warren Co, OH to WILLIAM HENRY EADS. Brkv lot 42. "ELIZABETH, his wife". Signed SAMUEL SIRING, ELIZABETH SIRING. Witness: JEREMIAH CORY (in OH) no rec date pp 228, 229

Deed dated 1814. WALTER TUCKER to JOHN BLUE. S 18, T 9, R 1W. "NANCY, his wife". Signed WALTER (x) TUCKER, NANCY (x) TUCKER. Witness: none. no rec date. pp 229, 230

Deed dated 1814. SAMUEL McCRAY to JOHN BLUE of Hamilton Co, OH. S 10, T 9, R 1W. Signed SAMUEL McCRAY ELIZABETH McCRAY. Witness: none. rec 1816. p 230

Deed dated 1814. JAMES WOOD to PETER VANDYKE of Hamilton Co, OH. S 5, T 9, R 1W. Signed JAMES WOODS, SARAH WOODS. Witness: none. no rec date. p 231

Deed dated 1815. WILLIAM NELSON to ISAAC UPDYKE of Fayette Co, PA. S 5, T 9, R 1W. Signed WILLIAM NELSON, BARBARY NELSON. Witness: PETER VANDYKE. rec 1815. p 231

Deed dated 1816. AMOS BUTLER to JOHN ADAIR of Dearborn Co. Brkv lot 30. Signed AMOS BUTLER, MARY BUTLER. Witness: none. rec 1816. p 232

Deed dated 1816. AMOS BUTLER to WILLIAM H. EADS. Brkv lot 31. Signed AMOS BUTLER, MARY BUTLER. Witness: none. rec 1816. pp 232, 233

Deed dated 1815. AMOS BUTLER to JOHN STRANGE. Brkv lot 53. Signed AMOS BUTLER, MARY BUTLER. Witness: none. rec 1816. pp 233, 234

Deed dated 1815. JAMES KNIGHT to STEPHEN C. STEPHENS. Brkv lots 13, 14. Signed JAMES KNIGHT, MARY KNIGHT. Witness: none. rec 1816. p 234

FRANKLIN COUNTY DEEDS: Book B

Deed dated 1816. JAMES NOBLE to STEPHEN C. STEPHENS. S 28, T 9, R 2. Signed JAMES NOBLE, MARY NOBLE. Witness: none. rec 1816. p 235

Deed dated 1816. ISAAC M. JOHNSON to BENJAMIN McCARTY. Brkv lot 39. "his wife ANNE". Signed ISAAC M. JOHNSON, ANNA JOHNSON. Witness: JOHN TEST. no rec date. p 236

Deed dated 1816. JEREMIAH CORY to JAMES A. PIATT. Brkv lots 61, 62. Signed JEREMIAH CORY, REBECAH CORY Witness: J. WINCHILL. rec 1816. p 237

Deed dated 1816. BENJAMIN SMITH to ENOCH D. JOHN. Brkv lots 47, 48. BENJAMIN SMITH, REBECCAH SMITH. Witness: NAT'L. FRENCH. no rec date. pp 238, 239

Deed dated 1815. WILLIAM SEIRS of Washington Co to EDWARD HAYMOND. S 10, T 8, R 1. Signed WILLIAM (x) SIERS. Witness: WILLIAM POPE (at Washington Co). rec 1816. p 240

Deed dated 1815. WILLIAM BUSTER & SARAH, his wife, of Washington Co to EDWARD HAYMOND. S 10, T 8, R 1. Signed WILLIAM BUSTER, SARAH BUSTER. Witness: BATIE BUSTER (at Washington Co). no rec date. pp 240, 241

Deed dated 1816. ISAAC SUMAN to THOMAS NEAL JR & LOUISA, his wife. "possession now being and to the heirs of the body of said LOUISA NEAL". S 24, T 10, R 2W. "to corner of WILLIAM GRAY". Signed ISAAC SERMAN, ELIZABETH SERMAN. Witness: none. rec 1816. pp 241, 242

Deed dated 1816. STEPHEN C. STEVENS to JOHN CARSON of Cincinnati, OH. S 28, T 9, R 2W. JOHN CORSON in text. Signed STEPHEN C. STEVENS. Witness: JOHN MAHARD, ANSON BOGGS (at Hamilton Co, OH) no rec date. pp 242, 243

Deed dated 1815. MICHAEL CLINE to JOHN CLINE, one of the sons & heirs-at-law of MICHAEL. S 7, T 10, R 1. "HANNAH, his wife". Signed MICHAEL CLINE, HANNAH (x) CLINE. Witness: JOHN WHITWORTH. rec 1816. pp 243, 244

Deed dated 1816. MARTIN JAMISON of Warren Co, OH to WALTER DICKINSON of Butler Co, OH. Brkv 30. Signed MARTIN JAMISON, BARBARY JAMISON. Witness: JOHN GREGG, ABRAM VANVECT (Warren Co, OH). rec 1816. pp 245, 246

Deed dated 1816. WALTER DICKINSON as above to ROBERT JOHN. Brkv lot 30. Signed WALTER DICKINSON. Witness

FRANKLIN COUNTY DEEDS: Book B

ENOCH D. JOHN. rec 1816. pp 246, 247

Sheriff's Sale dated 1815. ROBERT HANNA, Sheriff of Franklin Co, to JAMES KNIGHT. Property of JONES & HAMILTON seized in lawsuit. Brkv lots 45, 46 purchased at auction. Signed ROBERT HANNA, Sheriff. Witness: none. no rec date. p 248

Deed dated 1815. LEMUEL LEMMON of Butler Co, OH to DANIEL SHAFER SR of Northumberland Co, PA. S 4, T 9, R 1W. "SARAH, his wife." Signed LEMUEL LEMMON, SARAH LEMMON. Witness: none. no rec date. p 249

Deed dated 1815. JOHN HAGEMAN of Wayne Co to ABIAH HAYSE of Dearborn Co. S 19, T 8, R 1W. "HANNAH, his wife". Signed JOHN HAGEMAN, HANNAH HAGEMAN. Witness: SIMON GULLY, JOSEPH DORTON. rec 1816. p 250

Deed dated 1816. WILLIAM MULHALLAN of Hamilton Co, OH to ALEXANDER GARDNER. Brkv inlot 37. Unsigned. Witness: JOHN PENWELL, J. WINCHILL. No rec date p 251

Deed dated 1816. WILLIAM WILSON SR & HANNAH, his wife to JOHN WILSON. S 11, T 13, R 12E. Signed WILLIAM WILSON, HANNAH WILSON. Witness: JAMES WILSON, BENJ. WILSON. rec 1816. pp 251, 252

Deed dated 1816. DAVID MOORE to JAMES MOORE. Brkv lot 2. Signed DAVID MOORE. Witness: none. no rec date. p 252

Deed dated 1816. JOHN ALLEN SR to JACOB HUNT. Brkv lot 48. Signed JOHN ALLEN SR, REBECCAH (x) ALLEN. Witness: none. no rec date. p 253

Deed dated 1815. HENRY SCUDDER & MARGARET CROWEL, admrs of estate of JOHN CROWEL, dec, of Hamilton Co, OH to JOHN C. POUNER (PAWNER in text). S 32, T 9, R 1W. Signed HENRY SCUDDER, MARGARET (x) CROWEL. Witness: none. no rec date. pp 254, 255

Deed of partition dated 1816. BENJAMIN WILSON to WILLIAM WILSON SR. Land in S 21, T 10, R 2W bought jointly, now divided. WILLIAM to have south portion. Signed BENJAMIN WILSON, ELIZABETH WILSON. Witness: none. no rec date. p 256

Deed of partition dated 1816. WILLIAM WILSON SR to BENJAMIN WILSON. As above; BENJAMIN to have north. Signed WILLIAM WILSON, HANNAH WILSON. Witness: none. rec 1816. p 257

FRANKLIN COUNTY DEEDS: Book B

Deed dated 1816. WILLIAM WILSON SR to JAMES WILSON. S 21, T 10, R 2W. Signed WILLIAM WILSON, HANNAH WILSON. Witness: BENJAMIN WILSON no rec date. p 258, 259

Deed dated 1815. DAVID RICHARDSON to JOHN PENWELL. Brkv lot 17. Signed DAVID RICHARDSON. Witness: J. WINCHILL, ISRAEL W. BONAM. rec 1816. p 260.

Deed dated 1815. JAMES WILSON to DAVID KAUTZE of Cincinnati, Oh. Brkv lots 57, 58. Signed JAMES WILSON, ELIZABETH WILSON. Witness: none. rec 1816. p 261

Deed dated 1815. JOHN POWERS to GEORGE BUTLER, "his son-in-law lately married to MARY POWERS". S 31, T 10, R 1W. Signed JOHN POWERS. Witness: JOSHUA BUTLER, JOHN WHITWORTH. rec 1816. p 261, 262

Deed dated 1815. JAMES McCLERKIN & SUSANNA, his wife to ISRAEL HAMILTON. S 13, T 11, R 1W. Signed JAMES McCLERKIN, SUSANNA McCLERKIN. Witness: WILLIAM LEPER, JOHN WILEY. rec 1816. p 263

Deed dated 1816. THOMAS COOK to ISAAC HOLLINGSWORTH & CALEB WICKERSHEM, Overseers of Silver Creek Mtg. S 24, T 11, R 2W for a meetinghouse. "KEZIA, his wife" Signed THOMAS COOK, KEZIA COOK. Witness: HENRY HUNTER, JOHN HAVENRIDGE JR. no rec date. p 264

Deed of partition dated 1816. HUGH ABERNATHY to WILLIAM RUSING. Land purchased jointly in S 21, T 10, R 2W. HUGH to have east portion. Signed WILLIAM RUSING AGNES (x) RUSING. Witness: JAS. WILSON. rec 1816 p265

Deed dated 1816. JOHN ALLEN SR to JOSEPH ALLEN of Fayette Co, PA. Brkv lots 31, 36. Signed JOHN ALLEN REBECCA ALLEN. Witness: none. rec 1816. p 266

Deed dated 1816. JABEZ WINSHIP to JOSEPH SCHOONOVER. S 13, T 8, R 2W. Signed JOBEZ WINSHIP. Witness: ENOCH McCARTY. no rec date. p 267

Deed dated 1816. RALPH WILLIAMS to JACOB BLACKLIDGE. S 19, T 12, R 13E. "PATSY, wife of RALPH". Signed RALPH WILLIAMS, PATSY WILLIAMS. Witness: none. no rec date. p 268

Deed dated 1816. WILLIAM WILSON to JOSEPH W. MORRISON. S 13, T 10, R 3W. Signed WILLIAM WILSON, HANNAH (x) WILSON. Witness: SOLOMON ALLEN. rec 1816. p 269

Deed dated 1816. WILLIAM H. EADS to JONATHAN EADS. S 1, T 8, R 2W. Signed WILLIAM H. EADS, JANE EADS.

FRANKLIN COUNTY DEEDS: Book B

Witness: JOHN ADAIR.   no rec date.   p 270

Deed dated 1816.   WM. ARDERY of Harrison Co, KY to MOSES RARDEN. S 14, T 9, R 1W. Signed WILLIAM ARDRY. Witness: ELIJAH HOLTON, DAVID OSBORN, JAMES BARNETT (at Harrison Co).   no rec date.   p 271

Deed dated 1816. WILLIAM LINES to LEWIS DUESE. S 4, T 8, R 2W. "HANNA, wife of WILLIAM". Signed WILLIAM (x) LINES, HANNAH (x) LINES. Witness: ENOCH McCARTY. rec 1816.   p 272

Deed dated 1816. AMOS BUTLER to JAMES WINCHILL. No lot #; bounds given in Brkv. Signed AMOS BUTLER, MARY BUTLER. Witness: none. rec 1816. p 273

Deed dated 1815. THADIUS WHELAN to HARRISON ROBINSON. Brkv lot 3. Signed THADIUS WHELAN. Witness: S. C. STEVENS.   no rec date.   p 274

Deed dated 1816.   GEORGE DIKE of Warren Co, OH to DAVID DUNHAM of same. S 7, T 11, R 1W. Signed GEORGE DICK, ELIZABETH (x) DICK. Witness: GEORGE HARLAN, JACOB HAMPTON (at Warren Co). no rec date pp 275, 276

Deed dated 1815.   JOHN MILLER & NANCY, his wife, to THOMAS CAPPER. S 14, T 10, R 1W. Signed JOHN MILLER, NANCY (x) MILLER. Witness: ABRAHAM (x) HAMMON. rec 1816. p 277

Deed dated 1816. WILLIAM HENDERSON to BENJAMIN CHILDERS. S 33, T 9, R 2W. "ZILPHA, his wife." Signed WILLIAM HENDERSON, ZILPHA HENDERSON. Witness: none. rec 1816. p 278

Deed dated 1814.   JACOB BAKE & CATHARINE, his wife, to JOHN BAKE JR of Butler Co, OH. S 13, T 10, R 1W. Signed JACOB BAKE, CATHARINE (x) BAKE. Witness: JONAS JONES, WILLIAM BAKE. no rec date. pp 279, 280

Deed dated 1816.   ANTHONY HOLBERSTOLD to ZACARIAH COOKSEY. S 10, T 8, R 2W. Signed ANTHONY HOLBERSTADT SARAH (x) HOLBERSTADT. Witness: ENOCH McCARTY. rec 1816. p 281

Deed dated 1816.   DAVID HOLLINGSWORTH to ANNA BURNSIDES. S 7, T 11, R 1W. Signed DAVID HOLINGSWORTH. Witness: T. E. BURNSIDE, PAMELA BURNSIDE. rec 1816. p 282

Deed dated 1816. THADIUS WHELAN to JAMES A. PIATT. Brkv inlot 3. Signed THADIUS WHELAN. Witness: none.

FRANKLIN COUNTY DEEDS: Book B

no rec date. pp 282, 283

Deed dated 1813. RALPH WILDRIDGE & ELIZABETH his wife to SAMUEL ROCKEFELLAR. S 32, T 8, R 1W. Signed RALPH WILDRIDGE, ELIZABETH (x) WILDRIDGE. Witness: CHARLES VANCAMP. no rec date. p 284

Deed dated 1816. JOHN ALLEN SR to HUGH MAY. Brkv lot 56. Signed JOHN ALLEN, REBECCA (x) ALLEN. Witness: none. rec 1816. p 285

Deed dated 1816. JAMES McKINNY to HUGH MAY. Brkv lot 53. Signed JAMES McKINNEY, EDITH (x) McKINNEY. no rec date. p 286

Deed dated 1816. JOHN WILSON of Clermont Co, OH to D.B. & R. MULLIKIN of Baltimore Co, MD. "his wife, CELLA". Signed JOHN WILSON, CELLA (x) WILSON. Witness: ANDREW MEGRUE. no rec date. p 287

Deed dated 1816. JOSEPH ALLEN of Washington Twp, Fayette Co, PA to SAMUEL LOVEJOY of same. Brkv lots 9, 10. Signed JOSEPH ALLEN, ANN (x) ALLEN. Witness: GEORGE CROFFORD (in PA). rec 1816. pp 288, 289

Deed dated 1814. THOMAS MADEN to EBENEZER HOWE of Hamilton Co, OH. S 17, T 11, R 1W. Signed THOMAS MADDEN, RUTH MADDEN. Witness: JOHN MACLIN, E. HOLLINGSWORTH. rec 1816. p 290

Deed dated 1813. JOHN VANBLOSSOM to GEORGE RUDICEL. S 29, T 8, R 1W. Signed JOHN VANBLARICUM, MARYANN VANBLARICUM. Witness: JOHN HAGERMAN, ALLEN RAMSEY. rec 1816. p 291

Deed dated 1815. JOHN ALLEN SR to THOMAS BRADLY. Brkv lot 9. Signed JOHN ALLEN, REBECAH (x) ALLEN. Witness H. ROBINSON, H. BATES. rec 1816. pp 292, 293

Deed dated 1816. ANNA BURNSIDE to DAVID DUNHAM. "adj land of ..SAMUEL TOPPIN". S 27, T 11, R 1W. Signed ANNA (x) BURNSIDE. Witness: THOMAS E. BURNSIDES, EBENEZER HOWE. no rec date. p 294

Brookville outlots plat map dated 1816. Laid off by AMOS BUTLER. Signed SOLOMON ALLEN, surveyor. no rec date. p 295

Deed dated 1815. ROBERT GLIDEWELL to JAMES DRAKE. S 34, T 10, R 2W. "JOANA, his wife". Signed ROBERT (x) GLIDEWELL, JOANA (x) GLIDEWELL. Witness: JOHN HANNA, WILLIAM (x) BURNS. rec 1816. p 296

FRANKLIN COUNTY DEEDS: Book B

Deed dated 1816. JOHN H. ROCKEFELLAR & MARY his wife to WILLIAM HUDSON & MARY HUDSON. S 32, T 8 R 1W. Signed JOHN ROCKEFELLAR, MARY ROCKEFELLAR. Witness: SAMUEL ROCKEFELLER. no rec date. pp 297, 298

Deed dated 1816. JAMES JONES SR & REBECCA his wife of Dearborn Co to JOHN H. ROCKEFELLER. S 32, T 8, R 1W. Signed JAMES JONES, REBECCA (x) JONES. Witness: none. rec 1816. pp 299, 300

Greensburgh plat map dated 1816. "off Connersville Rd about 7 miles from Brkv". Laid off by JOHN NAYLOR & JAMES SHEARWOOD. Signed JOSEPH S. ALLEN, C.S.V. p 301

Deed dated 1816. THOMAS OWSLY to WILLIAM WILSON. S 23, T 12, R 13E. Signed THOMAS (x) OWSLY, DINA (x) OWSLY. Witness: JOHN TEST. no rec date. p 302

Deed dated 1816. JOHN GARRISON to THOMAS RISK of Millcreek Twp, Hamilton Co, OH. Brkv lots 63, 64. Signed JOHN GARRISON, SINA GARRISON. Witness: JAMES W. GAZLAY, HUGH MOORE (at Hamilton Co). Mortgage by THOMAS RISK: to HUGH MOORE, RICHARD POSDUCK, MEEKER & OGDEN,all of Cincinnati. no rec date. pp 303, 304

Deed dated 1816. JOHN NEAL to HENRY BROWN. S 3, T 11, R 13E. "to said HERVY BROWN". Signed JOHN NEAL ELIZABETH NEAL. Witness: JOHN FUGET. rec 1816. p 305

Deed dated 1816. JOHN ALLEN SR to LUTHER RUSSEL. Brkv lot 87. Signed JOHN ALLEN SR, REBECAH (x) ALLEN Witness: J. WINCHILL. rec 1816. p 306

Deed dated 1816. WILLIAM H. EADS to THOMAS CLERK. Brkv lot 42. Signed WILLIAM H. EADS, JANE EADS. Witness: none. no rec date. pp 307, 308

Quitclaim deed dated 1815. JOHN NORRIS & JANE, his wife to SAMUEL HANNA & JAMES C. HANNA. JANE NORRIS, heir of JOHN HANNA, dec, and other heirs are tenants in common of father's land: S 27, T 11, R 2W. Gave title to SAMUEL & JAMES. Signed JOHN NORRIS, JANE NORRIS. Witness: ROBERT SHAW. no rec date. pp 309,310

Union plat map date 1816. EBENEZER HOWE, proprietor. JAMES LEVISTON, surveyor. p 311

Deed dated 1816. JOHN RICHARDSON & POLLY, his wife, to WILLIAM HOPKINS. S 20, T 13, R 13E. Signed JOHN RICHARDSON, POLLY RICHARDSON. Witness: WM. HELM. no rec date. p 312

FRANKLIN COUNTY DEEDS: Book B

Emancipation dated 1816. EDE GILL, widow of JACOB, dec, knowing that husband intended to free SIMON GILL "a man of colour" upon her death, gave SIMON his freedom. Signed EDE (x) GILL. Witness: none. rec 1816. p 313

Mortgage deed dated 1816. JAMES SHARP of Warren Co, OH to CALEB B. CLEMENT of same. S 8, T 12, R 13E. debt to be paid by Nov, 1817 to void conveyance of title. Signed JAMES SHARP. Witness: THOMAS CORWIN, JACOB HARLAN. rec 1816. pp 313, 314, 315

Deed dated 1815. CHRISTOPHER SMITH & ANN, his wife, of Butler Co, OH to WILLIAM SMITH. S 23, T 10, R 1W. Signed CHRISTOPHER SMITH, ANN (x) SMITH. Witness: SAMUEL SHERWOOD, HENRY WEAVER (at Butler Co). no rec date. pp 316, 317

Gift dated 1816. JAMES ALBERT of Scott Co, VA, by "affection which I bear" to SARAH JONES, gave a "red cow and her increase now in care of .. SAMUEL ALLEY" for SARAH's use and benefit. Signed JAMES ALBERT. Witness: GEORGE WILSON, JP. no rec date. p 317

Deed dated 1815. JOHN FISHER to SAMUEL PATTERSON. S 25, T 11, R 1W. Signed JOHN FISHER, ISABEL (x) FISHER Witness: TOBIAS MILLER, JOHN PATTERSON. JP's note: JOHN FISHER & ISABELLA, his wife. no rec date. p 318

Deed dated 1816. ROBERT McGRUE of Williamsport, Washington Co, PA to ALEXANDER McGRUE of Cincinnati, OH. Brkv lots 34, 35. Signed ROBERT McGRUE. Witness: none. no rec date. pp 319, 320

Deed dated 1816. AARON STAUNTON to DAVID BERRY. S 20, T 11, R 1W. "LYDIA, his wife". Signed AARON STAUNTON, LYDIA STAUNTON. Witness: EBENEZER HOWE, JAMES STANON. rec 1816. p 321

Mortgage deed dated 1816. DAVID STIPPS to JOHN C. HARLEY. S 33, T 12, R 12E. Debt to be paid in full by Sept 1821 to void conveyance of title. Signed DAVIS STIPP. Witness: JOHN BRYSON, JOHN CAMPBELL. no rec date. pp 322, 323

Deed dated 1816. ROBERT McGRUE (Bk B, pp 319, 320) to ALEXANDER McGRUE (see same). Brkv lots 26, 27. Signed ROBERT McGRUE. Witness: none. rec 1816. p 324

Deed dated 1816. JOHN FREAD to JOHN ALISON. S 28, T 13, R 12. Signed JOHN FRED. Witness: WM. HELM. rec 1816. (p 325 blank) p 326

FRANKLIN COUNTY DEEDS: Book B

Deed dated 1816. PAUL DAVIS to GEORGE DAVIS. S 21, T 14, R 12E. "MARGARET, wife of PAUL". Signed PAUL DAVIS, MARGARET (x) DAVIS. Witness: none. no rec date. p 327

Deed dated 1816. DAVID BELL of "Waine" Co to CHARLES HARDY. S 8, T 9, R 2W. Signed DAVID BELL. Witness: none. no rec date. p 328

Deed dated 1816. GEORGE KEFFER to JACOB KINGERY, KATY KINGERY & GEORGE KINGERY, infant heirs of JOHN KINGERY, dec, who was a son & heir of JACOB KINGERY, also dec. S 35, T 11, R 1W. "EVE, wife of GEORGE". Signed GEORGE KEFFER, EVE (x) KEFFER. Witness: JOHN (x) RICHARDSON. rec 1816. pp 329, 330

Deed dated 1816. OBADIAH EASTES to PHILAMON HERVEY. S 33, T 10, R 2W. "FANNY, his wife". Signed OBADIAH EASTES, FANNY (x) EASTES. Witness: none. no rec date. p 331

Deed dated 1816. JAMES STAUNTON to LATHAM STAUNTON. S 17, T 11, R 2W. "MARY, his wife". Signed JAMES STAUNTON, MARY (x) STAUNTON. Witness: EBENEZER HOWE, AARON STAUNTON. rec 1816. p 332

Deed dated 1816. LEWIS DUESE to ABRAHAM LINBROOKE of PA & JAMES A. PIATT. "corner of..WILLIAM LYONS..incl. sawmill built by EZRA MOORE". No S-T-R; bounds only. "NANCY, his wife". Signed LEWIS DUESE, NANCY (x) DUESE. Witness: none. rec 1816. pp 333, 334

POA dated 1816. ABRAHAM GARRISON appted ENOCH GARRISON of Hamilton Co, OH to act on his behalf. Signed ABRAHAM GARRISON. Witness: none. rec 1816. p 335

Emancipation dated 1814. WILLIAM CUNNINGHAM JR as agent for JAMES BLAKELY of SC. In consideration of $300 pd by WILLIAM PALMER & ROBERT FLACK of Franklin Co, releases a "mulatto man otherwise WILLIAM TRAIL" from BLAKELY's ownership. Signed WILLIAM CUNNINGHAM. Witness: JAMES NOBLE. rec 1816. p 336

Deed dated 1816. ANTHONY HOBBERSTADT to JOHN HALBERSTADT. S 22, T 9, R 2W. Signed ANTHONY HALBERSTADT, SARAH (x) HALBERSTADT. Witness: ENOCH McCARTY. rec 1816. p 337

Deed dated 1816. JACOB SAILORS to ROYLY WOODWORTH. S34, T 9, R 2W. "NANCY, wife of JACOB". Signed JACOB (x) SAILORS, NANCY (x) SAILORS. Witness: ENOCH McCARTY. rec 1816. p 338

FRANKLIN COUNTY DEEDS: Book B

Deed and bill of sale dated 1816. JOHN MILLER & CHRISTIANA, his wife, to ISAAC MILLER of Montgomery Co, OH. S 12, T 11, R 1 & S 2, T 10, R 1. All household furniture, carpenter tools, horses, cattle, swine, farm tools, etc. Signed JOHANNES MILLER, CHRISTIANA (x) MILLER. Witness: WILLIAM DUBOISE, THOMAS HARPER. rec 1816. pp 339, 340

Deed dated 1816. JOHN T. McLINN to HUGH GLENN of Cincinnati, OH. S 18, T 11, R 1W. "together with his wife who relinquishes her right of dower". Signed J. T. McLINN (no wife's signature). Witness: JOHN CRAMNER, JOHN MAHARD (at Hamilton Co). rec 1816. p 341

Deed dated 1816. JOHN HEVENRIDGE to HUGH GLENN of Cincinnati, OH. S 19, T 11, R 1W. Signed JOHN HEVENRIDGE. Witness: as above. rec 1816. p 342

Deed dated 1816. DAVID EWING to JAMES TRUSLER. S 2, T 12, R 13E. "CASSEY, his wife". Signed DAVID EWING, CASSY (x) EWING. Witness: none. rec 1816. p 343

Deed dated 1816. JAMES NOBLE to STEPHEN C. STEVENS. S 28, T 9, R 2W. Signed JAMES NOBLE, MARY NOBLE. Witness: EDMUND HARRISON. rec 1816. p 344

Deed dated 1816. DAVID AGNEW to ALEXANDER GARDNER. Brkv lot 38. "SINA, his wife". Signed DAVID AGNEW, JOSINAH (x) AGNEW. rec 1816. p 345

Deed dated 1816. JAMES LOGAN to BENJAMIN McCARTY. S 21, T 9, R 2W. "SARAH, his wife". Signed JAMES LOGAN SARAH (x) LOGAN. Witness: ENOCH McCARTY. rec 1816. pp 346, 347

Springfield plat map dated 1816. Surveyed by JOSEPH ALLEN. WILLIAM SNODGRASS, Proprietor. rec 1816. p 348

Deed dated 1816. JOHN ALLEN SR to PETER VANDYKE. Brkv inlots 61, 66. Signed JOHN ALLEN SR, REBECCAH (x) ALLEN. Witness: none. rec 1817. p 349

Deed dated 1816. SOLOMON MANWARING & JANE, his wife, of Dearborn Co to RICHARD MANWARING. S 26, T 12, R 13E. Signed SOLOMON MANWARING, JANE MANWARING. Witness: GEORGE MILLIS, WILLIAM PARVIS. rec 1817. p 350

Deed dated 1816. CHARLES HENDERSON to SAMUEL WIER. S 18, T 8, R 1W. "SARAH, wife of CHARLES". Signed CHARLES HENDERSON, SARAH (x) HENDERSON. Witness: none. rec 1817. p 351

FRANKLIN COUNTY DEEDS: Book B

Deed dated 1816. WILLIAM S. WHITE of Dearborn Co TO JAMES HANLEY of Butler Co, OH. S 3, T 12, R 12E. "corner to JOHNSON CLARK". "MARY, his wife". Signed WILLIAM S. WHITE, MARY (x) WHITE. Witness: none. rec 1817. pp 352, 353

Deed dated 1817. ENOCH McCARTY to DAVID CASE of Butler Co, OH. No S-T-R; bounds "to LEWIS DEWEESE's line." Signed ENOCH McCARTY, ELIZABETH (x) McCARTY. Witness: JOHN QUICK, JP. rec 1817. p 354

Springfield addition plat map dated 1816. BENJAMIN ABRAMS, proprietor. Town is to be known as Fairfield, laid off by ABRAMS & SNODGRASS (see Bk B, p 181 and p 348). p 355

Deed dated 1817. AMOS BUTLER to SAMUEL SERRING of Warren Co, OH. Brkv inlot 38. Signed AMOS BUTLER, MARY BUTLER. Witness: none. rec 1817. p 356

New Trenton plat map dated 357. S 32, T 8, R 1W. Laid out by SAMUEL ROCKAFELLAR & RALPH WILDRIDGE. Surveyed by SOLOMON MANWARING. rec 1817. p 357

Deed dated 1814. DAVID BONER & MARGARET, his wife, to ROBERT CARR. S 34, T 11, R 1W. Signed DAVID BONER MARGARET (x) BONER. Witness: JAMES STAUNTON. rec 1817. pp 358, 359

Mortgage deed dated 1816. GEORGE TENUS to CHRISTOPHER HANSEL. S 36, T 10, R 1W. Land to be paid off by 1819 to void conveyance of title. Signed GEORGE (x) TENUS. Witness: ABRAHAM HARMON, CATHERINE (x) BAKE. rec 1817. pp 360, 361

Deed dated 1816. THOMAS KEENEY & NANCY, his wife, to JONATHAN KEENEY. S 29, T 14, R 14E. Signed THOMAS KEENEY, NANCY (x) KEENEY. Witness: none. rec 1817. p 362

Deed dated 1816. THOMAS KEENEY & NANCY, his wife, to JOHN KEENEY, SR. S 29, T 14, R 14E. Signed THOMAS KEENEY, NANCY (x) KEENEY. Witness: none. rec 1817. p 363

Deed dated 1816. JACOB RETTER of Preble Co OH to JOHN RETTER. S 13, T 11, R 1W. Land purchased jointly in 1812. JACOB & SALLY, his wife, gave quitclaim to JOHN. Signed JACOB RITTER, SALLY (x) RITTER. Witness: CATHERINE (x) BAKE, WILLIAM BAKE. rec 1817. p 364

Deed dated 1816. CHRISTOPHER HANSEL to GEORGE TENUS.

FRANKLIN COUNTY DEEDS: Book B

S 36, T 10, R 1W. "ELIZABETH, his wife". Signed CHRISTOPHER HANSEL, ELIZABETH (x) HANSEL. Witness: ABRAHAM HAMMON, CATHERINE (x) BAKE. rec 1817. p 365

Deed dated 1815. ARTHUR DICKSON to MARTIN JAMISON. Brkv lot 30. Signed ARTHUR DICKSON, SARAH DICKSON. Witness: JAMES NOBLE. rec 1817. p 366

Deed dated 1816. MARTIN JAMISON, late of Madison Co, KY, to ROBERT JOHN. Brkv 30. Signed MARTIN JAMISON, BARBARY (x) JAMISON. Witness: EDMUND HARRISON. rec 1817. p 367

Deed dated 1817. ABNER LEONARD to ROBERT BRADFORD of Butler Co, OH. S 29, T 9, R 1W. "HETTY, his wife." Signed ABNER LEONARD, HETTY (x) LEONARD. Witness: none. rec 1817. p 368

Deed dated 1817. ROBERT BRADFORD as above to ISAAC WAMSLY. No S-T-R; bounds given. "by deed from ABNER LEONARD." Signed ROBERT BRADFORD. Witness: ABNER LEONARD. JONATHAN STOUT, JP. rec 1817. p 369

Deed dated 1816. JOHN SHAW of Hamilton Co, Oh to JAMES THOMPSON. S 28, T 9, R 1W. "PHOEBE, his wife" Signed JOHN SHAW, PHEBE SHAW. Witness: PETER WILLIAMS JACOB (x) PETERS, ZACHARIAH GRAVES (all in Hamilton Co, OH). no rec date. p 370

Deed dated 1816. JOHN MILLER & PHOEBE, his wife, to JOHN GLASS. S 12, T 10, R 1W. Signed JOHN MILLER, PHOEBE (x) MILLER. Witness: none. JACOB BAKE, JP. rec 1817. p 371

Deed dated 1816. THOMAS ORANGE to NATHAN D. GALLION. Brkv lot 65. Signed THOMAS ORANGE. Witness: HARROD NEWLAND, JOSHUA HARLAN. rec 1817. p 372

Deed dated 1817. THOMAS CLARKE to NATHAN D. GALLION. Brkv lot 42. Signed THOMAS CLARKE, NANCY (x) CLARKE. Witness: JAMES WINCHILL, JP. no rec date. p 373

Deed dated 1817. DAVID STOOPS to MICHAEL CHRISS. S 33, T 12, R 13E. Signed DAVID STOOPS, ABIGAIL STOOPS Witness: SOLOMON ALLEN. rec 1817. p 374

Deed dated 1817. NICHOLAS CHRISS & BARBARA his wife, to DAVID STOOPS. S 5, T 12, R 13E. Signed NICHOLAS (x) CHRISS, BARBARA (x) CHRISS. Witness: none. rec 1817. p 375

Deed dated 1817. NATHAN D. GALLION & HANNAH his wife

FRANKLIN COUNTY DEEDS: Book B

to THOMAS CLARK. Brkv lot 65. Signed N. D. GALLION, HANNAH GALLION. Witness: none. rec 1817. p 376

Deed dated 1817. VINCENT COOPER to ALLEN CRISLER. S 22, T 13, R 12E. Signed VINCENT (x) COOPER. Witness: EDWARD WEBB. WILLIAM HELM, JP. rec 1817. p 377

Deed dated 1815. JAMES DRAKE to JAMES HARRIS. S 34, T 10, R 2W. "ELIZABETH, his wife". Signed JAMES DRAKE, ELIZABETH (x) DRAKE. Witness: JOHN HANNA JP & WM. MURRAY. rec 1817. pp 377, 378

Deed dated 1815. THOMAS SKINNER & ANNA, his wife, to THOMAS PEERS BRIGGS. S 7, T 9, R 2W. Signed THOMAS SKINNER, ANNA (x) SKINNER. Witness: ENOCH McCARTY. rec 1817. pp 378, 379

Deed dated 1816. ALEXANDER FULTON to JOSEPH ADAMS. Brkv lot 97. "SARAH, wife of ALEXANDER". Signed ALEXANDER FULTON, SARAH (x) FULTON. Witness: none. no rec date. pp 379, 380

Mortgage deed dated 1817. BENJAMIN SWEET to JOHN JOHNSON. S 4, T 10, R 2. "by JOSEPH HANNA's west".. "land of JAMES NUNNAM". Debt to be paid by Dec 1817 to void conveyance. Signed BENJAMIN SWEET. Witness: JOHN TEMPLETON. rec 1817. p 380

Mortgage deed dated 1817. BENJAMIN SWEET to JOHN JOHNSON. S 4, T 10, R 2. "by WILLIAM CUTTER's". Debt to be paid Dec 1817 to void conveyance. Signed BENJAMIN SWEET. Witness: JOHN TEMPLETON. rec 1817. p 380

Somerset town plat map dated 1816. Laid off by JAMES & EDWARD TONER. Surveyed by JOSEPH ALLEN. JOHN BRISON, JP. rec 1817. p 382

Deed dated 1817. WILLIAM DENNISTON & RACHEL his wife to ROBERT BROWN. S 14, T 10, R 1W. Signed WILLIAM DENNISTON, RACHEL DENNISTON. Witness: JAMES M. DORSEY, MARTHA DORSEY (at Butler Co, OH). no rec date. p 383

Deed dated 1817. JOHN CARSON & HANSON LOVE to WALTER TUCKER. S 23, T 9, R 2W. Signed JOHN CARSON, HANSON LOVE. Witness: WILLIAM CHILTON, B.F. MORRIS. rec 1817. p 384

Deed dated 1817. JAMES WINCHILL to HERVEY BATES. No S-T-R; land adj Brkv. Signed JAMES WHICHILL, ABIGAIL (x) WINCHILL. Witness: none. no rec date. p 385

FRANKLIN COUNTY DEEDS: Book B

Deed dated 1817. STEPHEN WINCHILL to WILLIAM H. EADS S 28, T 9, R 2W. "SARAH, his wife". Signed STEPHEN WINCHILL, SARAY WINCHILL. Witness: JAS. McKINNEY. rec 1817. p 386

Deed dated 1816. STEPHEN C. STEVENS to WILLIAM H. EADS. S 28, T 9, R 2W. Signed STEPHEN C. STEVENS. rec 1817. p 387

Deed dated 1817. ENOCH D. JOHN & NOAH NOBLE to WILLIAM H. EADS. Brkv lot 37. "ELOISE, wife of ENOCH". Signed ENOCH D. JOHN, ELOISE JOHN, N. NOBLE. Witness: EDM. HARRISON, JP. no rec date. p 388

Deed dated 1817, EDWARD HAYMAN to HENRY MORE. S 10, T 8, R 1. Signed EDWARD HAYMOND. Witness: WILLIAM SNODGRASS, LEONARD SPARKS, MATTHEW SPARKS JR. rec 1817. p 389

Deed dated 1817. EDWARD HAYMAN to MATHEW ROBERTSON. S 10, T 8, R 1. Signed EDWARD HAYMOND. Witness: WILLIAM SNODGRASS, LEONARD SPARKS, MATTHEW SPARKS JR. rec 1817. p 390

Deed dated 1816. DAVID GAYMON to ANDREW SHIRK. S 33, T 9, R 2W. "MARY, his wife". Signed DAVID GAYMAN, MARY (x) GAYMAN. Witness: SOLOMON ALLEN. rec 1817. p 391

Deed dated 1816. BENJAMIN SMITH to DAVID MUSSELMAN of Hamilton Co, OH. Brkv lot 34. Signed BENJAMIN SMITH, REBECCA (x) SMITH. Witness: none. rec 1817. pp 391, 392

Deed dated 1817. JOHN ALLEN SR & REBECCA, his wife, to JOHN SCOTT, printer. Brkv inlot 8. Signed JOHN ALLEN SR, REBECAH (x) ALLEN. Witness: JOHN TEST. rec 1817. pp 392, 393

Deed dated 1817. MOSES BAKER & MARY ANNE, his wife of Gallatin Co, KY to NICHOLAS PUMPHREY SR. S 12, T 13, R 12E. Signed MOSES BAKER, MARY ANNE BAKER. Witness: none. rec 1817. pp 393, 394

Deed dated 1817. SAMUEL FULLEN to NICHOLAS PUMPHREY. S 12, T 13, R 12. "ELIZABETH, his wife". Signed SAMUEL FULLEN, ELIZABETH (x) FULLEN. Witness: Wm. HELM, JP. rec 1817. p 395

Deed dated 1816. EBENEZER HEATON of Wayne Co & JOANNA, his wife, to ELI HEATON of same. S 21, T 14, R 13. Signed EBENEZER HEATON, JOANNA (x) HEATON.

FRANKLIN COUNTY DEEDS: Book B

Witness: none. rec 1817. pp 395, 396

Deed dated 1816. EBENEZER HEATON of Wayne Co & JOANNA, his wife, to ASA HEATON of same. S 21, T 14, R 13. Signed EBENEZER HEATON, JOANNA (x) HEATON. Witness: none. rec 1817. pp 396, 397

Deed dated 1817. FREDERICK FERRIS to HENRY BECKLEY of Hamilton Co, OH. S 11, T 9, R 2W. "SUSANNA, his wife". Signed FREDERICK FERRIS, SUSANNA FERRIS. Witness: none. rec 1817. p 397

Deed dated 1817. SAMUEL ROCKAFELLAR to AARON FOOTE. Trenton inlot 32. Signed SAMUEL ROCKAFELLAR, MARY ROCKAFELLAR. Witness: H. MAY. rec 1817. p 398

Deed dated 1817. SAMUEL ROCKAFELLAR to AARON FOOTE. Trenton inlot 29. Signed SAMUEL ROCKAFELLAR, MARY ROCKAFELLAR. Witness: H. MAY. rec 1817. p 399

Deed dated 1817. SAMUEL ROCKAFELLAR to AARON FOOTE. Trenton inlot 31. Signed SAMUEL ROCKAFELLAR, MARY ROCKAFELLAR. Witness: H. MAY. rec 1817. pp 399, 400

Deed dated 1817. WILLIAM WILSON to CHARLES COLLETT. S 33, T 12, R 13E. "FRANKEY, his wife". Signed WM. WILSON, FRANKEY WILSON. Witness: EDM. HARRISON, JP. rec 1817. p 400

Deed dated 1816. THADDIUS WHELAN to JOHN JACOBS, JAMES A. PIATT & B. F. MORRIS. Brkv lot 3. Signed THADDIUS WHELAN, SARAH WHELAN. rec 1817. p 401

Deed dated 1817. ZACHARIAH OWSLEY to LEWIS BISHOP. S 34, T 12, R 13. "ELIZABETH, wife of ZACARIAH". Signed ZACHRIAH (x) OWSLEY, ELIZABETH (x) OWSLEY. Witness: ISC. WILSON, CHARLES COLLETT. rec 1817. p 402

Deed dated 1817. RALPH WILDRIDGE to AARON FOOTE. New Trenton inlot 25. Signed RALPH WILDRIDGE, ELIZABETH WILDRIDGE. Witness: H. MAY. rec 1817. p 403

Deed dated 1816. JOHN HARRELL & ABAGAIL, his wife, to PHILLIP MASON. S 28, T 13, R 12. Signed JOHN HARRELL, ABIGAIL (x) HARRELL. Witness: WM. HELM, JP. rec 1817. pp 403, 404

Deed dated 1817. CHARLES DAILY to JOHN SHANK. Brkv 26. "SARAH, his wife". Signed CHARLES DAILY, SARAH DAILY. Witness: B. F. MORRIS, recorder, Franklin Co. rec 1817. p 404

FRANKLIN COUNTY DEEDS: Book B

Deed dated 1817. JOHN NORRIS of Butler Co, Oh to JOSEPH W. MORRISON. S 19, T 9, R 2W. "REBECCA, his wife". Signed JOHN NORRIS, REBECCA (x) NORRIS. Witness: SOLOMON ALLEN. rec 1817. p 405

Deed dated 1816. JAMES WILLSON to JAMES NOBLE. Fairfield lots 17, 18. "NANCY, his wife". Signed JAMES WILLSON, NANCY (x) WILSON. Witness: none. rec 1817 p 406

Greens Boroug(h) plat map dated 1817. Laid off by JOHN NAYLOR & JAMES SHERWOOD. Surveyed by JOSEPH ALLEN. Witness: none. rec 1817. p 407

Deed dated 1817. JOHN BATES to AZOR STURDWANT*. S 11 T 8, R 2W. "HARRIET, wife of JOHN". Signed JOHN BATES, HARRIET BATES. Witness: JOHN STAFFORD JR, JOHN STAFFORD SR, JAMES BACKHOUSE, JP. rec 1817. pp 407, 408 *original ledger appears to be STURDEVANT.

Deed dated 1817. JOHN ALLEN & SARAH, his wife, to JOSEPH RIDENOUR of Preble Co, OH. S 36, T 11, R 1W. JOHN ALLEN, SARAH (x) ALLEN. Witness: JAMES SMITH, JACOB BAKE, JP. rec 1817. pp 408, 409

Deed dated 1817. VINCENT COOPER to WILLIAM WHERRIT of Jessamin Co, KY. S 27, T 13, R 12E. Signed VINCENT COOPER. Witness: JOSEPH S. ALLEN. rec 1817 p 409, 410

Deed dated 1817. WILLIAM H. EADS to WILLIAM BRADLEY. Brkv lot 42. Signed WILLIAM H. EADS, JANES EADS. Witness: JOHN EADS. rec 1817. pp 410, 411

Mortgage deed dated 1817. JOHN BRIDGES to CHRISTOPHER MOSTELLER. S 20, T 13, R 12E. Debt to be paid by April 1819 to void conveyance. Signed JOHN BRIDGES. Witness: JOHN TEMPLETON. rec 1817. Recpt by MOSTELLER: paid in full, 2 May, 1818. p 411

Deed dated 1816. JOHN ALLEN SR to JAMES WINCHELL. Brkv inlot 64. Signed JOHN ALLEN SR, REBECAH (x) ALLEN. Witness: JOHN TEST. rec 1817. pp 411, 412

Deed dated 1817. JAMES McGINNIS to CORBLY HUDSON. Brkv lot 35. Signed JAMES McGINNIS, JANE McGINNIS. Witness: none. rec 1817. pp 412, 413

Darlington plat map, undated. No proprietor's name, no S-T-R. "stake at Connersville Rd .. thence by PILKEY's line". Map shows town on west fork of Whitewater River. pp 413, 414

FRANKLIN COUNTY DEEDS: Book B

Deed dated 1816. HENRY REMY & PATSY, his wife of Gallatin Co, KY to ABRAHAM BLEDSOE of same. S 27, T 9, R 1W. "one half of section where I am assignee of ROBERT SCANLAND, the other half...through the estate of my father, JOHN REMY, dec." Signed HENRY REMY, no wife's signature. Witness: JAMES REMY, LEVI SPARKS. Note dated 1817: above deed has since been signed by MARTHE REMY". no rec date. p 415

Deed dated 1816. HENRY REMY to ABRAHAM BLEDSOE of same. S 13, T 8, R 1W. "one half of...section where I am assignee of ROBERT SCANLAND, the other half... through the estate of my father, JOHN REMY, dec." Signed HENRY REMY. Witness: JAMES REMY, LEVI SPARKS. no rec date. pp 415, 416

Deed dated 1816. HENRY REMY & PATSY, his wife of Gallatin Co, KY to ABRAHAM BLEDSOE of same. S 28, T 9, R 1W. "half...through the estate of my father, JOHN REMY". Signed HENRY REMY, no wife's signature. Witness: JAMES REMY, LEVI SPARKS. Note dated 1817: above deed has since been signed by MARTHE REMY". rec 1817. pp 416, 417

Deed dated 1815. JAMES WILLSON to ABRAHAM C. ROLL of Hamilton Co, OH. Brkv lots 40, 41. Signed JAMES WILSON, ELIZABETH WILSON. Witness: none. rec 1817. p 417, 418

Deed dated 1817. GEORGE BUTLER of Butler Co, OH to JOHN SHAFER of same. S 31, T 10, R 1W. "MARY, his wife". Signed GEORGE BUTLER, MARY (x) BUTLER. Witness: JOB MULFORD, WM. HERVEY. rec 1817. pp 418, 419

Deed dated 1816. GEORGE KEFFER to JOHN RICHARDSON. S 35, T 11, R 1. Signed GEORGE KEFFER, EVE KEFFER. Witness: SILAS MILLER, JOSEPH KINGERY. rec 1817. pp 419, 420

Deed dated 1816. THOMAS SANHEY (pencil corrected to SANKEY) to EDWARD DWIRE. S 3, T 10, R 1W. "HANNAH, his wife". Signed THOMAS SANKEY, HANNAH SANKEY. Witness: THOS. MARTIN. rec 1817. pp 421, 422

Deed dated 1815. CHRISTOPHER SMITH & ANN, his wife, of Butler Co, OH to GIDEON JOHNSON. S 8, T 10, R 1W. Signed CHRISTOPHER SMITH, ANN (x) SMITH. Witness: SAMUEL SHIRAND, HENRY WEAVER (at Butler Co). rec 1817. pp 422, 423

Deed dated 1817. JAMES McGINNIS to JAMES BACKHOUSE & ROBERT BRACKENRIDGE. No S-T-R: bounds given

FRANKLIN COUNTY DEEDS: Book B

"beginning...at mills of JAMES McGINNIS...across field which JOSEPH RIPPEY leased". Signed JAMES McGINNIS, JANE McGINNIS. Witness: JAMES NOBLE. rec 1817. pp 423, 424

Sheriff's sale dated 1817. ROBERT HANNA, Sheriff of Franklin Co to ENOCH D. JOHN. Judgement against property of JOHN CARSON, rcvd by ROBERT SCOTT. Land in S 28, T 9, R 2 seized by Dep.Sheriff JONATHAN McCARTY Purchased at auction by ENOCH D. JOHN, the high bidder. Signed ROBERT HANNA, Sheriff. Witness: none. rec 1817. pp 424, 425

Deed dated 1817. JOHN FISHER to JAMES SMITH. S 25, T 11, R 1W. "ISABER, his wife". Signed JOHN FISHER, ISABEL (x) FISHER. Witness: JANE EADS, GEORGE EWING. rec 1817. p 420

Deed dated 1817. JOHN ALLEN to JAMES SMITH. S 36, T11 R 1W. Signed JOHN ALLEN, SARAH (x) ALLEN. Witness: SAMUEL PATTERSON, JACOB BAKE, JP. rec 1817. p 427

Deed dated 1816. ANDREW SHIRK JR to THOMAS W. COLESCOTT. Brkv lot 26. "MARY, his wife". Signed ANDREW SHIRK, MARY SHIRK. Witness: none. rec 1816. p 428

Deed dated 1817. PHILIP FRAKES to SAMUEL ELWELL. S 30, T 10, R 1. Signed PHILIP FRAKES, PHOEBE (x) FRAKES. Witness: JOSEPH S. ALLEN, JOHN ALLEN JR. rec 1817. pp 428, 429

Deed dated 1817. ENOCH D. JOHN to HENRY COSTIN. Brkv lot 38. Signed ENOCH D. JOHN, ELOISE JOHN. Witness: none. rec 1817. pp 429, 430

Deed dated 1817. HUGH ABERNATHY to JAMES ABERNATHY. S 32, T 13, R 13E. "MARY, his wife". Signed HUGH ABERNATHY, MARY (x) ABERNATHY. Witness: JOHN GAMBLE, JOHN HANNA. rec 1817. pp 430, 431

Performance bond dated 1817. ROBERT HANNA JR, DAVID G. HANNA, PHILLEMON HERVEY & THOMAS POWERS to Governor of Indiana. Bond for ROBERT HANNA as Sheriff of Franklin Co. Signed ROBERT HANNA JR, THOMAS POWERS, DAVID G. HANNA, PHILLEMON (x) HERVEY. Witness: none. rec 1817. p 431

Deed dated 1817. DAVID GARMAN & ANDREW SHIRK SR to ADAM NELSON. S 33, T 9, R 2W. "MARY GAMON, wife of DAVID, and MARTHA SHIRK, wife of ANDREW". Signed DAVID GAEMAN, ANDREW (x) SHIRK, MARY (x) SHIRK*, MARTHA (x) SHIRK. Witness: ROBERT JOHN, JP. rec

FRANKLIN COUNTY DEEDS: Book B

1817. p 432 *transcription error? MARY GARMAN?

POA dated 18--. CHRISTIAN KELLER & MARY, his wife, FRANCIS FORMAN & ANN ELIZABETH, his wife, of Baltimore Co, MD appt MARTIN BAUM of Cincinnati, OH to convey property title. Signed CHRISTIAN KELLER, MARY KELLAR, FRA. FORMAN, ANN E. FORMAN. Witness: OWEN DORSEY, JOHN F. HARRIS (in MD). no rec date. p 433 pp 434, 435, 436 blank: end of Book B

Book C

Deed dated 1817. CHRISTIAN KELLER et al as above by MARTIN BAUM to DAVID E. WADE of Cincinnati, OH. Brkv lots 15, 16, 5, 6. Signed CHRISTIAN KELLER, MARY KELLER, FRANCIS FORMAN, ANN E. FORMAN by att'y BAUM. Witness: ISAAC E. BARNET, J. PRINCE JR in Hamilton Co, OH. rec 1817. p 1

Deed dated 1814. ABRAHAM HETDRICK of North Middleton Twp, Cumberland Co, PA to WILLIAM HETRICK of same. S 7, T 9, R 1W. Signed ABRAHAM HEDRICH. Witness: A. BRECKINRIDGE, WM. RANNEY (in PA). rec 1817. p 2 (p 3 blank)

Deed dated 1817. WILLIAM H. EADS to CORBLY HUDSON. Brkv lot 31. Signed WILLIAM H. EADS, JANE EADS. Witness: none. rec 1817. p 4

Deed dated 1817. JOHN BROWN & wife SARAH to WILLIAM ROSE. S 35, T 11, R 2W. Signed JOHN BROWN, SARAH (x) BROWN. Witness: JOEL GARRISON, ROBERT DAVIES. rec 1817. pp 4, 5

Deed dated 1816. JOHN ROBERTS & SUSANNA, his wife, to WILLIAM ROSE, late of the state of New Jersey. S 26, T 11, R 2W. Signed JOHN ROBERTS, SUSANNA ROBERTS Witness: JOHN WHITWORTH, CHRISTOPHER DART. rec 1817. pp 5, 6

Deed dated 1817. WILLIAM VANDEMAN & POLLY, his wife, to MORGAN LARIMORE. S 13, T 13, R 12E. Signed WILLIAM VANDEMAN, MARY (x) VANDEMAN. Witness: WM. HELM, JP. rec 1817. p 6

Deed dated 1817. THOMAS E. SMITH to JOHN C. McMANNIS Brkv lot 58. "ISABELLA, his wife". Signed THOMAS C. SMITH, ISABELLA SMITH. Witness: EDMUND HARRISON, JP rec 1817. pp 6, 7

Deed dated 1817. JOHN ALLEN & SARAH his wife of Dearborn Co to ROBERTSON JONES. S 29, T 8, R 1W. Signed

FRANKLIN COUNTY DEEDS: Book C

JOHN ALLEN, SARAH ALLEN. Witness: JAMES BACKHOUSE, ALLEN WICOFF. rec 1817. pp 7, 8

Deed dated 1816. DAVID SUTTON & ANCHOR, his wife, to ABSALOM SUTTON. S 20, T 14, R 13E. Signed DAVID SUTTON, ANCHOR SUTTON. Witness: JAMES LEVISTON. rec 1817. pp 8, 9

Deed dated 1817. HENRY MILLAR & JANE, his wife of Dearborn Co to SARAH GREGG. S 29, T 9, R 1W. Signed HENRY MILLAR, JANE MILLAR. Witness: TIMOTHY BROWN, EDWARD BARRICHLOW (at Dearborn). rec 1817. p 9, 10

Deed dated 1817. RICHARD KEEN to PETER DUIT. S 25, T 9, R 2W. "NANCY, his wife". Signed RICHARD KEEN, NANCY (x) KEEN. Witness: EDM. HARRISON. rec 1817. pp 10, 11

Deed dated 1817. WILLIAM NORRIS SR & MARTHA, his wife to JOHN DUNLAP. S 28, T 11, R 2. Signed WILLIAM NORRIS, MARTHA (x) NORRIS. Witness: ROBERT (x) ABERNATHY SAMUEL LOGAN, WILLIAM NICKLES. rec 1814. pp 11, 12

Deed dated 1816. JAMES NOBLE & ENOCH D. JOHN to HARRISON ROBINSON. Brkv lot 38. Signed JAMES NOBLE, ENOCH D. JOHN, MARY NOBLE, ELOISE JOHN. Witness: B.F. MORRIS, Recorder, Franklin Co. rec 1817. pp 12, 13

Deed dated 1817. AMOS BUTLER to GEORGE L. MURDOCK. Brkv lot 34. Signed AMOS BUTLER, MARY BUTLER. Witness: ROBERT JOHN. rec 1817. pp 13, 14

Deed dated 1817. GEORGE L. MURDOCK to JEHU JOHN. Brkv lot, no #, bounds given. "ANN, his wife". Signed GEORGE L. MURDOCK, ANNA MURDOCK. Witness: WILLIAM B. HARDCASTLE, ROBERT JOHN. rec 1817. pp 14, 15

Deed dated 1817. JACOB HUNT of Hamilton Co to ENOCH D. JOHN & NOAH NOBLE. Brkv lot 48. Signed JACOB HUNT. Witness: none. rec 1817. p 15

Deed dated 1815. STEPHEN C. STEVENS to ENOCH D. JOHN & NOAH NOBLE. S 28, T 9, R 2W. Signed STEPHEN C. STEVENS. Witness: none. rec 1817. pp 15, 16

Deed dated 1816. JAMES NOBLE to NOAH NOBLE. Brkv lot 37. Signed JAMES NOBLE, MARY NOBLE. Witness: none. rec 1817. pp 16, 17

Deed dated 1816. JOHN EWING & CATHARINE HARLAND, admrs of estate of GEORGE HARLAND, dec, to JONATHAN KEENEY. GEORGE sold S 9, T 11, R 2W, but died prior

FRANKLIN COUNTY DEEDS: Book C

to drawing deed, left minor heirs. Court appted JOHN TEST, JAMES RARDIN & ROBERT HANNA as commissioners to convey title. Signed ROBERT HANNA, JOHN TEST, JAMES RARDEN. Witness: none. rec 1817. pp 17, 18

Deed dated 1817. ROBERT BROWN & RACHEL, his wife, to GEORGE SHELLHOUSE. S 20, T 14, R 13E. Signed ROBERT BROWN, RACHEL BROWN. Witness: none rec 1817 pp 17, 18

Deed dated 1816. JOHN GARRISON to ABRAHAM GARRISON. Brkv lots 44, 45. Signed JOHN GARRISON, SINA GARRISON Witness: none. rec 1817. p 19

Deed dated 1817. WILLIAM VANDEMAN & POLLY, his wife, to NICHOLAS PUMPHREY. S 13, T 13, R 12E. Signed WILLIAM VANDEMAN, MARY (x) VANDEMAN. Witness: none. rec 1817. pp 19, 20

Deed dated 1817. JOHN ALLEN SR to JOSHUA HADLEY. Brkv lot 69. Signed JOHN ALLEN SR, REBECAH (x) ALLEN. Witness: SOLOMON ALLEN. rec 1817. pp 20, 21

Deed dated 1817. JOHN DUNLAP & ELIZABETH, his wife, to ROBERT ABERNATHY. S 28, T 7, R 2W. Signed JOHN DUNLAP, ELIZABETH DUNLAP. Witness: MOSES LYON, WILLIAM MORRIS. rec 1817. pp 21, 22 ROBERT SWAN, JP

Deed dated 1817. JOHN SHANK to JACOB HERVEY. S 2, no T, R. "SUSAN, wife of JOHN". Signed JOHN SHANK, SUSAN (x) SHANK. Witness: J. WINCHILL. no rec date. p 22

Deed dated 1817. NICHOLAS CRISS to DAVID STOOPS. S 33, T 12, R 13E. "BARBARA, wife of NICHOLAS". Signed NICHOLAS CHRIST, BARBARY (x) CHRIST. Witness: none. rec 1817. p 23

Deed dated 1817. THOMAS C. SMITH to WILLIAM G. ROSE. Brkv lot 4. Signed THOMAS C. SMITH, ISABELLA SMITH. Witness: HERVEY BATES. rec 1817. pp 23, 24

Lease dated 1815. MARY KNIGHT to WILLIAM G. WADE. Brkv lot 29, term of 10 yrs. WADE to build house on lot by 1822 or contract is void. Signed MARY KNIGHT, WM. W. WADE. Witness: none. rec 1817. pp 24, 25, 26

Dunlapsville town plat map, undated. No S-T-R. JOHN DUNLAP, Proprietor. JAMES LEWISTON, surveyor. p 27

Fairfield town plat map, undated. S 21, T 10, R 2W. Laid out by THOMAS OSBORN, HUGH ABERNATHY, J. WILLSON & GEORGE JOHNSON. rec 1817. pp 28, 29

FRANKLIN COUNTY DEEDS: Book C

Deed dated 1817. JAMES BRANNON & MARY, his wife, to MARTIN McCRAY. S 19, T 14, R 13E. Signed JAMES BRANNON, MARY (x) McCRAY*. Witness: WM. HELM. rec 1817. p 29 *clerical error? should be BRANNON

Deed dated 1817. ROBERT BROWN & RACHEL, his wife, to MARTIN McCRAY. S 19, T 14, R 13E. Signed ROBERT BROWN, RACHEL BROWN. Witness: none. rec 1817. p 30

Deed dated 1816. JOHN PENWELL to REUBEN R. PENWELL. Brkv lot 17. "EASTHER, his wife". Signed JOHN PENWELL ESTHER PENWELL. Witness: JAMES WINCHILL. rec 1817. pp 30, 31

Deed dated 1817. WILLIAM ARNET to PURCY KITCHELL of Warren Co, OH. S 6, T 11, R 13 "except 2 acres...sold to DODRIDGE ALLEY." "SARAH, his wife". Signed WILLIAM ARNETT, SARAH ARNETT. Witness: HERVEY BATES, SYLVAN B. MORRIS. rec 1817. pp 31, 32

Mortgage deed dated 1817. PERCY KITCHELL as above to WILLIAM ARNETT. S 6, T 11, R 13. Land to be paid off by 1821 or title reverts to ARNETT. Signed PERCY KITCHELL. Witness: ENOCH McCARTY. rec 1817. pp 32, 33

Deed dated 1816. DANIEL HEATON & MARY, his wife, of Wayne Co to MICHAEL PETRO of OH. S 21, T14, R 13E. Signed DANIEL HEATON, MARY (x) HEATON. Witness: none rec 1817. p 33

Deed dated 1814. JEREMIAH CORY to GEORGE L. MURDOCK. Brkv lot 73. Signed JEREMIAH CORY, REBECCA CORY. Witness: JOHN TEST, E. D. JOHN. rec 1817. pp 34, 35

Deed dated 1817. WILLIAM ARNETT to ISAAC WILLSON. S 4 T 11, R 13E. Signed WILLIAM ARNETT, SARAH ARNETT. Witness: PERCY KITCHELL, JOHN FUGIT. rec 1817. pp 35, 36

Deed dated 1817. WILLIAM ARNETT to ISAAC WILLSON. S 4, T 11, R 13E. Signed WILLIAM ARNETT, SARAH ARNETT Witness: none. rec 1817. p 37

Deed dated 1815. CHRISTOPHER SMITH & ANN, his wife, of Butler Co, OH to JACOB MILLS. S 23, T 10, R1W. Signed CHRISTOPHER SMITH (german script), ANN (x) SMITH. Witness: SAMUEL SHERARD, HENRY WEAVER (in OH) rec 1817. pp 37, 38

Deed dated 1814. USA to JAMES KNIGHT JR of Dearborn Co. S 17, T 9, R 2W. p 38

FRANKLIN COUNTY DEEDS: Book C

Deed dated 1817. DAVID STOOPS to JOSEPH BRECKENRIDGE & ROBERT BRECKENRIDGE. S 33, T 12, R 13E. Signed DAVID STOOPS, ABIGAIL (x) STOOPS. Witness: ROBERT JOHN. rec 1817. p 39

Deed dated 1817. WILLIAM ARNETT to DODDRIDGE ALLEY. S 6, T 11, R 13E. Signed WILLIAM ARNETT, SARAH ARNETT. Witness: B. FELLOWS. rec 1817. pp 39, 40

Deed dated 1815. GEORGE L. MURDOCK to PETER LABOY-TEAUSE of Hamilton Co, OH. Brkv lot 35. Signed GEORGE L. MURDOCK, ANNA MURDOCK. Witness: JOSEPH MOORE, HENRY H. CASE. rec 1817. pp 40, 41

Deed dated 1817. MATTHEW BROWN & JANE, his wife, of Hamilton Co, OH to WILLIAM EWING. S 29, T 11, R 2W. Signed MATTHEW BROWN, JANE (x) BROWN. Witness: JAMES C. HANNA, DAVID BROWN. rec 1817. p 41, 42

Deed dated 1817. WILLIAM VANDEMAN & POLLY, his wife, to JAMES WEBSTER. S 13, T 13, R 12E. Signed WILLIAM VANDEMAN, MARY (x) VANDEMAN. Witness: none. rec 1817 p 42

Deed dated 1817. JESSE RUSSEL of Butler Co, OH to MOSES LYONS. S 2, T 13, R13E. "RHODA, his wife". Signed JESSE RUSSEL, RHODA RUSSEL. Witness: SARAH POTTINGER, CHARLES SWEARINGEN (at Butler Co) rec 1817. pp 42, 43

Deed dated 1817. AARON VANMETER & MARY, his wife, & JESSE ROSSELL & RHODA, his wife of Butler Co, OH to PHILLIP LOWDERBACK. S 3, T 13, R 13E. Signed JESSE ROSSELL, AARON VANMETER, MARY (x) VANMETER, RHODA (x) VANMETER. Witness: JAMES HEATON, ROBERT LYTLE JR (at Butler Co). rec 1817. pp 43, 44

Deed dated 1817. WILLIAM ARNETT & SARAH, his wife, to MATTHEW KERR. S 4, T 11, R 13E. Signed WILLIAM ARNETT SARAH ARNETT. Witness: JOHN FUGIT. rec 1817 pp 44, 45

Deed dated 1816. WILLIAM B. ALLEN & ELIZABETH, his wife, & JOHN ALLEN of Dearborn Co to MATTHEW SPARKS. S 11, T 8, R 1W. Signed WILLIAM ALLEN, ELIZABETH ALLEN, JOHN L. ALLEN. Witness: none. rec 1817. pp 45,46

Deed dated 1817. JACOB MILLS & MARY, his wife, to ROBERT BROWN. S 23, T 10, R 1W. Signed JACOB (x) MILLS, MARY (x) MILLS. Witness: WILLIAM BAKE, JACOB BAKE, JP. rec 1817. pp 46, 47

Deed dated 1817. WILLIAM DENNISTON & RACHEL, his wife

FRANKLIN COUNTY DEEDS: Book C

to ROBERT BROWN. S 23, T 10, R 1W. Signed WILLIAM DENNISTON, RACHEL DENISTON. Witness: WM. HELM, JP. rec 1817. p 47

Deed dated 1817. WILLIAM SMITH & LIDDY, his wife, to ROBERT BROWN. S 23, T 10, R 1W. Signed WILLIAM (x) SMITH, LYDIA (x) SMITH. Witness: GIDEON (x) JOHNSON, JAMES F. BROWN. rec 1817. p 48

Deed dated 1817. ELIJAH LYMPUS & LEDIA to LEVY LYMPUS. S 34, T 13, R 12E. Signed ELIJAH (x) LYMPUS, LYDIA (x) LYMPUS. Witness: WM. HELM, JP. rec 1817. p 49

Deed dated 1817. WILLIAM NORRIS & MARTHA, his wife, to WILLIAM McGREER. S 28, T 11, R 2W. Signed WILLIAM NORRIS, MARTHA (x) NORRIS. Witness: ISAAC PATTEN, ROBERT NORRIS. rec 1817. pp 49, 50

Deed dated 1812. USA to JOHN HENDERSON, assignee of MARTIN BAUM. S 33, T 11, R 2W. p 50

Deed dated 1817. JOHN HENDERSON to JAMES GLANDON. S 33, T 11, R 2W. "by land of ABBARELLA ORSBORN.. by land of GEORGE NORRIS". Signed JOHN HENDERSON. Witness: JOHN MATLOCK. rec 1817. pp 50, 51

Deed dated 1817. JOHN HENDERSON to WILLIAM McGREER. S 33, T 11, R 2W. "by ABERILLA OSBORN..by ADAM ELY... by ROBERT ABERNATHY. Signed JOHN HENDERSON. Witness: JOHN MATLOCK, ETHAN (?) HENDERSON. JP's note: "RACHEL HENDERSON...convey all my right of dower", signed ROBERT SWANN. rec 1817. pp 51, 52

Deed dated 1817. JOHN SHAW of Hamilton Co, OH to NIXON OLIVER. S 28, T 9, R 1W. "PHEBE, his wife". Signed JOHN SHAW, PHEBE SHAW. Witness: WILLIAM J. CARSON, GEORGE (x) THOMAS. rec 1817. pp 52, 53

Deed dated 1817. JOHN CLENDENNING to NIXON OLIVER. S 33, T 9, R 1. "ANNE, his wife". Signed JOHN CLENDENNING, ANN CLENDENNING. Witness: J. WINCHELL. rec 1817. pp 53, 54

Deed dated 1817. AMOS BUTLER to NIXON OLIVER. Brkv lot 69. Signed AMOS BUTLER, MARY BUTLER. Witness: ROBERT JOHN. rec 1817. pp 54, 55

Deed dated 1816. JOHN JAMES of Rising Sun, Dearborn Co, to MARY KNIGHT. Brkv inlots 28, 29. "MARTHA, his wife". Signed JOHN JAMES, MARTHA JAMES. Witness: none. rec 1817. pp 55, 56

FRANKLIN COUNTY DEEDS: Book C

Deed dated 1817. AMOS BUTLER to JOHN C. McMANNIS. Brkv lot 71. Signed AMOS BUTLER, MARY BUTLER. Witness: JAS. McKINNEY. rec 1817. p 56

Deed dated 1817. HENRY & JONATHAN REMY of Galaton Co, KY to FREDERICK HARTMAN of Hamilton Co, OH. S 32, T 9, R 2W. Signed HENRY REMY, JONATHAN REMY. Witness JAMES REMY, WILLIAM REMY. rec 1817. p 57

Deed dated 1815. HENRY REMY of Galatan Co, KY to JAMES REMY. S 13, T 8, R 1W. Signed HENRY REMY. Witness: ABRAHAM BLEDSOE, LEVI SPARKS rec 1817 pp 57, 58

Deed dated 1817. JAMES WEBSTER & MARTHA, his wife, to THOMAS SILVEY. S 13, T 13, R 12E. Signed JAMES WEBSTER, MARTHA (x) WEBSTER. Witness: WM. HELM. rec 1817. pp 58, 59

Deed dated 1817. JOSEPH W. MORRISON to JOHN HARRIS. S 13, T 10, R 3W. "MARY ANN, wife of JOSEPH". Signed J. W. MORRISON, MARY ANN (x) MORRISON. Witness: HUGH MORRISON. rec 1817. pp 59, 60

Deed dated 1817. JAMES McGINNIS to THOMAS WINSCOTT. Brkv lot 70. Signed JAMES McGINNIS, JANE (x) McGINNIS. Witness: B.F. MORRIS. rec 1817. pp 60, 61

Deed dated 1815. JEREMIAH FRENCH of Butler Co, OH to DAVID CAREL of Hamilton Co, OH. "land in Hamilton Co: R 1*, T 1, S 4." "HANNAH, his wife". Signed JEREMIAH FRENCH, HANNAH FRENCH. Witness: NATHANIEL FRENCH, SAMUEL FRENCH. rec 1817. p 91   *E or W not given

Deed dated 1817. STEPHEN CAREL & SARAH, his wife, of Hamilton Co, OH, to DAVID CAREL. S 4, T 1, R 1E*. "at EDWARD SMITH's corner". Signed STEPHEN (x) CAREL, SARAH (x) CAREL. Witness: BENAJAH AYRES, GARRET VOORHEES (in Hamilton Co, OH.) rec 1817. pp 62, 63
*if E is correct, then the land was in Hamilton Co

Deed dated 1817. RUGGLES WINCHILL to NATHANIEL WINCHILL. S 32, T 10, R 2W. "MARTHA, his wife". Signed RUGGLES WINCHILL, MARTHA (x) WINCHILL. Witness: ROBERT JOHN, ALESR. GARDNER. rec 1817. pp 63, 64

Deed dated 1817. WILLIAM CUNNINGHAM to JOHN JOHN. S 33, T 11, R 2W. Signed WILLIAM (x) CUNNINGHAM. Witness: JOSEPH KELY. rec 1817. pp 64, 65

Deed dated 1817. HUGH ABERNATHY to BENJAMIN ABERNATHY S 32, T 13, R 13E. "MARY, his wife". Signed HUGH ABERNATHY, MARY ABERNATHY. Witness: JOHN GAMBLE,

FRANKLIN COUNTY DEEDS: Book C

JOHN HANNA. rec 1817. pp 65, 66

Deed dated 1817. BENJAMIN ABERNATHY to WILLIAM RUSING. S 32, T 13, R 13E. Signed BENJ. (x) ABERNATHY. Witness: JESSE EMMERSON, GEORGE V. EWING. rec 1817. pp 66, 67

Deed dated 1817. GEORGE JOHNSON to WILLIAM RUSING. Fairfield lot 10. "SARAH, his wife". Signed GEORGE JOHNSON, SARAH JOHNSON. Witness: JOHN HANNA, BENJAMIN WILLSON. rec 1817. pp 67, 68

Deed dated 1817. HUGH ABERNATHY to WILLIAM RUSING. S 21, T 10, R 2W. Signed HUGH ABERNATHY, MARY (x) ABERNATHY. Witness: SAMUEL ST. JOHN, JACOB BLOYD. rec 1817. p 68

Deed dated 1817. CHATFIELD HOWELL & JOHN HOWELL to JAMES HOWELL. S 32, T 10, R 1W. "NANCY, wife of JOHN Signed CHATFIELD HOWELL, JOHN HOWELL, NANCY HOWELL. Witness: JOHN WHITWORTH, ABEL DARE. rec 1817. p 69

Deed dated 1817. MATTHEW BROWN & JANE, his wife, of Hamilton Co, OH to JAMES C. HANNA. S 29, T 11, R 2W. Signed MATTHEW BROWN, JANE (x) BROWN. Witness: DAVID BROWN, WILLIAM EWING. rec 1817. pp 69, 70

Deed dated 1816. ALEXANDER McGREW of Cincinnati, OH to DAVID FINLEY of Hardensburgh, Dearborn Co. Brkv lot 29. "AURELIA, his wife." Signed ALEXANDER McGREW, AURELIA McGREW. Witness: STEPHEN BARCLAY, E. STONE. rec 1817. pp 70, 71

Deed dated 1817. HUGH ABERNATHY to ZOPHAR COLEMAN. Fairfield lots 21, 28. Signed HUGH ABERNATHY, MARY (x) ABERNATHY. Witness: JOHN HANNA, JOHN NUGENT. rec 1817. pp 71, 72

Deed dated 1817. AMOS BUTLER to WILLIAM H. EADS. Brkv inlot 35. Signed AMOS BUTLER, MARY BUTLER. Witness: none. rec 1817. pp 72, 73

Deed dated 1817. HUGH ABERNATHY to ZOPHAR COLEMAN. Fairfield lot 23. Signed HUGH ABERNATHY, MARY (x) ABERNATHY. Witness: none. rec 1817. p 73

Deed dated 1817. ENOCH D. JOHN to THOMAS MORRIS of Clermont Co, OH. Brkv lot, no #, bounds given. Signed ENOCH D. JOHN, ELOISE JOHN. Witness: #1 illegible, JOSEPH D. CLEMENTS. rec 1817. p 74

Deed dated 1817. THOMAS MORGAN to JESSE STOUT of

FRANKLIN COUNTY DEEDS: Book C

Hamilton Co, OH. S 24, T 9, R 1W. "ELIZABETH, his wife". Signed THOMAS (x) MORGAN, ELIZABETH (x) MORGAN. Witness: ADOLPHUS GALLEY, JOHN BARTLOW. rec 1817. pp 74, 75, 76

Deed dated 1817. JOHN CONNER to DAVID GOBLE. S 11, T 8, R 2W. "VINA, wife of JOHN". Signed JOHN CONNER, LEVIA CONNER. Witness: none. rec 1817. p 76

Deed dated 1817. JOHN C. McMANNIS to MOSES GREEN. Brkv lots 6, 71. Signed JOHN C. McMANNIS. Witness: WILL CHILTON. rec 1817. p 77

Deed dated 1817. JOHN C. McMANNIS to HUGH MAY & THOMAS TERRILL. Brkv lot 58. "CATHERINE, his wife". Signed JOHN C. McMANNIS, CATHERINE McMANNIS. Witness: none. rec 1817. pp 77, 78

Deed dated 1816. MICHAEL JONES of Shawnee Town, Illinois Ter'ty & MARY, his wife, to JOHN GARRISON. Brkv lot 64. Signed MICHAEL JONES, MARY JONES. Witness: JOSEPH HAYES, JNO. MARSHALL. rec 1817. pp 78,79

Deed dated 1817. WILLIAM RUSON to THOMAS OSBORN. S 21, T 10, R 2W. "NANCY, wife of WILLIAM". Signed WILLIAM RUSING, AGNES (x) RUSING. Witness: JOHN HANNA, GEORGE JOHNSON. rec 1817. pp 79, 80

Connersville addition plat map, undated. JOSHUA HARLAN, proprietor. THOS. HINKSON, surveyor. rec 1817. p 81

Deed dated 1817. ABRAHAM C. ROLL of Cincinnati, OH to JACOB CAPP of same. Brkv lots 40, 41. "MARY, his wife". Signed ABRAHAM C. ROLL, MARY ROLL. Witness: J.C.TUNNIS, JNO. L. AVERY (in OH) rec 1817 pp 82, 83

Deed dated 1816. USA to ISAAC STELLE, assignee of EBER HOWMAN. S 20, T 14, R 13E. rec 1817. p 83

Deed dated 1817. ARTHUR DICKSON to WILLIAM C. DREW. Brkv lot 17. Signed ARTHUR DICKSON, SARAH DICKSON. Witness: B.F. MORRIS, ENOCH McCARTY. rec 1817. p 84

Deed dated 1817. MARY HUDSON to THOMAS TERRILL. Brkv lot 27. Signed MARY HUDSON. Witness: none. rec 1817 pp 84, 85

Deed dated 1817. HENRY BEEKLEY to JOSEPH FERRIS & ANDREW FERRIS of Hamilton Co, OH. S 11, T 9, R 2W. "ANN his wife". Signed HENRY BEEKLEY, ANN BEEKLEY. Witness GIDEON FERRIS, ROBERT BARNARD. rec 1817. pp 85, 86

FRANKLIN COUNTY DEEDS: Book C

Deed dated 1817. THOMAS HENDERSON to HERVEY BATES. S 34, T 13, R 13E. Signed THOMAS HENDERSON. Witness: HENRY NEWKIRK, N. NOBLE. rec 1817. p 86

Deed dated 1817. MATTHEW BROWN & JANE, his wife of Hamilton Co, OH to NATHANIEL HENDERSON. S 35, T 11, R 2W. Signed MATTHEW BROWN, JANE (x) BROWN. Witness: SAMUEL B. POOHER, THOMAS GOLDING. rec 1817. p 87

Deed dated 1817. AMOS BUTLER to PRUDY HUDSON. Brkv lot 22. Signed AMOS BUTLER, MARY BUTLER. Witness: none. rec 1818. pp 87, 88

Deed dated 1817. JAMES TONER to BENJAMIN MAPLE. S 9 T 12, R 12E. "patented to JAMES TONER, assignee of JAMES EAGAN, 1816". Signed JAMES TOMS. Witness: WM. HELM, ACK NYERL. rec 1818. pp 88, 89

Deed dated 1817. ENOCH McCARTY to CHARLES B. FINCH. Brkv lots 32, 38. Signed ENOCH McCARTY, ELIZABETH (x) McCARTY. Witness: B.F. MORRIS. rec 1818. p 89

Deed dated 1818. CHARLES B. FINCH to NOAH NOBLE & HERVEY BATES. Brkv lot 35. "ISABELLA, his wife". Signed CHARLES B. FINCH, ISABELLA (x) FINCH. Witness: CHARLES H. TEST, GEORGE HARRIS. rec 1818. p 90

Deed dated 1818. THOMAS WILLIAMS & DEBORAH his wife to JOHN STINSON. S 19, T 9, R 2W. Signed THOMAS WILLIAMS, DEBORAH (x) WILLIAMS. Witness: B.F. MORRIS, ROB'T. JOHN. rec 1818. pp 90, 91

Deed dated 1815. JOHN ALLEN SR to LUTHER RUSSELL. Brkv lot 100. Signed JOHN ALLEN SR. Witness: ROBERT JOHN, B. F. MORRIS. rec 1818. pp 91, 92

Deed dated 1817. HERVEY BATES & PATIENCE, his wife to THOMAS HALSTEAD. S 4, T 11, R 13E. Signed HARVEY BATES, PATIENCE (x) BATES. Witness: CHARLES COLLETT, PELEAD HONEYWELL. rec 1818. pp 92, 93

Deed dated 1818. N. D. GALLION to --HENDERSON. Brkv lot 44. Signed N. D. GALLION, HANNAH GALLION. Witness: none. rec 1818. pp 93, 94

Deed dated 1817. JOSHUA WYETH to JOHN CONNER. S 14, T 8, R 2W. "HANNAH, his wife." Signed JOSHUA WYETH, HANNAH WYETH. Witness: ROBERT JOHN. rec 1818. p 94

Deed dated 1818. JOHN CARSON SR & HANSON LOVE to JACOB VANDERYNE. Sec 23, T 9, R 2W. Signed JOHN CARSON, HANSON LOVE, POLLY (x) CARSON, POLLY (x) LOVE. Wit-

FRANKLIN COUNTY DEEDS: Book C

ness: WILLIAM H. EADS, HUGH MORRISON rec 1818 p94 1/2

Deed dated 1818. STEPHEN OLDHAM & REBECCA, his wife, to SAMUEL HILL. S 22, T 14, R 13E. Signed STEPHEN (x) OLDHAM, REBECKA (x) OLDHAM. Witness: OWEN STODDARD, SAM'L BELL. rec 1818. p 95

Deed dated 1817. SAMUEL HILL & MARY his wife to STEPHEN OLDHAM. S 22, T 14, R 13E. Signed SAMUEL HILL, MARY (x) HILL. Witness: none. rec 1818. pp 95, 96

Deed dated 1817. JOHN BROWN & SARAH his wife to JOEL GARRISON. S 35, T 11, R 2. Signed JOHN BROWN, SARAH (x) BROWN. Witness: WILLIAM ROSS, ROBERT DARE. rec 1818. pp 96, 97

Deed dated 1818. JOHN ALLEN SR to B. F. MORRIS. Brkv lot 59. Signed JOHN ALLEN SR. Witness: ROBERT JOHN. rec 1818. pp 97, 98

Deed dated 1817. LISMUND BASEY to WILLIAM TEMPLETON. Brkv outlot 2. "ELIZABETH, his wife". Signed LISMUND BASEY, ELIZABETH (x) BASEY. Witness: JOHN HANNA. rec 1818. p 98

Deed dated 1817. ROBERT TEMPLETON SR to WILLIAM TEMPLETON. S 28, T 10, R 2W. "MARY, wife of ROBERT". Signed ROBERT TEMPLETON, MARY (x) TEMPLETON. Witness: JOHN HANNA, ROBERT TEMPLETON JR. rec 1818. pp 98, 99

Deed dated 1817. WILLIAM WILLSON SR to WILLIAM DICKSON. S 24, T 10, R 3W. Signed WILLIAM WILLSON, HANNAH WILLSON. Witness: SOLOMON ALLEN, WILLIAM WILSON. rec 1818. pp 99, 100

Deed dated 1816. JAMES WILSON to WILLIAM DICKSON. Fairfield lots 33, 40. "NANCY, his wife". Signed JAS. WILSON, NANCY (x) WILSON. Witness: none. rec 1818. pp 100, 101

Deed dated 1817. WILLIAM WILSON SR to WILLIAM WILSON JR. S 24, T 10, R 3W. "HANNAH, his wife". Signed WILLIAM WILSON, HANNAH WILSON. Witness: SOLOMON ALLEN, WILLIAM DICKSON. rec 1818. pp 101, 102

Deed dated 1817. HUGH ABERNATHY to JACOB BLOYD. Fairfield lots 22, 27. Signed HUGH ABERNATHY, MARY (x) ABERNATHY. Witness: SAMUEL ST. JOHN, WILLIAM RUSING. rec 1818. pp 102, 103

Deed dated 1817. SAMUEL ROCKAFELLER to JONATHAN J. SMITH of Dearborn Co. New Trenton lot 13. Signed

FRANKLIN COUNTY DEEDS: Book C

SAMUEL ROCKAFELLAR, MARY ROCKAFELLAR. Witness: H. MAY, ENOCH SMITH. rec 1818. pp 103, 104

Deed dated 1818. ARCHIBALD GUTHERY to JAMES C. MORSELL & WILLIAM K. LAMDIN (LAMBDIN in text). Brkv lot 44. "RACHEL, his wife". Signed ARCH'D. GUTHERY, RCHL. GUTTRY. Witness: ARTHUR DICKSON, HUGH MORRISON rec 1818. pp 104, 105

Brookville addition plat map dated 1818. WILLIAM H. EADS, prop'r. SOLOMON ALLEN, surveyor. rec 1818 p 105

Deed dated 1817. JAMES A. PIATT to WILLIAM H. EADS. Brkv 38. "JEMIMA, his wife". Signed JAMES A. PIATT, JEMIMA PIATT. Witness: ROBERT JOHN. rec 1818. p 106

Deed dated 1818. WILLIAM H. EADS to JOHN FOUCH. S 3 T 12, R 12E. Signed WILLIAM H. EADS, JANE EADS. Witness: ROBERT JOHN. rec 1818. pp 106, 107

Deed dated 1817. ROBERT TEMPLETON SR to ROBERT TEMPLETON JR. S 4, T 12, R 2W. Signed ROBERT TEMPLETON, MARY (x) TEMPLETON. Witness: JOHN HANNA, WILLIAM TEMPLETON. rec 1818. pp 108, 109

Deed dated 1818. DAVID AGNEW to JOSHUA V. ROBINSON & Co. Brkv lot 38. Signed DAVID AGNEW, JOSINAH AGNEW. Witness: WILLIAM GOOSHORN, JOHN McLEAN. rec 1818. pp 108, 109

Deed dated 1818. JOHN ALLEN SR to JOHN B. WHITFORD. Brkv lot 80. Signed JOHN ALLEN SR. Witness: SAMUEL GOODWIN, JOHN WINCHILL. rec 1818. pp 109

Deed dated 1818. JACOB HEDRICK to JAMES TYLER. S 1, T 12, R 13E. "MARGARET, his wife". Signed JACOB HETRICK, MARGARET HETRICK. Witness: B.F. MORRIS. rec 1818. p 110

Deed dated 1818. JACOB HEDRICK to SAMUEL BROWN. S 1, T 12, R 13E. Signed JACOB HETRICK, MARGARET HETRICK. Witness: B.F. MORRIS. rec 1818. pp 110, 111

Quitclaim deed dated 1811. Heirs of JACOB REED SR to HARDEN REED & ASA HARPER. JACOB SR, REED & HARPER purchased (unspecified) land jointly, now being sold. Signed AARON BROYLES, DEWARD HARPER, JACOB REED, SALLY REED, ARCHIBALD REED, JAMES GAMBULL, JO. C. REED, GEORGE REED. rec 1818. p 111

Quitclaim deed dated 1817. CHATFIELD HOWELL to JOHN HOWEL. S 32, T 10, R1W. Land owned jointly, now sold

FRANKLIN COUNTY DEEDS: Book C

to JOHN. Signed CHATFIELD HOWEL. Witness: SAMUEL HOWEL, JOHN WHITWORTH. rec 1818. p 112

Deed dated 1817. ROBERT GREEN & ANNA, his wife, to RICHARD McMILLAN. S 8, T 10, R 1W. Signed ROBERT GREEN, ANNA (x) GREEN. Witness: JOHN WHITWORTH, PETER D. GREEN. rec 1818. pp 112, 113

Deed dated 1817. PETER D. GREEN & MARY, his wife, of Butler Co, OH to RICHARD McMILLAN. S 8, T 10, R 1W. Signed PETER D. GREEN, MARY (x) GREEN. Witness: JOHN WHITWORTH, THOMAS WRIGHT. rec 1818. pp 113, 114

Deed dated 1817. SIMON ELY SR & ELIZABETH, his wife to JAMES FISHER. S 5, T 10, R 2W. Signed SIMON ELY, ELIZABETH (x) ELY. Witness: SAM'L. ELY, JAMES CARWILE rec 1818. pp 114, 115

Deed dated 1817. JOHN PENWELL to HERVEY BATES. S 27, T 9, R 2W. Signed JOHN PENWELL, ESTHER PENWELL. Witness: SOLOMON ALLEN, JOHN ALLEN JR. rec 1818. pp 115, 116

Deed dated 1818. JAMES WILSON to WILLIAM H. EADS & THOMAS C. EADS. Fairfield lots 71, 72, 73, 74, 75, 76. Signed JAMES WILSON, NANCY WILSON. Witness: JOHN EWING. rec 1818. pp 116, 117

Deed dated 1818. JAMES WILSON to WILLIAM H. EADS & THOMAS C. EADS. S 21, no T-R. Signed JAMES WILSON, NANCY WILSON. Witness: JOHN EWING. rec 1818. pp 116, 117

Deed dated 1817. SAMUEL FULLEN to NICHOLAS PUMPHREY. S 12, T 13, R 12E. "ELIZABETH, his wife". Signed SAMUEL FULLEN, ELIZABETH (x) FULLEN. Witness:none. rec 1818. pp 118

Deed dated 1817. JOSEPH LEE & NANCY, his wife, to ROBERT BROWN. S 23, T 10, R 1W. Signed JOSEPH LEE, NANCY (x) LEE. Witness: JACOB BAKE, JOSEPH SMITH. rec 1818. pp 118, 119

Deed dated 1817. MOSES MAXWELL to JOHN G. HUMPHREY of VA. S 19, T 10, R 1W. Signed MOSES (x) MAXWELL. Witness: none. rec 1818. pp 119, 120

Deed dated 1815. CHRISTOPHER SMITH & ANN, his wife, of Butler Co, OH to HENRY BLOS. S 8, T 10, R 1W. Signed CHRISTOPHER SMITH (german script), ANN (x) SMITH. Witness: SAMUEL SHERARD, HENRY WEAVER. rec 1818. pp 120, 121

FRANKLIN COUNTY DEEDS: Book C

Deed dated 1818. AMOS BUTLER to ELI LEE. Brkv lots 44, 58, 59. Signed AMOS BUTLER, MARY BUTLER. Witness HUGH MORRISON, HENRY PARKER. rec 1818. pp 121, 122

Deed dated 1815. CHRISTOPHER SMITH & ANN, his wife, of Butler Co, OH to JOHN SMITH. S 8, T 10, R 1W. Signed CHRISTOPHER SMITH (german script), ANN (x) SMITH. Witness: SAMUEL SHERARD, HENRY WEAVER. rec 1818. pp 122, 123

Land contract dated 1818. STEPHEN C. STEVENS to ALEXANDER GARDNER. Brkv lot 36 to be paid off by 1822. Signed S. C. STEVENS. Witness: HERVEY BATES. Note of completed payments, signed A. GARDNER, 1821. rec 1818. p 124

Deed dated 1818. JOHN STINSON & ELIZABETH, his wife, to JOSEPH BRACKENRIDGE. S 19, T 9, R 2W. Signed JOHN STINSON, ELIZABETH (x) STINSON. Witness: ALEX'R GARDNER. rec 1818. p 125

Deed dated 1818. JOHN ALLEN SR to WILLIAM W. WADE. Brkv lot 75. Signed JOHN ALLEN SR. Witness: ROBERT JOHN. rec 1818. p 126

Deed dated 1818. JOHN DUNLAP to JAMES W. SCOTT. Dunlapsville lot 25. "ELIZABETH, his wife". Signed JOHN DUNLAP, ELIZABETH DUNLAP. Witness: WILLIAM NICKLS, ROSS SMILIE. rec 1818. pp 126, 127

Deed dated 1818. JOHN DUNLAP to JAMES W. SCOTT. Dunlapsville lot 15. Signed JOHN DUNLAP, ELIZABETH DUNLAP. Witness: WILLIAM NICKLS, ROSS SMILIE. rec 1818. pp 127, 128

Deed dated 1818. JOHN DUNLAP to JAMES W. SCOTT. Dunlapsville lot 11. Signed JOHN DUNLAP, ELIZABETH DUNLAP. Witness: WILLIAM NICKLS, ROSS SMILIE. rec 1818. pp 128, 129

Deed dated 1818. JOHN DUNLAP to JAMES W. SCOTT. Dunlapsville lot 38. Signed JOHN DUNLAP, ELIZABETH DUNLAP. Witness: WILLIAM NICKLS, ROSS SMILIE. rec 1818. pp 129, 130

Deed dated 1818. JOHN DUNLAP to ROSS SMILIE. Dunlapville lot 34. Signed JOHN DUNLAP, ELIZABETH DUNLAP. Witness: JAMES W. SCOTT, WILLIAM NICKLS. rec 1818. p 130

Deed dated 1818. JOHN DUNLAP to ROSS SMILIE. Dunlapv 31. Signed JOHN DUNLAP, ELIZABETH DUNLAP. Witness:

FRANKLIN COUNTY DEEDS: Book C

JAMES W. SCOTT, WILLIAM NICKLS. rec 1818. p 131

Deed dated 1818. AMOS BUTLER to ABRAHAM ELWELL. Brkv lot 54. Signed AMOS BUTLER, MARY BUTLER. Witness: HUGH MORRISON. no rec date. pp 131, 132

Deed dated 1817. HUGH GLEN of Cincinnati, OH to JOHN McKINNEY. S 19, T 11, R 1W. "MARY, his wife". Signed H. GLENN, M. GLENN. Witness: JOHN B. ENNISS, JOHN MAHARD (in OH). rec 1818. pp 132, 133

Deed dated 1818. MATHEW ROBERTSON of Wayne Co to BENJAMIN BROWN of Butler Co, OH. S 10, T 8, R 1W. "ELINOR, his wife". Signed MATTHEW ROBINSON, ELEANOR (x) ROBINSON. Witness: B. F. MORRIS. rec 1818. pp 133, 134

Deed dated 1818. AMOS BUTLER & MARY his wife to ENOCH McCARTY & WILLIAM C. DREW. Brkv lot, no #; bounds given. Signed AMOS BUTLER, MARY BUTLER. Witness: HUGH MORRISON, CLARK HARRIS. rec 1818. pp 134, 135

Mortgage deed dated 1818. ABRAM NEWKIRK to DANIEL POWERS. S 27, T 10, R 2W. Note due in 1820 to void conveyance. Signed ABRAM NEWKIRK, DANIEL POWERS. Witness: JOHN HANNA, JACOB BARCKMAN. rec 1818 pp 136, 137

Deed dated 1817. WILLIAM BRADLEY to DODDRIDGE ALLY. Brkv lot 42. "REBECCA, wife of WILLIAM". Signed WM. BRADLEY, REBECCA BRADLEY. Witness: WILLIAM H. EADS. rec 1818. pp 137, 138

Deed dated 1818. DODDRIDGE & JONATHAN ALLEY & JANE & CATHERINE, their wives, to JEHU JOHN. Brkv lot 42. Signed DODDRIDGE ALLEY, JONATHAN ALLEY, JANE (x) ALLEY, CATHERINE (x) ALLEY. Witness: ENOCH D. JOHN. rec 1818. pp 138, 139

Deed dated 1817. JAMES HAMILTON of Dearborn Co to JOHN HAMILTON of same. S 29, T 9, R 2W. Signed J. HAMILTON. Witness: JAMES DILE, JOHN JAMES (at Dearborn). rec 1818. pp 140, 141

Deed dated 1818. SAMUEL ROCKAFELLER to GEORGE W. KIMBLE. New Trenton lot 11. Signed SAMUEL ROCKAFELLAR, MARY ROCKAFELLAR. Witness: HENRY ROCKAFELLAR. rec 1818. pp 141, 142

Mortgage deed dated 1818. JAMES McGINNIS to HERVEY BATES. Brkv lot 24. Notes due in 12 months to void conveyance. Signed JAMES McGINNIS. Witness: ROBERT JOHN, ENOCH McCARTY. rec 1818. pp 142, 143

FRANKLIN COUNTY DEEDS: Book C

Deed dated 1818. NOAH NOBLE to WILLIAM ORR of Jefferson Co, KY. Brkv lot; bounds given, no #. Signed N. NOBLE. Witness: ROBERT JOHN, HERVEY BATES. rec 1818. pp 143, 144

Deed dated 1818. HERVEY BATES to NOAH NOBLE. Brkv lot 35. Signed HERVEY BATES. Witness: ROBERT JOHN. rec 1818. pp 144, 145

Deed dated 1815. WILLIAM NORRIS & MARTHA, his wife to GEORGE NORRIS. S 28, T 11, no R given. Signed WILLIAM NORRIS, MARTHA (x) NORRIS. Witness: ROBERT SWAN, JP & WILLIAM CUNNINGHAM. rec 1818. pp 145, 146

Deed dated 1817. PETER GRAY & MARY his wife, of Hamilton Co, OH to STEPHEN REEDER of Warren Co, OH. S 14, T 9, R 2W. Signed PETER GRAY, MARY (x) GRAY. Witness: JACOB G. REEDER, JAMES W. LANIER (in OH) rec 1818. pp 147, 148

Brookville outlot plat map dated 1818. Laid off by AMOS BUTLER. rec 1818. p 148

Deed dated 1817. JOHN HEDLEY to HENRY BERRY. S 26, T 9, R2W. Signed JOHN HEDLEY. Witness: ROBERT JOHN JP. rec 1818. p 149

Deed dated 1818. THOMAS OSBORN to WILLIAM L. ROSE. Fairfield lots 58, 63. Signed THOMAS OSBORN. Witness: JOHN EWING, EBENEZER (x) SPRIGGS. rec 1818. p 150

Deed dated 1818. AMOS BUTLER to WILLIAM C. DREW. Brkv lot 67. Signed AMOS BUTLER, MARY BUTLER. Witness HUGH MORRISON, E.W. THRUSTON. rec 1818. p 151

Deed dated 1818. AMOS BUTLER to JAMES BACKHOUSE & ROBERT BRACKENRIDGE. S 20, T 9, R 2W. Signed AMOS BUTLER, MARY BUTLER. Witness: ROBERT JOHN rec 1818. pp 152, 153

Deed dated 1817. GIDEON JOHNSTON & POLLY, his wife, to JOHN MILLER. S 8, T 10, R 1W. Signed GIDEON (x) JOHNSON, POLLY (x) JOHNSON. Witness: none. rec 1818. pp 153, 154

Deed dated 1817. ROBERT GLIDEWELL, SR to WILLIAM GLIDEWELL. S 24, T 10, R 2W. Signed ROBERT (x) GLIDEWELL. Witness: ENOCH McCARTY. rec 1818. pp 154, 155

Deed dated 1817. GEORGE FRAZIERE & ELIZABETH, his wife, to SOLOMON CLAYPOOL. S 23, T 14, R 12E. Signed GEORGE FRAZIER, ELIZABETH FRAZIER. Witness: none.

FRANKLIN COUNTY DEEDS: Book C

rec 1818. pp 155, 156

Deed dated 1811. HENRY COSTON to WILLIAM H. EADS. S 25, T 13, R 1 "in the tract appropriated for Military Bounties in the Territory of Illinois". "HANNAH, his wife". Signed HENRY COSTON, HANNAH (x) COSTON. Witness: none. rec 1818. pp 156, 157

Deed dated 1818. WILLIAM BREWEN to HENRY COSTON. S 25 T 13, R 1. "granted to said WILLIAM, a private in the late Army of the US". "MATILDA, wife of WM." Signed WILLIAM (x) BREWEN, MATILDA (x) BREWEN. Witness: N.FRENCH. rec 1818. p 157

Deed dated 1818. AMOS BUTLER to WILLIAM W. WADE. Brkv outlot 23. Signed AMOS BUTLER, MARY BUTLER. Witness: HUGH MORRISON. rec 1818. p 158

Deed dated 1818. THOMAS MORGAN to MICHAEL WILKINS. S 24, T 9, R 1W. "ELIZABETH, his wife". Signed THOMAS (x) MORGAN, ELIZABETH (x) MORGAN. Witness: JOHN LUSE, JP. rec 1818. p 159

Deed dated 1817. CHRISTIAN SWIFT & FRANCES, his wife to WILLIAM VINHORN McCOMBS. S 15, T 12, R 13E. Signed CHRISTIAN (x) SWIFT, FRANCES (x) SWIFT. Witness: HENRY CALFEE. rec 1818. pp 160, 161

Brookville outlots plat map dated 1818. Laid out by JOHN ALLEN SR. rec 1818. p 161

Mortgage deed dated 1818. JOHN ROCKAFELLAR to WILLIAM KNOWLES. S 32, T 8, R 1W. Debt to be paid by 1821 to void conveyance. Signed JOHN H. ROCKAFELLAR. Witness: THOMAS MANWARING. rec 1818. pp 161, 162

Deed dated 1818. THOMAS WATTERS & ELIZABETH his wife, late TEGARDEN, to NATHAN D. GALLION. S 3, T 12, R 13E Signed THOMAS WATTERS, ELIZABETH WATTERS. Witness: N. FRENCH, G.W. KIMBLE. rec 1818. pp 162, 163

Deed dated 1818. DODDRIDGE ALLEY & JONATHAN ALLEY to NATHAN DESHA GALLION. Brkv lot 42. "JANE, wife of DODDRIDGE & CATHERINE, wife of JONATHAN". Signed DODDRIDGE ALLEY, JONATHAN ALLEY, JANE (x) ALLEY, CATHERINE (x) ALLEY. Witness: JOHN PENWELL, ALLEN RAMSEY. rec 1818. p 163, 164

Deed dated 1818. LISMUND BASYE to NATHAN D. GALLION. S 3, T 9, R 2W. Signed LISMUND BASEY, ELIZABETH (x) BASEY. Witness: ROBERT JOHN, CALVIN RUSSELL. rec 1818. p 165

FRANKLIN COUNTY DEEDS: Book C

Deed dated 1818. JOHN BREWEN of Green Co, OH to WILLIAM H. EADS. S 28, T 14, R 5W "in a tract appropriated for Military Bounties in Illinois Territory". Signed JOHN W. (x) BREWEN. Witness: ROBERT JOHN, RICH CROAKE. rec 1818. p 166

Deed dated 1815. USA to LISMUND BASYE. S 3, T 9, R 2W. rec 1818. p 167

Deed dated 1817. JOEL BELK & JANE, his wife, to GABRIEL HENSLEY. S 29, T 10, R 2W. Signed JOEL BELK, JANE BELK. Witness: JOHN GAMBLE, JOHN EWING. rec 1818. pp 167, 168

Deed dated 1817. DAVID STOOPS to NICHOLAS CHRIST. S 5, T 12, R 13E. Signed DAVID STOOPS, ABIGAIL (x) STOOPS. Witness: none. rec 1818. pp 168, 169

Deed dated 1818. ENOCH D. JOHN & NOAH NOBLE to WILLIAM C. DREW. Brkv lot 48. Signed ENOCH D. JOHN, N. NOBLE, ELOISE JOHN. Witness: none. rec 1818. p 169

Deed dated 1818. B.F. MORRIS to JOSEPH B.F. MORRIS, (error? name in text is JOSEPH COXE). Brkv lot 59. "ELIZABETH , his wife". Signed B.F. MORRIS, ELIZABETH MORRIS. Witness: none. rec 1818. p 170

Deed dated 1818. AMOS BUTLER to WILLIAM HARLOW of Cincinnati, OH. Brkv lot 2. Signed AMOS BUTLER, MARY BUTLER. Witness: HERVEY BATES, ROBERT JOHN. rec 1818. pp 170, 171

Deed dated 1817. THOMAS MORGAN to THOMAS D. MATTHEWS S 24, T 9, R 1W. Signed THOMAS (x) MORGAN, ELIZABETH (x) MORGAN. Witness: JOHN BARTLOW, JOSEPH VANNESS, ADOLPHUS GULLEY, JP. rec 1818. pp 171, 172

Deed dated 1815. JAMES McGINNIS to JOHN GARRISON. Brkv lots 63, 64. Signed JAMES McGINNIS, JANE McGINNIS. Witness: BENJAMIN SMITH. rec 1818. pp 173, 174

Deed dated 1818. ENOCH D. JOHN & NOAH NOBLE to THOMAS GREENE & WILLIAM HARTLOW (THOMAS GREENE & Co.) S 28, T 9, R 2W. Signed ENOCH D. JOHN, N. NOBLE, ELOISA JOHN. Witness: ROBERT JOHN, JP. rec 1818. pp 174, 175

Deed dated 1818. JOHN ALLEN SR to THOMAS GREENE as above. S 29, T 9, R 2W. Signed JOHN ALLEN SR, POLLY ALLEN. Witness: ROBERT JOHN. rec 1818. pp 175, 176

Deed dated 1818. ENOCH D. JOHN & NOAH NOBLE to THOMAS GREENE & WILLIAM HARTLOW (THOMAS GREENE & Co.)

FRANKLIN COUNTY DEEDS: Book C

S 28, T 9, R 2. Signed ENOCH D. JOHN, N. NOBLE, ELOISE JOHN. Witness: ROBERT JOHN. rec 1818. pp176, 177

Deed dated 1818. ENOCH D. JOHN & NOAH NOBLE to THOMAS GREENE & WILLIAM HARTLOW (THOMAS GREENE & Co.) S 28, T 9, R 2. Signed ENOCH D. JOHN, N. NOBLE, ELOISE JOHN. Witness: ROBERT JOHN. rec 1818. pp 177, 178

Deed dated 1818. JOHN JACOBS to THOMAS BRADLEY. Brkv lot 33. "ELIZABETH, his wife". Signed JOHN JACOBS, ELIZABETH JACOBS. Witness: ROBERT JOHN. rec 1818. pp 178, 179

Deed dated 1818. JOSEPH STEVENS & JAMES STEVENS SR to JOHN STEVENS. S 36, T 10, R 2W. Signed JAMES (x) STEVENS, JOSEPH (x) STEVENS. Witness: JOHN HANNA, ALIGAH STEVENS. rec 1818. pp 179, 180

Deed dated 1818. WILLIAM HEAVENRIDGE to USUAL WARD. S 20, T 11, R 1W. "MARY, his wife". Signed WILLIAM HEAVENRIDGE, MARY HEAVENRIDGE. Witness: EBENEZER HOWE, CALVIN WARD. rec 1818. pp 180, 181

Mortgage deed dated 1818. JOHN JASON to OLIVER BENTON Debt to be paid in whiskey, delv'd at Cincinnati by March, 1819. S 14, T 8, R 2W held as security. Signed JOHN JASON, LUCY JASN. Witness: CONRAD SAILORS, JP. rec 1818. pp 181, 182

Deed dated 1818. WILLIAM HENDERSON to WILLIAM TYNER. S 32, T 9, R 2W. Signed WM. HENDERSON, ZILPHA (x) HENDERSON. Witness: B.F. MORRIS, C.D. MORRIS. rec 1818. pp 182, 183

Deed dated 1817. JOSEPH VANCE & JANE his wife to TIMOTHY L. BROWN. S 4, T 13, R 12E. Signed JOSEPH VANCE JANE VANCE. Witness: none. rec 1818. pp 183, 184

Deed dated 1817. JAMES WATERS to ROBERT RUSING. S 20 T 10, R 2W. Signed JAMES WATERS, ELIZABETH WATERS. Witness: JESSE EMERSON, JOHN HAMBLE. rec 1818. pp 184, 185

Deed dated 1817. WILLIAM RUSING to ROBERT RUSING. S 21, T 10, R 2W. "NANCY, his wife". Signed WILLIAM RUSING, AGNES (x) RUSING. Witness: CHARLES HARVEY, JOHN RUSING. rec 1818. pp 185, 186

Deed dated 1817. DAVID GOBLE & ALESEY, his wife to JOSHUA WYETH. S 11, T 8, R 2W. "lane between JOSHUA WYETH & JOHN LAFORGE". Signed DAVID GOBLE, ALESEY (x) GOBLE. Witness: ROBERT JOHN. rec 1818. pp 186, 187

FRANKLIN COUNTY DEEDS: Book C

Deed dated 1817. ALEXANDER McGREW of Cincinnati, OH to DAVID BROWN of same. S 11, T 8, R 2W. Signed ALEXANDER McGREW, AURELIA McGREW. Witness: BENJ. BASSETT, HEZEKIAH KNAPP (in OH). rec 1818. pp 187, 188

Deed dated 1818. AMOS BUTLER to HUGH BRISON. Brkv 45. Signed AMOS BUTLER, MARY BUTLER. Witness: HUGH MORRISON, JEREMIAH GOODWIN. rec 1818. pp 188, 189

Deed dated 1817. ABNER LEONARD to ABNER LEONARD JR. "at ROBERT BRADFORD's corner". S 29, T 9, R 1W. "MEHETABLE, his wife". Signed ABNER LEONARD, MEHETABLE (x) LEONARD. Witness: HEZEKIAH SAILORS, JACOB LIONS. rec 1818. pp 189, 190

Deed dated 1818. WILLIAM L. ROSE to JOHN MILLER. Fairfield lot 30. Signed WILLIAM L. ROSE. Witness: JOHN EWING, THOS. EADS. rec 1818. pp 190, 191

Deed dated 1818. THOMAS HARVEY to JOHN MILLER. Fairfield lot 30. "HANNAH, his wife". Signed THOMAS HARVEY, HANNAH HARVEY. Witness: JESSE EMERSON. rec 1818. pp 190, 191

Deed dated 1817. BENJAMIN ABRAMS to JOAB COMSTOCK of Hamilton Co, OH. S 1, T 8, R 1W. Signed BENJ. ABRAHAM. Witness: ROBERT LUSE, JOHN LUSE. rec 1818. pp 191, 192

Deed dated 1817. ISAAC MILLER of Montgomery Co, OH to JOHN R. MILLER of same. "ELIZABETH, his wife". S 2 & 12, T 11, R 1W. Included farm animals, household goods. Signed ISAAC MILLER, ELIZABETH (x) MILLER. Witness: DAVID (x) SHOCK, ANNY (x) WEAVER (in OH). rec 1818. pp 192, 193

Deed dated 1818. ROBERT GLIDEWELL SR to NASH GLIDEWELL. S 3, T 9, R 2W. Signed ROBERT (x) GLIDEWELL. Witness: ENOCH McCARTY. rec 1818. pp 193, 194

Deed dated 1817. AMOS BUTLER to JAMES JOHNSTON. Brkv lot 43. Signed AMOS BUTLER, MARY BUTLER. Witness: ROBERT JOHN. rec 1818. p 194

Quitclaim deed dated 1817. ELIJAH GARDNER, ARCHIBALD GARDNER & RUSSEL GARDNER, heirs of JOHN GARDNER, dec, to JOSEPH GARDNER. S 3, T 9, R 1W. Signed ELIJAH GARDNER, ARCHIBALD (x) GARDNER, RUSEL GARDNER. Witness: none. rec 1818. p 195

Deed dated 1818. JOSEPH GARDNER to WILLIAM McCAW. S 3, T 9, R 1W. Signed JOSEPH (X) GARDNER. Witness:

FRANKLIN COUNTY DEEDS: Book C

ROBT. LUCE, J. H. WHITE. rec 1818. pp 195, 196

Deed dated 1818. HUGH BRYSON to ROBERT BRECKENRIDGE. Brkv lot 45. "RUTH, his wife". Signed HUGH BRISON, RUTH (x) BRISON. Witness: none. rec 1818. pp 196, 197

Deed dated 1818. ALLISON C. LOOKER & RACHEL his wife of Ross Co, OH to WILLIAM H. EADS. Brkv lot 50. Signed A.C. LOOKER, RACHEL H. LOOKER. Witness: BENJ. HOUGH, A. McCLEAN (in OH). rec 1818.   pp 197, 198

Election of Connersville Library Ass'n officers dated 1818. Held at house of ABSALOM BURHAM. Chairman JAMES BROWNLEE; Sec'y JOHN BRADBURN; Directors JOHN CONNOR, WILLIAM HELMS, LEWIS JOHNSON, JOHN BRADBURN, ABIATHER HATHAWAY, JOHN FINCH & JAMES BROWNLEE. rec 1818. p 198

Deed dated 1818. HERVEY BATES to STEPHEN C. STEVENS Brkv lot, no # given. Signed HERVEY BATES. Witness: B.F. MORRIS, JOHN LATOURETTE. rec 1818. pp 198, 199

Deed dated 1818. JOHN ALLEN SR to SOLOMON ALLEN. Brkv lot 25. Signed JOHN ALLEN SR, POLLY ALLEN. Witness: ROBERT JOHN. rec 1818. pp 199, 200

Lease dated 1818. STEPHEN C. STEVENS to JOHN VANBLARICUM. No S-T-R: "farm east of Brkv". Signed STEPHEN C. STEVENS, JOHN VANBLARICUM. Witness: B.F. MORRIS rec 1818. pp 200, 201

POA dated 1818. JOHN LEWIS of Springfield Twp, Franklin, IN & ASAHEL LEWIS of Campbell Co, KY appt NOAH LEWIS as atty to settle estate of SELAH & HANNAH ALVORD of Springfield Twp, "being lawful heirs to estate". Signed JOHN LEWIS, ASAHEL LEWIS. Witness: STEPHEN DAVIS. rec 1818. p 201

Quitclaim dated 1818. JOHN LEWIS to NOAH LEWIS. JOHN sold share of HANNAH ALVORD's estate to NOAH "if the will of SELAH ALVORD doth prove & stand good." Signed JOHN LEWIS. Witness: STEPHEN DAVIS. rec 1818. p 201

Deed dated 1818. AMOS BUTLER to JAMES BARBER. Brkv lot 77. Signed AMOS BUTLER, MARY BUTLER. Witness: none. rec 1818. p 202

Deed dated 1818. JOHN ALLEN SR to JAMES SCOLESCOTT. Brkv lots 91, 92. Signed JOHN ALLEN SR, POLLY ALLEN. Witness: ROBERT JOHN. rec 1818. p 203

Deed dated 1818. JOHN B. WHITFORD to GEORGE W. KIMBLE

FRANKLIN COUNTY DEEDS: Book C

Brkv lot 80. Signed JOHN B. WHITFORD, PATSY (x) WHITFORD. Witness: THOMAS C. SMITH, HARRISON R. ROBINSON. rec 1818. pp 203, 204

Deed dated 1818. THOMAS POWERS to HANNAH CLARKE, widow of JOSHUA CLARKE, dec; CORNELIA VANMETER, dau of JOSHUA & wife of SAMUEL VANMETER, GEORGE CLARKE, RICHARD CLARKE, REBECA CLARKE, NANCY CLARKE, MASTERSON CLARKE, JOHN CLARKE & BENNETT CLARKE, chldrn of JOSHUA, dec. S 25, T 10, R 3W. Contract entered into; JOSHUA dec before deed conveyed, now passes to heirs. Signed THOMAS POWERS, MARY POWERS. Witness: ROBERT JOHN, SOLLOMON ALLEN. rec 1818. pp 204, 205

Deed dated 1818. JOHN ALLEN SR to SOLLOMON SHEPPERD JR. Brkv lot 103. Signed JOHN ALLEN SR, POLLY ALLEN. Witness: ROBERT JOHN. rec 1818. p 206

Deed dated 1818. JOHN ALLEN SR to JOSIAH ALLEN. Brkv lot 108. Signed JOHN ALLEN SR, POLLY ALLEN. Witness: ROBERT JOHN. rec 1818. pp 206, 207

Deed dated 1818. BARBARY CHRIST, dau of DANIEL T. GARDEN, & NICHOLAS CHRIST, her husband, to SOLLOMON SHEPHERD. S 5, T 12, R 13E. Signed BARBARY (x) CHRIST, NICHOLAS (x) CHRIST. Witness: HENRY T. GARDEN, ROBERT JOHN. rec 1818. pp 207, 208

Deed dated 1818. JOHN ALLEN SR to ELIPHALEL ALLEN. Brkv lot 104. Signed JOHN ALLEN SR, POLLY ALLEN. Witness: none. rec 1818. p 208

Deed dated 1818. HENRY HUNTER to JOHN HEAVENRIDGE. S 18, T 11, R 1W. "ISABELLA, his wife". Signed HENRY HUNTER, ISABELLA HUNTER. Witness: GEORGE W. CRIST, JOHN HUNTER. rec 1818. pp 209, 210

Deed dated 1818. WILLIAM REMY to CHITTENDON & PEARPONT of Hamilton Co, OH. S 24, T 8, R 1. "ELIZABETH, his wife". Signed WILLIAM REMY, ELIZABETH (x) REMY. Witness: SALLY REMY, MARY REMY. rec 1818. pp 210, 211

Deed dated 1818. NATHAN RICHARDSON & ANNA, his wife to JOHN ADAIR. S 36, T 16, R 12E. Signed NATHAN (x) RICHARDSON, ANNA (x) RICHARDSON. Witness: SOLLOMON MANWARING. rec 1818. pp 211, 212

Deed dated 1817. HUGH ABERCROMBIE to WILLIAM HARPER of OH. S 28, T 8, R 1W. "ROSANNA, his wife". Signed HUGH ABERCROMBIE, ROSANNA (x) ABERCROMBIE. Witness: HUGH ABERCROMBIE, JAMES ABERCROMBIE. rec 1818. p 212

FRANKLIN COUNTY DEEDS: Book C

Bond sale dated 1816. ENOCH D. JOHN & NOAH NOBLE to WILLIAM HARLOW. Bond to ensure transferring good deed to farm in Walper's Bottom, Boone Co, KY, below farm of ELIJAH HEASLEY, above land of DANIEL MORLEY & U. LEBECE, "the same which was left to JAMES NOBLE & LAZARUS by the late DAL. NOBLE." Signed ENOCH D. JOHN, NOAH NOBLE. Witness: AMOS LANE, THOMAS GREEN. rec 1818. pp 212, 213

Deed dated 1817. JACOB GIGER to PETER LENNON of Wayne Co. S 28, T 11, R 1W. Signed JACOB GIGER. Witness: none. rec 1818. pp 213, 214

Deed dated 1817. JACOB GIGER to SAMUEL LENNON. S 28, T 11, R 1W. Signed JACOB GIGER. Witness: none. rec 1818. p 214

Deed dated 1816. ENOCH McCARTY, CONRAD SAILORS & JACOB SAILORS as exec'rs of estate of JOHN MILHOLLAND to JOHN QUICK. During his lifetime, MILHOLLAND sold land in S 3, T 8, R 2W to QUICK, died before conveying title. Transaction now completed. Signed ENOCH McCARTY, CONRAD SAILORS, JACOB SAILORS. Witness: none. rec 1818. p 215

Deed dated 1818. WILLIAM HUDSON to PRUDENCE HUDSON. S 32, T 8, R 1W. Signed WILLIAM HUDSON. Witness: THOMAS MANWARING. rec 1818. p 216

Deed dated 1817. ENOS BOWLSBY & ABI, his wife, of Ross Twp, Butler Co, OH to JOHN BROWN of same. S 36, T 11, R 2W. Signed ENOS BOWLSBY, ABI BOWLSBY. Witness: ROBERT ANDERSON, MARTIN WINES (in OH). rec 1818. p 217

Deed dated 1818. MARY KNIGHT, Admr of estate of JAMES KNIGHT, dec, to WILLIAM McCLURY of Frederickstown, MD. Estate invty filed 30 Sept, 1817. Court found estate insufficient to pay debts, maintain children. Land in S 29, T 9, R 2 ordered sold at auction. Signed MARY KNIGHT, Admr of estate. Witness S.C. STEVENS, ROBERT JOHN. rec 1818. pp 217, 218, 219

Deed dated 1818. WILLIAM McCLURY as above to MARY KNIGHT. S 29, T 9, R 2. "ELEANOR, wife of WILLIAM". Signed WM. McCLURY, ELEANOR McCLURY. Witness: S.C. STEVENS, ROBERT JOHN. rec 1817. p 219, 220

Mortgage deed dated 1815. JOHN C. POWNES to HENRY SCUDDER & MARGARET CROWELL of OH. S 32, T 9, R 1W. Debt to be paid by 1817 to void conveyance. Signed JOHN C. POWNES. Witness: W.J. CARSON, ENOCH CARSON.

FRANKLIN COUNTY DEEDS: Book C

(in Hamilton Co, OH). rec 1818. pp 220, 221

Deed dated 1815. REMEMBER BLACKMAN & LOIS, his wife, to ALEXANDER DEARMOND of Butler Co, OH. S 19, T 8, R 1W. Signed REMEMBER BLACKMAN, LOIS BLACKMAN. Witness ADOLPHUS GULLEY. rec 1818. pp 221, 222

Deed dated 1818. HERVEY BATES to NATHANIEL HUNT & ABNER HUNT of Warren Co, OH. S 27, T 8, R 2W. Signed HERVEY BATES. Witness: THOMAS CORWIN, JACOBY HALLACK (in OH). rec 1818. pp 222, 223

Deed dated 1818. WILLIAM L. ROSE to CORNELIUS BURROWS Fairfield lot 63. Signed WILLIAM L. ROSE. Witness: none. rec 1818. pp 223, 224

Deed dated 1817. MATTHEW McCLURKIN to JOHN ELIOTT. S 34, T 11, R 1W. "MARY, his wife". Signed MATTHEW McCLURKIN, MARY McCLURKIN. Witness: THOS. SANKEY, THOS. METIN. rec 1818. pp 224, 225

Deed dated 1818. WILLIAM WRISK to OVID YOUNGS. S 32 T 13, R 13E. "PRUDENCE, his wife". Signed WILLIAM RISK, PRUDENCE (x) RISK. Witness: none. rec 1818. pp 225, 226

Deed dated 1813. DAVID BELL to THOMAS SKINNER JR. S 8, T 9, R 2W. Signed DAVID BELL. Witness: BENJAMIN SMITH. rec 1818. pp 226, 227

Deed dated 1818. JOHN SHORT & EVE, his wife, of Washington Co to GEORGE KEFFER JR. S 27, T 11, R 1W. Signed JOHN SHORT, EVE (x) SHORT. Witness: JNO. WOOLFINGTON, JOHN CURRY (in Washington Co) rec 1818. pp 227, 228

Deed dated 1818. ANTHONY HALBERSTADT to ADAM RICHEY of Butler Co, OH. S 22, T 9, R 2W. Signed ANTONY HALBERSTAT, SARAH (x) HALBERSTADT. Witness: WILLIAM C. DREW, B.F. MORRIS. rec 1818. pp 228, 229

Deed dated 1817. WILLIAM H. EADS to JOHN PEGG. Brkv 32. Signed WILLIAM H. EADS, JANE EADS. Witness: ROBERT JOHN. rec 1818. pp 229, 230

Deed dated 1818. JOHN ALLEN SR to SAMUEL SERRING of Warren Co, OH. Brkv lots 76, 77. Signed JOHN ALLEN SR, POLLY (x) ALLEN. Witness: ELIPHALEL ALLEN, ROBERT JOHN. rec 1818. pp 230, 231

Verona plat map dated 1818. Blooming Grove Twp. OBADIAH ESTES & PHILEMON ESTES, prop'rs. rec 1818. p 231

FRANKLIN COUNTY DEEDS: Book C

Deed dated 1817. AZOR STURDEVANT to ROSWELL STURDEVANT. S 11, T 8, R 2W. "FEAR, wife of AZOR". Signed AZOR STURDEVANT, FEAR STURDEVANT. Witness: WILLIS E. BROWN, ELISHA WYETH. rec 1818. p 232

Deed dated 1818. JOHN DUNLAP to WILLIAM HANNA. Dunlapsv'l lot 29. Signed JOHN DUNLAP, ELIZABETH DUNLAP. Witness: ROBERT SWAN, WILLIAM NICKELS. rec 1818 p 233

Deed dated 1818. JOHN THOMAS of Butler Co, OH to CHARLES W. LEE & JOHN B. WHITFORD. Land in Vincent Twp, Chester Co, lot 1; descended to THOMAS as co-partner & heir of HAZEL THOMAS, dec. Recd Chester Co PA deed book O.3. vol 62, p 551. Signed JOHN THOMAS, CATHERINE THOMAS. Witness: JAMES B. RAY, MARTIN M. RAY, ROBERT JOHN, JOHN RAINEY, WILLIAM MARTIN. rec 1818. pp 234, 235

Mortgage deed dated 1817. WILLIAM HARPER of Oh to ALEXANDER ABERCROMBIE. S 28, T 8, R 1W. Debt to be paid by 1819 to void conveyance. Signed WILLIAM HARPER. Witness: MICHAEL AYRES, SAMUEL WM. AYRES (in Butler Co, OH). rec 1818. p 236

Deed dated 1817. HUGH ABERCROMBIE & ROSANA his wife, to JAMES KENEDY. S 28, T 8, R 1W. Signed HUGH ABERCROMBIE, ROSANA (x) ABERCROMBIE. Witness: WILLIAM GULLY, BENJAMIN GULLY. rec 1818. p 237

Affidavit dated 1818. Fairfield prop'rs swore plat map Bk C, pp 28, 29 was "correct & compleat". Signed JAMES WILSON, THOMAS OSBORN, GEORGE JOHNSON & HUGH ABERNATHY. Witness: JOHN EWING, JP. rec 1818. p 238

Deed dated 1818. JOHN ALLEN SR to JAMES GLASS of Hamilton Co, OH. Brkv lots 95, 96. Signed JOHN ALLEN, MARY (x) ALLEN. Witness: ROBERT JOHN, ELIPHALEL ALLEN. rec 1818. pp 238, 239

Deed dated 1818. AMOS BUTLER to SAMUEL WIER. S 18, T 8, R 1W. Signed AMOS BUTLER, MARY BUTLER. Witness: HUGH MORRISON. rec 1818. pp 239, 240

Deed correction dated 1818. JAMES McGINNIS to JAMES NOBLE. Corrected bounds description. Signed JAMES NOBLE. Witness: none. rec 1818. p 240

Deed dated 1818. JAMES McGINNIS to JAMES NOBLE. S 29 T 9, R 2W. Signed JAMES McGINNIS, JAIN (x) McGINNIS Witness: none. rec 1818. pp 240, 241

Deed dated 1818. JOHN DUNLAP to ABIJAH SHIELDS. Dun-

FRANKLIN COUNTY DEEDS: Book C

lapsv'l lot 37. Signed JOHN DUNLAP, ELIZABETH DUNLAP. Witness: ROBERT SWAN, JOSEPH BIRGLAND. rec 1818. pp 241, 242

Deed dated 1817. JACOB MATTIX to JOSHUA NELSON. S 7 T 13, R 13E. Signed JACOB MATTIX, KATHERINE (x) MATTIX. Witness: none. rec 1818. pp 242, 243

Deed dated 1818. WILLIAM HENRY EADS to ARTHUR DICKSON. S 28, T 14, R 5W; tract for Military Bounties in Illinois Territory. Signed WILLIAM HENRY EADS, JANE EADS. Witness: N. FRENCH. rec 1818. pp 243, 244

Deed dated 1818. WILLIAM HENRY EADS to ARTHUR DICKSON. S 25, T 13, R 1E; tract for Military Bounties in Illinois Territory. Signed WILLIAM HENRY EADS, JANE EADS. Witness: N. FRENCH. rec 1818. pp 244, 245

Deed dated 1817. WILLIAM C. DREW to ARTHUR DICKSON. Brkv lot 17. Signed WILLIAM C. DREW. Witness: B.F. MORRIS, ENOCH McCARTY. rec 1818. p 245 Note: above mortgage satisfied June, 1820. Signed ARTHUR DICKSON

Fairfield plat map addition dated 1818. Laid off by W. H. & T. C. EADS. rec 1818. p 246

Deed dated 1818. GEORGE L. MURDOCK to ALEXANDER GARDNER. Brkv lot 34. Signed GEORGE L. MURDOCK, ANN (x) MURDOCK. Witness: HUGH MORRISON. rec 1818 pp 246, 247

Deed dated 1818. PETER LABOYTON of Hamilton Co, OH to ALEXANDER GARDNER. Brkv 35. Signed PETER J. LABOYTON. Witness: HUGH MORRISON. rec 1818. pp 247, 248

Deed dated 1818. JOHN HALBERSTADT to ADAM RICHEY. S 22, T 9, R 2W. "MARY, wife of JOHN". Signed JOHN HALBERSTADT, MARY (x) HALBERSTADT. Witness: WILLIAM C. DREW, ENOCH McCARTY. rec 1818. pp 248, 249

Deed dated 1818. BENJAMIN SCHOONOVER & LYDIA, his wife to JOHN TITUS. S 13, T 8, R 2W. Signed BENJAMIN (x) SCHOONOVER, LYDIA (x) SCHOONOVER. Witness: JOSEPH SCHOONOVER. rec 1818. pp 249, 250

Deed dated 1818. TIMOTHY T. BROWN to AARON OWENS of KY. S 4, T 13, R 12E. "SALLY, his wife". Signed TIMOTHY T. BROWN, SALLY (x) BROWN. Witness: ROBERT JOHN, EVAN MORGAN. rec 1818. pp 250, 251

Deed dated 1817. EDWARD TONER to URBAN EDGERTON & CHARLES FOSDICK. Somerset lot # 12."SUSAN, his wife". Signed EDWARD TONER, SUSAN (x) TONER. Witness:

FRANKLIN COUNTY DEEDS: Book C

ANDREW L. BABBETT, JAMES EGANS. rec 1818. pp 251, 252

Deed dated 1818. EDWARD TONER to ANDREW L. BABBITT. Somerset lot 22. Signed EDWARD TONER, SUSAN (x) TONER. Witness: URBAN EDGERTON, THOMAS COOPER. rec 1818. pp 252, 253

Deed dated 1818. NOAH BEAUCHAMP & ELIZABETH his wife to BENJAMIN TAYLOR or SAYLOR. S 24, T 14, R 12E. Signed NOAH BEAUCHAMP, ELIZABETH BEAUCHAMP. Witness: none. rec 1818. pp 253, 254

Deed dated 1817. JACOB MATTIX to BENJAMIN H. HANSON of Bracken Co, KY. S 11, T 13, R 13E. Signed JACOB MATTIX, KATHERINE (x) MATTIX. Witness: none. rec 1818. pp 254, 255

Deed dated 1818. JEHU JOHN to WILLIAM H. EADS. S 18 T 4, R 1E "lying in Butler Co, OH". Signed JEHU JOHN ELIZABETH JOHN. Witness: ROBERT JOHN, B.F. MORRIS. rec 1818. pp 255, 256

Deed dated 1818. WILSON WADAMS to WILLIAM H. EADS. S 20, T 13, R 12E. "LOISA, his wife". Signed WILLSON WADAMS, LOUISA WADAMS. Witness: ROBERT JOHN, DAN'L. RUICK. rec 1818. pp 256, 257

West Union plat map dated 1818. JAMES LEVISTON, surveyor "by order of (not named) proprietors". rec 1818. p 258 See acknowledgement, Bk C, p 298

Sheriff sale dated 1818. ROBERT HANNA, Sheriff of Franklin Co to JOSEPH EVANS. Court ordered levy on S 17, T 11, R 1W & New Washington town lots 7, 8, 12, 13, 14, 22, 23, 24, 26 to settle debts of THOMAS MADDEN & RUTH, his wife, to JOSEPH EVANS. Land sold at auction to EVANS, the highest bidder. Signed ROBERT HANNA. Witness: none. rec 1818. pp 259, 260

Deed dated 1816. PETER VANDIKE to SAMUEL SHIRK. Brkv lot 66. "ADY, his wife". Signed PETER VANDIKE,* ADY (x) VANDIKE. Witness: none. rec 1818. pp 260, 261

Deed dated 1818. EDWARD TONER to ANDREW S. BABBITT & JAMES TONER. Somerset lot 19. Signed EDWARD TONER, SUSANA TONER. Witness: JAMES COOPER. rec 1818. pp 261, 262

Deed dated 1818. JOHN C. McMANNIS to ALEXANDER DELORAC of OH. Brkv lots 60, 61. Signed JOHN C. McMANNIS Witness: BENJ. COLLETT. rec 1818. pp 262, 263

FRANKLIN COUNTY DEEDS: Book C

Deed dated 1818. JAMES L. COLESCOTT to HENRY WEBSTER Brkv lot 91. "LUCRETIA, his wife". Signed JAMES L. COLESCOTT, LUCRETIA (x) COLESCOTT. Witness: HUGH MORRISON. rec 1818. pp 263, 264

Deed dated 1818. THOMAS SHERWOOD to HENRY WEBSTER. Brkv lot 75. "CHARLOTTE, his wife". Signed THOMAS SHERWOOD, CHARLOTTE (x) SHERWOOD. Witness: HUGH MORRISON. rec 1818. pp 264, 265

Deed dated 1817. THOMAS W. COLESCOTT to HENRY WEBSTER. Brkv lot 26. Signed THOMAS W. COLESCOTT. Witness: N. FRENCH, H.A. REED. rec 1818. pp 265, 266

Deed dated 1818. DAVID MUSSLEMAN of Hamilton Co, OH to ADAM MOORE of same. Brkv lot 34. "MARGARET, his wife." Signed DAVID MUSSLEMAN, MARGARET (x) MUSSELMAN. Witness: DANIEL HEYWOOD, E. STONE. rec 1818. pp 266, 267

Deed dated 1818. ADAM MOORE of Cincinnati, OH to GEORGE ALDVID. Brkv lot 34. Signed ADAM MOORE. Witness: ROBERT JOHN, JOHN SCOTT. rec 1818. pp 267, 268

Deed dated 1818. GEORGE ALDVID to ADAM MOORE as above Brkv lot 34. Signed GEORGE ALDVID. Witness: ROBERT JOHN, JON SCOTT. rec 1818. pp 268, 269

Mortgage deed dated 1817. LINES D. WARD to WM. JAMES CRISSEY. Connersv'l lot 34. (S 25, T 14, R 12.) Term of mortgage unspecified. Signed LINES D. WARD, MARY WARD. Witness: none. rec 1818. pp 269, 270

Deed dated 1818. AMOS BUTLER to JOSEPH BRACKINRIDGE. Brkv lot 39. Signed AMOS BUTLER, MARY BUTLER. Witness: SOLOMON ALLEN. rec 1818. pp 270, 271

Deed dated 1818. S.C. STEVENS & JOHN WINCHILL, admrs of estate of JAMES WINCHILL, dec, to GRIFFIN TAYLOR. Brkv lot 13, sold to satisfy debts of estate. Signed S. C. STEVENS, JOHN WINCHILL. Witness: ROBERT JOHN, JOHN ALLEN SR. rec 1818. pp 271, 272

Deed dated 1818. S.C. STEVENS & JOHN WINCHILL, admrs of estate of JAMES WINCHILL, dec, to HERVEY BATES. Brkv lots 13, 18, 19, 24 sold to satisfy debts of estate. Signed S. C. STEVENS, JOHN WINCHILL. Witness: ROBERT JOHN, JOHN ALLEN SR. rec 1818. pp 272, 273

Deed dated 1818. HERVEY BATES to STEPHEN C. STEVENS. Brkv lots 13, 18, 19, 24. Signed HERVEY BATES. Witness: JOHN ALLEN SR, JOHN WINCHILL. rec 1818. p 274

FRANKLIN COUNTY DEEDS: Book C

Deed dated 1818. THOMAS BRADLEY to HERVEY BATES. Brkv lot 33. Signed THOMAS BRADLEY. Witness: SOLLOMAN ALLEN, HARRISON ROBINSON. rec 1818. p 275

Deed dated 1818. ABNER LEONARD to THOMAS SHAW. S 29 T 9, R 1W. Signed ABNER LEONARD. Witness: ALEXR. GARDNER, ROBERT JOHN. rec 1818. p 276

Mortgage deed dated 1818. JOHN VORHESS to THOMAS SHAW. S 29, T 9, R 1W. Debt to be paid by 1822 to void conveyance. "ELIZABETH, wife of JOHN". Signed JOHN VORHEES, ELIZABETH VOORHIS. Witness: ABRAHAM SIMONSON, ROB'T. LUCE. rec 1818. pp 277, 278

Deed dated 1818. JOHN ALLEN SR to HERVEY BATES. Brkv lot 67. Signed JOHN ALLEN SR, MARY ALLEN. Witness: ROBERT JOHN, THOMAS HAYNES. rec 1818. p 278

Deed dated 1818. WILLIAM SIMS JR to WM SIMS SR. S 2, T 11, R 13E. "ELIZABETH, his wife". Signed WILLIAM SIMS JR, ELIZABETH (x) SIMS. Witness: B.F. MORRIS, JOHN STINSON. rec 1818. p 279 Margin note: deed was not rec'd agreeably to original deed. No explanation given.

Deed dated 1817. WILLIAM SIMS JR to CHILTON FOSTER. S 2, T 11, R 13E. Signed WILLIAM SIMS JR, ELIZABETH (x) SIMS. Witness: B.F. MORRIS, JOHN STINSON. rec 1818. p 280

Deed dated 1818. HENRY COSTON to HARRISON J. ROBINSON Brkv 38. Signed HENRY COSTON, HANNAH (x) COSTON. Witness: ROBERT JOHN, SYLVAN B. MORRIS. rec 1818. p 281

Deed dated 1818. JOHN DUNLAP to WILLIAM NICKLES SR. Dunlapsv'l lot 9. Signed JOHN DUNLAP, ELIZABETH DUNLAP. Witness: ROBERT SWANN, WILLIAM HANNA. rec 1818. p 282

Deed dated 1818. JOHN DUNLAP to WILLIAM NICKLES SR. Dunlapsv'l lot 10. Signed JOHN DUNLAP, ELIZABETH DUNLAP. Witness: ROBERT SWANN, WILLIAM HANNA. rec 1818. p 283

Deed dated 1818. JOHN DUNLAP to WILLIAM NICKLES SR. Dunlapsv'l lot 27. Signed JOHN DUNLAP, ELIZABETH DUNLAP. Witness: ROBERT SWANN, WILLIAM HANNA. rec 1818. p 284

Deed dated 1818. JOHN DUNLAP to WILLIAM NICHOLS SR. Dnlsv'l lot 8. Signed JOHN DUNLAP, ELIZABETH DUNLAP. Witness: ROBERT SWANN, WILLIAM HANNA. rec 1818. p 285

FRANKLIN COUNTY DEEDS: Book C

Deed dated 1818. JOHN DUNLAP to WILLIAM NICKLES SR. Dnlsv'l lot 12. Signed JOHN DUNLAP, ELIZABETH DUNLAP Witness: ROBERT SWANN, WILLIAM HANNA. rec 1818. p 286

Deed dated 1818. JOHN DUNLAP to WILLIAM NICKLES SR. Dnlsv'l lot 35. Signed JOHN DUNLAP, ELIZABETH DUNLAP Witness: ROBERT SWANN, WILLIAM HANNA. rec 1818. p 287

Deed dated 1818. JONATHAN GILLAM to HANNAH CLARKE, widow of JOSHUA CLARKE dec, GEORGE CLARKE, RICHARD CLARKE, REBECCA CLARKE, NANCY CLARKE, MASTERSON CLARK JOHN CLARKE & BENNETT CLARK, chdrn of JOSHUA. S 25, T 10, R 3W contracted in JOSHUA'S lifetime. "MARY, his wife". Signed: JONATHAN (x) GILLAM, MARY (x) GILLAM. Witness: ROBERT JOHN. rec 1818. pp 287, 288, 289

Deed dated 1818. JOHN ALLEN SR to JACOB ROSS. Land adj Brkv, adj lots 89, 90 owned by JOSEPH SEAL & lot of JACOB ROSS. Signed JOHN ALLEN SR, MARY ALLEN. Witness: ROBERT JOHN. rec 1818. pp 289, 290

Deed dated 1818. JAMES **FERRILLE** to GEORGE BURGED. S 3, T 9, R 1W. Signed JAMES (x) **FERRIL,** ANNA (x) **FERRIL.** Witness: none. rec 1818. pp 290, 291

Deed dated 1818. GEORGE **BURGET** to WILLIAM WEBB of Stockbridge Co, VA. S 3, T 9, R 1W. Signed GEORGE (x) **BURGED,** CHARLOTTE (x) **BURGED.** Witness: none. rec 1818. p 291, 292

Deed dated 1818. HENRY BURGED of Butler Co, OH to GEORGE BURGED. S 3, T 9, R 1W. Signed HENRY (x) BURGED, CATHERINE (x) BURGED. Witness: none. rec 1818. pp 292, 293

Deed dated 1818. DAVID FINLEY of Hardinsburgh, Dearborn Co to JOSEPH JONAS of Cincinnati, OH. Brkv lots 26, 27. Signed DAVID FINLEY, NANCY FINLEY. Witness: WILLIAM STEVENS, BENJAMIN RENO (at Dearborn Co). rec 1818. pp 293, 294

Deed dated 1818. GEORGE FRAZIER SR to GEORGE FRAZIER JR. S 30, T 14, R 13E. "ELIZABETH, his wife". Signed GEORGE FRAZIER, ELIZABETH FRAZIER. Witness: ROBERT SWANN, JONATHAN HUNT. rec 1818. p 295

Deed dated 1818. WILLIAM McCAW to ANDREW HINES. S 3, T 9, R 1W. "NANCY, his wife". Signed WILLIAM McCAW, NANCY McCAW. Witness: none. rec 1818. p 296

Deed dated 1818. JAMES HOLLINGSWORTH to LEVI MEAD. S 20, T 11, R 1W. "SARAH, his wife". Signed JAMES

FRANKLIN COUNTY DEEDS: Book C

HOLLINGSWORTH, SARAH HOLLINGSWORTH. Witness: JAMES HOLLINGSWORTH JR. rec 1818. p 297

Affidavit dated 1818. WILLIAM GOE & ELI ADAMS swear West Union plat map, rec'd Bk C, p 258, is correct. rec 1818. BETHEL F. MORRIS, Recorder. p 298

Deed dated 1818. JAMES BARBER to OBADIAH BENNET & NEVI OGDEN. Brkv lots 77, 78. "MARGARET, wife of JAMES". Signed JAMES BARBER, MARGARET BARBER. Witness: ROBERT JOHN. rec 1818. pp 298, 299

Deed dated 1818. HARRISON J. ROBINSON to GEORGE W. KIMBLE. Brkv lot 3. Signed HARRISON J. ROBINSON. Witness: HERVEY BATES, JOHN D. GARRISON. rec 1818. pp 299, 300

Deed dated 1818. JOHN REED to JAMES McKNIGHT, both of Rockbridge Co, VA. "patent granted to DANIEL REED, father of said JOHN". S 6, T 9, R 1W. Signed JOHN REED. Witness: WM. SOMWELL, JOHN PAXTON, GEORGE WALKER (in VA). rec 1818. pp 300, 301

Connersville outlots plat map, dated 1818. JOSHUA HARLAN, Prop'r. THOMAS HINKSON, surveyor. rec 1818. pp 302, 303

Mortgage deed dated 1818. GEORGE W. KIMBLE to HARRISON J. ROBINSON. Brkv lots 38, 80. Debt to be paid by 1820 to void conveyance. Signed G. W. KIMBLE. Witness: HERVEY BATES, JOHN D. GARRISON. rec 1818. pp 304, 305

Deed dated 1818. JAMES WATTERS to BENJAMIN WILLSON. S 20, T 10, R 2W. Signed JAMES WATTERS, ELIZABETH WATTERS. Witness: JAMES WILLSON, WILLIAM DICKSON. rec 1818. pp 305, 306

Deed dated 1817. ROBERT HANNA SR to ROBERT HANNA JR. S 33, T 28, R 2W. Signed ROBERT HANNA SR, MARY HANNA Witness: none. rec 1818. pp 306, 307

Deed dated 1818. JOHN NUGENT to ROBERT HANNA JR. S 28, T 10, R 2W. "ELIZABETH, his wife". Signed JOHN NUGENT, ELIZABETH (x) NUGENT. Witness: JOHN HANNA. rec 1818. pp 307, 308

Deed dated 1818. JOHN SHAFOR of Butler Co, OH to ADAM C. KEYBOURN of FAYATTE Co, KY. S 31, T 10, R 1W Signed JOHN SHAFOR. Witness: ROBERT JOHN, JEHU JOHN rec 1818. pp 308, 309

FRANKLIN COUNTY DEEDS: Book C

Deed dated 1818. NATHAN D. GALLION & HANNAH his wife to JOHN H. PIATT, JOHN ARMSTRONG & PHILIP GRANDON of Hamilton Co, OH. S 3, T 12, R 13E. Signed N. D. GALLION, HANNAH GALLION. Witness: none. rec 1818. pp 309, 310

Deed dated 1818. JOHN ALLEN SR to B. F. MORRIS. Brkv lot 88. Signed JOHN ALLEN SR, POLLY ALLEN. Witness: JOSEPH L. ALLEN, ROBERT JOHN. rec 1818. pp 310, 311

Deed dated 1818. JOHN MORRIS of Butler Co, OH to LEMUEL SIMMON* of same. S 26, T 10, R 1W. "MARY, his wife". Signed JOHN MORRIS, MARY (x) MORRIS. Witness: HUGH MORRISON. rec 1818. pp 311, 312 *LEMMON in text

Deed dated 1818. THOMAS BRADLEY to JOHN JACOBS. Brkv inlot 9. Signed THOMAS BRADLEY. Witness: ROBERT JOHN. rec 1818. p 313

Deed dated 1818. GEORGE JOHNSON to CHRISTIAN MOSTEL-LER. Fairfield lot 8. Signed GEORGE JOHNSON, SARAH JOHNSON. Witness: JAMES OSBORN, BENNETT MICHAEL. rec 1818. p 314

Deed dated 1818. THOMAS HENDERSON to WILLIAM ARNETT. S 27, T 13, R 13E. Signed THOMAS HENDERSON. Witness: JEREMIAH CORY, ROBERT JOHN. rec 1818. p 315

Deed dated 1818. JOHN ALLEN SR to WILLIAM ALLEN. Brkv lot 109. Signed JOHN ALLEN SR, POLLY ALLEN. Witness: ROBERT JOHN. rec 1818. p 316

Deed dated 1818. JAMES MORROW & GEORGE MATLOCK of Orange Co to OBADIAH ESTES. S 27, T 13, R 13E. Signed GEORGE (x) MATLOCK, SARAH (x) MATLOCK, JAMES MORROW, SARAH ANN MORROW. Witness: JOHN MATLOCK, ROBERT HANNA, CHESLEY BAILEY. rec 1818. pp 316, 317

Deed dated 1818. IRA MEAD of Granville Twp, Licking Co, OH & CYNTHIA, his wife, to JOHN HARRIS of Washington Twp, Montgomery Co, Oh. S 27, T 10, R 1W. Signed IRA MEAD, SYNTHIA MEAD. Witness: SAMUEL BANCROFT, ISRAEL HARRIS (in Licking Co). rec 1818. p 318

Deed dated 1818. ELIPHALEL ALLEN to HERVEY BATES. Brkv lot 104. "ELIZABETH, his wife". Signed ELIPHALEL ALLEN, ELIZABETH (x) ALLEN. Witness: B.F. MORRIS rec 1818. pp 318, 319

Deed dated 1818. WILLIAM W. WADE to WILLIAM BURNET. Brkv lot 75. Signed WILLIAM W. WADE. Witness: ROBERT JOHN, J. W. MORRISON. rec 1818. pp 319, 320

FRANKLIN COUNTY DEEDS: Book C

Deed dated 1814. JOHN DUNLAP to WILLIAM NICHOLS. S 28, T 11, R 2W. Signed JOHN DUNLAP. Witness: JOHN WARD, JOHN WHITWORTH. rec 1818. pp 320, 321

Deed dated 1818. RUGGLES WINCHEL to NATHAN HOLMES. S 32, T 10, R 2W. Signed RUGGLES WINCHEL, MARTHA (x) WINCHEL. Witness: STEPHEN WINCHELL. rec 1818. p 322

Deed dated 1818. WILLIAM WILSON to CHILAN FOSTER. S 3, T 11, R 13E. Signed WILLIAM WILSON, FRANKY WILSON. Witness: ISAAC G. JOHN, ROBERT JOHN. rec 1818. p 323

Deed dated 1818. ITHAMER WHITE to JACOB GATES. S 29 T 9, R 1W. Signed I.H. WHITE, MARGERY (x) WHITE. Witness: ROBERT LUSE, JOHN LUSE. rec 1818. p 324

Deed dated 1817. MORRIS WITHAM & REBECKAH, his wife, to EDMUND BILLINGS. S 8, T 10, R 1W. Signed MORRIS WITHAM, REBECKAH (x) WITHAM. Witness: none. rec 1818. p 325

Deed dated 1817. JAMES HARRIS to JEREMIAH CORY. S 34, T 10, R 2W. "MARTHA, his wife". Signed JAMES HARRIS, MARTHA HARRIS. Witness: N. FRENCH, HUGH MORRISON. rec 1818. p 326

Deed dated 1818. JOHN CONNER to JOSHUA HARLAN. S 25, T 14, R 12E. Signed JOHN CONNER, LAVINA CONNER. Witness: none. rec 1818. p 327

Deed dated 1818. THOMAS HARVEY to WILLIAM THOMPSON. Fairfield lots 31, 32. Signed THOMAS HERVEY, HANNAH HERVEY. Witness: SAMUEL H. JOHN, L. BELDING. rec 1818. p 328

Deed dated 1818. THOMAS WILLIAMS to HANNAH CLARKE. widow of JOSHUA CLARKE dec, GEORGE CLARKE, RICHARD CLARKE, REBECCA CLARKE, NANCY CLARKE, MASTERSON CLARK JOHN CLARKE & BENNETT CLARK, children of JOSHUA. S 30, T 9, R 2W contracted in JOSHUA'S lifetime. Signed: THOMAS WILLIAMS, DEBORAH (x) WILLIAMS Witness: ROBERT JOHN. rec 1818. pp 328, 329, 330

Deed dated 1817. JAMES McCOY to STEPHEN JENKS. S 21 T 12 R 12E. Signed JAMES (x) McCOY, NANCY (x) McCOY. Witness: THOMAS BUSH, JANE BUSH. rec 1818. p 330

Deed dated 1818. JOSHUA HARLAN to ENOCH McCARTY. Connersv'l lot 67. Signed JOSHUA HARLAN, SALLY HARLAN. Witness: none. rec 1818. pp 330, 331

Deed dated 1818. JAMES SMITH to SAMUEL SMITH. S 36,

FRANKLIN COUNTY DEEDS: Book C

T 11, R 1W. Signed JAMES SMITH, ANN SMITH. Witness: none. rec 1818. pp 331, 332

Deed dated 1818. NOAH NOBLE to ENOCH D. JOHN. Brkv lot 37. Signed NOAH NOBLE. Witness: ANTHONY HALBERSTADT, ROBERT JOHN. rec 1818. pp 332, 333

Deed dated 1818. ROBERT JOHN to NOAH NOBLE of Dearborn Co. S 19, T 9, R 2W. "ASENATH, his wife". Signed ROBERT JOHN, ASENATH JOHN. Witness: HUGH MORRISON, MARIA RICHARDSON. rec 1818. pp 333, 334

Deed dated 1818. JOHN ALLEN to THOMAS GREEN. Brkv lots 71, 72. Signed JOHN ALLEN, POLLY ALLEN. Witness: ROBERT JOHN. rec 1818. pp 334, 335

Deed dated 1818. EDWARD TONER & his wife (no name) to WILLIAM WADAMS. Somerset lot 29. Signed EDWARD TONER, no wife's signature. Witness: none. rec 1818. pp 335, 336

Deed dated 1818. JOHN NORRIS of Dearborn Co to ROBERT JOHN. S 19, T 9, R 2W. "REBECKAH, his wife". Signed JOHN NORRIS, REBECCA (x) NORRIS. Witness: E. D. JOHN, HUGH MORRISON. rec 1818. p 336

Deed dated 1818. ENOCH D. JOHN to ROBERT JOHN. Brkv lot 38. Signed ENOCH D. JOHN, ELOISA JOHN. Witness: NOAH NOBLE, HUGH MORRISON. rec 1818. p 337

Deed dated 1818. LEVI HOLLINGSWORTH & CHARITY, his wife, to ELI & NATHANIEL HENDERSON. S 22, T 11, R 2W. Signed LEVI HOLLINGSWORTH, CHARITY (x) HOLLINGSWORTH. Witness: CARTER HOLLINGSWORTH, DAVID HOLLINGSWORTH. rec 1818. pp 337, 338

Deed dated 1818. NATHAN D. GALLION to WILLIAM H. EADS. S 3, T 9, R 2W. Signed N.D. GALLION, HANNAH GALLION. Witness: none. rec 1819. pp 338, 339

Connersville addition plat map dated 1818. S 24, T 14, R 12E. GEORGE WALKER, LYDNOR DALE, SAMUEL DALE, prop'rs. Witness: JOHN PERRIN, JP. rec 1819. p 339

Deed dated 1818. ROBERT GLIDEWELL JR to WILLIAM H. EADS. S 30, T 13, R 12E. Signed ROBERT GLIDEWELL, SARAH GLIDEWELL. Witness: ISAAC H. MORRIS. rec 1819. p 340

Deed dated 1818. JAMES LOGAN to WILLIAM H. EADS. S 10, T 9, R 2W. Signed JAMES LOGAN. Witness: J.A. PIATT, ROBERT JOHN. rec 1819. pp 340, 341

FRANKLIN COUNTY DEEDS: Book C

Deed dated 1818. DAVID LORING & FANNY, his wife, to WILLIAM H. EADS. Brkv lot 43. Signed DAVID LORING, FANNY LORING. Witness: HENRY P. THORNTON. JABEZ VIGERY (at Jefferson Co). rec 1819. pp 341, 342

Deed dated 1819. SAMUEL GOODWIN to ENOCH D. JOHN. Brkv lot 99. "ELEANOR, wife of SAMUEL". Signed SAMUEL GOODWIN, ELEANOR (x) GOODWIN. Witness: ROBERT JOHN, JOHN HENDERSON. rec 1819. p 343

Deed dated 1818. AMOS BUTLER to THOMAS SHEARWOOD. Brkv lots 74, 75, 81. Signed AMOS BUTLER, MARY BUTLER. Witness: HUGH MORRISON. rec 1819. p 344

Deed dated 1818. WILLIAM GOE to NICHOLAS PUMPHREY. S 21, T 13, R 13. Signed WILLIAM GOE. Witness: WM. HELM. rec 1819. pp 344, 345

Deed dated 1818. JAMES WILLSON to JAMES WEAMER. Fairfield lot 37. Signed JAMES WILSON, NANCY WILLSON. Witness: JESSE EMMERSON, G.W. WARD. rec 1819. pp 345, 346

Deed dated 1818. WILLIAM H. EADS & THOMAS C. EADS to ROBERT GLIDEWELL JR. Fairfield lots 99, 100, 117, 118 Signed WILLIAM H. EADS, JANE EADS, THOS. C. EADS, ANN B. EADS. Witness: ISAAC H. MORRIS, E.D. JOHN. rec 1819. pp 346, 347

Deed dated 1818. WILLIAM H. EADS & THOMAS C. EADS to WILSON WADHAM. Fairfield lots 103, 113. Signed WILLIAM H. EADS, THOMAS C. EADS. Witness: ROBERT JOHN. rec 1819. p 347

Deed dated 1819. NATHANIEL WINCHILL to GEORGE GITTNER. S 32, T 10, R 2W. "BARBARA, his wife". Signed NATHANIEL WINCHILL, BARBARA WINCHILL. Witness: JOHN HANNA, MARY (x) HANNA. rec 1819. p 348

Deed dated 1818. AMOS BUTLER to JAMES McGINNIS. Brkv lot 24. Signed AMOS BUTLER, MARY BUTLER. Witness: ROBERT JOHN. rec 1819. pp 348, 349

Deed dated 1819. JAMES McGINNIS & his wife (no name) to JOSEPH MOFFIT. Brkv inlot 24. Signed JAMES McGINNIS, JANE (x) McGINNIS. Witness: HUGH MORRISON, MARY HEDLEY. rec 1819. pp 349, 350

Deed dated 1817. GEORGE JOHNSON to JOHN NUGENT. Fairfield lot 50. Signed GEORGE JOHNSON, SARAH JOHNSON. Witness: JOHN HANNA, ROBERT HANNA JR. rec 1819. pp 350, 351

FRANKLIN COUNTY DEEDS: Book C

Deed dated 1817. JOHN HANNA to JOHN NUGENT. S 28, T 10, R 2W. Signed JOHN HANNA, SARAH (x) HANNA. Witness: JOHN JACOBS, ELIZABETH (x) JACOBS. rec 1819. pp 351, 352

Deed dated 1817. ROBERT HANNA JR to JOHN NUGENT. S 28, T 10, R 2W. Signed ROBERT HANNA, SALLY HANNA. Witness: ROBERT NUGENT. rec 1819. pp 352, 353

Deed dated 1818. RUGGLES WINCHILL & MARTHA, his wife to ROBERT HANNA JR & WILLIAM C. DREW. S 32, T 10, R 2W. Signed RUGGLES WINCHILL, MARTHA WINCHILL. Witness none. rec 1819. pp 353, 354

Sheriff's sale dated 1818. ROBERT HANNA, Sheriff of Franklin Co, to ANTHONY HALBERSTADT. BENJAMIN SMITH, confined to prison for debt, was released under An Act for Relief of Insolvent Debtors, required to file inventory of assets. Brkv lot 68 seized, sold at auction to ANTHONY HALBERSTADT. Signed ROBERT HANNA, Sheriff. Witness: none. rec 1819. pp 354, 355

Deed dated 1819. ROBERT WHITE to HENRY FRY. S 24, T 10, R 2W. "MARY, his wife". Signed ROBERT WHITE, MARY WHITE. Witness: JOHN HANNA, JOHN WHITE. rec 1819. pp 355, 356

Deed dated 1818. JOHN SMITH to HENRY FRY. S 25, T 10, R 2W. Signed JOHN SMITH. Witness: ROBERT JOHN, ISAAC G. JOHN. rec 1819. pp 356, 357

Deed dated 1818. ADAM ELY to SAMUEL MAZE & DAVID MAZE. S 18, T 13, R 14E. "ELIZABETH, his wife". Signed ADAM (x) ELY, ELIZABETH (x) ELY. Witness: ROBERT SWANN, NANCY SWANN. rec 1819. pp 357, 358

Deed dated 1818. BENJAMIN WILSON to JONATHAN BASSETT & Co of Hamilton Co, OH. No S-T-R: One acre adj Fairfield, formerly owned by JAMES WILSON. "ELIZABETH, his wife". Signed BENJAMIN WILSON, ELIZABETH WILSON. Witness: LUDOVICUS BELDING, NATHANIEL BASSETT. rec 1819. pp 358, 359

Deed dated 1818. GEORGE JOHNSON to JONATHAN BASSETT. Fairfield lot 12. Signed GEORGE JOHNSON, SARAH JOHNSON. Witness: LUDOVICUS BELDING, NATHANIEL BASSETT. rec 1819. p 359

Deed dated 1818. THOMAS OSBORN to JONATHAN BASSETT. Fairfield lot 15. Signed THOMAS OSBORN, MARY OSBORN. Witness: LUDOVICUS BELDING, NATHANIEL BASSETT. rec 1819. p 360

FRANKLIN COUNTY DEEDS: Book C

Deed dated 1818. THOMAS OSBORN to NATHANIEL BASSETT. Fairfield lots 1, 6. Signed THOMAS OSBORN, MARY OSBORN. Witness: WM. L. ROSE, L. BELDING. rec 1819. pp 360, 361

Mortgage deed dated 1818. WILLIAM FREED to WILLIAM KNOWLES. S 26, T 8, R 2W. Debt to be paid in 1819 to void conveyance. Signed WILLIAM (x) FREED. Witness: none. rec 1819. pp 361, 362

Deed dated 1817. THOMAS MADDEN to LATHAM STANTON. New Washington lots 8, 9, 10. Signed THOS. MADDEN, RUTH MADDIN. Witness: EBENEZER HOWE, LYDIA MAADEN. rec 1819. pp 362, 363

Deed dated 1818. SAMUEL ROCKAFELLAR & MARY, his wife to ROBERTSON JONES. New Trenton lot 9. Signed SAMUEL ROCKAFELLAR, MARY ROCKAFELLAR. Witness: THOMAS MANWARRING. rec 1819. pp 363, 364

Deed dated 1818. SAMUEL ROCKAFELLAR & MARY, his wife to ROBERTSON JONES. New Trenton lot 8. Signed SAMUEL ROCKAFELLAR, MARY ROCKAFELLAR. Witness: THOMAS MANWARRING. rec 1819. pp 363, 364

Deed dated 1819. ROBERT WHITE to JOHN WHITE. S 24, T 10, R 2W. Signed ROBERT WHITE, MARY WHITE. Witness JOHN HANNA, HENRY FRY. rec 1819. p 365

Deed dated 1818. ELI LEE of Monroe Co to JACOB GIGER. Brkv lot 44. Signed ELI LEE. Witness: ROBERT HANNA JR. rec 1819. pp 365, 366

Deed dated 1818. ELI LEE of Monroe Co to WILLIAM SIMS Brkv lot 58. Signed ELI LEE. Witness: A. GARDNER. rec 1819. pp 366, 367

Deed dated 1818. OBADIAH ESTES & FANNY, his wife, to WILLIAM ADAMS. S 33, T 10, R 2W. Signed OBADIAH (x) ESTES, FANNY (x) ESTES. Witness: none rec 1819 p 367

Deed dated 1818. ELI LEE of Monroe Co to JOSEPH D. CLEMENTS. Brkv lot 59. Signed ELI LEE. Witness: ROBERT HANNA JR. rec 1819. p 368

Mortgage deed dated 1818. SAMUEL TEST to WILLIAM McGREER. S 33, T 11, R 2W. "bounded by ...ABUVILLA OSBORN...by ADAM ELY...by ROBERT ABERNATHY". Debt to be paid by 1823 to void conveyance. Signed SAMUEL TEST, SARAH TEST. Witness: ROBERT SWANN, WILLIAM CHAMBERS. rec 1819. pp 368, 369. Margin note of full payment, signed WM. McGREER, dated 1821

FRANKLIN COUNTY DEEDS: Book C

Deed dated 1817. JOHN LEFFORGE & MARY, his wife, to JABEZ WINCHISS. S 10, T 8, R 2W. Signed JOHN LEFFORGE, MARY LEFFORGE. Witness: WILLIAM GOBLE, DAVID JASMON. rec 1819. pp 369, 370

Deed dated 1818. AQUILLA LOGAN of New Orleans to WILLIAM McCLURY. Brkv lots 26, 27. Signed AQUILLA LOGAN. Witness: HUGH MORRISON, CHARLES ROBINSON. rec 1819. pp 370, 371

Deed dated 1819. LEMUEL SNOW JR to WILLIAM GULLEY & SMITH GULLEY. "paid by ...JAMES ABERCROMBIE". S 27, T 8, R 1W. "LORINDA, wife of LEMUEL". Signed LEMUEL SNOW JR, LORINDA SNOW. Witness: LEMUEL SNOW JR, THOMAS MANWARRING. rec 1819. pp 371, 372

Mortgage deed date 1819. WILLIAM & SMITH GULLEY to JAMES ABERCROMBIE. S 27, T 8, R 1W. Debt to be paid by 1820 to void conveyance. Signed WILLIAM GULLY, SMITH GULLEY. Witness: THOMAS MANWARRING, LEMUEL SNOW. rec 1819. p 372

Deed dated 1818. GEORGE ANTHONY to JOSIAH WILCHER. S 35, T 9, R 2W. "KATHARINE, his wife". Signed GEORGE ANTHONY, KATHARINE (x) ANTHONY. Witness: HENRY BERRY, PHILLIP (x) ANTHONY. rec 1819. pp 372, 373

Deed dated 1814. WILLIAM LEIPER & GRIZZLE, his wife, to SILAS MILLAR. S 10, T 10, R 1W. Signed WILLIAM LEIPER, GRIZZLE (x) LEIPER. Witness: FRANCIS McCLELLAND, JAMES McCLURKIN. rec 1819. pp 373, 374

Deed dated 1818. WILLIAM SPARKS & MARY, his wife, to NOAH BEAUCHAMP. S 30, T 14, R 12E. Signed WILLIAM (x) SPARKS, MARY (x) SPARKS. Witness: none. rec 1819. pp 374, 375

Deed dated 1818. VOLLENTINE MOWERY & SUSANNA to HENRY BROWN. S 26, T 12. R 12E. Signed VOLLENTINE MOWERY (german script), SUSANNA (x) MOWERY. Witness: ROBERT HANNA JR, WILLIAM MOWERY. rec 1819 pp 375, 376

Deed dated 1819. SIMON ELY & ELIZABETH, his wife, to ADAM ELY. S 32, T 11, R 2W. Signed SIMON ELY, ELIZABETH (x) ELY. Witness: SAMUEL ELY, GEORGE NORRIS. rec 1819. pp 376, 377

Deed dated 1818. JAMES TANNER to ABRAHAM BURCKHALTER. S 2, T 11, R 2W. "NANCY, his wife". Signed JAMES TANNER, NANCY (x) TANNER. Witness: THOMAS CASON, WILLIAM CASON. rec 1819. pp 377, 378

FRANKLIN COUNTY DEEDS: Book C

Deed dated 1818. GEORGE WILLSON to HENRY BROWNE. S 26, T 12, R 2E. "MARY, his wife". Signed GEORGE (x) WILSON, MARY (x) WILSON. Witness: ARTEMIS D. WOODWORTH, JAMES BRISON. rec 1819. pp 378, 379

Deed dated 1818. JOHN ALLEN SR to WILLIAM BRADLEY. Brkv lot 43. Signed JOHN ALLEN SR, POLLY (x) ALLEN. Witness: ELIPHALEL ALLEN, ROBERT JOHN. rec 1819. pp 379, 380

Deed dated 1818. WILLIAM H. EADS to SAMUEL GOODWIN. S 28, T 9, R 2W. Signed WILLIAM H. EADS, JANE EADS. Witness: ROBERT JOHN, E.D. JOHN. rec 1819 pp 380, 381

Deed dated 1818. JOSEPH ADAMS to SAMUEL GOODWIN & ENOCH D. JOHN. Brkv lot 97. "LYDIA, his wife". Witness: ROBERT JOHN, RICHARD CROAKE. rec 1819. pp 381, 382

Deed dated 1818. JOHN ALLEN SR to SAMUEL GOODWIN. Brkv lot 99. Signed JOHN ALLEN SR, MARY ALLEN. Witness: ROBERT JOHN. rec 1819. p 382

Deed dated 1817. WILLIAM RUSON to BAILEY JOHNSON. S 29, T 10, R 2W. "FRANCY, his wife". Signed WILLIAM RUSING, AGNES (x) RUSING. Witness: JOHN EWING, URIAH ROSE. rec 1819. p 383

Deed dated 1815. DAVID HOLLINGWORTH to WILLIAM NORRIS JR. S 27, T 11, R 2W. Signed DAVID HOLLINGSWORTH. Witness: JOHN NORRIS, JONATHAN HOLLINGSWORTH. rec 1819. pp 383, 384

Deed dated 1817. MATTHEW BROWN of Hamilton Co, OH to EPHRAIM DORTON. S 35, T 11, R 2W. Signed MATTHEW BROWN, JANE (x) BROWN. Witness: ROBERT SWANN, JOHN BROWN SR. rec 1819. pp 384, 385

Deed dated 1818. JOHN McMANUS & CATHARINE, his wife of Butler Co, OH to ABRAHAM MILEY SR of same. Brkv lots 66, 71. Signed J. C. McMANUS, CATHARINE McMANUS Witness: JEREMIAH CREIN, GEORGE MILEY (in OH). rec 1819. pp 385, 386

Deed dated 1818. THOMAS HENDERSON to WILLIAM HENDERSON. S 33, T 9, R 2W. Signed THOMAS HENDERSON. Witness: SOLOMON ALLEN. rec 1819. pp 386, 387

Sheriff's sale dated 1818. ROBERT HANNA, Sheriff of Franklin Co to BARTHOLOMEW McCLARY. BENJAMIN SMITH* Brkv lots 53, 54 seized, sold at auction to McCLARY. Signed ROBERT HANNA, Sheriff. Witness: none. rec

FRANKLIN COUNTY DEEDS: Book C

1819. pp 387, 388 *see Bk C, pp 354, 355

Deed dated 1817. JOHN HAMILTON of Dearborn Co to STEPHEN C. STEVENS. Brkv lots 13, 14. Signed JOHN HAMILTON. Witness: CHARLES L. BRASHIER, A. LANE. rec 1819. pp 388, 389

Deed dated 1819. JOSEPH COX to JACOB HARTMAN. Brkv lot 59. Signed JOSEPH COX. Witness: ROBERT JOHN. rec 1819. pp 389, 390

Deed dated 1819. THOMAS SHANK & JACOB SHANK to JOHN CASE. S 11, T 8, R 2W. Signed THOMAS SHANK, JACOB SHANK. Witness: B.F. MORRIS, SAMUEL CASE. rec 1819 pp 390, 391

Deed dated 1815. HUGH REID & MARGARET, his wife, of Abbaville District, SC, to JAMES REID. S 19, T 11, R 1W. Signed HU REID, MARGARET REID. Witness: THOS. BROWNE, J. LEVISTON. rec 1819. pp 391, 392

Deed dated 1815. HUGH REID & MARGARET, his wife, of Abbaville District, SC, to JAMES REID. S 24. T 11, R 2W. Signed HU REID, MARGARET REID. Witness: THOS. BROWNE, J. LEVISTON. rec 1819. pp 392, 393

Deed dated 1818. JOHN BRIDGES to JOHN SMITH. S 20, T 13, R 12E. "CHARLOTTE, his wife". Signed JOHN BRIDGES, CHARLOTTE (x) BRIDGES. Witness: JOHN HANNA. rec 1819. p 393

Brookville outlots plat map dated 1819. JOHN ALLEN SR, prop'r. rec 1819. p 394

Deed dated 1816. ADAM ELY to JESSE W.L.H. ATKINS. S 18, T 13, R 14E. Signed ADAM (x) ELY, ELIZABETH (x) ELY. Witness: SAMUEL MAZE, DAVID MAZE. rec 1819. pp 394, 395

Mortgage deed dated 1818. JOSEPH SCOTT & JAMES NOBLE to JESSE W.L.H. ATKINS & LEVI MEAD. S 18. T 13, R 14E Debt to be paid in 1823 to void conveyance. Signed JOSEPH SCOTT, JANE (x) SCOTT, JAMES NOBLE, ELIZABETH (x) NOBLE. Witness: ROBERT SWANN, WILLIAM McGREER, HENRY H. BRANDENBURG. rec 1819. pp 395, 396

Deed dated 1819. ISAAC WOOD to SAMUEL GREY. S 25, T 9, R 1W. "ELIZABETH, his wife". Signed ISAAC (x) WOOD ELIZABETH (x) WOOD. Witness: JAMES BOARD, ABRAHAM LINCH. rec 1819. pp 396, 397

Deed dated 1819. WILLIAM H. EADS to THOMAS BARBER of

FRANKLIN COUNTY DEEDS: Book C

Marietta, OH. S 30, T 13, R 12E. Signed WILLIAM H. EADS, JANE EADS. Witness: ROBERT JOHN. rec 1819. pp 397, 398

Deed dated 1818. WILLIAM WILLSON JR to JOSEPH D. CLEMENTS. S 24, no T-R: "adj tract belonging to said CLEMENTS". Signed WILLIAM WILLSON JR, JANE (x) WILLSON. Witness: JOSEPH NICHOLLS. rec 1819. pp 398, 399

Deed dated 1819. JEREMIAH CORY to ROBERT HANNA JR & HERVEY BATES. Brkv lot 77. Signed JEREMIAH CORY, REBECAH CORY. Witness: HUGH MORRISON, FIRMAN SMITH. rec 1819. p 399

Quitclaim deed dated 1819. STEPHEN MARTIN to JOHN WELLS of Fayatte Co, PA. S 11, T 11, R 13E. "ANNAS, his wife". Signed STEPHEN MARTIN, ANNAS (x) MARTIN. Witness: ROBERT JOHN, T.E. BUSH. rec 1819. p 400

Deed dated 1819. JOHN JACOBS to GREEN B. LEAGUE. Brkv lots 48, 49. Signed JOHN JACOBS, ELIZABETH JACOBS. Witness: ROBERT JOHN. rec 1819. p 401

Quitclaim deed dated 1819. JOHN WELLS of Fayette Co, PA to STEPHEN MARTIN. S 11, T 11, R 13E. Signed JOHN WELLS, DEBORAH WELLS. Witness: ELI ALLEN, WILLIAM NORCROSS (in PA). rec 1819. pp 401, 402, 403

Mortgage deed dated 1819. GREEN B. LEAGUE to NATHAN D. GALLION. Brkv lot 48. Debt to be paid in 1820 to void conveyance. Signed GREEN B. LEAGUE, N. D. GALLION. Witness: WM. C.E. WESTON. rec 1819. pp 403, 404

Deed dated 1819. DAVID STIPP & MARY, his wife, to SILVANUS HOLSEY. S 4, T 11, R 12E. Signed DAVID STIPP, MARY STIPP. Witness: THOMAS HOW. rec 1819. pp 404, 405

Deed dated 1818. JOHN BROWN JR of Laurence Co, SC to THOMAS RITCHEY. S 25, T 11, R 2W. Signed JOHN BROWN. Witness: JAMES SNOWDEN, JACOB SNOWDEN (in SC). rec 1819. pp 405, 406

Partition deed dated 1819. JOSEPH J. ABBOTT to THOMAS RUNYAN. S 23, T 12, R 13E held as tenants in common. JOSEPH to have north half, THOMAS the south. Signed THOMAS RUNYAN, HANNAH (x) RUNYAN, JOSEPH J. ABBOTT, MARY ABBOTT. Witness: ROBERT JOHN. rec 1819. pp 406, 407

Deed dated 1819. EZRA STILES PIERPONT & LUCIUS CHITTENDEN, late of Hamilton Co, OH but now of Waterbury,

FRANKLIN COUNTY DEEDS: Book C

Newhaven Co, CT to JAMES PECK. S 24, T 8, R 1W. Signed EZRA S. PIERPONT, LUCIUS CHITTENDEN. Witness: CHARLES KINGSBURY, JOHN KINGSBURY (in CT). rec 1819. p 408

Deed dated 1819. JAMES PECK of Cincinnati, OH to JACOB WOLF of same. S 24, T 8, R 1W. Signed JAMES PECK. Witness: FRANCIS A. BLAKE, E. STONE (in OH). rec 1819. p 409

Deed dated 1818. JOHN WELLS of Fayette Co, PA to ISAAC HASTINGS. S 11, T 11, R 13E. Signed JOHN WELLS, DEBORAH WELLS. Witness: ELI ALLEN, WILLIAM NORCROSS (in PA). rec 1819. pp 409, 410

Deed dated 1819. GEORGE L. MURDOCK to ROBERT BRACKEN-RIDGE & JOSEPH BRACKENRIDGE. Brkv lot 52. Signed G.L. MURDOCK. Witness: WILLIAM C. DREW. rec 1819. p 411

Deed dated 1819. JOHN STEVENS to JOHN BAKER. S 36, T 10, R 2W. Signed JOHN (x) STEVENS, MARY (x) STEVENS Witness: none. rec 1819. p 412

Deed dated 1819. JOHN BAKER to JOHN STEVENS. S 36, T 10, R 2W. Signed JOHN BAKER. Witness: ROBERT JOHN rec 1819. pp 412, 413

Deed dated 1818. MARTINAS MILLSPAUGH of Hamilton Co, OH to HENRY MILE SR of same. S 34, T 9, R 1W. Signed MARTINAS MILLSPAUGH. Witness: TUBAL WILE, PATRICK SMITH (in OH). rec 1819. pp 413, 414
end of Book C

Book D

Deed dated 1817. WILLIAM SWAFFORD & NANCY, his wife, of Wayne Co to HUGH MAXWELL. S 4, T 11, R 1W. Signed WILLIAM SWAFFORD, NANCY (x) SWAFFORD. Witness: ISAAC JULIAN, JP, Wayne Co. rec 1819. p 1

Deed dated 1818. BENAJAH RICE of Boon Co, KY to AMOS BUTLER of Jefferson Co. S 19, T 9, R 2W. Signed BENAJAH RICE. Witness: ENOCH McCARTY, WILLIAM C. DREW. rec 1819. pp 1, 2

Deed dated 1818. JOHN WELLS of Fayette Co, PA to FIELDING JEATER. S 11, T 11, R 13E. Signed JOHN WELLS, DEBORAH WELLS. Witness: ELI ALLEN, WILLIAM NORCROSS (in PA). rec 1819. pp 2, 3

Deed dated 1818. THOMAS SHAW to JOHN L. VOORHEES. S 27, T 9, R 1W. Signed THOMAS SHAW, SARY (x) SHAW.

FRANKLIN COUNTY DEEDS: Book D

Witness: JACOB SIMONSON, ROB'T. LUCE. rec 1819 pp 3,4

Deed dated 1819. SAMUEL ROCKAFELLAR to THOMAS MANWARRING. New Trenton lots 33, 34. Signed SAMUEL ROCKAFELLAR, MARY ROCKAFELLAR. Witness: H. MAY. rec rec 1819. pp 4, 5

Deed dated 1818. THOMAS CULLY & ELIZABETH, his wife, to JOSEPH CULLY. S 3, T 11, R 2W. "natural love & affection..unto..JOSEPH, their son". Signed THOMAS CULLY, ELIZABETH CULLY. Witness: THOMAS CASON, JESSE CASON. rec 1819. pp 5, 6

Deed dated 1818. JAMES PIPER of Butler Co, OH to his son, WILLIAM PIPER of same. S 14, T 10, R 2W. Signed Signed JAMES PIPER. Witness: WM. ABRANDER, JONAS HUNT (in OH). rec 1819. pp 6, 7

Tax sale. ROBERT HANNA, Sheriff of Franklin Co, to GEORGE L. MURDOCK. Brkv lot 41. Signed ROBERT HANNA. rec 1819. p 7

Deed dated 1819. SAMUEL SERRING to JOSEPH MEEKS. Brkv lot 38. Signed SAMUEL SERRING, ELIZABETH SERRING. Witness: HUGH MORRISON, JOHN DAVIS. rec 1819. pp 7,8

Deed dated 1818. JAMES RAMY to WILLIAM RAMY. S 13, T 8, R 1W. "REBEKAH, wife of JAMES". Signed JAMES REMY, REBEKAH REMY. Witness: JOHN H. ROCKAFELLAR. rec 1819. pp 8, 9

Deed dated 1819. GREEN B. LEAGUE to LEWIS DEWEESE. Brkv lot 49. Signed GREEN B. LEAGUE, NANCY LEAGUE. Witness: JOHN QUICK, G.L. BENSON. rec 1819. pp 9,10

Deed dated 1818. VACHEL CLARY to GEORGE TAYLOR. S 34, T 13, R 13E. Signed VACHEL (x) CLARY, NANCY CLARY. Witness: J. M. JOHNSON, JAMES MORROW. rec 1819. pp 10, 11

Deed dated 1819. JACOB FAUSETT to REUBEN BRACKNEY. S 27, T 9, R 1W. "CATHERINE, his wife". Signed JACOB FAUSETT, CATHERINE FAUSETT. Witness: B.F. MORRIS. rec 1819. p 11

Deed dated 1818. WILLIAM CONNER of Boon Co, KY to ROBERT SCOTT. S 15, T 13, R 12E. "NELLY, his wife". Signed WILLIAM CONNER, NELLY CONNER. Witness: WILLIAM GRAVES (in KY). rec 1819. p 12

Deed dated 1819. JOHN ALLEN SR to ENOCH D. JOHN. Brkv lots 70, 73, 74, 81, 85, 86. Signed JOHN ALLEN SR,

FRANKLIN COUNTY DEEDS: Book D

MARY ALLEN. Witness: ROBERT JOHN. rec 1819. pp 12, 13

Deed dated 1817. JOHN HEALY to GEORGE ANTHONY. S 26 no T - R. Signed JOHN HEDLEY. Witness: JAMES WIN- CHILL, JACOB ANTHONY. rec 1819. pp 13, 14

Deed dated 1819. GEORGE ANTHONY to PETER HOCKENBERRY S 26 & 35, T 9, R 2W. "CATHARINE, wife of GEORGE". Signed GEORGE ANTHONY, CATHARINE (x) ANTHONY. Witness ROBERT JOHN, RICH'D CROOKE. rec 1819. pp 14, 15

Deed dated 1818. ROBERT BROWN to SKILMON ALGER of Butler Co, OH. S 23, T 12, R 1W. "RACHEL, his wife". Signed ROBERT BROWN, RACHEL BROWN. Witness: JEREMIAH BROWN, HARRELL HOLB. rec 1819. pp 15, 16

Deed dated 1818. ABRAHAM VANEATON to JOSEPH VANEATON S 14, T 11, R 2W. Signed ABRAHAM VANEATON. Witness: WILLIAM McGREW, MOSES LYONS. rec 1819. pp 16, 17

Easement dated 1819. AMOS BUTLER of Jefferson Co to President & trustees of Brookville. Permitted town to build aquaduct across S 20, T 9, R 2W & construct reservoirs to provide water to town. Brkv officials: ENOCH McCARTY, JOHN JACOB, SOLLOMON ALLEN, WILLIAM C. DREW, NATHANIEL FRENCH. Signed AMOS BUTLER. Witness: SAM'L LEWIS, JAS. BARBER. rec 1819. p 17

Deed dated 1819. THOMAS OSBORN to WILLIAM HAYS. Fair- field lots 57, 64. Signed THOMAS OSBORN, MARY OSBORN Witness: SAMUEL OSBORN, JAMES SHERRILL rec 1819. p 18

Deed dated 1819. JOHN ALLEN SR to HANNAH CLARK (widow of JOSHUA) GEORGE CLARK, RICHARD CLARK, REBECCA CLARK NANCY CLARK, MASTERSON CLARK, JOHN CLARK & BENNETT CLARK. Brkv lot 84. Signed JOHN ALLEN SR, MARY ALLEN. Witness: ROBERT JOHN. rec 1819. pp 18, 19

Deed dated 1819. BENJAMIN BROWN of Butler Co, OH to JOSEPH GROOMS of same. S 10, T 8, R 1W. Signed BEN- JAMIN BROWN, PHEBE (x) BROWN. Witness: ABIRHAM LOTTER, RACHEL (x) LOTTER (in OH). rec 1819. p 20

Deed dated 1819. JOHN ALLEN SR to HANNAH CLARK. Brkv lot 83. Signed JOHN ALLEN SR, MARY ALLEN. Witness: none. rec 1819. p 21

Deed dated 1819. JAMES HUSTON & SARAH, his wife, of Preble Co, OH to JACOB HUSTON. S 24, T 11, R 1W. Signed JAMES HUSTON, SARAH (x) HUSTON. Witness: JOHN HUSTON, ARTHUR CARR, JACOB KINGERY. rec 1819 pp 21, 22

FRANKLIN COUNTY DEEDS: Book D

Deed dated 1818. JOSEPH KINGERY of Preble Co, OH & EVA, his wife, to HENRY ICHELBERRY. S 23, T 11, R 1W. Signed JOSEPH KINGERY, EVA (x) KINGERRY. Witness: none. rec 1819. pp 22, 23

Deed dated 1818. RICHARD CONNER to HUGH MAY. S 18, T 8, R 1W. "including the cabbin DAVID WEBB lives in" "ELIZABETH, his wife". Signed RICHARD CONNER, ELIZABETH (x) CONNER. Witness: THOMAS MANWARRING. rec 1819. pp 23, 24

Quitclaim dated 1818. ABRAHAM HEATON & CATHARINE, his wife, of Wayne Co to MARY McCRAY of Butler Co, OH. CATHARINE, a dau of SAMUEL McCRAY, dec, relinquishes rightful claim to his estate. Signed ABRAHAM HEATON, CATHARINE HEATON. Witness: WILLIAM (x) NOBLE. rec 1819. p 24

Deed dated 1819. JAMES HUSTON & SARAH, his wife, of Preble Co, OH to JOHN HUSTON. S 14, T 11, R 1W. Signed JAMES HUSTON, SARAH HUSTON. Witness: JACOB HUSTON, JONATHAN CONN, JACOB KINGERY. rec 1819. pp 24, 25

Deed dated 1819. JEREMIAH CORY to JAMES DILL of Dearborn Co. S 8, T 9, R 2W. Signed JEREMIAH CORY, REBECCAH CORY. Witness: HUGH MORRISON, HENRY JENKINSON, GEORGE W. KIMBLE. rec 1819. pp 25, 26

Deed dated 1819. LEWIS BISHOP to WILLIAM C. DREW. S 34, T12, R 13E."MARY, his wife". Signed LEWIS BISHOP MARY (x) BISHOP. Witness: B.F. MORRIS. rec 1819. p26

Deed dated 1819. JESSE HUNT of Cincinnati, OH to THOMAS BROWN. S 30, T 11, R 1W. "ELIZA, his wife". Signed JESSE HUNT, ELIZA HUNT. Witness: SAMUEL F. HUNT, JOHN MAHARD (in OH). rec 1819. p 27

Deed dated 1819. WILLIAM SKINNER to JOHN KEEN. S 11, T 12, R 13E. Signed WILLIAM SKINNER, REBECCA (x) SKINNER. Witness: B.F. MORRIS, WM. RICHARDSON. rec 1819. pp 27, 28

Deed dated 1819. JOHN WOODS to PHILIP HARWOOD. S 13 T 8, R 1. Signed JOHN WOODS. Witness: ARCH'D GUTHREY H. MAY. rec 1819. pp 28, 29

Deed dated 1819. BENJAMIN SCHOONOVER & LYDA, his wife, to JAMES SCOFIELD. S 13, T 8, R2W. Signed BENJAMIN (x) SCHOONOVER, LYDIA (x) SCHOONOVER. Witness: NATHANIEL HYATT. rec 1819. p 29

FRANKLIN COUNTY DEEDS: Book D

Deed dated 1819. JOHN A. WHITE to HENRY FRY. S 24, T 10, R 2W. "MARY, his wife". Signed JOHN A. WHITE, MARY WHITE. Witness: RICHARD W. McMILLAN, JP, & HENRY (x) JOHNSTON. rec 1819. p 29, 30

Deed dated 1818. JEREMIAH CORY to JOHN JACOBS. S 8, T 9, R 2W. Signed JEREMIAH CORY, REBECCA CORY. Witness: ROBERT HANNA JR, ROBERT JOHN. rec 1819 pp 30,31

Deed dated 1819. JOHN LATOURETTE of Jennings Co to WILLIAM C. DREW. Brkv lot 43. Signed JOHN LATOURETTE. Witness: ROBERT JOHN. rec 1819. pp 31, 32

Deed dated 1819. JOHN ALLEN SR to SAMUEL GOODWIN. Brkv lot 79. Signed JOHN ALLEN SR, MARY ALLEN. Witness: B.F. MORRIS. rec 1819. pp 32, 33

Deed dated 1819. JOHN ALLEN SR to SAMUEL GOODWIN. Brkv lot 98. Signed JOHN ALLEN SR, MARY ALLEN. Witness: B.F. MORRIS. rec 1819. p 33

Partition deed dated 1818. SAMUEL SHIRK & ELIZABETH, his wife, to DAVID SHIRK. S 17, T 9, R 1W purchased jointly; north half to DAVID. Signed SAMUEL SHIRK, ELIZABETH SHIRK. Witness: none. rec 1819. pp 33, 34

Deed dated 1819. JAMES GLASS of Hamilton Co, OH to WILLIAM GLASS of same. Brkv lot 95. Signed JAMES GLASS, SOPHIA GLASS. Witness: SIMON SMITH, JOHN MAHARD (in OH). rec 1819. pp 34, 35

Deed dated 1818. SAMUEL LEE to ABRAHAM LEE. Brkv lot 55. Signed SAMUEL LEE, PHEBE (x) LEE. Witness: ROBERT LUSE, JP, MARY (x) LUSE. rec 1819. pp 35, 36

Deed dated 1819. ENOCH D. JOHN to WILLIAM W. WADE. Brkv lot 70. Signed ENOCH D. JOHN. Witness: JOHN JACOBS, B.F. MORRIS. rec 1819. p 36

Deed dated 1818. JACOB BELL of Butler Co, OH & SARAH his wife, to JOHN MILLER. S 22, T 10, R 1W. Signed JACOB BELL, SARAH (x) BELL. Witness: JACOB BAKE, ROBERT BROWN. rec 1819. pp 36, 37

Deed dated 1817. ROBERT BROWN & RACHEL, his wife, to WILLIAM DENISON. S 30, T 14, R 13E. Signed ROBERT BROWN, RACHEL BROWN. Witness: ROB'T. LONG, JEREMIAH BROWN. rec 1819. pp 37, 38

Deed dated 1818. STEPHE GARNER to JOHN CASSEDAY. S 36, T 10, R 2W. "NANCY, his wife". Signed STEPHEN (x) GARNER, NANCY (x) GARNER. Witness: JOHN HANNAH,

FRANKLIN COUNTY DEEDS: Book D

JOSEPH OSBORN. rec 1819. pp 38, 39

Deed dated 1818. THOMAS SKINNER SR to DANIEL SKINNER S 7, T 9, R 2W. "land of...CHARLES DAILY". "ANN, his wife". Signed THOMAS SKINNER, ANN (x) SKINNER. Witness: none. rec 1819. p 39

Deed dated 1819. SOLOMON TYNER to JEREMIAH FRENCH. S 27, T 9, R 2W. "JEMIMA, his wife". Signed SOLOMON (x) TYNER, JEMIMA (x) TYNER. Witness: none. rec 1819. pp 39, 40

Deed dated 1818. MARGARET KIMMY to JEREMIAH FRENCH. S 27, T 9, R 2W. Signed MARGARET (x) KIMMY. Witness: NATHANIEL FRENCH. rec 1819. pp 40, 41

Deed dated 1818. HENRY COSTEN to JEREMIAH FRENCH. Brkv lot 50. Signed HENRY COSTEN, HANNAH (x) COSTEN. rec 1819. pp 41, 42

Deed dated 1818. DANIEL POWERS to ABRAM NEWKIRK. S 27, T 10, R 2W. "ABIGAIL, his wife". Signed DANIEL POWERS, ABIGAIL POWERS. Witness: JOHN HANNA, JACOB BARSHMAN. rec 1819. pp 42, 43

Deed dated 1818. NATHANIEL HUNT & ABNER B. HUNT of Warren Co, OH to RALPH HUNT of same. S 27, T 8, R 2W. Signed NATHANIEL HUNT, ABNER B. HUNT. Witness: JAMES FUGATE, WM. CARTER. rec 1819. p 43

Deed dated 1818. RICHARD COLLIVER & MARY, his wife of Montgomery Co, KY to ENOCH TUCKER of Hamilton Co, OH. S 10, T 9, R 1W. Signed RICHARD COLLIVER, MARY COLL-IVER. Witness: THOS. HIGGINS, BENJAMIN TUCKER (in KY). rec 1819. pp 43, 44

Deed dated 1818. JOHN ALLEN SR to JACOB HETRICK. Brkv lot 106. Signed JOHN ALLEN, MARY ALLEN. Witness: ROBERT JOHN. rec 1819. pp 44, 45

Deed dated 1819. JAMES TYLER to JOHN FISHER. S 1, T 12, R 13E. "VILEY, his wife". Signed JAMES (x) TYLER, VILEY (x) TYLER. Witness: B.F. MORRIS, JOHN CONNER. rec 1819. pp 45, 46

Deed dated 1819. GEORGE W. KIMBLE to THOMAS W. COLE-SCOTT. Brkv lot 38. Signed G.W. KIMBLE. Witness: JEREMIAH CORY, ROBERT JOHN. rec 1819. pp 46, 47

Deed dated 1819. ZOPHAR COLEMAN to THOMAS HARVEY. Fairfield lot 21. Signed ZOPHAR COLEMAN. Witness: none. rec 1819. p 47

FRANKLIN COUNTY DEEDS: Book D

Deed dated 1819. ANDREW BURNSIDE & MARTHA CROSSAN to HENRY HUNTER. S 7, T 11, R 1W. Signed ANDREW BURNSIDE, MARTHA CROSSAN, JANE BURNSIDE. Witness: EBENEZER HOWE, AGNES (x) CROSSAN. rec 1819. pp 47, 48

Deed dated 1816. ANNA BURNSIDE to ANDREW BURNSIDE. S 7, T 11, R 1W. Signed ANNA (x) BURNSIDE. Witness: THOS. MADDEN. rec 1819. p 48

Deed dated 1816. EDGEHILL BURNSIDE to MARTHA CROSSAN S 7, T 11, R 1W. "corner of DAVID DUNHAM's land...of GEORGE WILLIAMS' land". Signed EDGEHILL BURNSIDE, PERMELA BURNSIDE. Witness: ANDREW BURNSIDE, JANE BURNSIDE, EBENEZER HOWE. rec 1819. p 49

Deed dated 1819. VINCENT COOPER & REBECA, his wife, to WILLIAM HELM. S 21, T 13, R 12E. Signed VINCENT (x) COOPER, REBECKA (x) COOPER. Witness: none. rec 1819. pp 49, 50

Deed dated 1818. JOEL BELK to JOHN RUSING. S 29, T 10, R 2W. Signed JOEL BELK, JANE BELK. Witness: JOHN EWING, GEORGE V. EWING. rec 1819. pp 50, 51

Deed dated 1819. JOHN PEGG to HERVEY BATES. Brkv lot 32. Signed JOHN PEGG, HANNAH G. PEGG. Witness: HUGH MORRISON, HENRY JENKINSON. rec 1819. p 51

Deed dated 1819. JOHN ALLEN SR to ARTHUR HENRIE of Hamilton Co, OH. Brkv lot 93. Signed JOHN ALLEN SR MARY ALLEN. Witness: B. F. MORRIS. rec 1819. p 52

Deed dated 1819. ARTHUR HENRIE as above to JOHN ALLEN SR. "land adj Brkv in S --, T 9, R 2W." Signed Signed ARTHUR HENRIE. Witness: ROBERT JOHN, E.D. JOHN. rec 1819. pp 52, 53

Brookville addition plat map dated 1819. JOHN ALLEN SR, prop'r. rec 1819. pp 53, 54

Brookville addition plat map dated 1819. ARTHUR HENRIE, prop'r. rec 1819. pp 54, 55, 56

Deed dated 1818. JAMES C. HANNA to WILLIAM HANNA. S 29, T 11, R 2. Signed JAMES C. HANNA, ELENOR HANNA. Witness: ROBERT SWANN, MARTHA ANDERSON, WILLIAM EWING rec 1819. pp 56, 57

Deed dated 18--. ARTHUR HENRIE of Hamilton Co, OH to HENRY PARKER. Brkv lot 113. Signed ARTHUR HENRIE, GRACE M. HENRIE. Witness: ROBERT JOHN, J. M. JOHNSON rec 1819. p 57

FRANKLIN COUNTY DEEDS: Book D

Mortgage deed dated 1819. JOHN PLICARD to ARTHUR HENRIE. Brkv lot 6, square 6. Debt to be paid in 1821 to void conveyance. Signed JOHN (x) PLICARD. Witness: THOS. SHARPLESS, ROBERT JOHN. rec 1819. p 58

Deed dated 1819. ARTHUR HENRIE of Hamilton Co, OH to WILLIAM SEAL. Brkv lot 122. Signed ARTHUR HENRIE, GRACE M. HENRY. Witness: ROBERT JOHN, N. D. GALLION. rec 1819. pp 58, 59

Deed dated 1819. ARTHUR HENRIE as above to DANIEL WILLISON (in text, WILSON). Brkv lot 6 square 2. Signed ARTHUR HENRIE, GRACE M. HENRIE. Witness: ROBERT JOHN, N.D. GALLION. rec 1819. pp 59, 60

Mortgage deed dated 1819. ROBERT DUNN to ARTHUR HENRIE. Brkv lot 4, square 4. Signed ROBERT DUNN. Witness: W. POUNDSFORD, P. SMITH. rec 1819. pp 60, 61

Mortgage deed dated 1819. DANIEL OWEN to ARTHUR HENRIE. Brkv lot 2, square 5. Signed DANIEL (x) OWEN. Witness: W. POUNDSFORD, P. SMITH. rec 1819. p 61

Mortgage deed dated 1819. GREEN B. LEAGUE to NATHAN D. GALLION. Brkv lot 48. Debt to be paid by 1820 to void conveyance. Signed GREEN B. LEAGUE, N.D. GALLION. Witness: illegible. rec 1819. pp 62, 63

Mortgage deed dated 1819. BENJAMIN NICHOLS to ARTHUR HENRIE. Brkv lot 2 in Square 8. Debt to be paid in 1822 to void conveyance. Signed BENJAMIN NICHOLS. Witness: PATRICK SMITH, ROBERT JOHN. rec 1819. p 63

Deed dated 1819. ARTHUR HENRIE as above to JOHN C. POWNES. Brkv lots 13, 14 in square 2. Signed ARTHUR HENRIE, GRACE M. HENRIE. Witness: ROBERT JOHN, ALFRED HARRISON. rec 1819. pp 63, 64

Mortgage deed dated 1819. JAMES HOLDERFIELD to ARTHUR HENRIE. Brkv lot 4, Square 6. Debt paid in 1822 to void conveyance. Signed JAMES (x) HOLDERFIELD. Witness: THOS. SHARPLESS, ROBERT JOHN. rec 1819. p 65,66

Mortgage deed dated 1819. ROBERT <u>ADKINSON</u> to ARTHUR HENRIE. Brkv lots 3, Square 2 & lot 8, Square 6. Debt to be paid in 1822 to void conveyance. Signed R. (x) <u>ACTKINSON.</u> Witness: ROBERT JOHN, N.D. GALLION rec 1819. pp 66, 67

Deed dated 1819. ARTHUR HENRIE as above to JOHN C. McGUIRE. Brkv lot 2, square 1. Signed ARTHUR HENRIE,

FRANKLIN COUNTY DEEDS: Book D

GRACE M. HENRIE. Witness: ROBERT JOHN, N.D. GALLION. rec 1819. pp 67, 68

Deed dated 1819. JOHN SMITH to WILLIAM SMITH. S 25, T 10, R 1W. "SARAH, his wife". Signed JOHN SMITH, SARAH (x) SMITH. Witness: JOHN HANNA. rec 1819. p 68

Deed dated 1819. THOMAS GREGG to THOMAS GLISSON*. S 20, T 9, R 1W. "DELILAH, his wife". Signed THOMAS GREGG, DELILAH GREGG. Witness: ROBERT LUSE, JAMES THOMPSON. rec 1819. pp 69, 70 *GLISTEN in deed text

Deed dated 1819. GEORGE GREGG to THOMAS GLISSON. S 20, T 9, R 1W. "MAHALAH, his wife". Signed GEORGE GREGG, MAHALAH (x) GREGG. Witness: ELI JAMES. rec 1819. p 70

Deed dated 1819. THOMAS GREGG to THOMAS GLISSON. S29 T 9, R 1. Signed THOMAS GREGG, DELILAH GREGG. Witness ROBERT LUSE, JAMES THOMPSON. rec 1819. pp 70, 71

Deed dated 1819. JOHN ALLEN SR to ELI JAMES. Brkv lot 63. Signed JOHN ALLEN SR, MARY ALLEN. Witness: HUGH MORRISON, JAMES D. MORRISON. rec 1819. pp 71,72

Deed dated 1819. LUDOVICUS BELDING to WILLIAM WADAMS of Butler Co, OH. Fairfield lots 35, 38. Signed LUDOVICUS BELDING, LYDIA BELDING. Witness: JOHN HANNA. rec 1819. pp 72, 73

Deed dated 1818. THOMAS SLAUGHTER to JAMES C. GINN. S 23, T 12, R 13E. "MARTHA, his wife". Signed THOMAS SLAUGHTER, MARTHA (x) SLAUGHTER. Witness: MARTIN CLARKE. rec 1819. pp 73, 74

Deed dated 1817. JOSHUA WYTHE & HANNAH, his wife to JOHN JASON. S 14, T 8, R 2W. Signed JOSHUA WYETH, HANNAH WYETH. Witness: ROBERT JOHN. rec 1819 pp 74,75

Relinquishment of dower rights, dated 1819. S 29, T 9, R 1W sold by ABNER LEONARD to THOMAS SHAW, now dec Deed unsigned by LEONARD's wife; now relinquishes claim to land. Signed MEHITABEL (x) LEONARD. Witness ROBERT JOHN. rec 1819. p 75

Deed dated 1819. AMOS BUTLER of Jefferson Co to THOMAS GREEN. Brkv lots 40, 41. Signed AMOS BUTLER, MARY BUTLER. Witness: EPHRAIM (x) DOTY. rec 1819. pp 75,76

Deed dated 1819. JOHN JASON & LUCY, his wife, to LEVI COY. S 14, T 8, R 2W. Signed JOHN JASON, LUCY JASON. Witness: CALEB DICKINSON, CHARLOTTE DICKINSON

FRANKLIN COUNTY DEEDS: Book D

rec 1819. pp 76, 77

Deed dated 1819. JOSIAH ALLEN to JOHN ALLEN JR. S 4, T 12, R 13E. "SARAH, wife of JOSIAH". Signed JOSIAH ALLEN, SARAH ALLEN. Witness: ROBERT JOHN, JOHN SHAW. rec 1819. pp 77, 78

Deed dated 1819. ARTHUR HENRIE of Hamilton Co, OH to JAMES SEALS. Brkv lots 15, 16 in square 2. Signed ARTHUR HENRIE, GRACE M. HENRIE. rec 1819. p 78

Deed dated 1819. MATTHEW SPARKS & PRUDENCE, his wife to JACOB FELTER of Hamilton Co, OH. S 4, T 8, R 1W. Signed MATTHEW SPARKS (german), PRUDENCE (x) SPARKS. Witness: ROBT. LUSE, MOSES RARDEN. rec 1819. p 78

Deed dated 1819. JOHN FISHER & ISABELLA, his wife to JONATHAN WRIGHT of Cincinnati, OH. S 23, T 13, R 13E. Signed JOHN FISHER, ISABELLA (x) FISHER. Witness: L. BELDING, JP & DAVID BASSETT. rec 1819. pp 79, 80

Deed dated 1819. JOHN HARRIS of KY to DAVID OLIVER. S 18, T 9, R 2W. Signed JOHN HARRIS. Witness: none. rec 1819. pp 80, 81

Mortgage deed dated 1819. WILLIAM HARLOW of Cincinnati, OH to JESSE EMBREE of same. Brkv outlot 2; debt to be paid by 1820 to void conveyance. Signed WM. HARLOW. Witness: CORNELIUS DUBOIS, JOHN MAHARD in OH rec 1819. pp 81, 82

Deed dated 1819. BLACKSLEE BARNS & ALMIRA BARNES of Berlin, Hartford Co, CT to THOMAS KENSETT & CHARLES SHELTON of Cheshier, New Haven Co, CT. S 7, T 9, R 2. Signed BLACKSLEE BARNS, ALMIRA BARNS. Witness: LUTHER BERKLEY, BENJ. CRONE (in CT). rec 1819. p 82

Deed dated 1818. JAMES FERRELL & ANNA, his wife, to WILLIAM FORBES & GEORGE ALLHANDS. S 3, T 9, R 1W. Signed JAMES (x) FERRELL, ANNA (x) FERRELL. Witness: JACOB BAKE, PETER BAKE. rec 1819. pp 83, 84

Deed dated 1819. RUGGLES WINCHELL to WILLIAM D. DREW S 28, T 9, R 2W. Signed RUGGLES WINCHELL, MARTHA (x) WINCHELL . Witness: E.W. THRISTON, GEORGE GITTNER. rec 1819. pp 84, 85

Deed dated 1819. JOHN ALLEN SR to DANIEL MASON. Brkv lot 30. Signed JOHN ALLEN SR, POLLY ALLEN. Witness: ROBERT JOHN. rec 1819. pp 85, 86

Deed dated 1819. THOMAS OSBORN to THOMAS C. EADS.

FRANKLIN COUNTY DEEDS: Book D

Fairfield lot 65. Signed THOMAS OSBORN, MARY OSBORN. Witness: JESSE EMERSON, JOHN EWING. rec 1819 pp 86,87

Deed dated 1819. WILLIAM H. EADS to OBADIAH BENNETT. Brkv lot 32. Signed WILLIAM H. EADS, JANE EADS. Witness: ROBERT JOHN. rec 1819. p 87

Deed dated 1819. WILLIAM C. DREW to NATHANIEL HUNT & ABNER B. HUNT of Warren Co, OH. S 28, T 9, R 2W. Signed WILLIAM C. DREW. Witness: M.C. EGLESTON, ROBERT JOHN. rec 1819. pp 87, 88

Deed dated 1819. USA to RUGGLES WINCHELL. S 28, T 9, R 2W. rec 1819. pp 88, 89

Deed dated 1819. ALEXANDER GARDNER to WILLIAM H. EADS. Brkv lot 37. Signed A. GARDNER, ELIZA (x) GARDNER. Witness: none. rec 1819. pp 89, 90

Deed dated 1819. WILLIAM H. EADS & THOMAS C. EADS of Dearborn Co to ROBERT HANNA JR. S 21, no T-R. Signed WILLIAM H. EADS, JANE EADS, THOMAS C. EADS, ANN B. EADS. Witness: R. TYNER. rec 1819. pp 90, 91

Deed dated 1819. THOMAS <u>REEDS</u> to THOMAS NEAL SR. S 18, T 10, R 1W. Signed THOS. <u>REED,</u> SARAH (x) REED. Witness: JOHN NEAL, ROBERT REEDS. rec 1819. p 91

Deed dated 1819. HENRY CAFFEE to GEORGE MARTIN. S 10 T 11, R 13E. Signed HENRY CAFFEE, NANCY (x) CAFFEE. Witness: B.F. MORRIS. rec 1819 p 92

Deed dated 1818. USA to JOSEPH J. ABBOTT & THOMAS RUNYAN, assignees of JACOB BLACKLEDGE. S 23, T 12, R 13E. rec 1819. p 93

Partition agreement dated 1819. THOMAS RUNYAN & JOSEPH <u>ABBOTT</u> as above. THOMAS to have south half, JOSEPH the north. Signed JOSEPH J. <u>ABBOT,</u> MARY ABBOT, THOMAS RUNYAN, HANNAH (x) RUNYAN. Witness: ROBERT JOHN. rec 1819. pp 93, 94

Deed dated 1819. GEORGE MARTIN to STEPHEN MARTIN. S 10, T 11, R 13E. "JANE, wife of GEORGE". Signed GEORGE MARTIN, JANE (x) MARTIN. Witness: ROBERT JOHN rec 1819. pp 94, 95

Deed dated 1818. KERIAN CAMPION & his wife (no name) of Louisville KY to SAMUEL ELWELL. S 30, T 10, R 1W Signed KERIAN CAMPION, MARY CAMPION. Witness: D. FITZHUGH (in KY). rec 1819. pp 95, 96

FRANKLIN COUNTY DEEDS: Book D

Deed dated 1818. ALEXANDER WHITE & NANCY his wife of Dearborn Co to WILLIAM WHITE. S 15, T 12, R 13E. Signed ALEXANDER WHITE, NANCY WHITE. Witness: GEORGE W. MILLIS. rec 1819. pp 96, 97

Deed dated 1818. WILLIAM HELM & ELIZABETH, his wife, to BENJAMIN SCHOONOVER. S 13, T 8, R 2W. Signed WILLIAM HELM, ELIZABETH (x) HELM. Witness: none. rec 1819. pp 97, 98

Deed dated 1818. BENJAMIN SCHOONOVER & LYDIA, his wife, to NATHANIEL HYATT. S 13, T 8, R2W. Signed BENJAMIN (x) SCHOONOVER, LYDIA (x) SCHOONOVER. Witness: DAVID HANNAH. rec 1819. pp 98, 99

Deed dated 1818. SAMUEL BROWN to DAVID ERB. S 1, T 12, R 13E. "SARAH, his wife". Signed SAMUEL BROWN, SARAH (x) BROWN. Witness: JAS. WILSON, JOHN EWING. rec 1819. p 99

Deed dated 1818. JAMES WILSON to DAVID ERB. Fairfield lots 34, 39. Signed JAMES WILSON, NANCY WILSON. Witness: JOHN FISHE, JOHN EWING. rec 1819. p 100

Deed dated 1819. WILLIAM RUSING to ROBERT NUGENT. Fairfield lot 10. Signed WILLIAM RUSING, AGNES (x) RUSING. Witness: THOMAS MORROW, JOHN EWING. rec 1819. pp 100, 101

Deed dated 1819. ROBT. BRACKENRIDGE & JOSEPH BRACKENRIDGE to JOHN H. PIATT, PHILIP GRANDISE & JOHN ARMSTRONG of Cincinnati, OH. S 33, T 12, R 13E. "JOSEPH with MARY, his wife". Signed ROBERT BRACKENRIDGE, JOS. BRACKENRIDGE, MARY BRACKENRIDGE. Witness: ROBERT JOHN. rec 1819. pp 101, 102

Deed dated 1818. WILLIAM L. ROSE to RICHARD TYNER. Brkv lot 4. Signed WILLIAM L. ROSE. Witness: THOMAS ADAMS, THOS. C. EADS. rec 1819. pp 102, 103

Deed dated 1819. PHILEMON HARVEY to JACOB J. CAPP of of Hamilton Co, OH. S 33, T 10, R 2W. Signed PHILEMON (x) HERVEY, SARAH HARVEY. Witness: PETER DUNKIN, JOHN HANNA. rec 1819. pp 103, 104

Deed dated 1819. JEREMIAH CORY to GEORGE W. KIMBLE. Brkv lot 77. Signed JEREMIAH CORY, REBECKAH CORY. Witness: HUGH MORRISON, JOHN PEGG. rec 1819. pp 104, 105

Deed dated 1819. LEWIS HARRISON to JOHNSON WHITAKER. S 25, T 1, R 5W in the state of IL. Signed LEWIS (x)

FRANKLIN COUNTY DEEDS: Book D

HARRISON. Witness: M.C. EDGERTON, A.S. BABBIT. rec 1819. p 105

Deed dated 1818. RALPH WILDRIDGE to WILLIAM HUDSON. New Trenton lot 38. Signed RALPH WILDRIDGE, ELIZABETH WILDRIDGE. Witness: THOMAS MANWARRING. rec 1819. p 106

Deed dated 1818. RALPH WILDRIDGE to CORBLY HUDSON & WILLIAM HUDSON. New Trenton lot 24. Signed RALPH WILDRIDGE, ELIZABETH WILDRIDGE. Witness: THOMAS MANWARRING. rec 1819. pp 106, 107

Deed dated 1819. SAMUEL GOODWIN to ENOCH D. JOHN. S 34, T 9, R 2W. Signed SAMUEL GOODWIN, ELEANOR (x) GOODWIN. Witness: none. rec 1819. pp 107, 108

Mortgage deed dated 1819. JOHN McLENE of Washington Co, PA to SAMUEL ARNETT. S 32, T 9, R 2W. Debt due 1823 to void conveyance. Signed JOHN McLENE. Witness: JAMES NOBLE. rec 1819. pp 108, 109

Deed dated 1818. THOMAS CULLY & ELIZABETH, his wife, to WILLIAM CLARK. S 3, T 11, R 2W. Signed THOMAS CULLY, ELIZABETH (x) CULLY. Witness: THOMAS CASON SR, JESSE ELSTON. rec 1819. p 110

Deed dated 1819. MOSES CRIST & ABRAHAM CRIST of Sycamore Twp, Hamilton Co, OH to LOCOVICK WELLER of Montgomery, Hamilton Co, OH. S 18, T 11, R 1W. "with CYNTHIA & MARGARET, their wives". Signed MOSES CRIST ABRAHAM CRIST, CYNTHIA CRIST (german script), MARGARET CRIST (german script). Witness: JOHN LONGHEAD, SALLY FELTER (in OH). rec 1819. pp 110, 111

Deed dated 1813. OBADIAH EASTUS to THOMAS POWERS. S 33, T 10, R 2W. "FANNY, his wife". Signed OBADIAH (x) EASTUS, FANNY (x) EASTUS. Witness: ROBERT JOHN, SOLOMON ALLEN. rec 1819. pp 111, 112

Deed dated 1819. WILLIAM R. MORRIS to THOMAS POWERS. Brkv lot 114. Signed WILLIAM R. MORRIS. Witness: HUGH MORRISON, JAMES B. RAY. rec 1819. p 113

Deed dated 1819. MARTIN M. RAY & JAMES B. RAY to THOMAS POWERS. Brkv lot 65. "NANCY, wife of MARTIN & MARY, wife of JAMES". Signed MARTIN M. RAY, NANCY RAY, JAMES B. RAY, MARY RAY. Witness: HUGH MORRISON. rec 1819. pp 113, 114

Deed dated 1819. MARTIN M. RAY & JAMES B. RAY to THOMAS POWERS. S 33, T 10, R 2W . Signed MARTIN M.

FRANKLIN COUNTY DEEDS: Book D

RAY, JAMES B. RAY. Witness: HUGH MORRISON, JOHN PENWELL. rec 1819. p 115

Deed dated 1819. GREEN B. LEAGUE to LEWIS DEWEESE. Brkv lot 49. Signed GREEN B. LEAGUE. Witness: THOMAS FOSTER, C. STONE. rec 1819. p 116

Deed dated 1819. JOHN ALLEN SR to ROBERT BRACKENRIDGE & JOSEPH BRACKENRIDGE. S 29, T 9, R 2W. Signed JOHN ALLEN SR, POLLY ALLEN. Witness: ROBERT JOHN, MARY CHURCHILL. rec 1819. pp 117, 118

Deed dated 1818. ISAAC HOLLINGSWORTH to WILLIAM HOLLINGSWORTH. S 14, T 11, R 2W. Signed ISAAC HOLLINGSWORTH. Witness: ROBERT SWAN. rec 1819. p 118

Deed dated 1819. ALEXANDER McGREW & AURELIA his wife to JOHN H. PIATT. Brkv lots 34, 35. Signed ALEXANDER McGREW, AURELIA McGREW. Witness: JOHN SMITH, E. STONE (in OH). rec 1819. p 119

Deed dated 1819. WILLIAM C. DREW & ROBERT HANNA JR to GURNSEY G. BROWN. S 32, T 10, R 2W. Signed WILLIAM C. DREW, MARY G. DREW, ROBERT HANNA JR, SALLY HANNA. Witness: B.F. MORRIS. rec 1819. p 120

Deed dated 1818. DAVID KAUTZ of Cincinnati, OH to ROBERT HANNA & JONATHAN McCARTY. Brkv lots 57, 58. Signed DAVID KAUTZ, MARY KAUTZ. Witness: none. rec 1819. p 121

Deed dated 1819. HUGH ABERNATHY to ROSS SMILEY. Fairfield lot 41. Signed HUGH ABERNATHY, MARY (x) ABERNATHY. Witness: ISAAC BUCKLEY, JOHN EWING. rec 1819 p 121

Deed dated 1818. WILLIAM BARR & WILLIAM RUFFIN of Hamilton Co, OH to SABBINA ADAMS & WILSON ADAMS, heirs of JOSEPH ADAMS, dec. S 17, T 9, R 2W. Signed W. BARR, MARY BARR, WILLIAM RUFFIN, ELIZABETH RUFFIN. Witness: MARY RUFFIN, JOHN B. RUFFIN (in OH). rec 1819. pp 122, 123

Deed dated 1818. THOMAS SKINNER SR to CHARLES DAILY. S 7, T 9, R 2W. Signed THOMAS SKINNER, ANNA (x) SKINNER. Witness: none. rec 1819. pp 123, 124

Deed dated 1819. B.F. MORRIS to DAVID MORRIS of Warren Co, OH. Brkv lot 87. Signed B.F. MORRIS, ELIZABETH MORRIS. Witness: ROBERT JOHN. rec 1819. pp 124, 125

Deed dated 1819. JOHN ALLEN SR to DAVID MORRIS of

FRANKLIN COUNTY DEEDS: Book D

Warren Co, OH. Brkv lots 100, 101. Signed JOHN ALLEN, MARY ALLEN. Witness: B.F. MORRIS. rec 1819 pp 125,126

Deed dated 1819. ROBERT HANNA & JONATHAN McCARTY to WILLIAM H. EADS. Brkv lots 57, 58. Signed ROBERT HANNA, SALLY HANNA, JONATHAN McCARTY, DESDEMONA McCARTY. Witness: none. rec 1819. pp 126, 127

Deed dated 1819. SABBINA ADAM of Concord Twp, NY & WILLSON ADAMS to JOHN TILLOTSON of Genoa, Cayuga Co, NY. S 17, T 9, R 2W. Signed G. L. MURDOCK, atty for SABBINA ADAMS, WILLSON ADAMS. Witness: HUGH MORRISON C.D. MORRIS. rec 1819. pp 127, 128

Quitclaim deed dated 1819. THOMAS TERREL & ELECTA, his wife to WILLSON ADAMS. S 17, T 9, R 2W. Signed THOMAS TERRILL, ELECTA TERRILL. Witness: HUGH MORRISON, ISAAC MORRIS. rec 1819. p 128

Deed dated 1818. SAMUEL VANSEL to THOMAS BURK of Butler Co, OH. "MARY, his wife". S 13, T 9, R 1W. Signed SAMUEL (x) VANSEL, MARY (x) VANSEL. Witness: ROBERT LUSE, JOHN BURK. rec 1819. pp 128, 129

Deed dated 1818. DANIEL SHAFOR SR of Butler Co, OH to JOHN SHAFOR. "being a deductive part...from the estate of ...DANIEL". S 4, T 9, R 1W. "his wife, MARY". Signed DANIEL SHAFOR (german script), MARY (x) SHAFOR. Witness: none. rec 1819. pp 129, 130

Deed dated 1819. PETER SHAFOR to JOHN SHAFOR. S 4, T 9, R 1W. Signed PETER (x) SHAFOR, REBECKAH (x) SHAFOR. Witness: ROBERT LUSE, ELEONER LANPHER. rec 1819. pp 130, 131

Deed dated 1819. JOHN SHAFOR to DANIEL SHAFOR. S 4,T 9, R 1W. Signed JOHN SHAFOR, CATTARIN SAFOR. Witness ROBERT LUSE, ELEONER LANPHER. rec 1819. pp 131, 132

Deed dated 1818. DANIEL SHAFOR SR of Butler Co, OH to DANIEL SHAFOR JR. "being a deductive part...from the estate of ...DANIEL". S 4, T 9, R 1W. Signed DANIEL SHAFOR (german script), MARY (x) SHAFOR. Witness: none. rec 1819. pp 132, 133

Deed dated 1818. ENOCH D. JOHN to EDWARD H. HUDSON. Brkv lot 73. Signed ENOCH D. JOHN. Witness: B.F. MORRIS, C.D. MORRIS. rec 1819. p 133

Deed dated 1819. ARTHUR HENRIE of Hamilton Co, OH to LOUIS BISHOP. Brkv lots 4, 5, sq 3. Signed ARTHUR HENRIE, GRACE M. HENRIE. Witness: I.M. JOHNSON,

FRANKLIN COUNTY DEEDS: Book D

ROBERT JOHN. rec 1819. p 134

Deed dated 1819. WILLIAM H. EADS & JANE, his wife to WILLIAM EVENS. S 3, T 12, R 12E. Signed WILLIAM H. EADS, JANE EADS. Witness: ROBERT JOHN. rec 1819. pp 134, 135

Deed dated 1819. WILLIAM BROWN to WILLIAM WRAY. S 25, T 11, R 1W. Signed WILLIAM BROWN, EVE BROWN. Witness JACOB HUSTON, SAMUEL KINGERY. rec 1819. pp 135, 136

Deed dated 1818. USA to ANDREW JACKSON, assignee of ELLIOT HERNDON. S 6, T 8, R 2W. rec 1819. p 136

Deed dated 1819. WILLIAM H. EADS to JAMES BARBER. Brkv lots 47, 48. Signed WILLIAM H. EADS, JANE EADS Witness: R. TYNER. rec 1819. p 137

Brookville outlot 5 plat map dated 1819. Now laid off into inlots 1, 2, 3, & 4. AMOS BUTLER, prop'r. SOLOMON ALLEN, surveyor. rec 1819. p 138

Deed dated 1819. ARTHUR HERNIE of Hamilton Co, OH to JOHN PLICARD. Brkv lot 6 in square 6. Signed ARTHUR HENRIE, GRACE M. HENRIE. Witness: ROBERT JOHN, N. D. GALLION. rec 1819. pp 138, 138

Deed dated 1818. LEMUEL SNOW to JOSHUA NYE. S 28, T 8, R 1W. Signed LEMUEL SNOW, LYDIA SNOW. Witness: MARY H. SNOW, SALOME SNOW. rec 1819. p 139

Deed dated 1818. JESSE W.L.H. ATKINS to JAMES SCOTT & JAMES NOBLE. S 18, T 13, R 14E. "HARRIET, his wife" Signed JESSE W.L.H. ATKINS, HARRIET ATKINS. Witness: ROBERT SWAN, WILLIAM McGREW. rec 1819. pp 139, 140

Deed dated 1819. ROBERT HANNA JR to JOHN ALLEN SR. S 33 & 28, T 10, R 2W. Signed ROBERT HANNA JR, SALLY HANNA. Witness: ROBERT JOHN, SAM'L. SHIRK. rec 1819 pp 140, 141

Deed dated 1819. STEPHEN MARTIN to JOSEPH D. CLEMENTS. S 11, T 11, R 13. Signed STEPHEN MARTIN, ANNES MARTIN. Witness: WILLIAM SIMS, ELD. WILLIAM WILSON. rec 1819. pp 141, 142

Deed dated 1818. WILLIAM WILSON SR to JOSEPH D. CLEMENTS. S 24, T 10, R 3W. "HANNAH, his wife". Signed Elder WILLIAM WILSON, HANNAH WILSON. Witness: WILLIAM DICKSON, WILLIAM SIMS. rec 1819. pp 142, 143

Deed dated 1819. JOHN MERIUM to JOSEPH D. CLEMENTS.

FRANKLIN COUNTY DEEDS: Book D

S 24, T 11, R 13. Signed JOHN MERIAM. Witness: ROBERT JOHN. rec 1819. pp 143, 144

Deed dated 1819. ARTHUR HENRIE of Hamilton Co, OH to SOLOMON ALLEN. Brkv lot 3 in square 1. Signed ARTHUR HENRIE, GRACE M. HENRIE. Witness: ROBERT JOHN, N. D. GALLION. rec 1819. p 145

Labanon plat map dated 1819. PETER VANDIKE & HENRY GROOBER, prop'rs. SOLOMON ALLEN, surveyor. rec 1819. pp 145, 146

Deed dated 1819. JOHN JACOBS to ROBERT BRACKENRIDGE & JOSEPH BRACKENRIDGE. S 8, T 9, R 2W. "ELIZABETH, his wife". Signed JOHN JACOBS, ELIZABETH JACOBS. Witness: ROBERT JOHN. rec 1819. pp 146, 147

Deed dated 1819. RICHARD W. McMILLAN of Butler Co, OH to ROWLEY McMILLAN SR. S 8, T 10, R 1W. Signed RICHARD W. McMILLAN. Witness: JANE HAMILTON, ROWLEY McMILLAN JR. rec 1819. pp 147, 148

Deed dated 1818. LEVI HOLLINGSWORTH to CARTER HOLLINGSWORTH. S 22, T 11, R 2W. "CHARITY, his wife". Signed LEVI (x) HOLLINGSWORTH, CHARITY (x) HOLLINGSWORTH. Witness: ROBERT SWAN, CHARITY (x) WHITE. rec 1819. pp 148, 149

Deed dated 1819. ROBERT HANNA JR & HERVEY BATES to JOHN PEGG. Brkv lot, no #; bounds given. Signed ROBERT HANNA, SARAH (x) HANNA, HERVEY BATES, SIDNEY BATES. Witness: ROBERT JOHN, ROBERT A. TEMPLETON. rec 1819. pp 149, 150

Deed dated 1819. GEORGE W. KIMBLE to JOHN PEGG. Brkv lot, no #; "half of a Tanyard". Signed G. W. KIMBLE, MARY KIMBLE. Witness: none. rec 1819. pp 150, 151

Deed dated 1819. HENRY TEGARDEN & VALERIAH, his wife of Wayne Co to JACOB A. HINES. S 21, T 12, R 13E. Signed HENRY TEGARDEN, VALERIAH TEGARDEN. Witness: ADAM BANKS, THOMAS BANKS. rec 1819. pp 151, 152

Deed dated 1819. HUGH ABERNATHY to JOSEPH NICHOLAS. Fairfield lot 44. Signed HUGH ABERNATHY, MARY (x) ABERNATHY. Witness: LUDOVICUS BELDING, PETER D. CLINE. rec 1819. p 152

Deed dated 1819. LEWIS DEWESE to ENOCH D. JOHN & NOAH NOBLE. S 4, T 8, R 2W. Signed LEWIS DEWEESE, NANCY(x) DEWEESE. Witness: ROBERT JOHN. rec 1819. pp 152,153

FRANKLIN COUNTY DEEDS: Book D

Deed dated 1819. HENRY WEBSTER of Fayette Co to ELIZABETH HOWARD. Brkv lot 75. Signed HENRY WEBSTER. Witness: HUGH MORRISON, J.A. ELDRED. rec 1819 pp 153,154

Deed dated 1818. JOAB BROOKS to SYLVERRUS WARD. S 9,T 11, R 1W. Signed JOAB BROOKS, HANNAH (x) BROOKS. Witness: ROBERT SWANN, NANCY SWANN. rec 1819. pp 154,155

Deed dated 1819. SAMUEL HOWELL to MARY COPELIN. S 18 T 10, R 1W. Signed SAMUEL HOWELL. Witness: LUDOVIDUS BELDING, JOHN WHITE. rec 1819. pp 155, 156

Deed dated 1819. PETER VANDYKE to CORNELIUS VICLEY of Hamilton Co, OH. S 5, T 9, R 1W. Signed PETER VANDYDK, ADY (x) VANDYKE. Witness: none. rec 1819. pp 156, 157

Deed dated 1819. THOMAS SHERWOOD & CHARLOTTE, his wife, to SAMUEL MOORE of PA. Brkv lot 74. Signed THOMAS SHERWOOD, CHARLOTTE (x) SHERWOOD. Witness: ROBERT JOHN. rec 1819. pp 157, 158

Deed dated 1819. THOMAS SHERWOOD & CHARLOTTE, his wife, to SAMUEL MOORE of PA. Brkv lot 11. Signed THOMAS SHERWOOD, CHARLOTTE (x) SHERWOOD. Witness: ROBERT JOHN. rec 1819. pp 158, 159

Deed dated 1819. GEORGE W. KIMBLE to AMOS W. HARRIS & GEORGE HARRIS. Brkv lot 38. Signed G. W. KIMBLE, MARY KIMBLE. Witness: E.M. MESSICK. rec 1819. pp 159, 160

Mortgage deed no date. JAMES ROSS GILLESPIE of Butler Co, OH to NIMROD BRACKNEY. S 33, T 9, R 1W. JAMES to pay notes given by W. D. JONES to ANN WYNN, by her signed over to GILLESPIE and by him, signed over to BRACKNEY. Debt to be paid by 1821 to void conveyance Signed J.R. GILLESPIE. Witness: ELI JAMES, JP. rec 1819. Margin note: mortgage satisfied, signed NIMROD BRACKNEY, dated 1849. pp 160, 161

Deed dated 1819. JOSEPH D. CLEMENTS to WILLIAM SIMS. S 24, T 10, R 3 & S 11, T 11, R 13. "MARY, his wife". Signed JOSEPH D. CLEMENTS, MARY CLEMENTS. Witness: HUGH MORRISON, JOHN ADAIR. rec 1819. pp 161, 162

POA dated 1818. MARY HUDSON to CORBLY HUDSON. S 18, T 8, R 1W entered by WILLIAM HUDSON. CORBLY to sell land to best advantage, MARY to receive half of money Signed CORBLY HUDSON. Witness: JEREMIAH GOODRICH, MICHAEL SHIRK. rec 1819. p 162

FRANKLIN COUNTY DEEDS: Book D

Deed dated 1819. ARTHUR HENRIE of Hamilton Co, OH to ROBERT ADKINSON. Brkv lot 3 in square 2 & lot 8, sq 6. Signed ARTHUR HENRIE, GRACE M. HENRIE. Witness: ROBERT JOHN, N. D. GALLION. rec 1819. pp 162, 163

Deed dated 1819. JOSEPH D. CLEMENTS to WILLIAM W. WILSON JR. S 11, T 11, R 13. Signed JOSEPH D. CLEMENTS, MARY CLEMENTS. Witness: WILLIAM SIMS, JP & STEPHEN MARTIN. rec 1819. pp 163, 164

Mortgage deed dated 1819. JOHN STIPP JR of Champaign Co, OH to JOHN MILLER. S 26, T ?, R 1W. Debt to be paid in 2 yrs to void conveyance. Signed JOHN STIP JR. Witness: none. rec 1819. p 164, 165

Deed dated 1819. JOHN GOLDTRAP of Hamilton Co, OH to WILLIAM GOLDTRAP of same. S 25, T 9, R 1W. "ANN, his wife". Signed JOHN GOLDTRAP, ANN GOLDTRAP. Witness: JONATHAN PITMAN, EZRA SPENCER. rec 1819. pp 165, 166

Deed dated 1819. ARTHUR HENRIE of Hamilton Co, OH to DANIEL OWENN. Brkv lot 2 in square 5. Signed ARTHUR HENRIE, GRACE M. HENRIE. Witness: ROBERT JOHN, N. D. GALLION. rec 1819. p 166

Mortgage deed dated 1817. EPHRAIM DORTON to MATHEW BROWN of Hamilton Co, OH. S 35, T 11, R 2W. "ANNA, his wife". Debt to be paid in 2 yrs to void conveyance. Signed EPHRAIM DORTON, ANNA DORTON. Witness: ROBERT SWANN. rec 1819. p 167

Deed dated 1819. SAMUEL SERING to URIAH SAMPLE. Brkv lot 76. Signed SAMUEL SERING, ELIZABETH SERING. Witness: ROBERT JOHN, ROBERT BARNARD. rec 1819. p 168

Deed dated 1818. GEORGE JOHNSON to JOHN BLACK. Fairfield lot 85. "SARY, his wife". Signed GEORGE JOHNSON SARAH J. JOHNSON. Witness: JOHN EWING, MARY OSBORN. rec 1819. pp 168, 169

Deed dated 1819. VINCENT COOPER & REBECCA, his wife to WILSON WADOMS. S 21, T 13, R 12. Signed VINCENT COOPER, REBECCA (x) COOPER. Witness: none. rec 1819. pp 169, 170

Mortgage deed dated 1819. JOHN STIP JR of Champaign Co, OH to JOSEPH MARMON. S 20, T 8, R 1W. Debt due in 2 yrs to void conveyance. Signed JOHN STIP JR. Witness: none. rec 1819. pp 170, 171

Deed dated 1819. JOHN BLUE to JACOB GRAUMLICK of Hamilton Co, OH. S 10, T 9, R 1W. "MARGARET, his

FRANKLIN COUNTY DEEDS: Book D

wife". Signed JOHN BLUE, MARGARET (x) BLUE. Witness: ELI JAMES. rec 1819. pp 171, 172

Quitclaim dated 1819. JOHN HARPER to WILLIAM HARPER. S 28, T 8, R 1W. Signed JOHN HARPER. Witness: JAMES HARTPENCE. rec 1819. p 172

Deed dated 1819. BLACKSLEE BARNS of Hartford Co, CT to GIDEON NORTON. S 9, T 9, R 2W. Signed BLACKSLEE BARNS. Witness: DANIEL DUNBAR, SEPHIOS PORTER (in CT) JP's note: ALMIRA BARNS, wife of BLACKSLEE. rec 1819. pp 172, 173

Mortgage deed dated 1819. SAMUEL PREWITT to JACOB ANTHONY. S 35, T 9, R 2W. Debt to be paid by JACOB & by GEORGE ANTHONY by 1821 to void conveyance. Signed SAMUEL (x) PREWITT. Witness: ROBERT JOHN. rec 1819. pp 173, 174, 175

Deed dated 1819. SAMUEL HOWELL to JOHN A. WHITE. S 18, T 10, R 1W. Signed SAMUEL HOWELL. Witness: LUDOVICUS BELDING, JP, LYDIA BELDING. rec 1819. pp 175, 176

Deed dated 1819. ITHAMER WHITE to JOSEPH C. DENNY of Butler Co, OH. S 26, T 9, R 1W. Signed I. A. WHITE. Witness: H.M. CLEHARD, JAMES McCLANE. rec 1819. pp 176, 177

Deed dated 1819. ITHAMER WHITE to ROBERT LUSE & THOMAS MATHEWS, tenants in common. S 26, T 9, R 1W. "his wife MARJORY". Signed I.H. WHITE, no wife's signature. Witness: ELI JAMES, ISAAC WARMSLEY. rec 1819. pp 177, 178

Deed dated 1820. ROBERT HANNA JR to ZOPHAR COLEMAN. Fairfield lots 69, 72. Signed ROBERT HANNA, SALLY (x) HANNA. Witness: none. rec 1820. pp 178, 179

Deed dated 1819. JOHN DUNLAP to JESSE EMERSON. Dunlapsv'l lots 2, 3. Signed JOHN DUNLAP, ELIZABETH DUNLAP. Witness: HENRY H. BRANDENBURG, WILLIAM MANLEY. rec 1820. pp 179, 180

Deed dated 1819. ABRAHAM FINBROOK to JAMES A. PIATT. No S-T-R; bounds "JOHN HALL's land...corner between WILLIAM LINES..on JACOB HACKLEMAN's line". Signed ABRAHAM FINBROOK, CATHARINE FINBROOK. Witness: ROBERT JOHN. rec 1820. pp 180, 181

Deed dated 1819. SARAH SKINNER, heir to estate of ELI SEATTEN, & THOMAS SKINNER, her husband, to EMERY SEATTEN. S 32, T 10, R 2W. Signed SARAH (x) SKINNER.

FRANKLIN COUNTY DEEDS: Book D

THOMAS SKINNER. Witness: ROBERT JOHN. rec 1820. pp 181, 182

Deed dated 1820. JOHN FLINT JR to WILLIAM HENRY EADS Brkv lots 21, 22. "CHARLOTTE, his wife". Signed JOHN FLINT JR, CHARLOTTE FLINT. Witness: R. S. TYNER. rec 1820. pp 182, 183

Deed dated 1819. JOHN PEGG to WILLIAM HENRY EADS. Brkv lot 77. "tanyard which formerly belonged to JER--MIAH CORY". Signed JOHN PEGG, HANNAH G. PEGG. Witness: HUGH MORRISON, JUZAL CORY. rec 1820. pp 183,184

Deed dated 1819. JACOB HOLLINGSWORTH to ISAAC COOK. S 23, T 11, R 2. "MARTHA, his wife". Signed JACOB HOLLINGSWORTH, MARTHA HOLLINGSWORTH. Witness: ROBERT SWANN, REBECCA HENDERSON. rec 1820. pp 184, 185

Deed dated 1819. JAMES HOLLINGSWORTH of Warren Co, OH to ISAAC COOK. S 24, T 11, R 2W. Signed JAMES HOLLINGSWORTH. Witness: EDWARD THOMAS, MARY THOMAS. rec 1820. pp 185, 186

Mortgage deed dated 1820. MICHAEL WHITEMIRE of Hamilton Co, OH to JOHN BLUE. S 10, T 9, R 1W. "said MICHAEL WITMIRE". Debt due by 1830 to void conveyance. Signed MICHAEL WHITEMIRE (german script). Witness: ELI JAMES. no rec date. p 186

Mortgage deed dated 1819. JACOB GROUMLICH of Hamilton Co, OH to JOHN BLUE. S 10, T 9, R 1W. Debt due by 1830 to void conveyance. Signed JACOB GROUMLICH. Witness: none. rec 1820. p 187

Deed dated 1820. JACOB HARTMAN to CHARLES HASSON of Conton Co, PA. Brkv lot 59. "RUTH, his wife". Signed JACOB HARTMAN, RUTH (x) HARTMAN. Witness: ROBERT JOHN, REUBEN BRACKNEY. rec 1820. pp 187, 188

Deed dated 1818. JAMES WILLSON to THOMAS TERRIL. Fairfield lot 20. Signed JAMES WILLSON, NANCY WILLSON Witness: JOHN EWING, JP & WILLIAM WILLSON. rec 1820. pp 188, 189

Deed dated 1820. STEPHEN RHODS to CLARK WHEELER. S 18, T 9, R 1W. Signed STEPHEN ROADS. Witness: ELI JAMES. rec 1820. p 189

Deed dated 1820. JOHN MILLAR to JESSE EMERSON & WILLIAM C. DREW. Fairfield lot 30. Signed JOHN MILLAR, ELIZABETH MILLAR. Witness: MARGARET THOMPSON. JOHN EWING. rec 1820. p 190

FRANKLIN COUNTY DEEDS: Book D

Deed dated 1819. REUBEN R. PENWELL to JOSEPH WINSHIP. Brkv lot 17. "SALLY, his wife". Signed REUBEN R. PENWELL, SALLY PENWELL. Witness: none. rec 1820. pp 190, 191

Deed dated 1818. JOHN ALLEN SR to GURNSEY G. BROWN. Brkv lot 11. Signed JOHN ALLEN SR, POLLY ALLEN. Witness: ROBERT JOHN. rec 1820. pp 191, 192

Deed dated 1820. ENOCH D. JOHN to SAMUEL JONES. Brkv lot 81. Signed ENOCH D. JOHN. Witness: ROBERT JOHN, J.D. MOORE. rec 1820. pp 192, 193

Deed dated 1819. STOPHEL WITTER to WILLIAM BROWN. S 25, T 11, R 1W. Signed STOPHEL WITTER (german) Witness: SAMUEL HUSTON, SAMUEL BELL. rec 1820 pp 193,194

Deed dated 1817. JONATHAN PITMAN of Hamilton Co, OH to SAMUEL TUCKER. S 35, T 10, R 1W. Signed JONATHAN PITTMAN, REBECCA (x) PITTMAN. Witness: JOHN McGILLIARD, ARTHUR COFFEND. rec 1820. pp 194, 195

Deed dated 1819. CHARLES B. FINCH to ALEXANDER GARDNER. Brkv lot, no #. "ISABELLA, his wife". Signed C. B. FINCH, ISABELLA (x) FINCH. Witness: ROBERT JOHN, ISAAC G. JOHN. rec 1820. pp 195, 196

Deed dated 1819. THOMAS HENDERSON to ALEXANDER GARDNER. S 33, T 9, R 2W. Signed THOMAS HENDERSON. Witness: ROBERT JOHN, WILLIAM C. DREW. rec 1820. p 196

POA dated 1820. LEONARD SAILORS of White Co, TN apptd ELIJAH ELMORE of the same to convey land title to HENRY CASE, TYRE GLEANTT & HENRY LYONS, collect money due from sale. Signed LEONARD SAYLORS. Witness none. rec 1820. p 197 (first page of that number)

Deed dated 1819. ROBERT GLIDEWELL to THOMAS CHESNEY. Fairfield lot 117. Signed ROBERT GLIDEWELL, SARAH (x) GLIDEWELL. Witness: JOHN EWING, JP & REBECCA EWING. rec 1820. pp 197, 197 (2 pages of same number)

Deed dated 1819. THOMAS OSBORN to THOMAS CHESNEY. Fairfield lots 78, 80. Signed THOMAS OSBORN, MARY OSBORN. Witness: JOHN EWING, JP & REBECCA EWING. rec 1820. pp 197 (2d page of that #), 198

Deed dated 1820. THOMAS CHESNEY to CHARLES SHIRER. Fairfield lots 78, 80. "HANNAH, his wife". Signed THOS. CHESNEY, HANNAH CHESNEY. Witness: JOHN HANNAH, BENNETT MICHAEL. rec 1820. pp 198, 199

FRANKLIN COUNTY DEEDS: Book D

Deed dated 1819. PERCY KITCHEL to JAMES JONES. S 6. T 11, R 13E. Signed PIERCY KITCHEL. Witness: WILLIAM C. JONES. rec 1820. p 199

Deed dated 1819. JAMES WILSON to JESSE EMERSON. Fairfield lot 23. Signed J. S. WILSON, NANCY WILSON. Witness: WILLIAM WILSON, JOHN EWING. rec 1820. p 200

Deed dated 1818. AMOS BUTLER of Jefferson Co to ENOCH McCARTY, WILLIAM C. DREW & ROBERT BRACKENRIDGE. S 29, T 9, R 2W. Signed AMOS BUTLER, MARY BUTLER. Witness: none. rec 1820. pp 200, 201, 202

Deed dated 1819. WILLIAM S. ROSE to WILLIAM C. DREW & JESSE EMERSON. Fairfield lot 58. Signed WILLIAM S. ROSE, REBECKAH (x) ROSE. Witness: WILLIAM POPENS, JOHN HANNA. rec 1820. p 202

Deed dated 1820. JOHN SCOT to WILLIAM C. DREW & DANIEL J. CASWELL. Brkv lot 8. "JANE, his wife". Signed JOHN SCOTT, JANE SCOTT. Witness: ROBERT JOHN. rec 1820. pp 202, 203

Deed dated 1820. WILLIAM C. DREW to JOSEPH CANBY of Warren Co, OH. Brkv lot 17. Signed WILLIAM C. DREW. Witness: B.F. MORRIS. rec 1820. pp 203, 204

Sheriff's sale dated 1819. ROBERT HANNA, Sheriff of Franklin Co to ENOCH D. JOHN & WILLIAM C. DREW. Property of JAMES McGINNIS seized for debt; suit brought by NATHAN D. GALION. Brkv lot 34 sold at auction to JOHN & DREW. Signed ROBERT HANNA, Sheriff. Witness: none. rec 1820. pp 204, 205

Sheriff's sale dated 1819. ROBERT HANNA, Sheriff of Franklin Co to JEREMIAH SCHOONOVER. Property of AZOR STURDEVANT seized for debt; suit brought by SCHOONOVER & Att'y DICKETT. S 11, T 8, R 2 sold at auction to SCHOONOVER. Signed ROBERT HANNA, Sheriff. Witness: none. rec 1820. pp 206, 207

Deed dated 1820. JOHN PEGG to JOHN DAVIS. S 3 & 10, T 9, R 2W. Signed JOHN PEGG, HANNAH G. PEGG. Witness ROBERT JOHN, SOLLOMON ALLEN. rec 1820. pp 207, 208

Deed dated 1819. JOHN ARNOLD to ANDREW S. BABBITT. S 10, T 12, R 12W*. Signed JOHN ARNOLD, DRUSILLA ARNOLD Witness: WILLIAM ARNOLD, JAMES EAGANS. rec 1820. pp 208, 209   *if W is correct, then in Illinois.

Deed dated 1818. LUTHER RUSSLE to B.F. MORRIS. Brkv lot 87. Signed LUTHER RUSSELL. Witness: ROBERT JOHN,

FRANKLIN COUNTY DEEDS: Book D

HARRISON J. ROBINSON. rec 1820. p 209

Deed dated 1815. JAMES REID to THOMAS COOK. S 24, T 11, R 2W. Signed JAMES REID, ANN REID. Witness: EBENEZER HOWE, WILLIAM NORRIS. rec 1820. pp 209, 210

Deed dated 1820. WILLIAM SIMS JR to DAVID MORRIS. S 2, T 11, R 13E. "ELIZABETH, his wife". Signed WILLIAM SIMS, ELIZABETH (x) SIMS. Witness: B.F. MORRIS. rec 1820. pp 210, 211

Deed dated 1819. GEORGE ANTHONY to HENRY ANTHONY. S 35, T 9, R 2W. Signed GEORGE ANTHONY, CATHARINE (x) ANTHONY. Witness: none. rec 1820. pp 211, 212

Deed dated 1819. BENJAMIN SCHOONOVER to JAMES DOTY. S 13, T 8, R 2W. "LYDIA, his wife". Signed BENJAMIN (x) SCHOONOVER, LYDIA SCHOONOVER. Witness: none. rec rec 1820. pp 212, 213

Mortgage deed dated 1816. WILLIAM G. TODD of Hamilton Co, OH to JOHN VANBLARICUM. S 29, T 8, R 1W. Debt to be paid by 1821 to void conveyance. Signed WILLIAM G. TODD. Witness: JOHN HARPER. rec 1820. pp 213, 214

Deed dated 1819. THOMAS OSBORN to URIAH ROSE. Fairfield lot 59. Signed THOMAS OSBORN, MARY OSBORN. Witness: JESSE EMERSON, JOHN EWING. rec 1820. p 214

Deed dated 1819. ADOLPHUS GULLY to BENJAMIN LEWIS. S 28, T 8, R 1W. Signed ADOLPHUS GULLEY, HARRIET GULLEY. Witness: B. GULLEY, WILLIAM GULLEY (in Dearborn Co). rec 1820. pp 215, 216

Deed dated 1819. JOHN DUNLAP to ROBERT S. NORRIS. Dunlapsv'l lot 43. Signed JOHN DUNLAP, ELIZABETH DUNLAP. Witness: J.W. SCOTT, JOHN KINTON. rec 1820. p216

Deed dated 1819. ARTHUR HENRIE of Hamilton Co, OH to MICHAEL WHITEHEAD of same. Brkv lot 13, square 5. Signed ARTHUR HENRIE, GRACE M. HENRIE. Witness: ROBERT JOHN, N. D. GALLION. rec 1820. p 217

Deed dated 1819. ARTHUR HENRIE of Hamilton Co, OH to ISAAC VANTRUSE of same. Brkv lot 12, square 5. Signed ARTHUR HENRIE, GRACE M. HENRIE. Witness: ROBERT JOHN, N. D. GALLION. rec 1820. pp 217, 218

Deed dated 1819. JOHN DUNLAP to JOHN HANNA. Dunlapsville lots 40, 41, 47. Signed JOHN DUNLAP, ELIZABETH DUNLAP. Witness: JOHN HANNA, JOHN KINTON. rec 1820. pp 219, 220

FRANKLIN COUNTY DEEDS: Book D

Deed dated 1819. ABRAHAM BURKHALTER to JAMES TANNER. S 2, T 11, R 2W. "ELIZABETH, his wife". Signed ABRAHAM (x) BURKHALTER. ELIZABETH (x) BURKHALTER. Witness THOMAS CULLY, JAMES ARMSTRONG. rec 1820. pp 220, 221

Deed dated 1820. DAVID HANSEL to ROBERT WHITE. S 24, T 10, R 1W. Signed DAVID (x) HANSEL. Witness: JOHN HANNA, ROBERT GLIDEWELL. rec 1820. pp 221, 222

Deed dated 1819. JOHN DUNLAP to ISAAC MOSS of Butler Co, OH. Dunlapsv'l lot 4. Signed JOHN DUNLAP, ELIZABETH DUNLAP. Witness: J.W. SCOTT, JOHN KINTON. rec 1820. pp 222, 223

Deed dated 1819. THOMAS GREEN of Franklin Co & WILLIAM HARLOW of Hamilton Co, OH to ANDREW WALLACE. S 28, T 9, R 2W. "to JOHN TEST's land". Signed THOMAS GREEN, WM. HARLOW. Witness: WILLIAM C. DREW. rec 1820. pp 223, 224

Deed dated 1819. THOMAS GREEN of Franklin Co & WILLIAM HARLOW of Hamilton Co, OH to ANDREW WALLACE. S 28, T 9, R 2W. Signed THOMAS GREEN, WM. HARLOW. Witness: WILLIAM C. DREW. rec 1820. pp 224, 225

Deed dated 1819. THOMAS GREEN of Franklin Co & WILLIAM HARLOW of Hamilton Co, OH to ANDREW WALLACE. S 28, T 9, R 2W. Signed THOMAS GREEN, WM. HARLOW. Witness: WILLIAM C. DREW. rec 1820. pp 225, 226

Deed dated 1819. THOMAS GREEN of Franklin Co & WILLIAM HARLOW of Hamilton Co, OH to ANDREW WALLACE. S 29, T 9, R 2W. Signed THOMAS GREEN, WM. HARLOW. Witness: WILLIAM C. DREW. rec 1820. pp 226, 227

Deed dated 1819. JOSHUA HARRIS to DEMEE TRUSTEE. S 27, T 10, R 1W. "money to ..HARRIS & to JOHN PIERCE" "RACHEL, his wife". Signed JOSHUA (x) HARRIS, RACHEL (x) HARRIS. Witness: SAMUEL ELWELL, JP & ISAAC ELWELL rec 1820. p 227

Deed dated 1819. GEORGE JELLARD of Dearborn Co to JEWELL* DAIGE CATER of same. S 34, T 8, R 1W. Signed GEORGE JELLARD. Witness: JOHN W. CALDWELL (in Dearborn). rec 1820. p 228 *JUEL in text; perhaps should have been JOEL?

Deed dated 1820. JAMES PECK of Cincinnati, OH to REBECCA PECK of Newhaven, CT. S 24, T 6, R 1W. "ANN, his wife". Signed JAMES PECK, ANN PECK. Witness: DANIEL ROE, C.T. BOSSON (in OH). rec 1820. pp 229, 230

FRANKLIN COUNTY DEEDS: Book D

Deed dated 1818. EDMOND HAMMAND to MALCOLM ANARE of Liberty Twp. Butler Co. OH. S 10, T 8. R 1W. Signed EDWARD HAYMOND. Witness: JOHN HAYMOND. JAMES A. LOWES rec 1820. p 230

Deed dated 1817. MARQUES D. MISNER of Butler Co. OH to DAVID LAROWE of Hamilton Co, OH. S 11, T 8, R 1W. "MILLY, his wife". Signed DENMARQ VIS MISNER, MILLY MISNER. Witness: H. MAY, JAMES A. LOWES. rec 1820. p 231

Sheriff's sale dated 1819. ROBERT HANNA, Sheriff of Franklin Co, to JOHN ROOP. Property of DAVID OLIVER & JOSEPH MOFFIT seized; suit brought by JOHN ALLEN SR Brkv outlot 12 in S 18, T 9. R 2 as laid out bv JOHN HARRIS. Sold at auction to ROOP. Signed ROBERT HANNA Sheriff. Witness: none. rec 1820. pp 231. 232

Deed dated 1819. JOHN LEWIS to NIMROD BRACKNEY. S29 T 9, R 1W. Signed JOHN LEWIS, POLLY LEWIS. Witness: ELI JAMES. rec 1820. pp 232. 233

Mortgage deed dated 1820. STEPHEN DAVIS to JOHN C. POUND of Hamilton Co, OH. S 32. T 9, R 1W. Debt due in 2 yrs to void conveyance. Signed STEPHEN DAVIS Witness: none. rec 1820. p 233

Deed dated 1820. HERVEY BATES to WILLIAM C. DREW. Brkv lot 32. Signed HERVEY BATES, SIDNEY BATES. Witness: D.E. ALLEN, ROBERT JOHN. rec 1820. pp 234,23

Deed dated 1817. WILLIAM H. EADS to JOHN PEGG. Brkv lot 32. Signed WILLIAM H. EADS, JANE EADS. Witness: ROBERT JOHN. rec 1818. pp 229. 230

Deed dated 1819. JOSEPH HOLLINGSWORTH of Butler Co. to (JOHN) HAYWORTH. S 27, T 11. R 2W. "HANNAH, his wife". Signed JOSEPH HOLLINGSWORTH. HANNAH HOLLINGSWORTH. Witness: HENRY H. BRANDENBURG. ROBERT SWAN. rec 1820. pp 234, 235

Deed dated 1818. JAMES WILSON to LUDOVICUS BELDING. Fairfield lot 35. Signed JAMES WILSON, NANCY WILSON. Witness: JOHN EWING. WILLIAM WILSON. rec 1820. pp 235 236

Deed dated 1819. HUGH ABERNATHY to JONATHAN BASSETT. S 21, T 10, R 2W. Signed HUGH ABERNATHY, MARY ABERNATHY. Witness: JOHN HANNA, ROBERT RUSING. rec 1820. pp 236, 237

Deed dated 1819. HUGH ABERNATHY to JONATHAN BASSETT.

FRANKLIN COUNTY DEEDS: Book D

S 21, T 10, R 2W.   Signed HUGH ABERNATHY, MARY (x) ABERNATHY. Witness: ROBERT DAVE, THOMAS ABERNATHY. rec 1820. pp 237, 238

Deed dated 1820. AMOS BUTLER of Jefferson Co to JOHN JACOBS & ENOCH D. JOHN. Brkv lots 18, 19. Signed AMOS BUTLER, MARY BUTLER. Witness: none. rec 1820. pp 238, 239

Deed dated 1820. DAVID POWERS of Butler Co, OH to GEORGE POWERS of same. S 23, T 10, R 2W. "SARAH, his wife". Signed DAVID POWERS, SARAH POWERS. Witness: JAMES HEATON, WILLARD M. SMITH. rec 1820. pp 239, 240

Deed dated 1820. RYALE SIMMONS & REBECCA, his wife to SAMUEL HOWELL. S 19, T ?, R 1W. "to JOHN FLINT's corner..at BENJAMIN FLOOD's corner". Signed RYALE (x) SIMMONS, REBECCA (x) SIMMONS. Witness: SAMUEL ELWELL ELIZABETH (x) ELWELL.   rec 1820. pp 240, 241

Deed dated 1819. ADAM C. REYBURN & ALSA, his wife of Fayette Co, KY to JACOB D. WILLIAMSON of Hamilton Co, OH.   S 31, T 10, R 1W. Signed ADAM C. REYBURN, ELSEY (x) REYBURN. Witness: J.C. RODES, JOHN SHAFOR (in KY) rec 1820. pp 241, 242

Deed dated 1818. BENEJAH RICE of Boon Co, KY to FREDERIC HARTMAN. S 19, T 9, R 2W. Signed BENEJAH RICE. Witness: WILLIAM C. DREW, JOHN STINSON. rec 1820. pp 242, 243

Deed dated 1819. WILLIAM HENDERSON to FREDERIC HARTMAN. S 33, T 9, R 2W. Signed WILLIAM M. HENDERSON, ZILPHA (x) HENDERSON. Witness: ROBERT JOHN, A. GARDNER. rec 1820. pp 243, 244

Deed dated 1820.   JAMES TONER to URBAN EDGERTON & CHARLES FOSDICK.   Somerset lot 8. Signed JAMES TONER, JANE (x) TONER. Witness: JAMES EGANS, JOHN ROGERS. rec 1820. pp 244, 245

Deed dated 1819. HENRY WEBSTER of Fayette Co to SAMUEL LEWIS. Brkv lot 26. "REBECCA, his wife". Signed HENRY WEBSTER, REBECCA (x) WEBSTER. Witness: WILLIAM C. DREW, FIELDING HAZLERIGG, JP. rec 1820. pp 245,246

Deed dated 1818. WILLIAM BRADLEY & REBECCA, his wife, to JOHN LATOURETTE. Brkv lot 43. Signed WILLIAM BRADLEY, REBECCA (x) BRADLEY. Witness: THOMAS BRADLEY, ROBERT JOHN. rec 1820. pp 246, 247

FRANKLIN COUNTY DEEDS: Book D

Deed dated 1818. JAMES ADAIR JR of Connersville to JOHN ADAIR of Brkv. S 25, T 14, R 12. "POLLY, his wife". Signed JAMES ADAIR JUN., POLLY (x) ADAIR. Witness: HUGH MORRISON, CHARLES ROBISON. rec 1820. pp 247, 248

Deed dated 1820. WILLIAM C. DREW to DAVID ALLEN. Brkv lots 67, 68. "MARY, his wife". Signed WILLIAM C. DREW, MARY G. DREW. Witness: ROBERT JOHN, ELIZA ARMSTRONG. rec 1820. p 248

Sheriff's sale dated 1819. ROBERT HANNA, Sheriff of Franklin Co. Suit brought by JOHN ALLEN against DAVID OLIVER. Brkv lot 48 seize, sold at auction to ABNER McCARTY & JAMES SCOTT. rec 1820. p 249

Deed dated 1820. ROBERT TEMPLETON to DAVID TEMPLETON S 4, T 9, R 2W. Signed ROBERT TEMPLETON, MARY (x) TEMPLETON. Witness: WILLIAM TEMPLETON, JAMES TEMPLETON. rec 1820. p 250

Deed dated 1820. WILLIAM BROWN to SAMUEL KINGERY. S 25, T 11, R 1W. Signed WILLIAM BROWN, EVE (x) BROWN. Witness: JANE HAMILTON, NANCY B. HAMILTON. rec 1820. pp 250, 251

Deed dated 1819. JAMES WILSON to ABRAHAM LOWDABACK. Fairfield lot, no #. Signed JAMES WILSON, NANCY WILSON. Witness: JOHNI SHERIR, BENJAMIN WILSON. rec 1820. pp 251, 252

Deed dated 1820. GEORGE W. KIMBLE to THOMAS W. COLESCOTT. Brkv lot 38. Signed GEORGE W. KIMBLE, MARY KIMBLE. Witness: ROBERT JOHN. rec 1820. pp 253, 254

Deed dated 1819. THOMAS GREEN, Merchant now of Cincinnati, OH to JESSE EMBREE of same. Brkv lot 71, 72, 40, 41. Signed THOMAS GREENE. Witness: ROBERT JOHN, ASENATH JOHN. rec 1820. pp 254, 255

Deed dated 1820. WILLIAM HARLOW of Cincinnati, OH & MARY, his wife, to JESSE EMBREE of same. Brkv outlot 2. Signed WM. HARLOW, MARY HARLOW. Witness: JONAS HARLOW, ISAAC G. BURNET (in OH). rec 1820. pp 255, 256

Deed dated 1820. JONATHAN BASSETT to JAMES LOPER. Fairfield lot, no #. Signed JONATHAN BASSETT. Witness: JOHN HANNA, JAMES LOPER SR. rec 1820. pp 256, 257

Deed dated 1820. HERVEY BATES of Fayette Co to JOHN JACOBS. Brkv lot 33. Signed HERVEY BATES, SIDNEY

FRANKLIN COUNTY DEEDS: Book D

BATES. Witness: FIELDING HAZLERIGG, JP & JAMES B. COLESCOTT. rec 1820. pp 257, 258

Deed dated 1820. NATHAN GARRETT & CASSEY, his wife, to RYALS SIMMONS. S 19, T ?, R 1W. "to JOHN DUNN's corner". Signed NATHAN GARRETT, CASSEY GARRETT. Witness: SAMUEL ELWELL, JP & THOMAS FLINT. rec 1820. pp 258, 259

Mortgage deed dated 1820. JOSEPH SCHOONOVER to WILLIAM METCALFE. S 13, T 8, R 2W. Debt to be paid in 1821 or land sold at public auction. Signed JOSEPH SCHOONOVER. Witness: B.F. MORRIS, WILLIAM H. EADS. rec 1820. pp 259, 260 Note: mortgage satisfied, signed WILLIAM METCALFE, dated 1823

Sheriff sale dated 1818. ROBERT HANNA, Sheriff of Franklin Co to JOSEPH EVANS. Court ordered levy on S 17, T 11, R 1W & New Washington town lots 6, 7, 8, 12, 13, 14, 22, 23, 24, 26 to settle debts of THOMAS MADDEN & RUTH, his wife, to JOSEPH EVANS. Land sold at auction to EVANS, the highest bidder. Signed ROBERT HANNA. Witness: none. rec 1818. pp 260, 261

Deed dated 1820. JOHN FLINT to NATHAN GARRETT. S 19, T 10, R1W. Signed JOHN FLINT. Witness: SAMUEL ELWELL THOMAS FLINT. rec 1820. pp 262

Deed dated 1820. JOSEPH SCHOONOVER to JOHN WARD. S 13, T 8, R 2W. Signed JOSEPH SCHOONOVER. Witness: WARD DAVIS, B.F. MORRIS. rec 1820. pp 262, 263

Deed dated 1819. JOSEPH EVANS & RACHEL, his wife, to BENJAMIN PADDOCK. S 17, T 11, R 1W: lots in New Washington. (see HANNA to EVANS above). Signed JOSEPH EVANS, RACHEL EVANS. Witness: ROBERT F. EVANS, JOHN MAHARD (in OH). rec 1820. pp 263, 264

Deed dated 1819. ARTHUR HENRIE of Hamilton Co, OH to WILLIAM McCOMBS. Brkv lot 4, square 2. Signed ARTHUR HENRIE, GRACE M. HENRIE. Witness: ROBERT JOHN, N.D. GALLION. rec 1820. pp 264, 265

Deed dated 1819. JOHN DUNLAP to HUGH McCULLOUGH of Fayette Co. Dunlapsv'l lot 16. Signed JOHN DUNLAP, ELIZABETH DUNLAP. Witness: J.W. LION, JOSEPH VERNON. rec 1820. pp 265, 266

Deed dated 1819. JOHN DUNLAP to JOSEPH VERNON of Fayette Co. Dunlapsv'l lot 48. Signed JOHN DUNLAP, ELIZABETH DUNLAP. Witness: J.W. SCOTT, ROBERT SWANN. rec 1820. p 266

FRANKLIN COUNTY DEEDS: Book D

Deed dated 1820. JOHN JACOBS to WILLIAM H. EADS. Brkv lot 9. "ELIZABETH, his wife". Signed JOHN JACOBS, ELIZABETH JACOBS. Witness: ROBERT JOHN. rec 1820. p 267

Deed dated 1819. JAMES CONWELL from JOHN WILLIAMS & SARAH, his wife, of Fayette Co. S 11, T 8, R 1W. Signed JOHN WILLIAMS, SARAH (x) WILLIAMS. Witness: none. rec 1820. pp 267, 268

Deed dated 1819. ISAAC HASTINGS to LEWIS BISHOP & WILLIAM BUNYARD, Trustees of West Fork Baptist Society. No S-T-R; bounds on West Fork of the Whitewater River. Signed ISAAC HASTINGS, MARTHA (x) HASTINGS. Witness: ROBERT JOHN. rec 1820. pp 269, 270

Deed dated 1820. WILLIAM H. EADS & THOMAS C. EADS of Dearborn Co to JACOB DUBOIS. Fairfield lots 105, 111, 112. Signed WILLIAM H. EADS, JANE EADS, THOMAS C. EADS. Witness: ROBERT JOHN. rec 1820. pp 270, 271

Deed dated 1820. THOMAS SACKET to JACOB DUBOIS. S 2, T 10, R 2W.) Signed THOMAS SACKET, MARGARY (x) SACKET. Witness: CHRISTOPHER MOSTELLER, JOHN EWING. rec 1820. p 271

Deed dated 1820. GEORGE KEFFER to LEONARD COFFMAN. S 26, T 11, R 1W. Signed GEORGE KEFFER, EVE (x) KEFFER Witness: JOHN PATTERSON, JANE HAMILTON. rec 1820. pp 271, 272

Deed dated 1818. JACOB BELL of Butler Co, Oh & SARAH his wife to WILLIAM BRADY. S 23, T 10, R 1W. Signed JACOB BELL, SARAH (x) BELL. Witness: ROBERT BROWAY, JOSEPH BRADY. rec 1820. pp 272, 273

Deed dated 1820. FRANCIS McCLELLAND to SAMUEL RIDENOUR of Preble Co, OH. S 2, T 10, R 1W. Signed FRANCIS McCLELLAND, ANN McCLELLAND. Witness: JANE HAMILTON, NANCY B. HAMILTON. rec 1820. pp 273, 274

Deed dated 1816. JAMES A. PIATT to ENOCH D. JOHN & NOAH NOBLE. Brkv lot 37. Signed JAMES A. PIATT, JEMIMA PIATT. Witness: EDMUND HARRISON. rec 1820. pp 274, 275

Deed dated 1820. JOHN VOORHIS to CORNELIUS SIMONSON. S 27, T 9, R 1W. Signed JOHN VOORHEIS. Witness: ROBERT LUSE, ISAAC CLARK. rec 1820. pp 275, 276

Deed dated 1820. JOHN MACCANNON to BENJAMIN LEWIS. S 9, T 8, R 1W. "ELENOR, wife of JOHN". Signed JOHN

FRANKLIN COUNTY DEEDS: Book D

(x) MACCANNON, ELENOR (x) MACCANNON.
Witness: JOHN STIPP, H. MAY. rec 1820. pp 276, 277

Deed dated 1819. USA to BENJAMIN LEWIS. S 34, T 8, R 1W. rec 1820. p 277

Deed dated 1819. SAMUEL KINGERY to SAMUEL McDILL. S 34, T 11, R 1W. "SARAH, his wife". Signed SAMUEL KINGERY, SARAH (x) KINGERY. Witness: JANE HAMILTON, NANCY B. HAMILTON. rec 1820. pp 277, 278

Deed dated 1819. HUGH ABERNATHY to ISAAC BULKREY. Fairfield lot 42. Signed HUGH ABERNATHY, MARY (x) ABERNATHY. Witness: none. rec 1820. p 279

Deed dated 1820. ABNER McCARTY & JAMES SCOTT to WILLIAM H. EADS. Brkv 45. Signed ABNER McCARTY, JAMES SCOTT. Witness: ROBERT JOHN. rec 1820. pp 279, 280

Deed dated 1820. AMOS BUTLER of Jefferson Co, to WILLIAM H. EADS. Brkv lots 26, 21, 23. Signed AMOS BUTLER, MARY BUTLER. Witness: none. rec 1820. pp 280, 281

Deed dated 1820. AMOS BUTLER of Jefferson Co, to WILLIAM H. EADS. Brkv lots 3, 6. Signed AMOS BUTLER, MARY BUTLER. Witness: none. rec 1820. pp 281, 290 (page numbers 282 through 289 skipped by clerks)

Deed dated 1819. MARY KNIGHT, Admr of estate of JAMES KNIGHT, dec, to WILLIAM McCLURY, late of Frederickstown, MD. Brkv lots 11, 8, 7, 2, 26, 25, 46, 45 sold at auction. Signed MARY KNIGHT. Witness: ROBERT JOHN, JOHN JAMES. rec 1820. pp 290, 291, 292

Deed dated 1819. MARY KNIGHT as above to WILLIAM McCLURY as above. Brkv lots 66, 5, 6, 9, 2. Signed MARY KNIGHT. Witness: ROBERT JOHN, JOHN JAMES. rec 1820. pp 292, 293, 294, 295

Deed dated 1819. WILLIAM McCLURY as above to MARY KNIGHT. Brkv lots 11, 8, 7, 1, 2, 25, 26, 45, 46, 66, 5, 6, 9, 1, 2, 23, 24 and 2 lots, no # given. "ELENOR wife of WILLIAM". Signed WILLIAM McCLURY, ELEANOR McCLURY. Witness: ROBERT JOHN, JOHN JAMES. rec 1820. pp 295, 296

Deed dated 1820. MARY KNIGHT as above to WILLIAM McCLEARY. Brkv lots 26, 27. Signed MARY KNIGHT. Witness: ROBERT JOHN, WILLIAM H. EADS. rec 1820. p 296

Deed dated 1819. JOHN JAMES of Dearborn Co to ELEANOR McCLURY, dau of JAMES KNIGHT, dec. S 17, T 9, R

FRANKLIN COUNTY DEEDS: Book D

2W. Signed JOHN JAMES, MARTHA JAMES. Witness: B. JAMES, JOEL DECAUNEY. rec 1820. pp 296, 297

Deed dated 1820. MARTIN M. RAY & JAMES B. RAY to WILLIAM NOBLE of Hamilton Co, OH. S 33, T 10, R 2W. "MARY, wife of JAMES". Signed MARTIN M. RAY, JAMES B. RAY, MARY RAY. Witness: HUGH MORRISON, W.R. MORRIS. rec 1820. pp 298, 299

Deed dated 1819. THOMAS POWERS to MARTIN M. RAY & JAMES B. RAY. S 33, T 10, R 2W. "MARY, his wife". Signed THOMAS POWERS, MARY POWERS. Witness: HUGH MORRISON, WILLIAM McCLURY. rec 1820. pp 299, 300

Deed dated 1819. ROBERT HANNA JR & JOHN NUGENT to ANDREW RAY. S 32, T 10, R 2W. Signed: ROBERT HANNA, SALLY (x) HANNA, JOHN NUGENT, ELIZABETH (x) NUGENT. Witness: ELIZABETH ANNE HANNA, JOHN HANNA. rec 1820. pp 300, 301

Deed dated 1820. WILLIAM HARPER to GEORGE TODD, SR of NJ. S 28, T 8, R 1W. "ELIZABETH, wife of WILLIAM" Signed WILLIAM HARPER, ELIZABETH (x) HARPER. Witness: GEORGE RUDISEL, JOSEPH BENNETT. rec 1820. pp 301, 302

Deed dated 1819. JAMES BRISON to JAMES NICKLES. S 21, T 11, R 2W. Signed JAMES BRISON, MARY BRISON. Witness: JAMES NICKLES, SR, ROBERT SWANN. rec 1820. pp 302, 303

Deed dated 1820. LEVI MEAD & MARY ANN, his wife,to LUTHER LEONARD. S 20, T 11, R 1W. Signed LEVI MEAD, MARY ANN MEAD. Witness: E. BURNSIDE. rec 1820. pp 303, 304

Deed dated 1819. JAMES BRYSON to WILLIAM NICKLES. S 21, T 11, R 2W. Signed JAMES BRYSON, MARY BRYSON. Witness: JAMES NICKLES, ROBERT SWANN. rec 1820. pp 304, 305

Deed dated 1819. JOHN DUNLAP to JAMES NICKLES SR. Dunlapsv'l lot 60. Signed JOHN DUNLAP, ELIZABETH DUNLAP. Witness: JAMES W. SCOTT, JOHN ISRAEL. rec 1820. pp 305, 306

Deed dated 1819. JOHN NUGENT to GEORGE W. CRIST. Fairfield lot 50. Signed JOHN NUGENT, ELIZABETH (x) NUGENT. Witness: JOHN HANNA, MARY (x) HANNA. rec 1820. pp 306, 307

Partition deed dated 1820. DANIEL ELLIOTT to ROBERT ELLIOT. S 12, T 11, R 1W. DANIEL to have north half,

FRANKLIN COUNTY DEEDS: Book D

ROBERT the south. "PEGGY, wife of DANIEL & BETSEY, wife of ROBERT". Signed ROBERT ELLIOTT, BETSEY ELLIOT, DANIEL ELLIOT, PEGGY ELLIOT. Witness: JOHN PINKERTON, HUGH LESLIE. rec 1820. pp 307, 308

Deed dated 1820. JOHN PENTICOST JR to JOHN PENTACOST SR. S 1, T 11, R 1W. Signed JOHN PENTECOST. Witness JANE HAMILTON, NANCY B. HAMILTON. rec 1820 pp 308,309

Deed dated 1819. GEORGE JOHNSON to ROBERT DARE. Fairfield lots 83, 86. Signed GEORGE JOHNSON, SARAH JOHNSON. Witness: JOHN HANNA, JONATHAN BASSETT. rec 1820. pp 309, 310

Deed dated 1818. WILLIAM HARPER to GEORGE TODD SR of NJ. S 28, T 8, R 1W. Signed WILLIAM HARPER (german script), ELIZABETH (x) HARPER. Witness: EDWARD BURRELL. rec 1820. pp 310, 311

Deed dated 1820. MARY KNIGHT, Admr of estate of JAMES KNIGHT, to WILLIAM McCLEERY. Brkv lots 23, 24. Signed MARY KNIGHT. Witness: ROBERT JOHN, WILLIAM H. EADS. rec 1820. pp 311, 312, 313

Deed dated 1820. WILLIAM McCLEERY to MARY KNIGHT. Brkv lots 23, 24. Signed WILLIAM McCLEERY, ELEANOR McCLEERY. Witness: ROBERT JOHN, WILLIAM H. EADS. rec 1820. pp 313, 314

Deed dated 1819. PETER VANDYKE to WILLIAM HETRICK. Lebanon lot 10. Signed PETER VANDYKE, ADY VANDYKE. Witness: none. rec 1820. pp 314, 315

Deed dated 1819. PETER VANDYKE to WILLIAM HETRICK. Lebanon lots 1, 2, 3. Signed PETER VANDYKE, ADY VANDYKE. Witness: none. rec 1820. pp 315, 316

Deed dated 1820. ELI STRINGER to OBADIAH EASTES. S 27, T 13, R 13E. "PEGGY, his wife". Signed ELI STRINGER, PEGGY (x) STRINGER. Witness: ROBERT JOHN, ROBERT HOBBS. rec 1820. pp 316, 317

Deed dated 1819. FREDERICK HARTMAN to BENJAMIN CHILDERS. S 33, T 9, R 2W. Signed FREDERICK HARTMAN. Witness: ROBERT JOHN, WILLIAM PREVOST. rec 1820. pp 317, 318

Deed dated 1817. THOMAS C. KELSEY of Butler Co, OH to NATHAN D. GALLION. Brkv lot 43. "LYDIA, his wife" Signed THOMAS C. KELSEY, LYDIA KELSEY. Witness: M. HUSTON, JAMES CRAMER. rec 1820. pp 318, 319

FRANKLIN COUNTY DEEDS: Book D

Mortgage deed dated 1820. JOHN WILLIAMS to JOSEPH WILLIAM. S 12, T 8, R 1W. Debt to be paid in 2 yrs to void conveyance. Signed JOHN WILLIAMS. Witness: ELI JAMES, JP. rec 1820. pp 319, 320

Deed dated 1820. JOHN ALLEN SR to ALEXANDER MOORE. Brkv lot 105. Signed JOHN ALLEN SR, POLLY ALLEN. Witness: JOHN HANNA, SAM'L. D. WOODWORTH. rec 1820. pp 320, 321

Deed dated 1820. SYLVANUS WARD to JANE WARD, widow. S 9, T 11, R1W. Signed SYLVANUS WARD. Witness: E. BURNSIDE, PERMELA BURNSIDE. rec 1820. pp 321, 322

Deed dated 1819. ROBERT HANNA JR & JOHN NUGENT to JOHN HANNA. S 32, T 10, R 2W. Signed ROBERT HANNA JR SALLY (x) HANNA, JOHN NUGENT, ELIZABETH (x) NUGENT. Witness: ELIZABETH ANNE HANNA, JOHN EWING. rec 1820. pp 322, 323

Deed dated 1820. DAVID S. VANBLARICUM & MARY, his wife, late MARY HEDLEY, to ALEXANDER GARDNER. S 26, T 9, R 2W "which descended from JOHN HEDLEY, dec, who died intestate, to said MARY"..."WILLIAM HEDLEY, ELIZABETH HEDLEY, JOHN HEDLEY, JEREMIAH HEDLEY & THOMAS HEDLEY, legal heirs...of JOHN, which they hold in coparcenary". Signed DAVID VANBLARICUM, MARY VANBLARICUM. Witness: ROBERT JOHN. rec 1820. pp 323, 324

Deed dated 1817. WILLIAM SPARKS & POLLY, his wife, to CALEB WICKERSHAM. S 20, T 7, R 1W. Signed WILLIAM (x) SPARKS, MARY (x) SPARKS. Witness: none. rec 1820. p 324

Deed dated 1820. ENOCH D. JOHN & NOAH NOBLE to LEWIS DEWESE. S 4, T 8, R 2W. Signed ENOCH D. JOHN, NOAH NOBLE, KITTY S. NOBLE. Witness: ROBERT JOHN, THO. G. NOBLE. rec 1820. pp 324, 325

Deed dated 1820. WILLIAM H. EADS to JOSEPH JONAS of Cincinnati, OH. Brkv lot 3. Signed WILLIAM H. EADS, JANE EADS. Witness: R. TYNER, ROBERT JOHN. rec 1820. pp 325, 326

POA dated 1820. SABBINA ADAMS & WILSON ADAMS apptd GEORGE L. MURDOCK as atty, convey deed to MOSES GREEN S 17, T 9, R 2W. Signed SABBINA ADAMS, WILSON ADAMS. Witness: ENOCH McCARTY. rec 1820. pp 326, 327

Deed dated 1819. ALEXANDER DEARMOND & ELIZABETH, his wife of Butler Co, OH to MOSES WHITNEY. S 19, T 8, R 1W. Signed ALEXANDER DEARMOND, ELIZABETH DEARMOND.

FRANKLIN COUNTY DEEDS: Book D

Witness: H. (HUGH) MAY, JP. rec 1820. pp 327, 328

Partition deed dated 1820. ROBERTSON JONES & BETSEY, his wife, to JAMES JONES of Hamilton Co, OH. JAMES & ROBERTSON, assignees of JOHN VANBLARICUM, bought S 30 T 8, R 1W. JAMES to have north half. Signed ROBERTSON JONES, ELIZA JONES. Witness: THOMAS MANWARING, W. KNOWLES. rec 1820. pp 328, 329

Partition deed dated 1820. JAMES JONES to ROBERTSON JONES. ROBERTSON to have south half of property above Signed JAMES JONES. Witness: THOMAS MANWARING, W. KNOWLES. rec 1820. pp 330, 331

Bond. To Governor of Indiana, guaranteeing performance of NOAH NOBLE, Sheriff of Franklin Co. Signed N. NOBLE, ROBERT HANNA JR, R. BRACKENRIDGE. Witness: ENOCH McCARTY, BENJAMIN McCARTY. rec 1820. p 331

Bond. To Governor of Indiana, guaranteeing performance of HENRY JENKINSON as Coroner. Signed HENRY JENKINSON, GEORGE L. MURDOCK, JAMES LEWIS. Witness: ENOCH McCARTY, BENJAMIN McCARTY. rec 1820. pp 331,332

Deed dated 1820. JAMES JONES SR of Hamilton Co, OH to JAMES JONES, JR. S 29, T 8, R 1W. Signed JAMES JONES. Witness: SOLOMON MANWARING, W. KNOWLES. rec 1820. pp 332, 333

Deed dated 1820. JEREMIAH CORY to ROBERT GLIDEWELL. S 34, T 10, R 2W. Signed JEREMIAH CORY, REBECAH CORY Witness: none. rec 1820. pp 333, 334

Deed dated 1819. USA to WILLIAM RICHARDSON of Warren Co (OH?). S 8, T 12, R 13E. rec 1820. pp 333, 334

Mortgage deed dated 1820. JOHN J. VORHESS to THOMAS SHAW. S 27, T 9, R 1W. "paid to said JOHN SHAW, admr of estate of THOMAS SHAW, dec." Debt due 1821 to void conveyance. Signed JOHN J. VOORHEES. Witness: none. rec 1820. pp 335, 336

Deed dated 1820. NOAH NOBLE to JEHU JOHN SR. S 19, T 9, R2W. "CATHERINE, wife of said NOBLE". Signed N. NOBLE, KITTY S. NOBLE. Witness: ROBERT JOHN. rec 1820. pp 336, 337

Deed dated 1820. RALPH WILDRIDGE to ROBERTSON JONES. New Trenton lot 22. Signed RALPH WILDRIDGE, ELIZABETH WILDRIDGE. Witness: JOHN H. ROCKAFELLAR, THOMAS MANWARRING. rec 1820. pp 337, 338

FRANKLIN COUNTY DEEDS: Book D

Apprenticeship dated 1820. MICHEAL ARMSTRONG with the consent of his father, ABBEL ARMSTRONG, apprentced himself to JAMES GIVENS of the city of "Philladelphia" to learn the trade of a laborer for a term of seven years. Signed MICHAEL (x) ARMSTRONG, JAMES GIVAN. Witness: H. BADGEN, ALEX'R WILLEY. (at Philladelphia Co, no state given) rec 1820. pp 338, 339

Deed dated 1820. HUGH MAY to JOSEPH C. COLLINGS. S 18, T 8, R 1W. Signed HUGH MAY. Witness: THOMAS MANWARRING, SAM'L ROCKAFELLAR. rec 1820. pp 339, 340

Deed dated 1820. RICHARD CONNER to JOSEPH C. COLLINGS S 18, T 8, R 1W. "ELIZABETH, wife of RICHARD" Signed RICHARD (x) CONNER, ELIZABETH (x) CONNER. Witness: none. rec 1820. p 340

Deed dated 1819. WILLIAM McGREAR to EZEKIEL JOHNSON of Butler Co, OH. S 28, T 11, R 2W. "wife SARAH". Signed WILLIAM McGREAR, SARAH McGREAR. Witness: BENJAMIN GREAVES, HENRY H. BRANDENBURG. rec 1820. pp 340, 341

Deed dated 1820. JAMES C. HANNA & ELLENDER, his wife WILLIAM HANNA & PHEBE, his wife, & JOHN HANNA to SAMUEL HANNA. S 16, T 11, R 2W. Signed JAMES C. HANNA, ELEANOR (x) HANNA, WILLIAM HANNA, PHEBE (x) HANNA, JOHN HANNA. Witness: ROBERT SWANN, ROBERT S. NORRIS. rec 1820. p 342

Deed dated 1819. ABNER LEONARD JR to ALEXANDER FLEMING of Hamilton Co, OH. S 29, T 9, R 1W. "at ROBERT BRADFORD's corner". "NANCY, his wife". Signed ABNER (x) LEONARD, NANCY (x) LEONARD. Witness: WILLIAM C. DREW, ELI JAMES. rec 1820. pp 342, 343

Deed dated 1819. ABNER LEONARD to ALEXANDER FLEMING as above. S 29, T 9, R 1W. "MEHITABLE his wife". Signed ABNER (x) LEONARD, MEHITABLE (x) LEONARD. Witness: MORGAN RUPE, ELI JAMES, WILLIAM COULSON, JP of Warren Co, OH. rec 1820. pp 343, 344

Deed dated 1819. WILLIAM H. EADS to JOHN PEGG. S 3 & 10, T 9, R 2W. Signed WILLIAM H. EADS, JANE EADS. Witness: ROBERT JOHN. rec 1820. p 345

Deed dated 1818. JACOB G. CAPP of Cincinncati, OH to JOHN PEGG. Brkv lots 40, 41. "MARGARET, his wife". Signed JACOB G. CAPP, MARGARET M. CAPP (german script). Witness: JOSEPH MASON, HENRY B. CAPP (in OH). rec 1820. pp 345, 346

FRANKLIN COUNTY DEEDS: Book D

Deed dated 1820. JEREMIAH CORY to JOHN PEGG. Brkv lot 77. Signed JEREMIAH CORY, REBECAH CORY. Witness: HUGH MORRISON, SOLOMON ALLEN. rec 1820. pp 346, 347

Deed dated 1820. ANDREW BURNSIDE & MARTHA CROSSON to SYLVANUS EVERETS & ELISHA ROBINSON. S 18, T 11, R 1W Signed MARTHA (x) CROSSON, ANDREW BURNSIDE, JANE BURNSIDE. Witness: HENRY R. BRANDENBURG, JP & EZEKIEL HOLLINGSWORTH. rec 1820. pp 347, 348

Deed dated 1819. JACOB MANAN to EDWARD JACKMAN. S 34 T 12, R 12E. "SARAH, his wife". Signed JACOB (x) MANAN, SARAH (x) MANAN. Witness: JOHN BRISON, JOSEPH WESTON. rec 1820. pp 348, 349

Mortgage deed dated 1820. SYLVANUS EVERTS & ELISHA ROBINSON to ANDREW BURNSIDES. Debt due in 2 yrs to void conveyance. No S-T-R; 25 acres in Union Twp, house & mills. Signed SYLVANUS EVERTS, ELISHA ROBINSON, SARAH ROBINSON. Witness: MORGAN MOORE, HENRY BRANDENBURGH. rec 1820. pp 349, 350

Deed dated 1819. JOSEPH D. CLEMENTS to JOSEPH MERIUM S 24, T 10, R 3W. "MARY, his wife". Signed JOSEPH D. CLEMENTS, MARY (x) CLEMENTS. Witness: ROBERT JOHN. rec 1820. pp 350, 351

Deed dated 1819. JOSEPH D. CLEMENTS to JOSEPH MERIUM S 24, no T or R & S 11, T 11, R 13. Signed JOSEPH D. CLEMENTS, MARY (x) CLEMENTS. Witness: ROBERT JOHN. rec 1820. pp 351, 352

Affidavit dated 1820. MATHIAS CORWIN JR, Clerk of Common Pleas Court, Warren Co, OH: JAMES FUGATE was a Warren Co JP at the time the acknowledgement of NATHAN HUNT & ABNER HUNT was taken. rec 1820. p 352 (see Bk D, p 43: HUNT & HUNT to RALPH HUNT)

Affidavit dated 1820. MATHIAS CORWIN JR, Clerk of Common Pleas Court, Warren Co, OH: BENJAMIN SAYRE was a Warren Co JP at the time the acknowledgement of HERVEY BATES was taken. rec 1820. pp 352, 353 (see Bk C, pp 222-223: BATES to HUNT & HUNT)

Deed dated 1820. THOMAS HERVEY to EBENEZER SPRIGG. Fairfield lot 21, "adj lot owned by JACOB BLOYD". Signed THOMAS HERVEY, HANNAH HERVEY. Witness: JAMES OSBORN, WILLIAM S. ROSE. rec 1820. pp 353, 354

Deed dated 1820. WILSON ADAMS, SABINA ADAMS & GEORGE L. MURDOCK to DAVID PRICE. S 17, T 9, R 2W.

FRANKLIN COUNTY DEEDS: Book D

"ELIZABETH, his wife". Signed WILLSON ADAMS, ELIZABETH (x) ADAMS, G. L. MURDOCK as atty for SABINA ADAMS. Witness: WILLIAM C. DREW, ROBERT JOHN. rec 1820. pp 354, 355

Deed dated 1820. DANIEL MASON to DAVID PRICE. Brkv lot 30. "DEBORAH, his wife". Signed DANIEL MASON, DEBORAH MASEN. Witness: ROBERT JOHN, EDWARD H. HUDSON. rec 1820. p 355

Bond dated 1816. SABINA ADAMS, WILSON ADAMS & GEORGE L. MURDOCK to JOSEPH MORRISON. Clear deed for S 17, T 9, R 2W must be given before Sept, 1818 to void bond. Signed GEORGE L. MURDOCK for SABINA ADAMS, WILLSON ADAMS. Witness: SOLOMON ALLEN. Assignment of claim dated 1820 from estate of JOSEPH W. MORRISON, dec, to ALEXANDER GARDNER. Signed ENOCH McCARTY, Admr of estate. Assignment of claim dated 1820 from GARDNER to DAVID PRICE. Signed ALEXANDER GARDNER. rec 1820. p 356

Deed dated 1820. PETER HANN & SARAH, his wife of Hamilton Co, OH to JOHN LOWES. S 14, T 8, R 1W. Signed PETER HANN, SARAH HANN. Witness: JAMES HARTPENCE, JP & JAMES A. LOWES. rec 1820. pp 356, 357

Deed dated 1820. ENOCH D. JOHN, surviving Admr of estate of JOSEPH W. MORRISON to NOAH NOBLE. S 19, T 9, R 2W. Signed ENOCH D. JOHN, Admr. Witness: ROBERT JOHN. rec 1820. pp 357, 358

End of Book D, dated 12 Oct, 1920

RANDOLPH COUNTY

RANDOLPH CO. - 1818

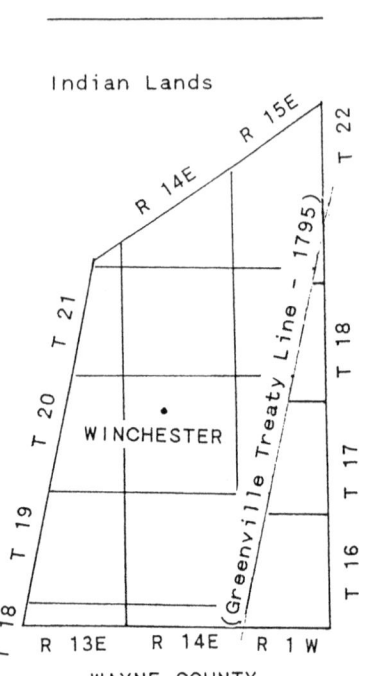

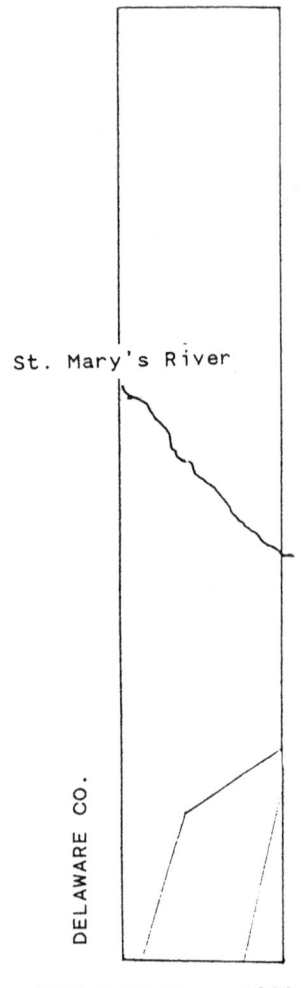

RANDOLPH CO. - 1820

bound on north by Michigan - land above St. Mary's River supposed to belong to Indians, but seldom respected by settlers. Shortly after 1820, Jay and Allen counties were formed, giving Randolph its present day boundaries.

RANDOLPH COUNTY: Original Land Entries Tract Book
FORMAT: Section - Purchaser - year - page;

In territorial days, a previous Randolph County existed, land now in southern Illinois. The present Randolph Co. was formed in 1818, latest of the "Gore" counties covered in this book, and taken entirely from Wayne Co. In 1820, Indiana claimed Indian lands to the Michigan border and included all of that strip in Randolph. This lasted a brief time; Jay and Allen counties were formed within a few years.

Township 18, Range 13

2 - JOSEPH HOLLINGSWORTH - 1818 - 35; 2 - JESSE COX 1817 - 35; 3 - HUGH BOTKIN - 1817 - 35; 3 - JOSHUA JAMES WRIGHT - 1817 - 35; 5 & 6 - WILLIAM SMITH -1817 35; 7 - ISAAC BARNES - 1815 - 36; 8 - CORNELIUS SHANE - 1815 - 36; 8 - JOHN E. HODGE - 1815 - 36; 8 THOS. CROFORD - 1816 - 36; 8 - WILLIAM BLUNT - 1815 36; 9 - JOHN COX - 1818 - 36; 9 - WILLIAM SMITH -1818 37; 9 - ACHILLIS MORRIS - 1817 - 37; 10 - E.L. WILLIAMS - 1817 - 37; 10 - JAMES & M. THORNBURGH - 1817 37; 10 - SETH RODEBAUGH - 1818 - 37; 11 - SAMUEL JONES - 1818 - 37; 11 - JOSEPH HOLLINGSWORTH - 1818 37; 11 & 13 - MOSES MARTINDALE - 1817 - 37; 12 THOMAS PHILLIPS - 1819 - 37; 12 - JAMES BURNS - 1817 37; 12 - ISAIAH RODGERS - 1818 - 37; 12 - JOSEPH RODGERS 1818 - 37; 13 - REUBEN NORCROSS - 1818 - 37; 14 - WILLIAM PEACOCK - 1818 - 37; 14 - MOSES MARTINDALE - 1817 - 38; 15 - JONATHAN COX - 1817 - 38; 17 JAMES MALCOLM - 1816 - 38; 17 - JOB HUDDLESTON - 1815 38; 17 - AMY HALL - 1815 - 38; 17 - DAVID MOORE 1816 - 38; 18 - JOHN JONES - 1815 - 38; 19 - JOHN JORDAN - 1815 - 38; 20 - WILLIAM LIFE - 1817 - 38; 20 - JOHN JORDAN - 1818 - 38; 20 - WILLIAM BARNES 1814 - 38.

Township 17, Range 1W

24 & 25 - WILLIAM CHENOWETH - 1817 - 41; 26 - ABRAHAM CHENOWETH - 1817 - 41; 35 - JOHN SMALL - 1818 - 42; 36 - JOHN FOSTER - 1817 - 42; 36 - COLLIER SIMPSON 1820 - 42.

Township 16, Range 1W

1 - PETER CRUMVIN - 1819 - 44; 2 - EPHRAIM BOWEN 1818 - 44; 3 - JOSHUA LANGERLY - 1819- 44; 10 - WILLIAM LATT - 1818 - 44; 10 - OBADIAH SMALL - 1817 - 45; 11 - PLEASANT WINSTON - 1817 - 45; 14 - EPHRAIM OVERMAN - 1816 - 46; 14 - STANTON BAILY - 1820 - 46; 23 ISAAC ELLIOTT - 1820 - 47; 27 - EPHRAIM OVERMAN 1814 - 48; 27 - NATHAN OVERMAN - 1815 - 48; 27

RANDOLPH COUNTY: Original Land Entries Tract Book
FORMAT: Section - Purchaser - year - page;

Township 16, Range 1W continued

ABSOLOM THOMAS - 1817 - 48; 28 - EPHRAIM BOWEN - 1814 48; 28 - CLARK WILCOTT - 1814 - 49; 29 - SAMUEL MANN 1816 - 49; 32 - THOMAS PARKER - 1814 - 49; 33 - JAMES CAMMACK - 1814 - 49; 33 - JOHN THOMAS - 1814 - 49; 33 ELI OVERMAN - 1814 - 49; 34 - AMBROY OSBORN - 1820 49; 34 - HENRY BAILY - 1817 - 49; 36 - GABRIEL ODELL 1817 - 49; 36 - ANDREW ARCHART - 1818 - 49.

Township 19, Range 13

3 -JEREMIAH RINARD - 1818 - 51; 3 - ZACHARIAH PUCKETT 1819 - 51; 9 - THOMAS GILLUM - 1818 - 52; 9 - JOSEPH HOLLINGSWORTH - 1819 - 52; 12 & 13 - ANDREW LYKINS 1817 - 53; 15 - JOHN ADAMSON - 1820 - 54; 21 - OLIVER WALKER - 1819- 55; 28 - OLIVER WALKER - 1819- 57; 28 JONAH HEATON - 1819 - 57; 32 - B. L. POWERS & WM. C. DREW - 1817 - 58; 33 - JOHN JACKSON - 1819 - 57.

Township 20, Range 13

3 - JOHN SAMPLE - 1817 - 60; 13 - JOSEPH SMITH -1819 63; 13 - JOHN CLARK - 1816 - 63; 13 - LEARTTON MORMAN 1816 - 63; 14 - DAVID FAIRFIELD & ROBERT ATHUNSON 1819 - 63; 22 - WILLIAM WAY - 1816 - 66; 22 - HENRY WAY - 1816 - 66; 22 - WILLIAM WAY JR -1817 - 66; 22 HENRY K. WAY - 1817 - 66; 23 - ALBERT BANTA - 1818 66; 23 - WILLIAM DIGGS - 1818 -66; 23 - ROLESON McINTYRE - 1819 - 66; 23 - WILLIAM WAY JR - 1816 66; 23 - ISAAC BARKER - 1817 - 66; 23 - JAMES MOORMAN 1817 - 66; 24 - WILLIAM DIGGS JR - 1816 - 66; 24 JOHN WRIGHT - 1817 - 66; 24 - JOSEPH WRIGHT - 1817 66; 24 - WILLIAM HAYWORTH - 1816 - 66; 25 - DANIEL PUCKETT - 1818 - 66; 25 - TARLETON HOOMAN - 1819- 66; 26 - THOMAS PACKETT - 1818 - 66; 26 - PAUL W. WAY 1818 - 66; 26 - GEORGE W. HAYWORTH - 1815- 66; 26 JOHN HAYWORTH - 1818 - 66; 27 - HENRY H. WAY - 1816 66; 27 - JESSE GREEN - 1816 - 66; 27 - JOHN BALLINGER 1816 - 67; 27 - THOMAS GILLIAN - 1816 - 67; 28 GODFRY SUMWALT - 1820 - 67; 28 - JESSE GREEN - 1820 67; 33 - WILLIAM & PHILLIP LARCH - 1820 - 68; 34 JESSE BALINGER - 1817- 68; 34 - JAMES SPRING JR- 1817 68; 34 - JOSEPH PUCKETT - 1819 - 68; 35 - JESSE MORMAN - 1819 - 68; 36 - JOSEPH CREW - 1819 - 68.

Township 21, Range 13

1 & 12 - MARSHACK LEWELLEN - 1817 - 70; 13 - SOLOMON HORNBY - 1817 - 73; 23 - JACOB SANDERS - 1817 - 75; 16 - H.H. EDWARDS & S.T. ORR - 1816 - 79; 16 - JACOB B. JONES - 1816- 79; 16 - JOHN FOX - UNDATED- 79; 16

RANDOLPH COUNTY: Original Land Entries Tract Book
FORMAT: Section - Purchaser - year - page;

Township 21, Range 13 continued

16 - ROBERT STEPHENS - UNDATED - 79; 16 - THOMAS HIGGINBOTHAM - UNDATED - 79; 16 - GEORGE DELOY UNDATED - 79.

Township 18, Range 14

1 - JESSE JOHNSON - 1818 - 80; 2 - JAMES FRAZIER 1816 - 80; 2 - DAVID HENARTHY - 1816 - 80; 2 - JESSE JOHNSON - 1816 - 80; 4 - JOSEPH HOCKETT - 1816 - 80; 4 - DAVID HAMMER - 1818 - 80; 4 - ISAAC HOCKETT 1817 - 81; 5 & 6 - EDWARD THORNBURG - 1819 - 81; 5 JOHN FOWLER - 1818 - 81; 5 - EDWARD THORNBURGHT 1818 - 81; 5 - STEPHEN HOCKETT - 1817 - 81; 5 WILLIAM HOCKETT - 1817 - 81; 6 - HAV HODGSON - 1817 81; 7 - HEZEKIAH HOCKETT - 1816 - 81; 7 - SAMUEL SMITH - 1818 - 81; 7 - NATHAN CASE - 1818 - 81; 8 STEPHEN HOCKETT - 1817 - 81; 8 - THOMAS HESTER - 1818 81; 8 - JOHN OSBORN - 1815 - 81; 8 - DANIEL OSBORN 1818 - 81; 9 - BURNET FROST - 1816 - 81; 9 - GEORGE FRAZIER - 1815 - 81; 9 - ISAAC COOK - 1816 - 81; 9 JOHN JOHNSTON - 1816 - 81; 10 - PAUL BEARD - 1815 81; 10 -THOMAS FRAZIER - 1818 - 81; 10 - FRANA ADCOCK 1814 - 81; 10 - OBADIAH HARRIS - 1815 - 81; 11 - PAUL BEARD - 1815 - 82; 11 - PETER MILLS (S.F. SHOEMACKER) 1818 - 82; 11 - CURTIS CLEMING - 1815 -82; 13 - PETER PEARSON - 1817 - 82; 14 - JAMES NORTON - 1820 - 82; 14 - FRANA ADCOCK - 1814 - 82; 14 - WM. MILNER -1817 82; 15 - OBADIAH HARRIS - 1815 - 82; 15 - SETH COOK 1816 - 82; 15 - ISAAC HUTCHINS - 1816 - 82; 16 SUSANNA WOODMAN - 1817- 83; 17 - MORDACAI MENDENHALL 1817 - 83; 17 - JOHN PEGG - 1816 - 83; 18 - ELEAZER SMITH - 1816- 83; 18 - MORGAN McQUAMY - 1818 - 83; 18 ZIMRI LEWIS - 1818 - 83; 18 - WILLIAM LEWIS -1818 -83

Township 19, Range 14

2 - N. LONGWORTH - 1819 - 84; 2 - WILLIAM KENNADY 1818 - 84; 3 - HENRY MONFORE - 1818 - 84; 3 - JESSE BROWN or BREWER - 1818 - 84; 3 - ALBERT BANTA - 1818 84; 5 - GEORGE W. HINES - 1818 - 85; 5 - M. BROOKS & N. LONGWORTH - 1818 - 85; 6 - JOHN ELTROTHE - 1818 85; 6 - THOMAS JARRED - 1819 - 85; 7 - ANDREW LYKINS 1817 - 85; 10 - ALBERT BANTA - 1818 - 86; 10 - HENRY WYSONG - 1818 - 86; 10 - MOSS BROOKS - 1818 - 86; 14 NICHOLAS LONGWORTH - 1818 - 87; 15 - ALBERT BANTA 1818 - 87; 18 - JAMES LYKINS - 1818 - 88; 27 STEPHEN MELTON - 1818 - 90; 27 - ENOCH PILSHER - 1817 90; 29 - JOSEPH GASS - 1817 - 91; 32 - WILLIAM REESE 1816 - 92; 32 - JONATHAN HASKINS - 1818 - 92; 32 JOSEPH WILLIS - 1819 - 92; 32 - JOSEPH THORNBURGH

RANDOLPH COUNTY: Original Land Entries Tract Book
FORMAT: Section - Purchaser - year - page;

Township 19, Range 14 continued

1819- 92; 33 - WILLIAM CONNER - 1817 - 92; 33 - CALEB REECE - 1818 - 92; 33 - JAMES ABSHIRE - 1819 - 92; 33 ISAAC PEARSON - 1818 - 92; 33 - NATHAN THORNBURGH 1816 - 92; 34 - JOHN BAXTER - 1817 - 92; 34 - A. & E. HUNT - 1817 - 92; 36 - DAVID FRAZIER - 1819 - 93.

Township 20, Range 14

9 - JAMES MAGUIRE - 1818 - 96; 10 - JOSEPH MOFFIT 1818 - 96; 13 - RICHARD MENDENHALL - 1818 - 97; 14 DANIEL HODGSON - 1817 - 97; 14 - ISAAC WRIGHT - 1817 97; 14 - JOHN COX - 1817 - 97; 15 - JOSHUA COX JR 1817 - 97; 15 - SAMUEL CHARLES - 1818 - 97; 15 - BENJAMIN COX - 1817 - 97; 15 - JOHN DODSON - 1817 - 97; 17 - JAMES WRIGHT - 1816 - 98; 17 - SOLOMON WRIGHT 1816 - 98; 17 - ANTIPAS THOMAS - 1816 - 98; 17 - WILLIAM HAUNTH - 1816 - 98; 18 - SHUBAL ELLIS - 1814 98; 18 - JOHN WAY - 1820 - 98; 18 - JOHN MOORE - 1816 98; 18 - ARMSBE DIGGS - 1817 - 98; 19 - LONGWORTH & BROOKS - 1818 - 98; 19 - JESSE MORMAN - 1817 - 98; 19 CHRISTOPHER HIATT - 1817- 98; 20 - JOHN WRIGHT - 1816 98; 20 - DAVID WRIGHT - 1816 - 98; 20 - CHARLES CONAWAY - 1817 - 98; 20 - DAVID STOUT - 1817 - 98; 21 JONATHAN HIATT - 1817 - 98; 21 - J. WRIGHT & L. PETTY 1817 - 99; 21 - CHRISTIAN SHILL - 1818- 99; 21- ISAAC EVERETT - 1817 - 99; 22 - JEREMIAH MOFFITT - 1817 99; 22 - JEREMIAH MEEK - 1817 - 99; 22 - ZACARIAH HYATT - 1818 - 99; 22 - MOSES HIATT - 1820 - 99; 24 RICHARD MENDENHALL - 1818- 99; 25 - JESSE BREWER 1818 100; 25 - BENJAMIN COX - 1818 - 100; 26 - RENE JULIAN 1818 - 100; 27 - ZACARIAH HIATT - 1818- 100; 27 -JOHN SMITH - 1817 - 100; 28 - JACOB MILLER - 1817 - 100; 28 - THOMAS LINARD - 1818 - 101; 29 - CHARLES CONAWAY 1817 - 101; 29 - JONATHAN EDWARDS - 1817 - 101; 29 CALEB WICKERSHAM - 1817 - 101; 29 - LONGWORTH & G. TAYLOR - 1818 - 101; 30 - LONGWORTH & TAYLOR - 1818 101; 30 - M. BROOKS - 1818 - 101; 31 - N. LONGWORTH 1818 - 101; 31 - THOMAS JARRARD - 1817 - 101; 32 WILLIAM HOCKETT - 1817 - 101; 32 - MASACK LEWELLIN 1817 - 101; 32 - VALENTINE WYSONG - 1818 - 101; 32 JOHN ELTRUTHE - 1818 - 101; 33 - N. LONGWORTH & M. BROOKS - 1818- 101; 33 - JOHN ELTZEWTHE - 1818 - 101; 33 - AMOS HODGSON - 1817 - 102; 35 - LONGWORTH & TAYLOR - 1818 - 102; 35 - VALENTINE WYSONG -1818 - 102.

Township 21, Range 14

7 - BENJAMIN LEUELLIN - 1817 - 104; 7 - JACOB GROVES 1817 - 104; 8 - DAN'L KITE - 1817 - 104; 8 - ROBERT TAYLOR - 1818 - 104; 8 - DANIEL KITE - 1817 - 104; 8

RANDOLPH COUNTY: Original Land Entries Tract Book
FORMAT: Section - Purchaser - year - page;

Township 21, Range 14 continued

JAMES & JOHN JACOBS - 1817 - 104; 9 - JOEL CASSADY 1817 - 104; 9 - JAMES REED - 1817 - 104; 9 - DAVID CONNER - 1817 - 104; 10 - JAMES WILSON - 1817 - 105; 10 - TENCE MASSEY - 1818 - 105; 11 - JAMES MASSEY 1818 - 105; 12 - ELI BLOUNT - 1819 - 105; 12 - DAN'L & ? RICHARDSON - 1817- 105; 13 - JAMES STRAINE - 1816 106; 14 - JOSEPH CRAVENS - 1819 - 106; 17 - JOSEPH HENSHAW - 1817 - 107; 17 - JOHN S. REED - 1817 - 107; 18 - JAMES JACOBS - 1817 - 107; 20 - MARTIN BOOTS 1820 - 107; 21 - RICHARD REISON - 1818 - 108; 21 WILLIAM JACKSON - 1819 - 108; 21 - SAMUEL CAIN - 1818 108; 24 - JAMES MASSEY - 1818- 109; 28 - JACOB WEAVER 1819 - 110; 28 - JOHN HALL - 1819 - 110; 28- JEREMIAH LINDSEY - 1819 - 110; 29 - HENRY HIZER - 1820 - 110.

Township 18, Range 15

18 - RICE PRICEN - 1817 - 113.

Township 20, Range 15

18 - JEREMIAH MOFFITT - 1812 - 118; 18 & 19 - JEREMIAH COX - 1818 - 118; 20 - CHRISTOPHER BAKER - 1819 119; 30 - ABRAHAM PEACOCK - 1818 - 119; 30 - HENRY HILL - 1818 - 119; 31 - AMOS PEACOCK - 1818 - 120; 31 BENONI HILL - 1818 - 120.

Township 21, Range 15

7 - JOHN ABERCROMBIE - 1816 - 122; 8 - JOHN C. DUNHAM - 1819 - 122; 20 - JOHN LARERTY - 1816 - 124.

End of Randolph Co land entries to & including 1820

*****

RANDOLPH COUNTY DEEDS

Few land records found in the first deed book of Randolph County are included in the time period being investigated (1803-1820). Deed book A was abstracted only for those pertinent to that period. While the early books are covered by a master index, Book A has its own index at the back, following the entries. Copies cannot be made directly from the fragile deed books, but are available from microfilm.

Bond dated 1818. DAVID WRIGHT, JOHN WRIGHT & CHARLES CONWAY to Governor. Performance bond of DAVID WRIGHT

RANDOLPH COUNTY: Deed Book A

as Sheriff. Signed DAVID WRIGHT, JOHN WRIGHT, CHARLES CONWAY. Witness: WILLIAM EDWARDS, JOHN WRIGHT. no rec date. p 1

Bond dated 1819. PAUL W. WAY to JAMES McCOOLE. Performance bond for WAY as County Agent. Signed PAUL W. WAY. Witness: JAMES WRIGHT. no rec date. p 1

Bond dated 1819. SOLOMON WRIGHT, JOHN WRIGHT & DAVID WRIGHT to Governor. Bond for performance of SOLOMON as Coroner. Signed SOLOMON WRIGHT, JOHN WRIGHT, DAVID WRIGHT. Witness: WILLIAM EDWARDS, JOHN WRIGHT

Certification dated 1819. JOHN WRIGHT & WILLIAM EDWARDS identified as Associate Judges of Randolph County Circuit Court. no rec date. p 2

Deed dated 1817. USA to CHARLES CONWAY. S 29, T 20, R 14E. no rec date. pp 2, 3

Deed dated 1820. PAUL W. WAY to ISAAC WRIGHT of Clinton Co, OH. Winchester town lot 6. Signed PAUL W. WAY, Agent. Witness: JAMES WRIGHT, SAMUEL PREBLE. no rec date. pp 3, 4

Deed dated 1820. PAUL W. WAY to ALBERT BANTA. Winchester lot 3. Signed PAUL W. WAY, Agent. Witness: JOHN WRIGHT, CHARLES CONWAY. no rec date. pp 4, 5

Deed dated 1820. JOHN ELTZROTH & ELIZABETH, his wife, to DAVID HEASTON. S 6, T 19, R 14. Signed JOHN ELTZROTH, ELIZABETH (x) ELTZROTH. Witness: WILLIAM WRIGHT, JACOB ROTHS. no rec date. pp 5, 6

Drawing, no date. DAVID HEASTON's plot. Signed PAUL W. WAY. no rec date. p 6

Deed dated 1820. JOHN ELTZROTH to JACOB ROTHS*. S 33, T 20, R 14E. In exchange for legacy expected by ROTHS' wife POLLY from her father, NICHOLAS ELZROTH. Legacy must be for $150 or more. Otherwise, JACOB will owe JOHN the difference. Signed JACOB ROTHS, POLLY (x) ROTHS. Witness: CHARLES CONWAY, County Recorder. no rec date. pp 6, 7 *see name in following deed; same property involved.

Deed dated 1820. JOHN ELTZROTH & ELIZABETH, his wife to JACOB ROADS*. S 33, T 20, R 14. Signed JOHN ELTZROTH, ELIZABETH (x) ELTZROTH. Witness: CHARLES CONWAY. no rec date. pp 7, 8. *see name in previous deed; same property involved.

RANDOLPH COUNTY: Deed Book A

Deed dated 1820. JOHN ELTZROTH & ELIZABETH, his wife, to JOHN IRVIN. S 6, T 19, R 14. Signed JOHN ELTZROTH, ELIZABETH (x) ELTZROTH. Witness: WILLIAM WRIGHT, JACOB ROTHS (in german script). no rec date. pp 8, 9

Deed dated 1819. PAUL W. WAY to HIRAM BALEY of Clinton Co, OH. Winchester lot 6. Signed PAUL W. WAY Agent. Witness: JAMES WRIGHT, SAMUEL RUBLE. no rec date. pp 9, 10

Deed dated 1819. CHARLES CONWAY to PAUL W. WAY. S 20, T 20, R 14E. For county use. "BETSEY, his wife". Signed CHARLES CONWAY, BETSEY (x) CONWAY. Witness: JOHN BALLINGER, PETER LASLEY. no rec date pp 10, 11
Bill of sale dated 1820. GEORGE W. HIGHT of Darke Co, OH to WILLIAM VANCE JR of same. Household goods, livestock, other chattels. Signed GEORGE W. HIGHT. Witness: MOSES SCOTT, BENJAMIN P. SOUTHWORTH. Full listing follows. no rec date. pp 11, 12, 13

Deed dated 1819. JAMES OLDHAM to PAUL W. WAY. Winchester outlot 2. Signed JAMES OLDHAM. Witness: PETER LASLEY, SIMS HILLIS. no rec date. pp 13, 14

Bond dated 1820. SOLOMON WRIGHT, DAVID WRIGHT, JOHN WRIGHT to Governor. Bond for performance of SOLOMON as Sheriff. Signed SOLOMON WRIGHT, DAVID WRIGHT, JOHN WRIGHT. Witness: JOHN WRIGHT, WILLIAM EDWARDS. no rec date. p 14

Bond dated 1820. PAUL W. WAY to JAMES McCOOL. Winchester lot 8 as security for performance of WAY as County Agent. Signed PAUL W. WAY. Witness: WILLIAM WRIGHT, -- MASSEY. no rec date. p 15

Deed dated 1820. GIDEON FRAZIER to ISAAC HOCKET. S 9, T 13?, R 14E. "ANN, his wife". Signed GIDEON FRAZIER, ANN FRAZIER. Witness: JESSE JOHNSON, WILLIAM CONNOR. no rec date. pp 15, 16

Deed dated 1819. PAUL W. WAY to THOMAS JARRET. Winchester lot 9. Signed PAUL W. WAY, Agent. Witness: JAMES OLDHAM, SOLOMAN HIATT. no rec date. p 17

Deed dated 1819. PAUL W. WAY to DAVID WYSONG. Winchester lot 16. Signed PAUL W. WAY, Agent. Witness: DAVID HEASTON, JOHN IRVIN. no rec date. p 18

Promissory note dated 1819. WILLIAM JONES to County Agent. Contract to purchase Winchester lot 14. Terms given. Signed WILLIAM (x) JONES. Witness:

RANDOLPH COUNTY: Deed Book A

JAMES OLDHAM, SOLOMON HIATT. no rec date. p 19

Deed dated 1820. ISAAC COOK to JOSEPH ROOKS. S 9, T 18, R 14. "MARY, his wife". Signed ISAAC (x) COOK, MARY (x) COOK. Witness: DAVID FRAZIER, HEZEKIAH HOCKETT. no rec date. pp 20, 21

Deed dated 1820. PAUL W. WAY to RICHARD BEASON. Winchester lot 17. Signed PAUL W. WAY, Agent. Witness: CHARLES CONWAY, ELI OVERMAN. no rec date. pp 27, 28

Deed dated 1820. PAUL W. WAY to DAVID HEASTON. Winchester lot 11. Signed PAUL W. WAY, Agent. Witness: SIMS HILLIS, JOHN IRVIN. no rec date. p 37

Deed dated 1820. JAMES FRAZIER to JOHN FRAZIER, his son. S 2, T 18, R 14. "SUSANNA, his wife". Signed JAMES FRAZIER, SUSANNA (x) FRAZIER. Witness: DAVID FRAZIER, ELIZABETH (x) FRAZIER. rec 1822. p 44

Deed dated 1817. USA to EPHRAIM OVERMAN of Wayne Co. S 27, T 16, R 1W. no rec date. p 84

Deed dated 1818. NATHAN OVERMAN of Wayne Co, to EPHRAIM OVERMAN of same. "line that divides 27th from 28th sections", T 16, R 1W. "THAMER, his wife." Signed NATHAN OVERMAN, THAMER (x) OVERMAN. Witness: ELI OVERMAN, DAVID BOWLES. rec 1824. p 86

Deed dated 1820. SETH COOK of Warren Co, OH to DAVID FRAZIER. S 15, T 18, R 14E. "RUTH, his wife". Signed SETH COOK, RUTH COOK. Witness: ELI OVERMAN, EPHRAIM OVERMAN. rec 1831. pp 444, 445

Deed dated 1820. FRANCIS FRAZIER SR to DAVID FRAZIER JR, "son of FRANCIS". S 10, T 18, R 14E. "ELIZABETH, his wife". Signed FRANCIS (x) FRAZIER, ELIZABETH (x) FRAZIER. Witness: ROBERT MENDENHALL, EPHRAIM BOWEN. rec 1831. p 446

End of Book A, 458 pp: last recording dated Oct, 1831

SWITZERLAND COUNTY

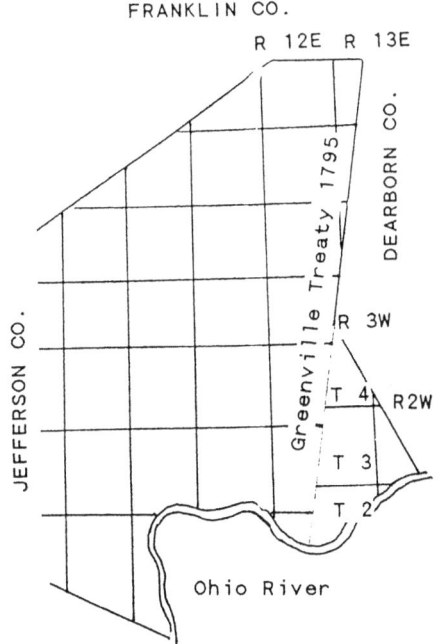

JEFFERSON COUNTY
1811

SE portion now
SWITZERLAND COUNTY.
Central and eastern
SWITZERLAND derived
from southern end
of Dearborn County.

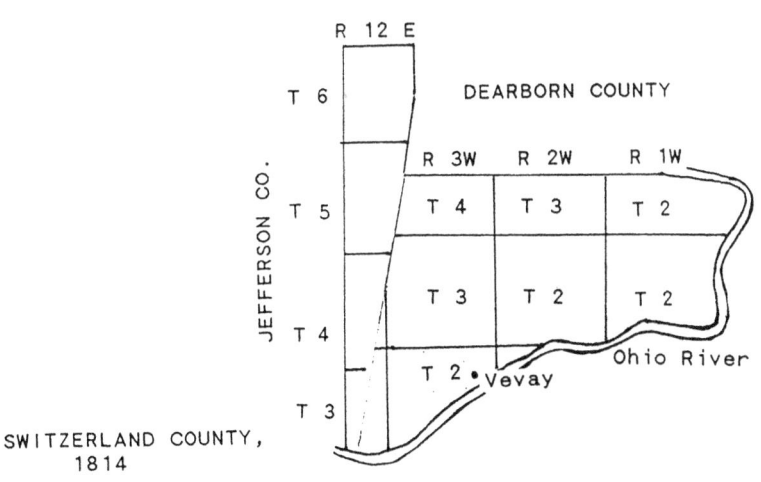

SWITZERLAND COUNTY,
1814

boundaries have changed
very little since formation

SWITZERLAND COUNTY: Original Land Entries Tract Book
FORMAT: Section - Purchaser - year - page;

Jefferson Co. was formed in 1811, partly from Dearborn. That section, plus more land from Dearborn, became Switzerland Co. in 1814. (Its west edge, lying outside the treaty line of 1795, was first Clark Co.) The first records of that small western area, never part of the Gore, based in Clark and Jefferson counties, are not included here. Names should be read with the French accent of the early settlers: see J. James Dufour, Bk A, pp 104, 105, 106.

Pages are out of order in the tract book, but have been entered in sequence here.

Township 1, Range 1W

5 & 6 - JOHN BUCKANAN & THM. PHILLIPS - 1804 - 1; 5, 6, 7 & 8 - OLIVER ORMSBY - 1806- 1; 18 - JOHN ANDREWS 1809 - 1; 31 - THOMAS HOPKINS - 1801 - 1.

Township 2, Range 1E

29, 30, 31 & 32 - PATRICK DONAHOE - 1804 - 1.

Township 2, Range 1W

1- THOMAS STEWART JR - 1816 - 1; 1 - JOHN QUIGLEY 1817 - 1; 1 - JOHN QUIGLEY - 1816- 1; 2 - ROBERT HAMILTON - 1818 - 1; 2 - SETH SAMSON - 1818 - 1; 2 - WM. CAMPBELL & WM. RIDGELY - 1817 - 1; 2 - EDW. HEPBURN & E. DIFFENDERFFER - 1818 - 1; 2 - JOHN VAN BOR--L 1817 - 1; 3 - SAM'L TRUESDELL & CHRISTOPHER JONES 1815 - 1; 3 - PINCKNEY JAMES - 1816 - 1; 3 - JAMES TRUESDELL - 1814 - 1; 3 - WILLIAM L--NE - 1816 - 1; 4 WILLIAM POWELL - 1817- 1; 4 - HENRY WEIST - 1816 - 1; 4 - DAVID PENWELL - 1816 - 1; 5 - FRANCIS HEES - 1816 1; 5 - JOHN BAYNE - 1817 - 1; 5 - JOHN D. COOK - 1817 1; 5 - ALA TAHLE - 1817 - 1; 6 - CALEB MOUNTS - 1812 2; 6 - ALEXANDER SCOTT - 1816 - 2; 6 - ROBERT HARRIS 1817 - 2; 7 - THOMAS DUGAN - 1816 - 2; 7 - JAMES HAMILTON - 1814 - 2; 8 - ELI PENWELL - 1816 - 2; 8 & 9 JOHN CUNNINGHAM - 1817 - 2; 8 - NOAH SMITH - 1815- 2; 9 - RODERICK & E. MOORE - 1817 - 2; 9 - JOHN McDOWELL 1817 - 2; 9 - HENRY JONES - 1817- 2; 10 & 11 - SAMUEL JACK - 1816 - 2; 10 - CHARLES WRIGHT - 1816 - 2; 10 COLIN McNUTT - 1817 - 2; 10 - WILLIAM McNUTT - 1817 2; 11 - SAMUEL WEST - 1818 - 2; 11 - LEMUEL SEAREY 1813 - 2; 11 - JAMES MURDOCK - 1815 - 2; 12 - JOHN QUIGLEY - 1813 - 2; 12 - JACOB SHERK - 1817 - 2; 12 JOSHUA PETTY - 1812 - 2; 12 - ROBERT GASTON - 1816 2; 13 - ELISHA WADE - 1813 - 2; 14 - JAMES MOREDOCK 1815 - 2; 14 - JAMES MOORE - 1817 - 2; 14 - JAMES McINTIRE - 1816 - 2; 14 - WILLIAM WADE - 1816 - 2; 15

SWITZERLAND COUNTY: Original Land Entries Tract Book
FORMAT: Section - Purchaser - year - page;

Township 2, Range 1W continued

AUSTIN AMES - 1818 - 2; 15 - JOHN PATTON - 1817 - 2; 15 - JOEL BRADFORD - 1818 - 2; 17 - EBENEZER HUMPHREY 1817 - 2; 17 - ZEALLY MOSS - 1816 - 2; 17 - LEWIS JONES - 1814 - 2; 18 - ZEALLY MOSS - 1817 - 2; 18 JACOB COOK - 1817 - 2; 18 - JOSEPH GROSE & A. EVELETE 1817 - 2; 19 - THOMAS BURKE - 1817 - 2; 19 - WILLIAM McGINNESS - 1815 - 2; 19 - THOMAS BURK - 1816 - 2; 20 WILLIAM SCOTT - 1814- 2; 20 - WILLIAM CAMPBELL - 1817 2; 20 - AMOS BROWN - 1814 - 2; 20 - WILLIAM CARVER 1815- 2; 21 - JOHN POTTER - 1814- 3; 21 - PETER SMITH 1818 - 3; 21 - ABRAHAM BLEDSOE - 1815 - 3; 22 - ETHEL R. LYON - 1818 - 3; 22 - HENRY WEIST - 1818 - 3; 22 WM. SHERMAN BUCK - 1818 - 3; 22 - GEORGE TAGUE - 1817 3; 23 - JACOB SHERK - 1818- 3; 23 - PETER BOAZ - 1818 3; 23 - ACKLIN DeHART - 1818 - 3; 23 - LEVI JAMES 1817 - 3; 23 - SAMUEL C. VANCE - 1818 - 3; 23 - LEVI HAMBLIN - 1818 - 3; 24 - WILLIAM LEGG - 1814 - 3; 25 JAMES TAYLOR - 1814- 3; 25 - DAVID McCLURE - 1813- 3; 26 & 35 - PATRICK DONAHOE - 1804 - 3; 27 - LEWIS JONES - 1805 - 3; 27 - AMOS BROWN - 1814 - 3; 27 WILLIAM PIERSON - 1814 - 3; 27 - WILLIAM JOHNSTON 1814 - 3; 28 - ZEALLY MOSS - 1814 - 3; 28 - CHRISTIAN CARVER - 1813 - 3; 28 - MARTIN HOLDER - 1813 - 3; 28 NICHOLAS KEITH - 1813 - 3; 29 - GEORGE TEAGUE - 1814 3; 29 - ROBT. WILSON - 1814 - 3; 29 - ELI PENWELL 1816 - 3; 29 - CALEB HARRIS - 1815- 3; 30 - CHRISTIAN COOPER - 1814 - 3; 30 - WM. McCRARY - 1816 - 3; 30 JOHN GILLILAND - 1818 - 3; 30 - WM. CAMPBELL - 1817 3; 30 - JESSE KIRK - 1816 - 3; 31 - LEVI JAMES - 1817 3; 31 - ALBERT COSSART - 1816 - 3; 31 - JOHN B. LINDSEY - 1815 - 3; 31 - BENJ. P. DRAKE & JAS. NELSON 1814 - 3; 32 - WILLIAM CAMPBELL - 1814 - 3; 33 - JAS. & JOHN NELSON - 1814 - 3; 34 - MARTIN BAUM - 1814 3; 36 - THOMAS HOPKINS - 1801 - 3.

Township 3, Range 1W

25 - WILLIAM CAMPBELL - 1814- 3; 26 - WILLIAM ENGLISH 1814 - 3; 27 - THOMAS NORTH - 1814 - 3; 28 - THOMAS MOUNTS - 1812 - 3; 28 - JAMES CURRY - 1812 - 3; 28 LEVI JAMES - 1819 - 4; 28 - THOMAS MOUNTS - 1814 - 4; 29 - PETER LOSTUTTER - 1815 - 4; 29 - EDWARD TYDINGS 1815 - 4; 29 - HENRY WALBICK - 1811 - 4; 29 - PETER LOSTUTTER - 1816 - 4; 30 - WILLIAM KELLY - 1817 - 4; 30 - ROBERT HEWITT - 1817- 4; 30 & 31 - CONRAD BUCK 1815 - 4; 30 - JOHN GIBBENS - 1817 - 4; 31 - MARTIN BAUM & JAS. FINDLAY - 1815 - 4; 31 - DAVID HISER 1813 - 4; 31 - DAVID WILSON - 1818 - 4; 32 - WILLIAM STEWART - 1815 - 4; 32 - JAMES HAMILTON - 1814 - 4; 32 - CORNELIUS S. HARRIS - 1817 - 4; 32 - C. SMITH

SWITZERLAND COUNTY: Original Land Entries Tract Book
FORMAT: Section - Purchaser - year - page;

Township 3, Range 1W continued

1817 - 4; 33 - CORNELIUS McPHAILL - 1817 - 4; 33 THOMAS STEWART JR - 1816- 4; 33 - JACOB POWELL - 1817 4; 33 - WILLIAM VANHISEL - 1817 - 4; 34 - LEWIS HAMMOND - 1815 - 4; 34 - JAMES DAVIS - 1817 - 4; 34 DAVID CLOSE - 1819 - 4; 35 - ARCHIBALD MERIT - 1816 4; 35 - JAMES BUTLER - 1815- 4; 36 - JOHN HAMILTON JR 1818 - 4; 36 - WILLIAM CAMPBELL - 1817 - 4; 36 PETER SHEETS - 1817 - 4.

Township 1, Range 2W

1 & 2 - JOHN F. DUFOUR - 1801 - 4; 3 - THOMAS HOPKINS 1801 - 4; 4 - JOHN GREENER - 1813- 4; 5 - JOHN BLANEY 1815 - 4; 5 - JOHN BOISSEAU - 1814 - 4; 5 - ELISHA GOLAY - 1815 - 4; 6 - SETH STODDER - 1816 - 4; 6 JAMES BURKE - 1814 - 4; 6 - JACOB MISNER - 1813 -4; 6 RICHARD FOLSOM - 1813 - 4; 7 & 18 - JOHN JAMES DUFOUR et al - 1804 - 4; 8 & 9 - CHAS. KRUTZ, CHS. SEARIGER & PETER MIRA - 1813 - 4.

Township 2, Range 2W

1 - JESSE EMBREE & EDW. HEPBURN - 1818 - 5; 1 - S. LOVELACE & A. RUTER - 1817 - 5; 1 - ROBERT BLACKER 1817 - 5; 2 - JACOB WHITE - 1817 - 5; 2 - JOHN H.O. NEAL - 1815 - 5; 2 - JOHN HAMILTON - 1817 - 5; 2 DAVID O. NEAL - 1816 - 5; 3 - EBENEZER MIXTER - 1815 5; 3 - GEORGE BERNARD - 1814 - 5; 3 - EBENEZER MIXTER & C.B. SEDAM - 1816 - 5; 3 - BENJAMIN M. STEPHENS 1814 - 5; 4 - NICHOLAS LONGWORTH - 1818 - 5; 4 - WILLIAM SMITH - 1814 - 5; 4 - ROBERT DRAKE - 1813 - 5; 4 JOHN DICKSON - 1814 - 5; 5 - NATHAN PLATT - 1814 - 5; 5 - CORNELIUS R. SEDAM - 1815 - 5; 5 - J. PUGH & C. MOORE - 1815 - 5; 5 & 6 - SAMUEL BUCK - 1817 - 5; 6 NICHOLAS BOYLAND - 1818 - 5; 7 - WILLIAM ANDERSON 1816- 5; 7 - JOHN CARTER - 1816- 5; 7 - MARVIN BACKUS 1816 - 5; 8 - WILLIAM DICKASON - 1814 - 5; 8 - THOMAS COOPER - 1818 - 5; 8 - AARON CHAMBERLAIN - 1818- 5; 9 JOHN SHERER - 1816 - 5; 9 - ROBERT BOVARD - 1817 - 5; 9 - GEORGE WOOLLEY - 1817 - 5; 10 - DANIEL DICKERSON 1817 - 5; 10 - JOHN SHERER - 1816 - 5; 10 - JOHN DICKSON - 1817 - 5; 10 - BENJAMIN M. STEPHENS - 1817 5; 11 - JESSE HUNT & ISAAC BATES - 1817 - 5; 11 LEWIS BOCOCK - 1817 - 5; 11 - WILLIAM CAMPBELL - 1817 5; 12 - E. ELLIS & A. COFFIN - 1817- 5; 12 - W. MEANS 1817 - 5; 12 - EDWARD BOCOCK or POCOCK - 1816 - 5; 12 S. LOVELACE & A. RUTER - 1817 - 5; 13 - JAMES POCOCK 1816 - 5; 13 - ROBERT CUNNINGHAM - 1818 - 5; 13 WILLIAM SCOTT - 1815 - 5; 13 - SAMUEL FENTON - 1818 5; 14 - WILLIAM GARD - 1816 - 6; 14 - LEVI JAMES

SWITZERLAND COUNTY: Original Land Entries Tract Book
FORMAT: Section - Purchaser - year - page;

Township 2, Range 2W continued

1817 - 6; 14 - WILLIAM McGARVEY - 1817 - 6; 14 - J. REEDER - 1818 - 6; 15 - HENRY SCUDDER SR - 1819 - 6; 17 - WILLIAM BARR - 1818 - 6; 17 - JOHN DAN'L MOREROD 1814 - 6; 17 - ZACARIAH MONTAYNE - 1817 - 6; 17 ROBERT BOVARD - 1817 - 6; 18 - JOHN F. DUFOUR - 1814 6; 18 - ELISHA GOLAY - 1814 - 6; 18 - ROBERT BOVARD 1817 - 6; 18 - ABRAHAM LINDLY - 1814 - 6; 19 - GEORGE SIMONTON - 1817 - 6; 19 - ENOS McILROY - 1817 - 6; 19 THEODORE F. TALBOT - 1818 - 6; 19 - BENJAMIN WARREN 1817 - 6; 20 - JONATHON SHUFF - 1818- 6; 20 - WILLIAM CAMPBELL - 1817 - 6; 20 - NOAH GATES - 1818 - 6; 20 SAMUEL LEWIS - 1818 - 6; 21 - JOHN JOHNSON - 1818- 6; 21 - JAMES BOYD - 1819 - 6; 21 - GEORGE TURNER - 1815 6; 21 - RILEY TRUITT - 1817 - 6; 22 - GEORGE MEDSKER 1816 - 6; 23 - ABRAHAM BURKDOLL - 1816- 6; 23 - CALEB HAYS - 1817 - 6; 23 - PETER VANBLARICUM - 1817 - 6; 23 - MARTIN CROWEL - 1815 - 6; 24 - JAMES CUNNINGHAM 1818 - 6; 24 - WILLIAM CAMPBELL - 1817 - 6; 24 CHARLES PHILLIPS - 1817 - 6; 24 - NATHAN & CHAS. NELSON - 1815 - 6; 25 - WILLIAM PHILLIPS - 1814 - 6; 25 SAMUEL FENTON - 1815 - 6; 25 - WILLIAM WHITE - 1809 6; 25 - LUKE WILES - 1816 - 6; 26 - CHARLES PHILLIPS 1815 - 6; 26 - WILLIAM RAYL - 1814 - 6; 26 - ANDREW JELLY - 1816 - 6; 26 - DAVID FULTON - 1815 - 6; 27 JAS. MOSLEY & SARAH HUTCHISON - 1814 - 6; 27 - WILLIAM McCULLOUGH - 1816 - 6; 27 - ABNER SCUDDER - 1815 6; 27 - HENRY LOUGHMAN - 1817 - 6; 28 - WILLIAM MARSH 1815 - 6; 28 - JOHN McCREARY - 1815 - 7; 28 - JOHN BOISSEAU - 1817 - 7; 28 - MORDECAI JACKSON - 1815- 7; 29 - SAMUEL KRALL - 1817 - 7; 29 - JOSEPH BENTLEY 1818 - 7; 29 - WILLIAM McCULLOUGH - 1816 - 7; 30 ROBERT McKIM - 1817- 7; 30 - JOHN BOSOW SR - 1818- 7; 30 - ISAAC LEVI - 1817 - 7; 30 - JOSEPH CRAWL - 1817 7; 30 - DUNCAN McCALLUM - 1815 - 7; 31 - PAUL FROMAN 1815 - 7; 31 - JAMES BATES SR - 1812 - 7; 32 - NEWTON H. TAPP - 1815 - 7; 32 - RICHARD WEAVER - 1816 - 7; 32 - SOLOMON NIGHSWONGER - 1815- 7; 32 - JAMES POCOCK 1816 - 7; 33 - DAVID McCORMICK - 1818 - 7; 33 - JAMES HADLOCK - 1817 - 7; 33 - JOSHUA COOK & BENJM. PICKETT 1814 - 7; 33 - DAVID McCORMICK - 1815 - 7; 33 - BRAZILLA CLARK - 1815 - 7; 34 - ROBT. GULLION & DAVID MILLER - 1816 - 7; 34 - THOMAS RAMSEY - 1818 - 7; 34 JAMES TAYLOR - 1814- 7; 35 - CHARLES BEATY -1816 - 7; 35 - LEMON DUSKY - 1817 - 7; 35 - DANIEL CRUME - 1812 7; 35 - JOHN GULLION - 1810 - 7; 36 - JOHN FENTON 1809 - 7; 36 - JOHN BONTA - 1816 - 7; 36 - JOSEPH McFALL - 1812 - 7; 36 - JOHN MILLER - 1813 - 7.

SWITZERLAND COUNTY: Original Land Entries Tract Book
FORMAT: Section - Purchaser - year - page;

Township 3, Range 2W

25 - JOHN REMER - 1818 - 7; 25 - JACOB GOODNER - 1817 7; 25 - JOHN RYDER - 1818 - 7; 26 - JOHN HUNTER -1817 7; 26 - JOHN ARMSTRONG & WM. KERR - 1817 - 7; 26 DAVID CUMMINS - 1818 - 7; 26 - WILLIAM BRINDLE - 1817 7; 27 - THOMAS BISHOP - 1816 - 7; 27 - ABRAHAM PARKER 1812 - 7; 27 - JN. P. & JONATHAN MIERS - 1818 - 7; 27 - STEPHEN STEWART & WM. MYERS - 1814 - 7; 28 JONATHAN MYERS - 1815 - 8; 28 - JOSEPH BELL - 1817 8; 28 - AMOS GILBERT - 1816 - 8; 28 - JACOB SUYDAM 1816 - 8; 29 - N. LONGWORTH & M. BROOKS - 1818 - 8; 29 - ISAAC JESSUP - 1817 - 8; 29 - SIMON MYERS - 1816 8; 29 - CHARLES McNUTT - 1816 - 8; 30 - WILLIAM BELL 1817 - 8; 30 - JUSTICE REYNOLDS - 1816 - 8; 30 HARMON LEEK - 1817 - 8; 31 - JOSEPH PUGH - 1815 - 8; 31 - JOEL CLARK - 1817 - 8; 31 - JESSE HUNT - 1815 8; 31 - WILLIAM T. CULLUM - 1817 - 8; 32 & 33 - JOHN SHERER - 1816 - 8; 32 - JANE MATHERAL - 1815 - 7; 32 JESSE HARRELL - 1815 - 8; 32 - PETER DEMMAREE - 1815 8; 33 - PETER DEMMAREE - 1816 - 8; 33 - MINOR ROBERTS 1815 - 8; 33 - JUSTSY CARLEY - 1816 - 8; 34 & 35 CALEB A. CRAFT - 1818- 8; 34 - BENJAMIN DUBOIS - 1816 8; 34 - DAVID CUMMINS - 1817 - 8; 34 - NICHOLAS LONG-WORTH - 1818 - 8; 35 - EDWARD WHITE - 1817 - 8; 35 HARDY ROPER & DAVID CUMMINS - 1817 - 8; 35 - JOSEPH McHENDRY - 1817 - 8; 36 - MATTHIAS & JOSHUA HAYNES 1818 - 8; 36 - JN. LEWIS & JN. COURTNEY - 1818 - 8; 36 - RALPH COTTON SR - 1818 - 8.

Township 1, Range 3W

5 & 6 - WILLIAM STANLEY - 1804 - 8.

Township 2, Range 3W

1 - RALPH & NATHANIEL COTTON - 1812 - 8; 1 - GEORGE WALTZ - 1814 - 8; 1 - JOHN GILLILAND - 1814 - 8; 1 PICKETT, McCREARY & KEETH - 1813 - 8; 2 - PETER LOCK 1811 - 8; 2 - STILLWELL, HEADY & GRIFFY DICKISON 1804 - 8; 2 - NATHAN PLATT - 1812 - 8; 3 - DEMEREE & DOTSON - 1813- 8; 3 - SETH STODDER - 1816- 8; 3- JOHN TEAGUE - 1812 - 8; 3 - JACOB BURNET & WILLIAM COTTON 1815 - 9; 4 - MARVUS BACCHUS - 1816 - 9; 4 - JAMES WHITAKER - 1817 - 9; 4 - SETH STODDAR - 1816 - 9; 4 BENJAMIN HEADY - 1816 - 9; 5 - SAMUEL LAMBERSON -1816 9; 5 - JOSEPH ORR - 1814 - 9; 5 - JOHN WILLIS - 1817 9; 5 - NICHOLAS DAVIS - 1815 - 9; 6 - GEORGE CRAIG 1816- 9; 6 - SAMUEL HEATH - 1814 - 9; 6 - BENJAMIN D. DAVIS - 1816 - 9; NICHOLAS DAVIS - 1816 - 9; 7 WILLIAM McKINSTREY - 1816 - 9; 7 - N. LONGWORTH & D.K. ESTE - 1817 - 9; 7 - HUGH MOORE - 1818 - 9; 8

SWITZERLAND COUNTY: Original Land Entries Tract Book
FORMAT: Section - Purchaser - year - page;

Township 2, Range 3W continued

JOHN VAN BRIGGLE - 1817 - 9; 8 - THOMAS WRIGHT - 1816 9; 8 - ROBERT BAKES - 1817 - 9; 9 - PETER VAN BRIGGLE 1815- 9; 9 - JOSEPH ORR - 1817 - 9; 9 - GEORGE CRAIG 1815 - 9; 9 - JACOB RAMSIERE - 1817 - 9; 10 - HIERAM OGLE - 1817 - 9; 10 - HUGH MOORE - 1816- 9; 10 - JOHN F. DUFOUR - 1814 - 9; 10 - JOHN BLANEY -1814 - 9; 11 - AMOS GILBERT - 1812 - 9; 11 - WM. & JN. DICKESON 1811 - 9; 11 - JOSEPH NOBLE - 1813 - 9; 11 - PHILO AVERILL - 1813 - 9; 12, 13, 14 & 15 - JOHN JAMES DUFOUR et al - 1802 - 9; 17 - ROBERT BAKE - 1816 - 9; 17 - JAMES ROUS - 1817 - 9; 17 - ROBERT BAKE - 1814 9; 17 - NIEL McCALLUM - 1815 - 9; 18 - JOHN MARLING 1817 - 9; 18 - PHILIP ROMERIE - 1817 - 9; 18 - DUNCAN McCALLUM - 1816 - 9; 18 - FRANCIS LOUIS DESERENS 1816 - 9; 19 - JOHN SHAW - 1816- 9; 19 - JOHN DENTRAZ 1817 - 9; 19 - HENRY PETERS - 1816 - 9; 19 - JAMES WHITAKER - 1817 - 9; 20 - FELIX BRANDT - 1817 - 9; 20 GEORGE CRAIG - 1818 - 9; 20 - GABRIEL PHILLIPS - 1817 10; 20 - CORNELIUS YOUELL - 1818 - 10; 20 - ZACARIAH COTTON - 1818 - 10; 21 - GEORGE P. TORRENCE & L. WHITEMAN - 1814- 10; 21 - EUGENE DOUTOIT - 1817 - 10; 21 - JOHN MILLS - 1814 - 10; 21 - DAVID LATHAM - 1818 10; 22, 23 & 27 - JOHN JAMES DUFOUR et al - 1802- 10; 28 - SAMUEL MENNET - 1812 - 10; 29 - FREDERICK L. THIEBAUD - 1817 - 10; 29 - MINOR ROBERTS - 1815 - 10; 29 - JN. JAMES & PHILIP SCHENK - 1817- 10; 29- GEORGE CRAIG - 1817 - 10; 30 - PETER PETEY - 1812 - 10; 30 JOSEPH BROWN - 1816 - 10; 30 - GEORGE CRAIG - 1814 10; 30 - THOMAS DAVIS - 1814- 10; 31- DUNCAN McCALLUM 1819 - 10; 31 - AARON CULVER - 1818 -10; 31 - ABISHA McCAY - 1810 -10; 31 - ROBERT McCAY - 1816 - 10; 32 & 33 - GEORGE CRAIG - 1809 - 10.

Township 3, Range 3W

1 - JOHN DICKINSON - 1818- 10; 1 - THOMAS SMITH -1817 10; 1 - NICHOLAS LONGWORTH - 1818 - 10; 2 - WM BARR & EDW. HEPBURN - 1818- 10; 2 - PRESLEY RENO - 1818- 10; 2 - JOHN RILEY - 1818- 10; 2 - ROBT. R. ANDREWS- 1817 10; 3 - HUGH GLENN & E. HEPBURN - 1818 - 10; 3 - JOHN DICKINSON - 1818 - 10; 3 - DAVID LEE - 1815 - 10; 3 STEPHEN PEABODY - 1817 - 10; 4 - ARTHUR ANDREWS -1818 10; 4 - WILLIAM RICHARDS - 1816- 10; 4 - WM. WHITMORE 1816 - 10; 4 - ETHAN A. BROWN - 1818 - 10; 5 - A.R. DUMONT - 1818 - 10; 5 - NICHOLAS LENTZ- 1818 - 10; 5 WILLIAM MITCHELL - 1818- 10; 6 -GABRIEL JOHNSTON 1818 11; 7 - JAMES McMANAMAN - 1815- 11; 8 - JAMES MAPES 1818 - 11; 8 - HENRY BURCH - 1818 - 11; 8 - CHARLES BREWER - 1815 - 11; 8 - JOHN SNOOK - 1816 - 11; 9 LIESTER & LIENTZ - 1818 - 11; 9 - ISAAC BACHUS/BACKUS

187

SWITZERLAND COUNTY: Original Land Entries Tract Book
FORMAT: Section - Purchaser - year - page;

Township 3, Range 3W continued

1818 - 11; 9 - RALPH COTTON - 1815 - 11; 9 - BROOKS & MAGUIRE - 1818 - 11; 10 - WILLIAM LAMBDIN & JOHN B. LINDSEY - 1815 - 11; 11 - CHARLES LEATHERBURG - 1817 11; 11 - WM. COTTON & J. BURNET - 1817 - 11; 11 ALLEN WILEY - 1815 - 11; 12 - PETER LOCK JR - 1815 11; 12 - JAMES E. BROWN - 1817 - 11; 12 - DEMAS MOSS 1816 - 11; 12 - JOHN TAGUE - 1817 - 11; 13 - MINOR CHAMBERS & JOHN PICKETT - 1816 - 11; 13 - JOHN COOMBS - 1818 - 11; 13 - STEPHEN PEABODY - 1817 - 11; 13 -JOHN TAGUE - 1814 - 11; 14 - GEORGE ARNOLD - 1816 11; 14 - WM. COTTON & J. BURNET - 1815- 11; 14 - A.B. DUMONT - 1818 - 11; 15 - JAS. RICHARDSON, assignee of JONATHAN BAIRE - 1817 - 11; 15 - HIRAM OGLE - 1816 11; 16 - HIRAM OGLE - 1815- 11; 17 - LEVI OREM - 1817 11; 17 & 20 - MICHAEL HILDIBRAND - 1816 - 11; 19 JOSEPH BRYANT - 1819 - 11; 19 - HENRY ROGERS - 1818 11; 19 - JOHN WRIGHT - 1817 - 11; 20 - GEORGE BUTCHER 1817 - 11; 20 - ROBERT TAYLOR - 1818- 11; 21 - JOSEPH COLE - 1817 - 11; 22 - JAMES RICHARDSON - 1817 - 12; 22 - MARTIN GILLESPY - 1818 - 12; 23 - JOHN HAYNES 1817- 12; 23 - CALEB WHITE & D. CUMMINS - 1818 - 12; 23 - NICHOLAS LIENTZ - 1815 - 12; 23 - JAMES DALMAZZO 1816 - 12; 24 - ABRAHAM LINDLEY - 1814 - 12; 24 LEWIS MICHOUD - 1816 - 12; 24 - JOSEPH NOBLE - 1815 12; 24 - JOHN NELSON - 1814 - 12; 25 - JOHN COCHRAN 1816 - 12; 25 - JONAS BALDWIN - 1815 - 12; 25 - SETH STODDER - 1816 - 12; 25 - ALLEN BURTON - 1815 - 12; 26 - WILLIAM T. HUFF - 1815 - 12; 26 - JACOB HESLER 1812 - 12; 26 - DANIEL PRATT - 1814 - 12; 26 - ANDREW STEPLETON - 1813 - 12; 27 - EDWARD COEN - 1814 - 12; 27 - R. ROSEBROUGH & FRED. GREENE - 1817 - 12; 27 WILLIAM COTTON - 1814 - 12; 27 - FRIEND THRALL - 1816 12; 28 - WEBSTER MARSH - 1817 - 12; 28 - SILAS BASCOM 1817 - 12; 28 - ADAM COLE - 1817 - 12; 28 - THOMAS DAVIS - 1818 - 12; 29 - SILAS SMITH - 1818 - 12; 30 STEPHEN ROGERS SR - 1817- 12; 30 - NICHOLAS LONGWORTH 1818 - 12; 30 - JAMES FARRAL - 1817 - 12; 30 - WM. JACKSON GRIFFITH - 1817 - 12; 31 - HUGH WILSON - 1816 12; 31 - JOHN GILLILAND - 1815 - 12; 31 & 32 - JOHN PRATSMAN - 1814- 12; 31 - THOS. GILLILAND - 1814- 12; 32 - ISAAC RICHARD - 1817 - 12; 32 - HENRY HANNAS 1817 - 12; 33 - JOHN SHAW - 1817 - 12; 33 - NICHOLAS DAVIS - 1817 - 12; 33 - NICHOLAS DAVIS - 1816 - 12; 34 - SETH STODDER - 1816 - 13; 34 - WILLIAM COTTON 1805 -13; 34 - ROBERT COTTON - 1816- 13; 35 -JONATHAN HUNTINGTON - 1814 - 13; 35 - JOSEPH NOBLE - 1813 -13; 35 - PAUL FROMAN - 1813 -13; 35 - HENRY EAVES - 1813 13; 36 - KIMBRAW LANDEY or LANDERS - 1814 - 13; 36 SOLOMON NIGHSWONGER JR - 1814- 13; 36 - ANDREW BAILEY 1814 - 13; 36 - SAMUEL McHENRY - 1814 - 13.

SWITZERLAND COUNTY: Original Land Entries Tract Book
FORMAT: Section - Purchaser - year - page;

Township 4, Range 3W

25 - WILLIAM BELL - 1818 - 13; 26 & 34 - N. LONGWORTH & MOSES BROOKS - 1818 - 13; 26 & 27 - N. LONGWORTH & K. ESTE - 1818- 13; 27 & 28 - WM. BARR & EDW. HEPBURN 1818 - 13; 27 - STEPHEN BURROWS - 1818 - 13; 27 -JOHN DICKINSON - 1818- 13; 29- JESSE EMBREE & EDW. HEPBURN 1818 - 13; 29 - JOHN MISNER - 1818 - 13; 30 - WILLIAM T. CULLOM - 1818- 13; 31 - FREDERICK SHAFF - 1818-13 32 - JOHN GRAY - 1818- 13; 32 & 33 - PETER LOCK -1818 13; 32 - ETHAN BROWN - 1818 - 13; 33 - JAMES STONE 1818 - 13; 33 - ISAAC RICHARDS - 1817 - 13; 33 - WILLIAM C. MITCHELL - 1818 - 13; 34 - N. LONGWORTH & MOSES BROOKS - 1818 - 13; 35 - JOEL TOWNSEND - 1817 14; 35 & 36 - SAMUEL STONE - 1817 - 14; 36 - AUSTIN CLARK - 1817 - 14; 36 - HUGH GLENN & E. HEPBURN 1818 - 14; 36 - JOHN DICKINSON - 1818 - 14.

Township 1, Range 4W

1 - JAMES McKAY - 1810 - 14; 2 - THOMAS THOMPSON 1804 - 14.

Township 2, Range 4W

1 - JACOB KARN - 1815 - 14; 12 - PHILIP ROMEREL 1816 - 14; 13 - JAMES WHITEAKER - 1817 - 14; 24 WILLIAM PIATT - 1816 - 14; 23 - LEWIS F. GOLAY - 1817 14; 25 - JOHN BRAY - 1811 - 14; 25 - ELISHA BORK & EDW. RAY - 1817 - 14; 25 - WILLIAM I. STEWART - 1816 14; 25 - GEORGE GILMORE - 1817 - 14; 26 - CHARLES JOHNSTON - 1816 - 14; 35 - EDWARD McINTIRE - 1817 14; 36 - HENRY LANHAM - 1814 - 14; 36 - WILLIAM JOHNSTON - 1816 - 14; 36 - CHARLES E. ROMERIL - 1818 14.

Township 3, Range 4W

25 & 26 - ROBERT RUTHERFORD - 1816 - 14; 36 - HENRY HANNAS - 1814 - 14.

Township 6, Range 12E

33 - ZEBULON BRINGEN - 1817 - 19; 33 - JOSHUA CHAPMAN 1817 - 19; 33 - JOHN HENNY - 1818 - 19; 33 - JOHN HALLGATH - 1817 - 19.

End of Switzerland Co land entries until and including 1820.

SWITZERLAND COUNTY DEEDS: Book A

Book A is dated "1815 - 1819" on the cover. However, deeds dated 1820 are included among the final entries. Since Book A spans the time period covered in this book, no later ledgers were abstracted. Recording dates were rarely given.

Deed dated 1815. ISAAC BLEDSOE of Gallatin Co, KY to ROBERT McKAY. R 3, T 1, S 5 "to STURMAN CRAIG's land ...to JAMES McKAY's corner". Signed ISAAC BLEDSOE. Relinquishment of dower rights by ELIZABETH BLEDSOE, wife of ISAAC. Witness: none. p 1.

Lease dated 1815. FRANCIS LOUIS RAYMOND to JOSHUA JONES. No S-T-R given. JONES to build cabin, kitchen & stable, clear 6 acres "bound by Indian Creek and JOHN MILL's land", dig a well & run a ferry crossing. RAYMOND to have free ferry use, land rent. Signed F. LOUIS RAYMOND, JOSHUA JONES. Witness: JOHN FRANCIS DUFOUR. p 2

Bill of Sale dated 1815. GEORGE SANGER to PETER MING. Cattle, horse, hogs, household goods and chattels. Signed GEORGE SANGER. Witness: CHAS. MURET. pp 3, 4

Bill of Sale dated 1815. ABRAHAM MILLER to JOHN MILLER. Cattle, household goods. Signed ABRAHAM (x) MILLER. Witness: ROBERT M. TROTTER. p 4

Assignment of deed rights. JOHN NISWONGER to JOHN G. FLUGEL. Vevay lot 115. Mortgage held by FREDERICK CHMIER. Lot 13 deed held as security. Signed JOHN NISWONGER, JOHN G. FLUGEL. Witness: none. pp 4, 5

Lease dated 1815. JOHN FRANCIS DUFOUR to ROBERT M. TROTTER. Vevay lot 155. TROTTER to build 2 story home, pay rent for 9 yrs. Signed JOHN FRANCIS DUFOUR, ROBERT M. TROTTER. Witness: none. pp 5, 6. rec 1815

Deed dated 1815. Commissioners of estate of CHARLES CAMPBELL to JOB TRUESDELL. S 26 & 35, T 2, R 1W. "corner of JOHN CAMPBELL". Signed (commissioners) WILLIAM CAMPBELL, JOHN CAMPBELL, WMS. PIERSON. Witness: WM. McCORKHILL, WMS. PIERSON JR. pp 8, 9

Deed dated 1815. WILLIAM JENNINGS JR & MARION, his wife of Jefferson Co, KY to EDWARD McINTIRE of Gallatin Co, KY. S 2, T 1, R 4W. "corner to JOSHUA KEEN.. bank of Tucker's Run..on bank of Ohio River opposite the mouth of the Kentucky River. Signed W. JENNINGS JR, MARION JENNINGS. Witness: none. pp 9, 10, 11

Deed dated 1815. WILLIAM JENNINGS JR & MARION, his

SWITZERLAND COUNTY DEEDS: Book A

wife of Jefferson Co, KY to JOSHUA KEEN. "corner to EDWARD McINTIRE..to Tucker's Run". Signed W. JENNINGS JR, MARION JENNINGS. Witness: none. pp 11, 12, 13

Affidavit dated 1814. JAMES CHENOWETH of Ross Co, OH: CHENOWITH, then living in VA, knew JEFFERY DAY, a free black man. DAY's mother was free as much as 15 yrs ago and all her family were considered free persons. Signed JAMES CHENOWETH. Rec 1814, Ross Co, OH. p 13

Assignment dated 1815. WILLIAM COTTON to JOHN FRANCIS DUFOUR. Assigned right to build a mill dam over Indian Creek at line dividing S 34, T 3, R 3 from S 3, T 2, R 3; gave right to build a public road. Signed WILLIAM COTTON. Witness: illegible #1, LUKE OBUSSIER. pp 14, 15

Deed dated 1815. ZEALY MOSS to BARNEY BARNUM. S 34, T 16, R 1. "being JAMES TRUESDELL's corner..with JOHN LANGLAY's line". Signed ZEALLY MOSS. Witness: WM. CAMPBELL, WM. McCORKHILL. pp 15, 16

Mortgage dated 1815. LUCIEN GEX to JOHN MILLS. Vevay lot 147. Signed LUCIEN GEX. Witness: JOHN F. DUFOUR. p 17

Deed dated 1815. JOHN BUCHANON & RACHEL his wife of Jefferson Co to BENJAMIN DRAKE. S 6, T 1, R 1. Signed JOHN BUCHANON, RACHEL (x) BUCHANON. Witness: GEORGE TEAGUE, AMOS BROWN. pp 18,19

Jacksonville plat map dated 1815. PETER HANIS, proprietor. Witness: JOHN GILLILAND, JP. pp 20, 21

Erie plat map dated 1815. EDWARD McINTIRE, proprietor. p 21

Assignment dated 1815. ROBERT M. TROTTER to STEPHEN LUDLOW of Lawrenceburg. Assigned rights to Vevay lot 155 as granted by JOHN FRANCIS DUFOUR. (see Bk A, pp 5, 6) Signed ROBERT M. TROTTER. LUDLOW then assigned rights back to DUFOUR. Signed STEPHEN LUDLOW. pp 22, 23

Agreement dated 1816. JOHN NIGHSWONGER to PAXTON W. TODD. Vevay lot 160 to be sold. Signed PAXTON W. TODD, JOHN NIGHSWONGER. Witness: JOHN FRANCIS DUFOUR. pp 25, 26

Allenville plat map dated 1816. PETER DEMAREE, proprietor. p 27

SWITZERLAND COUNTY DEEDS: Book A

Allenville outlots plat map dated 1816. PETER DEMAREE proprietor. p 27

Mt. Sterling plat map dated 1816. PHILO AVERIL, proprietor. p 29

Deed dated 1815. WILLIAM CAMPBELL & POLLY, his wife, to EVEN BROCK. S 32, T 2, R 1. Signed WM. CAMPBELL, POLLY CAMPBELL. Witness: ROBERT McCORKHILL, ELI RISLEY. pp 30, 31

Deed and bill of sale dated 1816. THOMAS STUART SR to "my son" THOMAS STUART JR. Household goods, livestock, etc, including land "now occupied" by STUART SR. No bounds or S-T-R given. Signed THOMAS (x) STUART. Witness: JOHN FRANCIS DUFOUR. pp 31, 32

Deed dated 1816. LEWIS GEX OBOUSSIER* & MARIANNE his wife, to JOHN PETER NAIRIN. S 27 & 22, T 2, R 3W. "corner between said GEX & RAYMOND's corner." Signed L. GEX OBOUSSIER, MARIANNE GEX. Witness: J.G. FLUGEL, JAMES DALMAZZO. pp 33, 34 *probably wife's family name, in old French tradition

Deed dated 1816. JOHN PETER NAIRIN & MARGARET PAULINA his wife to LEWIS GEX OBOUSSIER. S 22 & 27, T 3, R 3W. Signed JOHN P. NAIRIN, MARGUERITE PAULINA NAIRIN. Witness: J. G. FLUGEL, JAMES DALMAZZO. pp 35, 36, 37

Bond dated 1816. NATHANIEL HARRINGTON to ALEXANDER HOLTON. HOLTON to obtain deed to Vevay lot 17 upon paym't of his note to HARRINGTON. Signed NATHANIEL HARRINGTON. Witness: ROBERT M. TROTTER. pp 38, 39

Partition deed dated 1816. USA to CHARLES KRUTZ, GEORGE SANGER & PETER MING as Tenants in Common. S 8 & 9, T 1, R 2W. Land now being divided. Signed CHARLES F. KRUTZ, PETER MING. Witness: JOHN GREENER, WM. CORRY. pp 39, 40 (See Bk A, pp 58, 59, 60)

Mortgage dated 1816. JOHN G. FLUGEL to SAMUEL MENNET. MENNET paid debt owed by FLUGEL to ZELIM HUMBERT DROZ; household goods & sorrel mare held as security. Signed J. G. FLUGEL. Witness: LUCIEN GEX. pp 40, 41

Bond dated 1816. RAWLEIGH DAY to SETH STODDER of Baltimore, MD. DAY to deliver deed to Vevay lot 104 as soon as he receives it from J. F. DUFOUR. Signed RAWLEIGH DAY. Witness: JOHN GILLILAND, JOSEPH BENTLEY. pp 42, 43

POA dated 1816. JOHN GREENER of Cincinnati, OH apptd

SWITZERLAND COUNTY DEEDS: Book A

ELISHA GOLAY to collect rents on S 4 & 9, T 1, R 2W on GREENER's behalf. Signed JOHN GREENER. Witness: JOHN FRANCIS DUFOUR, L. GEX OBOUSSIER. pp 43, 44

Deed dated 1816. GEORGE SEANGER & DOROTHEA, his wife to JOHN GREENER. S 9, T 1, R 2W. Signed GEORGE SEANGER, DOROTHEA (x) SANGER. Witness: CHARLES F. KRUTZ, PETER MING. pp 44, 45, 46

Bill of sale dated 1816. JOHN NISWONGER to JOHN FRANCIS DUFOUR. Household chattels, cattle, Vevay outlot (no #). Signed JOHN NIGHSWONGER. Witness: ELISHA GOLAY. pp 46, 47, 48

Bond dated ?. CHARLES F. KRUTZ to JOSEPH HAYS. Deed on S 8, T 1, R 2 given when HAYS has made payment. Bound on east by GEORGE SEANGER & MORDECAI JACKSON (land previously sold by KRUTZ on SE corner of tract). Signed CHARLES F. KRUTZ. Witness: JOHN GILLILAND, THOMAS GILLILAND. pp 48, 49 (See Bk A, p 176)

Deed dated 1816. SAMUEL MENNET & SALLY, his wife, to ZELIM HUMBERT DROZ. S 28, T 2, R 3W. Signed SAMUEL MENNET, SALLY (x) MENNET. Witness: JOHN FRANCIS DUFOUR, ALLEN WILEY. pp 49, 50, 51

Deed dated 1816. BENJAMIN CRAIG SR & NANCY, his wife of Gallatin Co, KY to ISAAC BLEDSOE of same. S 6, T 1, R 3. Signed BENJAMIN CRAIG, NANCY (x) CRAIG. Witness: none. pp 51, 52, 53

Deed dated 1816. BENJAMIN CRAIG SR & NANCY, his wife & ISAAC BLEDSOE, all of Gallatin Co, KY, to STUMAN CRAIG. S 6 & 5, T 1, R 3W. Signed BENJAMIN CRAIG, NANCY (x) CRAIG, ISAAC BLEDSOE. Witness: none. pp 53, 54, 55

Deed dated 1816. ISAAC BLEDSOE of Gallatin Co, KY to ROBERT McKAY. S 6, T 1, R 3W. Signed ISAAC BLEDSOE. Witness: JOHN FRANCIS DUFOUR, JN. DAVID DUFOUR. pp 55, 56

Deed dated 1816. ROBERT McKAY to STUMAN CRAIG. S 5, T 1, R 3. Signed ROBERT (x) McKAY, POLLY (x) McKAY. Witness: JOHN GILLILAND. pp 56, 57

Partition deed dated 1816. GEORGE SEANGER & PETER MING to CHARLES KRUTZ. Original patent dated 1816 on S 8 & 9 T 1, R 2W. (see Bk A, pp 39, 40). Land now being divided. Signed GEORGE SEANGER, PETER MING. Witness: JOHN GREENER, WM. CORRY. pp 58, 59, 60

SWITZERLAND COUNTY DEEDS: Book A

Deed dated 1816. STUMAN CRAIG to ROBERT McKAY. S 6, T 1, R 3. Signed STUMAN CRAIG, ELIZABETH CRAIG. Witness: none. Note by GEORGE CRAIG, JP: ELIZABETH, wife of STUMAN. pp 60, 61, 62

Jacksonville outlot plat map dated 1817. WILLIAM GERARD, proprietor. p 62

Deed dated 1816. GEORGE LANGER to NICK LONGWORTH. S 8, T 1, R 2W. Signed GEORGE SEANGER. Witness: JOHN MAHARD, JOHN GREENER. pp 63, 64

Deed dated 1816. CHARLES F. KRUTZ to NICHOLAS LONGWORTH. S 8, T 1, R 2W. Signed CHARLES F. KRUTZ. Witness: JOHN MAHARD, JOHN GREENER. pp 65, 66

Bill of sale dated 1817. DANIEL BURCHAM to JOHN FRANCIS DUFOUR. Household chattels, real property & deed for Vevay lot 57. Signed DANIEL BURCHAM. Witness: JAMES DALMAZZO. pp 67, 68

Deed dated 1816. JOHN G. FLUGEL to JOHN GILLILAND. Vevay outlots 17, 27, inlots 24, 36. Sold by FLUGEL from estate of DAVID GOLAY, dec. Signed J. G. FLUGEL Witness: SILVANUS WALDON. p 69

Deed dated 1817. EVEN BROCK & BETSY, his wife, to JOSEPH NELSON. S 32, T 2, R 1. Signed EVAN BROCK, BETSY (x) BROCK. Witness: WM. CAMPBELL, JOHN (x) NELSON, SAM'L. BROWN. pp 70, 71

Deed dated 1817. DAVID P. GOLAY of Jefferson Co to JAMES DELMAZO. "my father the late DAVID GOLAY". No S-T-R given. Signed DAVID P. GOLAY. Witness: JOHN FRANCIS DUFOUR. pp 71, 72

Deed dated 1816. JOBE TRUESDELL to WILLIAM TRUESDELL. S 26 & 35, T 2, R 1W. Signed JOBE TRUESDELL. pp 72, 73

Receipt dated 1817. BARBARY PETERS to DENNIS ABBOTT. Sale of land in S 30, T 2, R 3 ordered by court. Signed BARBARY (x) PETERS. Witness: ALEX HANLIN, HENRY PETERS. p 73

Sheriff's sale dated 1817. JOHN FRANCIS SIBENTHAL, Sheriff, to THOMAS ARMSTRONG, ALEXANDER A. MEEK & HENRY P. THORNTON. JAMES COLLIER & JOHN S. RUTHERFORD received a judgement against JOHN G. FLUGEL; Vevay outlots 17, 27, inlots 36, 16 & 88, share of lot 108 seized, sold by sheriff to satisfy debt. (Vevay plat recorded in Jefferson Co, IN.) Signed J.

SWITZERLAND COUNTY DEEDS: Book A

F. SIBENTHAL, Sheriff. Witness: WM. C. KEEN, WILLIAM HENDRICKS, ALEX. HOLTON. pp 74, 75

Bill of sale dated 1817. JAMES BATES to CHARLES MURET. Household goods, horses, hogs, property on Plumb Creek - no S-T-R given. Signed JAMES BATES. Witness: none. pp 76, 77

Bill of sale dated 1817. JAMES BATES to NICHOLAS LENTZ. Household goods, standing crops & land on Plumb Creek - no S-T-R given. Signed JAMES BATES. Recpt of note from LENTZ, signed JAMES BATES. Witness: ELISHA GOLAY. pp 77, 78, 79

Bond dated 1815. JOHN G. FLUGEL to DAVID LORRING of Cincinnati, OH. FLUGEL to deliver deed of Vevay lot 101 before 1820. Signed J.G. FLUGEL. Witness: JOHN FRANCIS DUFOUR. p 79

Deed dated 1817. PETER LOCK SR to WILLIAM LOCK. S 2, T 2, R 3W. "corner to JOHN KEITH". Signed PETER (x) LOCK SR, RHODAY (x) LOCK. Witness: none. pp 80, 81

Deed dated 1817. JOHN JAMES DUFOUR to JAMES STEWART. S 15, T 2, R 3W. Signed J. DUFOUR. Witness: JOHN FRANCIS DUFOUR, JAMES DELMAZZO. pp 81, 82, 83

Deed dated 1817. JOHN JAMES DUFOUR to JOHN FRANCIS SIEBENTHAL. S 15 & 22, T 2, R 3. Signed J.J. DUFOUR. Witness: JOHN FRANCIS DUFOUR, HEZEKIAH B. HULL. pp 83, 84

Deed dated 1817. SIEBENTHAL to J. J. DUFOUR. Quitclaim on land granted to DUFOUR et al in 1802, per an agreement (in French) dated 1803. No S-T-R given. Signed JOHN FRANCIS SIEBENTHAL. Witness: JOHN FRANCIS DUFOUR, HEZEKIAH B. HULL. p 85

Deed dated 1817. JOHN JAMES DUFOUR to JOHN FRANCIS DUFOUR. S 15, T 2, R 3W. Signed J.J. DUFOUR. Witness: JOHN GILLILAND, JAMES DALMAZZO. pp 85, 86

Bond dated 1817. JOHN FRANCIS SIEBENTHAL, JOHN JAMES DUFOUR & JOHN GILLILAND to Gov'r of IN. Bond for SIEBENTHAL's service as Sheriff of Switzerland Co. Signed JOHN FRANCIS SIEBENTHAL, J. DUFOUR, JOHN GILLILAND. Witness: JOHN FRANCIS DUFOUR. pp 86, 87

Bond dated 1817. PHIL AVERILL, ANDREW STAPLETON & DAVID BEEBE to Gov'r of IN. Bond for AVERILL's service as Coroner of Switzerland Co. Signed PHILO AVERILL, ANDREW (x) STAPLETON, DAVID BEEBE. Witness:

SWITZERLAND COUNTY DEEDS: Book A

JOHN FRANCIS DUFOUR. p 87

Bond dated 1816. WILLIAM ROBINSON & JOSEPH NOBLE to ABM. B. DUMONT of Vevay, IN & JONATHAN HATHAWAY of NY for title to share of Vevay lot 103. Signed WILLIAM ROBINSON, JOSEPH NOBLE. Witness: JOHN DUMONT. p 88

New York* plat map dated 1817. BENJAMIN DRAKE, proprietor. Witness: WILLIAM C. KEEN. pp 88, 89
(*Bk A, pp 121, 122, 123 -- in S 6, T 1, R 1)

Deed dated 1817. PETER MING to CHARLES LOUIS MURET. S 8, T 1, R 2W. Signed PETER MING. Witness: ELISHA GOLAY, CHARLES F. KRUTZ. pp 89, 90, 91

Deed dated 1816. USA to SAMUEL JACK of KY. S 11, T 2, R 1W. p 91

Deed dated 1816. USA to SAMUEL JACK of KY. S 10, T 2, R 1W. pp 91, 92

Deed dated 1817. SAMUEL JACK of Gallatin Co, KY & ROSANNAH his wife to JOHN JACK of same. S 10, 11, T 2 R 1W. Signed SAMUEL JACK, ROSANNAH JACK. Witness:JAMES McCLURE, DAVID McCLURE, FRANCIS McCLURE. pp 92, 93

Sheriff's sale dated 1817. JOHN FRANCIS SIEBENTHAL to JOHN JAMES DUFOUR. Suits brought against BENJAMIN NORTON by DOUGLAS JOSEPHUS PUCKET & DAVID SHERWOOD. Vevay lot 119 & outlot 1 ordered sold to satisfy debt Purchased at auction by DUFOUR. Signed JOHN FRANCIS SIEBENTHAL. Witness: none. pp 93, 94, 95

Deed dated 1817. WILLIAM LOCK & NANCY, his wife, to MORDECAI REDD. S 2, T 2, R 3W. Signed WILLIAM LOCK, NANCY (x) LOCK. Witness: WILLIAM C. KEEN, THOMAS ARMSTRONG. pp 95, 96

Bond dated 1815. PETER HARRIS to JOHN T. DEMING. HARRIS to give title to lot adj Jacksonville by 1818. Signed PETER HARRIS. Witness: EBENEZER STARLIN. Reassigned by DEMING to RALPH B. COTTON dated 1816, witness EBENEZER STARLIN. Reassigned by RALPH to ROBERT COTTON dated 1817. Reassigned by ROBERT COTTON to WILLIAM BRANDENBURG dated 1817, witness PETER HARRIS. Reassigned by BRANDENBURG to JOHN B. MINOLA dated 1817, witness T.H. THOMAS. Reassigned by MINOLA to JACOB D. BREYFOGEL dated 1817. Reassigned by BREYFOGEL to JOHN J. REED dated 1817. Reassigned by REED to JOHN B. MINOLA dated 1817, witness SAMUEL MERRILL. Reassigned by MINOLA to CYPRIANA PULASKY dated Nov, 1817, witness DANIEL DUFOUR. pp 97, 98

SWITZERLAND COUNTY DEEDS: Book A

Bond dated 1815. PETER HARRIS to JOHN RUTHERFORD. HARRIS to provide deed to Jacksonville lot 9. Signed PETER HARRIS. Witness: P. AVERILL. Reassigned by RUTHERFORD to J.B. MINOLA, witness JOHN STAPLETON, WILLIAM BRANDENBURG. Reassigned by MINOLA to JACOB D. BREYFOGEL dated 1817, witness S. MERRILL, A.B. DUMONT. Reassigned by BREYFOGEL to JOHN J. REED dated 1817, witness SAMUEL MERRILL. Reassigned by REED to JOHN B. MINOLA dated 1817. Reassigned by MINOLA to CYPRIANA PULASKY, witness DANIEL DUFOUR. pp 98, 99

Bond dated 1815. PETER HARRIS to B. NORTON & J. NOBLE. HARRIS to provide deed to Jacksonville lot 10 before 1818. Signed PETER HARRIS. Witness: P. AVERILL. Reassigned by DR. B. NORTON to JOHN B. MINOLA, witness JOHN LATHAM. Reassigned by JOSEPH NOBLE to JOHN B. MINOLA dated 1816, witness CHARLES NEWTON. Reassigned by MINOLA to CYPRIANA PULASKY dated 1817, witness DANIEL DUFOUR. p 99

Deed dated 1817. JOHN JAMES DUFOUR to ABNER CLARKSON of SC & JOHN HUNT of Jefferson Co. Vevay inlot 136. Signed J. J. DUFOUR. Witness: JOHN FRANCIS DUFOUR, ELISHA GOLAY. pp 100, 101

Agreement dated 1818. DANIEL DUFOUR with FRANCIS BARNES & NATHAN M. WHITMORE. Terms of partnership setting up distillery near Vevay. Signed DANIEL DUFOUR, FRANCIS BARNES, NATHAN M. WHITMORE. Witness: JOHN MARLINS, WILLIAM C. KEEN. pp 101, 102, 103

Quitclaim dated 1818. JOHN FRANCIS DUFOUR & POLLY, his wife, to JOHN JAMES DUFOUR. No S-T-R given. Signed JOHN FRANCIS DUFOUR, POLLY DUFOUR. Witness: ELISHA GOLAY, J. F. SIEBENTHAL. pp 103, 104

Deed dated 1818. JOHN JAMES DUFOUR, late of Montreus, Vaud Canton, Republic of Switzerland & now of Vevay to JOHN FRANCIS DUFOUR, brother to said JOHN JAMES. S 14 & 23, T 2, R 3W except Vevay lots 136 & 145. Signed J.J. DUFOUR. Witness: ELISHA GOLAY, J. F. SIEBENTHAL. pp 104, 105, 106

Deed dated 1818. JOHN FRANCIS DUFOUR & POLLY, his wife, to THOMAS ARMSTRONG. Vevay inlots 168, 148. Signed JOHN FRANCIS DUFOUR, POLLY DUFOUR. Witness: WILLIAM C. KEEN, TRUMAN RICHARD. pp 106, 107

Deed dated 1818. JOHN FRANCIS DUFOUR & POLLY, his wife to JONATHAN McGUIRE, assignee of PHILIP FRY of Gallatin Co, KY. Vevay lot 166. Signed JOHN FRANCIS DUFOUR, POLLY DUFOUR. Witness: WILLIAM C. KEEN,

SWITZERLAND COUNTY DEEDS: Book A

THOS. ARMSTRONG. pp 107, 108

Deed dated 1818. JOHN FRANCIS DUFOUR & POLLY, his wife, to TRUMAN RICHARDS, att'y, late of NY state, now of Vevay. Vevay lot 167. Signed JOHN FRANCIS DUFOUR, POLLY DUFOUR. Witness: WILLIAM C. KEEN, THOMAS ARMSTRONG. pp 108, 109, 110

Deed dated 1817. CHARLES F. KRUTZ & ELIZABETH, his wife, to GEORGE ROTE. S 8, T 1, R 2W. Signed CHARLES F. KRUTZ, ELIZABETH KRUTZ. Witness: none. pp 110, 111

Deed dated 1818. JOHN JAMES DUFOUR to JOSEPH MALIN. S 13, T 2, R 3. Signed J. J. DUFOUR. Witness: TRUMAN RICHARDS, JOHN FRANCIS DUFOUR. pp 111, 112

Deed dated 1860. SAMUEL MENNET & SALLY, his wife, to EDWARD VIOLET SR. S 28, T 2, R 3W. Signed SAMUEL MENNET, SALLY (x) MENNET. Witness: none. pp 113, 114

Deed dated 1818. JOHN FRANCIS DUFOUR & POLLY, his wife, to JOHN BLANEY. Vevay lot 8. Signed JOHN FRANCIS DUFOUR, POLLY DUFOUR. Witness: WILLIAM C. KEEN, LUCIEN GEX. pp 114, 115

Deed dated 1817. USA to JAMES RICHARDSON as assignee of JONATHAN BAIRD, late a forage master in the corps of Canadien Volunteers. S 15, T 3, R 3W. p 115

Deed dated 1818. JAMES RICHARDSON & HANNAH his wife, late of NY state, now of SC, to JOHN STICKLER, late of OH, now of SC. S 22, T 3, R 3W. Signed JAMES RICHARDSON, HANNAH RICHARDSON. Witness: WILLIAM C. KEEN. pp 115, 16

Deed dated 1818. JOHN FRANCIS DUFOUR & POLLY his wife, to JAMES H. McCLURE of Shippingsburg, Cumberland Co, PA. Vevay lot 62. Signed JOHN FRANCIS DUFOUR, POLLY DUFOUR. Witness: MICHAEL LENTZ, ELISHA GOLAY. pp 117, 118

Deed dated 1818. JOHN FRANCIS DUFOUR & POLLY his wife, to DAVID COWAN of Ghent, Gallatin Co, KY. Vevay lot 48. Signed JOHN FRANCIS DUFOUR, POLLY DUFOUR. Witness: TRUMAN RICHARDS, JOSEPH TODD. pp 118, 119

Deed dated 1818. JOHN FRANCIS DUFOUR & POLLY his wife, to ABNER K. STARR of Butler Co, OH. Vevay lots 123, 183. Signed JOHN FRANCIS DUFOUR, POLLY DUFOUR. Witness: TRUMAN RICHARDS, JOSEPH TODD. pp 119, 120

SWITZERLAND COUNTY DEEDS: Book A

Bond dated 1816. PETER HARRIS to HENRY STOUT of Hamilton Co, OH. HARRIS to deliver deed to Jacksonville lot 11 before 1818. Signed PETER HARRIS. Witness: WM. MATTHEWS. Reassigned by STOUT to MICAL FOULON, dated 1818, witness J. H. THOMAS. p 121

Deed dated 1818. BENJAMIN DRAKE & HANNAH, his wife, to HARRY PIERSON. New York town lots S 6, T 1, R 1. Signed BENJAMIN DRAKE, HANNAH (x) DRAKE. Witness: MARTIN ADKINS, ROBERT McCORKLE. pp 121, 122, 123

Deed dated 1818. JOHN FRANCIS DUFOUR & POLLY, his wife, to ABNER CLARKSON & J. & N. HUNT as tenants in common. Vevay lot 133. Signed JOHN FRANCIS DUFOUR, POLLY DUFOUR. Witness: TRUMAN RICHARDS, JOHN GILLILAND. pp 123, 124

Deed dated 1818. JOHN FRANCIS DUFOUR & POLLY his wife to JAMES C. MORSELL & WILLIAM K. LAMBDIN. Vevay lot 107. Signed JOHN FRANCIS DUFOUR, POLLY DUFOUR. Witness: TRUMAN RICHARDS, JOHN GILLILAND. pp 124, 125

Deed dated 1818. STEPHEN C. STEPHENS of Franklin Co to JOSEPH L. McGEE. Vevay lot 126. Signed S. C. STEPHENS. Witness: TRUMAN RICHARDS, JOHN GILLILAND. pp 126, 127

Agreement dated 1815. JOHN FRANCIS DUFOUR, acting as agent for JOHN JAMES DUFOUR, to CHARLES RICKETTS. Vevay outlot 28. RICKETTS to make payment by Sept, 1816. Signed JOHN FRANCIS DUFOUR, CHARLES (x) RICKETTS. Witness: JOHN T. DEMING, JOHN BADOLLET. RICKETTS reassigned right to WILLIAM J. STEWART dated 1815, witness PETER VAN BRIGGLE. pp 127, 128, 129

Deed dated 1818. JOHN JAMES DUFOUR to WILLIAM J. STEWART, assignee of CHARLES RICKETS. S 13, T 2, R 3. Signed J. J. DUFOUR. Witness: TRUMAN RICHARDS, WILLIAM C. KEEN. pp 129, 130

Affidavit dated 1818. In 1815, HENRY BLUNT prepared a bill of sale for PRESTON HAMPTON to give JOSEPH GOODWIN for the purchase of a black woman PEGGY. He was told GOODWIN had set PEGGY free. Signed HENRY BLUNT, Pendleton Co, KY. Certification by WILLIAM CAMPBELL: In 1816, GOODWIN of Gallatin Co, KY brought PEGGY across the Ohio River and set her free in CAMPBELL's presence. p 131

Deed dated 1818. JOHN JAMES DUFOUR to EBENEZER STARLIN. S 13, T 2, R 3. Signed J. J. DUFOUR. Witness: WILLIAM C. KEEN. pp 131, 132, 133

SWITZERLAND COUNTY DEEDS: Book A

Deed dated 1818. JOHN FRANCIS DUFOUR & POLLY his wife, to STEPHEN C. STEPHENS & LAURENCE NIKELL, tenants in common. Vevay lot 34. Signed JOHN FRANCIS DUFOUR, POLLY DUFOUR. Witness: TRUMAN RICHARDS, WILLIAM C. KEEN. pp 133, 134, 135

Deed dated 1818. JOHN FRANCIS DUFOUR & POLLY, his wife, to STEPHEN C. STEVENS, late of Franklin Co. Vevay outlot 32. Signed JOHN FRANCIS DUFOUR, POLLY DUFOUR. Witness: TRUMAN RICHARDS, WILLIAM C. KEEN. pp 135, 136

Bond dated 1816. JOHN FRANCIS DUFOUR to JAMES DALMAZZO. DUFOUR to give deed for Vevay lot 68 by 1820. Signed JOHN FRANCIS DUFOUR. Witness: DANIEL DUFOUR. DALMAZZO reassigned title (in French) to ANTOINE GUIBERT dated 1817, witness SIMEON JOHN DUFLON, JEAN DESPOUYS. GUIBERT reassigned title (in French) to PHILIPE AUGUSTE SANDOZ & ERNESTE SANDOZ dated 1817, witness DAVID MATILE, CHARLES ULMER. pp 136, 137

Bond dated 1815. DANIEL DUFOUR BLANC* to BENJAMIN NORTON. DUFOUR to give title to Vevay lot 119 by 1820. Signed D'L. DUFOUR BLANC. Witness: J.G. FLUGEL. NORTON reassigned to WILLIAM C. KEEN & JOHN B. MINOLA, dated 1818, witness JOHN DUMONT. MINOLA reassigned to KEEN, dated 1817, witness DANIEL DUFOUR p 137   *BLANC possibly wife's family name, in old French tradition, used to increase social standing. Signature appears with and without BLANC usage. (See Bk A, p 192, 193: Vevay lot sale without BLANC)

Bond dated 1814. LUCIEN GEX to JOHN GODFREY FLUGEL. GEX to give title to Vevay lot 113 by 1820. Signed LUCIEN GEX. Witness: JOHN FRANCIS DUFOUR, JAMES DALMAZZO. FLUGEL reassigned rights to ALLEN L. WOODNUT of Cincinnati, OH. Witness: LUKE OBOUSSIER. p 138

POA dated 1817. PHILLIPE AUGUSTE SANDOZ of Philadelphia, PA appted DANIEL DUFOUR to act on his behalf. Signed PHILIPE A. SANDOZ. Witness: HEZEKIAH B. HULL. pp 138, 139

Deed dated 1818. JOSEPH MALIN & NANCY his wife to STEPHEN C. STEVENS. S 13, T 2, R 3. Signed JOSEPH MALIN, NANCY MALIN. Witness; JOSEPH BENTLEY, WILLIAM C. KEEN. pp 139, 140, 141

Deed dated 1818. JOHN FRANCIS DUFOUR & POLLY, his wife, to STEPHEN C. STEVENS. Vevay lot 176. Signed JOHN FRANCIS DUFOUR, POLLY DUFOUR. Witness: TRUMAN RICHARDS, JOHN GILLILAND. pp 141, 142, 143

SWITZERLAND COUNTY DEEDS: Book A

Deed dated 1818. HENRY COTTON, RAWLEIGH DAY & SALLY, his wife, to STEPHEN C. STEVENS. S 13, T 2, R 3W. Signed HENRY COTTON, RAWLEIGH DAY, SALLY DAY. Witness JOSHUA H. BROWN, WILLIAM C. KEEN. pp 143, 144

Deed dated 1817. JAMES CURRY to ELIAKAM JONES. S 28, T 3, R 1W. Signed JAMES CURRY, SALLY (x) CURRY. Witness: SAMUEL JELLEY, CALEB A. CRAFT. pp 144, 145, 146

Bond dated 1817. DANIEL DUFOUR to PHILLIPE AUGUSTE SANDOZ. DUFOUR to give title to Vevay lot 119 by 1820. Signed D'L. DUFOUR. Witness: WALTER ARMSTRONG THOMAS ARMSTRONG. pp 146, 147

Deed dated 1817. JAMES TRUESDELL & NANCY, his wife, to JOHN SMITH. Land in Posey Twp, bounds given. Signed JAMES TRUESDELL, NANCY (x) TRUESDELL. Witness: JOHN McCLURE, ETHAN STONE, RICHARD WOOD, WMS. PIERSON. pp 147, 148

Deed dated 1818. JOHN FRANCIS DUFOUR & POLLY, his wife, to JOHN SHAFFER of Montgomery Co, OH. Vevay lot 11. Signed JOHN FRANCIS DUFOUR, POLLY DUFOUR. Witness: TRUMAN RICHARDS, JOHN GILLILAND. pp 149, 150

Deed dated 1818. JOHN JAMES DUFOUR to JOHN SHAFFER of Germantown, Montgomery Co, OH. S 13, T 2, R 3. Signed JOHN JAMES DUFOUR. Witness: WILLIAM C. KEEN, G. COGGSHELL. pp 150, 151

Deed dated 1817. ZEALLY MOSS, JENNY MOSS, BARNA BARNUM & POLLY, his wife, to JOHN SMITH. Bounds given in Posey Twp, no S-T-R. Signed ZEALLY MOSS, JANET MOSS, BARNA BARNUM, POLLY BARNUM. Witness: RICHARD WOODS, WMS. PEIRSON. pp 152, 153

Bond dated 1814. F. LOUIS RAYMOND to JOHN GODFREY FLUGEL of Cincinnati. RAYMOND to give title to Vevay lot 112 by 1820. signed F. LOUIS RAYMOND. Witness: GEORGE COGGSHELL, JOHN FRANCIS DUFOUR. pp 153, 154

Deed dated 1818. HENRY COTTON to THOMAS ARMSTRONG. Vevay lot 34. Signed HENRY COTTON. Witness: WILLIAM C. KEEN. pp 154, 155

Bond dated 1817. HUGH COEN to EDWARD COEN & MARGARET his wife. HUGH to provide food, shelter & burial for EDWARD & MARGARET. Signed HUGH (x) COEN. Witness: JOHN GILLILAND. p 156

Bond dated 1817. WILLIAM ROSS to LARKIN COOK. ROSS to give deed (no S-T-R, only bounds) before 1822.

SWITZERLAND COUNTY DEEDS: Book A

Signed WILLIAM ROSS. Witness: ROBERT RAY, JAMES WILSON. pp 156, 157

Deed dated 1818. PAXTON W. TODD & MARTHA, his wife, to ABNER CLARKSON. Vevay lot 167. Signed P.W. TODD, MARTHA Y. or Z. TODD. Witness: TRUMAN RICHARDS, WM. C. KEEN. pp 157, 158

Deed dated 1818. JOHN FRANCIS DUFOUR & POLLY, his wife, to JOHN McCLUTCHE, assignee of JONATHAN REEDER. Vevay lot 9. Signed JOHN FRANCIS DUFOUR, POLLY DUFOUR. Witness: WM. C. KEEN, ROBERT BURCHFIELD. pp 158, 159, 160

Quitclaim dated 1818. AIME' DUFOUR to JOHN JAMES DUFOUR. Land granted by USA to JJD, no S-T-R. Signed AIME' DUFOUR. Witness: JOHN FRANCIS DUFOUR. p 160

Deed dated 1818. JOHN JAMES DUFOUR to AIME' DUFOUR, brother of JOHN JAMES. S 2, T 1, R 2. Signed JOHN JAMES DUFOUR. Witness: JOHN FRANCIS DUFOUR, WILLIAM KEEN. pp 160, 161, 162

Deed dated 1818. JOHN JAMES DUFOUR to STEPHEN C. STEVENS. S 12, T 2, R 3. "surveyed by JOHN GILLI-LAND for JOHN DAVID DUFOUR...to NATHAN PEAK's eastern boundary". Signed JOHN JAMES DUFOUR. Witness: TRUMAN RICHARDS, JOHN FRANCIS DUFOUR. pp 162, 163, 164

Quitclaim deed dated 1818. JOHN DAVID DUFOUR to JOHN JAMES DUFOUR, his brother. All land granted to JOHN JAMES DUFOUR by USA, to allow JJD to give clear deed to STEPHEN C. STEVENS. Signed J'N. DAVID DUFOUR. Witness: JOHN FRANCIS DUFOUR, TRUMAN RICHARDS. pp 164, 165

Deed dated 1817. ELISHA WADE & NANCY, his wife, to JOSHUA PETTY. S 13, no T - R. Signed ELISHA WADE, NANCY (x) WADE. Witness: WILLIAM W. WARNER, ROBERT McCORKLE. pp 165, 166

Deed dated 1818. JACOB SHIRK & MARY, his wife, to JOSHUA PETTY. S 12, T 2, R 1. Signed JACOB SHIRK, MARY (x) SHIRK. Witness: JAMES ROBERTSON, ARCHIBALD MERIT. pp 166, 167

Deed dated 1818. JOHN FRANCIS DUFOUR & POLLY, his wife to THOMAS EVINS. Vevay lot 54. Signed JOHN FRANCIS DUFOUR, POLLY DUFOUR. Witness: TRUMAN RICHARDS, JOHN GILLILAND. pp 168, 169

SWITZERLAND COUNTY DEEDS: Book A

Deed dated 1813. USA to JOHN GREENER of Cincinnati, OH. S 4, T 1, R 2W. p 169

Deed dated 1818. JOHN GREENER of Cincinnati, OH to SAMUEL McCORMICK of Montgomery Co, OH. S 4 & 9, T 1, R 2W. "AUGUSTA, his wife". Signed JOHN GREENER, AUGUSTA GREENER. Witness: ROBERT McCLEARY, RALPH McCORMICK, JOHN MAHARD. pp 169, 170, 171

Lease dated 1818. S.C. STEVENS to JOHN PERNET. "land purchased of JOHN DAVID DUFOUR"; no S-T-R. Signed S.C. STEVENS, J. PERNET. Witness: J. J. DUFOUR, THOMAS ARMSTRONG. pp 171, 172, 173, 174

Deed dated 1818. JOHN FRANCIS DUFOUR & POLLY, his wife to JOHN DUMONT. Vevay lot 83. Signed JOHN FRANCIS DUFOUR, POLLY DUFOUR. Witness: TRUMAN RICHARDS, WILLIAM C. KEEN. pp 174, 175

Bond revocation dated 1818. JOSEPH HAYS to CHARLES F. KRUTZ. Quitclaim on 1816 bond on S 8, T 1, R 2. Signed JOSEPH HAYS. Witness: CHS. MURET. p 176

Deed dated 1818. AMOS GILBERT & SALLY, his wife, to SAMUEL FINTON. S 11, T 11, R 3W. Signed AMOS GILBERT SALLY (x) GILBERT. Witness: JOHN GILLILAND, JOHN PROTSMAN. pp 176, 177, 178

Deed dated 1818. AMOS GILBERT & SALLY, his wife, to GABRIEL JOHNSON. S 11, T 2, R 3W. Signed AMOS GILBERT SALLY (x) GILBERT. Witness: JOHN GILLILAND, JOHN PROTSMAN. pp 178, 179, 180

Bequest dated 1818. WILLIAM SHARP to JOHN IVY, "beloved stepson". Bequeathed all land & property of WILLIAM & wife ANNA upon their deaths to JOHN. Signed WILLIAM (x) SHARP. Witness: THOMAS EVINS, JAMES D. DAUGHERTY. p 180

Deed dated 1818. JAMES RICHARDSON & HANNAH his wife late of NY, now of SC, to WILLIAM COTTON. S 15, T 3, R 3W. Signed JAMES RICHARDSON, HANNAH RICHARDSON. Witness: WILLIAM C. KEEN. pp 181, 182

Deed dated 1818. HARMAN LEEK & ELIZABETH, his wife, to JACOB KERN. Vevay lot 136. Signed HARMAN LEEK, ELIZABETH LEEK. Witness: JOSEPH PUGH, CONRAD (x) LEEK. pp 182, 183

Deed dated 1818. NATHAN PLATT, late of SC, to MORDECAI REDD. S 2, T 2, R 3. "corner of ARMSTRONG & CUNNINGHAM's land...to DAVID BEEBE's corner". Signed

SWITZERLAND COUNTY DEEDS: Book A

NATHAN PLATT. Witness: DAVID BEEBE, WM. C. KEEN.
pp 183, 184, 185

Quitclaim dated 1818. DANIEL DUFOUR to JOHN JAMES DUFOUR. Released all claim to land granted JJD by USA in exchange for deed to land on which DANIEL lived, granted to JJD in 1803. Signed DANIEL DUFOUR. Witness: none. pp 185, 186

Deed dated 1818. JOHN JAMES DUFOUR to DANIEL DUFOUR, his brother. S 14 & 15, T 2, R 3. "on line between DANIEL & JOHN FRANCIS DUFOUR, his brother". Signed JOHN JAMES DUFOUR. Witness: JOHN GILLILAND, JOHN SHEETS. pp 186, 187, 188

Deed dated 1818. DANIEL DUFOUR BLANC & FANNY DUFOUR, his wife, to JOHN SHEETS of Jefferson Co. S 14 & 23, T 2, R 3W. Signed DANIEL DUFOUR BLANC, FANNY DUFOUR BLANC. Witness: JOHN GILLILAND, SALLY PARKINSON. pp 188, 189

Vevay addition plat dated 1818. DANIEL DUFOUR BLANC & JOHN SHEETS, proprietors. pp 190, 191

Deed dated 1818. JOHN FRANCIS DUFOUR & POLLY, his wife to RAWLEIGH DAY. Vevay lots 99, 139. Signed JOHN FRANCIS DUFOUR, POLLY DUFOUR. Witness: TRUMAN RICHARDS, WILLIAM C. KEEN. pp 191, 192

Bond dated 1818. DANIEL DUFOUR to JACOB FRED. To deliver title to Vevay additon 72 by 1820. Signed DANIEL DUFOUR. Witness: JOHN GAVIT. FRED assigned rights to J. DUMONT in 1818, signed JACOB (x) FREDE. pp 192, 193

Agreement dated 1819. Conditions of sale of Vevay addition lots. Signed DANIEL DUFOUR BLANC, JOHN SHEETS. Witness: none. pp 193, 194

Deed dated 1818. JOHN FRANCIS DUFOUR & POLLY his wife to WILLIAM SMITH, late of Erie Co, PA. Vevay lot 58. Signed JOHN FRANCIS DUFOUR, POLLY DUFOUR. Witness: JAMES DALMAZZO, WILLIAM C. KEEN. pp 194, 195

Release dated 1818. JOHN TREAT DEMING to JOHN JAMES DUFOUR. Grants right of way on Vevay lot 41. Signed JOHN T. DEMING. Witness: none. pp 195, 196

Deed dated 1818. JOHN FRANCIS DUFOUR & POLLY, his wife to SALEM POCOCK, late of OH. Vevay lot 97. Signed JOHN FRANCIS DUFOUR, POLLY DUFOUR. Witness: WILLIAM C. KEEN. pp 196, 197

SWITZERLAND COUNTY DEEDS: Book A

Deed dated 1818. JOHN FRANCIS DUFOUR & POLLY, his wife to DANIEL POCOCK, late of OH. Vevay lot 180. Signed JOHN FRANCIS DUFOUR, POLLY DUFOUR. Witness: WILLIAM C. KEEN. pp 197, 198, 199

Deed dated 1817. USA to JOHN MARLING of Cincinnati, OH. S 18, T 2, R 3. p 199

Deed dated 1818. JOHN JAMES DUFOUR to HENRY COTTON. S 13, T 2, R 3. Signed JOHN JAMES DUFOUR. Witness: TRUMAN RICHARDS, JOHN FRANCIS DUFOUR. pp 200, 201

Deed dated 1818. WILLIAM J. STEWART & SUSANNAH, his wife, to RAWLEIGH DAY & HENRY COTTON. S 13, T 2, R 3. Signed WILLIAM J. STEWART, SUSANNAH (x) STEWART. Witness: WILLIAM C. KEEN. pp 201, 202, 203

Deed dated 1818. THOMAS ARMSTRONG to STEPHEN C. STEVENS. S 13, T 2, R 3. Signed THOMAS ARMSTRONG, MARGRET (x) ARMSTRONG. Witness: WILLIAM C. KEEN, JONAS BALDWIN. pp 203, 204, 205

Deed dated 1819. JOHN FRANCIS DUFOUR & POLLY, his wife to FRANCIS BONNER. Vevay lot 10. Signed JOHN FRANCIS DUFOUR, POLLY DUFOUR. Witness: AIME' DUFOUR ELISHA GOLAY. pp 205, 206

Deed dated 1818. NATHAN PLATT to DAVID BEEBE. S 2, T 2, R 3. Signed NATHAN PLATT. Witness: WILLIAM C. KEEN, RAWLEIGH DAY. pp 206, 207, 208

Deed dated 1819. JOHN DETRAZ to JEANNE DETRAZ. S 19, T 2, R 3W. "issued under patent to name JOHN DENTRAZ dated 5 May, 1818". Signed JN. DETRAZ. Witness: JOHN FRANCIS DUFOUR. pp 208, 209

Deed dated 1819. JOHN JAMES DUFOUR to FRANCIS LOUIS DIZERENS. S 27, T 2, R 3. Signed J.J. DUFOUR. Witness: TRUMAN RICHARDS, JOHN FRANCIS DUFOUR, WM. C. KEEN. pp 209, 210, 211

Deed dated 1818. JOHN FRANCIS DUFOUR & POLLY, his wife to ABRAHAM B. DUMONT. Vevay lot 103. Signed JOHN FRANCIS DUFOUR, POLLY DUFOUR. Witness: JOHN GILLILAND, RAWLEIGH DAY. pp 211, 212

Deed dated 1818. ANDREW STAPLETON & BARBARY his wife to JOHN HARCOURT. S 26, T 3, R 3W. Signed ANDREW (x) STAPLETON, BARBARY (x) STAPLETON. Witness: JOHN GILLELAND, ABNER CLARKSON. pp 212, 213, 214

Deed dated 1818. JOHN STAPLETON & POLLY his wife to

SWITZERLAND COUNTY DEEDS: Book A

PETER HARPER. S 26, T 3, R 3W. Signed JOHN STAPLETON, POLLY (x) STAPLETON. Witness: JOHN GILLILAND, JOSEPH MALIN. pp 214, 215, 216

Deed dated 1818. JOHN TREAT DEMING & DEBORAH, his wife, to JOHN FRANCIS DUFOUR. S 13, T 2, R 3. Signed JOHN T. DEMING, DEBORAH DEMING. Witness: JAMES DUGAN, TRUMAN RICHARDS. pp 216, 217

Deed dated 1818. JOHN FRANCIS DUFOUR & POLLY, his wife to STEPHEN C. STEVENS. Vevay lot 61. Signed JOHN FRANCIS DUFOUR, POLLY DUFOUR. Witness: TRUMAN RICHARDS, WILLIAM C. KEEN. pp 218, 219

Deed dated 1815. JOHN BUCKHANEN & RACHEL, his wife, to WILLIAM PHILIPS. S 6, T 1, R 1. Signed JOHN BUCHANEN, RACHEL (x) BUCKHANEN. Witness: JOHN GILLILAND JACOB SHORT. pp 219, 220

Bond dated 1818. DANIEL DUFOUR, JOHN FRANCIS SIEBENTHAL, JOHN JAMES DUFOUR to Gov'r of IN. Performance bond for SIEBENTHAL as Sheriff. Signed JOHN FRANCIS SIEBENTHAL, DANIEL DUFOUR, JOHN JAMES DUFOUR. Witness: JOHN FRANCIS DUFOUR. p 221

Bond dated 1818. CHARLES F. KRUTZ, WILLIAM BRADLEY & THOMAS ARMSTRONG to Gov'r. of IN. Performance bond for KRUTZ as Coroner. Signed CHARLES F. KRUTZ, WM. BRADLEY, THOS. ARMSTRONG. Witness: JOHN FRANCIS DUFOUR. pp 221, 222

Deed dated 1819. JOHN QUIGLEY of Posey Twp to DENNIS QUIGLEY. S 13, T 2, R 1W. Dower rights waived by MARY QUIGLEY, wife of JOHN. Signed JOHN (x) QUIGLEY, MARY (x) QUIGLEY. Witness: ROBERT McCORKHILL, JACOB WIGAL. pp 222, 223

Certificate dated 1816. JOHN QUIGLEY purchased S 1, T 2, R 1 at the Cincinnati Land Office. Signed DANIEL SYMMES, Register of Land Office. QUIGLEY assigned rights to JACOB WIGAL in 1819. Witness: PATRICK DONOHOE. pp 223, 224

Quitclaim dated 1819. JOHN DANIEL MOREROD & ANTOINETTE, his wife, JOHN FRANCIS SIEBENTHAL & JEANNE MARIE, his wife, PHILIPE BETTENS & ROSE, his wife, to JOHN JAMES DUFOUR. Land purchased from USA in 1801. Deeds given to ELISHE GOLAY, FREDERICK SCHMIDT; land sold to CHARLES MURET & WILLIAM STOUT. Signed PH. BETTENS, ROSE BETTENS, JOHN F. SIEBENTHAL. J. MARIE SIEBENTHAL, JEAN MOREROD, ANTOINETTE MOREROD. Witness: JOHN FRANCIS DUFOUR, WM. C. KEEN. pp 225, 226

SWITZERLAND COUNTY DEEDS: Book A

Deed dated 1819. JOHN JAMES DUFOUR to PHILIP BETTENS. S 15 & 23, 14 & 22, T 2, R 3. "to DAVID GOLAY". Signed JOHN JAMES DUFOUR. Witness: JOHN FRANCIS DUFOUR, WILLIAM C. KEEN. pp 226, 227, 228

Deed dated 1817. USA to JOHN JAMES DUFOUR & associates (not named). S 7 & 18, T 1, R 2. pp 228, 229

Deed dated 1817. USA to JOHN JAMES DUFOUR & associates (not named). 2 12 & 14, T 2, R 3. pp 229, 230

Deed dated 1819. BENJAMIN DRAKE & HANNAH, his wife, to WILLIAM CAMPBELL. New York town lots 1, 2, 7, 13, 18, 30, 31, 32, 33, 34, 35, 36, 38, 45, 46, 47, 48, 49, 50, 51, 52, 57, 60, 61, 64. Signed BENJAMIN DRAKE, HANNAH (x) DRAKE. Witness: JOHN GILLILAND, ELIZABETH (x) ADKINS. pp 230, 231, 232

Deed dated 1819. HENRY HANNIS & HANNAH, his wife, to JAMES BELL. S 36, T 3, R 4W. "to SARAH BELL". Signed HENERY HANNIS, HANNAH (x) HANNIS. Witness: JOSEPH GILLILAND, JOSEPH TODD. pp 232, 233

Deed dated 1818. DANIEL DUFOUR & FANNY ELIZABETH. his wife, to STEPHEN C. STEVENS. Vevay lot 25. Signed DANIEL DUFOUR, FANNY ELIZABETH BLANC. Witness: TRUMAN RICHARD, WM. C. KEEN. pp 233, 234, 235

Deed dated 1819. JOHN JAMES DUFOUR to FREDERICK SCHMIDT, late "citizen of Canton of Bern &...now of Switzerland Co". S 7 & 8, T 1, R 2W. Signed JOHN JAMES DUFOUR. Witness: WM. C. KEEN, J.R. WHITEHEAD. pp 235, 236, 237

Deed dated 1818. JOHN FRANCIS DUFOUR & POLLY. his wife to FREDERICK SCHMIDT. Vevay lot 93. Signed JOHN FRANCIS DUFOUR, POLLY DUFOUR. Witness: TRUMAN RICHARDS, JONAS BALDWIN. pp 237, 238

Deed dated 1819. JOHN JAMES DUFOUR to JOHN DANIEL MORREROD, "late of Montreux, Canton of Vaud, republic of Switzerland, now of Vevay". S 15, 14 & 23, T 2, R 3. Signed J. J. DUFOUR. Witness: JOHN FRANCIS DUFOUR, WILLIAM C. KEEN. pp 238, 239, 240, 241

Deed dated 1818. DANIEL DUFOUR & FANNY ELIZABETH his wife to STEPHEN C. STEVENS. Vevay outlot bounded by JOHN DUMONT & MARTHA DYER MANVILLE. Signed DANIEL DUFOUR, FANNY DUFOUR. Witness: JAMES ROUS, WM. C. KEEN. pp 241, 242, 243

Agreement dated 1819. STEPHEN C. STEVENS, MOSES GRAY

SWITZERLAND COUNTY DEEDS: Book A

& LEWIS HOUGHMAN. S 10, T 2, R W. Lists work to be done by GRAY & HOUGHMAN for lease of land lately occupied by WILLIAM BRANDENBURGH. Signed S.C. STEVENS, MOSES GRAY, LEWIS (x) HUFFMAN. Witness: E. S. HARRELL. pp 243, 244

Deed dated 1818. JOHN FRANCIS DUFOUR & POLLY, his wife to JOHN BROWN, shoemaker. Vevay lot 179. Signed JOHN FRANCIS DUFOUR, POLLY DUFOUR. Witness: TRUMAN RICHARDS, WM. C. KEEN. pp 244, 245, 246

Deed dated 1819. FRANCIS BARNES & HENRIETTA, his wife, to JOHN BROWN. Vevay lot 179, to be paid in (listed) dry goods. Signed FRANCIS BARNES, HENRIETTA BARNES. Witness: TRUMAN RICHARDS, WM. C. KEEN. pp 246, 247, 248

Deed dated 1818. JOHN JAMES DUFOUR to STEPHEN C. STEVENS. Vevay outlot 33. Signed J.J. DUFOUR. Witness: WM. C. KEEN. pp 248, 249

Deed dated 1818. JOHN FRANCIS DUFOUR & POLLY, his wife to NATHANIEL P. PORTER & WILLIAM E. YOUNG of Gallatin Co, KY. Vevay lot 56. Signed JOHN FRANCIS DUFOUR, POLLY DUFOUR. Witness: TRUMAN RICHARDS, THOMAS ARMSTRONG. pp 249, 250, 251

Indenture dated 13 Jan, 1819. SAMUEL EVANS, son of RACHEL EVANS, age 11 yrs, 2 mo, 2 days, "father of SAMUEL being dead", was apprenticed to STEPHEN C. STEVENS for 9 yrs, 9 mo. Terms & conditions given, trade not specified. Signed SAMUEL (x) EVANS, RACHEL (x) EVANS, S. C. STEVENS. Witness: WILLIAM C. KEEN. pp 251, 252

Deed dated 1819. WILLIAM CAMPBELL & POLLY, his wife, to JOHN MOORE. S 11, T 2, R 2W. Signed WILLIAM CAMPBELL, POLLY CAMPBELL. Witness: JOHN GILLILAND, JENNET CAMPBELL. pp 252, 253, 254

Deed dated 1818. JOHN FRANCIS DUFOUR & POLLY, his wife to SAMUEL FALLIS. Vevay lot --. Signed JOHN FRANCIS DUFOUR, POLLY DUFOUR. Witness: JN. DAVID DUFOUR, WM. C. KEEN. pp 254, 255

Indenture dated 5 Feb, 1819. RACHEL EVANS, dau of RACHEL EVANS, age 7 yrs, 5 mo, 26 days (her father being dead), was apprenticed to STEPHEN C. STEVENS for 10 yrs, 6 mo. Signed RACHEL (x) EVANS, RACHEL (x) EVANS, S. C. STEVENS. Witness: WILLIAM C. KEEN. pp 255, 256

SWITZERLAND COUNTY DEEDS: Book A

Deed dated 1818. JOHN FRANCIS DUFOUR & POLLY, his wife to JOSHUA BROWN, assignee of JOHN HAWKINS of Clermont Co, OH. Vevay lot 70. Signed JOHN FRANCIS DUFOUR, POLLY DUFOUR. Witness: THOMAS ARMSTRONG, PETER VAN BRIGGLE. pp 257, 258

Deed dated 1818. JOSHUA BROWN of Clermont Co, OH to PETER VAN BRIGGLE. Vevay lot 70. Signed JOSHUA BROWN. Witness: WM. C. KEEN, CHARLES F. KRUTZ. pp 258, 259

Deed dated 1818. BENJAMIN DRAKE & HANNAH, his wife, to WILLIAM CAMPBELL. S 6, T 1, R 1W. "patented to WILLIAM PHILIPS & JOHN BUCKHANON". Signed BENJAMIN DRAKE, HANNAH (x) DRAKE. Witness: JOHN GILLILAND, JOSEPH NELSON. pp 259, 260, 261

Deed dated 1819. JOHN NELSON & IBBERELLA, his wife, and JOSEPH NELSON & NANCY, his wife, to WILLIAM CAMPBELL. S 33, T 2, R 1W. Signed JOHN (x) NELSON, IBBERELLA (x) NELSON, JOSEPH NELSON, NANCY (x) NELSON. Witness: JOHN GILLILAND, NICHOLAS KEITH, SAMUEL LINEBACK, LEVINA NELSON. pp 261, 262, 263

Deed dated 1815. WILLIAM PHILIPS & MARY, his wife, to JOHN BUCHANON of Jefferson Co. S 36, T 1, R 1. Signed WILLIAM (x) PHILIPS, MARY (x) PHILIPS. Witness: JOSEPH NELSON, BENJAMIN DRAKE. pp 263, 264

Deed dated 1818. CHARLES F. KRUTZ to JOSEPH HAYS. S 8, T 1, R 2W. Bounds: by PETER MING, GEORGE LINGER or SINGER & GEORGE ROTES. Signed CHARLES F. KRUTZ. Witness: CHAS. MURET. pp 265, 266

Deed dated 1818. NATHAN PLATT & POLLY, his wife, to THOMAS ARMSTRONG & RICHARD ARMSTRONG. S 2, T 2, R 3W. Signed NATHAN PLATT, POLLY PLATT. Witness: JAMES FISLAR, JOHN PRATHER. pp 266, 267, 268

Deed dated 1819. HARMAN LEEK & ELIZABETH, his wife, to CATHARINE ANDERSON. Vevay lot 135. Signed HARMAN LEEK, ELIZABETH LEEK. Witness: HENREY MONTOOTH, CYRUS MOORE. pp 268, 269

Deed dated 1819. JOSIAH WOODRUFF & POLLY, his wife, to SEARS B. MOTT. "corner of JOHN MOORE's land"; no S-T-R given. Signed JOSIAH WOODRUFF, POLLY WOODRUFF. Witness: HERMAN LEEK, HENREY MONTOOTH. pp 269, 270

Deed dated 1818. BENJAMIN DRAKE & HANNAH, his wife, to HUGH McNULTY of Hamilton Co, OH. New York town lots 54, 55. Signed BENJAMIN DRAKE, HANNAH (X) DRAKE Witness: HARRY PIERSON, RALPH COLE. pp 270, 271

SWITZERLAND COUNTY DEEDS: Book A

Deed dated 1818. ZACHARIAH GARTON & POLLY, his wife, to CALEB HAYS. S 34, T 2, R 1W. Signed ZACHARIAH GARTON, POLLY (x) GARTON. Witness: none. pp 271, 272

Deed dated 1818. BENJAMIN DRAKE & HANNAH, his wife, to MARTIN ADKINS. New York town lots 8 & 24. Signed BENJAMIN DRAKE, HANNAH (x) DRAKE. Witness: HARRY PIERSON, HUGH McNULTY. pp 272, 273

Bill of sale dated 1819. JOHN QUIGLEY of Posey Twp to JACOB WIGAL. Household goods, implements & cattle. Signed JOHN (x) QUIGLEY. Witness: ROBERT GASTON, JAMES (x) SMITH. pp 274, 275

Deed dated 1819. JOHN FRANCIS DUFOUR & POLLY, his wife to JOSHUA SMITHSON, assignee of JOHN G. FLUGEL. Vevay lot 64. Signed JOHN FRANCIS DUFOUR, POLLY DUFOUR. Witness: TRUMAN RICHARDS, WM. C. KEEN. pp 254, 255

Bill of sale dated 1819. THOMAS STITH to ZACHARIAH McKAY. One bay mare. Signed THOMAS STITH. Witness; none. pp 276, 277

Deed dated 1819. DANIEL DUFOUR & FANNY, his wife, to ABRAHAM B. DUMONT. Vevay lot 74. Signed DANIEL DUFOUR, FANNY DUFOUR BLANC. Witness: SAMUEL FALLIS, WM C. KEEN. pp 277, 278

Quitclaim dated 1819. AUGUSTUS VAIRIN & SOPHIA, his wife, to JUSTUS VAIRIN of Gallatin Co, KY. "estate of JOHN PETER VAIRIN, dec, of Switzerland Co...as a son of JOHN PETER, S 27 & 22, T 2, R 3 plus household goods & animals of estate". Signed A. VAIRIN, SOPHIA VAIRIN nee PERNET. Witness: JOHN F. DUFOUR, L. GEX OBOUSSIER. pp 278, 279, 280, 281, 282

Deed dated 1819. JOHN MENDENHALL to LEWIS CRAIG of Ghent, Gallatin Co, KY. Vevay lot 172. Signed JNO. MENDENHALL. Witness: JOS. CRAIG, JAMES O'NEAL. pp 282, 283

POA dated 1817. SETH STODDER of Orleans in state of Orleans appt'd JOHN GILLILAND as atty to lease or sell property: Vevay lot 104; S 25 & 34, T 3, R 3W; S 3 & 4, T 2, R 3W; S 6, T 1, R 2; cash in the hands of FETRARCH FOHL or FALL of Laughery, Dearborn Co. Signed SETH STODDER. pp 283, 290 (284 through 290 missed in page numbering)

POA dated 1818. ENOS ELLIS appt'd JAMES SMITH to sell or lease S 12, T 2, R 2W. Signed ENOS ELLIS.

SWITZERLAND COUNTY DEEDS: Book A

Witness: none. pp 290, 291

Deed dated 1819. JOHN MARLING & MARGARET, his wife, to WILLIAM BRANDENBURGH. S 18, T 2, R 3W. Signed JOHN MARLING, MARGARET (x) MARLING. Witness: WM. C. KEEN, ELIJAH MARLING. pp 291, 292, 293

Deed dated 1819. JOHN SHEETS of Jefferson Co to THOMAS DOUGLAS of same. Vevay outlots 106, 115, 121. Signed JOHN SHEETS, ANN G. SHEETS. Witness: ELIZABETH GARDNER, JOHN MEEK. pp 293, 294

Deed dated 1819. WILLIAM BRANDENBURGH & POLLY, his wife, to JOSEPH MALIN. S 18, T 2, R 3W. Signed WILLIAM BRANDENBURGH, POLLY (x) BRANDENBURG. Witness: JOSEPH PUGH, JOSEPH CULP, CYRUS MOORE. pp 294, 295, 296

Deed dated 1819. AIME' DUFOUR to JOHN FRANCIS DUFOUR. S 2, T 1, R 2. Signed AIME' DUFOUR. Witness: WILLIAM C. KEEN, JOHN F. SIEBENTHAL. pp 296, 297

Deed dated 1819. JOHN FRANCIS DUFOUR & POLLY, his wife to FREDERICK WALDOW. Vevay lots 144, 185, 188. Signed JOHN FRANCIS DUFOUR, POLLY DUFOUR. Witness: WM. C. KEEN, CHARLES HENDERSON. pp 297, 298, 299

Deed dated 1819. HENRY HANNIS & HANNAH, his wife, to SARAH BALL. S 36, T 3, R 4W. Signed HENRY HANNAS, HANNAH (x) HANNIS. Witness: JOHN GILLILAND, JOSEPH TODD. pp 299, 300, 301

Deed dated 1819. RICHARD CUNNINGHAM & CATHERINE, his wife, to THOMAS ARMSTRONG. S 2, T 2, R 3. "corner to WILLIAM SMITH". Signed RICHARD CUNNINGHAM, CATHARINE CUNNINGHAM. Witness: WILLIAM C. KEEN, ROBERT BONNER. pp 301, 302

Deed dated 1818. JOHN FRANCIS DUFOUR & POLLY, his wife to BARZILLA CLARK JR. Vevay lot 53. Signed JOHN FRANCIS DUFOUR, POLLY DUFOUR. Witness: JOHN GILLILAND, JAMES DALMAZZO. pp 303, 304 Note: word JUNIOR was interlined before signing.

Mortgage dated 1818. BARZILLA CLARK JR & SUSANNAH, his wife, to JOHN FRANCIS DUFOUR. Vevay lot 53. Signed BARZILLA CLARK, SUSANNAH (x) CLARK. Witness: JOHN GILLILAND, JAMES DALMAZZO. pp 304, 305, 306

Deed dated 1818. NATHAN PLATT to WILLIAM SMITH. S 2, T 2, R 3. "DAVID BEEBE's line". Signed NATHAN PLATT. Witness: RAWLEIGH DAY. pp 306, 307, 308 Deed

SWITZERLAND COUNTY DEEDS: Book A

dated 1818. AMOS GILBERT & SALLY, his wife, to JOHN PROTSMAN. S 11, T 2, R 3. "corner to GABRIEL JOHNSON." Signed AMOS GILBERT, SALLY (x) GILBERT. Witness: JOHN GILLILAND, LYMAN GILBERT. pp 308, 309, 310

Deed dated 1819. JOHN FRANCIS DUFOUR & POLLY, his wife to ELIZA D. CARTMELL, formerly ELIZA D. McGEE of KY. Vevay lot 67. Signed JOHN FRANCIS DUFOUR, POLLY DUFOUR. Witness: SAMUEL FALLIS, ELISHA GOLAY. pp 310, 311

Mortgage dated 1818. DAVID COWAN to FITTER & HUGHES of Jefferson Co, KY. Vevay inlot 148. Signed DAVID COWAN. Witness: H.B. HULL, THOS. ARMSTRONG. p 312

Deed dated 1819. SAMUEL MENNET & SALLY, his wife, to LYDIA DUTOIT. S 28, T 2, R 3W. Signed SAMUEL MENNET SALLY MENNET. Witness: WM. C. KEEN, ROBERT PHILIPS. pp 312, 313, 314

Deed dated 1819. ROBERT NICHOLSON & ANNE, his wife, of Bourbon Co, KY to JOHN LOWARDS of Scott Co, KY. S 26, T 2, R 2. Signed ROBERT F. NICHOLSON, ANN (x) NICHOLSON. Witness: none. pp 314, 315, 316

Deed dated 1819. JOHN JAMES DUFOUR to ELISHA GOLAY, late a citizen of the Canton of Vaud (Republic of Switzerland), now of Switzerland Co. S 18 & 7, T 1, R 2W. Signed JOHN JAMES DUFOUR. Witness: TRUMAN RICHARDS, WM. C. KEEN. pp 316, 317, 318

Deed dated 1818. JOHN FRANCIS DUFOUR & POLLY, his wife to JONATHAN REEDER. Vevay lot 103. Signed JOHN FRANCIS DUFOUR, POLLY DUFOUR. Witness: TRUMAN RICHARDS, WM. C. KEEN. pp 318, 319

Deed dated 1818. JOHN FRANCIS DUFOUR & POLLY, his wife to ABRAHAM LINDLEY of OH. Vevay lot 138. Signed JOHN FRANCIS DUFOUR, POLLY DUFOUR. Witness: TRUMAN RICHARDS, WM. C. KEEN. pp 319, 320, 321

Agreement dated 1818. HUGH COWEN to EDWARD COEN & MARGARET, his wife. HUGH to provide for EDWARD & MARGARET during their lifetimes. Signed HUGH (x) COEN Witness: JOHNSTON BROWN. p 321

Deed dated 1819. EDWARD McINTIRE to JAMES ARMSTRONG JR of Baltimore, MD. S 35, T 2, R 4W. Signed EDWARD McINTIRE. Witness: WM. C. KEEN, TRUMAN RICHARDS. pp 322, 323

SWITZERLAND COUNTY DEEDS: Book A

Deed dated 1816. PETER MING to JOHN GREENER of Cincinnati, OH. S 8, T 1, R 2W. Signed PETER MING. Witness: CHARLES F. KRUTZ, JOHN MAHARD. pp 323, 324, 325

Deed dated 1819. JOHN MARLING & MARGARET, his wife, to WILLIAM DOW of Jefferson Co. S 18, T 2, R 3W. Signed JOHN MARLING, MARGARET (x) MARLING. Witness: SAMUEL MERRILL, WM. C. KEEN. pp 325, 326, 327

Deed dated 1819. JOHN FRANCIS DUFOUR & POLLY, his wife to JOHN HARPER, assignee of DAVIS HARRISON of KY Vevay lot 98. Signed JOHN FRANCIS DUFOUR, POLLY DUFOUR. Witness: TRUMAN RICHARDS, WM. C. KEEN. pp 327, 328

Deed dated 1819. WILLIAM KEITH & CATHERINE, his wife to BARNABAS NEWKIRK. S 1, T 2, R 3W. Signed WILLIAM KEITH, CATHARINE KEITH. Witness: JOHN GILLILAND, JOHN DUMONT. pp 328, 329, 330

Deed dated 1819. JOHN DUMONT & JULIA LOUISA his wife to JOSEPH DOW. S 3, T 2, R 3W. Signed JOHN DUMONT, JULIA L. DUMONT. Witness: JOHN GILLILAND, JOSHUA SMITHSON. pp 330, 331, 332

Deed dated 1818. JOHN FRANCIS DUFOUR & POLLY, his wife to PAXTON W. TODD. Vevay lot 167. Signed JOHN FRANCIS DUFOUR, POLLY DUFOUR. Witness: THOMAS ARMSTRONG, WM. C. KEEN. pp 332, 333, 334

Deed dated 1819. JOHN FRANCIS DUFOUR & POLLY, his wife to JOHN DANIEL MORROOD. Vevay lot 154. Signed JOHN FRANCIS DUFOUR, POLLY DUFOUR. Witness: TRUMAN RICHARDS, WM. C. KEEN. pp 334, 335

Sheriff's sale dated 1818. JOHN F. SIEBENTHAL, Sheriff, to THOMAS ARMSTRONG. JOHN ROBINSON recovered debt in Dearborn Co Circuit Court against JOHN JORDAN & his securitor, JOHN DEMOSS. Vevay lot 122 seized, sold at auction to ARMSTRONG. Signed J. F. SIEBENTHAL, Sheriff. Witness: H. B. HULL, TRUMAN RICHARDS. pp 335, 336, 337

Deed dated 1819. JOSEPH MALIN & NANCY, his wife, to WILLIAM DOW JR of Jefferson Co. S 18, T 2, R 3W. Signed JOSEPH MALIN, NANCY MALIN. Witness: WM. C. KEEN, THOMAS ARMSTRONG. pp 340, 341

Deed dated 1819. WILLIAM C. KEEN to JAMES HOLE of Hamilton Co, OH. S 24, T 3, R 3W. Signed WILLIAM C. KEEN. Witness: R.T. GODARD, JOHN GILLILAND. pp 341, 342

SWITZERLAND COUNTY DEEDS: Book A

Promissory note dated 1820. THOMAS BRADLEY & ANN, his wife, to STEPHEN C. STEPHENS. Vevay lot 126. Signed THOMAS BRADLEY, WILLIAM BRADLEY. Mortgage signed THOMAS BRADLEY, ANN BRADLEY. pp 342, 343, 345

Deed dated 1820. STEPHEN C. STEVENS & JANE, his wife to JOHN DAVID DUFOUR. "all land purchased from JOHN JAMES DUFOUR, excepting parcel sold WILLIAM H. EADS" & Vevay outlots 33 & 34. Signed S. C. STEVENS, JANE STEVENS. Witness: TRUMAN RICHARDS, WM. J. STEWERT. pp 345, 346, 347

Sheriff's sale dated 1818. JOHN F. SIEBENTHAL, Sheriff, to JOHN DAVID DUFOUR. Suit brought by DUFOUR against JOHN P. HOGAN. Vevay lot 82 seized, sold at auction to DUFOUR. Signed J. F. SIEBENTHAL, Sheriff. Witness: none. pp 347, 348, 349

Sheriff's sale dated 1820. JOHN F. SIEBENTHAL, Sheriff, to CHARLES L. VATZ. Suit brought by JOHN DEVOR against JOHN G. FLUGEL. Vevay lot 115 seized, sold at auction to VATZ. Signed J. F. SIEBENTHAL, Sheriff. Witness: JOHN FRANCIS DUFOUR, GEORGE G. KNOX. pp 349, 350, 351

Deed dated 1819. JOHN SHEETS of Jefferson Co to RICHARD VERBRYCK. Vevay addition lot 104. Signed JOHN SHEETS, ANN G. SHEETS. Witness: ELIZABETH GARDNER, JOHN MEEK. pp 351, 352, 353

Deed dated 1817. FREDERIC LINEBACK to NICHOLAS KEITH. S 28, T 2, R 1W. "that MARTIN HELDER entered". Signed FREDERICK LINEBACK, SALLY (x) LINEBACK. Witness: ROBERT McCORKHILL, ARCHIBALD SCOTT, THOS. WADE, (illegible) FLUM. pp 353, 354

Deed dated 1819. JOHN JAMES DUFOUR to LEWIS GEX OBOUSSIER. S 22, T 2, R 3. Signed J. J. DUFOUR. Witness: PETER D. BORRALLY, WM C. KEEN. pp 354, 355, 356

Deed dated 1819. JOHN FRANCIS DUFOUR & POLLY, his wife to RAWLEIGH DAY. Vevay lot 104. Signed JOHN FRANCIS DUFOUR, POLLY DUFOUR. Witness: AIME' DUFOUR, ELISHA GOLAY. pp 356, 357, 358

Deed dated 1819. JOHN FRANCIS DUFOUR & POLLY, his wife to WILLIAM BRADLEY. Vevay lot 155. Signed JOHN FRANCIS DUFOUR, POLLY DUFOUR. Witness: SAMUEL FALLIS, JOHN GILLILAND. pp 358, 359, 360

Deed dated 1818. USA to WILLIAM WHITMORE of PA. S 4, T 3, R 3. p 360

SWITZERLAND COUNTY DEEDS: Book A

Deed dated 1818. EVAN BROOK & BETSEY, his wife, to AMOS BROWN. S 32, T 2, R 1. Signed EVIN BROCK, BETS (x) BROCK. Witness: ROBERT McCORKHILL, SAMUEL BROWN. pp 361, 362

Deed dated 1819. JOHN FRANCIS SIEBENTHAL & JANE MARIE, his wife, to BARNARD WARDEN. S 15, T 2, R 3W. Signed JOHN F. SIEBENTHAL, J. MARIA SIEBENTHAL. Witness: SAM'L. FALLIS, A. B. DUMONT, WM. C. KEEN. pp 363, 364

Deed dated 1819. JOHN FRANCIS DUFOUR & POLLY, his wife to JONATHAN ABBETT & WILLIAM ABBETT of Henry Co, KY. Vevay lot 46. Signed JOHN FRANCIS DUFOUR, POLLY DUFOUR. Witness: JOHN GILLILAND JAMES DALMAZZO, RICHARD GAINS. pp 365, 366

Payment dated 1819. Ordered to S. C. STEPHENS. Signed HUGH & JAM. GLENN. p 366

Deed dated 1819. STEPHEN C. STEPHENS & JANE, his wife to WILLIAM H. EADS. Bounds given, no S-T-R. Signed S. C. STEPHENS, JANE STEPHENS. Witness: none. pp 367, 368

Deed dated 1809. USA to JOHN JAMES DUFOUR of KY. S 1 & 2, T 1, R 2. p 368

Deed dated 1819. DANIEL DUFOUR & JOHN FRANCIS DUFOUR to JAMES NOBLE & ENOCH D. JOHN of Franklin Co. Vevay lots 163, 164. Signed DANIEL DUFOUR, JOHN F. DUFOUR, POLLY DUFOUR, FANNY DUFOUR. Witness: JOSHUA PETTY, WM. C. KEEN. pp 368, 369, 370

Deed dated 1819. JOHN DUMON & JULIA LOUISA, his wife, to WILLIAM TURNER. S 3, T 2, R 3W. Signed JOHN DUMONT, JULIA L. DUMONT. Witness: JOHN GILLI-LAND, JOSEPH DOW. pp 371, 372

Deed dated 1809. USA to JOHN JAMES DUFOUR. S 22, 27 & 15, T 2, R 3W. pp 372, 373

Deed dated 1819. WILLIAM TURNER & TABITHA, his wife, to SMITH TURNER. S 3, T 2, R 3W. Signed WILLIAM (x) TURNER, TABITHA (x) TURNER. pp 373, 374

Deed dated 1820. CALEB MOUNTS of Posey Twp to JOSEPH RITCH. S 6, T 2, R 1. Signed CALEB MOUNTS, JANE MOUNTS. Witness: SAMUEL RAVENSCROFT, WILLIAM RICKETS. pp 375, 376

Deed dated 1820. PETER HARPER & MARY, his wife, to

SWITZERLAND COUNTY DEEDS: Book A

WILLIAM HARPER of Woodford Co, KY. S 26, T 3, R 3W. Signed PETER HARPER, MARY (x) HARPER. Witness: JOHN GILLILAND, FRANCIS (x) NELSON. pp 377, 378

Deed dated 1819. JOHN MOORE & SARAH, his wife, to SEARS B. MOTT. S 11, T 2, R 2. Signed JOHN MOORE, SARAH MOORE. Witness: WILLIAM GARD, JOSEPH PUGH, HENRY MONTOOTH. pp 379, 380

Deed dated 1819. JOHN JAMES DUFOUR to JOHN FRANCIS SIEBENTHAL. S 7, T 1, R 2. Signed J.J. DUFOUR. Witness: JOHN F. DUFOUR, WM. C. KEEN. pp 380, 381

Deed dated 1819. DANIEL DUFOUR & FANY, his wife, to THOMAS BRADLEY. Vevay outlot 161. Signed DANIEL DUFOUR, FANY DUFOUR. Witness: WM. C. KEEN, JOHN RIDDLE. pp 382, 383

Deed dated 1819. JOHN BROWN & BETSY, his wife, to FRANCIS BARNES. Vevay lot 179. Signed JOHN BROWN, BETSY BROWN. Witness: TRUMAN RICHARDS, WM. C. KEEN. pp 383, 384, 385

Deed dated 1819. ALEXANDER A. MEEK & MARTHA, his wife to JOHN SHEETS. Vevay lot 108. Signed ALEX A. MEEK, MARTHA MEEK. Witness: JOHN MEEK, JAMES F. D. LAURIER. pp 385, 386

Deed dated 1819. JOHN FRANCIS DUFOUR & POLLY, his wife to ISRAEL R. WHITEHEAD. Vevay lot 40. Signed JOHN FRANCIS DUFOUR, POLLY DUFOUR. Witness: TRUMAN RICHARDS, JOHN GILLILAND. pp 386, 387, 388

Deed dated 1819. ABRAHAM B. DUMONT to JAMES K. OGDEN & MOSES L. MEEKER of OH. Vevay lot 84. Signed A. B. DUMONT. Witness: JOHN GILLILAND, JOHN F. DUFOUR. pp 388, 389, 390

Deed dated 1819. JOHN JAMES DUFOUR to ABRAM DUMONT. S 13, T 2, R 3. Signed J. J. DUFOUR. Witness: TRUMAN RICHARDS, WM. C. KEEN. pp 392, 393

Deed dated 1819. BENJAMIN FARNER & MARY, his wife, of Cincinnati, OH to STEPHEN BURROWS of same. Vevay lot 187. Signed BENJ'N. FARNER, MARY FARNER. Witness: WILLIAM NEWELL, THEO SIMONTON. pp 394, 395, 396

Deed dated 1819. JOHN FRANCIS DUFOUR & POLLY, his wife to JAMES DALMAZZO. Vevay lot 90. Signed JOHN FRANCIS DUFOUR, POLLY DUFOUR. Witness: JOHN GILLILAND TRUMAN RICHARDS. pp 396, 397, 398

SWITZERLAND COUNTY DEEDS: Book A

Deed dated 1819. JOHN FRANCIS DUFOUR & POLLY, his wife to JAMES DALMAZZO. Vevay lot 128. Signed JOHN FRANCIS DUFOUR, POLLY DUFOUR. Witness: JOHN GILLILAND TRUMAN RICHARDS. pp 398, 399

Deed dated 1819. BARZILLA CLARK & SUSANNAH his wife to SAMUEL MERRILL. Vevay lot 53. Signed BARZILLA CLARK, SUSANNAH (x) CLARK. Witness: WM. C. KEEN, SOLOMON WASHER. pp 399, 400, 401

Deed dated 1819. BENJAMIN DRAKE & HANNAH, his wife to ANDREW KETCHUM of Cincinnati, OH. New York lot 56. Signed BENJAMIN DRAKE, HANNAH (x) DRAKE. Witness: HARRY PIERSON, WM. CAMPBELL. pp 401, 402

Deed dated 1819. JONATHAN McGUIRE & ELIZABETH, his wife, to WILLIAM BRADLEY. Vevay lot 166. Signed JONATHAN McGUIRE, ELIZABETH (x) McGUIRE. Witness: JOHN GILLILAND, J.J. WELCH. pp 403, 404

Deed dated 1819. F. LOUIS RAYMOND to FRANCIS LOUIS DIZEREUS, ADDAM KLEIN, JAMES TODD. Land willed by father in will dated 1811, rec Jefferson Co: no S-T-R given. Signed F. LOUIS REYMOND. Witness: CHARLES F. KRUTZ. pp 405, 406

Deed dated 1820. JOHN FRANCIS DUFOUR & POLLY, his wife to AMOS GILBERT. Vevay lot 181. Signed JOHN FRANCIS DUFOUR, POLLY DUFOUR. Witness: TRUMAN RICHARDS. pp 406, 407

Mortgage dated 1820. AMOS GILBERT to JOSEPH McFALL. On Vevay lot 181. Signed AMOS GILBERT. Witness: I. R. WHITEHEAD, W. C. KEEN. pp 408, 409

Deed dated 1819. ABRAHAM B. DUMONT to IZRAEL R. WHITEHEAD. S 13, T 2, R 3. Signed A.B. DUMONT. Witness: WM. C. KEEN, GEORGE W. WELCH. pp 410, 411, 412

Deed dated 1819. JAMES CLANCY & NANCY, his wife, to DAVID WAGONER. New York town lot 45. Signed JAMES CLANCY, NANCY CLANCY. Witness: CHRISTIAN COOPER, MARTIN ADKINS. pp 412, 413, 414

Deed dated 1819. JAMES CLANCY & NANCY, his wife, to COONROD WAGONER. New York town lot 46. Signed JAMES CLANCY, NANCY CLANCY. Witness: CHRISTIAN COOPER, MARTIN ADKINS. pp 414, 415

Deed dated 1819. JAMES CLANCY & NANCY, his wife, to CHRISTIAN COOPER. New York town lot 32. Signed JAMES CLANCY, NANCY CLANCY. Witness: MARTIN ADKINS.

SWITZERLAND COUNTY DEEDS: Book A

pp 416, 417, 418

Deed dated 1819. JOHN FRANCIS DUFOUR & POLLY, his wife to WALTER ARMSTRONG of Lawrenceburgh. Vevay lot 111. Signed JOHN FRANCIS DUFOUR, POLLY DUFOUR. Witness: JOHN GILLILAND, TRUMAN RICHARDS. pp 418, 419

Deed dated 1819. JOHN FRANCIS DUFOUR & POLLY, his wife to JOAB MADISON, assignee of RICHARD DUMONT. Vevay lot 45. Signed JOHN FRANCIS DUFOUR, POLLY DUFOUR. Witness: JOHN GILLILAND, TRUMAN RICHARDS. pp 420, 421

Deed dated 1819. WILLIAM CAMPBELL & POLLY, his wife, to WILLIAM McCORKHILL. S 20, T 2, R 1W. Signed WM. CAMPBELL, POLLY CAMPBELL. Witness: ALEXANDER SEBASTEN, AMOS BROWN. pp 421, 422, 423

Deed dated 1819. JOHN FRANCIS DUFOUR & POLLY, his wife, to BENJAMIN FARNER of Cincinnati, OH. Vevay lot 187. Signed JOHN FRANCIS DUFOUR, POLLY DUFOUR. Witness: TRUMAN RICHARDS, JOHN GILLILAND. pp 423, 424, 425

Agreement dated 1819. SIDNEY STEPHEN & JOSEPH DOW. S 3, T 2, R 3 to be purchased. Signed SIDNEY STEPHEN, JOSEPH DOW. Witness: THURSTON J. GOSLIN, EDW. H. HALL. pp 425, 426

Deed dated 1820. STEPHEN C. STEVENS to THOMAS BRADLEY. Vevay lot 176 & chattels. Signed S.C. STEVENS, JANE STEVENS. Witness: WILLIAM BRADLEY, JOHN GILLILAND. pp 426, 427, 428

Deed dated 1819. JOHN SHEETS of Jefferson Co to SOLOMON WASHER JR. Vevay lot 122. Signed JOHN SHEETS, ANN SHEETS. Witness: I. R. WHITEHEAD, JOHN MEEK. pp 429, 430

Deed dated 1818; USA to ELIJAH GRIMES, assignee of THOMAS EVANS. S 15, T 4, R 12E. p 430

Deed dated 1819. BARNARD WARDEN to RAWLEIGH DAY. S 15, T 2, R 3W. Signed BARNARD WARDEN. Witness: WM. C. KEEN, DAVID McCORMICK. pp 431, 432, 433

Deed dated 1819. JOHN JAMES DUFOUR to JANE TODD, widow of OWEN TODD. S 22, T 2, R 3. Signed J. J. DUFOUR. Witness: TRUMAN RICHARDS, ELISHA GOLAY. pp 433, 434, 435

Deed dated 1819. WILLIAM McCORKHILL & PEGGY his wife

SWITZERLAND COUNTY DEEDS: Book A

to WILLIAM CAMPBELL. S 34, T 2, R 1W. Signed WILLIAM McCORKHILL, PEGGY (x) McCORKHILL. Witness: ALEXANDER SEBASTEN, AMOS BROWN. pp 435, 436, 437

Deed dated 1820. JOHN SHEETS & ANN, his wife, to FRANCIS BARNS. Vevay addition lots 135, 136. Signed JOHN SHEETS, ANN SHEETS. Witness: JOHN MEEK, DANIEL DUFOUR. pp 437, 438, 439

Deed dated 1818. JOHN FRANCIS DUFOUR & POLLY, his wife to FRANCIS BARNS. Vevay lot 100. Signed JOHN FRANCIS DUFOUR, POLLY DUFOUR. Witness: TRUMAN RICHARDS, WM. C. KEEN. pp 439, 440

Deed dated 1820. ELIZABETH SEARCY of Posey Twp. to MOSES SEARCY. S 11, T 2, R 1W. Signed ELIZABETH SEARCY. Witness: ROBERT McCORKHILL, BERRY SEARCY. pp 441, 442

Deed dated 1820. LUCIEN GEX & ELIZABETH, his wife, to WILLIAM CAMPBELL. Vevay lot 137. Signed LUCIEN GEX, ELIZABETH GEX. Witness: WM. C. KEEN, JAMES DALMAZZO. pp 442, 443

Deed dated 1819. GEORGE CRAIG & JANE B., his wife, to ROBERT McKAY the third. S 30, T 2, R 3. Signed GEORGE CRAIG, JANE B. CRAIG. Witness: WM. J. STEWART, CHARLES B. FELLMAN. pp 443, 444, 445

Deed dated 1819. JONATHAN REEDER & SALLY, his wife, to JAMES HOLE of OH. Vevay lot 103. Signed JONATHAN REEDER, SALLY REEDER. Witness: THOMAS BRADLEY, WM. C. KEEN. pp 445, 446, 447

Deed dated 1818. FRANCIS BARNES & HENRIETTA, his wife, to WILLIAM McKINSTRY. Vevay lot 100. Signed FRANCIS BARNES, HENRIETTA BARNES. Witness: WM. C. KEEN, WILLIAM KEITH. pp 447, 448, 449, 450

Dissolution of partnership dated 1820. DANIEL DUFOUR & FRANCIS BARNS of Switzerland Co & NATHAN M. WHITTEMORE of Cincinnati, OH were formerly in the distillery business together. Signed DANIEL DUFOUR, FRANCIS BARNES, N. M. WHITTEMORE. Witness: S. C. STEVENS. pp 450, 451, 452, 453

Deed dated 1820. SELATHIEL THOMAS to WILLIAM BRADLEY Vevay addition lot 120. Signed SELATHIEL THOMAS. Witness: JOHN GILLILAND. pp 453, 454, 455

Deed dated 1819. JOHN FRANCIS DUFOUR & POLLY, his wife to THOMAS ARMSTRONG, assignee of JOSEPH McFALL.

SWITZERLAND COUNTY DEEDS: Book A

Vevay lot 177. Signed JOHN FRANCIS DUFOUR, POLLY DUFOUR. Witness: JOHN GILLILAND, TRUMAN RICHARDS. pp 455, 456, 457

Deed dated 1819. FREDERICK WALDOW & MIRIAM, his wife to JOSEPH McGEE. Vevay lot 188. Signed FREDERICK WALDOW, MIRIAM WALDOW. Witness: HOLLIS KELLOGG, WM. C. KEEN. pp 457, 458, 459

Deed dated 1819. THOMAS EVINS & LEANER IVINS, his wife, to ABIJAH GRIMES. S 15, T 4, R 12. Signed THOMAS EVINS, LEANOR (x) EVINS. Witness: JOHN GILLILAND, JOHN (x) WASHBURN. pp 459, 460, 461

Deed dated 1819. THOMAS EVINS & LEANER, his wife, to HENRY COTTON. S 15, T 4, R 12. Signed THOMAS EVINS, LEANOR (x) EVINS . Witness: JOHN GILLILAND, JACOB KERN. pp 461, 462, 463

Deed dated 1819. JOHN FRANCIS DUFOUR & POLLY, his wife to JOSEPH MALIN. Vevay lot 171. Signed JOHN FRANCIS DUFOUR, POLLY DUFOUR. Witness: WM. C. KEEN, TRUMAN RICHARDS. pp 464, 465

Deed dated 1819. DANIEL DUFOUR & FANNY, his wife, to LAWRENCE NIHILL. Vevay lot 117. Signed DANIEL DUFOUR, FANNY DUFOUR BLANC. Witness: WM. C. KEEN, JOHN JACOB GOETZ. pp 465, 466, 467

Deed dated 1819. DANIEL DUFOUR & FANNY, his wife, to ANDREW JACKSON JOHNSON. Vevay lot 117. Signed DANIEL DUFOUR, FANNY DUFOUR BLANC. Witness: WM. C. KEEN, JOHN JACOB GOETZ. pp 467, 468, 469

Bond dated 1818. JAMES BOLENS to PHILO AVERILL. Bond on lots in town of Mt. Sterling, S 35, T 3, R 3W. Lots sold to GEORGE W. SAMPSON, BENJAMIN HEADY, JACOB L. CARLOW, CALDWELL HINES, ALEXANDER HATTON, JOHN PROTSMAN SR, JOHN DUMONT, SAMUEL ROBERTS, JOHN DUNSROTH, GEORGE COGGSHELL, P.D. MANVILLE, SAMUEL DAVIS. Signed J. BOLENS. Witness: WM. C. KEEN, JOHN BROWN. pp 469, 470

Deed dated 1820. ELIJAH GRIMES & JANE MILLER, his wife, to SKELTON FOWLER. S 15, T 4, R 12E. Signed ELIJAH GRIMES, JANE GRIMES. Witness: WM. C. KEEN, JOHN GILLILAND. pp 470, 471

Deed dated 1820. JOSEPH McFALL & POLLY, his wife, to HENRY WEBB. S 36, T 2, R 2W. Signed JOSEPH McFALL. POLLY (x) McFALL. Witness: MOS. LYON, ARCHIBALD SCOTT, SAMUEL FENTON. pp 472, 473

SWITZERLAND COUNTY DEEDS: Book A

Deed dated 1820. ELIJAH GRIMES & JANE, his wife, to ISAAC HARKERSMITH of Jessamine Co, KY. S 15, T 4, R 12E. ELIJAH GRIMES, JANE GRIMES. Witness: WM. C. KEEN, JOHN GILLILAND. pp 473, 474, 475

Deed dated 1820. FREDERICK WALDO & MIRIAM, his wife, to IZRAEL R. WHITEHEAD. Vevay lot 147. Signed FREDERICK WALDO, MIRIAM (W.) WALDOW. Witness: WM. C. KEEN, NEWTON H. TAPP. pp 475, 476, 477

Deed dated 1819. WILLIAM CAMPBELL & POLLY, his wife, to MARTIN ADKINS. S 30, T 2, R 1W. Signed WILLIAM CAMPBELL, POLLY CAMPBELL. Witness: CHRISTIAN COOPER, JAMES CLANCY, ROBERT McCORKHILL. pp 477, 478, 479

Deed dated 1819. WILLIAM CAMPBELL & POLLY, his wife, to JAMES CLANCY. S 6, T 1, R 1W. Signed WILLIAM CAMPBELL, POLLY CAMPBELL. Witness: CHRISTIAN COOPER, MARTIN ADKINS. pp 479, 480, 481

Deed dated 1819. JAMES CLANCY & NANCY, his wife, to GEORGE HUTCHISON. New York town lot 7. Signed JAMES CLANCY, NANCY CLANCY. Witness: ROBERT McCORKHILL. GEORGE CLANCY. pp 481, 482, 483

Deed dated 1819. JAMES CLANCY & NANCY, his wife, to LUIS GORDON. New York town lot 31. Signed JAMES CLANCY, NANCY CLANCY. Witness: MARTIN ADKINS, ROBERT McCORKHILL. pp 483, 484, 485

Deed dated 1819. BENJAMIN DRAKE & HANNAH, his wife, to LUIS GORDON. New York town lot 15. Signed BENJAMIN DRAKE, HANNAH (x) DRAKE. Witness: JAMES CLANCY, NATHANIEL MIX. pp 485, 486, 487

Deed dated 1819. WILLIAM CAMPBELL & POLLY, his wife, to JAMES CLANCY. New York lots 32, 33, 34, 35, 36, 38, 45, 46, 47 48, 49, 50, 51, 52, 57, 60, 61, 65. Signed WILLIAM CAMPBELL, POLLY CAMPBELL. Witness: CHRISTIAN COOPER, MARTIN ADKINS. pp 487, 488, 489

Deed dated 1820. JOHN DUMONT & JULIA L., his wife, to A.B. DUMONT. Vevay lot 26. Signed JOHN DUMONT, JULIA L. DUMONT. Witness: S. MERRILL, JOHN GILLILAND. pp 489, 490, 491

Deed dated 1820. ANDREW STAPLETON & BARBARY, his wife, to WILLIAM CHARLES KEEN. S 26, T 3, R 3W. Signed ANDREW (x) STAPLETON, BARBARY (x) STAPLETON. Witness: JOHN GILLILAND, ELIZABETH (x) STAPLETON. pp 492, 493, 494

SWITZERLAND COUNTY DEEDS: Book A

Deed dated 1819. JOHN JAMES DUFOUR to FRANCIS LOUIS RAYMOND. S 22, T 2, R 3. "to JOHN TODD's widow's tract". Signed J.J. DUFOUR. Witness: TRUMAN RICHARDS, ELISHA GOLAY. pp 494, 495, 496, 497

Deed dated 1817. USA to JAMES POCOCK of Butler Co, OH. S 13, T 2, R 2W. p 497

Deed dated 1819. BENJAMIN DRAKE & HANNAH, his wife, to TIMOTHY LYONS. New York town lot 27. Signed BENJAMIN DRAKE, HANNAH (x) DRAKE. Witness: JAMES LYON, ROBERT McCORKHILL. pp 498, 499

Deed dated 1820. LUCIEN GEX & ELIZABETH, his wife, to FREDERICK WALDO, assignee of HENRY HUCKLEBERRY, assignee of JOHN MILLS. Vevay lot 147. Signed LUCIEN GEX, ELIZABETH GEX. Witness: OTIS WALDO, JOHN GILLILAND. pp 499, 500

Deed dated 1820. BENJAMIN DRAKE & HANNAH his wife to CHRISTIAN COOPER. New York town lot 22. Signed BENJAMIN DRAKE, HANNAH (x) DRAKE. Witness: ROBERT McCORKHILL, JAMES MANSELL. pp 501, 502

Deed dated 1820. JOHN MILLER & CATY, his wife, to WILLIAM CAMPBELL. S 36, T 2, R 2W. Signed JOHN MILLER, CATY (x) MILLER. Witness: JOHN GILLILAND, JOHN DUMONT. pp 502, 503, 504

Deed dated 1819. JAMES CLANCY & NANCY, his wife, to JOHN GIBSON. New York town lot 16. Signed JAMES CLANCY, NANCY CLANCY. Witness: GEORGE CLANCY, ROBERT McCORKHILL. pp 504, 505, 506

Deed dated 1819. USA to PETER LOSTUTTER. S 29, T 3, R 1W. pp 506, 507

Deed dated 1820. DANIEL <u>MISER</u> of Posey Twp to WILLIAM RICKETTS. S 31, T 3, R 1W. Signed DANIEL (x) <u>HIZER</u> MARY (x) <u>HIZER.</u> Witness: SAMUEL RAUCHCRAFT, CALEB MOUNTS. pp 507, 508, 509

Deed dated 1820. BENJAMIN DRAKE & HANNAH, his wife, to AMOS BROWN. New York town lot 29. Signed BENJAMIN DRAKE, HANNAH (x) DRAKE. Witness: ROBERT McCORKHILL, SAMUEL LOWREY. pp 510, 511

Deed dated 1819. JOHN FRANCIS DUFOUR & POLLY, his wife to PETER DANIEL BORRALLY of Garrard Co, KY. Vevay lot 14. Signed J. F. DUFOUR, POLLY DUFOUR. Witness: JAMES McCLURE, TRUMAN RICHARDS. pp 512, 513
END OF SWITZERLAND COUNTY DEED BOOK A

UNION COUNTY: Original Land Entries Tract Book
FORMAT: Section - Purchaser - year - page;

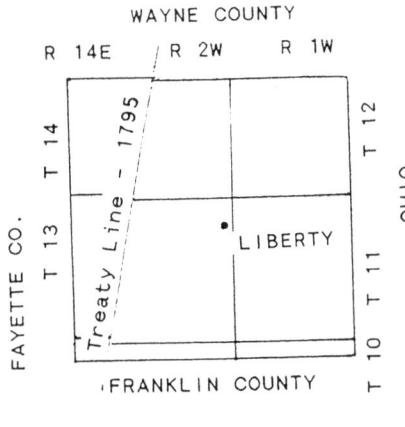

UNION COUNTY IN 1821

Union County was not formed until 1821, taken almost equally from Franklin and Wayne counties.

Unlike Ohio County, Union was formed in time to have a land tract book copied ca 1845 by the office of the Secretary of State. The County Recorder has a duplicate ledger copied again in 1923. The original ledger is no longer available for public use.

The Treaty Line Museum, a collection of log cabins, is an historical site south of the county seat, Liberty. Each year in May and again over the Labor Day weekend, the public may attend a recreation of late 18th/early 19th Century village life and a re-enactment of Indian conflicts. For a few days, the old settlement comes to life again.

Township 10, Range 1W

1 - CORNELIUS WILEY - 1804 - 1; 1 - JOSEPH HARTER 1813 - 1; 1 - JOHN MILLER - 1810 - 1; 2 - THOMAS McCLELLAND - 1814 - 1; 2 - JACOB DARST - 1807 - 1; 2 TOBIAS MILLER - 1814 - 1; 3 - MATTHEW McCLURKIN -1809 1; 3 - THOMAS SANKEY - 1811 - 1; 3 - THOMAS HARPER 1811 - 1; 4 - WILLIAM OGLE - 1813 - 1; 4 - WILLIAM MILLER - 1813 - 1; 5 - JOSEPH HAUGH - 1814 - 1; 5 ROBERT FLACK - 1806 - 1; 5 - WILLIAM MILLER - 1814 1; 6 - JAMES DAVIS - 1806 - 1; 6 - SAMUEL SHANNON 1806 - 1; 6 - SAMUEL SHANNON - 1813 - 1; 7 - JAMES FORDYCE - 1814 - 1; 7 - JAMES RAY - 1813 - 1; 7 PETER DAVIS - 1806 - 1; 7 - WILLIAM COE - 1814 - 1; 8 - MORRIS WITHAM - 1812 - 1; 8 - JOSHUA WILLIAMS 1812 - 1; 8 - CHRISTOPHER SMITH - 1814 - 1; 8 - PETER DAVIS - 1816 - 1; 9 - JOHN KELL - 1814 - 1; 9 - JAMES & THOMAS R. SMILEY - 1814 - 1; 9 - JOHN McCLURKIN 1811 - 1; 9 - WILLIAM DENNISTON - 1814- 1; 10 - CLOSS THOMPSON - 1814 - 2; 10 - WILLIAM LEAPER - 1810 - 2; 10 - JAMES CURRIE - 1813 - 1; 10 - JOHN SPEAR - 1816 2; 11 - THOMAS HARPER - 1811 - 2; 11 - DAVID BLACK 1814- 2; 12 - JOHN MILLER - 1805- 2; 12 - JOHN MILLER

UNION COUNTY: Original Land Entries Tract Book
FORMAT: Section - Purchaser - year - page;

Township 10, Range 1W continued

1810 - 2; 12 - ABRAHAM DARST - 1807 - 2; 13 - JOHN DENMAN - 1808 - 2; 13 - WILLIAM CRAWFORD - 1806 - 2; 13 - ABRAHAM HAMMOND - 1806- 2; 13 - JACOB BAKE -1806 2; 14 - JOHN MILLER - 1810 - 2; 14 - WILLIAM STEPHENS 1810- 2; 14 - WILLIAM DENNISTON - 1809 - 2; 14 -ISAAC COON - 1810 - 2; 15 - BENONI GOBLE - 1815 - 2; 15 ABNER GOBLE - 1815 - 2; 17 - JOHN McCORD - 1814 - 3; 17 - JAMES STEWART - 1815 -3; 17 - JONATHAN W. POWERS 1814 - 3; 17 - JAMES SMITH - 1814 - 3; 18 - SAM'L. HOWELL - 1806 - 3; 18 - JAMES REEDS - 1806 - 3; 18 JOHN HATFIELD - 1813- 3; 18- JOSEPH NELSON -1806 - 3.

Township 11, Range 1W

1 - ANTHONY WILLIAMS - 1806 - 4; 1 - JOHN PENTECOST 1808 - 4; 1 - JOHN PENTECOST - 1808 - 4; 1 - DAVID LANDIS - 1807 - 4; 2 - JAMES EGGERS - 1813 - 4; 2 STEPHEN HAYDEN & BENJAMIN GARD - 1813 - 4; 2 - GEORGE BRIDGED - 1813 - 4; 2 - EPHRAIM BROWN - 1813 - 4; 3 WILLIAM EATON - 1814 - 4; 3 - WILLIAM MILLER - 1813 4; 3 - THOMAS A.R. EATON - 1815 - 4; 3 - MATTHEW EATON - 1815 - 4; 4 - RICHARD MINER - 1806 - 4; 4 ISAAC SWAFFORD - 1808 - 4; 4 - WILLIAM SWAFFORD -1808 4; 4 - VINCENT CROMWELL - 1808 - 4; 5 -JACOB SKILLMAN 1807 - 4; 5 - SAM'L LAFUZE & JOSEPH VANMETER - 1813 4; 5 - THOMAS MILLER - 1813 - 4; 5 - JONAS & JOHN HUNT - 1813 - 4; 6 - RICHARD ARNOLD - 1814 - 4; 6 AARON STANTON - 1815 - 4; 6 - JAMES SNODGRASS - 1815 4; 7 - GEORGE DIHR - 1811 - 4 (margin note - DIEK or DIKE); 7 - GEORGE CRIST - 1814 - 4; 7 - DAVID HOLLINGSWORTH - 1814 - 4; 7 - GEORGE WILLIAMS -1814 4; 8 - RUTH CRANE - 1807 - 4; 8 - SAM'L. TAPPIN -1807 4; 8 - ZEPHANIAH BURT - 1814 - 4; 8 - JONATHAN CRANE 1807 - 4; 9 - JOHN WRIGHT - 1814 - 4; 9 - IDEL BROOKS - 1813 - 4; 9 - HENRY HOLLINGSWORTH - 1814 4; 9 - UZAL WOOD - 1813 - 4; 10 - WILLIAM CARTWRIGHT 1815 - 5; 10 - LATHAN STANTON - 1814 - 5; 10 - WILL-IAM MILLER - 1814 - 5; 10 - ISAAC GARDNER - 1817 -5; 11 & 14 - ASA TOLER - 1814 - 5; 11 - JACOB MAXWELL 1814 - 5; 11 - SAM'L. McDILL - 1814 - 5; 11 - THOMAS MILLER - 1814 - 5; 12 - ROBERT & DAN'L. ELLIOTT 1814 - 5; 12 - JOHN MILLER - 1813 - 5; 12 - JOHN WILEY - 1810 - 5; 12 - SAM'L. RALTER - 1807 - 5; 13 JAMES McCLERKIN - 1813 - 5; 13 - ISAAC and JOHN RITTER - 1811 - 5; 13 - ROBERT M. MILLER - 1818 - 5; 13 - CHRISTOPHER WITTER - 1806 - 5; 14 - PETER LEMAN - 1818 - 5; 14 - JOSEPH KINGERY - 1813 - 5; 14 JAMES BURTON - 1813- 5; 15 - BENJAMIN JOHNSON - 1818 5; 15 - WILLIAM MACY - 1818 - 5; 15 - BENJAMIN JOHNSON - 1810 - 5; 15 - DAVID SWAIN - 1817 - 5;

UNION COUNTY: Original Land Entries Tract Book
FORMAT: Section - Purchaser - year - page;

Pages 6 & 7 are the same sheet in the copied ledger.

17 - EDGHILL HOLLINGSWORTH - 1817 - 6/7; 17 - THOMAS MADDEN - 1811 - 6/7; 17 - JAMES STANTON - 1811 - 6/7; 18 - EBENEZER HOWELL - 1813 - 6/7; 18 - JOHN MACKLIN 1811 - 6/7; 18 - HENRY HUNTER - 1814 - 6/7; 18 HENRY HUNTER - 1813 - 6/7; 18 - DANIEL PALMER - 1808 6/7; 19- JOHN HEAVENRIDGE - 1811- 6/7; 19 - HUGH REED 1807 - 6/7; 19 - REUBEN SCARLOCK - 1813 - 6/7; 19 JAMES GUIDER & THOMAS BROWN - 1813 - 6/7; 20 - ELIAB GARDNER - 1811 - 6/7; 20 - JAMES HOLLINGSWORTH - 1813 6/7; 20 - AARON STANTON - 1812- 6/7; 20 - W.S. PARKS 1809 - 6/7; 21 - URIAH STARBUCK - 1817 - 6/7; 21 ROWLAND COLEMAN - 1815 - 6/7; 21 - ISAAC GARDNER 1817 - 6/7; 21 - ISAAC GARDNER - 1815 - 6/7; 22 JOEL HAWORTH - 1816 - 6/7; 22 - LOT TALBERT 1822 - 6/7; 22 - MOSES MARTINDALE - 1817 - 6/7; 22 SYLVANUS SWAIN - 1815 - 6/7; 23 - JOSEPH KENNY - 1814 6/7; 23 - CHRISTOPHER WITTER - 1810 - 6/7; 23 - ABRAHAM MYER - 1810 - 6/7; 23 - JOHN MYER - 1809 - 6/7; 24 - JOHN BROWN - 1814 - 6/7; 24 - WM. BROWN - 1805 6/7; 24 - SAM'L. BELL - 1814 - 6/7; 24 - JOHN WITTER 1806 - 6/7; 25 - CHRISTOPHER WITTER - 1816 - 8; 25 SAMUEL KINGERY - 1813 - 8; 25 - JOHN FISHER - 1805 8; 25 - JOHN FISHER - 1813 - 8; 26 - JOSEPH KINGERY 1815 - 8; 26 - MARTIN KINGERY - 1809 - 8; 26 - HENRY BRANDENBURG - 1810 - 8; 26 - GEORGE KEFFER - 1806 -8; 27 - SAM'L. & PETER LEMON - 1815 - 8; 27 - JOHN SHORT 1808 - 8; 27 - DAVID PRIESTLY - 1808 - 8; 28 - JAMES MARTIN - 1814 - 8; 28 - JONATHAN HUDDLESTON - 1815 8; 28 - JACOB GIGER - 1814 - 8; 28 - WM. BEARD - 1815 8; 29 - AARON STANTON - 1813 - 8 (margin note: JONATHAN HUDDLESTON, assignee); 29 - JOHN FURNAS - 1814 8; 29 - HUGH MAXWELL - 1813- 8; 30 - ARAHAM HOLLINGSWORTH - 1808 - 8; 30 - THOMAS BROWN - 1810- 8 (resold 1816 to JESSE HUNT); 30 - JOHN CREEK - 1815 - 8; 30 SOLOMON BEACH - 1816 - 8; 31 & 32 - JOHN CREEK - 1808 8; 31 & 32 - JOHN CREEK - 1810 - 8; 31 - JOHN CREEK 1814 - 8; 31 - ROBERT GOBLE - 1814 - 8; 32 - THOMAS WRIGHT - 1814 - 8; 32 - JOSEPH HOUGH - 1814 - 8; 33 SAM'L. BONNER - 1814 - 9; 33 - DAVID BONNER - 1813 9; 33 - SAM'L. McDILL - 1814 - 9; 33 - ANDREW NIXON 1817 - 9; 34 - JACOB KINGERY SR - 1806 - 9; 34 MATTHEW McCLERKIN - 1809 - 9; 34 - ADAM RICHEY - 1806 9; 34 - WM. OGLE - 1813 - 9; 35 - WM. BEARD - 1817 9; 35 - GEORGE KEFFER - 1806 - 9; 35 - ISAAC GARDNER & WM. BEARD - 1817 - 9; 35 - WILLIAM RAMSEY JR - 1808 9; 36 - JOHN MYERS - 1806 - 9; 36 - JOHN ALLEN - 1815 9; 36 - CHRISTIAN KINGERY - 1805 - 9; 36 - JOSEPH RIGHNOUR - 1815 - 9.

UNION COUNTY: Original Land Entries Tract Book
FORMAT: Section - Purchaser - year - page;

Township 12, Range 1W

7 & 8 - THOS. BURKE - 1806 - 10; 7 - JOHN SMITH -1816 10; 7 - WM. HOLEMAN - 1809 - 10; 7 - JOHN WILLIAMS 1809 - 10; 8 - JOSEPH POWERS - 1808 - 10; 8 - WALTER S. BURGESS - 1811 - 10; 8 - JOSEPH HOLEMAN - 1806 10; 9 - ABRAHAM LEWIS - 1811 - 10; 9 - JOHN STARR 1809 - 10; 9 - HENRY HOOVER - 1807 - 10; 9 - ABRAHAM LEWIS - 1812 - 10; 10 - JACOB ESTEP - 1808 - 10; 10 MAJOR DODSON - 1811 - 10; 10 - ISAAC METCALF, RICHARD SEDGWICK & WILLIAM BROWN - 1808 - 10; 10 - ZACARIAH STANLEY - 1811 - 10; 11 - JOEL MOON - 1810 - 10; 11 ABRAHAM LEWIS - 1811 - 10; 11 - ANDREW JONES - 1813 10; 11 - METCALF, SEDGWICK & BROWN - 1808 - 10; 12 JOHN JORDAN - 1812- 10; 12 - SAM'L DRULEY - 1814 -10; 12 - JOHN THOMPSON - 1814 - 10; 12 - DAVID BROWN 1817 - 10; 13 - CHARLES GORDON - 1816 - 10; 13 JACOB HOWSE - 1816 - 10; 13 - HENRY VAN MIDDLESWORTH 1818 - 10; 14 - WM. WYATT - 1814 - 10; 14 - DAVID WYANT - 1814 - 10; 14 - JOHN STANLEY - 1812 - 10; 14 JAMES BEDWELL -1812 - 10; 15 - ANTHONY MALBITT - 1814 10; 17 - PHILLIP WOODS - 1812 - 11; 17 - WILLIAM HUNT 1808 - 11; 17 - THOMAS BRADBURY - 1814 - 11; 17 THOMAS JOB - 1807 - 11; 19 - JOHN STARR - 1807 - 11; 19 - JOHN HARLAN - 1813 - 11; 19 - WM. FARLOW - 1818 11; 18 - ANDREW FOUTZ - 1806 - 11; 18 - BEALE BUTLER 1806 - 11; 18 - JOHN BEARD - 1806 - 11; 18 - JESSE HENLEY - 1806 - 11; 20 - DAVID F. WYATT - 1814 - 11; 20 - ROBT. BENNETT - 1814 - 11; 20 - JOHN McEURN (McEWEN?) - 1815 - 11; 20 - ROBERT BENNETT - 1808 11; 21 -JOHN RICHARDSON - 1817 - 11; 22 - JACOB STRAW 1818 - 11; 23 - JACOB HOWSE - 1814 - 12; 23 - JAMES DAVIS - 1814 - 12; 23 - LOT GARD - 1815 - 12; 23 JOHN McEWEN - 1815 - 12; 24 - MICHAEL SNIDER - 1808 12; 24 - WM. MOSS - 1814 - 12; 24 - WM. MOSS - 1808 12; 25 - PHILIP LYBROOK - 1808 - 12; 25 - JACOB KINGERY - 1808 - 12; 26 - JACOB KINGERY - 1814 - 12; 26 JAMES SULSER - 1816 - 12; 26 - HENRY LYBROOK - 1816 12; 26 - JACOB ROWSH - 1816 - 12; 27 - ROBT. HARVEY 1808 - 12; 27 - FRANCIS HARVEY - 1813 - 12; 27 - JOHN KENNADY - 1814 - 12; 27 - AARON GARD - 1814 - 12; 28 WM. FOX - 1808 - 12; 28 - DAVID DREEMAN - 1815 - 12; 28 - JOSEPH NELSON - 1813 - 12; 28 - JOHN PLUMMER 1808 - 12; 29 - WM. DUNBAR - 1814 - 12; 29 - SAM'L. KITCHELL - 1815 - 12; 30 - EBENEZER HOWE - 1814 - 12; 30 - DAN'L MILLER - 1808 - 12; 30 - ASA ELLIOT - 1818 12; 30 - GEORGE FALL - 1817 - 12; 31 - HENRY PEARSON 1816 - 13; 31 - JOHN REILEY - 1815 - 13; 31 - DAVID DUNHAM - 1816 - 13; 31 - MICHAEL CULVER (corrected from COLVIN) - 1813 - 13; 32 - ROBERT WADDELL - 1813 13; 32 - JOSEPH BRADWAY - 1814 - 13; 32 - JACOB SKILLMAN - 1807 - 13; 33 - MARY MINER - 1806 - 13; 33

UNION COUNTY: Original Land Entries Tract Book
FORMAT: Section - Purchaser - year - page;

Township 12, Range 1W continued

JACOB FOUTS - 1808 - 13; 33 - BENJAMIN NUTTER - 1816 13; 33 - ANTIPAS THOMAS - 1814 - 13; 34 - NATHAN & JEREMIAH REEDER - 1814 - 13; 34 -JOSEPH SPENCER -1811 13; 34 - DAVID GOODING - 1814 - 13; 34 - JOHN CARTWRIGHT - 1806 - 13; 35 - BENJAMIN THOMAS - 1814 - 13; 35 - WM. ELDER - 1814 - 13; 35 - DANNIEL EGGERS 1813 - 13; 35 - ENOCH BOLING - 1814 -13; 36 - PHILIP LYBROOK - 1806 - 13; 36 - JOSEPHUS GARD - 1806 - 13.

Township 10, Range 2W

1 - HENRY SHAEFFER - 1813 - 14; 1 - EBENEZER HAYWARD 1814 - 14; 1 - ABRAHAM ROSE - 1814 - 14; 1 - JAMES & JOHN G. GRAY - 1816 - 14; 2 - WILLIAM DUNKIN - 1815 14; 2 - JAS. DEACONS - 1814 - 14; 2 - DAVID ARCHER 1815 - 14; 2 - THOMAS SACKETT - 1815 - 14; 3 - SETH H. BATES - 1815 - 14; 3 - JOHN SAMPLE - 1813 - 14; 3 JOHN BRIDGES - 1814 - 14; 3 - WM. CARTER - 1807 - 14; 4 - WM. NEWMAN - 1815 - 14; 4 - JOHN TEMPLETON - 1804 14; 4 - JOHN JOHNSON - 1814 - 14; 5 - DAVID STANTON 1807- 14; 8 - THOMAS THOMAS - 1816 - 14; 9 - JOSEPH HANNA - 1804 - 14; 9 - GEORGE HOLLINGSWORTH - 1806 14; 9 - JAS. TAYLOR - 1804 - 14; 10 - WM. ABERNATHY 1815 - 14; 10 - GEORGE HOLLINGSWORTH - 1806 - 14; 11 WM. DUBOIS - 1806 - 14; 11 - JACOB DUBOIS - 1811- 14; 11 - JOHN DICKSON - 1806 - 14; 12 - DAN'L WILLSON 1811 - 14; 12 - AMASIAH ELWELL - 1808 - 14; 12 - WILLIAM COOMS - 1814 - 14; 12 - ALEXANDER & ISAAC DUBOIS 1806 - 14; 13 - CLARK BATES/BALES - 1814 - 15; 13- CLARK BATES - 1810 - 15; 13 - JAS. PIPER & JOEL WILLIAMS - 1806 - 15; 14 - JAS. PIPER - 1812 - 15; 14 - WM. POPENSE - 1814 - 15; 14 - JOHN WHITWORTH & JOHN REILEY - 1814 - 15; 14 - JACOB NEWKIRK - 1815 15; 15 - EDGEHILL ROSE (margin note: EZEKIEL ROSE) 1818 - 15; 15 - WITIE POWELL - 1818 - 15; 15 - JAMES OSBORN - 1818 - 15; 15 - WM. H. EADS - 1818 - 15; 17 JACOB BLOYD - 1806 - 15; 17 - JOHN EWING - 1805 - 15; 17 - MATTHEW BROWN - 1816 - 15.

Township 11, Range 2W

1 - JACOB HOMER - 1814 - 16; 1 - BYRD STILES - 1813 16; 1 & 2 - WM. CASON - 1814 - 16; 2 - HENRY BECK 1814 - 16; 2 & 3 - THOMAS CULLY - 1814 - 16; 2 - JAS. TANNER -1811 - 16; 3 - J. ANDREWS & R. & E. BURBRIDGE 1814 - 16; 4 - ZACARIAH FERGUSON - 1815 - 16; 9 GEORGE HARLAN - 1807 - 16; 10 - ROBERT SWANN & JOS. NICHOLS - 1814 - 16; 10 - JOHN CAMPBELL - 1817 - 16; 10 & 12 - JACOB HOMER - 1814 - 16; 10 - JAS. SNOWDEN

UNION COUNTY: Original Land Entries Tract Book
FORMAT: Section - Purchaser - year - page;

Township 11, Range 2W continued

1815 - 16; 11 - JOSHUA PALMER - 1814 - 16; 11 - ABEL BURKHALTER - 1810 - 16; 11 - JOSHUA PALMER SR - 1807 16; 11 - JONATHAN HOLLINGSWORTH - 1807 - 16; 12 WRIGHT COOK - 1813 - 16; 12 - JAS. ARMSTRONG - 1814 16; 12 - GEORGE CRIST - 1814 - 16; 13 & 13 - THOMAS COOK - 1813 - 16; 13 - ISAAC COOK - 1814 - 16; 13 JONATHAN HOLLINGSWORTH - 1814- 16; 14 - JOHN HOLLINGSWORTH - 1814 - 16; 14 - JOSHUA HARLAN - 1807- 16; 14 ISAAC HOLLINGSWORTH - 1813 - 16; 14 - JONATHAN HOLLINGSWORTH - 1807 - 16; 15 - WM. McMAHAN - 1816 - 17; 15 - WM. RING - 1814 - 17; 15 - WM. GREENE - 1814 17 (margin note: CALEB WICKERSHAM, assignee); 15 JOHN CAMPBELL - 1814 - 17; 16 - JOHN HANNA & JOHN LIVINGSTON - 1804- 17; 20 - THOMAS NICKELS - 1815- 17 (margin note: JAMES BOYSON, assignee); 21 - WM. BOTKIN & JOHN McCUTCHEON- 1804- 17; 22 - WM. LOGAN -1807 17; 22 - WM. McGREER - 1814 - 17; 22 - LIN HOLLINGSWORTH - 1806 - 17; 22 - ROBT. SWANN - 1805 - 17; 23 JACOB HOLLINGSWORTH - 1806 - 17; 23 - RICHARD HOLLINGSWORTH - 1815 - 17; 23 - JAS. MARDOCK - 1814 - 17; 23 - NATHANIEL HENDERSON - 1814 - 17; 24 - HUGH REID 1807 - 17; 24 - JAMES HOLLINGSWORTH - 1813 - 17; 24 ELI HENDERSON - 1807 - 17; 25 - ELIAB GARDNER - 1811 17; 25 - ELI HENDERSON - 1807 - 17; 25 - JOHN CREEK 1815 - 17; 25 - JOHN BROWN JR - 1813 - 17; 26 WILLIS KELLY - 1813 - 17; 26 - WM. NORRIS -1814 -17; 26 - THOS. BROWN - 1806 - 17; 26 - DAN'L. ERVING or EWING - 1813 - 17; 27 - DAVID HOLLINGSWORTH - 1806 17; 27 - JOHN HANNA - 1804 - 17; 27 - JOSEPH HOLLINGSWORTH - 1806 - 17; 27 - JOHN HANNA - 1814 - 17; 28 WM. NICHOLS - 1806 - 18; 28 - JAMES NICHELL - 1806 18; 28 - WM. NORRIS - 1806 - 18; 28 - MORDECAI McKINZEY - 1807 - 18; 29 - WM. ERVING or EWING - 1806 - 18 (margin note: -- BROWN, assignee); 32 - SAMUEL HARTER 1807 - 18 (margin note: HUSTON); 33 - ROBT. A. TEMPLETON - 1815 - 18; 33 - WM. CUNNINGHAM - 1814 -18; 33 GEORGE NORRIS - 1814 - 18; 33 - MARTIN BAUM - 1806 18; 34 - WILLIAM SPARKS - 1809 - 18; 34 - ABRAHAM BUCKLES - 1815 - 18; 34 - JACOB CASE or CARE - 1813 18; 34 - ARTHUR FERGUSON - 1816- 18 (margin note: WM. MAXWELL); 35 - JOHN BROWN - 1813 - 18; 35 - MATTHEW BROWN - 1806 - 18; 35 - JOHN BURNS - 1818 - 18; 35 BENNETT LANGSTON - 1810- 18; 36 - SOLOMON BEACH -1814 18; 36 - JAMES SNOWDEN - 1814 - 18; 36 - ENOS BOWLSLY 1814 - 18.

Township 12, Range 2W

10 & 14 - ABRAHAM NAVE - 1806 - 19; 11 - RICH'D DENNY 1811 - 19; 11 - THOMAS LEWIS - 1806 - 19; 11 -

UNION COUNTY: Original Land Entries Tract Book
FORMAT: Section - Purchaser - year - page;

Township 12, Range 2W continued

ISAAC WILEY - 1814- 19 (margin note: ISAAC NEELEY); 12 - SMITH HUNT - 1808 - 19; 12 & 13 - CHARLES HUNT 1807 - 19; 12 - HENRY MARTIN - 1811 - 19; 13 - BENJAMIN BOWNE - 1808 - 19; 13 - ADAM ELY - 1817 - 19; 13 - CHARLES GORDON - 1811 - 19; 14 - JOHN SENEY 1815 - 19; 14 - HENRY MARTIN - 1814 - 19; 14 - WM. MARSH - 1815 - 19; 15 - JOSEPH COX & WILLIAM LEWIS 1806 - 19; 22 - THOMAS HUGHES - 1809 - 19; 23 - SAM'L CUNNINGHAM - 1817 - 19; 23 - JOHN SHELLEY - 1814 -19; 23 - MICHAEL SNYDER - 1813 - 19; 23 - JOHN EMMETT 1816 - 19; 24 - MICHAEL SNYDER - 1812 - 19; 24 - JOHN MYERS - 1808 - 19; 24 - HENRY MILLER - 1807 - 19; 25 WHITELY WRIGHT - 1814 - 19; 25 - WILLIAM FALL - 1807 19; 25 - JACOB HOOVER - 1807 - 19; 25 - WM. KNOTT 1807 - 19; 26 - PETER EMMOND - 1809 - 20; 26 FRANCES HARVEY - 1815 - 20; 26 - DAVID CANADAY - 1815 20; 26 - HENRY BECK - 1813 - 20; 27 - THOMAS MARTIN 1816 - 20; 28 - ABNER CHENARETT or CHENAULT - 1813 20; 33 - JAMES OLDHAM - 1815 - 20; 34 - WM. RIDDLE 1815 - 20; 34 - JOHN D. CASTERLINE - 1815 - 20; 34 JOEL KENNEDAY - 1815 - 20; EDWARD J. SWANSON & MICHAEL CULVER - 1813 - 20; 35 - WHITELY WRIGHT 1814 - 20; 35 - DAVID DUNHAM - 1816 - 20; 35 JOSEPH FERGUSON - 1814 - 20; 36 - SOLOMON BECK - 1813 20; 36 - RICHARD RING - 1816 - 20; 36 - JOHN CROMWELL 1806 - 20.

Township 13, Range 13E

1 - HENRY NICHOLS - 1814 - 21; 1 - JEREMIAH WOODS 1814 - 21; 1 - JOHN FISHER - 1815 - 21; 1 - MARTIN GLIDEWELL - 1814 - 21; 12 - SILAS ANDERSON - 1814 21; 12 - NATHAN CROOKSHANK - 1815 - 21; 12 - WM. KIRKPATRICK - 1811 - 21; 12 - JOHN NORRIS - 1814 21; 13 - DAVID NOBLE JR - 1816 - 21; 13 - HARROLD NEWLAND - 1814 - 21; 13 - SAM'L & DAVID MAZE - 1811 21; 13 - ALEXANDER McCOWN - 1814 - 21; 24 - JOHN MATTOCKS - 1813 - 21; 24 - JOHN HUFF - 1814 - 21; 24 WM. CLAREY - 1814 - 21; 24 - JOHN HOWELL or HARRELL 1817 - 21; 25 - JOHN CAMPBELL - 1815 - 21; 36 ABRAHAM LOUDERBACK - 1816 - 21.

Township 13, Range 14E

6 - JOHN WARD - 1814 - 21; 7 - JOHN HANNA SR - 1811 21; 18 & 19 - ADAM ELI & SAM'L MAZE - 1812 - 21.

Township 14, Range 13E

1 - DAVID THOMAS - 1816 - 22; 1 - EPHRAIM THOMAS
Township 14, Range 13E continued

UNION COUNTY: Original Land Entries Tract Book
FORMAT: Section - Purchaser - year - page;

1815 - 22; 12 - JAS. DUNGAN - 1817 - 22; 12 - WM. LEWIS - 1813- 22; 12 - ZADOCK STEPHENSON - 1817 - 22; 13 - MICHAEL SNYDER, assignee of THOS. BRUMBLEY- 1815 22; 13 - JOHN RANCK - 1817 - 22; 13 - THOMAS MADDEN 1814 - 22; 13 - WM. HOLLINGSWORTH - 1815 - 22; 24 JAS. CONAWAY - 1815- 22; 24 - JOHN HARLAN - 1815 -22; 24 - SAM'L. LITTERET or LUTTREL - 1814- 24; 24 - JOHN CREEK - 1814 - 22; 25 - WM. McMAHAN - 1816 - 22; 25 JAMES CONAWAY - 1815 - 22; 25 - ISAAC ODELL - 1814 22; 25 - JOHN ELLERLEY - 1814 - 22; 36 - JOHN McMAHAN 1814 - 22; 36 - WILLIAM WILSON - 1805 - 22; 36 - WM. NICHOLS - 1814 - 22; 36 - HUGH BELL - 1814 - 22.

Township 14, Range 14E

4 & 5 - BENJAMIN McCARTY - 1812 - 23; 6 - POWELL SCOTT - 1817 - 23; 6 - JOHN STARR - 1811 - 23; 6 SAMUEL WALKER - 1817 - 23; 7 - JOHN MYERS - 1811 -23; 7 - GEORGE PARIS - 1814 - 23; 7 - JOHN SUMEY - 1811 23; 7 - WM. LEWIS - 1813 - 23; 8 - JAS. BOLTON - 1814 23; 17 - ZACARIAH FERGUSON - 1815 - 23; 18 - AARON ASHBROOK - 1811 - 23; 18 - RICHARD BROCK - 1814 - 23; 18 - CHAS. McGLOTHLIN - 1811- 23; 18 - DAVID HOLLINGWORTH - 1811 - 23; 19 - JAS. LEVISTON - 1811 - 23; 19 JOSHUA HARLAN - 1811 - 23; 19 - JOHN NORRIS - 1811 23; 19 - SAM'L LITTEREL or LUTTEREL - 1811 - 23; 20 & 29 - GEORGE HARLAN - 1811 - 23; 30 - WHITELY WRIGHT 1817 - 23; 30 - JAS. McKINNEY - 1815 - 23; 30 JOSEPH KEENEY - 1814 - 23; 30 - JOHN ELY - 1817- 23; 30 - JAMES NOBLE - 1817 - 23; 31 & 32 - ABIJAH SHEILDS - 1816 - 23.

Township 15, Range 14E

28 & 33 - THOS. MOFFITT - 1811 - 24; 29 - THOS. B. CHUNN - 1817 - 24; 29 - HENRY WHITINGER - 1815 - 24; 29 - JOHN WHITINGER - 1814 - 24; 30 - JOSEPH SHELBY - 1813 - 24; 30 - JOEL HILL - 1817 - 24; 31 - ALEXANDER WOOD SR - 1818- 24; 31 - BENJAMIN McCARTY - 1816- 24; 32 - JOHN MYERS - 1811 - 24; 32 - WM. WALKER - 1817 24; 32 - SAMUEL STOVER - 1811 - 24; 32 - JOHN MILLER 1814 - 24.

END OF UNION CO LAND ENTRIES TO & INCLUDING 1820

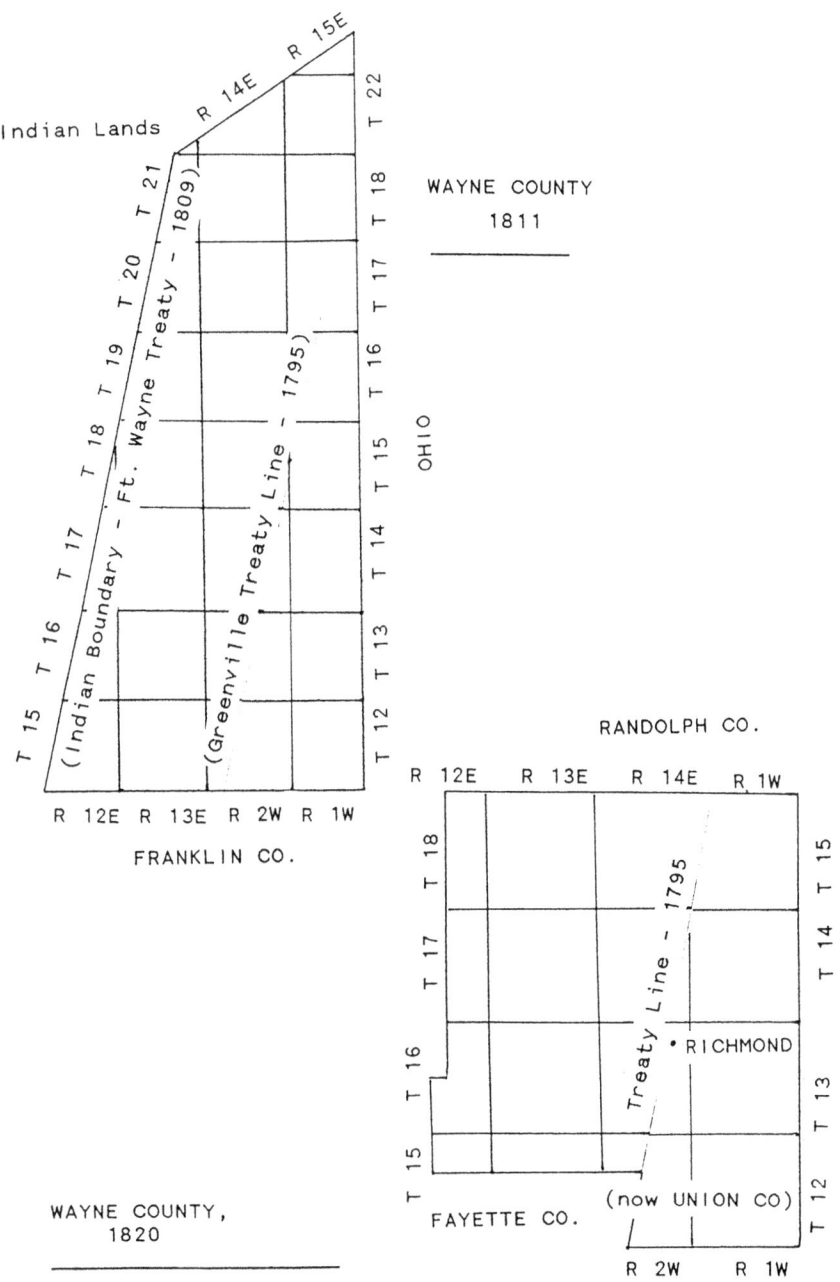

WAYNE COUNTY: Original Land Entries Tract Book
FORMAT: Section - Purchaser - year - page;

Wayne County was one of the first two separated from the original Dearborn County. It has since lost land to Randolph, Fayette and Union counties.

Wayne County was settled to a great extent by Quakers from the Carolinas, coming north on the "Quaker Trace". The Quaker meetings, at first centrally located, spread into the area which later became Randolph County. All Wayne county connections should be researched in Hinshaw and Heiss' genealogical records of the Society of Friends, available in most libraries. A Quaker background can be pure gold for the researcher, proving several generations in a single afternoon. Richmond's Morrison-Reeves Library has an extensive genealogy collection, emphasizing local history and records. The Quaker Society's Earlham College Library in Richmond is also available for public use. Both will reply to written requests for information.

Two tract books are available at the Recorder's office, , both apparently transcriptions of the original 1844 ledger. Comparison of entries show only variations in spelling the buyer's name. If the difference is significant, both versions are given. Pages refer to the copy labeled Land Entry Book #1"; out of order pages have been put into the proper township/range sequence here.

Township 12, Range 1W

1 - JOHN THOMPSON - 1814 - 2; 1 - BRYAN SEANEY - 1814 2; 1 - WM. S. JONES - 1814 - 2; 1 - WM. K. McBOON 1817 - 2; 2 - JOHN & DANIEL SAWMAN - 1817 - 2; 2 ISAAC CONLEY - 1816 - 2; 2 - THOMAS WYATT - 1811 - 2; 2 - BENJ. WHITE - 1813 - 2; 3 - DAVID FISHER - 1813 2; 3 - WM. FOUTS - 1806 - 2; 3 - MAJOR DODSON - 1813 2; 3 - OWEN SENEY - 1808 - 2; 4 - PETER MELENDOSE 1813 - 2; 4 - ISAAC ELSTED - 1807 - 2; 4 - ABRAHAM LEWIS - 1811 - 2; 4 & 5 - SAMUEL JOB - 1813 - 2; 5 EDWARD CLAWSON - 1814- 2; 5 - THOMAS BURKE -1806 - 2; 5 - JACOB LITTLE SR - 1807- 2; 6 - LEWIS LITTLE -1807 2; 6 - PETER SMITH - 1806 - 2; 6 -JOHN HUNT -1813 -2.

Township 12, Range 2W

1 - PETER SMITH - 1805 - 4; 1 - CHARLES HUNT - 1807 4; 1 - GEORGE HUNT - 1807 - 4; 2 - DAVID RAILSBACK 1807 - 4; 2 - TIMOTHY HUNT - 1814 - 4; 2 & 3 - JOS. & JOHN COX - 1814 - 4.

WAYNE COUNTY: Original Land Entries Tract Book
FORMAT: Section - Purchaser - year - page;

Township 13, Range 1W

1 - PETER FLEMING - 1805 - 6; 1 - MATTHEW FLANAGAN 1805 - 6; 1 - BENJAMIN SMALL - 1805 - 6; 2 - WM. ELLERMAN - 1806 - 6; 2 - JOHN SMITH - 1806 - 6; 2 THOMAS HILL - 1806 - 6; 3 - NATHAN OVERMAN - 1813 6; 3 - JOHN HARVEY - 1807 - 6; 3 - ELARON HILL - 1807 6; 4 - JAMES JOHNSON - 1813 - 6; 4 - THOMAS ROBERTS 1806 - 6; 4 - EPHRAIM OVERMAN - 1813 - 6; 4 - JOHN TOWNSEND - 1807 - 6; 5 - JOHN SMITH - 1806 - 6; 5 JEREMIAH COX - 1806 - 6; 5 - JOHN ROGERS (changed to BOYERS) - 1806 - 6; 6 - JONAS RANDALL - 1806 - 6; 6 JEREMIAH MEEK - 1806 - 6; 6 - SAMUEL McKINLEY - 1806 6; 6 - JOHN MEEK - 1806 - 6; 7 - JOSEPH WOODCOCK 1806 - 6; 7 - DAVID HARMAN - 1813 - 6; 7 - SAMUEL McHENRY - 1817 - 6; 7 - DAVID GALBREATH - 1817 - 6; 8 JOHN DAVIDSON - 1807 - 6; 8 - DANIEL TRINDLE/ TRIMBLE 1806 - 6; 8 - JEREMIAH S. MEEK - 1812 - 6; 9 SAMUEL WALKER - 1806 - 6; 9 - JOHN MEEKS JR & ISAAC MEEKS -1806 - 6; 9 - WM. SCARCE - 1806 - 6; 9 - MARY EASTON - 1805 - 6; 10 - SAMUEL HOLMES - 1813 - 6; 10 JOHN McLEAN SR - 1815 - 6; 10 - NATHANIEL McCLURE 1808 - 6; 10 - JASPER KOONSE - 1808- 6; 11 -NATHANIEL SMALL - 1808 - 6; 11 - JAMES JACOBS - 1808 - 6; 11 JACOB FOUTS - 1816 - 6; 11 - JESSE DAVENPORT - 1806 6; 12 - SAMUEL WALKER - 1808 - 6; 12 - AMOS HIGGINS 1806 - 6; 12 - JACOB FOUTS - 1806 - 6; 13 - WM. FOUTS 1806 - 7; 13 - WM. FOUTS - 1807 - 7; 13 - THOMAS WADE 1806 - 7; 13 - THOMAS BULLA - 1806 - 7; 14 - THOMAS BULLA - 1814 - 7; 14 - JOHN HOWARD - 1814 - 7; 14 JOHN WATTS - 1807 - 7; 14 - NATHAN PEARSON -1813 - 7; 15 - JOHN DOUGAN - 1816 - 7; 15 - NATH. McCLURE JR 1816 - 7; 17 - GEORGE HOLMAN - 1804 - 7; 17 - JOHN TURNER - 1804 - 7; 17 - JEREMIAH MEEK - 1805 - 7; 17 RICHARD RUE - 1804 - 7; 18 - MARGARET McCOY -1805 -7; 18 - DANIEL & ANDREW HARMON - 1814 - 7; 18 - SAMUEL ARNET - 1805 - 7; 19 - THOMAS McCAISLEY - 1807 - 7 (note: resold 1812 to THOS. SHOOP); 19 - SAMUEL HENDERSON - 1804 - 7; 19 - JOHN COLLINS - 1808 - 7; 19 PETER WEAVER - 1807- 7; 20 - VINCENT STEPHENSON -1812 7; 20 - WM. REYNOLDS - 1813 - 7; 20 - HENRY WINFIELD 1806 - 7; 20 - JOSHUA MEEK - 1813- 7; 21 - WM. WILLIAMS - 1814 - 7; 21 - ABR. GAAR - 1817 -7; 22 - DANIEL CLARK - 1815- 7; 22 - WM. FOUTS - 1808 -7; 22 - JEREMIAH PARKER - 1818 - 7; 23 - DAVID BAILEY 1807 -8; 23 JOHN WATTS - 1813 - 8; 23 - JAMES HARTUP - 1806 - 8; 23 - CATHERINE PRICE - 1813 - 8; 24 - JOHN HARDIN 1805 - 8; 24 - ADAM ZEEK - 1813 - 8; 24 - JOHN RAPER 1811 -8; 24 - WM. MILNER - 1813 - 8; 25 - THOMAS HOLLETT - 1814 - 8; 25 - MARK HOLLETT - 1814 - 8; 25 GEORGE HOLLETT - 1814 - 8; 26 - WM. JONES - 1806- 8; 26 - JACOB KESSLING - 1809- 8; 26 - GEORGE JONES-1806

WAYNE COUNTY: Original Land Entries Tract Book
FORMAT: Section - Purchaser - year - page;

Township 13, Range 1W continued

8; 26 - JACOB KESSLING - 1812- 8; 27 - BENJAMIN HODGE 1812 - 8; 27 - GEORGE JONES - 1806 -8; 27 & 28 -JACOB KESSLING -1808 - 8; 28 - DANIEL HART - 1815 - 8; 28 - WM. & J. GRIMES - 1813 - 8; 28 - ELIZABETH MILLER 1811 - 8; 29 - HUGH CULL - 1806 - 8; 29 - BASIL MEEK 1807 - 8; 29 - WASHINGTON ELLIOTT - 1817 - 8; 29 ISAAC BEESON - 1806 - 8; 30 - AARON MARTIN -1806 - 8; 30 - ABR. GARR - 1807 - 8; 30 - RICHARD RUE - 1805 8; 30 - JOHN HUNT - 1806 -8; 31 - JACKSON RAMBO -1809 8; 31 - LAZARUS WHITEHEAD - 1805 - 8; 31 - DANIEL OSBORN - 1814 - 8; 31 - JOHN WHITEHEAD - 1811 - 8; 32 BENJAMIN BROWN - 1813 - 8; 32 - JOHN WHITEHEAD - 1814 8; 32 - ABNER ACRES -1815 -8; 32 - WASHINGTON ELLIOTT 1814 - 8; 33 - JOHN JORDAN - 1814- 8; 33 - JOHN TOWNSEND - 1813- 8; 33 - WM. JONES - 1808 - 8; 34 -GEORGE HOLMAN - 1807 - 8; 34 - PETER DEMAREE - 1807 - 8; 34 WM. HOLMAN - 1806 - 8; 34 - JOSEPH HOLMAN - 1806 -8; 35 -JOHN JORDAN - 1814 - 9; 35 - GEORGE HOLMAN -1807 9; 35 - ABSOLOM RAMBO - 1813 - 9; 36 - AARON HARDING 1814 - 9.

Township 13, Range 2W

1 - JOHN TOWNSEND - 1808 - 10; 12 - SUSANNA BUTLER 1806 - 10; 12 - ISAAC ELLIOTT - 1811 - 10; 11 & 12 CALEB HARVEY - 1808 - 10; 13 - SHADRACK HENDERSON 1806 - 10; 13 - HUGH ENDSLEY - 1808 - 10; 14 - DAVID FISHER - 1815 - 10; 23 - BEALE BUTLER - 1806 - 10; 24 JACOB LEE - 1814 - 10; 24 - ALEXANDER MILLER - 1812 10; 24 - PETER FLEMING - 1804 - 10; 24 - JOHN COX 1806 - 10. 25 - JOSEPH WASSON - 1804 - 10; 25 - DAVID NORTON - 1806 - 10; 25 - ANDREW ENDSLEY - 1805 - 10; 26 - DAVID PARSON/ CARSON - 1807 - 10; 26 - ABNER MARTIN - 1814 - 10; 26 - LAZARUS WHITEHEAD - 1806 10; 26 - WILLIAM REED - 1812 - 10; 35 - JOHN READ 1806 - 10; 35 - JOHN ELLIS - 1814 - 10; 35 - DAVID RAILSBACK - 1810 - 10; 36 - JOHN ENDSLEY - 1805 - 10; 36 - JOHN LEE - 1806 - 10; 36 - JAMES C. MORRIS 1806 - 10; 36 - LAZARUS WHITEHEAD - 1806 - 10.

Township 14, Range 1W

1 - SAMUEL HENDERSON - 1808 - 14; 1 - ROBERT MORRISON - 1810 - 14; 1 - ISAAC COMMONS - 1813 - 14; 2 ISAAC HIATT - 1816 - 14; 2 - JOHN WHITE - 1816 -14; 2 - ISAAC BOSWELL - 1814 - 14; 2 - ZACARIAH HIATT 1814 - 14; 3 - ENOS GROVE - 1816 - 14; 3 - WM. HIATT 1813 - 14; 3 - JOHN THOMAS - 1816 - 14; 4 - BENJAMIN HARRIS - 1807 - 14; 4 - MICHAEL LEWELLEN - 1813 - 13; 4 - WM. STARBUCK - 1808 - 14; 4 - JOSEPH ADDINGTON

WAYNE COUNTY: Original Land Entries Tract Book
FORMAT: Section - Purchaser - year - page;

Township 14, Range 1W continued

1813 - 14; 5 - JAMES MORRISON - 1813 - 14; 5 - TEUCE MASSEY - 1817 - 14; 5 - BENJAMIN COX - 1807 - 14; 5 & 7 - JACOB HAMPTON - 1816 - 14; 6 - ANDREW HAMPTON 1817 - 14; 8 - THOMAS ADDINGTON - 1807 - 14; 8 - SAMEUL CHARLES - 1815 - 14; 8 - JOHN ADDINGTON - 1806 14; 8 - ISAAC PARKER - 1808 - 14; 9 - PAUL STARBUCK 1816 - 14; 9 - THOMAS ROBERTS - 1812 - 14; 9 - ISAAC PARKER - 1817 - 14; 9 - JOHN ADDINGTON -1807 - 14; 10 LIBNI HUNT - 1814 - 14; 10 - JAMES WRIGHT - 1814- 14; 10 - ALEXANDER MOORE - 1816 - 14; 11 - HENRY NULL 1806 - 14; 11 - MARION BOSWELL - 1818 - 14; 11 & 11 TABITHA WHITE - 1806 - 14; 12 - CHRISTIAN PETTIFISH 1806 - 14; 12 - JEREMIAH COX - 1808 - 14; 12 - CONRAD ROBERT - 1816 - 14; 12 - BLADEN ASHBY - 1812 - 14; 13 WM. ALEXANDER - 1811- 14; 13 - JOSEPH PEMBERTON -1816 14; 13 - ISAAC JESSUP - 1814 - 14; 13 - BENJAMIN SMITH - 1813 - 14; 14 - JOHN MORROW - 1813 -14; 14 MORDECAI CARTER - 1806- 14; 14 - JOHN MEEK -1814 -15; 14 - ANDREW HOOVER - 1817- 15; 15 -WILLIAM BOND -1816 15; 15 - THOMAS STAFFORD - 1813 - 15; 15 - ISAAC VORE 1816 - 15; 17 - JOHN ADDINGTON -1806 -15; 17 -SUSANNA BUTLER - 1806 - 15; 17 - WM. MEEK - 1815 - 15; 18 ISAAC HAMPTON - 1816 - 15; 18 - ISAAC COOK - 1814- 15 18 - ISAAC MARTIN - 1815 - 15; 19 - JONATHAN MILLER 1814 - 15; 19 - JOHN SUTHERLAND & WM. W. PHARRIS JR 1816 - 15; 19 - HARDY & JOS. CAIN - 1814 - 15; 20 JOSHUA PIGGOT - 1808- 15; 20 - PHINEAS ROBERTS - 1812 15; 20 - ABIJAH CAIN - 1813 - 15; 20 - BENJAMIN PEARSON - 1811 - 15; 21 - ABNER CLAWSON - 1817 - 15; 21 - WM. BROWN - 1817 - 15; 21 -JOSIAH CLAWSON - 1813 15; 21 - WM. CLAWSON - 1813 - 15; 22 - JESSE CLARK 1813 - 15; 22 - ALEXANDER MOON - 1817- 15; 23 - JOHN WHEELER - 1814 - 15; 23 - GRIFFITH MENDENHALL - 1815 15; 23 - THOMAS KENDALL - 1817 - 15; 23 - WM. THORNBOROUGH - 1813 - 15; 24 - JONATHAN WRIGHT & WM. COOK 1813 - 15; 24 - JOHN ALEXANDER - 1807 - 15; 24 ARCHIBALD WOOD - 1813 - 15; 24 - ISAAC JESSUP - 1814 15; 25 - ANDREW BAILEY - 1814 - 15; 25 - CONRAD ROBERT - 1817 - 15; 25 - JOHN DRAKE - 1807 - 15; 25 JOSEPH WAYSON - 1806 - 15; 26 - BENJAMIN HILL - 1817 13; 26 - JAC. & WM. JESSUP - 1817 - 13; 26 - BENJ. HILL - 1808 - 13; 26 - JOHN WASSON - 1807 - 13; 27 RALPH WRIGHT - 1807- 13; 27, 28 & 29 - ANDREW HOOVER 1806 - 13; 27 - SAMUEL WOODS - 1806 - 13; 27 - WM. FOUTS - 1806 - 13; 28 - JOHN SMALL - 1807 - 13; 29, 32 & 33 - JOHN SMITH - 1806 - 13; 29 - MOSES KELLEY 1806- 13; 30 - THOMAS RANDALL - 1807 -13; 30 - THOMAS LAMB - 1813 - 13; 30 - WM. PRICE - 1814 - 13; 30 - JONAS RANDALL - 1806 - 13; 31 - ENNIS SHOEMAKER 1812 - 13; 31 - MARY & CHARITY COOK - 1807 - 13; 31

WAYNE COUNTY: Original Land Entries Tract Book
FORMAT: Section - Purchaser - year - page;

Township 14, Range 1W continued

JONATHAN ROBERTS - 1806 - 13; 31 - JESSE BOND -1813 13; 32 - JOHN MEEK - 1805 - 13; 33 - JOHN HAWKINS 1807 - 13; 33 - JEREMIAH COX - 1807 - 13; 33 - JOHN MEEK - 1806 - 13; 34 - AMOS HAWKINS - 1807 - 13; 34 HEZEKIAH WITS - 1817 - 13; 34 - B. MORGAN & B. MODLIN 1807 - 13; 34 - JOHN HARVEY - 1807 - 13; 35 - ROBERT CONNER - 1807 - 13; 35 - BENJ. HILL -1814 - 13; 35 ROBERT HILL - 1806 - 13; 35 -JOHN & THOS. POOL - 1807 13; 36 - ROBERT MAXWELL - 1805 - 13; 36 - JAMES ALEXANDER - 1805 -13; 36 - JOHN IRELAND - 1805 - 13.

Township 14, Range 2W

13 & 24 - JULAIN & HARRY COX - 1808 - 16; 25 - NATHAN MORRIS - 1813 - 16; 36 - THOMAS NEELEY - 1814 - 15.

Township 15, Range 1W

1 - JAMES COMPTON - 1817 - 22; 2 - ISAAC HOFFMAN 1817 - 22; 2 - JOHN SHARP - 1818 - 22; 2 - WM. ODELL 1817 - 22; 3 - JOHN PEARSON - 1817 - 22; 4 - WILLIAM NIXON - 1817 - 22; 4 - SAMUEL NIXON - 1818 - 22; 5 JOHN LONGFELLOW - 1813- 22; 8 - JOHN HARRIES & MALACH MOORE - 1811 - 22; 9 - FRANCIS THOMAS - 1817 - 22; 9 JAMES MENDENHALL - 1817 - 22; 9 - BENJAMIN MORGAN 1818 - 22; 9 - BENJ. THOMAS - 1815 - 22; 10 - JAMES HARRIS - 1819 - 22; 10 - ARCHILAUS MOOREMAN - 1817 22; 10 - THOMAS WILEY - 1818 - 22; 10 - SAMUEL SYMONS 1817 - 22; 11 - SAMUEL THOMSON - 1816 - 22; 12 - VALENTINE HARLAN - 1816 - 23; 12 - ELISHA HARLAN - 1816 23; 12 - DENNIS SPRINGER - 1817 - 23; 12 - JOSHUA HARLAN - 1816 - 23; 13 - NATHANIEL ELLIOTT - 1816 23; 13 - EDWARD STARBUCK - 1818- 23; 13 - JAMES WHITE 1816 - 23; 13 & 14 - TABITHA WHITE - 1817 - 23; 14 EDWARD STARBUCK - 1818 - 23; 17 - WM. STAFFORD - 1811 23; 17 - JAMES DWIGGINS - 1810- 23; 19 - BENJAMIN THOMAS - 1811 - 23; 20 - ISAAC THOMAS - 1817 - 23; 20 SOLOMON THOMAS - 1814 - 23; 22 - WM. ADDLEMAN - 1818 24; 23 - THOMAS MASON - 1817 - 24; 23 - RICHARD WILLIAMS - 1817 - 24; 23 - SAMUEL WILLIAMS - 1817 - 24; 23 - HENRY GARRET - 1817 - 24; 24 - JOHN WHITE - 1816 24; 24 - BENJAMIN PARKER & JO. SKINNER - 1819 - 24; 24 - RICHARD BUNCH - 1817 - 24; 24 - THOMAS MASON 1815 - 24; 25 - HENRY NEWTON - 1814 - 24; 25 - WM. HUNT - 1816 - 24; 25 - JAMES NEWTON - 1816 - 24; 25 JOB ELLIOTT - 1814 - 24; 26 - JOB ELLIOTT - 1817- 24; 26 - GABRIEL HARRELL - 1816 - 24; 27 - NATHAN FISHER 1817 - 24; 24 - EDWARD STARBUCK - 1817 - 24; 28 HENRY DETEROW - 1818 - 24; 28 - WM. HUNT - 1817 - 24;

WAYNE COUNTY: Original Land Entries Tract Book
FORMAT: Section - Purchaser - year - page;

Township 15, Range 1W continued

28 - PETER DETEROW - 1818 - 24; 29 - SAMUEL SANDERS - 1818 - 24; 29 - MATTHEW ALDEMAN - 1814 - 24; 29 STEPHEN MENDENHALL - 1817- 24; 29 - STEPHEN THOMAS SR 1816 - 24; 30 - CHARLES BALDWIN - 1813 - 25; 32 ENOS GRAVE - 1816 - 25; 32 - JONATHAN GROVE - 1816 25; 32 - JOHN TURNER - 1808 - 25; 33 - THOMAS FISHER 1817 - 25; 33 - WM. STARBUCK - 1808 - 25; 33 - JAMES JOHNSON - 1814 - 25; 34 - JOSEPH BROWN - 1818 - 25; 34 - JOHN VENNARD - 1816 - 25; 35 - JAMES WICKERSHAM 1817- 25; 35 - JAS. BROWN - 1818 - 25; 35 - ZACHARIAH HIATT - 1816 - 25; 35 - JOHN NICHOLSON - 1818 - 25; 36 - JOHN ZIMMERMAN - 1814 - 25; 36 - ELLIOTT PEARSON 1814 - 25; 36 - SAM'L. G. MITCHELL - 1808 - 25; 36 HENRY PAYLIN - 1814 - 25.

Township 15, Range 12E

1 - JAMES ROGERS - 1811 - 26; 1 - ISAAC WILLETS 1811 - 26; 1 - JACOB BURNET - 1811 - 26; 1 - JAS. & JOHN CONNOVER - 1811 - 26; 2 - DANIEL GOUNT - 1811 26; 2 - RICHARD WILLIAMS- 1811- 26; 2 - DEBOLT HICKLE 1811 - 26; 2 - JAMES HOLSCLAW - 1815 - 26; 3 & 12 JOHN KNIPE - 1811 - 26; 3 - WM. REYNOLDS - 1816- 26; 3 - MOSES COOPER - 1817 - 26; 3 - PETER MARTS - 1816 26; 10 - JAMES CATHCART - 1817 - 26; 10 - JOHN BELL 1817 - 26; 10 - REUBEN BROWNSON - 1814 - 26; 10 DAVID SHAY - 1817 - 26; 11 & 13 - NIMROD FERGUSON 1811- 26; 11 - JOHN BELL - 1815 - 26; 11, 12 & 14 JAMES SHAW - 1811 - 26; 11 - JOHN WALLACE - 1813 26; 12 - THOMAS BEARD - 1811 - 26; 13 - WM. WILSON 1811 - 26; 13 - STEPHEN GRIFFITH - 1811 - 26; 13 THOMAS HARDIN - 1811 - 26; 14 - JOHN WALLACE - 1812 26; 14 - JAMES JACKSON - 1817 - 26; 15 - RICHARD WILLIAMS - 1816 - 26; 15 - THOMAS THOMAS - 1813 26; 15 - JOSEPH VAN METER - 1811 - 26; 22 - JACOB BLOYD - 1814 - 26; 22 - THOMAS GILLIAN - 1813 - 26; 22 - JOSEPH WILLIAMS - 1813 - 26; 22 - SOLOMON BYRHILL - 1815 - 26; 23 - SAMUEL EASTON - 1814 - 26; 23 - WM. HATHCLAW - 1814 - 26; 23 - SAMUEL McGEORGE 1813 - 26; 23 - JOSEPH FLINT - 1814 - 26; 24 - JOSEPH SPENCER - 1811 - 26; 24 - BENJAMIN BEASON - 1812 26; 24 - ISAAC WILSON - 1811 - 27; 24 - JOEL WRIGHT 1814 - 27; 25 - NIMROD FERGUSON - 1811 - 27; 25 THOMAS BEARD - 1811 - 27; 25 - WM. ROSS - 1814 - 27; 26 - JOHN BAKER - 1813 - 27; 26 - ISAAC WILSON 1813 - 27; 26 - THOMAS NEAL - 1814- 27; 26 - E. BROWN 1814 - 27; 27 - ABRAHAM VAN METER - 1811 - 27; 27 SAMUEL SANDERS - 1812 - 27; 27 - ADAM BANKS - 1813 27; 27 - ADAM JACK - 1814 - 27.

WAYNE COUNTY: Original Land Entries Tract Book
FORMAT: Section - Purchaser - year - page;

Township 15, Range 13E

1 - LEWIS THOMAS - 1816 - 30;   1 - HENRY RYAN - 1811 30; 1 - JOB HUDDLESTON - 1816 - 30; 1 - THOS. DANBY & A. BAILEY - 1814 - 30;   2 - JOHN KNIPE - 1811 - 30; 2 PETER BANTA - 1816 - 30; 2 - ELISHA DENNIS - 1814 30; 2 - THOMAS McCOY - 1811- 30; 3 - JOSEPH GILLESPIE & SAMUEL BOCK - 1817 - 30; 3 - JOHN PATTERSON - 1811 30; 4 - JOB McCARTHY - 1816 - 30; 4 - JESSE WILLETS 1816 - 30; 4 - MARTIN FISHER - 1816 - 30; 4 - JESSE & ELISHA WILLETS - 1814 - 30; 5 - SAMUEL BLACK - 1811 30; 5 - WM. WILLETS - 1811 - 30; 5 & 6 - LEVI WILLETS 1811- 30; 6 - JOHN KILLONER - 1811- 30; 6 - ALEXANDER GRAY - 1811 - 30;   6 - JOHN WALLACE - 1811 - 30; 7 SAM'L. C. VANCE - 1818 - 30; 7 - WM. H. HARRISON 1814 - 30;   7 - ANDREW CROUCH - 1811 - 30; 7 - JOHN ANDREWS - 1817 - 30; 8 - ISAAC WATERS & WM. CUMMINGS 1814 - 30; 8 - ABRAHAM MILLER - 1811 - 30; 8 - JAMES A. CHAMBERS - 1811 - 30; 8 - SAMUEL BEELER - 1814 30; 9 - WM. M. LUCAS - 1818 - 30; 9 - JAMES McGREW 1811 - 30;   9 - PETER GITHRO (corrected to GITTRO) 1811 - 30; 9 - SILAS DUNN - 1813 - 30; 10 - WILLIAM BEESON - 1811 - 30; 10 - DANIEL NOLAND - 1811 - 30; 10 - WRIGHT LANCASTER - 1811 - 30; 10 - JACOB LITTLE 1811 - 30;   11 - JOHN SPAHR - 1811 - 30;   12 - JOHN JONES - 1816 - 31; 12 - JOHN DODDRIDGE - 1813 - 31; 12 - WM. BLACK - 1816 - 31; 13 - HENRY HENDRICKS 1815 - 31; 13 - PHINEAS McCREA/McCRAY - 1813 - 31; 13 DAVID DAY - 1815 - 31;   14 - JOHN HEWOOD - 1812 - 31; 14 - JOHN SPAHR - 1811 - 31; 14 - JOHN COMLEY/ CONLEY 1812 - 31; 15 - WRIGHT LANCASTER - 1811 - 31;   15 JOHN POST - 1811 - 31; 15 - PHILIP DODRIDGE - 1814 31;   17 - DAVID STEVENSON - 1814 - 31;   17 - GEORGE FARLOW - 1814 - 31; 17 - JOHN MILLER - 1814 - 31; 17 STEPHEN GRIFFITH - 1817 - 31;   18 - RICHARD KENDRY / HENDRY - 181-- 31;   18 - JOHN FOX - 1811 - 31; 18 SAMUEL BROWN - 1813 - 31; 18 - DAVID LAMB - 1811- 31; 19 - GEORGE MILLER - 1811- 31; 19 & 20 - THOMAS BEARD 1811 - 31;   19 - ISAAC MILLER - 1814 - 31;   19 - JOHN DODSON - 1816 - 31; 20 - SIMMONS & FARLOW - 1812- 31; 20 - JOSEPH FLINT - 1811 - 31;   20 - WM. MONTGOMERY 1814 - 31;   21 - JONATHAN GILBERT - 1811 - 31;   21 SAMUEL STERCET - 1811 - 31; 21 - THOMAS BEARD & JACOB WEYMIRE - 1812 - 31; 21 - PHILIP FOX - 1811 - 31; 22 DAVID JENKINS - 1812 - 31; 22 - WM. WALTER - 1814 31; 22 - THOMAS ENDSLEY & EDWARD HUNT - 1814 - 31; 23 JOHN SHETTERLEY & GEORGE MISOR - 1818 - 31; 23 - JOHN SPAHR - 1813 - 31; 23 - JOHN BENEFIELD - 1814 - 32; 23 - DAVID JENNINGS - 1813 - 32; 34 - WM. GARRETT 1817 - 32; 24 - JOHN DODDRIDGE - 1814- 32; 24 - JAMES McCLAIN - 1816 - 32; 24 - SMITH LANE - 1817 - 32; 26 ROBERT BENEFIELD - 1814 - 32;   26 - SIMEON SUMMERS

WAYNE COUNTY: Original Land Entries Tract Book
FORMAT: Section - Purchaser - year - page;

Township 15, Range 13E continued

1815 - 32; 26 - JONAS HUFFAMAN - 1814 - 32; 26 - JOHN SUMMERS - 1815- 32; 27 - PLATT MONTGOMERY - 1814- 32; 27 - JOSIAS LAMBERT - 1814 - 32; 27 - JOHN SIMMONS 1814 - 32; 27 - JOHN SIMMONS - 1814 - 32; 27 - WM. DYER - 1814 - 32; 28 - JOHN FOX - 1811 - 32; 28 JOSEPH HONET - 1816 - 32; 28 - WM. SHAW - 1811 - 32; 28 - THOMAS CLARK - 1813 - 32; 29 - ROBERT MONTGOMERY 1812 - 32; 29 - JOSEPH WATTS - 1811 - 32; 29 - MATTHIAS PARSONS - 1812 - 32; 30 - ASA GREENWELL - 1814 32; 30 - JONATHAN HIGGINS - 1816- 32; 30 - HUGH MOORE 1817 - 32; 30 - RALPH WRIGHT - 1811 - 32.

Township 15, Range 14E

3, 34, 16 & 14 - HIRAM & BEAL BUTLER - 1816 - 33; 4 ZACARIAH DICKS - 1816 - 33; 4 - THOMAS CAMPBELL/ CARNELL - 1816 - 33; 5 - WM. BUTLER - 1817 - 33; 5 - WM. JENKINS - 1817 - 33; 6 - ALEXANDER C. BLACK - 1816 33; 6 - ISAAC WILLIAMS - 1847 - 33; 6 - JOHN JONES JR 1817 - 33; 7 - WM. JONES - 1816 - 33; 8 - GEORGE JARRETT - 1817 - 33; 8 - LAURENCE BRANNON - 1818- 33; 8 - LEVI JARRETT - 1817 - 33; 8 - JOSEPH ALLAN PRYOR 1817 - 33; 9 & 10 - MOSES ROBBINS - 1817 - 33; 17 DAVID RAILSBACK - 1812 - 33; 17 - WM. JARRETT - 1817 33; 17 - GABRIEL FENDER - 1815 - 33; 18 - EDMUND JONES - 1817 - 33; 18 - JOHN ELLIS - 1815 - 33; 18 SPENCER STEPHENS - 1815 - 33; 19 - DANIEL CLEVENGER 1816 - 34; 19 - JEREMIAH ALLEN - 1814 - 34; 20 - JEREMIAH ALLEN - 1816 - 34; 20 - HENRY LONG - 1817 - 34; 20 - BENSON MINOR - 1815 - 34; 20 - DAN'L. ALEXANDER 1815 - 34; 21 - HENRY FENDER - 1813 - 34.

Township 16, Range 12E

1 - JOHN SUMMERS - 1811 - 36; 2 & 3 - GEORGE IRVIN 1815 - 36; 11 - DAVID ODEM - 1814 - 36; 11 - BENJAMIN ROBERTS - 1815 - 36; 11 - JOSEPH EVANS - 1811 - 36; 11 - JOHN POOL - 1815 - 36; 12 - DANIEL NOLAND - 1811 37; 12 - ELIJAH SPENCER - 1814 - 37; 12 - ATTERILL WARRALL - 1811 - 37; 12 - SARAH & LYDIA SYMONS - 1812 37; 13 - WM. BROWN - 1812- 37; 13 - JEHOSAPHAT MOORIS 1811 - 37; 13 - WM. THOMAS - 1811 - 37; 14 - ROBERT DICKERSON - 1811 - 37; 22 - THOMAS SIMONS - 1811 -38; 23 - JOHN NIXON - 1811 - 38; 23 - JOHN HOOVER - 1811 38; 23 - GEORGE VAN BUSKIRK -1814 - 38; 24 -WM. THORN 1811 - 38; 24 - JESSE BEARD - 1811 - 38; 24 - HENRY BROWN - 1811 - 38; 25 - JOHN SHORTRIDGE - 1811 - 38; 26 - WILLIAM WILLETS - 1811 - 38; 26 - SIMON POWELL 1814 - 38; 26 - LEVI W. WILLETS - 1811 - 38; 26 GEORGE ISHE - 1812 - 38; 27 & 28 - JOHN HAWKINS

WAYNE COUNTY: Original Land Entries Tract Book
FORMAT: Section - Purchaser - year - page;

Township 16, Range 12E continued

1811 - 38; 34 - JOHN BELL - 1811 - 39; 34 - THOMAS STAFFORD - 1811 - 39; 34 - BOAZ THORPE/ THARP - 1811 39; 34 - SAMUEL DRURY - 1814 - 39; 35 - GEORGE GLAZE/ GLASS - 1811 - 39; 35 - THOMAS SIMONS - 1811 - 39; 35 DANIEL YOUNT - 1811 - 39; 35 - JOHN CONNOR - 1811 39; 36 - ISAAC WILSON -1811 - 39; 36 - SAMUEL BEELER 1811 - 39; 36 - NATHAN RICHARDSON - 1811 - 39; 36 GEORGE GLASS - 1811 - 39.

Township 16, Range 13E

1 - JONATHAN CLOUD - 1814 - 40; 1 - JOHN HARVEY SR 1815 - 40; 1 - WILLIAM PIKE - 1814 - 40; 1 - ELI BROWN - 1816 - 40; 2 - ABSOLOM WILLIAMS - 1814 - 40; 2 - ISAAC MENDENHALL - 1814 - 40; 2 - WM. FRASIER 1815 - 40; 2 - NATHAN HILL - 1818 - 40; 3 - HENRY HOOVER - 1811 - 40; 3 - JOHN FINCHER - 1811 - 40; 3 PETER HOOVER - 1811- 40; 4 - JOHN FINCHER - 1817- 40; 4 - SAMUEL LEONARD - 1816 - 40; 4 - WILLIAM FINCHER 1811- 40; 4 - JOHN HARVEY JR - 1815 - 40; 11 - ROBERT GALBREATH - 1815 - 40; 12 - JOHN GARRETT - 1815 - 41; 12 - NATHAN GARRETT - 1817- 41; 12 - JOSEPH COX -1814 41; 12 - WM. HOSIER - 1817 - 41; 13 - JONATHAN JESSUP 1814 - 41; 13 - N. COOK & J. MARTIN - 1816 - 41; 13 WM. HOSIER - 1816 - 41; 13 - WM. CUMMINS - 1811 - 41; 14 - NATHAN HILL - 1816 - 41; 14 - ROBERT HILL - 1815 41; 14 - CHARLES GORDON - 1816 - 41; 14 - SUSAN REED 1815 - 41; 15 - WM. HOSIER - 1814 - 41; 15 - JOSEPH EVANS - 1811 - 41; 15 - JACOB REED - 1814 - 41; 15 JOHN HARVEY - 1814- 41; 17 - RICHARD L. LEASON - 1816 41; 17 - THOMAS I. WORMAN - 1811 -41; 17 - J. SHANK & W. LANE - 1816 - 41; 17 - JAMES DOHERTY/DOUGHERTY 1816 - 41; 18 & 18 - JOHN McKEE - 1811- 41; 18 - ASA PREVO - 1814 - 41; 18 - DAVIS EMBIER - 1811 - 41; 19 - WM. THORNE - 1811 - 41; 19 - J. PERSONETT & J. DAVIS - 1816 - 41; 20 - ISAAC WILLETS - 1816 - 41; 20 ISAAC MORRIS - 1815 - 41; 20 - BENJ. MORGAN - 1815 41; 20 - JOSIAH BUNDY - 1815 - 41; 21 - LEWIS HOSIER 1811 - 41; 21 - ISAAC WILLETS - 1811 - 41; 21 - WM. THORNE - 1811 - 41; 22 - EZEKIAL COMMONS - 1814- 41; 22 - JOHN BECK - 1814 - 41; 22 - GEORGE BROWN - 1815 41; 22 -SAMUEL BOYD - 1811- 41; 23 -JOHN HARVEY -1816 42; 23 - NATHAN COMMONS - 1817 - 42; 23 - ZACARIAH HIATT - 1816 - 42; 24 - JOHN HARVEY - 1811 - 42; 24 NATHAN HILL - 1814 - 42; 24 - WM. HARVEY - 1811 42; 24 - GREENBERRY CORNELIUS - 1813 - 42; 25 ROBERT BLAIR - 1812 - 42; 25 - WM. IRVIN - 1811 42; 25 - ISAAC JULIAN - 1811 - 42; 25 - JOHN McINTYRE 1811 - 42; 26 - ISAAC JULIAN - 1817 - 42; 26 - H. HARVEY -1817 - 42; 26 - JOHN McINTIRE -1812 - 42; 27

WAYNE COUNTY: Original Land Entries Tract Book
FORMAT: Section - Purchaser - year - page;

Township 16, Range 13E continued

DANIEL STONE - 1816 - 42; 27 - REUBEN WAGGONER - 1814 42; 27 - JOEL REED - 1816- 42; 27 - ISAAC HICKS -1814 42; 28 - ISAAC WILLETTS - 1811- 42; 28 - JOHN WOODARD 1814 - 42; 28 - EDWARD DRURY -1811 - 42; 29 - JOHN LACY - 1814 - 42; 29 - AARON MANN - 1814 - 42; 29 GEORGE ISH - 1815 - 42; 29 - RICHARD WHARLTON - 1814 42; 30 - WM. THORNE -1811 -42; 30 - WM. G. REYNOLDS 1816 - 42; 30 - ANDREW WOODS - 1811 - 42; 31 - GEORGE SHORTRIDGE - 1812 - 42; 31 - SAMUEL BEELER - 1811 42; 31 - JOS. HOBSON/ HOLLSON - 1812 - 42; 32 - JOHN CONNOVER -1815 - 42; 32 - JACOB OLDAKER - 1815 - 42; 32 - EDWARD DRURY - 1811 - 42; 32 - GEORGE ISH -1812 42; 33 - SAMUEL SHORTRIDGE - 1816 - 42; 33 - WILLIAM CAMPBELL - 1811 -42; 33 - HENRY BRYAN - 1816 - 43; 34 JAMES TUCKER - 1814 - 43; 34 - SAMUEL C. VANCE - 1818 43; 34 - HOOK & MISOR - 1817 - 43; 34 - BUNNEL WRIGHT 1814 - 43; 35 - JOHN HARVEY - 1811 -43; 35 - THOMAS McCOY - 1811 - 43; 36 - HARMON WAIRAM - 1812 - 43; 36 HENRY BRYAN - 1811 - 43; 36 - ROBERT BLACK - 1813 43.

Township 16, Range 14E

2 & 11 - THOMAS LAMB - 1815 - 44; 3 - PATRICK MOON/ MOORE - 1817 - 44; 3 - WM. DAVIS - 1817 - 44; 3 - WM. RIDER/ REIDER - 1817 - 44; 3 & 4 - SAM'L. MILLIKIN & JOS. HOUGH - 1816 - 44; 4 - ASA PREVO - 1815 - 44; 4 MILLIKIN & HOUGH - 1816 - 44; 4 - JOHN KING - 1817 44; 5 - HENRY BAILEY - 1811 - 44; 5 - JOSEPH HOLMAN 1815 - 44; 5 - JOSEPH KING - 1816 - 44; 5 - JOHN COPELAND - 1814 - 44; 6 - ROBERT GALBREATH - 1815 44; 6 - THOMAS NIXON - 1814 - 44; 6 - EXUM ELLIOTT 1815 - 44; 6 - HENRY BAILEY - 1814 - 44; 7 - JOSEPH HOLMON & ELI OWEN - 1812 - 44; 7 - BENJAMIN MODLIN 1813 - 44; 7 - WM. HASTINGS - 1811 - 44; 7 - HENRY BAILY - 1815 - 44; 8 - ARCHIBALD BEALL - 1816 - 44; 8 DANIEL KING - 1816 - 44; 8 - FRANCIS CULBERTSON 1814 - 44; 8 - JACOB GRIFFIN - 1814 - 44; 9 - ALEX. McCALLISTER - 1815 - 44; 9 - WM. BEALL - 1816 - 44; 9 JAMES BLACK - 1815 - 44; 9 - JOSHUA ELIASSON - 1814 44; 10 - PATRICK MOORE/ MOON - 1817 - 44; 10 - DAVID DAVIS - 1815 - 44; 10 - WM. DAVIS - 1817 - 44; 10 JAMES BLACK - 1813 - 44; 14 & 15 - J. SUTHERLAND & WM ERWIN & F. SLOO, JR - 1812 - 44; 17 - JOHN MAXWELL 1811 - 44; 17 - NATHAN GARRETT - 1811 - 44; 17 - JOHN BELL - 1812 - 44; 17 - JOHN HARVEY - 1812 - 44; 18 WM. PATTERSON - 1811 - 44; 18 - JAMES TOWNSEND - 1811 44; 18 - GARRETT & GALBREATH - 1811 - 45; 18 - ROBERT HARVEY - 1811 - 45; 19 - JACOB SINKS - 1811 - 45; 19 WM. HOSIER - 1811 - 45; 19 - ETHAN STONE - 1811 - 45;

WAYNE COUNTY: Original Land Entries Tract Book
FORMAT: Section - Purchaser - year - page;

Township 16, Range 14E continued

19 - NATHAN OVERMAN - 1811 - 45;   20 - JACOB BURNET 1811 - 45;   20 - ENNIS SHOEMAKER - 1813 - 45;   20 ISRAEL ELLIOTT - 1813 - 45; 21 - EUELE KINDELL & JOHN TURNER - 1812 - 45;   21 - ELI BUTLER - 1814 - 45;   21 JAMES THOMPSON - 1817 - 45; 21 - JOSEPH KIBBEY/ KILBY 1814 - 45;   22 - JOHN SMITH - 1811 - 45; 27 - SAMUEL WALKER - 1813 - 45;   28 - P.S. SYMMS - 1815 - 45;   28 JESSE THOMAS - 1817 - 45; 28 - JOHN LAUGH - 1816- 45; 29 - SAMUEL KING - 1814 - 45; 29 - JAMES BLACK - 1814 45; 29 - ELISHA KING - 1814 - 45; 29 - SPENCER FREE (a free negro) - 1813 - 45;   30 - CHRISTOPHER RODDY (to ISAAC JULIAN, assignee) - 1814 - 45;   30 - ROBERT CULBERTSON - 1814 - 45; 30 - DANIEL GALBREATH - 1813 45; 30 - JAMES JENKINS - 1813 - 45;   31 - ARCHIBALD BEALL - 1814 - 45;   31 - JOHN GALBREATH - 1813 - 45; 31 & 32 - ENOS BUTLER - 1816 - 45;   31 - LEWIS THOMAS 1815 - 45;   32 - SPENCER FREE (a free negro) - 1815 45; 32 - JOSEPH AIKEN/ ALLEN - 1814 - 45; 32 - HIRAM BUTLER - 1816 - 45;   33 - MOSES MARTINDALE - 1817 45;   33 - SOLOMON MADDEN - 1817 - 45.

Township 17, Range 12E

1 - JOHN HAWORTH & A. ELLMORE - 1817 - 48; 12 - JACOB VIRGIL - 1815 - 48; 13 & 14 - JOSEPH HANCOCK - 1815 48;   23 - BARTLETT WOODWARD - 1813 - 49;   24 - JAMES REEDER - 1817 - 49; 24 - SAMUEL HAYES - 1817 - 49; 24 HORREL/ HOWELL CAMPBELL - 1817 - 49; 24 - PHILIP BAL-TIMORE - 1816 - 49; 25 - ENOS VEAL - 1817 - 49;   25 WM. CODDINGTON - 1817 - 49; 25 - JAMES STURGIS - 1817 49;   25 & 26 - CALEB BARRETT - 1816 - 49;   35 - JOHN CLARK - 1817 - 50;   36 - ELISHA HARLAN - 1816 - 50; 36 - JOHN W. BERRY - 1817 - 50;   36 - PETER RUNION 1817 - 50.

Township 17, Range 13E

1 - WM. BALLINGER - 1816 - 52; 1 - SETH WAY - 1817 52; 1 - THOMAS LILLEY - 1820 - 52; 2 - JOSHUA BALLIN-GER - 1815 - 52;   2 - LUKE DILLON - 1815 - 52;   3 JESSE DILLON - 1815 - 52; 3 - JOHN BAILEY - 1815 -52; 4 - HENRY STEDDON/ STEDHAM - 1818 - 52;   4 - JOHN W. BERY - 1817 - 52;   5 - JAMES FERRILL - 1816 - 52;   5 JACOB FRENCH - 1812 - 52; 5 - HEZEKIAH MANNING - 1816 52; 5 - JOHN MOUNTS - 1816 - 52; 6 - SOLOMON HODGSON 1816 - 52;   6 - WM. WILLIAMS - 1816 - 52;   6 - DILWIN BALES - 1816 - 52; 6 - NATHAN WILLIAMS - 1816 - 52; 7 DILWIN BALES - 1815- 52; 7 - JAMES MOORE - 1816 - 52; 8 - WM. MURRAY - 1816 - 52; 9 - JAMES PORTER - 1814

WAYNE COUNTY: Original Land Entries Tract Book
FORMAT: Section - Purchaser - year - page;

Township 17, Range 13E continued

52; 10 - WM. ELLIOTT - 1816 - 53; 10 - JOHN CAIN 1814 - 53; 10 - WM. DEMMITT - 1815 - 53; 10 - SAMUEL SMITH - 1813 - 53; 11 - HENRY OHLER - 1814 - 53; 11 JOSHUA ALLISON - 1815 - 53; 12 - WM. DEMMITT - 1814 53; 12 - MOSES MARTINDALE - 1817 - 53; 13 - DANIEL CLARK -1811 - 53; 13 - WM. UNDERHILL - 1814 - 53; 13 SAMUEL JONES - 1816- 53; 13 - DAVID BROWN -1817 - 53; 14 - GEORGE RENBERGER / RENLINGER - 1816 - 53; 15 THOMAS DEMMITT - 1816 - 53; 15 - ARCHIBALD BEALE 1814 - 53; 15 - ANDREW HOOVER - 1815 - 53; 17 -JOSIAS LAMBERT - 1815 - 53; 17 - MICHAEL FOUTS - 1811 - 53; 17 & 18 - SAMUEL McCULLOUGH - 1816 - 53; 17 -ISAAC HARVEY - 1811 - 53; 18 - BONHAM RUNYAN - 1816 - 54; 19 - JAMES HILL - 1815 - 54; 19 - JOHN MELL - 1820 54; 19 - JAMES PORTER - 1811 - 54; 19 - MATTHIAS PEARSON JR - 1816 - 54; 20 - JOHN MOON/ MOORE - 1815 54; 20 - JACOB GALYEAU - 1811 - 54; 20 - JACOB HUGHOLL - 1812 - 54; 20 - THOMAS GALYEAU - 1811 - 54; 21 - JOSIAH BRADBERRY - 1814 - 54; 21 - JONATHAN SHAW SR - 1815 - 54; 21 - WM. YOUNG - 1815- 54; 21 -DANIEL BRADBERRY - 1814 - 54; 22 - JOHN SUTTON - 1818 - 54; 22 - AARON R. SAYERS - 1817 - 54; 22 - JOSHUA BINNEY 1816 - 54; 22 - ENOS VEAL - 1817 - 54; 23 - HENRY GARRETT - 1817 - 54; 23 - WM. BULLA - 1815 - 54; 23 WM. FOX - 1811 - 54; 23 - JAMES SPRAY - 1815 - 54; 24 JEREMIAH & ABNER ELLIOTT - 1811 - 54; 24 - HENRY GARRETT - 1811 - 54; 24 - JAMES ODELL - 1811 - 54; 25 STEPHEN GULLIFER - 1813 - 54; 25 - ABRAHAM ELLIOTT JR 1812 - 54; 25 - NATHAN HILL - 1814 - 54; 25 - JESSE ALBERTSON - 1814 - 54; 26 - ABEL JENNEY - 1811 - 54; 26 - THOMAS HATFIELD - 1812 - 54; 26 - JAMES MARTIN-DALE - 1811 - 54; 26 - JOSEPH HATFIELD - 1811 - 54; 27 - SAMUEL EVANS - 1817 - 54; 27 - ENOS VEAL - 1817 54; 27 - MILES DEMMITT - 1816- 54; 27 - MASON FITHIAN 1817 - 54; 28 - CALEB MORRIS - 1815 - 54; 28 - MILES MURPHY - 1815 - 54; 28 - NATHAN MORRIS - 1815 - 55; 29 - JAMES ODELL - 1811 - 55; 29 - JOHN MARTINDALE 1811 - 55; 29 - JEREMIAH COX - 1811 - 55; 29 - JOHN HARVEY - 1811 - 55; 30 - ROBERT EWING - 1811 - 55; 30 WM. MARTINDALE - 1816 - 55; 30 - SAMUEL BALDRIDGE 1816 - 55; 30 - HUGH ALLEN - 1818 - 55; 31 - ETHAN STONE - 1811 - 55; 31 - JAMES WILCOX - 1817 - 55; 31 PETER CUSSANT - 1812 - 55; 31 - JAMES RALSTON - 1817 55; 32 - JAMES HOLLIDAY - 1812 - 55; 32 - NATHAN LEONARD - 1814 - 55; 32 - JOHN SCOTT - 1812 - 55; 32 EPHRAIM CLARK - 1812 - 55; 33 - CORNELIUS RATLIFF 1814 - 55; 33 - WM. STEELE - 1818 - 55; 33 - DAVID HOOVER (son of JACOB) - 1816 - 55; 33 - JOHN SCOTT 1815 - 55; 34 - THOMAS KERSEY - 1811 - 55; 34 - DAVID PEACOCK - 1817 - 55; 34 - ELI MILLIKEN - 1811 - 55;

WAYNE COUNTY: Original Land Entries Tract Book
FORMAT: Section - Purchaser - year - page;

Township 17, Range 13E continued

34 - JOHN FOLAND - 1814 - 55; 35 - JAMES MARTINDALE 1811 - 55; 35 - PETER QUACKENBUSH - 1811 - 55; 35 JESSE BOND - 1814 - 55; 35 - JACOB JULIAN - 1811 55; 36 - JACOB THORNBOROUGH - 1816 - 55; 36 - CORNELIUS RATLIFF - 1814 - 55; 36 - ELI FRAZER - 1816 55; 36 - WM. McDOUGHTY - 1820 - 55.

Township 17, Range 14 East

1 - GEO. SHUGART & JONATHAN HOUGH - 1811 - 56; 2 ABRAHAM HAMPTON - 1817 - 56; 2 - THOMAS POTTER - 1817 56; 2 - JOS. WOODY & J. HURST/ HUNT - 1817 - 56; 2 ABIJAH JONES - 1814 - 56; 3 - HARTSHON WHITE - 1819 56; 3 - TRISTRAM CROGGESHALL - 1815 - 56; 3 - DAVID BOWLES/ BOULES - 1817 - 56; 5 - SETH WAY - 1811 - 56; 5 - JOHN TERRELL/ TERIELT - 1811 - 56; 5 - STEPHEN JOHNSON - 1815 - 56; 5 - JAMES ODELL - 1811 - 56; 6 THOMAS CRANON/ CRANER - 1813 - 56; 6 - HENRY WAY 1815 - 56; 6 - SETH WAY - 1813 - 56; 7 - JOHN LEWIS 1811 - 56; 7 - JAMES LINDLEY - 1811- 56; 7 - ANTHONY CHAMNESS -1811 - 56; 6 - RICHARD LEWIS - 1811 - 56; 8 JOSHUA CRANON/ CRANER - 1815 - 56; 8 - JACOB FRENCH 1811 - 56; 8 - JAMES HARRIS - 1818 - 56; 8 - JOHN LEWIS - 1815 - 56; 9 - HENRY CATEY - 1820 - 56; 9 NATHAN JESSUP - 1816 - 56; 9 - WILLIS WHITSON - 1818 56; 10 - TRISTRAM COGGESHALL / TRISTAN CROGGERHALL 1815 - 56; 10 - JOHN STEDHAM / STUDDAN - 1817 - 56; 10 - ZACARIAH HIATT - 1817 - 56; 10 - JACOB JESSUP 1817 - 56; 11 - THOMAS THORP/ THARP - 1811 - 56; 11 JOSIAH LAMB - 1815 - 56; 11 - OBADIAH HARRIS - 1817 56; 11 - DANIEL BALDWIN - 1813 - 56; 12 - FRANCIS THOMAS - 1811 - 57; 13 - JONATHAN MARINE - 1817 - 57; 14 - JONATHAN MARINE - 1811 - 57; 14 - THOMAS BALDWIN 1812 - 57; 14 - JOHN BALDWIN - 1811 - 57; 15 - ISA HOUGH - 1816 - 57; 15 - JOHN SCOTT - 1816 - 57; 15 JOSEPH BOND - 1811- 57; 17 - JOHN SCROGGY - 1817- 57; 17 - JOSEPH LEWIS - 1817- 57; 17 - EDWARD BOND - 1817 57; 17 - JOHN BEVERLIN - 1815 - 57; 18 - MICAJAH SIMMONS - 1811 - 57; 18 - RICHARD LEWIS - 1811 - 57; 18, 19 & 20 - JOSEPH EVANS - 1811 - 57; 18 - JOHNSON & MURPHY - 1811 - 57; 21 - JOSEPH TEAGLE - 1817 57; 21 - THOMAS T. TEAGLE - 1817 - 57; 21 - WALLS & HOWARD - 1817 - 57; 21 - H. HAWKINS - 1817 - 57; 22 WM. THORNE 1811 - 57; 22 - SAMUEL BOND - 1814 - 57; 22 - EDWARD BOND - 1811 - 57; 22 - BENJAMIN EVANS 1811 - 57; 23 - ISAAC JESSUP - 1816 - 57; 23 & 24 JACOB HAMPTON - 1816 - 57; 26 - JOHN STEDHAM & JOHN JAY - 1817 - 57; 27 - STEPHEN CONNER/ COMER - 1813 57; 27 - WILLIS WHITSON - 1811 - 57; 27 - NATHAN HAWKINS - 1813 - 57; 28 - ISAAC JESSUP JR - 1816

WAYNE COUNTY: Original Land Entries Tract Book
FORMAT: Section - Purchaser - year - page;

Township 17, Range 14 East continued

57; 28 - THOMAS CASON - 1816 - 57; 28 - HENRY HAWKINS 1814 - 57; 28 - WM. THORNBORO -1816 - 57; 29 - JOSEPH EVANS - 1811 - 58; 29 - RICHARD W. CHEESEMAN - 1811 58; 29 - MIRION NIXON - 1815 - 58; 29 - WM. COMMONS 1814 - 58; 30 - JOHN McCLAIN SR - 1814- 58; 30 - JOHN PIERSON - 1815 - 58; 30 - THOMAS CASON JR - 1816 -58; 30 - MARTIN MARTINDALE - 1815 - 58; 31 - ARCHIBALD BEALE - 1814 - 58; 31 - EDWARD BENBO - 1814 - 58; 31 - D. BAILEY & THOMAS NIXON - 1813 - 58; 32 - WM. McCLAIN -1817 - 58; 32 - TIMOTHY JESSUP - 1815 - 58; 32 - ROBERT CULBERTSON - 1814 - 58; 32 - JOHN McCLAIN 1817 - 58; 33 - BENJAMIN EVANS - 1811 - 58; 33 JOHN KING - 1814 - 58; 33 - BENJAMIN HARVEY - 1814 58; 33 - WM. McLEAN - 1811 - 58; 34 - MICHAEL HARVEY 1813 - 58; 34 - WM. HARVEY - 1813 -58; 34 - BENJAMIN HARVEY - 1816 - 58; 34 - REUBEN OVERMAN - 1813 - 58; 35 - JOSEPH CANBY - 1818 - 58.

Township 18 Range 12 East

25 & 36 - LEONARD STAMP - 1816 - 61.

Township 18 Range 13 East

19 - JOHN JORDAN - 1815 - 64; 20 - WM. FIFE - 1817 64; 20 - JOHN JORDAN - 1818 - 64; 20 - WM. BARNES 1814- 64; 20 - GEORGE HODSON - 1816 - 64; 21 - THOMAS MARSHALL - 1815- 64; 21 - THOMAS CRAWFORD - 1815 -64; 21 - ELIAS SWAYNE - 1815 - 64; 21 - SAMUEL BALDRIDGE 1814 - 64; 23 - ISAAC MILLS - 1816 - 64; 23 - JOHN MILLS - 1816 - 64; 25 - WM. COOK - 1817 - 64; 26 WM. BURROUGHS - 1816 - 64; 26 - JESSE BALDWIN - 1819 64; 27 - WM. LOCK - 1818- 65; 28 - ISAAC MILLS - 1814 65; 28 - JOHN BAILEY - 1814 - 65; 28 - SAMUEL MOORE 1816 - 65; 28 - HENRY & MOSES MILLS - 1814 - 65; 29 ROBERT CANADAY - 1815- 65; 29 - NATHAN STOCKER -1817 29 - RICHARD WILLIAMS - 1811 - 65; 29 - WM. BLOUNT/ BLUNT - 1814 - 65; 30 - WALTER THORNBURGH - 1814- 65; 30 - RICHARD MILLS - 1815 - 65; 30 - GUINN & MILES 1814 - 65; 31 - DAVID OSBORNE - 1815 - 65; 31 - J. GREENSTREET - 1815 - 65; 31 - JESSE PUGH - 1815 - 65; 31 - JASON HOWELL - 1817 - 65; 32 - JESSE WILLETTS/ WILLIS - 1815 - 65; 32 - WM. BLUNT - 1814 - 65; 32 JAMES WARREN - 1813 - 65; 33 - JOHN CANADY - 1818 65; 33 - HEZEKIAH WILLIAMS - 1814 - 65; 34 - JOHN HAWORTH & ARCHILAUS ELMORE - 1817 - 65; 34 - SAMUEL JAY - 1817 - 65; 34 - JOHN DAVIS - 1817 - 65; 35 CHARLES W. STARR - 1819 - 65; 35 - ELI GAPEN - 1815 65; 36 - ABRAHAM ELLIOTT - 1816 - 65; 36 - JACOB STUDY - 1818 - 66; 36 - NATHAN REILLY - 1816 - 66.

245

WAYNE COUNTY: Original Land Entries Tract Book
FORMAT: Section - Purchaser - year - page;

Township 18, Range 14 East

20 - J. POOL & M. HENLEY - 1816 - 68; 20 - ELIJAH BROCK - 1818 - 68; 20 - WM. MILLS JR - 1818 - 68; 20 ELEAZER SMITH - 1816 - 68; 21 - THOMAS MOORMAN - 1814 68; 21 - ISAAC GARDNER - 1814- 68; 21 - THOMAS THORP 1814 - 68; 21 - JOHN PEGG - 1814 - 68; 22 - THOMAS MOORMAN - 1818 - 68; 22 - HULDAY WAY - 1815 - 68; 22 DANIEL BALDWIN - 1818 - 68; 22 - CLARK WOLCOTT/ WILCUTT - 1818 - 68; 23 - MOSES PARK - 1819 - 68; 23 STEPHEN WILLIAMS - 1818 - 68; 23 - ELIAS MORTON 1819 - 68; 23 - GEORGE WILSON - 1819 - 68; 23 - JOHN MOORMAN - 1817 - 68; 24 - JOHN BARNES - 1820 - 68; 24 CHARLES MARINE - 1819 - 68; 24 - JAMES MOORMAN - 1819 68; 25 - JOHN JAMES - 1818 - 68; 25 - JOHN FISHER 1817 - 68; 25 - THOMAS KNIGHT - 1814 - 68; 25 - JOHN PIELE/ PEALE - 1816 - 68; 26 - JOHN ROBERTSON - 1817 68; 26 - WM. LACY - 1817 - 68; 27 - JOHN KENWORTHY 1818 - 68; 27 - JOHN LACY & THOMAS MILLS - 1818 - 68; 28 - JOHN FRAZER - 1814 - 69; 28 - ISAAC HUTCHINS 1811 - 69; 28 - SAMUEL CHARLES - 1813 - 69; 29 ISAIAH CASE - 1819 - 69; 29 - PAUL WAY - 1817 - 69; 29- ISAIAH CASE - 1811 - 69; 30 - JOHN PIERSON - 1819 69; ELIJAH WRIGHT - 1818 - 69; 30 - TRISTRAM STARBUCK 1816- 69; 30 - JEREMIAH STEGALL - 1819- 69; 30 - JOHN BARNES - 1820 - 69; 31 - JOSEPH LADD - 1815 - 69; 31 BENJAMIN HUTCHINS - 1814 - 69; 32 - HENRY WAY - 1811 69; 32 - ABEL LOMAX - 1815 - 69; 32 - CHARLES MOFFATT 1811 - 69; 32 - JAMES MORRISON - 1811 - 69; 33 - JOHN BALDWIN - 1817 - 69; 33 - HENRY WAY - 1814 - 69; 33 LEVI HORNER - 1818 - 69; 33 - ISAAC GARDNER - 1814 69; 34 - JOEL JEFFERY - 1820 - 69; 34 - JACOB COOK 1817 - 69; 34 - JOHN JEFFERY - 1820 - 69; 35 - THOMAS PRICE - 1817 - 69; 35 - SAMUEL HOOVER - 1818 - 69; 35 JOB HOOVER - 1817 - 69; 35 - JOB L. JEFFERY - 1817 69; 36 - STEPHEN THOMAS - 1814 - 69.

Township 18 Range 15 East

19, 30 & 31 - JOSEPH COX - 1816 - 70.

End of Wayne Co land entries to & including 1820

WAYNE COUNTY DEEDS: Book A

Salisbury was the original county seat (grant, Bk A, p 9, 10) recorded in many of the following deeds. According to the Wayne Co Surveyor's office, no one is quite sure where Salisbury was located. Salisbury Road runs south from the western edge of Richmond, verifying the location shown on the 1811 map on page 231.

Deed dated 1811. JOHN TOWNSEND & ELVIRA, his wife, to SAMUEL WOODS. R 2W, T 13, S 1. Signed JOHN TOWNSEND, ELVIRA (x) TOWNSEND. Witness: JONATHAN TOWNSEND, WILLIAM TOWNSEND. rec 1811. pp 1, 2

Deed dated 1811. JOHN TOWNSEND & ELVIRA, his wife, to WILLIAM S. WILLIFORD. R 2W, T 13, S 1. Signed JOHN TOWNSEND, ELVIRA (x) TOWNSEND. Witness: JOSEPH (x) ADDINGTON. rec 1811. pp 2, 3

Deed dated 1811. JOHN IRELAND to ROBERT HILL. S 36, T 14, R 1W. Signed JOHN IRELAND, MARY (x) IRELAND. Witness: JAMES WRIGHT, JONATHAN JESSOP. rec 1811. pp 4, 5

Deed dated 1811. ROBERT HILL to JOHN IRELAND. S 35, T 14, R 1W. Signed ROBERT HILL, SUSANNAH HILL. Witness: JAMES WRIGHT, JONATHAN JESSOP. rec 1811. pp 5, 6, 7

Deed dated 1812. GEORGE HOLMAN & ELIZABETH his wife to JOHN PARKER & JOHN WILLETE, assignee of MICHAEL COLLIER of Shelby Co, KY. "beginning at JAMES HOLMES'." No S-T-R given. Signed GEORGE HOLMAN. No wife's signature. Witness: none. rec 1812. pp 7,8

Deed dated 1812. SAMUEL WOODS to PETER FLEMING, President of Court of Common Pleas, Wayne Co. R 2W, T 13, S 1 "originally granted to JOHN TOWNSEND in 1809" for a permanent seat of Justice. Signed SAMUEL WOODS POLLY WOODS. Witness: G. HUNT. rec 1812. pp 9, 10

Deed dated 1811. WILLIAM S. WILLIFORD to BENJAMIN EVANS of Warren Co, OH. R 2W, T 13, S 1. Signed W. S. WILLIFORD. Witness: THOMAS EVANS, DAVID EVANS. rec 1812. pp 10, 11, 12

Deed dated 1812. JACOB LITTLE SR & HANNAH, his wife, to GASPAR LITTLE. S 5, T 12, R 1W. Signed JACOB (x) LITTLE, HANNAH (x) LITTLE. Witness: BETSEY ESTELE, ISAAC ESTELE. rec 1812. pp 12, 13

Deed dated 1812. WILLIAM LEWIS & HANNAH, his wife, to SUSANNA HUGHS. S 15, T 12, R 2W. Signed WILLIAM

WAYNE COUNTY DEEDS: Book A

LEWIS, HANNAH LEWIS. Witness: G. HUNT, SUMER COLETE. rec 1812. pp 13, 14, 15

Deed dated 1812. WILLIAM FOUTS to THOMAS WARD of Chatham Co, NC. S 13, T 12, R 1W. "SARAH, his wife". Signed WILLIAM FOUTS, SARAH FOUTS. Witness: DANIEL CLARK, ABRAHAM ELLIOTT. rec 1813. pp 15, 16

Deed dated 1812. JACOB LITTLE SR & HANNAH, his wife, to JOSEPH POWER. S 5, T 12, R 1W. Signed JACOB (x) LITTLE, HANNAH (x) LITTLE. Witness: G. HUNT, JASPER LITTLE. rec 1813. pp 16, 17

Deed dated 1812. LEWIS LITTLE & ELIZABETH, his wife, to JOSIAH ELSTON. S 6, T 12, R 1W. Signed LEWIS (x) LITTLE, ELIZABETH (x) LITTLE. Witness: RACHEL JOB, ISAAC ESTELE. no rec date. pp 18, 19

Deed dated 1813. DAVID RAILSBACK & SALLY, his wife, to GABRIEL FENDER. S 2, T 12, R 2W. Signed DAVID RAILSBACK, SALLY RAILSBACK. Witness: JAMES WHITE, JONATHAN HUNT. rec 1813. pp 19, 20, 21

Deed dated 1813. JACOB FOUTS JUN. to WILLIAM FOUTS. S 12, T 13, R 1W. "ELENOR, his wife". Signed JACOB FOUTS, ELENOR FOUTS. Witness: EDWARD BOND, JESSE DAVENPORT. rec 1813. pp 21, 22

Deed dated 1813. JESSE DAVENPORT to JAMES JACOBS. S 11, T 13, R 1W. "REBEKAH, his wife". Signed JESSE DAVENPORT, REBEKAH DAVENPORT. Witness: JACOB FOUTS, WILLIAM FOUTS. rec 1813. pp 22, 23, 24

Deed dated 1813. JESSE DAVENPORT to NATHANIEL McCLURE. S 11, T 13, R 1W. Signed JESSE DAVENPORT, REBEKAH DAVENPORT. Witness: JACOB FOUTS, JAMES JACOBS. rec 1813. pp 24, 25

Deed dated 1813. JESSE DAVENPORT to JACOB FOUTS JR. S 11, T 13, R 1W. Signed JESSE DAVENPORT, REBEKAH DAVENPORT. Witness: WILLIAM FOUTS, JAMES JACOBS. rec 1813. pp 26, 27

Deed dated 1813. PETER FLEMING, Pres. of Common Pleas Court, Wayne Co, to LEWIS MARTIN of KY. Salisbury lot 110. Signed PETER FLEMING. Witness: none. rec 1813. pp 27, 28

Deed dated 1813. PETER FLEMING, Pres., Common Pleas Court, Wayne Co, to JOHN McKEE. Salisbury lot 4. Signed PETER FLEMING. Witness: G. HUNT. rec 1813. pp 28, 29

WAYNE COUNTY DEEDS: Book A

Deed dated 1813. PETER FLEMING, Pres. of Common Pleas Court, Wayne Co, to JEREMIAH MEEK. Salisbury lot 73. Signed PETER FLEMING. Witness: none. rec 1813. pp 29, 30

Deed dated 1813. WILLIAM WILLIFORD & RUTHA, his wife to EVAN SHOEMAKER. R 2W, T 13, S 1. Signed W.S. WILLIFORD, RUTHA (x) WILLIFORD. Witness: ENOS BUTLER. rec 1813. pp 29, 30

Deed dated 1813. BENJAMIN BOON of Lincoln Co, TN to JONATHAN HUNT. S 13, T 12, R 2W. Signed BENJAMIN BOON Witness: CHARLES HUNT SR. rec 1813. pp 31, 32

Deed dated 1813. PETER QUACKENBUSH of Chatham Co, NC to JEREMIAH COX. S 35, T 17, R 13E. Signed PETER QUACKENBUSH. Witness: ABRAHAM ELLIOTT. rec 1813. pp 32, 33, 34

Deed dated 1813. JEREMIAH COX to JOHN CLARK & FREDE-RICK HOOVER, Overseers of the Monthly Meeting of the Friends of Whitewater. S 33, T 13, R 1W. Signed JEREMIAH COX, CATHARINE COX. Witness: CORNELIUS RATLIFF, ROBERT HILL. rec 1813. pp 34, 35, 36

Deed dated 1813. THOMAS McCOY, exec of estate of MARGARET McCOY, dec, to WILLIAM BLOUNT. S 18, T 13, R 1W. Signed THOMAS McCOY. Witness: none. rec 1813 pp 36, 37

Deed dated 1812. SAMUEL JOB & RACHEL, his wife, to THOMAS BRADBURY. S 17, T 12, R 1W. Signed SAMUEL JOB, RACHEL JOB. Witness: G. HUNT. rec 1813. pp 37, 38

Deed dated 1813. JEREMIAH COX to JESSE BOND. S 35, T 17, R 3E. Signed JEREMIAH COX. Witness: JOHN STUART. rec 1813. pp 39, 40

Deed dated 1812. RICHARD RUE to JOSEPH COX. S 30, T 13, R 1. Signed RICHARD RUE, BETSY RUE. Witness: ISAAC BUSON, SAMUEL MARTIN. rec 1813. pp 40, 41

Deed dated 1813. SAMUEL McKINLY & ELIZABETH, his wife, to VALENTINE PEGG. S 6, T 13, R 1W. Signed SAM'L McKINLY, ELIZABETH McKINLY. Witness: ZIMRI COOK, ANDREW HOOVER. (written at Jefferson Co) rec 1813. pp 41, 42

Deed dated 1813. PETER FLEMING, Pres. of Common Pleas Court, Wayne Co, to JOHN C. KIBBEY. Salisbury lot 40. Signed PETER FLEMING. Witness: none. rec 1813. pp 42, 43

WAYNE COUNTY DEEDS: Book A

Deed dated 1813. PETER FLEMING, Pres. of Common Pleas Court, Wayne Co, to LEVI KERNS of Claborn Co, TN. Salisbury lot 68. Signed PETER FLEMING. Witness: none. rec 1813. p 43

Mortgage dated 1813. CHRISTOPHER RODDEY to ELI BUTLER & JESSE BUZAN. $239 owed on S 11 & 12, no T-R given. Signed CHRISTOPHER RODDEY. Witness: SAM'L. CASS, SARAH (x) CASS. rec 1813. p 44

Deed dated 1813. EVAN SHOEMAKER & EVE, his wife, to ELI BUTLER. R 2W, T 13, S 1. Signed EVANS SHOEMAKER, EVE SHOEMAKER. Witness: DAVID F. LACKEL, ENOS BUTLER. rec 1813. pp 44, 45, 46

Deed dated 1813. JOHN SMITH to JESSE MORRIS. S 2, T 13, R 1W. "LATYCHY, his wife". Signed JOHN SMITH, LISHE (x) SMITH. Witness: ELI OVERMAN, JESSE HILL. rec 1813. pp 46, 47

Deed dated 1813. JOHN SMITH to JOHN POOL. S 2, T 13, R 1W. Signed JOHN SMITH, LATYCHY SMITH. Witness: ELI OVERMAN, JESSE HILL. rec 1813. pp 47, 48, 49

Deed dated 1813. JESSE HILL to NATHAN HILL. S 2, T 13, R 1W. Signed JESSE HILL, MABEL (x) HILL. Witness: WM. DUNMAN. rec 1813. pp 49, 50

Deed dated 1813. NATHAN HILL to MICAJAH HENLY. S 3, T 13, R --W. "ELIZABETH, his wife" Signed NATHAN HILL, ELIZABETH HILL. Witness: JEHOSHAPHAT MORRIS. rec 1813. pp 51, 52

Deed dated 1813. PETER FLEMING, Pres. of Common Pleas Court, Wayne Co, to JOHN RUTHERFORD of Butler Co, OH. Salisbury lots 93, 46. Signed PETER FLEMING. Witness: none. rec 1813. pp 52, 53

Deed dated 1813. PETER FLEMING, Pres., Common Pleas Court, Wayne Co, to THOMAS SHOE of Hamilton Co, OH. Salisbury lots 9, 10, 19, 20, 22, 23, 24, 34, 35 58. Signed PETER FLEMING. Witness: none. rec 1813. pp 53, 54

Deed dated 1813. PETER FLEMING, Pres. of Common Pleas Court, Wayne Co, to ALEXANDER MILLER. Salisbury lot 122. Signed PETER FLEMING. Witness: none. rec 1813. p 54

Deed dated 1813. RICHARD MAXWELL to PETER FLEMING. S 36, T 14, R 1W. Signed RICHARD MAXWELL, MARY ANNE MAXWELL. Witness: DAVID PURVIANCE, JOHN PURVIANCE.

WAYNE COUNTY DEEDS: Book A

rec 1814. pp 55, 56

Deed dated 1813. GEORGE SMITH to THOMAS LAMB. S 30, T 14, R 1W. Signed GEORGE SMITH, SARAH SMITH. Witness: DAVID HOOVER. rec 1814. pp 56, 57, 58

Deed dated 1813. PETER FLEMING, Pres. of Common Pleas Court, Wayne Co, to SAMUEL WALKER. Salisbury lot 94. Signed PETER FLEMING. Witness: none. rec 1813. p 58

Deed dated 1813. PETER FLEMING, Pres. of Common Pleas Court, Wayne Co, to JOHN WALKER. Salisbury lot 121. Signed PETER FLEMING. Witness: none. rec 1813. pp 28, 29

Deed dated 1813. WILLIAM LEWIS & HANNAH, his wife, to JOHN ARMSTRONG. R 2W, T 12, S 15. Signed WILLIAM LEWIS, HANNAH LEWIS. Witness: R. WRIGHT. rec 1814. pp 59, 60

Deed dated 1813. PETER FLEMING, Pres. of Common Pleas Court, Wayne Co, to JOHN SMITH. Salisbury lot 61. Signed PETER FLEMING. Witness: none. rec 1813. p 61

Deed dated 1813. JOSEPH COX to ISAAC BEESON. S 30, T 13, R 1W. Signed JOSEPH COX. Witness: RICHARD RUE, SAMUEL MARTIN, LEVI COLEMAN. rec 1814. JP's note: "acknowledged by MARY COX, party thereto, to be her act of Deed". pp 61, 62

Deed dated 1814. WILLIAM BLOUNT to SAWYER McFADDEN of Franklin Co, PA. S 18, T 13, R 1W. Signed WILLIAM (x) BLOUNT, MARY (x) BLOUNT. Witness: none. rec 1814. pp 63, 64

Deed dated 1812. USA to ISAAC ESTELE of KY. S 4, T 12, R 1W. rec 1814. pp 64, 65

Deed dated 1812. USA to ISAAC ESTELE of Dearborn Co. S 10, T 12, R 1W. rec 1814. pp 65, 66

Deed dated 1813. PETER FLEMING, Pres. of Common Pleas Court, Wayne Co, to ROBERT SMITH. Salisbury lot 33. Signed PETER FLEMING. Witness: none. rec 1813. p 66

Deed dated 1814. WILLIAM COX to SHUBAL JULIAN. Brkv (Franklin Co) lot 38. Signed WILLIAM COX, ELIZABETH COX. Witness: none. rec 1814. pp 67, 68

Deed dated 1813. SUSANNA BUTLER to DAVID HARMAN & ANDREW HARMAN. S 12, T 13, R 2W. Signed SUSANNA BUTLER. Witness: BEALE BUTLER. rec 1814. pp 68, 69

WAYNE COUNTY DEEDS: Book A

Deed dated 1813. PETER FLEMING, Pres. of Common Pleas Court, Wayne Co, to WILLIAM WHITEHEAD. Salisbury lots 2, 13. Signed PETER FLEMING. Witness: none. rec 1814. pp 69, 70

Deed dated 1813. JOSEPH COX to JOSEPH PRATHER. S 30, T 13, R 1W. Signed JOSEPH COX. Witness: PETER IMEL, WILLIS WRIGHT. pp 70, 71

Deed dated 1813. SPENCER FREE to JOHN JORDAN. S 34, T 13, R 1W. Signed SPENCER (x) FREE. Witness: WILLIAM MEEK, JOHN WINGFIED. rec 1814. pp 72, 73

Deed dated 1813. PETER FLEMING, Pres. of Common Pleas Court, Wayne Co, to JOSEPH COX. Salisbury lots 109, 113. Signed PETER FLEMING. Witness: none. rec 1814. pp 73, 74

Deed dated 1813. PETER FLEMING, Pres. of Common Pleas Court, Wayne Co, to JAMES WHITE. Salisbury lots 32, 39. Signed PETER FLEMING. Witness: none. rec 1814. p 74

Deed dated 1813. PETER FLEMING, Pres. of Common Pleas Court, Wayne Co, to JOHN HUNT. Salisbury lot 81. Signed PETER FLEMING. Witness: none. rec 1814. pp 74, 75

Deed dated 1813. PETER FLEMING, Pres. of Common Pleas Court, Wayne Co, to JOHN WHITEHEAD. Salisbury lot 41. Signed PETER FLEMING. Witness: none. rec 1814. pp 75, 76

Deed dated 1814. ANDREW ENDSLEY to HENRY WHITINGER of Butler Co, OH. S 25, T 13, R 2W. Signed ANDREW ENDSLEY. Witness: JOHN TURNER. rec 1814. pp 76, 77

Deed dated 1813. PETER FLEMING, Pres. of Common Pleas Court, Wayne Co, to EUEEL KINDALL. Salisbury lots 42, 45. Signed PETER FLEMING. Witness: none. rec 1814. pp 77, 78

Deed dated 1813. PETER FLEMING, Pres. of Common Pleas Court, Wayne Co, to ELIJAH SPENCER. Salisbury lot 86. Signed PETER FLEMING. Witness: none. rec 1814. pp 78, 79

Deed dated 1813. PETER FLEMING, Pres. of Common Pleas Court, Wayne Co, to ABNER MARTIN of KY. Salisbury lot 60. Signed PETER FLEMING. Witness: none. rec 1814. p 79

WAYNE COUNTY DEEDS: Book A

Deed dated 1813. PETER FLEMING, Pres. of Common Pleas Court, Wayne Co, to NATHAN SMITH. Salisbury lot 74. Signed PETER FLEMING. Witness: none. rec 1814. p 80

Deed dated 1813. JOHN TOWNSEND to JOHN MEEK. S 1, T 13, R 2W. Signed JOHN TOWNSEND, ELVIRA TOWNSEND. Witness: JONATHAN TOWNSEND. rec 1814. pp 80, 81, 82

Deed dated 1814. CALEB HARVEY & MARY, his wife, to JOHN SUTHERLAND. "beginning of ENOS BUTLER's corner on SAMUEL WOODS' line...CHRISTOPHER RODDY's corner". S 12, T 13, R 2W. Signed CALEB HARVEY, MARY HARVEY. Witness: ABRAHAM ELLIOTT, ANDREW WOODS. rec 1814. pp 82, 83, 84

Deed dated 1814. ANDREW ENDSLEY SR to JAMES LAMB. S 25, T 13, R 2W. Signed ANDREW ENDSLEY. Witness: WM. WHITEHEAD, SAMUEL HUNT. rec 1814. pp 84, 85

Deed dated 1813. SAMUEL CARR to JOHN HART. Salisbury lots 85, 103, 106. Signed SAMUEL CARR, SARAH CARR. Witness: HIRAM BUTLER, ANDREW HARMAN. rec 1814. pp 85, 86

Deed dated 1814. ANDREW ENDSLEY SR to WILLIAM RHODE. S 25, T 13, R 2W. Signed ANDREW ENDSLEY. Witness: JOSEPH RIPPEY, JOHN WILKINS. no rec date. pp 86, 87, 88

Deed dated 1813. PETER FLEMING, Pres. of Common Pleas Court, Wayne Co, to HARMAN WARRAM. Salisbury lot 11. Signed PETER FLEMING. Witness: none. rec 1814. p 88

Deed dated 1813. PETER FLEMING, Pres. of Common Pleas Court, Wayne Co, to JOHN JACKSON of Dearborn Co. Salisbury lot 5. Signed PETER FLEMING. Witness: none. rec 1814. p 89

Deed dated 1813. CALEB HARVEY & MARY, his wife, to CHRISTOPHER RODDY. S 11 & 12, T 12, R 2W. Signed CALEB HARVEY, MARY HARVEY. Witness: JOHN SUTHERLAND JR, ANDREW WOODS, ABRAHAM ELLIOTT. rec 1814. pp 89, 90, 91

Deed dated 1814. JOHN MEEK to EUELL KINDALL. S 1, T 13, R 2W. Signed JOHN (x) MEEK. Witness: G. HUNT. JP's note: "grantor & his wife, PEGGY". rec 1814. pp 91, 92

Deed dated 1813. JOHN HARVEY to JESSE BOND. S 6, T 13, R 1W. Signed JOHN HARVEY, JANE HARVEY. Witness:

WAYNE COUNTY DEEDS: Book A

SAMUEL JONES, JEREMIAH COX. rec 1814. pp 92, 93, 94

Deed dated 1814. PETER FLEMING, First Judge of the Circuit Court of Wayne Co to BENJAMIN HARVEY. Salisbury lot 83. Signed PETER FLEMING. Witness: none. rec 1814. pp 94, 95

Deed dated 1814. PETER FLEMING, First Judge of the Circuit Court of Wayne Co to JOSEPH MARTIN of KY. Salisbury lots 31, 123. Signed PETER FLEMING. Witness: none. rec 1814. p 95

Deed dated 1814. PETER FLEMING, First Judge of the Circuit Court of Wayne Co to GIBBONS BRADBURY of OH. Salisbury lot 70. Signed PETER FLEMING. Witness: none. rec 1814. p 96

Deed dated 1814. PETER FLEMING, First Judge of the Circuit Court of Wayne Co to JOB GINN. Salisbury lot 98. Signed PETER FLEMING. Witness: none. rec 1814. pp 96, 97

Deed dated 1814. PETER FLEMING, First Judge of the Circuit Court of Wayne Co to DAVID RAILSBACK. Salisbury lots 50, 56, 59. Signed PETER FLEMING. Witness: none. rec 1814. pp 97, 98

Deed dated 1814. PETER FLEMING, First Judge of the Circuit Court of Wayne Co to WILLIAM HUNT. Salisbury lot 87. Signed PETER FLEMING. Witness: none. rec 1814. pp 98, 99

Deed dated 1814. CHARLES HUNT SR to JONATHAN HUNT. "love and good will to his dutiful son, JONATHAN". S 8, T 13, R 2W. Signed CHARLES HUNT. Witness: none. rec 1814. pp 99, 100

Deed dated 1814. CHARLES HUNT SR to JAMES HUNT. "love and good will to his dutiful son, JAMES". S 8, T 12, R 2W. Signed CHARLES HUNT. Witness: none. rec 1814. pp 100, 101

Deed dated 1814. CHARLES HUNT SR to TIMOTHY HUNT. "love and good will to his dutiful son, TIMOTHY". S 1, T 12, R 2W. Signed CHARLES HUNT. Witness: none. rec 1814. pp 101, 102

Deed dated 1814. CHARLES HUNT SR to JOHN HUNT. "love and good will to his dutiful son, JOHN". S 1, T 12, R 2W. Signed CHARLES HUNT. Witness: none. rec 1814. pp 102, 103

WAYNE COUNTY DEEDS: Book A

Deed dated 1813. JOHN HARVEY to SAMUEL CHARLES. S 3, T 13, R 1W. "JANE, his wife". Signed JOHN HARVEY, JANE HARVEY. Witness: SAMUEL JONES, JEREMIAH COX. rec 1814. pp 103, 104, 105

Deed dated 1814. SAMUEL CARR to ELIJAH SPENCER. Salisbury lots 103, 106. Signed SAM'L. CARR. Witness: none. rec 1814. pp 105, 106

Deed dated 1814. BENJAMIN NUTTER & ELIZABETH, his wife, to CHARLES WRIGHT. S 33, T 12, R 1W. Signed BENJAMIN (x) NUTTER, ELIZABETH (x) NUTTER. Witness: none. rec 1814. pp 106, 107

Deed dated 1813. GEORGE HOLMAN & ELIZABETH, his wife to JOHN JORDAN. S 34, T 13, R 1W. Signed GEORGE HOLDMAN, ELIZABETH HOLDMAN. Witness: BENJAMIN HODGES ISAAC CONLEY. rec 1814. pp 107, 108, 109

Deed dated 1814. CHRISTOPHER RODDY to JOHN SUTHERLAND JR. S 12 & 11, T 13, R 2W. Signed CHRISTOPHER RODDY, ISABELLA (x) RODDY. Witness: ABRAHAM ELLIOTT, BEALE BUTLER. rec 1814. pp 109, 110, 111

Deed dated 1814. LEWIS LITTLE to JAMES LITTLE. "goodwill toward his dutiful son (JAMES)". S 6, T 12, R 1. Signed LEWIS (x) LITTLE, BETSY (x) LITTLE. Witness: none. rec 1814. pp 111, 112

Deed dated 1813. PETER FLEMING, Pres. of Common Pleas Court, Wayne Co, to JOEL FERGUSON. Salisbury lot 47. Signed PETER FLEMING. Witness: none. rec 1814. pp 112, 113

Deed dated 1813. PETER FLEMING, Pres. of Common Pleas Court, Wayne Co, to NIMROD FERGUSON of NC. Salisbury lots 91, 55. Signed PETER FLEMING. Witness: none. rec 1814. pp 113, 114

Deed dated 1814. JOHN HUNT to JOHN SUTHERLAND JR. Salisbury lot 81. Signed JOHN HUNT, POLLY HUNT. Witness: none. rec 1814. pp 114, 115

Deed dated 1814. PETER FLEMING, First Judge of the Circuit Court of Wayne Co to JAMES DILL of Dearborn Co. Salisbury lot 43. Signed PETER FLEMING. Witness: none. rec 1814. pp 115, 116

Deed dated 1814. PETER FLEMING, First Judge of the Circuit Court of Wayne Co to WILLIAM SUTHERLAND. Salisbury lot 30. Signed PETER FLEMING. Witness: none. rec 1814. pp 116, 117

WAYNE COUNTY DEEDS: Book A

Deed dated 1813. JEHOSHAPHAT MORRIS to JONATHAN MORRIS. S 13, T 16, R 2W. Signed JEHOSHAPHAT MORRIS. Witness: NATHAN HILL, ROBERT HILL. rec 1814. pp 117, 118

Deed dated 1813. JOHN NIXON SR to JOHN NIXON JR. S 23, T 16, R 12E. Signed JOHN NIXEN. Witness: ELI OVERMAN, GEORGE BOWLES. rec 1814. pp 118, 119

Deed dated 1813. ROBERT MORRISON to HENRY PALIN. S 1, T 14, R 1W. Signed ROBERT MORRISON, JENNY MORRISON. Witness: ASA HUNT, MICAJAH JONES. rec 1814. JP's note: "his wife JANE MORRISON". pp 120, 121

Deed dated 1813. JAMES JACOBS to JOHN HOWARD. S 11, T 13, R 1W. "POLLY, his wife". Signed JAMES JACOBS, POLLY JACOBS. Witness: none. rec 1814. pp 121, 122, 123

Deed dated 1813. BENJAMIN MAUDLIN to ROBERT HILL. S 34, T 14, R 1W. "LEAH, his wife". Signed BENJAMIN (x) MAUDLIN, LEAH (x) MAUDLIN. Witness: WILLIAM HASTINGS, NATHAN HILL, JONATHAN MORRIS. rec 1814. pp 123, 124, 125

Deed dated 1814. ELI BUTLER & JANE, his wife, to DAVID J. P. FLEMING. R 2W, T 13, S 1. Signed ELI BUTLER, JANE BUTLER. Witness: none. rec 1814. pp 125, 126, 127

Deed dated 1814. PETER FLEMING, First Judge of the Circuit Court of Wayne Co to ROBERT LEVEL. Salisbury lot 19. Signed PETER FLEMING. Witness: none. rec 1814. p 127

Deed dated 1814. THOMAS McCOY & PEGGY, his wife, to JAMES LAMB. S 25, T 13, R 2W. Signed THOMAS McCOY, PEGGY (x) McCOY. Witness: BEALE BUTLER, JP. rec 1814. pp 128, 129

Deed dated 1814. ANDREW FOUTS & SALLY, his wife, to JAMES LAMB. S 13, T 12, T 2W. Signed ANDREW FOUTS, SALLY FOUTS. Witness: none. rec 1814. pp 129, 130

Deed dated 1814. JACOB GRIFFIN to JOHN POOL. S 35, T 14, R 1W. "MARY GRIFFIN, his wife". Signed JACOB GRIFFIN, MARY (x) GRIFFIN. Witness: none. rec 1814. pp 130, 131, 132

Deed dated 1813. PETER FLEMING, Pres. of Common Pleas Court, Wayne Co, to SMITH HUNT. Salisbury lot 69. Signed PETER FLEMING. Witness: none. rec 1814. pp

WAYNE COUNTY DEEDS: Book A

132, 133

Deed dated 1814. JOHN HUNT & POLLY, his wife, to LEWIS LITTLE. S 6, T 12, R 1W. Signed JOHN HUNT, POLLY HUNT. Witness: none. rec 1814. pp 133, 134

Deed dated 1813. USA to JOHN SHAW. S 11, T 15, R 12E. rec 1814. pp 134, 135

Deed dated 1814. JOHN SMITH to JOHN SUTHERLAND JR. Salisbury 61. Signed JOHN SMITH, LEAH (x) SMITH. Witness: none. rec 1814. pp 135, 136

Deed dated --. SAMUEL WOODS & POLLY, his wife, to JOHN SUTHERLAND. Salisbury lot 88. Signed SAMUEL WOODS, POLLY WOODS. Witness: none. rec 1814. p 137

Deed date 1814. SAMUEL WOODS & MARY, his wife, to NATHAN SMITH. Salisbury lot 95. Signed SAMUEL WOODS, POLLY WOODS. Witness: none. rec 1814. pp 138, 139

Deed dated 1815. BENJAMIN HARVEY to JEREMIAH MANSUR. Salisbury lot 83. Signed BENJAMIN HARVEY. Witness: none. rec 1815. pp 139, 140

Deed dated 1814. AARON MARTIN, First Associate Judge of Circuit Court of Wayne Co to CATHARINE RODDY. Salisbury lot 82. Signed AARON MARTIN. Witness: none. rec 1814. pp 140, 141

Deed dated 1814. HENRY HOOVER & ELIZABETH, his wife, to JOSEPH SPENCER. S 28, T 12, R 1W. Signed HENRY HOOVER, ELIZABETH HOOVER. Witness: none. rec 1814. pp 141, 142

Deed dated 1814. HENRY HOOVER & ELIZABETH, his wife, to JOSEPH SPENCER. S 9, T 12, R 1W. Signed HENRY HOOVER, ELIZABETH HOOVER. Witness: none. rec 1814. pp 142, 142 (2 pages of same number)

Deed dated 1811. USA to DANIEL FOUTS, assignee of ANDREW FOUTS. S 18, T 12, R 1W. rec 1814. pp 142, 143

Deed dated 1812. USA to DANIEL FOUTS, assignee of BEALE BUTLER. S 18, T 12, R 1W. rec 1814. pp 143, 144

Deed dated 1815. ELIJAH FOX to WILLIAM K. NUTT. S 9, T 16, R 13. "SUSANNA, his wife" Signed ELIJAH (x) FOX, SUSANNA (x) FOX. rec 1815. pp 144, 145

Deed dated 1813. JOHN HARVEY to JOHN HAWKINS. S 34, T 14, R 1W. "JANE, his wife". Signed JOHN HARVEY,

WAYNE COUNTY DEEDS: Book A

JANE HARVEY. Witness: DAVID HOOVER, WILLIAM HAWKINS, JOHN DAVIDSON. rec 1815. pp 146, 147

Deed dated 1813. JEREMIAH COX to CHARLES MOFFIT. S 33, T 14, R 1W. "CATHARINE, his wife". Signed JEREMIAH COX, CATHARINE COX. Witness: none. rec 1815. pp 148, 149

Deed dated 1813. JOHN SMITH to JEREMIAH COX. S 32, T 14, R 1W. Signed JOHN SMITH, LEAH SMITH. Witness: JACOB HOOVER, JACOB ELLIOTT. rec 1815. pp 149, 150, 151

Deed dated 1814. WILLIAM HASTINGS to BENJAMIN MAUDLIN. S 7, T 6, R 14. Signed WILLIAM HASTINGS. Witness: ISAAC JACKSON, JOSEPH HOLMAN. rec 1815. pp 151, 152, 153

Deed dated 1814. JOHN POOL to JACOB GRIFFIN. S 35, T 14, R 1W. "ELIZABETH, his wife". Signed JOHN POOL ELIZABETH POOL. Witness: none. rec 1815. pp 153, 154

Deed dated 1814. JAMES HARTUP to RICHARD WATTS of Butler Co, OH. S 23, T 13, R 1W. Signed JAMES HARTUP, MARY HARTUP. Witness: BENJAMIN MOORE, JESSE DAVENPORT. rec 1815. pp 155, 156

Deed dated 1814. ROBERT HILL to JOHN HORNEY of Preble Co, OH. S 34, T 14, R 1W. "on the south by BENJAMIN MORGAN". Signed ROBERT HILL, SUSANNA HILL. Witness: DAVID JONES, NATHAN HILL. rec 1815. pp 156, 157, 158

Deed dated 1814. JOHN DAVIDSON to JOSIAH GILBERT. S 8, T 13, R 1W. JOHN DAVIDSON, MARY DAVIDSON. Witness: ABRAHAM ELLIOTT, JOHN TOWNSEND. rec 1815. pp 158, 159

Deed dated 1815. JESSE BOND to JEHU STEWART. S 6, T 13, R 1W. Signed JESSE BOND, PHEBE BOND. Witness: D. HOOVER, VALENTINE PEGG. rec 1815. pp 160, 161

Deed dated 1815. AARON MARTIN, First Associate Judge of Circuit Court of Wayne Co to THOMAS NEELY. Salisbury lot 82. Signed AARON MARTIN. Witness: none. rec 1815. pp 161, 162

Deed dated 1815. THOMAS NEELY TO JAMES NOBLE. Salisbury lot 82. "ELIZABETH, his wife". Signed THOMAS (x) NEELY, ELIZABETH (x) NEELY. Witness: ABEL JANNEY rec 1815. pp 162, 163, 164

Deed dated 1815. JOHN SMITH to ROBERT SMITH. S 33, T 14, R 1W. "TISHE, wife of JOHN". Signed JOHN SMITH

WAYNE COUNTY DEEDS: Book A

TISHE SMITH. Witness: ROBERT MORRISON. rec 1815. pp 164, 165

Deed dated 1815. JEREMIAH COX to ROBERT SMITH. S 33, T 14, R 1W. Signed JEREMIAH COX, CATHARINE COX. Witness: none. rec 1815. pp 165, 166, 167

Deed dated 181. SAMUEL WOODS & POLLY, his wife, to JOZIAH DAVISSON. Salisbury lot 90. Signed SAMUEL WOODS, POLLY WOODS. Witness: none. rec 1815. pp 167, 168

Deed 1815. SOLOMON HORNEY to ISAAC VAN METER. S 34. T 15, R 12E. Signed SOLOMON HORNEY, ELIZABETH HORNEY. Witness: none. rec 1815. pp 168, 169

Deed dated 1815. LEVI KERNS of Claborn Co, TN to JEHU KERNS & JOSIAH KERNS, his sons, of the same place. Salisbury lots 68, 115. Signed LEVI KERNS. Witness: none. rec 1815. pp 169, 170, 171

Deed dated 1813. JOHN PLUMMER & ISABELLA, his wife, to JOSEPH SPENCER SR. S 28, T 12, R 1W. Signed JOHN PLUMMER, ISABELLA PLUMMER. Witness: none. rec 1815. pp 171, 172, 173

Deed dated 1815. MARY MINER to WILLIAM NELSON. Sec 33, T 12, R 1W. Signed MARY MINER. Witness: none. rec 1815. pp 173, 174

Deed dated 1815. FREDERICK SUMMY & RACHEL, his wife, to PHILEMON PLUMMER. S 33, T 12, R 1W. Signed FREDERICK SUMMY, RACHEL SUMMY. Witness: none. rec 1815. pp 175, 176

Deed dated 1813. WILLIAM FOUTS to EDWARD BOND. S 13, T 13, R 1W. "his wife, SARAH". Signed WILLIAM FOUTS, SARAH FOUTS. Witness: JESSE DAVENPORT, JACOB FOUTS. rec 1815. pp 176, 177, 178

Deed dated 1814. ELIJAH WADE to DANIEL SHANER or SHAVER. S 13, T 13, R 1W. "MARY, his wife". Signed ELIJAH WADE, MARY WADE. Witness: WILLIAM FOUTS, JOHN RAPER. rec 1815. pp 178, 179, 180

Deed dated 1815. ELI BUTLER & JANE, his wife, to ALEXANDER DICKEY of KY. S 21, T 16, R 14. Signed ELI BUTLER, JAIN BUTLER. Witness: none. rec 1815. pp 180, 181

Deed dated 1814. FRANCIS THOMAS to Overseers of the New Garden Meeting. R 14, T 17, S 12. "LYDIA, his

WAYNE COUNTY DEEDS: Book A

wife". Signed FRANCIS THOMAS, LYDIA THOMAS. Witness: JOHN THOMAS, BENJAMIN THOMAS. rec 1815. pp 182, 183

Deed dated 1813. USA to JOHN BALDWIN. S 14, T 17, R 14E. rec 1815. pp 183, 184

Deed dated 1814. BENJAMIN PEARSON & ESTHER his wife of Miami Co, OH to CORNELIUS RATLIFF. S 20, T 14, R 1W. Signed BENJAMIN PEARSON, ESTHER PEARSON. Witness: JAMES HAYWORTH, AARON HAYWORTH (at Miami Co, OH). rec 1815. pp 184, 185, 186

Deed dated 1815. JAMES JACOBS to NATHANIEL McCLURE. S 11, T 13, R 1W. "POLLY, his wife". Signed JAMES JACOBS, POLLY (x) JACOBS. Witness: none. rec 1815. pp 187, 188

Deed dated 1815. JOSEPH COX to NATHANIEL WAYNE. Salisbury lot 113. "POLLY, his wife". Signed JOSEPH COX, MARY COX. Witness: none. rec 1815. pp 188, 189

Deed dated 1815. HENRY MILLER to PETER MILLER. S 25, T 12, R 2W. Signed HENRY MILLER, ESTHER (x) MILLER. Witness: JOSEPH COX, DAVID COX. rec 1815. pp 189, 190

Deed dated 1815. JOEL FERGASON to JOHN HUNT. Salisbury lot 47. Signed JOEL FERGESON, LIDIA FERGESON. rec 1815. p 191

Deed dated 1814. JOHN HARVY to WILLIAM HARVY JR. S 3, T 13, R 1W. Signed JOHN HARVY, JEAN HARVY. Witness: none. rec 1815. JP's note: JOHN HARVY & JANE his wife. p 192

Deed dated 1815. JOHN IRELAND of Preble Co, OH to JAMES FLEMING. S 35 & 36, T 14, R 1W. Signed JOHN IRELAND, POLLY (x) IRELAND. Witness: JAMES IRELAND, DAVID MASON. rec 1815. pp 193, 194, 195

Deed dated 1815. ANDREW WOODS to SAMUEL FLEMING. S 1, T 13, R 1W. "wife JANE WOODS". Signed ANDREW WOODS, JANE WOODS. Witness: none. rec 1815. pp 195, 196

Deed dated 1815. SAMUEL WOOD to THOMAS McCARTNEY. Lot adj town of Salisbury; no S-T-R. Signed SAMUEL WOODS, POLLY WOODS. Witness: none. rec 1815. pp 196, 197

Deed dated 1815. SAMUEL WOODS to HUGH HALL of Cincinnati, OH. Salisbury lot 76. Signed SAMUEL WOODS, POLLY WOODS. Witness: none. rec 1815. pp 197, 198

WAYNE COUNTY DEEDS: Book A

Deed dated 1815. ANDREW WOODS to PEGGY BROWN, wife & relick of JAMES BROWN, dec, ALEXANDER BROWN & JAMES BROWN JR. S 1, T 13, R 1W. Signed ANDREW WOODS, JANE WOODS. Witness: none. rec 1815. pp 198, 199

Deed dated 1815. SAMUEL WOODS to HENRY HARMON. Lot adj town of Salisbury. Signed SAMUEL WOODS. POLLY WOODS. Witness: none. rec 1815. pp 199, 200

Deed dated 1815. SAMUEL WOODS to JOHN DAVIDSON. Lot adj town of Salisbury. Signed SAMUEL WOODS, POLLY WOODS. Witness: none. rec 1815. pp 200, 201, 202

Deed dated 1815. SAMUEL WOODS to CHRISTOPHER RODDEY. Lot adj town of Salisbury. Signed SAMUEL WOODS. POLLY WOODS. Witness: none. rec 1815. pp 202, 203

Deed dated 1815. JOHN DAVIDSON to VINCENT STEPHENSON. S 8, T 12, R 1W. Signed JOHN DAVIDSON, POLLY DAVIDSON. Witness: none. rec 1815. pp 203, 204

Deed dated 1815. SAMUEL WOODS to VINCENT STEPHENSON. Salisbury lot 75. Signed SAMUEL WOODS, POLLY WOODS. Witness: none. rec 1815. pp 204, 205

POA dated 1815. ANDREW WOODS & his wife JANE appt ASA PREVO as atty to sell S 6, T 16, R 13E to JOSEPH CHARLES. Signed ANDREW WOODS, JANE WOODS. Witness: none. rec 1815. p 206

Deed dated 1815. SAMUEL WOODS to PEGGY BROWN. "land on the waters of Clear Creek"; no S-T-R. Signed SAMUEL WOODS, POLLY WOODS. Witness: none. rec 1815. pp 206, 207

Deed dated 1815. SAMUEL WOODS to GEORGE HUNT, JOHN HUNT & SMITH HUNT. Bounds given; no S-T-R. Signed SAMUEL WOODS, POLLY WOODS. Witness: none. rec 1815. pp 207, 208, 209

Deed dated 1815. PETER FLEMING, First Judge of the Circuit Court of Wayne Co to SAMUEL FLEMING. Salisbury lot 80. Signed PETER FLEMING. Witness: none. rec 1814. p 209

Deed dated 1815. JOSEPH PRATHER to ISAAC BEESON. S 30, T 13, R 1W. "BETSY, his wife". Signed JOSEPH PRATHER, BETSY PRATHER. Witness: none. rec 1815. pp 210, 211

Deed dated 1815. NATHANIEL McCLURE to SAMUEL HOLMES. S 11, T 13, R - W. Signed NATHANIEL McCLURE, JANE

WAYNE COUNTY DEEDS: Book A

(x) McCLURE. Witness: none. rec 1815. pp 211, 212

Deed dated 1815. JOHN MEEK to EWEL KINDALL. S 1, T 13, R 2W. Signed JOHN MEEK, PEGGY MEEK. Witness: none. rec 1815. pp 212, 213

Deed dated 1814. PENNINAH HILL to NATHAN HILL. S 2, T 13, R 1W. "her part of her father's land" Signed PENNIAH HILL. Witness: JONATHAN JESSOP, ROBERT HILL. rec 1815. pp 214, 215

Deed dated 1815. WILLIAM TOWNSEND to HENRY CARSMORE of Hamilton Co, OH. S 13, T 13, R 2W. Signed WILLIAM (x) TOWNSEND. Witness: JOHN WHITEHEAD. rec 1815. pp 215, 216

Deed dated 1815. WILLIAM YOUN to ABIJAH CAIN. S 30. T 14, R 1W. Signed WILLIAM YOUNG. Witness: ABRAHAM ELLIOTT, HENRY GARRET. rec 1815. pp 216, 217

Deed dated 1815. PETER FLEMING, First Judge of the Circuit Court of Wayne Co to DAVID J. P. FLEMING. Salisbury lot 120. Signed PETER FLEMING. Witness: none. rec 1815. p 218

Deed dated 1815. WILLIAM FINCHER of Miami Co, OH to VALENTINE FOLAND of Rockingham Co, VA. S 4, T 16, R 13E. Signed WILLIAM FINCHER, SUSANNA (x) FINCHER. Witness: HENRY HOOVER, JOHN (x) FOLAND. rec 1815. pp 218, 219, 220

Deed dated 1815. GEORGE GLAZE & ELIZABETH, his wife, of Pickaway Co, OH to SAMUEL McCRAY. S 1, T 14, R 12. Signed GEORGE GLAZE, ELIZABETH (x) GLAZE. Witness: JOHN LUDWIG, THOMAS WHITING (in OH). rec 1815. pp 221, 222, 223

Deed dated 1815. PETER FLEMING, First Judge, Circuit Court of Wayne Co to JESSE ELSTON. Salisbury lot 53. Signed PETER FLEMING. Witness: none. rec 1815. pp 223, 224

Deed dated 1815. PETER FLEMING, First Judge of the Circuit Court of Wayne Co to JOHN SCANLAND of KY. Salisbury lot 55. Signed PETER FLEMING. Witness: none. rec 1815. p 224

Deed dated 1815. SAMUEL WOODS to MILBURN JACOBS. Lot adj SALISBURY; no S-T-R. Signed SAMUEL WOODS. POLLY WOODS. Witness: none. rec 1815. p 225

Deed dated 1815. OBADIAH HARRIS to OBADIAH HARRIS JR

WAYNE COUNTY DEEDS: Book A

S 11, T 17, R 14 Signed OBADIAH HARRIS, MIRIAM HARRIS Witness: JOHN THOMAS, GEORGE SHUGART. ISAAC THOMAS. rec 1815. pp 226, 227

Deed dated 1815. PETER FLEMING, First Judge of the Circuit Court of Wayne Co to FRANCIS KENDALL & WILLIAM KENDALL. Salisbury lot 105. Signed PETER FLEMING. Witness: none. rec 1815. p 227

Deed dated 1815. JOHN HARVEY to JOSEPH COOK. S 6, T 13, R 1. Signed JOHN HARVEY, JANE HARVEY. Witness: none. rec 1815. pp 228, 229

Deed dated 1815. AMOS HIGGINS of Preble Co. OH to JAMES STAFFORD. S 12, T 13, R 1W. "BETSEY, his wife". Signed AMOS HIGGINS, BETSEY (x) HIGGINS. Witness: WILLIAM FOUTS. rec 1815. pp 229, 230

Deed dated 1815. HENRY HARMAN to JAMES JONES. Salisbury lot, # not given. Signed HENRY HARMAN, POLLY (x) HARMAN. Witness: none. rec 1815. pp 230, 231

Deed dated 1815. OBADIAH HARRIS to JACOB COOK. R 14, T 17, S 11. "with FRANCIS THOMAS' line". Signed OBADIAH HARRIS, MIRIAM HARRIS. Witness: JOHN THOMAS. GEORGE UHRGART, ISAAC THOMAS. rec 1815 pp 231-232-233

Deed dated 1815. PETER FLEMING, First Judge of the Circuit Court of Wayne Co to ANDREW HARMAN. Salisbury lot 101. Signed PETER FLEMING. Witness: none. rec 1815. p 233

Deed dated 1815. PETER FLEMING, as above, to ANDREW HARMAN. Salisbury lots 38, 49 & 52. Signed PETER FLEMING. Witness: none. rec 1815. p 234

Deed dated 1815. PETER FLEMING, First Judge of the Circuit Court of Wayne Co to ANDREW HARMAN. Salisbury lot 89. Signed PETER FLEMING. Witness: none. rec 1815. pp 234, 235

Deed dated 1815. ANDREW HARMAN to JOSEPH DAVISON of OH. Salisbury lot 101. Signed ANDREW HARMAN. Witness: none. rec 1815. pp 235, 236

Deed dated 1815. ELIJAH SPENCER to JOHN C. KIBLEY. Salisbury lots 103, 106, 86. Signed ELIJAH SPENCER. Witness: ABRAHAM ELLIOTT, ANDREW HOOVER. rec 1815. pp 236, 237

Deed dated 1815. ROBERT HILL to JOHN POOL, BENJAMIN HILL & JOHN HORNEY, School Trustees. Gave 1 acre "on

WAYNE COUNTY DEEDS: Book A

the line that separates JOHN POOL & ROBERT HILL" for use of a school. Signed ROBERT HILL. Witness: none. rec 1816. p 237

Deed dated 1812. USA to JOSEPH CHARLES, assignee of JOHN & ISAAC MEEK. S 9, T 13, R 1. rec 1815. p 238

Deed dated 1815. USA to JAMES HUNT, assignee of HENRY MARTIN. S 12, T 12, R 2W. rec 1816. pp 238, 239

Deed dated 1815. ROBERT HILL to JOHN POOL. S 2. T 13, R 1W. Signed ROBERT HILL, SUSANNAH HILL. Witness: none. rec 1816. pp 239, 240

Deed dated 1815. PETER FLEMING, First Judge of the Circuit Court of Wayne Co to JEREMY MONSURE. Salisbury lot 65. Signed PETER FLEMING. Witness: none. rec 1815. pp 240, 241

Deed dated 1815. JAMES JACOB to JACOB FOUTS. S 11. T 13, R 1W. Signed JAMES JACOB, POLLY (x) JACOB. Witness: none. rec 1816. pp 241, 242

Deed dated 1812. USA to WILLIAM FOUTS of Dearborn Co. S 13, T 13, R 1W. rec 1816. pp 242, 243

Deed dated 1811. USA to WILLIAM FOUTS of Montgomery Co (OH or KY?). S 13, T 13, R 1W. rec 1816. p 243

Deed dated 1815. JOHN MARTENDALE to WILLIAM FOUTS. S 29, T 17, R 13E. Signed JOHN MARTENDALE. Witness: none. rec 1816. pp 244, 245

Deed dated 1815. NATHAN OVERMAN to THOMAS MOOR. S 3. T 13, R 1W. Signed NATHAN OVERMAN, TAMER (x) OVERMAN Witness: CORNELIUS RATLIFF, SAMUEL CHARLES. rec 1816. pp 245, 246

Deed dated 1815. HENRY MILLER to SOLOMON BECK. S 25, T 12, R 2W. Signed HENRY MILLER, ESTHER (x) MILLER. Witness: JOSEPH COX, PETER (x) MILLER. rec 1816. pp 246, 247

Deed dated 1815. JOSEPH COOK to JAMES PEGG. S 6. T 13, R 1W. "to JESSE BOND's corner". Signed JOSEPH COOK, LYDIA (x) COOK. Witness: JOHN C. KIBBEY, JOHN HARVEY. rec 1816. pp 248, 249

Deed dated 1815. (HENRY) STEDDOM of Warren Co. OH to ROBERT HILL. S 2, T 13, R 1W. Signed HENRY STEDDOM. Witness: NATHAN HILL. rec 1816. pp 249, 250

WAYNE COUNTY DEEDS: Book A

Deed dated 1815. SAMUEL WOODS to MORGAN WILSON & THOMAS McCARTNEY. Lot adj Salisbury. Signed SAMUEL WOODS, POLLY WOODS. Witness: none. rec 1816. pp 250, 251

Deed dated 1813. PETER FLEMING, President of Court of Common Pleas, Wayne Co, to JOHN DAVIDSON. Salisbury lot 71. Signed PETER FLEMING. Witness: none. rec 1816. pp 251, 252

Deed dated 1816. JOHN DAVIDSON & POLLY, his wife. to JOHN WILKINSON of St. Clair Twp, Butler Co, OH. Salisbury lot 71 and lot adj town. Signed JOHN DAVIDSON POLLY (x) DAVIDSON. Witness: JOHN NILSON. rec 1816. pp 252, 253

Deed dated 1813. JEREMIAH COX to THOMAS LEWIS. S 32, T 14, R 1W. Signed JEREMIAH COX, CATHARINE COX. Witness: ISAAC COOK. rec 1816. pp 253, 254

Deed dated 1815. PETER FLEMING, First Judge of the Circuit Court of Wayne Co to JOHN SUTHERLAND & WILLIAM PHERES. Salisbury lots 7, 8. Signed PETER FLEMING. Witness: none. rec 1816. pp 254, 255

Deed dated 1815. AARON MARTIN, First Associate Judge Circuit Court of Wayne Co to JOHN SUTHERLAND. Salisbury lots 102 & illeg. Signed AARON MARTIN. Witness: none. rec 1816. p 255

Deed dated 1815. WILLIAM McLUCAS of Montgomery Co, OH to ROBERT RUSELL of the same. S 9. T 15, R 13E. Signed WILLIAM McLUCAS. Witness: JAMES RUSSELL. ELIZABETH (x) RUSSELL (in OH). rec 1816. pp 256. 257

Deed dated 1815. JOSEPH EVANS of Warren Co. OH to WILLIAM EVANS, "son of said JOSEPH". S 20. no T-R. Signed JOSEPH EVANS, LYDIA EVANS. Witness: PAUL LEWIS, JUBAL WATERS (in OH). rec 1816. pp 257, 258. 259

Deed dated 1815. ANDREW HOOVER to EDWARD BOND. S 14, T 14, R 1W. Signed ANDREW HOOVER, ELIZABETH HOOVER. Witness: none. rec 1816. pp 260, 261

Deed dated 1815. SILAS GREGG of Preble Co. OH to HARMAN GREGG & JOHN GREGG. S 7, T 14, R 13E. "RHODA. his wife". Signed SILAS GREGG, RHODA GREGG. Witness: RICHARD HALL, MERCER BROWN, SUSANNA HALL (in OH). rec 1816. pp 261, 262, 263

Deed dated 1816. WILLIAM THORN of Green Co, OH to

WAYNE COUNTY DEEDS: Book A

THOMAS WARMAN. S 18, T 16, R 13E. Signed WILLIAM THORN, RACHEL THORN. Witness: MOSES COLLIER. ELIZA COLLIER (in OH). rec 1816. pp 263, 264

Deed dated 1815. OBADIAH HARRIS SR to JOSIAH LAMB. R 14, T 17, S 11. "to THOMAS THARP's corner". Signed OBADIAH HARRIS, MIRIAM HARRIS. Witness: OBADIAH HARRIS JR, JACOB COOK. rec 1816. pp 264, 265

Deed dated 1815. -- STAFFORD to HENRY BEASON of Highland Co, OH. S 12, T 13, R 1W. Signed THOMAS STAFFORD, ELIZABETH (x) STAFFORD. Witness: none. rec 1816. pp 265, 266.

Deed dated 1815. JOHN HARVEY to SAMUEL CHARLES. S 3, T 13, R 1W. Signed JOHN HARVEY, JANE HARVEY. Witness: ISAAC JULIAN, JOHN COPELAND. rec 1816. pp 266, 267

Deed dated 1815. JAMES SHAW & MARY, his wife. to THOMAS BURESS. S 12, T 15, R 12E. Signed JAMES SHAW MARY SHAW. Witness: CHARLES ROYSTER. rec 1816. pp 268, 269

Deed dated 1815. PETER FLEMING, First Judge of the Circuit Court of Wayne Co to NATHANIEL WAYNE. Salisbury lots 112, 124, 125. Signed PETER FLEMING. Witness: none. rec 1816. pp 269, 270

Deed dated 1816. ABNER MARTIN to NATHAN SMITH. Salisbury lot 60. Signed ABNER MARTIN, MARY MARTIN. Witness: none. rec 1816. p 270

Deed dated 1815. PETER FLEMING, First Judge of the Circuit Court of Wayne Co to JOHN WALKER, assignee of SAMUEL McGEORGE. Salisbury lot 100. Signed PETER FLEMING. Witness: none. rec 1816. p 271

Deed dated 1816. ANDREW HARMON to DAVID HARMON. Salisbury lot 19. Signed ANDREW HARMON. Witness: none. rec 1816. pp 271, 272

Deed dated 1816. ANDREW HARMON to DAVID HARMON. S 12, T 13, R 2W. Signed ANDREW HARMON. Witness: none. rec 1816. pp 272, 273

Deed dated 1816. PETER FLEMING, First Associate Judge of the Circuit Court of Wayne Co to NATHAN SMITH. Salisbury lots 51, 62, 67. Signed PETER FLEMING. Witness: none. no rec date. p 273

Deed dated 1816. GEORGE HUNT as exec of will of

WAYNE COUNTY DEEDS: Book A

DANIEL FOUTS, dec. to NOAH FOUTS. S 18, T 12, R 1W. Signed G. HUNT, exec of D. FOUTS, dec. Witness: none. rec 1816. p 274

Deed dated 1815. EBENEZER HEATON to DANIEL HEATON. S 17, T 14, R 13. Signed EBENEZER HEATON, JOANNA HEATON. Witness: CHARLES ROYSTER, EBENEZER GOBLE. rec 1816. pp 274, 275, 276

Quitclaim dated 1816. JAMES LAMB, having written a will held by WILLIAM McCASH near Cincinnati, OH, but desiring to avoid family dispute after his passing, gave a quitclaim on land "now in possession of my son-in-law SMITH HUNT". Land deeded to LAMB by THOMAS McCOY & ANDREW ENDSLEY. Signed JAMES LAMB. Witness: none. rec 1816. p 276

Deed dated 1815. WILLIAM BOND to JOSEPH BOND. S 14, T 14, R 1W. Signed WILLIAM BOND, CHARLOTTE BOND. Witness: none. rec 1816. pp 276, 277

Deed dated 1815. JOB GINN to JOSIAH DAVISSON of OH. Salisbury lot 98. Signed JOB GINN, SARAH (x) GINN. Witness: JOHN NILSON. rec 1816. p 278

Deed dated 1816. PETER FLEMING, First Associate Judge of the Circuit Court of Wayne Co to THOMAS McCARTNEY. Salisbury lots 18, 25, 37, 44. Signed PETER FLEMING. Witness: none. rec 1816. pp 278, 279

Deed dated 1811. USA to GEORGE HUNT of Clermont Co. (probably OH). S 1, T 12, R 2W. rec 1816. p 279

Deed dated 1816. JAMES MARTINDALE & ELIZABETH, his wife, to JESSE BOND. S 35, T 17, R 13E. Signed JAMES MARTINDALE, ELIZABETH MARTINDALE. Witness: THOMAS HATFIELD, ABRAHAM ELLIOTT. rec 1816. pp 280, 281

Deed dated 1816. HARMAN WARRAM & EDITH, his wife, to GEORGE MISOR. S 36, T 16, R 13. Signed HARMAN WARRAM EDITH WARRAM. Witness: none. rec 1816. pp 281, 282

Deed dated 1816. SAMUEL FLEMING to NATHAN SMITH. Salisbury lot 80. Signed SAMUEL FLEMING. Witness: none. rec 1816. pp 282, 283

Deed dated 1816. GEORGE HUNT to THOMAS T. LEWIS. Salisbury lots 7, 10. Signed G. HUNT, POLLY HUNT. Witness: none. rec 1816. pp 283, 284

Deed dated 1816. GEORGE HUNT to JONAS HAVENS of Hamilton Co, OH. Salisbury lot 11. Signed G. HUNT. no

WAYNE COUNTY DEEDS: Book A

wife's signature. Witness: none. rec 1816. JP's note: "GEORGE HUNT & PATSY, his wife". See previous deed. pp 284, 285

Deed dated 1816. WILLIAM HUNT to JOHN SUTHERLAND JR. Salisbury lot 87. Signed WILLIAM HUNT. BETSY HUNT. Witness: none. rec 1816. pp 285, 286

Deed dated 1815. EDWARD BOND to JOSHUA BOND. S 14, T 14, R 1W. "his wife, ANNE". Signed EDWARD BOND, ANNE BOND. Witness: none. rec 1816. pp 286, 287

Deed dated 1816. GEORGE HUNT, JOHN HUNT & SMITH HUNT to SAMUEL WOODS of KY. "EWEL KINDALL's line...to JOHN DAVIDSON...CHRISTOPHER RODDEY's line...PEGGY BROWN's line...to JOHN SUTHERLAND's.." Signed G. HUNT, PATSY HUNT, JOHN HUNT, POLLY HUNT, SMITH HUNT, ELIZABETH HUNT. Witness: none. rec 1816. pp 287, 288, 289

Deed dated 1815. JOSEPH COOK to JOHN STEWART. S 6, T 13, R 1. Signed JOSEPH COOK, LYDIA COOK. Witness: none. rec 1816. pp 289, 290

Deed dated 1815. PETER FLEMING, First Judge of the Circuit Court of Wayne Co to MILBURN JACOBS. Salisbury lot 119. Signed PETER FLEMING. Witness: none. rec 1816. p 291

Deed dated 1815. JAMES JACOBS to THOMAS COOK. S 18, T 13, R 1W. Signed JAMES JACOBS, POLLY JACOBS. Witness: none. rec 1816. pp 291, 292, 293

Deed dated 1816. GEORGE GLAZE & ELIZABETH, his wife of Pickaway Co, OH to BENJAMIN IDDINGS of Miami Co. OH. S 36, T 16, R 12E. Signed GEORGE GLAZE, ELIZABETH GLAZE. Witness: JONATHAN BALLINGER, JOHN LUDWIG (in OH). rec 1816. pp 293, 294, 295

Deed dated 1816. ANDREW WOODS & JANE, his wife, to JOSEPH CHARLES. S 6, T 16, R 13E. Signed ANDREW WOODS, JANE WOODS. Witness: none. rec 1816. pp 295, 296, 297

Deed dated 1815. USA to TIMOTHY HUNT. S 2, T 12, R 2W. rec 1816. pp 297, 298

Deed dated 1816. SUSANNA BUTLER to ANDREW WOODS. S 12, T 13, R 2W. Signed SUSANNA BUTLER. Witness: JOHN NILSON, DAVID HARMAN. rec 1816. pp 298, 299

Deed dated 1816. PETER FLEMING, First Judge of the Circuit Court of Wayne Co to REBECAH CORNELL. Salis-

WAYNE COUNTY DEEDS: Book A

bury lot 26. Signed PETER FLEMING. Witness: none. rec 1816. pp 299, 300

Deed dated 1816. SUSANNA BUTLER to JOHN SUTHERLAND SR, JOHN SUTHERLAND JR & WILLIAM PHARES. S 12, T 13, R 2W. Signed SUSANNA BUTLER. Witness: none. rec 1816. pp 300, 301

Deed dated 1816. EWEL KINDALL & ELIZABETH, his wife, & JOHN TURNER & SARAH, his wife, to JESSE BUZAN. S 21, T 16, R 14. Signed EWEL KINDALL, ELIZABETH KINDALL, JOHN TURNER, SARAH TURNER. Witness: none. rec 1816. pp 301, 302

Deed dated 1816. ALEXANDER MILLER to THOMAS McCARTNEY. Salisbury lot 122. ALEXANDER MILLER, MARY MILLER. Witness: none. rec 1816. p 303

Deed dated 1816. ALEXANDER MILLER to NATHAN SMITH. S 24, T 13, R 2W. Signed ALEXANDER MILLER, MARY MILLER. Witness: none. rec 1816. pp 304, 305

Agreement dated 1816. JOSEPH SPENCER SR to DIANA SPENCER, wife of said JOSEPH. Unhappy differences arose & the Spencers agreed to separate. JOSEPH to pay $160 as wife's share of property. DIANA, being content, relinquished all her rights to any property JOSEPH now has or will acquire. Signed JOSEPH SPENCER, DIANA (x) SPENCER. Witness: JOSEPH SPENCER, ISAAC MEDCALF. rec 1816. pp 305, 306

Deed dated 1816. JOSEPH SPENCER SR to JAMES SPENCER. "for $1": land in S 9, T 12, R 1W. Signed JOSEPH SPENCER. Witness: none. rec 1816. p 307

Deed dated 1816. JOSEPH SPENCER SR to ISAAC MEDCALF. S 28, T 12, R 1W. Signed JOSEPH SPENCER. Witness: none. rec 1816. pp 308, 309

Deed dated 1816. JOSEPH SPENCER SR to WILLIAM SPENCER. S 28, T 12, R 1W. Signed JOSEPH SPENCER. Witness: none. rec 1816. pp 309, 310

Deed dated 1816. JOSEPH SPENCER SR to JOSEPH SPENCER JR. S 9, T 12, R 1W. Signed JOSEPH SPENCER. Witness: none. rec 1816. pp 310, 311

Deed dated 1816. JOSEPH SPENCER SR to ROZZEL SPENCER. S 28, T 12, R 1W. Signed JOSEPH SPENCER. Witness: none. rec 1816. pp 311, 312

Deed dated 1816. ANTHONY CHAMNESS & MARTHA, his

WAYNE COUNTY DEEDS: Book A

wife, to JOHN LEWIS. S 7, T 7, R 14E. Signed ANTHONY CHAMNESS, MARTHA (x) CHAMNESS. Witness: RICHARD LEWIS, JOSEPH LEWIS. rec 1816. pp 313, 314, 315

Deed dated 1816. JOHN LEWIS & SARAH. his wife. to JOSEPH LEWIS. S 7, T 17, R 14E. Signed JOHN LEWIS. SARAH LEWIS. Witness: BENJAMIN HARRIS. RICHARD LEWIS. rec 1816. pp 315, 316, 317

Deed dated 1816. USA to SAMUEL BEELOR. S 8, T 15. R 13E. no rec date. p 318

Deed dated 1816. JOSEPH HOLMAN to JOHN MILLER. S 34, T 13, R 1W. Signed JOSEPH HOLMAN, LYDIA HOLMAN. Witness: WILLIAM HASTING, WM. McCLAIN. rec 1816. pp 319, 320

Deed dated 1816. ISAAC CONLEY to THOMAS WARD. S 34. T 13, R 1W. Signed ISAAAC CONLEY, MARY CONLY. Witness: DANIEL CLARK. rec 1816. pp 320, 321. 322

Deed dated 1816. THOMAS CLARK to THOMAS WARD. S 23, T 13, R 1W. Signed THOMAS CLARK, JANE CLARK. Witness: DANIEL CLARK, JONATHAN BRATTAIN. rec 1816. pp 322, 323, 324

Deed dated 1816. JAMES SPENCER & ANNA, his wife. to WILLIAM MABBETT. S 9, T 12, R 1W. "with his wife and his mother DIANA SPENCER who relinquishes her right". Signed JAMES SPENCER, ANNA SPENCER. DIANNA SPENCER. Witness: ANTHONY MABBETT. rec 1816. pp 324, 325

Deed dated 1816. PETER FLEMING, First Associate Judge of the Circuit Court of Wayne Co to GEORGE HUNT. Salisbury lots 1. 2, 3. 12, 13, 14, 16, 17, 26, 27. Signed PETER FLEMING. Witness: none. rec 1816. p 326

Deed dated 1816. PETER FLEMING. First Judge of the Circuit Court of Wayne Co to GEORGE DILL of Green Co. OH. Salisbury lots 116, 117. Signed PETER FLEMING. Witness: none. rec 1816. p 327

Deed dated 1813. SAMUEL JOB & his wife (not named) JOB to JAMES GORDON. S 17, T 12, R 1W. Signed SAMUEL JOB, RACHEL JOB. Witness: GEORGE HUNT. rec 1816. pp 328, 329

Deed dated 1816. JONAS HAVENS of Hamilton Co, OH to GEORGE HUNT. Salisbury lot 11. Signed JONAS HAVENS. Witness: none. rec 1816. p 330

WAYNE COUNTY DEEDS: Book A

Confirmation of deed dated 1816. TABITHA WHITE to DANIEL KAMP of Madison Twp, Butler Co, OH. TABITHA WHITE & BLADEN ASHBY, execs of will of JAMES WHITE, late of Butler Co, OH, sold land in S 17, T 2, R 4E (Butler Co) on 17 Oct, 1806 by assignment to KAMP. Good title could not be made as not all JAMES' heirs had attained 21 yrs. Land in S 11, T 14, R 1W purchased by TABITHA for use of heirs. SE & SW sections (except those partioned for use of heirs JAMES WHITE & THOMAS GRAY) now mortgaged to KAMP. Minor heirs to give quitclaims as they come of age; mortgage to be released. Signed TABITHA (x) WHITE. Witness: JACOB KAMP, JONAS JONES. rec 1817. pp 331, 332, 333

Deed dated 1812. USA to JOHN WHITEHEAD. S 31, T 13, R 1W. rec 1817. p 334

Deed dated 1810. USA to LAZARUS WHITEHEAD. S 31, T 13, R 1W. rec 1817. p 335

Deed dated 1812. USA to WILLIAM WHITEHEAD, asn'ee of LAZARUS WHITEHEAD. S 36, T 13, R 2W. rec 1817. p 336

Deed dated 1816. SAMUEL JOB to BENJAMIN JARVIS. S 4, T 12, R 1W. "RACHEL, his wife". Signed SAMUEL JOB RACHEL JOB. Witness: none. rec 1816. pp 337, 338

Deed dated 1816. GASPER LITTLE & ANNA LITTLE to BRYAN LEARY. S 5, T 12, R 1W. Signed JASPER LITTLE, ANNA LITTLE. Witness: none. JP's note: "GASPER LITTLE & ANNA, his wife". rec 1816. pp 338, 339, 340

Deed dated 1817. VINCENT STEPHENSON to JOHN SUTHERLAND JR. No S-T-R. Bounds: "SAMUEL WOOD's corner... SUTHERLAND's original line". "SUSANNA, his wife". Signed VINCENT STEPHENSON, SUSANNA STEVENSON. Witness: none. rec 1816. pp 340, 341

Deed dated 1816. JOSEPH DAVISSON of Green Co, OH to WILLIAM McBROOM. Salisbury lot 90. Signed JOSEPH DAVISSON. Witness: none. rec 1816. p 342

Deed dated 1816. JEREMIAH COX to JOHN MENDINGHALL. Plainfield lot 14. Signed JEREMIAH COX. Witness: none. rec 1816. pp 343, 344

Deed dated 1816. CHRISTOPHER RODDEY to GEORGE HUNT. Salisbury lot, no #: "conveyed by SAMUEL WOODS in 1815". Signed CHRISTOPHER RODDEY, ISABELLA (x) RODDEY. Witness: none. rec 1816. pp 344, 345

Deed dated 1816. GEORGE HUNT to CHRISTOPHER RODDEY.

WAYNE COUNTY DEEDS: Book A

Salisbury lot 1. Signed G. HUNT, PATSY HUNT. rec 1816. pp 345, 346

Deed dated 1816. PETER FLEMING, First Associate Judge of the Circuit Court of Wayne Co to NATHANEIL WAYNE. Salisbury lot 112. Signed PETER FLEMING. Witness: none. rec 1816. p 347

Deed dated 1816. NATHANIEL WAYNE to ABRAHAM LEWIS & THOMAS T. LEWIS. Salisbury lot 112. Signed NATHANIEL WAYNE, ESTHER (x) WAYNE. Witness: none. rec 1816 p348

Deed dated 1816. THOMAS T. LEWIS to NATHANIEL WAYNE. S 9, T 12, R 1W. Signed THOMAS T. LEWIS. Witness: none. rec 1816. pp 349, 350

Deed dated 1816. WILLIAM COX to JOHN SUTHERLAND JR. S 24, T 14, R 2W. Signed WILLIAM COX, ELIZABETH COX. Witness: none. rec 1816. JP's note: "WILLIAM COX & ELIZABETH, his wife". pp 350, 351

Deed dated 1816. JACOB MEEK to JEREMIAH L. MEEK & WILLIAM MEEK. S 9, T 13, R 1W. Signed JACOB MEEK, EL-ENOR MEEK. Witness: none. rec 1816. pp 352, 353, 354

Deed dated 1817. JOHN COLLINS to VINCENT STEPHENSON. S 19, T 13, R 1W. Signed JOHN COLLINS, JANE COLLINS. Witness: none. JP's note: "JOHN COLLINS & JANE, his wife". rec 1817. pp 354, 355

Deed dated 1817. JOHN COLLINS to PETER WEAVER. S 19, T 12, R 1W. Signed JOHN COLLINS, JANE COLLINS. Witness: none. rec 1817. pp 355, 356

Deed dated 1817. DAVID RAILSBACK to JAMES LAMB. S 35, T 13, R 2W. Signed DAVID RAILSBACK, SARAH RAILS-BACK. Witness: none. rec 1817. pp 356, 357

Deed dated 1817. WILLIAM TOWNSEND to JESSE HODGES. S 13, T 13, R 2W: "corner of HENRY PARSMORE's land". Signed WILLIAM (x) TOWNSEND. Witness: SMITH HUNT, SAM'L. CARR. rec 1817. pp 357, 358, 359

Deed dated ROBERT LEAVELL to ITHAMAR WARNER. Jacksonburgh lot 22. "SALLY, his wife". Signed ROBERT LEAV-ELL, SALLY LEAVELL. Witness: T.J. WARMAN, (illegible) BEARD. rec 1817. pp 359, 360

Deed dated 1817. JOSEPH SPENCER to JOEL MOORE. S 9, T 12, R 1W. "JOSEPH SPENCER & JANE, his wife, & DIANNA SPENCER...and JOSEPH SPENCER JR for himself". Signed JOSEPH SPENCER, JANE (x) SPENCER, DIANA (x)

WAYNE COUNTY DEEDS: Book A

SPENCER. Witness: J. WHITEHEAD, WASHINGTON ELLIOTT. rec 1817. pp 361, 362

Deed dated 1817. PETER FLEMING, First Associate Judge of the Circuit Court of Wayne Co to MARK HOLLETT. Salisbury lots 107, 108. Signed PETER FLEMING. Witness: none. rec 1817. pp 362, 363

Deed dated 1817. PETER FLEMING, First Associate Judge of the Circuit Court of Wayne Co to JOHN WALKER. Salisbury lot 100. Signed PETER FLEMING. Witness: none rec 1817. pp 363, 364

Deed dated 1817. JAMES WHITE to THOMAS McCARTNEY. Salisbury 32, 39. Signed JAMES WHITE. Witness: none rec 1817. pp 364, 365

Deed dated 1817. PETER FLEMING, First Associate Judge of the Circuit Court of Wayne Co to THOMAS McCARTNEY. Salisbury lot 57. Signed PETER FLEMING. Witness: none. rec 1817. pp 365, 366

Deed dated 1817. JOHN DUEY to WILLIAM CUMMENS. S 21 R 13, T 15E (transposition of T & R?). "ELIZABETH, his wife". Signed JOHN DUEY, ELIZABETH DUEY. Witness JOSEPH FLINT, POLLY DUEY. rec 1817. pp 366, 367, 368

Deed dated 1816. ANDREW CROUCH & ELENOR, his wife of Ross Co, OH to DANIEL AUSTIN of the same. S 7, T 15, R 13E. Signed ANDREW CROUCH, ELENOR CROUCH. Witness JAMES BURN, ANDREW IRWIN (in OH). rec 1817. pp 369, 370, 371

Deed dated 1809. USA to CHARLES HUNT, assignee of JOHN HUNT. S 30, T 13, R 1W. rec 1817. pp 371, 372

Deed dated 1812. USA to RICHARD SEDGEWICK, assignee of WILLIAM BROWN & ISAAC MEDCALF. S 11, T 12, R 1W. rec 1817. pp 372, 373

Deed dated 1812. USA to WILLIAM HUNT of Dearborn Co. S 17, T 12, R 1W. rec 1817. pp 373, 374

Deed dated 1816. USA to THOMAS BRADBERRY. S 17, T 12, R 1W. rec 1817. pp 374, 375

Deed dated 1817. THOMAS BRADBURY to BARNET STARR. S 17, T 12, R 1W. Signed THOMAS BRADBURY, CATY BRADBURY. Witness: none. rec 1817. pp 376, 377

Deed dated 1817. THOMAS CARTER to ISAAC VANMETER. S 36, T 15, R 12E. "NANCY, his wife". Signed THOMAS

WAYNE COUNTY DEEDS: Book A

CARTER, NANCY (x) CARTER. Witness: ADAM BAKS, BENJAMIN RUCHER. rec 1817. pp 377, 378

Deed dated 1817. JAMES JONES to JOHN LAUMAN. Lot adj Salisbury: "deed from GEORGE HUNT". "PHEBE, his wife". Signed JAMES (x) JONES, PHEBE (x) JONES. Witness: JOHN NILSON. rec 1817. pp 379, 380

Deed dated 1817. JACOB WEIMIRE & ELIZABETH, his wife from THOMAS BEARD. S 21, T 15, R 13. Signed THOMAS BEARD. Witness: PATRICK BEARD, JOHN BEARD. rec 1818 pp 380, 381, 382

Deed dated 1816. RICHARD DUEY & CATHARINE, his wife, to HENRY DUEY. S 11, T 12, R 2W. Signed RICHARD (x) DUEY, CATHARINE (x) DUEY. Witness: THOMAS WILES. rec 1817. pp 383, 384

Deed dated 1816. HENRY GARRETT & POLLY, his wife, to HENRY DUEY. S 11, T 12, R 2W. Signed HENRY GARRETT, MARY GARRETT. Witness: none. rec 1817. pp 384, 385

Deed dated 1817. EWEL KENDALL & ELIZABETH, his wife, to DAVID HARMAN. Salisbury lot 45. Signed EWEL KENDAL, ELIZABETH (x) KENDALL. Witness: none. rec 1817. pp 385, 386

Deed dated 1817. DAVID HARMAN & REBECKAH, his wife, to REUBEN BRATTAIN. Salisbury lot 45. Signed DAVID HARMAN, REBECKAH HARMAN. Witness: none. rec 1817. pp 386, 387

Deed dated 1817. FREDERICK LONG to BARNET STARR. S 18, T 12, R 1W. "RACHEL, wife of FREDERICK". Signed FREDERICK (x) LONG, RACHEL (x) LONG. Witness: none. rec 1817. pp 387, 388

Deed dated 1817. JAMES GORDEN to BARNET STARR. S 17, T 12, R 1W. Signed JAMES GORDEN, MARY GORDEN. Witness: none. rec 1817. pp 388, 389

Deed dated 1816. THOMAS CLARK to JONATHAN BRATTAIN. S 33, T 13, R 1W. "JANE, his wife". Signed THOMAS CLARK, JANE CLARK. Witness: DANIEL CLARK, PETER MELANDER, THOMAS WARD. rec 1817. pp 389, 390

Deed dated 1817. GEORGE GRAHAM & MARGARET, his wife, to JAMES DELAP. S ?, T 15, R 13E. Signed GEORGE GRAHAM, MARGARET GRAHAM. Witness: none. rec 1817. pp 390, 391

Deed dated 1816. JOHN SMITH to WILLIAM BOND.

WAYNE COUNTY DEEDS: Book A

Richmond lot 14. Signed JOHN SMITH. Witness: none. rec 1817. pp 391, 392

Deed dated 1812. USA to SAMUEL CHARLES, assignee of JOHN SMITH. S 32, T 14, R 1W. rec 1817. p 392

Deed dated 1817. SAMUEL CHARLES to "my son" JOHN CHARLES. S 32, T 14, R 1W. "GULIELMI, wife of SAMUEL." Signed SAMUEL CHARLES, GULIELMI CHARLES. Witness: MARTHA SACKETT. rec 1817. pp 392, 393

Deed dated 1816. RICHARD MAXWELL of Knox Co & ANNA, his wife, to JOHN GAY (GUY in text). S 36, T 14, R 1W. Signed RICHARD MAXWELL, ANNA MAXWELL. Witness: J. BLACK, BENJAMIN BYRAM (in Knox Co). rec 1817. pp 393, 394, 395

Deed dated 1817. JOHN SMITH to JOHN GAY. S 7, T 12, R 1W. Signed JOHN SMITH. Witness: STEPHEN HOLLOWAY SAMUEL SMITH. rec 1817. p 395

Deed dated 1817. JOHN SMITH to JOHN C. KIBBEY. S 22, T 16, R 14E. Signed JOHN SMITH. Witness: DANIEL LAMM, WILLIAM DALHOUN. rec 1817. p 396

Deed dated 1817. ROBERT LEAVELL to JOHN GINN. Jacksonburgh lots 3, 8. Signed ROBERT LEAVELL, SALLY (x) LEAVELL. Witness: THOMAS J. WARMAN, SALLY WARMAN. rec 1817. p 397

Deed dated 1816. SAMUEL WOODS of Giles Co, TN to DAVID IRELAND of Preble Co, OH. S 26, T 14, R 1W. Signed SAMUEL WOODS. Witness: JOHN IRELAND, LEVI PURVIANCE, WILLIAM IRELAND, WILLIAM GORDON. rec 1817. p 398

Deed dated 1817. MARY MINER to JAMES WADDELL. S 33, R 1, T 12. Signed MARY MINER. Witness: JOHN COX, JP rec 1817. p 399

Deed dated 1817. REUBEN BRATTAIN to PATRICK JUSTICE. Salisbury lot 45. Signed REUBEN BRATTAIN, JAIN BRATTAIN. Witness: none. rec 1817. p 400

Deed dated 1816. THOMAS WARMAN to JOSIAH BUNDY JR. S 17, T 16, R 13E. "SARAH, his wife". Signed THOMAS WARMAN, SARAH WARMAN. Witness: JOHN C. KIBBEY, WILLIAM LEWIS. rec 1817. pp 400, 401

Deed dated 1817. NIMROD FERGUSON to WILLIS PARKISON. Salisbury lots 91, 54. Signed NIMROD FERGUSON. Witness: none. rec 1817. p 402

WAYNE COUNTY DEEDS: Book A

Deed dated 1817. BENJAMIN MAUDLIN to JOSEPH HOLEMAN. S 7, T 16, R 14E. Signed BENJAMIN (x) MAUDLIN, LEAH (x) MAUDLIN. Witness: WRIGHT MAUDLIN. rec 1817. pp 402, 403

Deed dated 1813. USA to THOMAS STAFFORD. S 34, T 16, R 12E. rec 1817. pp 403, 404

Deed dated 1817. THOMAS STAFFORD to THOMAS PEARSON. S 34, T 16, R 12E. "his wife, ELIZABETH". Signed THOMAS STAFFORD, ELIZABETH (x) STAFFORD. Witness: none. rec 1817. pp 404, 405

Deed dated 1817. LUKE DILLON of Clinton Co, OH to JOSEPH LEWIS. S 2, T 17, R 13E. "CHARITY, his wife". Signed LUKE DILLON, CHARITY (x) DILLON. Witness: ELI GARKILL, WILLIAM WRIGHT (in OH). rec 1817. pp 405, 406, 407

Deed dated 1817. ETHAN STONE of Cincinnati to JOHN MAXWELL, JAMES JUNKINS, WILLIAM SUMNER, JEREMIAH MEEK & JOB HUDDLESTON, Trustees for town of Cntrv. Land in S 19, T 16, R 14E; no use specified. "ABIGAIL MARIA STONE, his wife". Witness: FRANCIS CARR, DAVID KIAERLEY. rec 1817. pp 407, 408, 409

Quitclaim dated 1817. MALACHI MOON to SAMUEL CHARLES. MOON & CHARLES, assignee of JOHN HAINS, obtained patent for S 8, T 15, R 1W. MOON yielding interest in land. "MARY, his wife". Signed MALACHI MOON, MARY MOON. Witness: ELI OVERMAN, JOHN FISHER. rec 1817. pp 409, 410

Deed dated 1816. ANDREW CROUCH & ELENOR, his wife of Ross Co, OH to JAMES McKINNEY of the same. S 7, T 15, R 13E. Signed ANDREW CROUCH, ELENOR (x) CROUCH. Witness: EZEKIEL BUNN, THOMAS AUSTIN (in OH). rec 1817. pp 410, 411, 412

Deed dated 1817. ROBERT LEAVELL to JOSIAH BUNDY SR. Jacksonburgh lots 1, 10. Signed ROBERT LEAVELL, SALLY (x) LEAVELL. Witness: THOMAS P. WARMAN, JOHN GINN. rec 1817. pp 412, 413

Deed dated 1817. ROBERT LEAVELL to JOHN BUNDY. Jacksonburgh lot 15. Signed ROBERT LEAVELL, SALLY (x) LEAVELL. Witness: THOMAS P. WARMAN, JOHN GINN. rec 1817. p 413

Deed dated 1817. WILLIAM THORN & RACHEL, his wife, of Green Co, OH to MORRIS NIXON of Pasquotank Co, NC.

WAYNE COUNTY DEEDS: Book A

S 19, T 16, R 13E. Signed WILLIAM THORN, RACHEL THORN Witness: THOMAS EMBREE, WILLIAM SAINT. rec 1817. pp 414, 415

Deed dated 1817. WILLIAM THORN & RACHEL, his wife, of Green Co, OH to JOSHUA MORRIS of Pasquotank Co, NC. S 19, T 16, R 13E. Signed WILLIAM THORN, RACHEL THORN. Witness: THOMAS EMBREE, WILLIAM SAINT. rec 1817. pp 415, 416

Deed dated 1816. USA to JOHN McEOWAN of Butler Co, OH. S 23, T 12, R 1W. rec 1817. pp 416, 417

Deed dated 1816. JAMES FLEMING of Bourbon Co, KY to ANDREW IRELAND of the same. S 35, T 14, R 1W. "VIOLINDA, his wife". Signed JAMES FLEMING, VIOLINDA FLEMING. Witness: JOHN CAMPBELL, ELOM IRELAND (in KY). rec 1817. pp 417, 418, 419

Deed dated 1817. JONATHAN HILL to WILLIAM COX. S 2, T 13, R 1W. Signed JONATHAN HILL. Witness: PHILIP HACKET. rec 1817. p 419

Deed dated 1817. JOHN SUTHERLAND JR to THOMAS CLIFFORD of Green Co, OH. Salisbury lot 84. Signed JOHN SUTHERLAND, JANE SUTHERLAND. Witness: none. JP's note: "JANE, his wife". rec 1817. p 420

Deed dated 1817. GEORGE SHUGURT to JONATHAN HOUGH. S 1, T 17, R 14E. "MARY, his wife". Signed GEORGE SHUGART, MARY (x) SHUGART. Witness: none. rec 1817. pp 420, 421

Deed dated 1816. EDWARD BENBOW to JOHN NIXON. S 5, T 16, R 14E. Signed EDWARD BENBOW, MARY (x) BENBOW. Witness: ABSOLOM HARVEY, WILLIAM McCLAIN. rec 1817. pp 422, 423

Deed dated 1817. GEORGE SHORTRIDGE of Clark Co, KY to WILLIAM G. RENOLDS. S 31, T 16, R 13E. Signed GEORGE SHORTRIDGE. Witness: ELI GASSIN, HENRY WARMAN. rec 1817. pp 423, 424

Deed dated 1817. JACOB ELLIOTT & ANN, his wife, to OVID BOONE. S 12, T 13, R 2W. Signed JACOB ELLIOTT, ANN (x) ELLIOTT. Witness: JESSE DAVENPORT, JOHN SUTHERLAND. rec 1817. pp 425, 426

Deed dated 1817. GEORGE MANLOVE or MANLOW & MARY, his wife, to DANIEL TRIPLETT. S 28, T 15, R 12. Signed GEORGE MANLOVE/MANLOW, MARY MANLOVE/MANLOW. Witness: ADAM BANKS, JOHN COOK. rec 1817 pp 426, 427

WAYNE COUNTY DEEDS: Book A

Deed dated 1817. GEORGE MANLOVE or MANLOW & MARY, his wife, to WILLIAM MANLOVE/MANLOW. S 28, T 15, R 12. Signed GEORGE MANLOVE/MANLOW, MARY MANLOVE/MANLOW. Witness: ADAM BANKS, JOHN COOK. rec 1817 pp 427

Deed dated 1816. JOHN ARMSTRONG & LUTESHA, his wife, of Orange Co to DAVID T. WYATT. R 2W, T 12, S 15. Signed JOHN ARMSTRONG, LUTESHA ARMSTRONG. Witness: THOMAS MOFFETT, JAMES ARMSTRONG (in Orange Co). rec 1817. pp 428, 429

Deed dated 1816. SETH WAY & SARAH, his wife, to WILLIAM JOHNSON. S 6, T 17, R 14E. Signed SETH WAY, SARAH (x) WAY. Witness: P.J.H. WAY, RICHARD LEWIS. rec 1817. pp 429, 430

Agreement dated 1817. JOHN PATTERSON gave 2 cows & calves, 15 head of hogs, 1 box hardware as security to WILLIAM SHAW & JONATHAN HIGGINS; debt not specified. Signed JOHN PATTERSON. rec 1817. p 431

Deed dated 1817. JOHN LEWIS to EDWARD THOMAS of Warren Co, OH. S 8, T 17, R 14E. "SARAH, his wife". Signed JOHN LEWIS, SARAH LEWIS. Witness: ABSALOM THOMAS, RICHARD LEWIS. rec 1817. pp 431, 432

Deed dated 1817. JOSHUA BOND to DANIEL NORTH. S 14, T 14, R 1W. "his wife RUTH". Signed JOSHUA BOND, RUTH BOND. Witness: none. rec 1817. pp 432, 433, 434

Deed dated 1817. ISRAEL ELLIOTT to JOHN JONES. Centerville lot 59. "WELLMET, wife of ISRAEL". Signed ISRAEL ELLIOTT, WELLMET (x) ELLIOTT. Witness: JOHN MAXWELL, JOHN McCLANE. rec 1817. pp 434, 435

Deed dated 1817. JOSEPH POWERS & SALOMEY, his wife, to ISAAC LEWIS. S 5, T 12, R 1W. Signed JOSEPH POWERS, SALOME (x) POWERS. Witness: BENJAMIN (x) PARSONS. rec 1817. pp 435, 436

Deed dated 1817. JOHN JONES to PETER RINGO. Cntrv lot 59. Signed JOHN JONES, SARAH JONES. Witness: WILLIAM BLACK, RUTH (x) JONES. rec 1817. pp 436, 437

Deed dated JOSEPH WORLD to ALLEN WILLIAMS. S 5, T 16, R 13E. "NANCY, his wife". Signed JOSEPH WORL, NANCY (x) WORL. Witness: JOHN MARTINDALE, CHARLES ROE. rec 1817. pp 438, 439

Deed dated 1817. JEHOSHAPHAT MORRIS & SARAH, his wife, to GEORGE BUNDY & JONATHAN JUSTICE, Overseers of the West Union Meeting of the Society of Friends.

WAYNE COUNTY DEEDS: Book A

S 19, T 16, R 13E for use as a meeting house. Signed JEHOSHAPHAT MORRIS, SARAH MORRIS. Witness: HENRY DARBY, THOMAS P. WARMAN. rec 1817. pp 439, 440

Deed dated 1817. WILLIAM THORN & RACHEL his wife, of Green Co, OH to GEORGE BUNDY. S 24, T 16, R 12E. Signed WILLIAM THORN, RACHEL THORN. Witness: JOSEPH HAMILL, MOSES COLLIER (in OH). rec 1817 pp 440, 441, 442

Deed dated 1817. JOSEPH EVANS of Warren Co, OH to SAMUEL EVANS, son of said JOSEPH. S 19, T 17, R 14E. Signed JOSEPH EVANS, LYDIA EVENS. Witness: JOHN BLAIR, JOB EVENS. rec 1817 (in OH). pp 442, 443, 444

Deed dated 1815. USA to RICHARD HENDRAY of Ross Co. (probably OH). S 18, T 15, R 13E. rec 1817. p 444

Deed dated 1817. RICHARD HENDRAY of Ross Co (see above) to WILLIAM PHARES. S 18, T 15, R 13E. Signed RICHARD HENDRAY. Witness: JOHN C. KIBBEY, H. T. LAUMAN. rec 1817. pp 444, 445

Deed dated 1817. CHRISTOPHER RODDEY to SUTHERLAND, PHARES & CO. Salisbury lot 1. Signed CHRISTOPHER RODDEY, ISABELLA (x) RODDEY. Witness: none. rec 1817. pp 445, 446

Deed dated 1817. HENRY HOLLAND to CHARLES HUBBARD. S 15, T 14, R 13E. "JANE, his wife". Signed HENRY HOLLAND, JANE HOLLAND. Witness: PEGGY MONTGOMERY, JOSEPH FLINT. rec 1817. pp 446, 447

Deed dated 1817. ISAAC LEWIS & PATSEY, his wife, to JOHN RIFE. S 4, T 12, R 1W. Signed ISAAC LEWIS, PATSEY (x) LEWIS. Witness: none. rec 1817. pp 447, 448

Deed dated 1817. WM. CRAWFORD & MARTHA, his wife, to (page torn). "unto their son, JAMES CRAWFORD". S 25, T 16, R 13. Signed WILLIAM CRAWFORD, MARTHA (x) CRAWFORD. Witness: none. rec 1817. pp 448, 449

Deed dated 1815. THOMAS KERSEY & REBECCA, his wife of Clinton Co, OH to HENRY STEDDOM of Warren Co, OH. S 34, T 17, R 13e. Signed THOMAS KERSEY, REBECKAH KERSEY. Witness: JOHN KERSEY, SAM'L. H. HALL (at Clinton Co). rec 1817. pp 449, 450, 451

Deed dated 1817. JAMES CRAWFORD to JOHN HARVEY. S 25, T 16, R 13. Signed JAMES CRAWFORD. Witness: none. rec 1817. pp 451, 452

Bond dated 1817. JOSEPH HOLEMAN & WILLIAM SUMNER

WAYNE COUNTY DEEDS: Book A

bound to THOMAS J. WARMAN, THOMAS BEARD & JAMES ODELL Wayne Co Commissioners for $4000, security for lots to be sold in town of Cntrv. Signed JOSEPH HOLEMAN, WM. SUMNER. Witness: WILLIAM HARVEY, D. HOOVER. rec 1817. pp 452, 453

Deed dated 1817. ISAAC JULIAN to JAMES CRAWFORD. S 25, T 216, R 13. Signed ISAAC JULIAN, REBECKAH JULIAN. Witness: none. rec 1817. pp 453, 454

Deed dated 1817. ISRAEL ELLIOTT to WILLIAM SUMNER & JOHN McCLAIN. S 20, T 16, R 14, for use of town of Cntrv, reserving lots 39, 46, 47, 58, 59. Signed ISRAEL ELLIOTT, WELLMET (x) ELLIOTT. Witness: JOHN MAXWELL, JOHN JONES. rec 1817. pp 454, 455

Deed dated 1817. JOHN MAXWELL, JAMES JUNKINS, WILLIAM SUMNER, JEREMIAH MEEK & JOB HUDDLESTON to Commisioners of Wayne Co. To remove seat of Justice from Salisbury to Cntrv. 30 acres in S 19, T 16, R 14E for use of town of Cntrv. Signed JOHN MAXWELL, JAMES JUNKEN, JEREMIAH MEEK, JOB HUDDLESTON. Witness: DAVID HOOVER, BEALE BUTLER, LEWIS THOMAS. rec 1817. pp 455, 456

Mortgage dated 1817. JOHN WILKINSON to JOHN SUTHERLAND. Salisbury lot 71. WILKINSON to pay SUTHERLAND $107.75 + interest in 1 yr to void mortgage. Signed JOHN WILKINSON. Witness: ADISON SMITH, DAVID HOOVER. rec 1817. pp 456, 457

Deed dated 1817. JOHN PATTERSON & CHRISTIAN, his wife, to MATTHEW LONGWILL. S 3, T 15, R 13E. Signed JOHN PATTERSON, CHRISTIAN PATTERSON. Witness: WILLIAM FARLOW, JOHN MULLINS. rec 1817. p 458

Sheriff's sale dated 1817. JOHN TURNER, Sheriff of Wayne Co, to PHILIP PENNYWIT JR of Hamilton Co, OH. RUFFNER & PENNYWIT, assignees of JOB HUDDLESTON, recovered at law against JOHN PATTERSON & SAMUEL PATTERSON. Auction held on JOHN's land in S 3, T 15, R 13; PENNYWIT the high bidder. Signed JOHN TURNER. Witness: none. prec 1817. pp 458, 459, 460

Deed dated 1817. DAVID FISHER to THOMAS McCARTNEY. Salisbury lot 15, 28. Signed DAVID FISHER. Witness: D.F. SACKETT. rec 1817. p 460

Bill of Sale dated 1817. CHRISTOPHER RODDEY to LAURENCE H. BRANNON. Blacksmith tools in exchange for RODDEY's debt to "NATHAN JOHNSON and others" to be paid by BRANNON. Signed CHRISTOPHER RODDEY, LAURENCE

WAYNE COUNTY DEEDS: Book A

H. BRANNNON. Witness: L. REYNOLDS. rec 1817. p 461

Deed dated 1817. JOHN HART to JOHN & WILLIAM SUTHERLAND. Salisbury lots 85, 103. Signed JOHN HART. Witness: ANDREW WOODS. rec 1817. pp 461, 462

Deed dated 1817. PETER FLEMING, First Associate Judge of the Circuit Court of Wayne Co to PEGG BROWN, ALEXANDER BROWN & JAMES BROWN. Salisbury lot 96. Signed PETER FLEMING. Witness: none. rec 1818. p 462

Deed dated 1817. BENJAMIN ROBERTS to JESSE ROBERTS. S 11, T 16, R 12E. Signed BENJAMIN ROBERTS. Witness: JOHN GINN, JAS. DOUGHERTY. rec 1818. p 463

Deed dated 1818. SUSANNA BUTLER to PHINEAS ROBERTS. S 17, T 14, R 1W. Signed SUSANA BUTLER. Witness: ELI BUTLER. rec 1818. pp 463, 464

Deed dated 1818. SUSANNA BUTLER to LEVI BUTLER. S 17, T 14, R 1W. Signed SUSANA BUTLER. Witness: ELI BUTLER. rec 1818. pp 464, 465

Deed dated 1818. PHINEAS ROBERTS to ISRAEL CLARK. S 20, T 14, R 1. Signed PHINEAS ROBERDS. Witness: JOHN WHITE, BENJAMIN CARRELL. rec 1818. pp 465, 466

Deed dated 1818. PHINEAS ROBBERDS to JOHN WHITE. S 20, T 14, R 1. Signed PHINEAS ROBERTS. Witness: ISRAEL CLARK, BENJAMIN CARRELL. rec 1818. pp 466, 467

Deed dated 1817. HENRY DUEY & NANCY, his wife, to SAMUEL LANDIS of Green Co, OH. S 11, T 12, R 2W. Signed HENRY DUEY, NANCY (x) DUEY. Witness: none. rec 1818. pp 468, 469

Deed dated 1817. JOHN WILLIAMS to JAMES ANDREWS. S 7, T 12, R 1W. "REBECCA, his wife". Signed JOHN WILLIAMS, REBECCA WILLIAMS. Witness: none. rec 1818. pp 469, 470

Deed dated 1818. ANDREW ENDSLEY SR to ABRAHAM ENDSLEY. S 25, T 13, R 2W. Signed AND'W. ENDSLEY SR. Witness: ZACARIAH HIATT. rec 1818. p 470

Deed dated 1817. Commissioners of Wayne Co to JOSEPH HOLEMAN & WILLIAM SUMNER. H & S to build courthouse in Cntry, receive 30 acres in S 19, T 16, R 14E. Signed JAMES ODELL, THOMAS BEARD. Witness: DAVID HOOVER, JOHN C. KIBBEY. rec 1818. pp 471, 472

WAYNE COUNTY DEEDS: Book A

Deed dated 1813. JOHN BEARD to FREDERICK LONG. S 18, T 3, R 1W. "POLLY, his wife". Signed JOHN BEARD, POLLY BEARD. Witness: WILLIAM WHITEHEAD, ROBERT GALBRAITH. rec 1818. pp 472, 473, 474

Deed dated 1817. ZADOCK SMITH to WILLIAM JONES. S 18, T 14, R 13E. Signed ZADOCK SMITH. Witness: JOSEPH FLINT, DANIEL HEATON. rec 1818. pp 474, 475

Quitclaim dated 1817. MARGARET McCLELLAND JR, AGNES McCANDLESS & WILLIAM McCANDLESS, ELIZABETH DUNLAP & JAMES DUNLAP, JANE McCLELLAN, POLLY BAIN & JAMES BAIN, heirs of WILLIAM McCLELLAN dec, of Green Co, OH to WILLIAM McCLELLAN. Father WM died; son WM not of age. Brownsville (IN) lots 70, 44, 10 & 4- were purchased. Young WM to receive all free of claim. Signed MARGARET McCLELLAN, AGNES McCANLESS, WILLIAM McCANLESS, ELIZABETH DUNLAP, JAMES DUNLAP, JEAN McCLELLAN, MARY BAIN, JAMES BAIN. Witness: MARGARET McCLELLAN, DAVID LONGHEAD (in OH). rec 1818. pp 475, 476, 477

Deed dated 1818. ISRAEL ELLIOTT & WELLMET, his wife, to LAURENCE H. BRANNON. Cntrv lot 47. Signed ISRAEL ELLIOTT, WELMET (x) ELLIOTT. Witness: DAVID SACKETT, NATHAN JOHNSON. rec 1818. pp 477, 478

Deed dated 1818. ISRAEL ELLIOTT & WELLMET, his wife, to CALEB LEWIS. Cntrv lot 46. Signed ISRAEL ELLIOTT, WELMET (x) ELLIOTT. Witness: DAVID SACKETT, NATHAN JOHNSON. rec 1818. p 478

Bond dated 1818. JESSE WILLITS, LEVI WILLITS & THOMAS JONES bound to WILLIAM SUMNER, LAURENCE H. BRANNON & LARKIN REYNOLDS for $10,000; to provide material & labor to build courthouse at Cntrv. Signed JESSE WILLITS, THOMAS JONES, LEVI WILLITS. Witness: CALEB LEWIS, CALEB REYNOLDS. rec 1818. p 479

Deed dated 1818. PHINEAS McCREA & SARAH his wife, of Franklin Co, to JOHN INGELS of the same. S 13, 5 15, R 13E. Signed PHINEAS (x) McCREA, SARAH (x) McCAE. Witness: JOHN CONNER, J. FLINT. rec 1818. pp 479, 480

Deed dated 1817. JOHN GINN of Mercer Co, KY to LAURENCE GINN SR of the same. Jacksonburgh lots 3, 8. Signed JOHN GINN. Witness: WM. WORTHINGTON, WM. BRONAUGH. rec 1818. p 481

Deed dated 1817. THOMAS THOMAS of Franklin Co to MICAJAH FERGUSON. S 15, T 15, R 12E. Signed THOMAS THOMAS. Witness: ADAM BANKS, THOMAS BANKS. no rec date. p 482

WAYNE COUNTY DEEDS: Book A

Deed dated 1816. TABITHA WHITE to JONATHAN L. GRAVE. S 11 & 14, T 14, R 1W. Signed TABITHA (x) WHITE. Witness: none. rec 1818. p 483

Bill of Sale dated 1818. CHRISTOPHER RODDEY to SPENCER FREE. Blacksmith tools & others "too tedious to mention". Signed CHRISTOPHER (x) RODDEY. Witness: CALEB LEWIS, ABEL JOHNSON. Additional condition imposed by LAURENCE H. BRANNON to whom both RODDEY & FREE owe bond: that RODDEY will not drink spiritous liquors for two years from 16 March, 1818. If he does so, then FREE is to have no other damages beyond the tools. RODDEY & FREE to set up blacksmith business next June at Cntrv. Signed CHRISTOPHER (x) RODDEY, SPENCER (x) FREE. Witness as above. rec 1818. pp 484, 485

Deed dated 1818. LAURENCE H. BRANNON to THOMAS JONES Cntrv lot 47. Signed LAURENCE H. BRANNON. Witness: WM. SUMNER, ROBERT GALBRAITH. rec 1818. pp 485, 486

Deed dated 1817. HENRY BEESON of Highland Co, OH to JOSIAH DRAPER of same. S 12, T 13, R 1W. Signed HENRY BEESON, REBECCA (x) BEESON. Witness: JACOB WORLEY FRANCIS WORLEY (in OH). rec 1818. pp 486, 487

Deed dated 1818. LEVI BUTLER to PHINEAS ROBERDS. S 17, T 14, R 1W. Signed LEVI BUTLER. Witness: D.F. SACKETT. rec 1818. p 488

Deed dated 1818. JOHN BECK & SARAH, his wife, of Montgomery Co, OH to CHARLES CANADAY. S 22, T 16, R 13E. Signed JOHN BECK, SARAH (x) BECK. Witness: JAMES RUSSELL, JOHN RUSSELL (in OH). rec 1818. pp 488, 489, 490

Deed dated 1817. WM. McBROOM to JOHN LAUMAN. Salisbury lots 90, 101. Signed WILLIAM McBROOM, BETSY (x) McBROOM. Witness: none. rec 1818. pp 490, 491

Deed dated 1817. JEREMIAH COX to ROBERT MORRISON. Richmond lot 6. Signed JEREMIAH COX. Witness: none. rec 1818. pp 491, 492

Deed dated 1817. JEREMIAH COX to ROBERT MORRISON. Richmond lot 16. Signed JEREMIAH COX. Witness: none. rec 1818. pp 492, 493

Deed dated 1816. JOHN SMITH to ADAM BOYD. Richmond lot 7. Signed JOHN SMITH. Witness: none. rec 1818. p 493

WAYNE COUNTY DEEDS: Book A

Deed dated 1816. JOHN SMITH to ELI BROWN. Richmond lot 16. Signed JOHN SMITH. Witness: EDMOND GROVER. rec 1818. p 494

Deed dated 1817. JOHN SMITH to ROBERT HILL. S 5, T 13, R 1W. Signed JOHN SMITH. Witness: DAVID HOOVER, JESSE PEGG. rec 1818. pp 494, 495

Deed dated 1818. JOSEPH HOLEMAN to WILLIAM SUMNER. Cntrv lot in S 19, T 16, R 14E. Signed JOSEPH HOLEMAN, LYDIA HOLEMAN. Witness: LAURENCE H. BRANNON, LEVI JONES. rec 1818. pp 495, 496

Deed dated 1818. JOHN McCLAIN to WILLIAM SUMNER. Cntrv lots in S 20, T 16, R 14E, reserving lots 39, 46, 47, 58, 59. Signed JOHN McCLAIN, CATHERINE McCLAIN. Witness: LAURENCE H. BRANNON, LEVI JONES. rec 1818. p 497

Deed dated 1818. HENRY BRYAN & JANE, his wife, to SAMUEL CRAWFORD. S 36, T 16, R 13E. Signed HENRY BRYAN, JANE BRYAN. Witness: JOHN JONES, WILLIAM CRAWFORD. rec 1818. p 498

Deed dated 1818. JOHN HARVEY SR to AARON MILLER & BENJAMIN HARDMAN. S 29, T 17, R 13E. Signed JOHN HARVEY, JEAN HARVEY. Witness: SETH BALES. rec 1818. pp 498, 499

Deed dated 1818. PETER FLEMING & ELIZABETH, his wife to SAMUEL FLEMING. S 1, T 13, R 1W. Signed PETER FLEMING, ELIZABETH FLEMING. Witness: none. rec 1818. pp 499, 500

Deed dated 1818. JESSE ROBERTS to WILLIAM BUNDY. S 11, T 16, R 12E. "his wife, EMEY". Signed JESSE ROBERTS, EMEY ROBERTS. Witness: WILSON (x) ROBERTS. rec 1818. pp 500, 501

Deed dated 1818. PETER FLEMING & ELIZABETH, his wife to DAVID WASSON of Preble Co, OH. S 36, T 14, R 1W. Signed PETER FLEMING, ELIZABETH FLEMING. Witness: none. rec 1818. pp 501, 502

Deed dated 1817. ALEXANDER DICKEY of Bourbon Co, KY to ARCHIBALD BELL of same. S 21, T 16, R 14. Signed ALEXANDER DICKEY, BETSY DICKEY. Witness: THOS. JONES VAL PEERS (in KY). rec 1818. pp 502, 503, 504

Deed dated 1818. ARCHIBALD BELL of Bourbon Co, KY to THOMAS CULBERTSON of Clark Co, KY. S 31, T 16, R

WAYNE COUNTY DEEDS: Book A

14E. Signed ARCH'D. BELL, MILLY BELL. Witness: none rec 1818. pp 504, 505

Deed dated 1818. ARCHIBALD BELL of Bourbon Co, KY to WILLIAM BELL of same. S 31, T 16, R 14E. Signed ARCH'D. BELL, MILLY BELL. Witness: none. rec 1818. pp 505, 506

Deed dated 1817. CHARLES McGLOTHLEN & JANE, his wife to ABNER CHENAULT & WILLIAM FURGERSON, Trustees of Union Church. Land upon which the meeting house sits in S 18, T 14, R 14E. Signed C. McGLOTHLEN, JANE McGLOTHLIN. Witness: none. rec 1818. pp 506, 507

Deed dated 1818. JOHN MILLER to GEORGE HINDLE. S 34, T 13, R 1W. Signed JOHN MILLER, CHRISTENA MILLER. Witness: none. rec 1818. pp 507, 508

Deed dated 1818. JAMES RICHARDSON of Switzerland Co to MORGAN McMAHAN. S 21, T 12, R 1W. "patented to RICHARDSON, assignee of ANNANIAS E. STAFFORD in 1817" Signed JAMES RICHARDSON. Witness: none. rec 1818. pp 508, 509

Deed dated 1817. ISAAC MILLER to GEORGE MILLER. S 19 T 15, R 13. Signed ISAAC MILLER, MARTHA MILLER. Witness: JOHN MILLER, JOSEPH FLINT. rec 1818. pp 509,510

Deed dated 1818. THOMAS BEARD to GEORGE JOHN ISAAC & ABRAHAM MILLER. (in text, commas between names: GEORGE, JOHN, ISAAC) T 15, R 13, S 19. Signed THOMAS BEARD. Witness: JOHN WILSON, JOSEPH LOWER. rec 1818. pp 510, 511

Deed dated 1818. NATHAN SMITH to JOHN GORDEN of Preble Co, OH. S 24, T 13, R 2W. Signed NATHAN SMITH, MARY SMITH. Witness: none. rec 1818. JP's note: MARY, his wife. pp 511, 512

Deed dated 1817. GEORGE MILLER to JOHN MILLER. S 19, T 15, R 13E. "LYDIA, wife of GEORGE". Signed GEORGE MILLER, LYDIA MILLER. Witness: ISAAC MILLER, MARTHA MILLER. rec 1818. pp 512, 513

Deed dated 1818. JOHN SMITH to STEPHEN COX. Richmond lot 60. Signed JOHN SMITH. Witness: none. rec 1818. pp 513, 514

Deed dated 1817. HENRY PALIN to JOSEPH ASHTON. S 1, T 14, R 1W. "SARAH, wife of HENRY". Signed HENRY PALIN, SARAH (x) PALIN. Witness: none. rec 1818. pp 514, 515

WAYNE COUNTY DEEDS: Book A

POA dated 1818. LOT PUGH & MICAJAH F. WILLIAMS, both of Cincinnati, OH, appt ARTHUR HENRIE of Miami town, Hamilton Co, OH to convey deeds for Cntrv lots. Signed L. PUGH, M.F. WILLIAMS. Witness: TH. M. BORRON, E. STONE. no rec date. p 515

Deed dated 1818. JONATHAN JUSTICE & ELIZABETH, his wife, to AARON WHITE of Pasquatank Co, NC. S 2, T 15, R 12. Signed JONATHAN JUSTICE, ELIZABETH JUSTICE. Witness: ISAIAH DRURY, JONATHAN WINSLOW. rec 1818. pp 515, 516

Deed dated 1818. THOMAS SYMONS & HANNAH, his wife, to JOHN BELL. S 35, T 16, R 12E. Signed THOMAS SYMONS, HANNAH SYMONS. Witness: MARY HODG, LANCELOT BELL. rec 1818. pp 516, 517, 518

Deed dated 1818. ROBERT HILL to WILLIAM COX. S 2, T 13, R 1W. Signed ROBERT HILL, SUSANNAH HILL. Witness: NATHAN HILL. rec 1818. pp 518, 519

Deed dated 1818. NATHAN HILL to WILLIAM COX. S 2, T 13, R 1W. Signed NATHAN HILL, ELIZABETH HILL. Witness: PETER EDWARDS. rec 1818. pp 519, 520

Deed dated 1818. NATHAN HILL to WILLIAM COX. S 2, T 13, R 1W. Signed NATHAN HILL, ELIZABETH HILL. Witness: PETER EDWARDS. rec 1818. pp 520, 521

Deed dated 1818. WM. SUMNER & NANCY, his wife to MARTIN MARTINDALE. Cntrv lot 68. Signed WM. SUMNER, NANCY SUMNER. Witness: JOHN JONES. rec 1818. p 522

Deed dated 1818. CALEB LEWIS to ROBERT BLACK. Cntrv lot 46. Signed CALEB LEWIS. Witness: WILLIAM CRAWFORD, JAMES BLACK JR. rec 1818. p 523

Deed dated 1818. JAMES BLACK JR to WILLIAM SUMNER. Cntrv lot in S 29, T 16, R 14W. Signed JAMES BLACK JR. Witness: JOHN GORDEN. rec 1818. p 524

Deed dated 1818. WM. SUMNER & NANCY, his wife, to MOSES MARTINDALE. Cntrv lot 61. Signed WM. SUMNER, NANCY SUMNER. Witness: ELIZABETH ALLISON. rec 1818. p 525

Deed dated 1817. JAMES SHAW & MARY, his wife, to JOHN BEARD JR. S 12, T 15, R 12. Signed JAMES SHAW, MARY (x) SHAW. Witness: JOHN BEARD, JOHN FRAIZER. rec 1818. pp 526, 527, 528

WAYNE COUNTY DEEDS: Book A

Deed dated 1817. THOMAS BEARD to JOHN BEARD JR. T 15, R 12, S 12. Signed THOMAS BEARD. Witness: JOHN BEARD, ELI WRIGHT. rec 1818. pp 528, 529, 530

Deed dated 1817. THOMAS BEARD to PHILEMON PLUMMER. S 25, T 15, R 12E. Signed THOMAS BEARD. Witness: PATRICK BEARD, JOHN BEARD. rec 1818. pp 530, 531, 532

Deed dated 1817. THOMAS BEARD to WILLIAM BEARD. S 25 T 15, R 12E. Signed THOMAS BEARD. Witness: PATRICK BEARD, JOHN BEARD. rec 1818. pp 532, 533

Deed dated 1818. ADAM JACK of Warren Co, OH to WILLIAM VANMETRE of Franklin Co. S 27, T 15, R 12E. Signed ADAM JACK, HANNAH JACK. Witness: ROBERT LEE, NATHAN LUSE (in OH). rec 1818. pp 533, 534, 535

Deed dated 1817. MARTIN MARTINDALE to JOHN JONES. Cntrv lot 68. "ELIZABETH, his wife". Signed MARTIN MARTINDALE, ELIZABETH MARTINDALE. Witness: WILLIAM SUMNER, BARCLAY BENBOW. rec 1818. pp 536, 537, 538

Deed dated 1818. PHILIP LYBROOK to JOHN LYBROOK. "JOHN as a lawful heir of PHILIP is gifted granted donated the above" S 25, T 12, R 1W. Signed PHILIP LYBROOK, ANY (x) LYBROOK. Witness: none. rec 1818. pp 538, 539, 540

Deed dated 1818. PHILIP LYBROOK to JACOB LYBROOK. "JACOB as a lawful heir of PHILIP is gifted granted donated the above" S 25, T 12, R 1W. Signed PHILIP LYBROOK, ANY (x) LYBROOK. Witness: none. rec 1818. pp 540, 541, 542

Deed dated 1818. PHILIP LYBROOK to BALTZER LYBROOK. "BALTZER as a lawful heir of PHILIP is gifted granted donated the above" S 36, T 12, R 1W. Signed PHILIP LYBROOK, ANY (x) LYBROOK. Witness: none. JP's note: ANA LYBROOK, wife of PHILIP. rec 1818. pp 542, 543, 544

Deed dated 1817. JOHN SMITH to ALICK THORNBURY of Highland Co, OH. Richmond lot 52. Signed JOHN SMITH. Witness: STEPHEN HOLLOWAY, JOSIAH DRAPER JR. rec 1818. p 544

Deed dated 1818. SETH MILLS & CHARITY, his wife, & JOHN GWIN & CHARITY, his wife, to MOSES ROBERTS of Knox Co, TN. S 30, T 18, R 13E. Signed SETH MILLS, CHARITY MILLS, JOHN GWIN, CHARITY GWIN. Witness: MILES MARSHILL, JOHN JORDAN, ISAAC MILLS. rec 1818. pp 545, 546

WAYNE COUNTY DEEDS: Book A

Deed dated 1817. JOHN HOOVER JR of Miami Co, OH to HENRY PALIN. S 23, T 16, R 12E. "ELIZABETH, his wife". Signed JOHN HOOVER JR, ELIZABETH HOOVER. Witness: CALEB NIXON, HENRY HOOVER (in OH). rec 1818. pp 546, 547, 548, 549

Deed dated 1818. ARTHUR HENRIE & GRACE, his wife, LOT PUGH & RACHEL, his wife, MICAJAH F. WILLIAMS & HANNAH, his wife, all of Hamilton Co, OH, to SAMUEL CAMMACK. Cntrv lot 9, 11, 26. Signed ARTHUR HENRIE, RACHEL A. PUGH, GRACE M. HENRIE, MICAJAH F. WILLIAMS, L. PUGH, HANNAH L. WILLIAMS. Witness: J. EMBREE, A. J. WHEELER. rec 1818. pp 549, 550

Deed dated 1817. JOHN SMITH to WILLIAM JUSTICE. Richmond lot 55. Signed JOHN SMITH. Witness: none. rec 1818. pp 550, 551

Deed dated 1818. JEREMIAH COX to STEPHEN THOMAS & WILLIAM JUSTICE. Richmond lot 14. Signed JEREMIAH COX. Witness: GEORGE SHUGART. rec 1818. pp 551, 552

Deed dated 1818. WILLIAM SUMNER to NATHAN JOHNSON. Cntrv lot 57. Signed WM. SUMNER, NANCY SUMNER. Witness: D.F. SACKETT, SAMUEL LOUTHAIN. rec 1818. pp 552, 553

Deed dated 1818. NATHAN JOHNSON to SAMUEL LOUTHAIN. Cntrv lot 57. Signed NATHAN JOHNSON. Witness: D.F. SACKETT, MARTHA SACKETT. rec 1818. p 554

Deed dated 1818. JONATHAN JESSOP to JESSE HILL. S 2, T 13, R 1W. "ELIZABETH, his wife" Signed JONATHAN JESSOP, ELIZABETH (x) JESSOP. Witness: MARTHA SACKETT. rec 1818. pp 555, 556

Receipt dated 1818. Cincinnati Land Office to SAMUEL McGEORGE. Full pay't for S 23, T 15, R 12E. Signed "for PEYTON S. SYMMES, Register, D. F. CARNEY". p 556

Assignment dated 1818. SAMUEL McGEORGE to WILLIAM PHILIPS, assignee. Rights to land in deed above. Signed SAMUEL McGEORGE. p 556.

End of Wayne County Book A.

Book B

Deed dated 1816. USA to RICHARD W. CHEESEMAN. S 29, T 17, R 14E. rec 1818. p 3

WAYNE COUNTY DEEDS: Book B

Deed dated 1818. WM. SUMNER & NANCY, his wife, to CALEB LEWIS. Cntrv lot 69. Signed WM. SUMNER, NANCY SUMNER. Witness: LAURENCE H. BRANNON. rec 1818. p 3

Deed dated 1818. ARTHUR HENRIE & GRACE, his wife, LOT PUGH & RACHEL, his wife, MICAJAH T. WILLIAMS & HANNAH, his wife, all of Hamilton Co, OH, to THOMAS CASON. Cntrv lots 17, 18. Signed ARTHUR HENRIE, RACHEL A. PUGH, GRACE M. HENRIE, MICAJAH T. WILLIAMS, LOT PUGH, HANNAH J. WILLIAMS. Witness: J. EMBREE, A.J. WHEELER. rec 1818. pp 1 & 5

Deed dated 1818. ADAM JACK of Warren Co, OH to WILLIAM VANMETRE of Franklin Co. S 27, T 15, R 12E. Signed ADAM JACK, HANNAH JACK. Witness: ROBERT LEE, NATHANIEL LUSE. rec 1818. pp 5, 6

Deed dated 1818. ETHAN STONE of Cincinnati, OH to ARTHUR HENRIE, LOT PUGH & MICAJAH T. WILLIAMS. S 19, T 16, R 14E. Signed ETHAN STONE, ABIGAIL M. STONE. Witness: MARY FARRAR, JOHN MAHARD (in OH). rec 1818. pp 6, 7

Deed dated 1818. ARTHUR HENRIE & GRACE, his wife, LOT PUGH & RACHEL, his wife, MICAJAH T. WILLIAMS & HANNAH, his wife, all of Hamilton Co, OH, to ROBERT HILL & ROBERT MORRISON. Cntrv lots 41 through 54 inclusive, 65 through 80 inclusive. Signed ARTHUR HENRIE, RACHEL A. PUGH, GRACE M. HENRIE, MICAJAH T. WILLIAMS, LOT PUGH, HANNAH J. WILLIAMS. Witness: J. EMBREE, A.J. WHEELER. rec 1818. pp 7, 8

Deed dated 1818. ARTHUR HENRIE & GRACE, his wife, LOT PUGH & RACHEL, his wife, MICAJAH T. WILLIAMS & HANNAH, his wife, all of Hamilton Co, OH, to ISAAC BEESON. Cntrv lot 25. Signed ARTHUR HENRIE, RACHEL A. PUGH, GRACE M. HENRIE, MICAJAH T. WILLIAMS, LOT PUGH, HANNAH J. WILLIAMS. Witness: J. EMBREE, A.J. WHEELER. rec 1818. pp 8, 9

Deed dated 1818. ARTHUR HENRIE & GRACE, his wife, LOT PUGH & RACHEL, his wife, MICAJAH T. WILLIAMS & HANNAH, his wife, all of Hamilton Co, OH, to DANIEL STONE. Cntrv lot 25. Signed ARTHUR HENRIE, RACHEL A. PUGH, GRACE M. HENRIE, MICAJAH T. WILLIAMS, LOT PUGH, HANNAH J. WILLIAMS. Witness: J. EMBREE, A.J. WHEELER. rec 1818. pp 9, 10

Deed dated 1818. ARTHUR HENRIE & GRACE, his wife, LOT PUGH & RACHEL, his wife, MICAJAH T. WILLIAMS & HANNAH, his wife, all of Hamilton Co, OH, to LEVI JONES. Cntrv lot 31. Signed ARTHUR HENRIE, RACHEL

WAYNE COUNTY DEEDS: Book B

A. PUGH, GRACE M. HENRIE, MICAJAH T. WILLIAMS, LOT PUGH, HANNAH J. WILLIAMS. Witness: J. EMBREE, A.J. WHEELER. rec 1818. p 10

Deed dated 1818. ARTHUR HENRIE & GRACE, his wife, LOT PUGH & RACHEL, his wife, MICAJAH T. WILLIAMS & HANNAH, his wife, all of Hamilton Co, OH, to JOHN McLAIN. Cntrv lot 3. Signed ARTHUR HENRIE, RACHEL A. PUGH, GRACE M. HENRIE, MICAJAH T. WILLIAMS, LOT PUGH, HANNAH J. WILLIAMS. Witness: J. EMBREE, A.J. WHEELER. rec 1818. pp 10, 11

Deed dated 1818. ARTHUR HENRIE & GRACE, his wife, LOT PUGH & RACHEL, his wife, MICAJAH T. WILLIAMS & HANNAH, his wife, all of Hamilton Co, OH, to JOSEPH COOK. Cntrv lot 40. Signed ARTHUR HENRIE, RACHEL A. PUGH, GRACE M. HENRIE, MICAJAH T. WILLIAMS, LOT PUGH, HANNAH J. WILLIAMS. Witness: J. EMBREE, A.J. WHEELER. rec 1818. pp 11, 12

Deed dated 1818. ARTHUR HENRIE & GRACE, his wife, LOT PUGH & RACHEL, his wife, MICAJAH T. WILLIAMS & HANNAH, his wife, all of Hamilton Co, OH, to MARTIN MARTINDALE. Cntrv lot 2. Signed ARTHUR HENRIE, RACHEL A. PUGH, GRACE M. HENRIE, MICAJAH T. WILLIAMS LOT PUGH, HANNAH J. WILLIAMS. Witness: J. EMBREE, A.J. WHEELER. rec 1818. pp 12, 13

Deed dated 1818. ARTHUR HENRIE & GRACE, his wife, LOT PUGH & RACHEL, his wife, MICAJAH T. WILLIAMS & HANNAH, his wife, all of Hamilton Co, OH, to JOHN HUFF. Cntrv lot 34. Signed ARTHUR HENRIE, RACHEL A. PUGH, GRACE M. HENRIE, MICAJAH T. WILLIAMS, LOT PUGH, HANNAH J. WILLIAMS. Witness: J. EMBREE, A.J. WHEELER rec 1818. p 13

Deed dated 1818. ARTHUR HENRIE & GRACE, his wife, LOT PUGH & RACHEL, his wife, MICAJAH T. WILLIAMS & HANNAH, his wife, all of Hamilton Co, OH, to NATHAN COMMONS. Cntrv lot 7. Signed ARTHUR HENRIE, RACHEL A. PUGH, GRACE M. HENRIE, MICAJAH T. WILLIAMS, LOT PUGH, HANNAH J. WILLIAMS. Witness: J. EMBREE, A.J. WHEELER. rec 1818. pp 13, 14

Deed dated 1818. ARTHUR HENRIE & GRACE, his wife, LOT PUGH & RACHEL, his wife, MICAJAH T. WILLIAMS & HANNAH, his wife, all of Hamilton Co, OH, to NATHAN JOHNSON. Cntrv lots 19, 20. Signed ARTHUR HENRIE, RACHEL A. PUGH, GRACE M. HENRIE, MICAJAH T. WILLIAMS, LOT PUGH, HANNAH J. WILLIAMS. Witness: J. EMBREE, A.J. WHEELER. rec 1818. pp 14, 15

WAYNE COUNTY DEEDS: Book B

Deed dated 1818. ARTHUR HENRIE & GRACE, his wife, LOT PUGH & RACHEL, his wife, MICAJAH T. WILLIAMS & HANNAH, his wife, all of Hamilton Co, OH, to WILLIAM GENTRY. Cntry lot 23. Signed ARTHUR HENRIE, RACHEL A. PUGH, GRACE M. HENRIE, MICAJAH T. WILLIAMS, LOT PUGH, HANNAH J. WILLIAMS. Witness: J. EMBREE, A.J. WHEELER. rec 1818. pp 15, 16

Deed dated 1818. ARTHUR HENRIE & GRACE, his wife, LOT PUGH & RACHEL, his wife, MICAJAH T. WILLIAMS & HANNAH, his wife, all of Hamilton Co, OH, to LAURENCE H. BRANNON. Cntry lots 5, 27, 28. Signed ARTHUR HENRIE, RACHEL A. PUGH, GRACE M. HENRIE, MICAJAH T. WILLIAMS, LOT PUGH, HANNAH J. WILLIAMS. Witness: J. EMBREE, A.J. WHEELER. rec 1818. pp 16, 17

Deed dated 1818. ARTHUR HENRIE & GRACE, his wife, LOT PUGH & RACHEL, his wife, MICAJAH T. WILLIAMS & HANNAH, his wife, all of Hamilton Co, OH, to CALEB REYNOLDS. Cntry lot 30. Signed ARTHUR HENRIE, RACHEL A. PUGH, GRACE M. HENRIE, MICAJAH T. WILLIAMS, LOT PUGH, HANNAH J. WILLIAMS. Witness: J. EMBREE, A.J. WHEELER. rec 1818. p 17

Deed dated 1818. ARTHUR HENRIE & GRACE, his wife, LOT PUGH & RACHEL, his wife, MICAJAH T. WILLIAMS & HANNAH, his wife, all of Hamilton Co, OH, to WILLIAM CRAWFORD. Cntry lot 21. Signed ARTHUR HENRIE, RACHEL A. PUGH, GRACE M. HENRIE, MICAJAH T. WILLIAMS, LOT PUGH, HANNAH J. WILLIAMS. Witness: J. EMBREE, A.J. WHEELER. rec 1818. pp 17, 18

Deed dated 1818. JAMES PORTER to JOHN HARDMAN of Montgomery Co, OH. S 19, T 17, R 13. "his wife, MARGARET." Signed JAMES PORTER, MARGARET PORTER. Witness: DAVID MARTINDALE, JACOB GALYEAN. rec 1818. pp 18, 19

Deed dated 1817. JOHN SHORTRIDGE to ELISHA SHORTRIDGE S 25, T 16, R 12. "MARGARET, his wife". Signed JOHN SHORTRIDGE, MARGET SHORTRIDGE. Witness: THOMAS J. WARMAN, JOHN BEARD. rec 1818. pp 19, 20

Deed dated 1818. JOHN HUFF to ELISHA SHORTRIDGE. Cntry lot 35. Signed JOHN (x) HUFF. Witness: WILLIAM LUNKEN. rec 1818. p 20

Deed dated 1818. ROBERT LEAVELL to LORING A. WALDO. Jacksonburgh lots 5, 6. Signed ROBERT LEAVELL, SALLY (x) LEAVELL. Witness: none. rec 1818. pp 20, 21

Deed dated 1817. THOMAS BEARD FROM JACOB WEIMIRE &

WAYNE COUNTY DEEDS: Book B

ELIZABETH, his wife. T 15, R 13, S 21. Signed JACOB (x) WEIMIRE, ELIZABETH WEIMIRE. Witness: WILLIAM FARLOW, SIMEON FARLOW. rec 1818. pp 21, 22

Deed dated 1817. THOMAS BEARD FROM ELI WIGHT. T 15, R 12, S 24. Signed ELI WRIGHT, ELIZABETH (x) WRIGHT. Witness: JOHN BEARD, WM. BEARD. rec 1818. p 22

Deed dated 1818. WILLIAM THORN & RACHEL, his wife, of Green Co, OH to WILLIAM SAINT. S 24, T 16, R 12. Signed WILLIAM THORN, RACHEL THORN. Witness: THOMAS EMBREE, ESTHER EMBREE. rec 1818. p 23

Deed dated 1817. LAURENCE GINN SR of Mason Co, KY to EZEKEL LEAVELL. Jacksonburgh lots 3, 8. Signed LAURENCE GINN. Witness: ELI GASSEN, THOMAS J. WARNER. rec 1818. pp 23, 24

Sheriff's sale dated 1817. JOHN TURNER, Sheriff of Wayne Co to PHILIP PENNYWITT of Hamilton Co, OH. PENNYWITT recovered at law against JOHN PATTERSON & THOMAS PATTERSON. Sheriff ordered to sell goods & land of JOHN PATTERSON & SAMUEL PATTERSON. S 3, T 15, R 13E sold at auction to PENNYWITT. Signed JOHN TURNER, Sheriff. Witness: none. rec 1818. pp 24, 25

Deed dated 1818. HENRY HOOVER to BOWATER CANADAY. S 10, T 16, R 13. "ELIZABETH, his wife". Signed HENRY HOOVER, ELIZABETH (x) HOOVER. Witness: none. rec 1818. pp 25, 26

Deed dated 1818. JOSIAH ELSTON SR & REBECKAH, his wife, to JOSIAH ELSTON JR. S 6, T 12, R 1W. Signed JOSIAH ELSTON, REBECKAH ELSTON. Witness: none. rec 1818. pp 26, 27

Deed dated 1818. BENJAMIN BROWN of Harrison Twp to JOSEPH PRATHER. S 32, R 1W in Harrison Twp. "FANNY, his wife". Signed BENJAMIN (x) BROWN, FANNY (x) BROWN. rec 1818. p 27

Deed dated 1817. JOHN DODDRIDGE & AVIS, his wife, to MORDICA MORGAN. S 24, T 15, R 13. Signed JOHN DODDRIDGE, AVIS DODDRIDGE. Witness: MONTGOMERY M. CALL, ELIZABETH FLINT. rec 1818. p 28

Deed dated 1818. GEORGE ISH & MARIUM ISH to ISRAEL ABRAHAMS. S 32, T 16, R 13E. Signed GEORGE ISH, MARIUM ISH. Witness: JAMES CONOVER, WM. G. REYNOLDS rec 1818. p 29

WAYNE COUNTY DEEDS: Book B

Deed dated 1818. NATHAN JOHNSON to JAMES BAILEY. Cntrv lot 19. Signed NATHAN JOHNSON. Witness: KINCHEN JOHNSON. rec 1818. pp 29, 30

Deed dated 1818. ROBERT LEAVELL to JOHN McKEE. Jacksonburgh lots 23, 24, 33, 36. Signed ROBERT LEAVELL, SALLY (x) LEAVELL. Witness: none. rec 1818. p 30

Deed dated 1818. JOSEPH OVERMAN to WILLIAM COX. S 2, T 13, R 1W. "HULDAH, his wife". Signed JOSEPH OVERMAN, HULDAH OVERMAN. Witness: ABNER OVERMAN. rec 1818. pp 30, 31

Deed dated 1818. JEREMIAH COX to JOHN HILL. Richmond lot 14. Signed JEREMIAH COX. Witness: FRANCIS CLARK. rec 1818. p 31

Deed dated 1818. ENOS GRAVE & BETTY, his wife, to NATHAN GRAVE. S 23, T 14, R 1W. Signed ENOS GRAVE, BETTY GRAVE. Witness: ADAM BOYD. rec 1818. pp 31, 32

Deed dated 1818. JONATHAN L. GRAVE & LYDIA, his wife to ENOS GRAVE. S 14, T 14, R 1W. Signed JONATHAN L. GRAVE, LYDIA GRAVE. Witness: ADAM BOYD. rec 1818. p 32

Deed dated 1818. ENOS GRAVE & BETTY, his wife, to JACOB GRAVE. S 13, T 14, R 1W. Signed ENOS GRAVE, BETTY GRAVE. Witness: ADAM BOYD. rec 1818. p 33

Deed dated 1818. ENOS GRAVE & BETTY, his wife, to JONATHAN L. GRAVE. S 3, T 14, R 1W. Signed ENOS GRAVE, BETTY GRAVE. Witness: ADAM BOYD, THOMAS HATTON. rec 1818. pp 33, 34

Deed dated 1817. TABITHA WHITE to JONATHAN L. GRAVE. S 11, T 14, R 1W. Signed TABITHA (x) WHITE. Witness: DAVID HOOVER, ABNER CLAWSON. rec 1818. p 34

Deed dated 1818. NATHAN JOHNSON to LAURENCE H. BRANNON. Cntrv lot 57. Signed NATHAN JOHNSON. Witness: SYLVAN B. MORRIS, ELIAS WILLITS. rec 1818. pp 34, 35

Deed dated 1817. HENRY GARRETT & MARY, his wife, of Perry Twp to DANIEL LANDIS. S 11, T 12, R 2W. "tract granted to ISAAC NEELEY...1815...conveyed to NATHANIEL REYAN". Signed HENRY GARRETT, MARY (x) GARRETT. Witness: ABEL LOMAX, RICHARD LEWIS. rec 1818. pp 35, 36

Deed dated 1818. NATHAN JOHNSON to LAURENCE H. BRANNON. Cntrv lot 57. Signed NATHAN JOHNSON. Witness:

WAYNE COUNTY DEEDS: Book B

JOHN LEWIS, JOHN GALBREATH. rec 1818. pp 36, 37
Deed dated 1818. NATHAN JOHNSON to JOHN LEWIS. Cntrv lot 57. Signed NATHAN JOHNSON. Witness: LAURENCE H. BRANNON, JOHN GALBREATH. rec 1818. pp 37, 38

Deed dated 1817. JOSEPH COX to HENRY LAUMAN. Salisbury lot 109. "MARY, his wife". Signed JOSEPH COX, MARY (x) COX. Witness: JOSEPH DEUEY, MOSES COX. rec 1818. p 38

Deed dated 1818. LAURENCE H. BRANNON to JAMES BLACK SR. Cntrv lot 47. Signe LAURENCE H. BRANNON. Witness: D. F. SACKETT. rec 1818. pp 38, 39

Deed dated 1818. NATHAN JOHNSON to ABEL JOHNSON. Cntrv lot 57. Signed NATHAN JOHNSON. Witness: D. F. SACKETT. rec 1818. p 39

Deed dated 1818. WM. SUMNER & NANCY, his wife, to LAURENCE H. BRANNON. Cntrv lots 56, 16, 5, 113, 98, 30, 103, 107, 110, 81, 60, 67, 15, 206 through 209, 106, 137, 138, 139, 141, 142, 116, 177, 178, 197, 198, 199, 223, 224, 225, 218, 219, 141, 118, 119. Signed WM. SUMNER, NANCY SUMNER. Witness: LEVI JONES, JOHN RALSTON. rec 1818. pp 39, 40

Deed dated 1818. WM. SUMNER & NANCY, his wife, to LAURENCE H. BRANNON. Cntrv lots 1, 2, 65, 66, 70, 38. Signed WM. SUMNER, NANCY SUMNER. Witness: LEVI JONES, JOHN RALSTON. rec 1818. pp 40, 41

Deed dated 1818. WM. SUMNER & NANCY, his wife, to JOHN LEWIS & JESSE WILLIAMS. Cntrv lot 74. Signed WM. SUMNER, NANCY SUMNER. Witness: MARTHA SACKETT. rec 1818. p 41

Deed dated 1818. WM. SUMNER & NANCY, his wife, to JOHN ROLSTON. Cntrv lot 75. Signed WM. SUMNER, NANCY SUMNER. Witness: LAURENCE H. BRANNON. rec 1818. p 42

Deed dated 1818. WM. SUMNER & NANCY, his wife, to JOHN SLATER. Cntrv lot 23. Signed WM. SUMNER, NANCY SUMNER. Witness: JAMES (x) JONES. rec 1818. p 42

Deed dated 1818. WM. SUMNER & NANCY, his wife, to CALEB REYNOLDS. Cntrv lots 26, 27. Signed WM. SUMNER, NANCY SUMNER. Witness: MARTHA SACKETT. rec 1818. p 43

Deed dated 1818. ISRAEL ELLIOTT to THOMAS JONES. S 20 T 16, R 14. Signed ISRAEL ELLIOTT, WELMET (x) ELLIOTT

WAYNE COUNTY DEEDS: Book B

Witness: none. rec 1818. pp 43, 44

Deed dated 1817. CALEB EASTERLING & MARTHA his wife, of Clinton Co, OH to JOHN A. RANCK of Montgomery Co, OH. S 11, T 12, R 2W. "CALEB...assignee of THOMAS LEWIS...in 1810". Signed CALEB EASTERLING, MARTHA EASTERLING. Witness: M. ROBINSON, JAMES BACKLES. rec 1818. pp 44, 45

Deed dated 1817. WM. TOWNSEND of Knox Co to OVID BOON. S 13, T 13, R 2W. Signed WILLIAM TOWNSEND. Witness: JOHN C. KIBBEY, JESSE BURK. JP's note: SARAH, wife of WILLIAM. rec 1818. pp 45, 46

Deed dated 1818. PETER LENNEN of Franklin Co to ISAAC GARDNER of same. "at FREDERICK SUMNER's corner.. with P. SUMMIE & SARAH MINER". S 33, T 12, R 1W. Signed PETER (x) LENNON, BARBARA (x) LENNON. Witness: PAUL GARDNER, DAVID GARDNER. rec 1818. pp 46, 47

Deed dated 1817. MARY MINER to PETER LENON. S 33, T 12, R 1W. Signed MARY (x) MINER. Witness: A. ESTEP. rec 1818. pp 47, 48

Deed dated 1818. ROBERT COMMONS to NATHAN HILL. S 13 T 16, R 13E. "RUTH, his wife". Signed ROBERT COMMONS, RUTH COMMONS. Witness: none. rec 1818. p 48

Deed dated 1818. SAMUEL JONES to DAVID YOUNG. T 16, R 13, S 7. Signed SAMUEL JONES. Witness: none. rec 1818. p 49

Deed dated 1818. DAVID YOUNG to JOHN McKEE. S 7, T 16, R 13E. Signed DAVID YOUNG. Witness: RENNY JULIAN. rec 1818. p 49

Deed dated 1818. DAVID YOUNG to SHUBAL JULIAN. S 7, T 16, R 13E. "SARAH, his wife". Signed DAVID YOUNG, SARAH YOUNG. Witness: RENNY JULIAN. rec 1818. p 50

Deed dated 1818. HENRY LYBROOK of Preble Co (OH?) to EDWIN MOSS. S 26, T 12, R 1W. Signed HENRY LYBROOK, HANNAH (x) LYBROOK. Witness: JACOB KINGERY, REBECKAH (x) ELDER. rec 1818. pp 50, 51

Deed dated 1816. USA to JACOB SINKS. S 19, T 16, R 14. rec 1818. p 51

Deed dated 1818. USA to ISAAC JULIAN, assignee of CHRISTOPHER RODDEY. S 31, T 16, R 14E. pp 51, 52

Deed dated 1818. JONATHAN HIGGINS & MARGARET, his

WAYNE COUNTY DEEDS: Book B

wife, to JACOB COZAD of Green Co, OH. S 33, T 15, R 13E. Signed JONATHAN (x) HIGGINS, MARGARET (x) HIGGINS. Witness: ELI HEATON. rec 1818. pp 52, 53

Deed dated 1818. JAMES TOWNSEND to JOHN MAXWELL & JACOB ELLIOTT, Overseers of the West Grove Meeting. S 18, T 16, R 14. Signed JAMES TOWNSEND, ROSANNA (x) TOWNSEND. Witness: WILLIAM HASTINGS, JOSEPH COX. rec 1818. p 53

Deed dated 1816. JEREMIAH COX to STEPHEN MACY of Montgomery Co, OH. Richmond lot 25. Signed JEREMIAH COX. Witness: ROBERT MORRISON. rec 1818. pp 53, 54

Deed dated 1818. JOSEPH SPENCER to ELIJAH WADDLE. S 34, T 12, R 1W. Signed JOSEPH SPENCER. Witness: none. rec 1818. p 54

Deed dated 1817. JOEL MOORE & POLLY, his wife, to EDWARD CLANTON. S 5, T 12, R 1W. Signed JOEL MOORE, POLLY (x) MOORE. Witness: NANCY ESTELL. rec 1818. pp 54, 55

Deed dated 1818. ISAAC JULIAN to ARCHIBALD BELL of Bourbon Co, KY. S 30, T 16, R 14E. Signed ISAAC JULIAN, REBECKAH JULIAN. Witness: none. rec 1818. pp 55, 56

Deed dated 1818. JOSEPH SPENCER to BENJAMIN NUTTER. S 35, T 12, R 1W. Signed JOSEPH SPENCER. Witness: none. rec 1818. p 56

Deed dated 1818. JAMES BEADWELL SR & HESTER his wife to GEORGE RINKER JR of Preble Co, OH. S 14, T 12, R 1W. Signed JAMES (x) BEADWELL, HESTER (x) BEADWELL. Witness: none. rec 1818. pp 56, 57

Deed dated 1818. THOMAS T. LEWIS to JOHN RIFE. S 9, T 12, R 1W. "SARAH, his wife". Signed THOMAS T. LEWIS, SARAH LEWIS. Witness: none. rec 1818. p 57

Deed dated 1818. WILLIAM SMITH of Lincoln Co TN to CALEB MORRIS of Pasquotank Co, NC. S 14, T 16, R 12E. Signed WILLIAM SMITH. Witness: SAMUEL WOODS, JEHOSHAPHAT MORRIS. rec 1818. pp 57, 58

Deed dated 1818. THOMAS CLIFFORD of Green Co, OH to WILLIAM & DAVID SUTHERLAND. Salisbury lot 84. Signed THOMAS CLIFFORD. Witness: REUBEN STRONG, BARBARY (x) STRONG (in OH). rec 1818. pp 58, 59

Deed dated 1818. JAMES MARTINDALE to THOMAS HATFIELD

WAYNE COUNTY DEEDS: Book B

S 26, T 17, R 13E. "ELIZABETH, his wife". Signed JAMES MARTINDALE, ELIZABETH (x) MARTINDALE. Witness: LISMUND BASYE, PHILIP RENBERGER. rec 1818. pp 59, 60

Deed dated 1818. JAMES MARTINDALE to THOMAS HATFIELD S 26, T 17, R 13E. Signed JAMES MARTINDALE, ELIZABETH (x) MARTINDALE. Witness: JOHN MARSHILL, JOHN (x) LITTLE. rec 1818. p 60

Deed dated 1818. AMOS HIGGINS of Preble Co. OH to WILLIAM EDWARDS. S 12, T 13, R 1W. Signed AMOS HIGGINS, BETSY (x) HIGGINS. Witness: none. rec 1818. pp 60, 61

Deed dated 1818. JOSEPH EVANS of Warren Co, OH to JOSEPH EVANS JR "son of said JOSEPH". S 19, T 11, R 14E. Signed JOSEPH EVANS, LYDIA EVANS. Witness: MARTHA HOMAN, WYLLYS PIERSON. rec 1818. pp 61, 62

Deed dated 1818. NATHAN HILL to BENJAMIN HILL. S 14, T 16, R 13E. Signed NATHAN HILL, ELIZABETH HILL. Witness: none. rec 1818. pp 62, 63

Deed dated 1818. JOSEPH LEWIS & PEGGY, his wife. to NICHOLAS DRULY. S 11, T 12, R 1W. Signed JOSEPH (x) LEWIS, PEGGY (x) LEWIS. Witness: none. rec 1818. pp 63, 64

Deed dated 1817. EDWARD CLANTON & RACHEL, his wife, to NICHOLAS DRULY. S 5, T 12, R 1W. Signed EDWARD CLANTON, RACHEL (x) CLANTON. Witness: ISAAC ESTELE, ISAAC LEWIS. rec 1818. p 64

Deed dated 1818. ISAAC LEWIS & PATSEY, his wife, to HENRY CUPPEY. S 5, T 12, R 1W. Signed ISAAC LEWIS, PATSEY LEWIS. Witness: ISAAC ESTELE. rec 1818. pp 64, 65

Deed dated 1818. USA to JAMES JUNKIN. S 30, T 16, R 14E. rec 1818. p 65

Deed dated 1818. SAMUEL LOUTHAIN to LAURENCE H. BRANNON. Cntry lot 57. Witness: none. rec 1818. pp 65, 66

Deed dated 1818. ISAAC JULIAN to LAURENCE H. BRANNON Cntry lots 162, 163. "REBECKA, his wife". Signed ISAAC JULIAN, REBECKAH JULIAN. Witness: none. rec 1818. p 66

Deed dated 1818. ISAAC JULIAN to WILLIAM SUMNER. S 30 T 16, R 14E. Signed ISAAC JULIAN, REBECKAH JULIAN. Witness: none. rec 1818. pp 66, 67

WAYNE COUNTY DEEDS: Book B

POA dated 1817. JACOB BEELER SR of Sullivan Co, TN apptd "my son" JACOB BEELER JR to sell land in R 13, T 15, S 8. Signed JACOB BEELER. Witness: none. rec 1818. p 67

Quitclaim dated 1818. WILLIAM ROSS, late of Wayne Co, dec, by will dated 8 March, 1817, left land to nephews WILLIAM ROSS, son of MOSES ROSS (bro of dec) & to JEHILL LAMPSON/SAMPSON, son of AMOS LAMPSON/ SAMPSON (bro/n/law of dec). Each to have equal half of S 25, T 15, R 12E; legatees to pay money due on land. ROSS' share bought by JEHILL. Signed WILLIAM ROSS. Witness: DAN'L. ROE, JOHN MAHARD (in OH). rec 1818. pp 67, 68

Deed dated 1818. JACOB GRIFFIN to JEREMIAH MOFFIT of Ross Co, OH. S 35, T 14, R 1W. "his wife, MARY". Signed JACOB GRIFFIN, MARY (x) GRIFFIN. Witness: WILLIAM HASTINGS, JOSEPH MOFFIT. rec 1818. pp 68, 69

Deed dated 1818. JOSEPH WAY to REUBEN LOY. S 32, T 18, R 14E. "ALICE, his wife". Signed JOSEPH WAY, ALICE WAY. Witness: JOHN HUNT JR, ROBERT MURPHY, JOHN MARSHILL. rec 1818. pp 69, 70

Bond dated 1818. LARKIN REYNOLDS to LAURENCE H. BRANNON & WILLIAM SUMNER. To build Courthouse in Cntrv by 10 May, 1819. Signed L. REYNOLDS. Witness: JESSE WILLITS. rec 1818. p 70

Deed dated 1818. NATHAN GARRETT to JOHN KING of Clark Co, OH. S 17, T 16, R 14. "CASSA, his wife". Signed NATHAN GARRETT, CASSA GARRETT. Witness: none. rec 1818. p 71

Bond dated 1818. JOSEPH LADD & WILLIAM BEVERLIN to Gov'r of IN. Performance bond for SETH WAY as Coroner of Wayne Co. Signed SETH WAY, JOSEPH LADD. WILLIAM (x) BEVERLIN. rec 1818. p 71

Deed dated 1817. ANDREW THARP to JACOB MILLER. S 31, T 15, R 13E. Signed ANDREW THARP, REBECCA THARP. Witness: STEPHEN GRIFFITH, DAVID DRUMMOND. rec 1818. pp 71, 72

Deed dated 1818. ELIJAH FOX to HENRY COFFETT. S 9, T 16, R 13E. Signed ELIJAH (x) FOX, SUSANNA (x) FOX. Witness: none. rec 1818. pp 72, 73

Deed dated 1818. ROBERT HARVEY to HENDERSON HARVEY*. S 27, T 12, R 1W. Signed ROBERT HARVEY, ELIZABETH (x) HARVEY. Witness: JOHN PLUMMER, FRANCIS HARVEY. JP's

WAYNE COUNTY DEEDS: Book B

note: his wife, ELIZABETH. rec 1818. pp 73, 74
*referred to in text as HENDERSON HARVEY JR.

Deed dated 1818. THOMAS GALYAN SR to JACOB GALYAN. S 20, T 17, R 13E. "PEGGY, his wife". Signed THOMAS (x) GALYAN, PEGGY (x) GALYAN. Witness: WILLIAM GALYAN, PEGGY GALYAN JR. rec 1818. p 74

Deed dated 1818. MICHAEL CULVER of Butler Co, OH to JOHN CULVER of same. S 31, T 12, R 1W. Signed MICHAEL CULVER. Witness: CHAS. STOVE, ALEX. T. DELORAE. rec 1818. pp 74, 75

Deed dated 1818. SAMUEL SANDERS of Chesterfield Co, SC to JAMES LOGAN. S 27, T 15, R 12E. Signed SAMUEL SANDERS. Witness: JESSE PEGG. rec 1818. pp 75, 76

Deed dated 1818. ROBERT RUSSELL & SARAH, his wife of Montgomery Co, OH to JOHN NORCROSS of same. S 9, T 15, R 13E. Signed ROBERT RUSSELL, SARAH (x) RUSSELL. Witness: JOHN RUSSELL, JAMES RUSSELL, WIAN RUSSELL. rec 1818. pp 76, 77

Deed dated 1818. JOSEPH WATTS to JOHN HURST. S 29, T 15, R 13E. Signed JOSEPH WATTS, JEMIMA (x) WATTS. Witness: WILLIAM FARLOW, ANDREW ENDLEY. rec 1818. p 77

Deed dated 1818. LAURENCE H. BRANNON to SAMUEL LOUTHAIN. Cntrv lot 163. "SINTHY, his wife". Signed LAURENCE H. BRANNON, SINTHY BRANNON. Witness: WILLIAM LUNKEN. rec 1818. p 78

Deed dated 1818. CRISTEN PRICE & NANCY, his wife, to JOSEPH LOWER. T 15, R 12E, S 24. Signed CRISTEN (x) PRICE, NANCY PRICE. Witness: SAMUEL M'GEORGE, CADER CARTER. rec 1818. pp 78, 79

Deed dated 1818. NATHANIEL WAYN & ESTHER, his wife, to AARON STANLEY of Clearmont Co, OH. S 9, T 12, R 1W. Signed NATHANIEL WAYNE, ESTHER (x) WAYNE. Witness: none. rec 1818. p 79

Deed dated 1818. LAURENCE H. BRANNON to WILLIAM LUNKEN. Cntrv lot 67. Signed LAURENCE H. BRANNON, SINTHY BRANNON. Witness: CALEB LEWIS. rec 1818. p 80

Deed dated 1818. ANDREW ENDSLEY SR to STEPHEN G. HUNT. "corner of ABRAHAM GARR...line of JAMES LAMB". No S, T 13 "at a stone on the line dividing R 1 & R 2W. Signed ANDW. ENDSLEY, SARAH ENDSLEY. Witness: none. rec 1818. pp 80, 81

WAYNE COUNTY DEEDS: Book B

Bond dated 1818. ELIJAH FISHER, SHADRICK HENDERSON, WM. GRIMES, HUGH CULL & D. FISHER to Gov'r of IN. Bond for performance of ELIJAH FISHER as Sheriff of Wayne Co. Signed ELIJAH FISHER, SHADRICK HENDERSON, WM. GRIMES, HUGH CULL, DAVID FISHER. Witness: DAVID HOOVER. rec 1818. p 81

Deed dated 1818. JOHN C. IRVIN of Butler Co, OH to EPHRAIM CLARK. T 16, R 13, S 7. Signed JOHN C. IRVIN BETSEY IRVIN. Witness: DAVID MORRIS, JAMES M. DORSEY (in OH). rec 1819. pp 81, 82

Deed dated 1818. SAMUEL LANDIS of Green Co, OH to DANIEL LANDIS. S 11, T 12, R 2W. Signed SAMUEL LANDIS. rec 1819. p 82

Deed dated 1818. DANIEL LANDIS to SAMUEL LANDIS as above. S 11, T 12, R 2W. "his wife, FANNY". Signed DANIEL LANDIS, FANNY (x) LANDIS. Witness: none. rec 1819. pp 82, 83

Deed dated 1818. LEMER COBB to DANIEL FOSHER. S 11, T 12, R 2W. "his wife, HESTER COBB". Signed LEMER COBB, ESTHER COBB. Witness: none. rec 1819. p 83

Deed dated 1818. WILLIAM SUMNER to WILLIAM BULLA. Cntrv lots 62, 63, 45. Signed WM. SUMNER, NANCY SUMNER. Witness: none. rec 1819. p 84

Deed dated 1818. WILLIAM SUMNER to JOHN LEWIS & JESSE WILLIAMS. Cntrv lot 74. Signed WM. SUMNER, NANCY SUMNER. Witness: none. rec 1819. p 84

Deed dated 1818. WILLIAM SUMNER to JAMES JONES. Cntrv lot 22. Signed WM. SUMNER, NANCY SUMNER. Witness: none. rec 1819. pp 84, 85

Deed dated 1818. THOMAS HATFIELD to LISMUND BASYE. Washington town lot 14 in S 26, T 17, R 13E. Signed THOMAS HATFIELD, SARAH (x) HATFIELD. Witness: none. rec 1819. p 85

Deed dated 1818. THOMAS HATFIELD to JOHN RUSSELL. Washington town lot 13 in S 26, T 17, R 13E. Signed THOMAS HATFIELD, SARAH (x) HATFIELD. Witness: LISMUND BASYE, REUBEN MACY. rec 1819. pp 85, 86

Deed dated 1816. JAMES WHITE to DAVID SUTHERLAND. Salisbury lot 39. Signed JAMES WHITE. Witness: JOHN NILSON. rec 1819. p 86

Deed dated 1818. WILLIAM KENDALL of Green Co, OH to

WAYNE COUNTY DEEDS: Book B

DAVID W. SUTHERLAND. Salisbury lot 105. Signed WILLIAM KENDAL. Witness: ISAIAH DAVISSON. rec 1819. p 87

Deed dated 1819. LAURENCE H. BRANNON to THOMAS CASON JR of Franklin Co. Cntrv lot 163. Signed LAURENCE H. BRANNON, SINTHY BRANNON. Witness: ELIAS WILLITS. rec 1819. p 87

Deed dated 1818. CHARLES McLAUGHLIN & JANE his wife, to JAMES KNOTT. S 18, T 14, R14E. Signed CHARLES McGLOTHLEN, JANE McGLOTHLEN. Witness: none. rec 1819. p 88

Deed dated 1818. PATRICK JUSTICE to FREDERICK STANTON of Warren Co, OH. Richmond lot 26. Signed PATRICK JUSTICE. Witness: JOHN SUTHERLAND JR, JOHN BROWN JR. rec 1819. pp 88, 89

Deed dated 1819. WILLIAM SUMNER to CALEB LEWIS. Cntrv lots 115, 116. Signed WM. SUMNER, NANCY SUMNER. Witness: LAURENCE H. BRANNON. rec 1819. p 89

Deed dated 1819. ABEL JOHNSON to JOHN LEWIS. Cntrv lot 57. Signed ABEL JOHNSON. Witness: JESSE WILLIAMS. rec 1819. pp 89, 90

Deed dated 1818. THOMAS PEARSON & NANCY, his wife to JACOB DICKARD. S 34, T 16, R 12E. Signed THOMAS PEARSON, NANCY (x) PEARSON. Witness: JOHN STROUD, JAMES CONOVER. rec 1819. p 90, p 100 (pp 91 to 99 missing in page numbering.)

Deed dated 1816. USA to JOSEPH HOLEMAN in his own right & BENJAMIN MAUDLIN, assignee of ELI OVERMAN. S 7, T 16, R 14E. Land partition agreement signed BENJAMIN (x) MAUDLIN, JOSEPH HOLEMAN. Witness: DAVID F. SACKETT, NATHAN OVERMAN. rec 1819. p 100

Deed dated 1819. WILLIAM SUMNER to DAVID F. SACKETT. Cntrv lots 95, 96. Signed WM. SUMNER, NANCY SUMNER. Witness: LAURENCE H. BRANNON. rec 1819. pp 100, 101

Deed dated 1819. ISAAC JULIAN to WM. SUMNER. S 30, T 16, R 14E. Signed ISAAC JULIAN, REBECKA JULIAN. Witness: none. rec 1819. p 101

Deed dated 1819. JACOB ELLIOTT to JAMES BLACK SR. S 12, T 13, R 2. "ANN, his wife". Signed JACOB ELLIOTT, ANN (x) ELLIOTT. Witness: MARTHA SACKETT, D. F. SACKETT. rec 1819. p 102

Deed dated 1818. THOMAS HATFIELD to BARTON PEARSON.

WAYNE COUNTY DEEDS: Book B

Washington town lot 11. Signed THOMAS HATFIELD, SARAH (x) HATFIELD. Witness: REUBEN MACY, HANNAH BARNAR. rec 1819. pp 102, 103

Deed dated 1818. WILLIAM JARRETT to ELI JARRETT. S 24, T 15, R 13E. "NANCY, his wife". Signed WILLIAM JARRETT, NANCY JARRETT. Witness: JESSE JARRETT, WILLIAM JONES. rec 1819. p 103

Deed dated 1818. USA to ANTHONY MABBETT. S 15, R 12, R 1W. rec 1819. pp 103, 104

Deed dated 1818. JOHN NIXON to EDWARD BENBOW. S 5, T 16, R 14E. "MARIAM, his wife". Signed JOHN NIXON, MARIAM (x) NIXON. Witness: WM. BROWN, JOHN BROWN. rec 1819. p 104

Deed dated 1818. USA to JAMES WICKERSHAM. S 35, T 15, R 1W. rec 1819. pp 104, 105

Deed dated 1818. EDWARD STARBUCK to MICAJAH HENLY. S 17, T 15, R 1W. "SARAH, his wife". Signed EDWARD STARBUCK, SARAH (x) STARBUCK. Witness: JESSE PEGG, WM. COOK. rec 1819. p 105

Deed dated 1818. AMOS HAWKINS of Warren Co, OH & JOHN HAWKINS of Wayne Co, IN as execs of estate of JOHN HAWKINS, dec, to AMOS HAWKINS, heir of ISAAAC HAWKINS, dec. JOHN HAWKINS, dec, had agreed to sell land in T 16, R 12, S 27 & 28 to ISAAC, also now dec. Estate execs convey title to ISAAC's heir, AMOS HAWKINS SR. Signed AMOS HAWKINS, JOHN HAWKINS. Witness: none. rec 1819. p 106

Deed dated 1818. AMOS HAWKINS of Warren Co, OH & JOHN HAWKINS of Wayne Co, IN as execs of estate of JOHN HAWKINS, dec, to ISAAC GREGORY, heir of ISAAAC HAWKINS, dec. JOHN HAWKINS, dec, had agreed to sell land in T 16, R 12, S 27 & 28 to ISAAC, also now dec. Estate execs convey title to ISAAC's heir, ISAAC GREGORY. Signed AMOS HAWKINS, JOHN HAWKINS. Witness: none. rec 1819. pp 106, 107

Deed dated 1818. JACOB BLOYD of Franklin Co, to MATTHEW SYMONS. S 22, T 15, R 12E. "HANNAH, his wife". Signed JACOB BLOYD, HANNAH (x) BLOYD. Witness: THOMAS SYMONS, DANIEL HARTY. rec 1819. pp 107, 108

Deed dated 1819. WILLIAM SUMNER to ELIAS WILLITS. Cntrv lot 117. Signed WM. SUMNER, NANCY SUMNER. Witness: THERESA BOOKER. rec 1819. p 108

WAYNE COUNTY DEEDS: Book B

Deed dated 1819. JAMES MARTINDALE to JOHN RUSSELL. Lot adj town of Washington in S 26, T 17, R 13E. "ELIZABETH, his wife". Signed JAMES MARTINDALE, ELIZABETH MARTINDALE. Witness: CHARLES THARP, JOHN WATKINS. rec 1819. pp 108, 109

Deed dated 1818. CHARLES McGLOTHLEN & JANE his wife, to THOMAS CONSTANT & EVAN MORGAN. S 18, T 14, R 14E. Signed CHARLES McGLOTHLEN, JANE (x) McGLOTHLEN. Witness: JAMES LIVINGSTON, GARRET ELKIN. rec 1819. pp 109, 110

Deed dated 1818. CHARLES McGLOTHLEN & JANE his wife, to THOMAS CONSTANT of Green Co, oh. S 18, T 14, R 14E. Signed CHARLES McGLOTHLEN, JANE (x) McGLOTHLEN. Witness: JAMES LIVINGSTON, GARRET ELKIN. rec 1819. pp 110, 111

Deed dated 1819. JOHN HARVEY to JESSE HILL. S 10 & 15, T 16, R 12. Signed JOHN HARVEY, JANE (x) HARVEY. Witness: REBECKA COX. rec 1819. pp 111, 112

Deed dated 1818. SAMUEL GREWELL to JOHN HARTER of Preble Co, OH. S 31, T 15, R 13E. "JANE, his wife". Signed SAMUEL GREWELL, JANE (x) GREWELL. Witness: JOHN HOWARD, LAURENCE GRUWELL. rec 1819. p 112

Deed dated 1816. JOHN SMITH to BARNABAS SPRINGER. Richmond lot 36. Signed JOHN SMITH. Witness: none. rec 1819. pp 112, 113

Deed dated 1819. THOMAS McCOY to JAMES HAYS SR. S 2, T 15, R 13E. "MARGARET, his wife". Signed THOMAS McCOY, MARGARET (x) McCOY. Witness: SETH WAY. rec 1819. p 113

Deed dated 1819. JOSEPH HOLEMAN to SALLY SLATER. Conveyed during SALLY's "continuance on the land", then to her four eldest sons, ELIJAH OLIVER, ELIAL OLIVER, JOSEPH OLIVER & ELUM OLIVER, equally divided. S 7, T 16, R 14E. Signed JOSEPH HOLEMAN, LYDIA HOLEMAN. Witness: ISAAC ELLIOTT, RACHEL ELLIOTT. rec 1819. pp 113, 114

Deed dated 1816. USA to JOHN SUTHERLAND, WILLIAM IRWIN & THOMAS SLOE JR. S 14 & 15, T 16, R 14E. p 114

Deed dated 1819. WILLIAM IRWIN of Cincinnati, OH to JOHN SUTHERLAND of Hamilton, OH. S 14 & 15, T 16, R 14E. "MARY, his wife". Signed WILLIAM IRWIN, MARY IRWIN. Witness: THOMAS SLOE JR, J.A. SIMPSON. rec 1819. pp 114, 115

WAYNE COUNTY DEEDS: Book B

Deed dated 1818. LOT PUGH & RACHEL his wife, MICAJAH WILLIAMS & HANNAH his wife, all of Cincinnati, OH, to THOMAS SLOE JR of the same. S 19, T 14, R 16E. Signed L. PUGH, R.A. PUGH, MICAJAH T. WILLIAMS, HANNAH J. WILLIAMS. Witness: JOEL WRIGHT JR, JOHN MAHARD. rec 1819. pp 116, 117

Deed dated 1819. BENIAH WHITE & MARY, his wife, to ENOCH WITT. S 2, T 12, R 1W. Signed BENIAH WHITE, MARY (x) WHITE. Witness: JOSEPH WYATT. rec 1819. p 117

Deed dated 1819. JOSEPH WATTS to DICKSON HURST of Warren Co, OH. S 29, T 15, R 13E. Signed JOSEPH WATTS, JEMIMA WATTS. Witness: JOHN HURST, EDE. HARDING. rec 1819. pp 117, 188

Deed dated 1819. LAURENCE H. BRANNON to CALEB REYNOLDS. Cntry lot 38. Signed LAURENCE H. BRANNON, CINTHY BRANNON. Witness: CALEB LEWIS. rec 1819. pp 118, 119

Deed dated 1814. USA to DAVID BRADBERY of Butler Co S 21, T 17, R 13E. rec 1819. p 119

Deed dated 1818. DAVID BRADBERY & SUSANA, his wife of Butler Co, OH to JOHN TULLIS of same. S 21, T 17, R 13E. Signed DAVID BRADBERY, SUSANA BRADBERY. Witness; FREEMAN CONKLIN, THOMAS McADAMS. rec 1819. pp 119, 120

Deed dated 1819. JOHN SUTHERLAND & WM. SUTHERLAND to OVID BOONE. Salisbury lot 85. "JOHN...& JANE, his wife, & WILLIAM...& JULIAN, his wife". Signed JOHN SUTHERLAND, WILLIAM SUTHERLAND, JANE SUTHERLAND, JULIAN SUTHERLAND. Witness: none. rec 1819. p 120

Deed dated 1819. LEVI JONES to GEORGE CORNELIUS. S 18, T 16, R 14E. "MARY, his wife". Signed LEVI JONES, MARY (x) JONES. Witness: JOHN CHARLES. rec 1819. pp 120, 121

Deed dated 1819. JEREMIAH COX SR to JOHN McCLAIN SR & PETER JOHNSON. Richmond lots 42 through 53 inclusive. Signed JEREMIAH COX. Witness: W. PUGH. rec 1819. p 121

Deed dated 1819. JEREMIAH COX SR to JOHN McCLAIN JR. Richmond lot 12. Signed JEREMIAH COX. Witness: W. PUGH. rec 1819. p 122

Deed dated 1819. JEREMIAH COX SR to PETER JOHNSON.

WAYNE COUNTY DEEDS: Book B

Richmond lot 22. Signed JEREMIAH COX. Witness: JOHN REED. rec 1819. p 122

Deed dated. WILLIAM NEEL to PETER JOHNSON. Richmond lot 37. Signed WILLIAM NEAL, ANNA (x) NEAL. Witness: JESSE PEGG. JP's note: ANNA, his wife. rec 1819. p 123

Deed dated 1819. SAMUEL CAMMACK to EDWARD KENADAY. Richmond lot 31. Signed SAMUEL CAMMACK. Witness: W.J. PUGH. rec 1819. p 123

Deed dated 1819. JEREMIAH COX to ROBERT MORRISON. Richmond lot 127. Signed JEREMIAH COX. Witness: none. rec 1819. pp 123, 124

Deed dated 1818. STEPHEN THOMAS & WILLIAM JUSTICE to JOHN MELLENDEY of Butler Co, OH. Richmond lot 15. Signed STEPHEN THOMAS, WILLIAM JUSTICE. Witness: JESSE PEGG, WILLIAM NEAL. rec 1819. p 124

Deed dated 1818. JESSE BREWER to ROBERT HILL. S 3, T 13, R 1W. Signed JESSE (x) BREWER, CHRISTENY (x) BREWER. Witness: ELIJAH (x) MUNDEN, THOMAS (x) SPEARS. JP's note: CHRISTENY, wife of JESSE. rec 1819. pp 124, 125

Deed dated 1818. NATHAN OVERMAN to JESSE BREWER. S 3, T 13, R 1W. S 3, T 13, R 1W. Signed NATHAN OVERMAN, THAMER OVERMAN. Witness: ELI OVERMAN, JOSEPH OVERMAN. rec 1819. pp 125, 126

Deed dated 1816. JOHN SMITH to WILLIAM NEEL of Preble Co, OH. Richmond lot 8. Signed JOHN SMITH. Witness: none. rec 1819. p 126

Deed dated 1819. SAMUEL CAMMACK to WILLIAM NEAL. Richmond lot 31. Signed SAMUEL CAMMACK. Witness: W. PUGH. rec 1819. pp 126, 127

Deed dated 1818. JEREMIAH COX to WILLIAM NEAL. Richmond lot 30. Signed JEREMIAH COX. Witness: none. rec 1819. p 127

Deed dated 1819. THOMAS ALBRED to WILLIAM NEAL. Richmond lot 5. Signed THOMAS ALBRED. Witness: JESSE PEGG. rec 1819. pp 127, 128

Deed dated 1819. ADAM BOYD to WILLIAM NEAL. Richmond lot 7. Signed ADAM BOYD. Witness: WILLIAM PUGH. rec 1819. p 128

WAYNE COUNTY DEEDS: Book B

Deed dated 1818. WILLIAM McLUCAS & MARY, his wife of Montgomery Co, OH to JAMES RUSSEL of the same. S 9, T 15, R 13. Signed WILLIAM McLUCAS, POLLY (x) McLUCAS. Witness: BIFLYALUS LARAY, ROBERT RUSSELL. rec 1819. pp 128, 129

Deed dated 1817. WILLIAM STARBUCK of Gifford Co, NC to EDWARD STARBUCK of the same. S 17, T 15, R 1W. Signed WILLIAM STARBUCK. Witness: WILLIAM STARBUCK JR, ANNA HUITH, PHEBE STARBUCK (in NC). rec 1819. pp 129, 130

Deed dated 1817. USA to STEPHEN MENDENHALL. S 29, T 15, R 1W. rec 1819. p 130

Deed dated 1818. ISAAC MENDENHALL to STEPHEN MENDENHALL SR. S 2, T 16, R 13E. "MARY, his wife". Signed ISAAC MENDENHALL, MARY (x) MENDENHALL. Witness: WM. WHITE, STEPHEN MENDENHALL JR. rec 1819. pp 130, 131

Deed dated 1818. JAMES LITTLE to NATHAN SMITH. S 6, T 12, R 1W. "his wife, SUSANNA". Signed JAMES LITTLE SUSANNA (x) LITTLE. Witness: none. rec 1819. pp 131, 132

Deed dated 1818. BRYAN SEANY to NATHAN SMITH. S 5, T 12, R 1W. "SALLY, his wife". Signed BRYAN SEANY, SALLY (x) SEANY. Witness: none. rec 1819. p 132

Deed dated 1819. WILLIAM WYATT & MARY, his wife, to JOSEPH WYATT. S 14, T 12, R 1W. Signed WILLIAM WYATT MARY (x) WYATT. Witness: none. rec 1819. pp 132, 133

Deed dated 1818. NICHOLAS DRULY & SALLY, his wife, to JOSEPH LEWIS. S 10, T 12, R 1W. Signed NICHOLAS (x) DRULY, SARAH (x) DRULY. Witness: none. rec 1819. p 133

Deed dated 1818. JOHN SMITH to JOHN McCLAIN. Richmond lot 15. Signed JOHN SMITH. Witness: none. rec 1819. pp 133, 134

Deed dated 1819. THOMAS HATFIELD to PAUL HAYWARD. Washington town lot 4, T 17, R 13E. Signed THOMAS HATFIELD, SARAH (x) HATFIELD. Witness: JOHN RUSSELL, ABEL JANNEY. rec 1819. p 134

Deed dated 1819. THOMAS HATFIELD to CHARLES THARP. Washington town lot 15, T 17, R 13E. Signed THOMAS HATFIELD, SARAH (x) HATFIELD. Witness: JOHN RUSSELL, ABEL JANNEY. rec 1819. pp 134, 135

WAYNE COUNTY DEEDS: Book B

Deed dated 1818. LEWIS LITTLE to NATHAN SMITH. "at JAMES LITTLE's line...JOHN HUNT's corner". S 6, T 12, R 1W. "ELIZABETH, his wife". Signed LEWIS (x) LITTLE, ELIZABETH (x) LITTLE. Witness: none. rec 1819. p 135

Deed dated 1819. THOMAS HATFIELD to JOHN HAGUE. Washington town lot 26, T 17, R 13E. Signed THOMAS HATFIELD, SARAH (x) HATFIELD. Witness: none. rec 1819. pp 135, 136

Deed dated 1819. THOMAS HATFIELD to BYROM CADWALADER. Washington town lot 30, T 17, R 13E. Signed THOMAS HATFIELD, SARAH (x) HATFIELD. Witness: none. rec 1819. p 136

Deed dated 1819. JEREMIAH COX to JOHN MENDENHALL. Richmond lot 41. Signed JEREMIAH COX. Witness: none. rec 1819. pp 136, 137

Deed dated 1816. GEORGE P. TORRENCE & MARY, his wife of Cincinnati OH to GEORGE HUNT. S 32, T 15, R 13E. Signed GEORGE P. TORRENCE, MARY B. TORRENCE. Witness: JOHN MAHARD, TH. D. CARNELL (in OH). rec 1819. pp 137, 138

Partition deed dated 1819. ROBERT ANDREW to BENJAMIN SMITH. Land purchased jointly in S 13, T 14, R 1W. Quitclaim now given. "MARY, his wife". Signed ROBERT ANDREW, MARY (x) ANDREW. Witness: MARTHA SACKETT. rec 1819. pp 138, 139

Partition deed dated 1819. BENJAMIN SMITH to ROBERT ANDREW. Land purchased jointly in S 13, T 14, R 1W. Quitclaim now given. "TAMAR, his wife". Signed BENJAMIN SMITH, TAMAR (x) SMITH. Witness: MARTHA SACKETT. rec 1819. p 139

Deed dated 1819. WILLIAM SUMNER to Wayne Co Commissioners THOMAS J. WARMAN, ENOS GRAVE, BEALE BUTLER. Cntry lot 49. Signed WM. SUMNER, NANCY SUMNER. Witness: JAMES CORNELIUS, JESSE WILLITS. rec 1819. p 140

Deed dated 1818. BARNET STARR to MORGAN McMAHAN. S 17, T 12, R 1W. Signed BARNET STARR, MARGARET STARR. Witness: none. JP's note: BARNET STARR & his wife MARGARET. rec 1819. p 141

Deed dated 1819. JOSEPH COX to JOHN COX SR. S 2 & 3, T 12, R 2W. "MARY, his wife". Signed JOSEPH COX, MARY (x) COX. Witness: ABSALOM CORNELIUS. rec 1819. pp 141, 142

WAYNE COUNTY DEEDS: Book B

Deed dated 1819. JOHN COX SR & CATHARINE, his wife, to JOSEPH COX. S 2 & 3, T 12, R 2W. Signed JOHN COX, CATHARINE (x) COX. Witness: ABSALOM CORNELIUS. rec 1819. p 142

Deed dated 1819. THOMAS GALYAN SR to WILLIAM GALYAN. S 20, T 17, R 13E. Signed THOMAS GALYAN, PEGGY GALYAN. Witness: JACOB GALYAN, PEGGY GALYAN, JOHN JORDAN. rec 1819. pp 142, 143

Bond dated 1817. GRIFFIN TREADWAY of Montgomery Co, KY to WILLIAM STARK. Land in S 33, T 16, R 13E first entered by SAMUEL SHORTRIDGE now conveyed to STARK; title to be given when issued by USA. Signed GRIFFIN TREADWAY. Witness: JOHN STARK. rec 1819. p 143

Deed dated 1818. ORR SCOFIELD & LYDIA, his wife, to PETER COX. S 13, T 17, R 13E. Signed ORR SCOFIELD, LIDIA SCOFIELD. Witness: WM. FOX, JOHN LITTLE. rec 1819. pp 143, 144

Deed dated 1819. WILLIAM SUMNER to WILLIAM DUNMAN. Cntrv lot 99. Signed WILLIAM SUMNER, NANCY SUMNER. Witness: none. rec 1819. pp 144, 145

Deed dated 1819. WILLIAM SUMNER to JOSEPH VAN BUSKIRK. Cntrv lots 112 & 14. Signed WM. SUMNER, NANCY SUMNER. Witness: D.C. SMITH. rec 1819. p 145

Deed dated 1817. JOHN TURNER to ALEXANDER GRIMES. S 17, T 13, R 1W. "at GEORGE HOLEMAN's". "SARAH, his wife." Signed JOHN TURNER, SARAH (x) TURNER. Witness: JOHN NILSON. rec 1819. pp 145, 146

Deed dated 1819. THOMAS HATFIELD to BYROM CADWALADER Washington town lot 23, T 17, R 13E. Signed THOMAS HATFIELD, SARAH (x) HATFIELD. Witness: LISMUND BASYE rec 1819. p 146

Deed dated 1818. JOHN DUEY & ELIZABETH, his wife, to THOMAS W. WALLACE. S 28, T 15, R 13E. Signed JOHN (x) DUEY, ELIZABETH (x) DUEY. Witness: J. FLINT, WILLIAM SHAW. rec 1819. pp 146, 147

Deed dated 1819. JOHN WALLACE & MARY, his wife, to THOMAS W. WALLACE. S 6, T 15, R 13E. Signed JOHN WALLACE, MARY (x) WALLACE. Witness: JACOB WILSON, THOMAS BANKS. rec 1819. pp 147, 148

Deed dated 1818. MARTIN FISHER & RACHEL, his wife, to SAMUEL HANNAH. S 4, T 15, R 13E. Signed MARTIN FISHER, RACHEL (x) FISHER. Witness: SALLY WILLITS,

WAYNE COUNTY DEEDS: Book B

SALLY WILLITS. rec 1819. pp 148, 149

Deed dated 1818. JAMES BOYD to JOHN BOYD. S 9, T 16, R 13E. "PEGGY, his wife". Signed JAMES BOYD, PEGGY BOYD. Witness: none. rec 1819. p 149

Deed dated 1819. WILLIAM SUTHERLAND & DAVID SUTHERLAND to LYDIA SUTHERLAND. Salisbury lot 84. Signed DAVID W. SUTHERLAND, WILLIAM SUTHERLAND, JULIAN SUTHERLAND. Witness: none. rec 1819. pp 149, 150

Deed dated 1818. JESSE HENLEY & POLLY, his wife of Clark Co to JASPER STARR. S 18, T 12, R 1W. Signed JESSE HENLEY, POLLY HENLEY. rec 1819. pp 150, 151

Deed dated 181. BARNET STARR to FREDERICK LONG. S 17, T 12, R 1W. Signed BARNET STARR, MARGARET STARR. Witness: none. rec 1819. p 151

Deed dated 181. BARNET STARR to FREDERICK LONG. S 18, T 12, R 1W. Signed BARNET STARR, MARGARET STARR. Witness: none. rec 1819. pp 151, 152

Deed dated 1818. JOSEPH WORL to ROBERT WORL. S 5, T 16, R 13E. "NANCY, his wife". Signed JOSEPH WORL, NANCY WORL. Witness: none. rec 1819. p 152

Deed dated 1818. NATHAN RICHARDSON & ANNA his wife of Franklin Co to JOHN ADAIR of same. S 36, T 16, R 12E. Signed NATHAN (x) RICHARDSON, ANNA (x) RICHARDSON. Witness: SOLOMON MANWARING. rec 1819. p 153

Deed dated 1818. JOHN ADAIR & SARAH his wife of Franklin Co to LARKIN REYNOLDS. S 36, T 16, R 12E. Signed JOHN ADAIR, SARAH ADAIR. Witness: HUGH MORRISON, ISAIAH DRURY. rec 1819. pp 153, 154

Deed dated 1819. WILLIAM SUMNER & NANCY, his wife, to JOSEPH EVANS of Cincinnati, OH. Cntrv lots 55, 12, 29, 88, 89, 91, 92, 108, 111, 161, 134, 135, 136, 143, 144, 145, 179, 180, 181, 194, 195, 196, 226, 227, 228, 229, 214, 215, 216, 217, 220, 221, 222. Signed WM. SUMNER, NANCY SUMNER. Witness: JOHN DRURY CALEB LEWIS. rec 1819. pp 154, 155

Deed dated 1819. WM. SUMNER & NANCY, his wife, to RICHARD CHEESEMAN of Springfield, OH. Cntrv lot, # not given. Signed WM. SUMNER, NANCY SUMNER. Witness: JOHN DRURY, CALEB LEWIS. rec 1819. pp 155, 156

Deed dated 1819. WM. SUMNER & NANCY, his wife, to

WAYNE COUNTY DEEDS: Book B

LAURENCE H. BRANNON. Cntrv lots, 113, 98, 103, 107, 110, 81, 206, 207, 208, 209, 160, 137 through 141, 176, 177, 178, 197, 198, 199, 223, 224, 225, 218, 219, 239, 240, 118, 119. Signed WM. SUMNER, NANCY SUMNER. Witness: JOHN DRURY, CALEB LEWIS. rec 1819. pp 156, 157

Deed dated 1819. JESSE MONDON to JOHN NIXON. S 15, R 12E, no T given. "MARY, his wife". Signed JESSE MUNDON, MARY (x) MUNDON. Witness: none. rec 1819. p 157

Deed dated 1819. FRANCIS CULBERTSON to JOHN MAXWELL. S 8, T 16, R 14E. "ANNA, his wife". Signed FRANCIS (x) CULBERTSON, ANNA (x) CULBERTSON. Witness: none. rec 1819. pp 157, 158

Deed dated 1819. JOHN McKEE to ELI GASSEN. S 18, T 16, R 13E. "MILLA, his wife". Signed JOHN McKEE, MILLINDA McKEE. Witness: WM. BROWN, EZEKIEL LEAVELL rec 1819. pp 158, 159

Deed dated 1819. SAMUEL W. BEELER of Butler Co, OH to SAMUEL C. BEELER, GEORGE W. BEELER & THOMAS BEELER minor sons of BENJAMIN BEELER, dec. "love & good will toward his grandsons". S 36, T 16, R 12E. Signed SAMUEL W. BEELER. Witness: J.M. DORSEY, MARTHA DORSEY. rec 1819. pp 160

Deed dated 1819. JOHN SMITH to ELEAZER HIATT. Richmond lot 17. Signed JOHN SMITH. Witness: none. rec 1819. p 161

Deed dated 1819. JOHN SMITH to ACHILLES WILLIAMS. Richmond lot 32. Signed JOHN SMITH. Witness: none. rec 1819. p 161

Deed dated 1819. JOHN SMITH to ELIAS JESSOP. Richmond lot 102. Signed JOHN SMITH. Witness: ADAM BOYD rec 1819. pp 161, 162

Deed dated 1818. WM. BLUNT to THOMAS R. STANFORD. S 29, T 18, R 13E. Signed WILLAM (x) BLUNT, MARY (x) BLUNT. Witness: WM. JORDAN, RACHEL JORDAN, JOHN JORDAN. JP's note: MARY, his wife. rec 1819. p 162

Deed dated 1819. DAVID ODOM to JOHN LAUMAN. S 11, T 16, R 12E. "ELIZABETH, his wife". Signed DAVID (x) ODOM, ELIZABETH (x) ODOM. Witness: none. rec 1819. p 163

Deed dated 1819. SAMUEL WOODS to THOMAS McCARTNEY.

WAYNE COUNTY DEEDS: Book B

Bounds given; no S-T-R. "POLLY, his wife". Signed SAMUEL WOODS, POLLY WOODS. Witness: none. rec 1819. pp 163, 164 (see following deed)

Deed dated 1819. SAMUEL WOODS to JOHN SUTHERLAND. S 1, T 13, R 2W. Signed SAMUEL WOODS, POLLY WOODS. Witness: none. rec 1819. p 164

Deed dated 1819. JOSHUA SHELBY & SUSANNA, his wife to JOHN SHELBY. S 25, T 15, R 13E. Signed JOSHUA SHELBY, SUSANNA (x) SHELBY. Witness: none. rec 1819 pp 164, 165

Deed dated 1818. JOHN SMITH to CAREY A. WESTERFIELD. Richmond lot 65. Signed JOHN SMITH. Witness: STEPHEN HOLLAWAY, JAMES PEGG. rec 1819. pp 165, 166

Deed dated 1817. JOSIAH CLAWSON to JOSEPH STOVVER. S 12, T 17, R 13. "REBECKAH, his wife." Signed JOSIAH CLAWSON, REBECKAH (x) CLAWSON. Witness: none. rec 1819. p 166

Deed dated 1819. JOHN DUEY to WILLIAM SHAW. S 28, T 15, R 13. Signed JOHN (x) DUEY, ELIZABETH (x) DUEY. Witness: WM. GUNN. rec 1819. pp 166, 167

Deed dated 1819. JAMES BLACK SR to GWYN BLACK. S 9, T 16, R 14E. "ELIZABETH, his wife". Signed JAMES (X) BLACK SR, ELIZABETH (x) BLACK. Witness: DUDLEY C. SMITH, JOHN LEWIS. rec 1819. pp 167, 168

Deed dated 1819. JAMES BLACK SR to JOHN BLACK. S 10, T 16, R 14E. Signed JAMES (X) BLACK SR, ELIZA- BETH (x) BLACK. Witness: DUDLEY C. SMITH, JOHN LEWIS. rec 1819. p 168

Deed dated 1819. JEREMIAH COX to ROBERT SMITH. S 33, T 14, R 1W. Signed JEREMIAH COX. Witness; none. rec 1819. pp 168, 169

Deed dated 1819. JAMES MARTINDALE to LISMUND BASYE. S 26, T 17, R 13E. "line of JONAS HATFIELD, dec". Signed JAMES MARTINDALE, ELIZABETH (x) MARTINDALE. Witness: none. rec 1819. p 169

Deed dated 1816. ANDREW HOOVER to WM. BULA. S 28, T 14, R 1W. Signed ANDREW HOOVER. Witness: JOHN MORROW, DAVID HOOVER. rec 1819. pp 169,170

Deed dated 1819. ABEL JANNEY to LISMUND BASYE. S 26, T 17, R 13E. Signed ABEL JANNEY, PEGGY JANNEY. Witness: none. rec 1819. pp 170, 171

WAYNE COUNTY DEEDS: Book B

Deed dated 1819. THOMAS HATFIELD to LISMUND BASYE. Washington town lots 17 & 24. Signed THOMAS HATFIELD SARAH (x) HATFIELD. Witness: B. CADWALADER. rec 1819. p 171

Deed dated 1819. JOHN SMITH to HENRY HODGSON. Richmond lot 59. Signed JOHN SMITH. Witness: none. rec 1819. pp 171, 172

Deed dated 1817. JOHN SMITH to HENRY HODGSON. Richmond lot 34. Signed JOHN SMITH. Witness: STEPHEN HOLLAWAY, SAMUEL SMITH. rec 1819. p 172

Deed dated 1817. JOHN SMITH JR to NATHAN SMITH. S 22, T 16, R 14E. Signed JOHN SMITH, JANE SMITH. Witness: none. JP's note: JANE SMITH, wife of JOHN. rec 1819. pp 172, 173

Deed dated 1818. JOHN SMITH to HENRY HODGSON. Richmond lot 18. Signed JOHN SMITH. Witness: EDWARD L. FROST, STEPHEN HOLLOWAY. rec 1819. p 173

Deed dated 1819. EDWARD STARBUCK to JACOB VORE. S 5, T 14, R 1W. Signed EDWARD STARBUCK, SARAH (x) STARBUCK. Witness: JACOB VORE JR. rec 1819. p 174

Deed dated 1819. ISAAC JULIAN to JOHN ROLSTEN. Cntry lot 83. ISAAC JULIAN, REBECKA JULIAN. Witness: none. rec 1819. p 174

Deed dated 1819. EDWARD DRURY & JANE, his wife, to WILLIAM DRURY. S 28, T 16, R 13E. Signed EDWARD DRURY, JANE (x) DRURY. Witness: none. rec 1819. pp 175, 176

Deed dated 1819. SAMUEL DRURY of Washington Twp & VIOLET, his wife, to GIDEON MYERS of same. S 34, T 16, R 12. Signed SAMUEL DRURY, VIOLET (x) DRURY. Witness: none. rec 1819. p 176

Deed dated 1819. JOHN COX SR to JOHN A. RANCK of Montgomery Co, Oh. Abington lots 37, 48. "CATHARINE his wife". Signed JOHN COX, CATHARINE (x) COX. Witness: none. rec 1819. p 177

Deed dated 1819. JOSEPH COX to JOHN A. RANCK of Montgomery Co, Oh. S 2 & 3, T 12, R 2W. "from THOMAS MOFFET". "MARY, his wife". Signed JOSEPH COX, MARY (x) COX. Witness: none. rec 1819. pp 177, 178

Deed dated 1819. THOMAS MOFFET to JOHN A. RANCK of Montgomery Co, Oh. S 10, T 12, R 2W. "MARY, his

WAYNE COUNTY DEEDS: Book B

wife". Signed THOMAS MOFFET, MARY (x) MOFFET. Witness: none. rec 1819. p 178

Deed dated 1819. MORDICA MENDINGHALL & ELENDER, his wife, to HENRY GARRETT. S 24, T 17, R 13E. Signed MORDECAI MENDENHALL, ELLENERT MENDENHALL. Witness: #1 illegible, WM. BROWN, ABRAHAM ELLIOT. rec 1819. pp 178, 179

Deed dated 1819. JOHN DODDREDGE & AVIS, his wife, to JOHN WINGLEY. S 12, T 15, R 13E. Signed JOHN DODDRIDGE, AVIS DODDRIDGE. Witness: JOHN JONES. rec 1819. pp 179, 180

Deed dated 1819. WILLIAM SUMNER to DUDLEY C. SMITH. Cntrv lot 93. Signed WM. SUMNER, NANCY SUMNER. Witness: CALEB REYNOLDS. rec 1819. pp 180, 181

Deed dated 1817. Successors of PETER FLEMING of Court of Common Pleas to DAVID SACKETT. Salisbury lots 63, 64. Signed JAMES ODELL, THOMAS BEARD. Witness: none. rec 1819. p 181

Deed dated 1819. JACOB BEELER JR to SAMUEL WILLITS SR. S 8, T 15, R 13E. "patented to SAMUEL BEELER, dec". "ESTHER, his wife". Signed JACOB BEELER, ESTHER (x) BEELER. Witness: LEVI WILLITS, JAMES CONOVER. rec 1819. pp 181, 182

Deed dated 1816. USA to SAMUEL WILLITS of Piqua (OH) assignee of WILLIAM WILLETS. S 26, T 16, R 12E. rec 1819. p 182

Deed dated 1818. USA to SAMUEL WILLITS, assignee of ABRAHAM MILLER. S 8, T 15, R 13E. rec 1819. pp 182, 183

Deed dated 1818. JOHN HAWKINS to CHARLES MOFFET. S 33, T 14, R 1W. "LYDIA, his wife". Signed JOHN HAWKINS, LYDIA HAWKINS. Witness: none. rec 1819. p 183

Deed dated 1819. THOMAS HATFIELD to JOHN SMITH. Washington lots 44 & 45, S 26, T 17, R 13E. Signed THOMAS HATFIELD, SARAH (x) HATFIELD. Witness: BARNEY McMANUS. rec 1819. p 184

Deed dated 1818. ANDREW IRELAND of Preble Co, OH to AMOS HAWKINS JR. S 36 & 35, T 14, R 1W. "corner to JAMES ALEXANDER". Signed ANDW. IRELAND, BETSEY IRELAND. Witness: none. rec 1819. pp 184, 185

Deed dated 1819. JOHN SMITH to JOHN CLARK. Richmond

WAYNE COUNTY DEEDS: Book B

lot 124. Signed JOHN SMITH. Witness: JESSE PEGG, SAMUEL SMITH. rec 1819. pp 185, 186

Deed dated 1819. JOHN SMITH to BARNABUS SPRINGER. Richmond lot 120. Signed JOHN SMITH. Witness: S. W. SMITH, JOB SWAIN. rec 1819. p 186

Deed dated 1819. ANTHONY MABBETT & SUSANNA, his wife, to JOHN MABBETT. S 15, T 12, R 1W. Signed ANTHONY (x) MABBETT, SUSANNA (x) MABBETT. Witness: none. rec 1819. pp 186, 187

Deed dated 1816. JEREMIAH COX to ZIMRI COOK. Richmond lot 24. Signed JEREMIAH COX. Witness: none. rec 1819. p 187

Deed dated 1817. VALENTINE PEGG & MARY, his wife to ZIMRI COOK. S 6, T 13, R 1W. Signed VALENTINE PEGG, MARY (x) PEGG. Witness: D.F. SACKETT. rec 1819. pp 187, 188

Deed dated 1819. VALENTINE PEGG & MARY, his wife to ZIMRI COOK. S 6, T 13, R 1W. Signed VALENTINE PEGG MARY (x) PEGG. Witness: none. rec 1819. pp 188, 189

Deed dated 1819. JOHN McCLAIN JR & PETER JOHNSON to AMOS HAWKINS. Richmond lot 49. Signed JOHN McCLAIN, PETER JOHNSON. Witness: ELEAZAR HIETT. rec 1819 p 189

Deed dated 1819. JEREMIAH L. MEEK & REBECCA his wife & WILLIAM MEEK & PATSY his wife to HEZEKIAH HAM. S 9, no T or R: bounds given. Signed JEREMIAH L. MEEK, REBECCA (x) MEEK, WILLIAM MEEK, PATSY MEEK. Witness: JEHU STUART. rec 1819. pp 189, 190

Deed dated 1819. JOHN SLATER to ELIJAH OLIVER. Cntry lot 23. "his wife, SALLY". Signed JOHN SLATER, SARAH (x) SLATER. Witness: WINDSOR PIPES, JOHN FLAMING. rec 1819. pp 190, 191

Deed dated 1818. BENJAMIN HUTCHENS & HANNAH his wife of Montgomery Co, Oh to JACOB BRENSON. S 28, T 18, R 14E. Signed BENJAMIN HUTCHINS, HANNAH HUTCHINS. Witness: JAMES JOHNSON, JOHN HOUGH (in OH). rec 1819. pp 191, 192

Deed dated 1819. THOMAS WYATT & NANCY, his wife, to BARTON WYATT. S 2, T 12, R 1W. Signed THOMAS WYATT, NANCY (x) WYATT. Witness: none. rec 1819. pp 192, 193

Deed dated 1819. ROBERT LEAVELL to JOSIAH BRADBURY.

WAYNE COUNTY DEEDS: Book B

Jacksonburgh lots 11, 20. Signed ROBERT LEAVELL, SALLY (x) LEAVELL. Witness; THOMAS GINN JR, ZADOCK DOUGHERTY. rec 1819. p 193

Deed dated 1819. JOHN HARDING to JOHN HOWARD. S 29, T 15, R 13E. Signed JOHN HARDING, ANN (x) HARDING. Witness: JOHN SMITH, WM. MONTGOMERY. rec 1819. pp 193, 194

Deed dated 1819. JOHN HARVEY to SAMUEL HARVEY. S 15, T 16, R 13E. "JANE, his wife." Signed JOHN HARVEY, JEAN HARVEY. Witness: none. rec 1819. p 194

Deed dated 1819. NATHAN SMITH to JOHN SUTHERLAND of Butler Co, OH. S 22, T 16, R 14E. "to ARMSTRONG GRIME's corner". Signed NATHAN SMITH, MARY SMITH. Witness: none. rec 1819. pp 194, 195

Deed dated 1819. THOMAS HATFIELD to JAMES BYRNS. Washington town lot 8, T 17, R 13E. Signed THOMAS HATFIELD, SARAH (x) HATFIELD. Witness: none. rec 1819. pp 195, 196

Deed dated 1819. GEORGE ISH of Jackson Twp & MARIAM, his wife, to SOLOMON REES. S 32, T 16, R 13E. Signed GEORGE ISH, MARIAM ISH. Witness: JAMES CONNOVER, CHARLES REYNOLDS. rec 1819. pp 196, 197

Deed dated 1819. JAMES MARTINDALE to THOMAS HATFIELD S 26, T 17, R 13E. Signed JAMES MARTINDALE, ELIZABETH (x) MARTINDALE. Witness: JOSIAH BINNEY. rec 1819. p 197

Deed dated 1818. THOMAS HATFIELD to SAMUEL LOGAN. Washington town lot 26, T 17, R 13E. Signed THOMAS HATFIELD, SARAH (x) HATFIELD. Witness: REUBEN MORRIS, JESSE BOND. rec 1819. pp 197, 198

Deed dated 1818. THOMAS HATFIELD to SAMUEL LOGAN. Washington town lot 2, T 17, R 13E. Signed THOMAS HATFIELD, SARAH (x) HATFIELD. Witness: REUBEN MORRIS, JESSE BOND. rec 1819. pp 198, 199

Deed dated 1818. THOMAS HATFIELD to THOMAS LOGAN. Washington town lot 3, T 17, R 13E. Signed THOMAS HATFIELD, SARAH (x) HATFIELD. Witness: none. rec 1819. p 199

Deed dated 1819. WM. SUMNER to ARCHIBALD BELL of Bourbon Co, KY. Cntrv lot 4. Signed WM. SUMNER, NANCY SUMNER. Witness: none. rec 1819. pp 199, 200

WAYNE COUNTY DEEDS: Book B

Deed dated 1819. WM. SUMNER to ARCHIBALD BELL of Bourbon Co, KY. Cntrv lot 17. Signed WM. SUMNER, NANCY SUMNER. Witness: none. rec 1819. p 200

Deed dated 1819. EZEKIEL LEAVELL & NANCY, his wife, to THOMPSON JONES. Jacksonburgh lots 3, 8. Signed EZEKIEL LEAVELL, NANCEY LEAVELL. Witness: LORING A. WALDO, STEPHEN GASSIN. rec 1819. pp 200, 201

Deed dated 1818. ITHAMAR WARNER to THOMPSON JONES. Jacksonburgh lot 22. Signed ITHAMAR WARNER. Witness: JOHN NORRIS, JONAS BELL. rec 1819. p 201

Deed dated 1819. SAMUEL LOUTHAIN to THOMPSON JONES. Cntrv lot 57. Signed SAMUEL LOUTHAIN. Witness: JOEL REED, ABSALOM LOUTHAIN. rec 1819. pp 201, 202

Deed dated 1819. JOHN COX & CATHARINE, his wife, to DAVID RAILSBACK. S 2 & 35, T 12 & 13, R 2W. Signed JOHN COX, CATHARINE (x) COX. Witness: none. rec 1819 pp 202, 203

Deed dated 1819. JEREMIAH COX to JAMES R. MENDENHALL Richmond lot 93. Signed JEREMIAH COX. Witness: none. rec 1819. p 203

Deed dated 1818. USA to GREENBURY CORNELIUS. S 24, T 16, R 13E. rec 1819. p 203

Quitclaim deed dated 1819. SAMUEL JONES to WILLIAM YOUNG. Both held title to S 24, T 17, R 13E as assignees of JEREMIAH & ABR. ELLIOTT. YOUNG to have title to South half of property. Signed SAMUEL JONES REBECKAH JONES. Witness: none. rec 1819. p 204

Deed dated 1819. THOMAS MOFFETT to JOHN A. RANCK of Montgomery Co, OH. S 10, T 12, R 2W. "MARY, his wife" Signed THOMAS MOFFETT, MARY MOFFETT. Witness: JOSEPH COX, JAMES LEVISTON. rec 1819. pp 204, 205

Deed dated 1819. JOSEPH COX to JOHN A. RANCK of Montgomery Co, OH. S 10, T 12, R 2W. Signed JOSEPH COX, MARY COX. Witness: JAMES LEVISTON. rec 1819. pp 205, 206

Deed dated 1819. JOSEPH COX to JOHN A. RANCK of Montgomery Co, OH. Abington lot 49. Signed JOSEPH COX, MARY (x) COX. Witness: JAMES LEVISTON. rec 1819. p 206

Deed dated 1819. JOSEPH COX to THOMAS MANNING of Montgomery Co, OH. S 2, no T-R: bounds given. Signed

WAYNE COUNTY DEEDS: Book B

JOSEPH COX, MARY (x) COX. Witness: MATHIAS FOSHER. rec 1819. pp 206, 207

Deed dated 1819. JOSEPH COX to THOMAS MANNING of Montgomery Co, OH. Abington lot 95. Signed JOSEPH COX, MARY (x) COX. Witness: none. rec 1819. p 207

Deed dated 1819. JOSEPH COX to JOHN DRUCK. Abington lots 109, 110. Signed JOSEPH COX, MARY (x) COX. Witness: MATHIAS FOSHER. rec 1819. p 208

Deed dated 1818. JOHN McCLAIN to JOSIAH MOORE. S 10, T 13, R 1W. "MARGARET, his wife". Signed JOHN McCLANE, MARGARET McCLANE. Witness: D. HOOVER, WILLIAM SCEARCE. rec 1819. pp 208, 209

Deed dated 1818. THOMAS HATFIELD to JESSE BOND. Washington town lot 27: S 26, T 17, R 13E. Signed THOMAS HATFIELD, SARAH (x) HATFIELD. Witness: REUBEN MORRIS, WILLIAM (x) KNUTT. rec 1819. p 209

Deed dated 1816. JEREMIAH COX to SAMUEL CAMMACK. Richmond lots 29, 31. Signed JEREMIAH COX. Witness: none. rec 1819. pp 209, 210

Deed dated 1816. THOMAS McCOY to JOHN SMITH. S 18, T 13, R 1W. "MARGARET, his wife". Signed THOMAS McCOY, MARGARET McCOY. Witness: none. rec 1819. p 210

Mortgage dated 1819. SAMUEL CAMMACK to EDWARD L. FROST. Richmond 29 held as security on debt to FROST Signed SAMUEL CAMMACK. Witness: THOMAS CARRALL. rec 1819. pp 210, 211

Deed dated 1819. WM. SUMNER to THOMAS CULBERTSON of Clark Co, KY. Cntrv lot 21. Signed WM. SUMNER, NANCY SUMNER. Witness: none. rec 1819. pp 211, 212

Deed dated 1819. WM. SUMNER to ARCHIBALD BELL of Bourbon Co, KY. Cntrv lot 70. Signed WM. SUMNER, NANCY SUMNER. Witness: none. rec 1819. p 212

Deed dated 1817. JOHN SMITH to JACOB FOUTS. Richmond lot 57. Signed JOHN SMITH. Witness: none. rec 1819. p 212

Deed dated 1818. JACOB FOUTS JR to JOB SPRINGER. Richmond lot 57. Signed JACOB FOUTS. Witness: none. rec 1819. p 213

Deed dated 1819. THOMPSON JONES to THOMAS ALEXANDER. Jacksonburgh lot 22. Signed THOMPSON JONES. Witness:

WAYNE COUNTY DEEDS: Book B

JOB GINN, ABSALOM LOUTHAIN. rec 1819. p 213

Deed dated 1819. LAURENCE H. BRANNON to SAMUEL E. SHORTRIDGE. Cntrv lot 163. Signed LAURENCE H. BRANNON, CINTHY BRANNON. Witness: none. rec 1819. pp 213, 214

Deed dated 1819. JOHN TURNER to PETER WEAVER. S 17, T 13, R 1W. Signed JOHN TURNER. Witness: JOHN SUTHERLAND, EWEL KENDAL, JOSEPH COX. rec 1819. pp 214, 215

Deed dated 1819. JOHN McCLANE & PETER JOHNSON to LEWIS BURK. Richmond lot 14. Signed JOHN McCLANE, PETER JOHNSON. Witness: WILLIAM SUTHERLAND. rec 1819. p 215

Deed dated 1818. JASPER LITTLE to JAMES BEDWELL. S 1, T 12, T 1W. "ANNA, wife of JASPER". Signed JASPER LITTLE, ANNA LITTLE. Witness: none. rec 1819. pp 215, 216

Deed dated 1818. JASPER LITTLE to JONATHAN BEDWELL. S 1, T 12, T 1W. Signed JASPER LITTLE, ANNA LITTLE. Witness: none. rec 1819. p 216

Deed dated 1819. ROBERT LEAVELL to JOB GINN. Jacksonburgh lots 34, 35. Signed ROBERT LEAVELL, SALLY (x) LEAVELL. Witness: JOSIAH BRADBURY, THOMAS GINN JR. rec 1819. pp 216, 217

Deed dated 1818. JOHN WHITINGER & ELIZABETH, his wife, to ALBERT MURPHY. S 29, T 15, R 14E. Signed JOHN WHITINGER, ELIZABETH (x) WHITINGER. Witness: THOMAS R. CHUNN, JOSEPH DUEY. rec 1819. p 217

Deed dated 1819. VINCENT STEPHENSON to DANIEL LAUMAN S 1, T 13, R 2E. "SUSANNA, his wife". Signed VINCENT STEPHENSON, SUSANNA STEPHENSON. Witness: JEREMY MANSUR, JNO. SUFFRINS. rec 1819. p 218

Deed dated 1819. JACOB KESLING to WILLIAM IRELAND. S 27, T 13, R 1W. "his wife PHEBE". Signed JACOB KESLING, PHEBE (x) KESLING. Witness: WILLIAM CLARK, JOHN (x) KESLING. rec 1819. pp 218, 219

Mortgage dated 1819. LARKIN REYNOLDS to WILLIAM REYNOLDS. Land in S 36, T 16, R 12 held as security on debt to WILLIAM. Signed LARKIN REYNOLDS. Witness: MOSES COOPER, CHARLES REYNOLDS. rec 1819. pp 219, 220 Margin note: mortgage satisfied 28 Aug, 1820.

Mortgage dated 1819. HENRY GARRETT to ANDREW MORROW

WAYNE COUNTY DEEDS: Book B

of Preble Co, Oh. S 23, T 17, R 13E: land, mill & houses held as security in debt to MORROW. Signed HENRY GARRETT. Witness: RICHARD WARNOCK, OWEN McMANUS. rec 1819. pp 220, 221

Deed dated 1819. JACOB WILLIAMS & REBECCA, his wife to THOMAS SYMONS. S 35, T 16, R 12E. Signed JACOB WILLIAMS, REBECCA (x) WILLIAMS. Witness: ELIZABETH BANKS, THOMAS BANKS. rec 1819. pp 221, 222

Deed dated 1819. HENRY PEARSON to JOHN BRADWAY JR. S 31, T 12, R 1W. "wife ABIGAIL". Signed HENRY PEARSON ABIGAIL (x) PEARSON. Witness: SAMUEL HAVENRIDGE. rec 1820. pp 222, 223

Deed dated 1819. JOSIAH BRADWAY to JOHN BRADWAY. S 32, T 12, R 1W. Signed JOSIAH BRADWAY. Witness: HENRY PEARSON, SAMUEL HAVENRIDGE. rec 1820. pp 223, 224

Deed dated 1819. ROBERT WADDELL & LEVINA, his wife, to SAMUEL HAVENRIDGE. S 32, T 12, R 1W. Signed ROBERT WADDELL, LEVINA (x) WADDELL. Witness: JOSIAH BRADWAY, HENRY PEARSON. rec 1820. pp 224, 225

Deed dated 1819. THOMAS HATFIELD to JACOB HOOVER. Washington town lot 26, S 26, T 17, R 13E. Signed THOMAS HATFIELD, SARAH (x) HATFIELD. Witness: JACOB JULIAN, MATHEW ELLIOTT. rec 1820. p 225

Deed dated 1818. HENRY HOOVER to JACOB HOOVER. S 10, T 16, R 13E. "ELIZABETH, his wife". Signed HENRY HOOVER, ELIZABETH (x) HOOVER. Witness: JACOB JULIAN, MATHEW ELLIOTT. rec 1820. pp 225, 226

Deed dated 1819. ISAAC WILSON to GRINER WILSON. S 26, T 15, R 12E. "SARAH, wife of ISAAC". Signed ISAAC WILSON, SARAH (x) WILSON. Witness: JOHN WILLSON, THOMAS HARDIN. rec 1820. pp 226, 227

Deed dated 1819. JEREMIAH COX to EZRA BOSWELL. Richmond lot 12. Signed JEREMIAH COX. Witness: none. rec 1820. p 227

Deed dated 1819. JEREMIAH COX to EZRA BOSWELL. Richmond lot 35. Signed JEREMIAH COX. Witness: none. rec 1820. pp 227, 228

Deed dated 1819. JEREMIAH COX to EZRA BOSWELL. Richmond lot 3. Signed JEREMIAH COX. Witness: none. rec 1820. p 228

Deed dated 1820. LAURENCE H. BRANNON to ROBERT WADE

WAYNE COUNTY DEEDS: Book B

of Clark Co, KY. Cntrv lot 57. Signed LAURENCE H. BRANNON, CINTHY BRANNON. Witness: JOHN MAXWELL, JOHN JONES. rec 1820. pp 228, 229

Deed dated 1818. USA to JAMES PORTER. S 9, T 17, R 13. rec 1820. p 229

Deed dated 1819. JAMES PORTER to WILLIAM ELLIOTT. S 9, T 17, R 13E. Signed JAMES PORTER, MARGARET (x) PORTER. Witness: none. rec 1820. pp 229, 230

Deed dated 1820. THOMAS CASON JR of Franklin Co to PHILIP MISER. Cntrv lot 163. Signed THOMAS CASON, MARY CASON. Witness: none. rec 1820. p 230

Deed dated 1819. NOAH FOUTS to DAVID T. WYATT. S 18, T 12, R 1W. Signed NOAH FOUTS, PHEBE FOUTS. Witness: none. rec 1820. pp 230, 321

Deed dated 1819. JOHN SMITH to AMOS WILKINS. S 18, T 13, R 1W. Signed JOHN SMITH, JANE SMITH. Witness: none. rec 1820. p 231

Deed dated 1819. THOMAS BEARD & MELINDA, his wife, to RACHEL FRAIZAR, dau of THOMAS. "unto RACHEL & the heirs of her own body." S 20, T 15, R 13E. Signed THOMAS BEARD, MELINDA BEARD. Witness: THOMAS R. IRVIN, JOHN BEARD. rec 1820. pp 231, 232

Deed dated 1819. JESSE TOMPKINS to NICHOLAS DRULY. S 2, T 12, R 1W. Signed JESS (x) TOMPKINS. Witness: ISAAC ESTELE. no rec date. pp 232, 233

Deed dated 1819. JOHN SUTHERLAND to JOHN McBROOM. S 13 & 24, T 14, R 2W. Signed JOHN SUTHERLAND, JANE SUTHERLAND. Witness: none. rec 1820. p 233

Deed dated 1820. JOSEPH TEAGLE to JOHN TEAGLE. S 21, T 17, R 14E. "RUTH, his wife". Signed JOSEPH (x) TEAGLE, RUTH (x) TEAGLE. Witness: none. rec 1820. pp 233, 234

Deed dated 1819. WILLIS PARKINSON to JAMES RARIDEN. Salisbury lot 54. "HARRIOTT, his wife". Signed WILLIS PARKINSON, HARRIET PARKINSON. Witness: none. rec 1820. p 234

Deed dated 1819. WILLIS PARKINSON to ELIJAH FISHER. Salisbury lot 54. Signed WILLIS PARKINSON, HARRIET PARKINSON. Witness: none. rec 1820. p 235

Deed dated 1819. ROBERT LEAVELL to EZEKIEL LEAVELL.

WAYNE COUNTY DEEDS: Book B

Jacksonburgh lots 14, 17, 18, 32. Signed ROBERT LEAVELL, SALLY (x) LEAVELL. Witness: THOMAS GINN SR, JOSIAH BRADBURY. rec 1820. pp 235, 236

Deed dated 1819. ROBERT LEAVELL to STEPHEN GASSEN. Jacksonburgh lot 2. Signed ROBERT LEAVELL, SALLY (x) LEAVELL. Witness: EZEKIEL LEAVELL, ZADOCK DOUGHERTY rec 1820. p 236

Deed dated 1819. ROBERT LEAVELL to STEPHEN GASSEN. Jacksonburgh lot 21. Signed ROBERT LEAVELL, SALLY (x) LEAVELL. Witness: EZEKIEL LEAVELL, ZADOCK DOUGHERTY. rec 1820. pp 236, 237

Deed dated 1820. JOHN SUTHERLAND & JANE his wife, & WILLIAM SUTHERLAND & JULIANN his wife, to PETER VAN DERVEER. Salisbury lot 85. Signed JOHN SUTHERLAND, JANE SUTHERLAND, WILLIAM SUTHERLAND, JULIANN SUTHERLAND. Witness: JOHN C. KIBBEY. rec 1820. p 237

Deed dated 1819. JEHU STUART to BENJAMIN EDWARDS. S 6, T 13, R 1W. Signed JEHU STUART, SARAH STUART. Witness: ABRAHAM STUART. rec 1820. pp 237, 238

Deed dated 1819. NATHAN SMITH to JOSEPH ABRAHAM of Clearmoun (Clermont) Co, OH. S 5, T 12, R 1W. Signed NATHAN SMITH, MARY (x) SMITH. Witness: MATTHEW DORON. rec 1819. p 238

Affidavit dated 1820. Notes held by JACOB BEELER JR against SAMUEL WILLITS were lost or misplaced. WILLITS signed replacements. Signed JACOB BEELER. Witness: D.F. SACKETT, LEVI WILLITS. rec 1820. p 239

Deed dated 1819. JOHN BLACK & BARBARY, his wife, to LEVI WILLITS. S 5, T 15, R 13E. Signed JOHN BLACK, BARBARY (x) BLACK. Witness: JOSEPH FLINT, L. REYNOLDS. rec 1820. pp 239, 240

Deed dated 1820. ROBERT WADE to LEWIS THOMAS. Cntry lot 57. Signed ROBERT WADE. Witness: LAURENCE H. BRANNON. rec 1820. p 240

Deed dated 1819. HENRY MILLS & HANNAH, his wife & MOSES MILLS & ELIZABETH, his wife, to CHARLES OSBORN. S 28, T 18, R 13E. Signed HENRY MILLS, HANNAH MILES, MOSES MILLS, ELIZABETH MILLS. Witness: ELIHU SWAIN, JOHN UNDERHILL. rec 1820. pp 240, 241

Deed dated 1819. JOHN C. IRVIN of Butler Co, OH to ABRAHAM ELLIOTT. T 16, R 13E, S 7. Signed JOHN C. IRVIN, BETSEY IRVIN. Witness: HENRY P. IRVIN,

WAYNE COUNTY DEEDS: Book B

LEWIS P. HUNT (in OH). rec 1820. pp 241, 242

Deed dated 1820. ISAAC BARKER & MARY, his wife, to JOHN COMER. S 9, T 14, R 1W. Signed ISAAC BARKER, MARY BARKER. Witness: none. no rec date. p 242

Deed dated 1820. JOSEPH COX to JONATHAN HILL. Abington lots 107, 108. Signed JOSEPH COX, MARY (x) COX. Witness: CHARLES H. STANLEY. rec 1820. pp 242, 243

Deed dated 1819. JOHN COX to JONATHAN HILL. Abington lot 41. Signed JOHN COX, CATHARINE (x) COX. Witness: BENSON MINER, DAVID COX. rec 1820. p 243

Deed dated 1820. LAURENCE H. BRANNON to DAVID F. SACKETT. Cntrv lot 103. Signed LAURENCE H. BRANNON, CINTHY BRANNON. Witness: PHILIP MIZER. rec 1820. pp 243, 244

Deed dated 1820. LAURENCE H. BRANNON to SIMON YANDES of Fayette Co. Cntrv lots 27, 28. Signed LAURENCE H. BRANNON, CINTHY BRANNON. Witness: PHILIP MIZER. rec 1820. p 244

Deed dated 1820. LAURENCE H. BRANNON to RACHEL NEEL. Cntrv lot 70. Signed LAURENCE H. BRANNON, CINTHY BRANNON. Witness: PHILIP MIZER. rec 1820. pp 244, 245

Deed dated 1819. GEORGE ISH & MARIAM, his wife, to ELI SIBBIT or TIBBIT of Warren Co, OH. S 29, T 16, R 13E. Signed GEORGE ISH, MARIAM ISH. Witness: WM. BROWN, JOSEPH (x) McCLANHAN. rec 1820. p 245

Deed dated 1819. JOHN MORROW & MARY, his wife, to DAVID MOORE. S 10, T 14, R 1W. Signed JOHN MORROW, MARY MORROW. Witness: JAMES CLARK. rec 1820. pp 245, 246

Deed dated 1820. JOHN THOMAS to JAMES PIERCE THOMAS. S 3, T 14, R 1W. "in JONATHAN L. GRAVE's line..to WILLIAM HIETT's line". "ELIZABETH, his wife". Signed JOHN THOMAS, ELIZABETH THOMAS. Witness: CHARLES TEAS ISAAC COMMONS, JACOB GRAVE. rec 1820. pp 246, 247

Deed dated 1820. THOMAS ALEXANDER to ABRAHAM ELLIOT. Jacksonburgh lot 22. Signed THOMAS ALEXANDER. Witness JAS. GILMORE, UMPHREY SUTTON. rec 1820. pp 247, 248

Deed dated 1820. ROBERT LEAVELL & SALLY, his wife, to ABRAHAM ELLIOT. Jacksonburgh lot 12. Signed ROBERT LEAVELL, SALLY (x) LEAVELL. Witness: DANIEL BRADBERRY, JOSIAH BRADBERRY. rec 1820. p 248

WAYNE COUNTY DEEDS: Book B

Deed dated 1819. JOHN TOWEL of Orange Co to STEPHEN JOHNSON. S 5, T 17, R 14E. Signed JOHN TOWEL. Witness BARNEY McMANUS, OWEN McMANUS. rec 1820. pp 248, 249

Deed dated 1820. STEPHEN JOHNSON to WILLIAM JOHNSON. S 5, T 17, R 14E. Signed STEPHEN JOHNSON. Witness: JOSEPH WAY, BARNEY McMANUS. rec 1820. pp 249, 250

Deed dated 1820. DAVID ODOM from JOHN SUMMERS. S 1, T 16, R 12. "ABIGAIL, his wife". Signed JOHN SUMMERS ABIGAIL (x) SUMMERS. Witness: WM. BROWN, ROBERT A. SUMERS. rec 1820. p 250

Deed dated 1819. JOSEPH PICKET to JOSEPH HOLEMAN. S 7, T 16, R 14E. "PRISCILLA, his wife". Signed JOSEPH PICKET, PRISCILLA (x) PICKET. Witness: ISOM HARVEY. rec 1820. pp 250, 251

Deed dated 1820. THOMAS HATFIELD to ISAAC MENDENHALL Washington town lot 35. Signed THOMAS HATFIELD, SARAH (x) HATFIELD. Witness: THOMAS LOGAN. rec 1820. p 251

Deed dated 1819. ISAAC MESSICK of Preble Co, OH to JOHN HALE. Richmond lot 48. Signed ISAAC MESSICK. Witness: none. rec 1820. pp 252, 253

Deed dated 1819. JOHN BURGES & SARAH, his wife, to JOHN HALE. Richmond lot, no #. Signed JOHN (x) BURGES, SARAH (x) BURGES. Witness: none. rec 1820. p 253

Deed dated 1819. WILLIAM JUSTICE to JOHN HALE. Richmond lot 55. Signed WILLIAM JUSTICE, HANNAH (x) JUSTICE. Witness: W. PUGH. rec 1820. pp 253, 254

Deed dated 1820. JOEL WRIGHT & SALLY, his wife, to NATHAN DOAN. S 24, T 15, R 12E. Signed JOEL WRIGHT, SALLY (x) WRIGHT. Witness: BENJAMIN BEESON, FRANCES (x) PEARCY. rec 1820. pp 254, 255

Deed dated 1820. JOEL WRIGHT & SALLY, his wife, to BENJAMIN BEESON. S 24, T 15, R 12E. Signed JOEL WRIGHT, SALLY (x) WRIGHT. Witness: NATHAN DOAN, FRANCES (x) PEARSEY. rec 1820. pp 255, 256

Emancipation certificate dated 1816. HENRY, late a slave of ALEXANDER BLACK, dec, was emancipated in BLACK's will, recorded April 1816 at Paris, Bourbon Co, KY. rec 1820. p 256

Deed dated 1818. THOMAS MOFFET & MARY, his wife, to ISAAC SHELBY. S 28, T 15, R 14. Signed THOMAS MOFFET MARY MOFFET. Witness: THOMAS R. CHUNN, JOSEPH DEWEY.

WAYNE COUNTY DEEDS: Book B

rec 1820. pp 256, 257

Deed dated 1817. USA to JAMES BLACK. S 9, T 16, R 14E. rec 1820. p 257

Deed dated 1818. ISRAEL HOUGH to JAMES EVANS. New Liberty lot 9. "MARTHA, his wife". Signed ISRAEL HOUGH, MARTHA HOUGH. Witness: none. rec 1820. pp 257, 258

Deed dated 1816. USA to JAMES BLACK. S 10, T 16, R 14E. rec 1820. p 258

Deed dated 1819. NATHAN SYMONS to JOHN NIXON. S 22, T 16, R 12. "JANE, his wife". Signed NATHAN SYMONS, JANE (x) SYMONS. Witness: WM. BROWN, JOHN BROWN. rec 1820. pp 258, 259

Deed dated 1820. ANDREW ENDSLEY SR to STEPHEN G. HUNT. S 25, T 13, R 2W. "SARAH, his wife". Signed ANDREW ENDSLEY, SARAH ENDSLEY. Witness: none. rec 1820. pp 259, 260

Deed dated 1819. JOHN McLANE JR to ISAAC M. JOHNSON of Franklin Co. Richmond lot 2. Signed JOHN McLANE, CATHARINE McLANE. Witness: JNO. SUFFRINS, ADAM BOYD. Rec 1820. p 260

Deed dated 1819. THOMAS BEARD & MELINDA, his wife, to JEANE BREAKS, dau of THOMAS. "to JEANE BREAKS & the heirs of her own body." S 20, T 15, R 13E. Signed THOMAS BEARD, MELINDA BEARD. Witness: JOHN BEARD, THOMAS R. IRVIN. rec 1820. p 261

Deed dated 1820. ABRAHAM ELLIOTT to THOMAS SYMONS. Jacksonburgh lot 12. Signed ABRAHAM ELLIOTT. Witness: JAMES GILMORE, EZEKIEL LEAVELL. rec 1820. pp 261, 262

Deed dated 1819. THOMAS PEARSON to ABRAHAM SYMONS. T 16, R 12E, S 34. "NANCY, my wife". Signed THOMAS (x) PEARSON, NANCY (x) PEARSON. Witness: MATTHEW SYMONS, WM. BROWN. rec 1820. pp 262, 263

Deed dated 1820. JACOB DICKARD to ABRAHAM SYMONS. S 34, T 16, R 12E. "ELIZABETH, his wife". Signed JACOB (x) DICKARD, ELIZABETH (x) DICKARD. Witness: JACOB HOOVER. rec 1820. pp 263, 264

Deed dated 1819. USA to JOHN JORDAN. S 13, T 13, R 1. rec 1820. p 264

WAYNE COUNTY DEEDS: Book B

Deed dated 1820. JOHN JORDAN to WILLIAM BRATTAIN. S 33, T 13, R 1W. Signed JOHN JORDAN, RACHEL JORDAN. Witness: JOHN GIBSON, WILLIAM HUNT. rec 1820. pp 264, 265

Deed dated 1820. JOHN JORDAN to CHRISTIAN HINDEL. S 33, T 13, R 1W. Signed JOHN JORDAN, RACHEL JORDAN. Witness: JOHN GIBSON, WILLIAM HUNT. rec 1820. p 265

Deed dated 1816. USA to ROBERT BLACK. S 36, T 16, R 13. rec 1820. pp 265, 266

Deed dated 1820. SAMUEL WALKER to THOMAS WALKER. S 27, T 16, R 14. "corner of SAMUEL WALKER SR". Signed SAMUEL WALKER. Witness: none. rec 1820. p 266

Deed dated 1819. LARKIN REYNOLDS to CHARLES REYNOLDS S 36, T 16, R 12. Signed LARKIN REYNOLDS. Witness: JACOB HOOVER, ISAIAH DRURY. rec 1820. pp 266, 267

Deed dated 1816. USA to JAMES BLACK JR. S 29, T 16, R 14E. rec 1820. pp 267, 268

Bill of sale dated 1820. ABRAHAM ELLIOTT to JOSIAH BRADBURY. Household goods, horses, cattle, surveyor's instruments, "corn coming from HUMPHREY SUTTON for rent of place belonging to heirs of JAMES BROWN, dec", etc. Signed ABRAHAM ELLIOTT. Witness: JAMES GILMORE, EZEKIEL LEAVELL. rec 1820. pp 268, 269

Report dated 1820. Commissioners apptd by State to select permanent Wayne Co Seat of Justice were equally divided in choice of a site, left county without accomplishing object. Signed JESSE DURHAM, SAM'L. CARR, ADAM DAVIS, WILLIAM LOWE. rec 1820. p 269

Deed dated 1820. LAURENCE H. BRANNON to LEWIS THOMAS. Cntry lot 57. Signed LAURENCE H. BRANNON, CINTHY BRANNON. Witness: none. rec 1820. pp 269, 270

Deed dated 1820. WILLIAM WILLIAMS to ELIAZAR HIATT. Richmond lot 24. Signed WILLIAM WILLIAMS. Witness: none. rec 1820. p 270

Deed dated 1820. NATHAN HOCKET & ELIZABETH, his wife to WILLIAM WILLIAMS. Richmond lot, no #. Signed NATHAN HOCKET, ELIZABETH HOCKET. Witness: none. rec 1820. pp 270, 271

Deed dated 1816. JOHN SMITH to WILLIAM WILLIAMS. Richmond lot 24. Signed JOHN SMITH. Witness: none. rec 1820. p 271

WAYNE COUNTY DEEDS: Book B

Deed dated 1819. JOHN SMITH to JESSE BALDWIN. Richmond lot 31. Signed JOHN SMITH. Witness: none. rec 1820. pp 271, 272

Deed dated 1818. JEREMIAH COX to JOHN REED. Richmond lot 38. Signed JEREMIAH COX. Witness: none. rec 1820. p 272

Deed dated 1818. JEREMIAH COX to JOHN REED of Fayette Co, PA. Richmond lot 21. Signed JEREMIAH COX. Witness: PETER JOHNSON. rec 1820. p 272

Deed dated 1818. JOHN CHARLES to JOHN REED. S 32, T 14, R 1W. Signed JOHN CHARLES, ELVY (x) CHARLES. Witness: JESSE PEGG. rec 1820. pp 272, 273

Deed dated 1819. JOHN HARDEN to DANIEL SHAFFER. S 24, T 13, R 1W. Signed JOHN HARDING, ANN (x) HARDING Witness: JOHN HOWARD, J. FLINT. rec 1820. pp 273, 274

Deed dated 1817. JOHN SMITH to JOHN WILLIAMS. Richmond lot 79. Signed JOHN SMITH. Witness: none. rec 1820. p 274

Deed dated 1820. ISAAC VORE to THOMAS STAFFORD. S 15, T 14, R 1W. "RUTH, his wife". Signed ISAAC VORE RUTH VORE. Witness: none. rec 1820. pp 274, 275

Deed dated 1816. JOHN SMITH to THOMAS STAFFORD. Richmond lot 43. Signed JOHN SMITH. Witness: none. rec 1820. p 275

Deed dated 1820. ISAAC HARVEY to WILLIAM BROWN. S 17, T 17, R 13E. Signed ISAAC HARVEY, REBECKA HARVEY Witness: WM. BROWN, JOHN BROWN. rec 1820. pp 275, 276

Deed dated 1820. ROBERT LEAVELL & SALLY, his wife, to JAMES GILMORE. Jacksonburg lot 2. Signed ROBERT LEAVELL, SALLY (x) LEAVELL. Witness: THOMAS ALEXANDER, ABRAHAM HENDRICKS. Rec 1820. pp 276, 277

Deed dated 1820. STEPHEN GASSEN & HARRIET, his wife, to JAMES GILMORE. Jacksonburg lot 2. Signed STEPHEN GASSEN, HARRIET GASSEN. Witness: ENOCH DART, DANIEL BRADBERRY. rec 1820. p 277

Deed dated 1819. JOHN WOODARD to JOHN SUTHERLAND. S 22, T 16, R 13E. "with RACHEL, his wife". Signed JOHN WOODARD, RACHEL (x) WOODARD. Witness: none. rec 1820. pp 277, 278

Deed dated 1820. HENRY GARRETT & (MARY) his wife to

WAYNE COUNTY DEEDS: Book B

WILLIAM YONG. S 24, T 17, R 13E. Signed HENRY GARRETT, MARY (x) GARRETT. Witness: ENOS VEAL. rec 1820. p 278

Deed dated 1820. WILLIAM SUMNER to CHARLES F. REED & LOVISE FOYE. Cntry lot 74. Signed WM. SUMNER, NANCY SUMNER. Witness: none. rec 1820. pp 278, 279

Deed dated 1820. WILLIAM SUMNER to LEVI JONES, PETER RINGO & JACOB N. BOOKER. Cntry lot 9 donated by SUMNER for burying ground, to erect a meeting house & a "Simenary of learning". Signed WM. SUMNER, NANCY SUMNER. Witness: CHARLES F. REED. rec 1820. pp 279, 280

Deed dated 1819. DANIEL LANDES to HENRY LANDES of Preble Co, OH. S 11, T 12, R 2W. "his wife, FANNY". Signed DANIEL LANDES, FANNY (x) LANDES. Witness; none. rec 1820. p 280

Deed dated 1820. JOHN C. KIBBEY to DAVID W. SUTHERLAND. Salisbury add'n lot 7. Signed JOHN C. KIBBEY, MARY KIBBEY. Witness: none. rec 1820. pp 280, 281

Deed dated 1820. JOHN ROLSTEN to SAMUEL D. DAVIS. Cntry lot 83. "SARAH, his wife". Signed JOHN ROLSTEN SALLY ROLSTEN. Witness: SAMUEL BECK, L. REYNOLDS, KESIAH J. BRANNON. rec 1820. p 281

Deed dated 1819. DAVID IRELAND & NANCY, his wife of Preble Co, OH to WILLIAM GORDON. S 26, T 14, R 1W. Signed DAVID IRELAND, NANCY (x) IRELAND. Witness: none. rec 1820. pp 281, 282

Deed dated 1820. JOHN WHITINGER to JOHN WILLIAMS. S 29, T 15, R 14. "his wife, ELIZABETH". Signed JOHN WHITINGER, ELIZABETH WHITINGER. Witness: ROBERT BEATY, SAMUEL DAWSON. rec 1820. pp 281, 282

Deed dated 1819. LAURENCE H. BRANNON to JESSE WILLIAMS. Cntry lots 208, 209. Signed LAURENCE H. BRANNON, CINTHY BRANNON. Witness: LEWIS THOMAS. rec 1820. p 283

Deed dated 1819. ISAAC SHELBY to JOHN A. RANCK of Montgomery Co, OH. S 28, T 15, R 14E. Signed ISAAC SHELBY. Witness: JOSEPH COX. rec 1820. pp 283, 284

Deed dated 1819. RICHARD RUE to JOHN HUNT. S 30, T 13, R 1. "ELIZABETH, his wife". Signed RICHARD RUE, ELIZABETH RUE. Witness: none. rec 1820. p 284

Deed dated 1819. JACOB GALYAN to JACOB LAD, "a man

WAYNE COUNTY DEEDS: Book B

of color". S 20, T 17, R 13E. Signed JACOB GALYAN, POLLY GALYAN. Witness: JOHN TULLIS, LISMUND BASYE. rec 1820. p 285

Deed dated 1819. ANDREW ENDSLEY to JOSEPH LAMB. S 25, T 13, R 2W. Signed ANDREW ENDSLEY, SARAH ENDSLEY Witness: none. rec 1820. pp 285, 286

Deed dated 1820. BENJAMIN HUTCHENS to THOMAS HUTCHENS S 31, T 18, R 14. Signed BENJAMIN HUTCHENS, MARTHA (x) HUTCHENS. Witness: WILLIAM LADD, GEORGE JOHNSON. rec 1820. pp 286, 287

Deed dated 1820. MAJOR DODSON to ELIJAH DODSON. S 10, T 12, R 1W. "AMY, his wife". Signed MAJOR DODSON AMY DODSON. Witness: none. rec 1820. p 287

Deed dated 1820. DANIEL LAUMAN to WILLIS PARKISON of Green Co, OH. S 1, T 13, R 2W: "at JEREMIAH MANSUR's corner". Signed DANIEL LAUMAN. Witness: none. rec 1820. pp 287, 288

Deed dated 1820. DAVID FISHER to WILLIAM LOWRY & WILLIS PARKISON of OH. S 14, T 13, R 2W: "corner of ISAAC RAMBO's land". "his wife, ELIZABETH". Signed DAVID FISHER, ELIZABETH M. FISHER. Witness: none. rec 1820. p 288

Deed dated 1820. ABRAHAM ELLIOTT & JANE, his wife to ROBERT BRECKENRIDGE & JOSEPH BRECKENRIDGE of Franklin Co. S 7, T 16, R 13E. Signed ABRAHAM ELLIOTT, JANE ELLIOTT. Witness: JOSIAH BRADBURY, JAMES GILMORE. rec 1820. p 289

Deed dated 1819. EWEL KENDALL to HENRY RUE. S 17, T 13, R 1W. Signed EWEL KENDALL, ELIZABETH KENDALL. Witness: HIRAM KENDALL. rec 1820. p 290

Deed dated 1819. JOHN SMITH to STEPHEN THOMAS. Richmond lot 21. Signed JOHN SMITH. Witness: none. rec 1820. pp 290, 291

Deed dated 1819. JEREMIAH COX to STEPHEN THOMAS. Richmond lot 17. Signed JEREMIAH COX. Witness: WM. PUGH. rec 1820. p 291

Deed dated 1820. HENRY GARRETT & (MARY) his wife to DAVID YONG. S 24, T 17, R 13E. Signed HENRY GARRETT MARY (x) GARRETT. Witness: THOMAS MARSHILL. rec 1820. pp 291, 292

Deed dated 1820. SAMUEL WALKER to JOHN WALKER. S

WAYNE COUNTY DEEDS: Book B

12, T 13, R 1W. Signed SAMUEL WALKER. Witness: JOHN JOHN C. KIBBEY. rec 1820. p 292

Deed dated 1820. SAMUEL JOB to BENJAMIN JARVIS. S 4, T 13, R 1W. Signed SAMUEL JOB, RACHEL JOB. Witness: none. rec 1820. p 293

Deed dated 1817. JAMES JOHNSON to GEORGE RUSSELL. S 4, T 13, R 1W. "MIRIAM, his wife". Signed JAMES JOHNSON, MIRIAM JOHNSON. Witness: CHARLES JOHNSON, ROBERT BRATTAIN. rec 1820. pp 293, 294

Deed dated 1819. THOMAS BURROUGHS & LETTY, his wife to JOHN WILSON. "sold by JAMES SHAW". S 12, T 15, R 12E. Signed THOMAS BURROUGHS, LETTY BURROUGHS. Witness: THOMAS BEARD, JOHN WILSON, MELINDA BEARD. rec 1820. pp 294, 295

Deed dated 1819. JOEL FERGUSON & LYDIA, his wife to JOHN WILSON. S 11, T 15, R 12E. Signed JOEL FERGUSON, LYDIA FERGUSON. Witness: JONATHAN JUSTICE, JOHN WILSON, SETH WILSON. rec 1820. p 295

Deed dated 1818. JOHN SMITH to JOHN MOORE. Richmond lot 29. Signed JOHN SMITH. Witness: THOMAS CLAR, JOSEPH (x) BRAHAIN. rec 1820. pp 295, 296

Deed dated 1820. WILLIAM SWAFFORD to WILLIAM G. REYNOLDS, RICHARD WHARTON & DANIEL NOWLAND, trustees apptd by Christian Society in the Walnut (illegible). S 6, T 15, R 13 for a non-denominational meeting house & graveyard. Signed WILLIAM SWAFFORD, NANCY (x) SWAFFORD. Witness: EDWARD EMERSON, ASA BREWER. rec 1820. pp 296, 297

Deed dated 1820. ISAAC WILLIAMS to JAMES GRIMES. S 9, T 13, R not given. "JANE, his wife". Signed ISAAC WILLIAMS, JANE (x) WILLIAMS. Witness: none. rec 1820. p 297

Deed dated 1819. THOMAS HATFIELD to ALLEN WILLIAMS. Washington town lot 49. Signed THOMAS HATFIELD, SARAH HATFIELD. Witness: none. rec 1820. pp 297, 298

Deed dated 1819. JESSE BOND & PHEBE, his wife, to ISAAC WALKER. S 31, T 14, R 1W. Signed JESSE BOND, PHEBE (x) BOND. Witness: WILLIAM HOOVER, CATHARINE HOOVER. rec 1820. p 298

Deed dated 1820. JOHN SMITH & JANE, his wife, to HEZEKIAH WILLIAMS. Richmond lot 94. Signed JOHN SMITH, JANE SMITH. Witness: none. rec 1820. p 299

WAYNE COUNTY DEEDS: Book B

Mortgage deed dated 1820. BENJAMIN BASSETT, BENJAMIN CUSHMAN & NATHANIEL PIERCE of Jefferson Co, NY to HEZEKIAH WILLIAMS. Richmond lot 94. To be paid in full by 1 Jan, 1821 to void conveyance. Signed BENJAMIN BASSETT, BENJAMIN CUSHMAN, NATHANIEL PIERCE. Witness: none. rec 1820. pp 299, 300

Deed dated 1820. JOHN HURST to HENRY ROCKEFALLER of Wayne Co & ELI HEATON of Fayette Co. S 29, T 15, R 13E. "ELIZABETH, his wife". Signed JOHN HURST, ELIZABETH HURST. Witness: J. C. HUNT, JOSEPH FLINT. rec 1820. pp 300, 301

Deed dated 1820. THOMAS SYMONS to NATHAN SYMONS. S 22, T 16, R 12E. Signed THOMAS SYMONS, HANNAH SYMONS. Witness: JOHN ROLSTEN. rec 1820. pp 301, 302

Deed dated 1820. HEZEKIAH WILLIAMS & REBECKA, his wife, to BENJAMIN BASSETT, BENJAMIN CUSHMAN & NATHANIEL PIERCE of Jefferson Co, NY. Richmond lot 94. Signed HEZEKIAH WILLIAMS, REBECKA WILLIAMS. Witness: none. rec 1820. pp 302, 303

Deed dated 1820. JOHN WILLIAMS & MARY, his wife, to ISAAC MARTIN. Richmond lot 79. Signed JOHN WILLIAMS MARY (x) WILLIAMS. Witness: none. rec 1820. p 303

Deed dated 1820. THOMAS SLOO JR & REBECA, his wife, to THOMAS D. CARWEL, WILLIAM IRWIN & NICHOLAS LONGWORTH. S 14 & 15, T 16, R 14E & Salisbury lots 10, 19, 20, 23, 24, 35 & S 19, T 14, R 16 excepting land in town of Cntry & Cntry lots 4, 8, 14, 15, 16, 22, 33, 36, 37, 38, 55 through 64 inclusive. Signed THO. SLOO JR, REBECCA SLOO. Witness: H. T. SLOO, JOHN MAHARD. (written at Hamilton Co. OH) rec 1820. pp 303, 304

Deed dated 1820. ELIAS WILLITS to JONATHAN KIDWELL. Cntry lot 5. Signed ELIAS WILLITS. Witness: SAM'L. P. BOOKER. rec 1820. pp 304, 305

Deed dated 1820. PATRICK JUSTICE to DAVID W. SUTHERLAND. Richmond lot 26. "KATHARINE, his wife". Signed PATRICK JUSTICE, KATHARINE JUSTICE. Witness: none. rec 1820. p 305

Deed dated 1820. WILLIAM HOLLINGSWORTH & MARY, his wife (formerly COOK) of Butler Co, OH & JESSE GREEN & CHARITY his wife (formerly COOK) of Preble Co, Oh to JAMES PERVAL. S 31, T 14, R 1W. Signed WILLIAM HOLLINGSWORTH, MARY HOLLINGSWORTH, JESSE GREEN, CHARITY GREEN. Witness: JOSEPH HOLLINGSWORTH, ASA PREVO (in

WAYNE COUNTY DEEDS: Book B

OH). rec 1820. pp 306. 307

Deed dated 1820. NATHAN COMMONS & MARTHA his wife to THOMAS COMMONS. Cntry lot 7. Signed NATHAN COMMONS, MARTHA (x) COMMONS. Witness: none. rec 1820. p 307

Deed dated 1819. ABNER SHENAULT & (MARY), his wife, to JOHN FERGUSON. Land in Franklin Co. S 27, T 12, R 2W. Signed ABNER (x) CHENAULT, MARY (x) CHENAULT. Witness: nonw. rec 1820. pp 307, 308

Deed dated 1820. THOMAS LAMB to JOHN LAMB of Perquimons Co, NC. S 2 & 11, T 16, R 14E. "SARAH, his wife." Signed THOMAS LAMB, SARAH (x) LAMB. Witness: none. rec 1820. pp 308, 309

Deed dated 1819. ABNER CHENAULT to WILLIAM FERGUSON. S 27, T 12, R 2W. Signed ABNER (x) CHENAULT, MARY (x) CHENAULT. Witness: none. rec 1820. pp 309. 310

Deed dated 1820. BENJAMIN EDWARDS of Preble Co. OH to WILLIAM COOK. S 6, T 13, R 1W. Witness: none. rec 1820. p 310

Deed dated 1820. JOSEPH SHELBY to JOSHUA SHELBY. S 30, T 15, R 14E. Signed JOSEPH SHELBY, ELIZABETH (x) SHELBY. Witness: JOHN P. WILLIAMS, JOHN WILLIAMS SR rec 1820. pp 310, 311

Deed dated 1819. DAVID IRELAND & NANCY, his wife of Preble Co to ELOM IRELAND of same. S 26, T 14, R 1W. Signed DAVID IRELAND, NANCY (x) IRELAND. Witness: none. rec 1820. pp 311, 312

Deed dated 1819. STEPHEN THOMAS & WILLIAM JUSTICE to JOHN SUFFRINS. Richmond lot 15. Signed STEPHEN THOMAS WILLIAM JUSTICE. Witness: WM. PUGH. rec 1820. p 312

Deed dated 1820. JOHN MENDENHALL to JOHN SUFFRINS. Richmond lot 14. Signed JOHN MENDENHALL. Witness: JOB SPRINGER. rec 1820. pp 312, 313

Deed dated 1820. THOMAS STAFFORD to EDWARD BOND. S 15, T 14, R 1W. Signed THOMAS STAFFORD, ELIZABETH (x) STAFFORD. Witness: none. rec 1820. p 313

Deed dated 1820. JOHN HALE & POLLY, his wife, to CALEB COWGILL. Richmond lot 55. Signed JOHN (x) HALE, POLLY HALE. Witness: none. rec 1820. pp 313. 314

Deed dated 1819. ROBERT LEAVELL to JOHN SCOTT,

WAYNE COUNTY DEEDS: Book B

JOHN McKEE & RICHARD LEESON on behalf of the Christian Church. Jacksonburg lot, no #, given solely and forever for church use. Signed ROBERT LEAVELL, SALLY (x) LEAVELL. Witness: L. A. WALDO, WILLIAM ELLIOTT. rec 1820. p 314, 315

Deed dated 1820. ELIZABETH MILLER to MICHAEL MILLER. S 28, T 13, R 1W. Signed ELIZABETH MILLER. Witness: LUDWIG --- (german script). rec 1820. pp 315, 316

Deed dated 1819. THOMAS HATFIELD to CALEB COPE. Washington town lot 33. Signed THOMAS HATFIELD, SARAH (x) HATFIELD. Witness: none. rec 1820. p 316

Deed dated 1820. LARKIN REYNOLDS & CHARLES REYNOLDS to ENOCH WARMAN of Monongahala Co, VA. S 36, T 16, R 12E. "SARAH, wife of LARKIN; POLLY, wife of CHARLES" Signed LARKIN REYNOLDS, SARAH REYNOLDS, C. REYNOLDS, POLLY (x) REYNOLDS. Witness: ELI GASSEN, LEVI WILLITS. rec 1820. pp 316, 317

Deed dated 1820. LOVISE FOYE to CHARLES F. REED. Cntry lot 74. Signed LOVISE FOYE. Witness: none. rec 1820. pp 317, 318

Right of Way dated 1819. JOSEPH COX to JOHN A. RANCK of Montgomery Co, OH. Sold right to build dam in S3, T 12, R 2W & build a race to RANCK's property through COX's land. Signed JOSEPH COX. Witness: MATTHIAS FOSHER, DANIEL LANDES. rec 1820. p 318

Deed dated 1819. WILLIAM VANMETRE to OTHO & ELI RENCH of Fayette Co. S 27, T 15, R 12E. "PHEBE, his wife" Signed WILLIAM VANMETRE, PHEBE VANMETRE. Witness: HENRY GORDEN, THOMAS BANKS. rec 1820. pp 318, 319

Deed dated 1820. WILLIAM SUMNER to JOHN SMITH. Cntry lot 74. Signed WM. SUMNER, NANCY SUMNER. Witness: JAMES CORNELIUS. rec 1820. p 319

Bill of sale dated 1820. ARMSTRONG GRIMES to ROBERT GRIMES. Household goods, horses, cattle, sheep & hogs. Signed ARMSTRONG GRIMES. Witness: ALEXANDER GRIMES, GEORGE GRIMES. rec 1820. p 320

Deed dated 1819. THOMAS HATFIELD to PHILIP RENBERGER Washington town lot 38 in S 26, T 117, R 13E. Signed THOMAS HATFIELD, SARAH HATFIELD. Witness: none. rec 1820. pp 320, 321

Deed dated 1820. PHILIP RENBERGER to JOHN MURDOCK. Washington town lot 38. "ANNA, his wife". Signed

WAYNE COUNTY DEEDS: Book B

PHILIP RENBERGER, ANNA RENBERGER. Witness: JACOB HOOVER, SAMUEL LOGAN. rec 1820. p 321

Deed dated 1820. WILLIAM SMITH JONES to THOMAS CUPPY S 1, T 12, R 1W. "NANCY, his wife". Signed WILLIAM SMITH JONES, NANCY (x) JONES. Witness: none. rec 1820. pp 321, 322

Deed dated 1820. CALEB REYNOLDS to SAM'L. P. BOOKER. Cntry lots 26, 27. Signed CALEB REYNOLDS, CHARITY REYNOLDS. Witness: LAURENCE BRANNON. rec 1820. p 322

Deed dated 1819. HENRY LAUMAN to ALFRED LAUMAN. Salisbury lot 109. Signed H. LAUMAN. Witness: JOHN MILLER, DANIEL LAUMAN. rec 1820. pp 322, 323

Deed dated 1820. AARON COOK & TEMPERANCE, his wife, to HENRY EMMIL. S 13, T 13, R 1W (Harrison Twp). Signed AARON COOK, TEMPERANCE (x) COOK. Witness: JOHN WHITEHEAD, JOSEPH JACKSON. rec 1820. p 323

Deed dated 1819. EVAN CHALFANT to PETER JOHNSON. Richmond lot 27. Signed EVAN CHALFANT. Witness: WM. PUGH. rec 1820. p 324

Deed dated 1820. WILLIAM SMITH JONES to JOSEPH CRAVENS. S 1, T 12, R 1W. Signed WILLIAM SMITH JONES. NANCY (x) JONES. Witness: none. rec 1820. p 324

Deed dated 1820. JOSHUA SHELBY & SUSANNA, his wife, to JOSIAH EASTWOOD. Bethlehem lot 80. Signed JOSHUA SHELBY, SUSANNA (x) SHELBY. Witness: ISAAC SHELBY. rec 1820. p 325

Deed dated 1820. PATRICK JUSTICE to FREDERICK STANTON of Warren Co, Oh. Richmond lot 26. Signed PATRICK JUSTICE, KATHARINE (x) JUSTICE. Witness: none. rec 1820. pp 325, 326

Deed dated 1819. JOHN SMITH to CHARITY, ZIMRI, WILLIAM, MARTHA, ISAAC, SARAH, DAVID, KETURAH, ELIZABETH & THOMAS LEWIS, heirs of THOMAS LEWIS, dec. S 32, T 14, R 1W sold to THOMAS in his lifetime now conveyed to his heirs. Signed JOHN SMITH, JANE SMITH. Witness: STEPHEN HOLLAWAY, JESSE PEGG. rec 1820. p 326

Deed dated 1820. JOHN SMITH & JANE, his wife to SAMUEL BUTTERWORTH of Warren Co, OH. Richmond lot 35. Signed JOHN SMITH, JANE SMITH. Witness: none. rec 1820. pp 326, 327

Deed dated 1820. JACOB KEESLING & PHEBE, his wife.

WAYNE COUNTY DEEDS: Book B

to WILLIAM FOUTS. S 27 & 28, T 13, R 1. Signed JACOB KESLING, PHEBE (x) KESLING. Witness: THOS. M. MOUS, JOHN BANKS. rec 1820. pp 327, 328

Deed dated 1820. JOHN C. KIBBEY to WILLIAM SUTHERLAND Salisbury lot 17. Signed JOHN C. KIBBEY, MARY KIBBEY Witness: PTR. V. DERVEER, JAMES CLAYTON. rec 1820. pp 328, 329

Deed dated 1819. JONATHAN BRATTAIN to JACOB MEEK. S 33, T 13, R 1W. "ANNA, his wife". Signed JONATHAN BRATTAIN, ANNA BRATTAIN. Witness: WILLIAM MEEK. JOHN WINGFIELD. rec 1820. p 329

Deed dated 1815. JOHN JORDAN to DANIEL BONINE. S 34, T 13, R 1W. "RACHEL, his wife". Signed JOHN JORDAN, RACHEL JORDAN. Witness: GEORGE HOLDMAN, WILLIAM BIRK. rec 1820. pp 329, 330

Deed dated 1819. SPENCER FREE "a free man of color" to DAVID BONINE. S 34, T 13, R 1W. Signed SPENCER (x) FREE, AMY (x) FREE. Witness: none. JP's note: came AMY FREE, his wife. rec 1820. pp 330, 331

Deed dated 1820. EDWARD BOND to ABRAHAM JEFFRIES. S 14, T 14, R 1W. "ANN, his wife". Signed EDWARD BOND, ANN (x) BOND. Witness: none. rec 1820. p 331

Deed dated 1820. WILLIAM BOND to ABRAHAM JEFFRIES. S 14, T 14, R 1W: "to JOSEPH BOND's corner". "CHARLOTTE, his wife". Signed WILLIAM BOND, CHARLOTTE BOND. Witness: none. rec 1820. p 332

Deed dated 1820. WILLIAM NEAL to EPHRAIM LACY. Richmond lot 8. Signed WILLIAM NEAL, ANNA (x) NEAL. Witness: ROBERT MORRISON, ELIJAH LACY. rec 1820. pp 332, 333

Deed dated 1820. BLADEN ASHBY to JACOB GRAVE. S 12. T 14, R 1W "to JONATHAN L. GRAVE's corner". "CATHARINE, his wife." Signed BLADEN ASHBY, CATHARINE ASHBY. Witness: none. rec 1820. p 333

Deed dated 1820. JAMES FISHER to JACOB TALBOT. S 3. T 12, R 1W. "SARAH, his wife" Signed JAMES FISHER, SARAH (x) FISHER. Witness: RUTH ESTELE. ISAAC ESTELE. rec 1820. pp 333, 334

Deed dated 1820. JOHN NICHOLSON & ESTHER, his wife. to CHARLES TEAS. S 35, T 15, R 1W. Signed JOHN NICHOLSON, ESTHER NICHOLSON. Witness: GABRIEL HARRELL. BENJAMIN ELLIOTT. rec 1820. pp 334, 335

WAYNE COUNTY DEEDS: Book B

Deed dated 1820. JOHN H. FRYAR to ABSALOM STUART. S 14, T 13, R 1W. "PEGGY, his wife". Signed JOHN H. FRYAR, PEGGY (x) FRYAR. Witness: BENJAMIN B. MOORE, JONATHAN EDWARDS. rec 1820. p 335

Deed dated 1820. DAVID OSBORN to RICHARD MILLS. S 31, T 18, R 13E. Signed DAVID OSBORN, ELIZABETH OSBORN. Witness: OWEN McMANUS. rec 1820. pp 335, 336

Deed dated 1820. AARON COOK & TEMPERANCE, his wife, to WILLIAM JACKSON SR. S 13, T 13, R 1W. Signed AARON COOK, TEMPERANCE (x) COOK. Witness: JOHN WHITEHEAD, JOSEPH JACKSON. rec 1820. pp 336, 337

Deed dated 1820. JOSEPH LEWIS to BARTLEMEY BURROUGHS of Preble Co, OH. S 10, T 12, R 1W. Signed JOSEPH LEWIS, MARGARET (x) LEWIS. Witness: NICHOLAS (x) DRULY, JOHN ESTEB. rec 1820. p 337

Deed dated 1820. NICHOLAS DRULY to JOSEPH WYATT. S 5, T 12, R 1W. Signed NICHOLAS (x) DRULY, SALLY (x) DRULY. Witness: BENJAMIN (x) JARVES. rec 1820. pp 337, 338

Deed dated 1820. SAMUEL DRULY to JEREMIAH STANLEY. S 12, T 12, R 1W. "wife ANN". Signed SAMUEL (x) DRULY, ANN (x) DRULY. Witness: none. rec 1820. p 338

Deed dated 1819. THOMAS HATFIELD to ISAAC RENBARGER. Washington town lot 39. Signed THOMAS HATFIELD, SARAH HATFIELD. Witness: none. rec 1820. pp 338, 339

Deed dated 1820. HENRY FENDER to WILLIAM DYE. S 21, T 15, R 14E. "ELIZABETH, his wife". Signed HENRY (x) FENDER, ELIZABETH (x) FENDER. Witness: none. rec 1820. p 339

Deed dated 1819. ROBERT LEAVELL to ZADOCK DOUGHERTY. Jacksonburg lot 19. Signed ROBERT LEAVELL, SALLY (x) LEAVELL. Witness: THOMAS GIN JR, JOSIAH BRADBERRY. rec 1820. p 340

Deed dated 1820. JOHN SMITH to JAMES BALLARD. Washington town lots 44, 45. "REBECKA, his wife". Signed JOHN SMITH, REBECKA SMITH. Witness: ABSALOM (x) FRASIER, JAMES BRADBERRY. rec 1820. pp 340, 341

Deed dated 1820. JOHN SMITH to JAMES BALLARD. Cntrv lot 74. Signed JOHN SMITH, REBECKA SMITH. Witness: ABSALOM (x) FRAZER. rec 1820. p 341

Deed dated 1820. PETER WEAVER & MARTHA, his wife, to

WAYNE COUNTY DEEDS: Book B

THOMAS M. PENDLETON. S 17, T 13, R 1W. Signed PETER WEAVER, MARTHA (x) WEAVER. Witness: none. rec 1820. pp 341, 342

Sheriff's sale dated 1820. ABRAHAM ELLIOTT, Sheriff of Wayne Co, to THOMAS M. PENDLETON. Writ issued against property to JOHN TURNER, PETER WEAVER, THOMAS McCARTNEY, DAVID HARMAN, THOMAS T. LEWIS by Gov'r of IN. Land in S 17, T 13, R 1W bought at auction by PENDLETON. Signed ABRAHAM ELLIOTT, Sheriff. Witness: JAS. GILMORE, THOMAS ALEXANDER. rec 1820. pp 342, 343

Deed dated 1819. JEREMIAH MANSUR to THOMAS M. PENDLETON. Salisbury lot 71. "JANE, his wife". Signed JEREMIAH MANSUR, JANE MANSUR. Witness: none. rec 1820. pp 343, 344

Sheriff's sale dated 1820. ABRAHAM ELLIOTT, Sheriff, to PETER WEAVER. Clerk of Court DAVID HOOVER directed Sheriff to seize estates of JOHN TURNER & HENRY STRADER; judgement granted to MARY KNIGHT against TURNER. Land in S 17, T 13, R 1W bought at auction by WEAVER. Signed ABRAHAM ELLIOTT, sheriff. Witness: ENOS HULBART, THOMAS ALEXANDER. rec 1820. pp 344, 345

Deed dated 1820. JOSEPH COX to JAMES MILLS. S 19, 30 & 31, T 18, R 15E. "DIANNA, his wife". Signed JOSEPH COX, DINAH (x) COX. Witness: none. rec 1820. p 345

Deed dated 1819. JAMES WICKERSHAM & RACHEL, his wife to WILLIAM HUNT. S 35, T 15, R 1W. Signed JAMES WICKERSHAM, RACHEL WICKERSHAM. Witness: GABRIEL HARREL, JOHN UNTHANK, BENJAMIN ELLIOTT. rec 1820. pp 345, 346

Deed dated 1820. JOHN SMALL & MARY his wife to JESSE WILLIAMS of Warren Co, OH. S 29, T 14, R 1W. Signed JOHN SMALL, MARY SMALL. Witness: ELEAZAR HIATT, M.T. WILLIAMS. rec 1820. pp 346, 347

Deed dated 1820. ROBERT WORL & PHEBE, his wife, to ENOS HURLBUT. S 5, T 16, R 13E. Signed ROBERT (x) WORL, PHEBE (x) WORL. Witness: ABRAHAM ELLIOTT, DANIEL BRADBERRY. rec 1820. pp 347, 348

Deed dated 1820. ALLEN WILLIAMS & CHARITY, his wife, to ENOS HURLBUT. S 5, T 16, R 13E. Signed ALLEN WILLIAMS, CHARITY (x) WILLIAMS. Witness: JOSIAH BRADBERRY, HENRY BRYAN. rec 1820. pp 348, 349

Deed dated 1820. WILLIAM SUMNER to LEWIS THOMAS. Cntry lots 20, 40. Signed WM. SUMNER, NANCY SUMNER.

WAYNE COUNTY DEEDS: Book B

Witness: none. rec 1820. pp 349, 350

Deed dated 1819. SAMUEL WALKER to JAMES WALKER. S 27, T 16, R 14E. Signed SAMUEL WALKER. Witness: none. rec 1820. p 350

Deed dated 1820. SAMUEL BROWN to JOSEPH BROWN. S 18, T 15, R 13E. Signed SAMUEL (x) BROWN, JANE (x) BROWN. Witness: LEBAN GARNER, WILLIAM HUTCHESON. rec 1820. p 351

Deed dated 1819. JOHN WILKISON to JEREMIAH MANSUR. Salisbury lot 70. "POLLY, his wife". Signed JOHN WILKINSON, MARY WILKINSON. Witness: none. rec 1820 pp 351, 352

Deed dated 1819. JOHN STARR to DANIEL PUTERBAUGH. S 19, T 12, R 1W. "RACHEL, his wife". Signed JOHN STARR RACHEL (x) STARR. Witness: none. rec 1820. p 352

Deed dated 1820. ASA GRUWELL to ANDREW HOLSON. S 30, T 15, R 13E. Signed ASA GRUWELL. Witness: WILLIAM MONTGOMERY, MARGARET MONTGOMERY. rec 1820. pp 352, 353

Deed dated 1820. WILLIAM PIKE to JAMES PERKINS. S 1, T 13, R 2W. "RACHEL, his wife". Signed WILLIAM PIKE, RACHEL PIKE. Witness: none. rec 1820. pp 353, 354

POA dated 1820. JOHN W. WHITE apptd AARON WHITE his atty to collect rent, sell land, etc. Signed JOHN W. WHITE. Witness: none. no rec date. p 354

Deed dated 1819. ASA WHITE to NICHOLAS DRULY. S 9, T 12, R 1W. "wife POLLY". Signed ASA WHITE, MARY (x) WHITE. Witness: none. rec 1820. pp 354, 355

Deed dated 1820. JOHN McCLAIN SR to PETER JOHNSON. Richmond lots 52, 53. Signed JOHN McCLAIN, CATHARINE McCLAIN. Witness: EZRA BOSWELL. rec 1820. p 355

Deed dated 1820. JOHN McCLAIN SR to PETER JOHNSON. S 1, T 14, R not given; "bound on East by Richmond...on West by JOHN CHARLES". Signed JOHN McCLAIN, CATHARINE McCLAIN. Witness: EZRA BOSWELL. rec 1820. pp 355, 356

Deed dated 1820. ROBERT HILL to JESSE BREWER. S 7, T 15, R 13E. Signed ROBERT HILL, SUSANNA HILL. Witness: THOMAS HILL SR, THOS. D. BUNDY. rec 1820. pp 356, 357

WAYNE COUNTY DEEDS: Book B

Deed dated 1820. JONATHAN JESSOP to CHARLES GORDEN & JOHN MAXWELL, Overseers of West Grove Meeting. S 13, T 16, R 13E: "benefit of the Society of Friends for a Meeting House, school and other purposes". "his wife ELIZABETH". Signed JONATHAN JESSOP, ELIZABETH JESSOP Witness: none. rec 1820. pp 357, 358

Deed dated 1820. JOSEPH PICKETT to WILLIAM HASTINGS. S 7, T 16, R 14E. Signed JOSEPH PICKETT, PRISCILLA PICKETT. Witness: none. rec 1820. pp 357. 358

Deed dated 1820. HEZEKIAH WILLIAMS to AZARIAH WILLIAMS. S 33, T 18, R 13. Signed HEZEKIAH WILLIAMS, REBECCA WILLIAMS. Witness: none. rec 1821 pp 358, 359

Deed dated 1820. SAMUEL LOGAN to WILLIAM OSBORN. S 2 & 7, T 17, R 13E. "his wife XENIA". Signed SAMUEL LOGAN, ZENOLIA LOGAN. Witness: none. rec 1821. p 359

Deed dated 1819. THOMAS HATFIELD to JOHN PAXSON. Washington town lot 37, S 26, T 17, R 13E. Signed THOMAS HATFIELD, SARAH HATFIELD. Witness: none. rec 1820. pp 359, 360

Deed dated 1820. SAMUEL WALKER SR to SAMUEL WALKER JR. S 27, T 10 (#16 written above in pencil) in R 14. "east corner of JAMES WALKER's land". Signed SAMUEL WALKER. Witness: none. rec 1821. p 360

Deed dated 1821. EDWARD L. FROST to DANIEL P. WIGGINS of Queens Co, NY. S 3, T 17, R 13E. Signed EDWARD L. FROST. Witness: none. rec 1821. pp 360, 361

Deed dated 1821. JOHN SMITH & JANE, his wife, to EDWARD L. FROST. Richmond lot 9. Signed JOHN SMITH, JANE SMITH. Witness: none. rec 1821. p 361

Deed dated 1821. JOHN SMITH & JANE, his wife, to EDWARD L. FROST. Richmond lot 78. Signed JOHN SMITH, JANE SMITH. Witness: none. rec 1821. pp 361, 362

Deed dated 1821. JOHN SMITH & JANE, his wife, to EDWARD L. FROST. Richmond lot 40. Signed JOHN SMITH, JANE SMITH. Witness: none. rec 1821. p 362

Deed dated 1821. JOSIAH GRINSLADE to EDWARD L. FROST Richmond lot 104. Signed J. GUNSLADE. Witness: none. rec 1821. pp 362, 363

Deed dated 1821. JOHN SMITH & JANE, his wife, to JOSIAH GUNSLADE. Richmond 104. Witness: none. rec 1821. p 363

WAYNE COUNTY DEEDS: Book B

Deed dated 1821. ELIAS WILLITS to THOMAS COMMONS & PHILIP SAVILL. Cntry outlot 117. Signed ELIAS WILLITS. Witness: none. rec 1821. pp 363, 364

Deed dated 1820. JEHU STUART to WILLIAM EDWARDS. S 6, T 13, R 1W. "SARAH, his wife". Signed JEHU STUART SARAH STUART. Witness: none. rec 1821. p 364

Deed dated 1820. ISAIAH DRURY & PRISCILLA his wife, & WILLIAM G. REYNOLDS & SARAH his wife, to JACOB CROLL. S 1, T 15, R 12E. Signed ISAIAH DRURY, PRISCILLA DRURY, WILLIAM G. REYNOLDS, SARAH REYNOLDS. Witness: WM. DRURY, RACHEL WILLITS. rec 1821. pp 364, 365

Deed dated 1818. WILLIAM THORN of Green Co, OH & RACHEL, his wife, to MICAJAH CHAMNYS (CHAMNESS in text.) S 30, T 16, R 13E. Signed WILLIAM THORN, RACHEL THORN. Witness: THOMAS EMBREE, IGAL BEESON. (in OH). rec 1821. pp 365, 366

Deed dated 1820. ELISHA SHORTRIDGE to BRADY WILLITS. S 25, T 16, R 12: "corner of JOHN SHORTRIDGE". Signed ELISHA SHORTRIDGE, ESTHER SHORTRIDGE. Witness: JOSIAH BRADBURY, DANIEL BRADBURY, ABEL H. LORD. rec 1821. pp 366, 367

Deed dated 1820. BENJAMIN HODGES to JOHN McCOMBS. S 27, T 13, R 1W. "JANE, his wife". Signed BENJAMIN HODGES, JANE HODGES. Witness: DANIEL HART, ELLIOT McCOMBS, JAMES HORNEY. rec 1821. pp 367, 368

Mortgage deed dated 1820. HENRY PASMORE of Butler Co OH to BENJAMIN HODGES. S 13, T 13, R 2W. Due March 1821 to void conveyance. Signed HENRY PASMORE. Witness: ABRAHAM ELLIOTT, ABNOR CATON. rec 1821. p 368

Deed dated 1820. JAMES JOHNSON to CHARLES JOHNSON. S 33, T 15, R 1W. "MARIAM, wife of JAMES". Signed JAMES JOHNSON, MARIAM JOHNSON. Witness: JOSIAH JOHNSON, PRUDENCE JOHNSON. rec 1821. pp 368, 369

Deed dated 1819. BLADEN ASHBY to JOHN NICHOLSON. S 12, T 14, R 1W. Signed BLADEN ASHBY, CATHARINE ASHBY Witness: none. rec 1821. p 369

Deed dated 1819. NICHOLAS DRULY to ENOCH WITT. S 2, T 14, R 1W. Signed NICHOLAS DRULY, SALLY (x) DRULY. Witness: none. rec 1821. p 370

Deed dated 1819. THOMPSON JONES to RENNEY JULIAN. Cntry lot 57. Signed THOMPSON JONES. Witness: DANIEL UNDERHILL, EZEKIEL LEAVELL. rec 1821. p 370 Deed

WAYNE COUNTY DEEDS: Book B

dated 1819. USA to ELI BROWN. S 1, T 16, R 13E rec 1821. pp 370, 371

Deed dated 1820. ROBERT LEAVELL & SALLY, his wife, to SHUBAL JULIAN. Jacksonburg lot 13. Signed ROBERT LEAVELL, SALLY (x) LEAVELL. Witness: JAS. GILMORE, JOSIAH BRADBURY. rec 1821. p 371

Deed dated 1821. JOHN CHARLES to ROBERT MORRISON. S 32, T 14, R 1W. Signed JOHN CHARLES. Witness: none. rec 1821. pp 371, 372

Deed dated 1821. JOHN CHARLES to ROBERT MORRISON. S 32, T 14, R 1W. Signed JOHN CHARLES. Witness: none. rec 1821. p 372

Deed dated 1820. JOHN H. FRYAR to JONATHAN EDWARDS. S 14, T 13, R 1W. Signed JOHN H. FRYAR, PEGGY (x) FRYAR. Witness: BENJAMIN B. MOORE, ABSALOM STUART. rec 1821. pp 372, 373

Deed dated 1820. MATHEW ALMOND to THOMAS WILLENTS. S 36, T 18, R 14E. Signed MATHEW ALMOND. Witness: ELLICK BEAUCHAMP. rec 1821. p 373

Deed dated 1820. STEPHEN THOMAS to MATTHEW ALMOND. S 36, T 18, R 14E. Signed STEPHEN THOMAS, HANNAH THOMAS. Witness: ELIJAH THOMAS, SOLOMON THOMAS. rec 1821. pp 373, 374

Deed dated 1820. STEPHEN THOMAS to ELIJAH THOMAS. S 36, T 18, R 14E. Signed STEPHEN THOMAS, HANNAH THOMAS. Witness: DANIEL PUCKETT, MATTHEW ALMOND. rec 1821. p 374

Deed dated 1820. STEPHEN THOMAS to JOSEPH WOODY. S 36, T 18, R 14E. Signed STEPHEN THOMAS, HANNAH THOMAS. Witness: MATTHEW ALMOND, SOLOMON THOMAS. rec 1821. p 375

Deed dated 1820. SOLOMON BURKIT & wife SALLY to ELI ELWELL of Clinton Co, OH. S 22, T 15, R 12E. Signed SOLOMON BURKIT, SALLY BURKIT. Witness: THOMAS ASHER, HENRY SPRAY. rec 1821. pp 375, 376

Deed dated 1820. SOLOMON BURKIT & wife SALLY & THOMAS ASHER & SALLY his wife to ELI ELWELL of Clinton Co, OH. S 22, T 15, R 12E. Signed SOLOMON BURKIT, SALLY (x) BURKIT, THOMAS (x) ASHER, SALLY (x) ASHER. Witness: HENRY SPRAY, JOSEPH HOLTZCLAW. rec 1821. pp 376, 377

WAYNE COUNTY DEEDS: Book B

Deed dated 1820. HENRY MILLER & ESTHER his wife to EDMOND MOSS. S 24, T 12, R 1W. Signed HENRY MILLER, ESTHER (x) MILLER. Witness: WILLIAM SPENCER, WILLIAM MOSS. rec 1821. pp 377, 378

Deed dated 1818. JEREMIAH COX to NATHAN BALLARD of Montgomery Co, OH. Richmond lot 36. Signed JEREMIAH COX. Witness: none. rec 1821. p 378

Deed dated 1821. JOHN McCLAIN & CATHARINE, his wife, to JONATHAN BEALS. Richmond lot 29. Signed JOHN McCLAIN JR, CATHARINE McCLAIN. Witness: none. rec 1821. pp 378, 379

Deed dated 1818. WILLIAM FOUTS of Preble Co, OH & SARAH, his wife, to SAMUEL SHUTE. S 12 & 13, T 13, R 1W. Signed WILLIAM FOUTS, SARAH (x) FOUTS. Witness: WILLIAM CURRY, JAMES CURRY (in OH). rec 1821. pp 379, 380

Deed dated 1821. SAMUEL SHUTE & SYBIL, his wife, to BENJAMIN B. MOORE. S 11, T 13, R 1W: "the still house sold before to LEVI FOUTS excepted". Signed SAMUEL SHUTE, SYBIL SHUTE. Witness: none. rec 1821. pp 380, 381

Deed dated 1821. LEVI FOUTS & SARAH, his wife, to BENJAMIN B. MOORE. S 11, T 13, R 1W. Signed LEVI FOUTS, SARAH (x) FOUTS. Witness: none. rec 1821. pp 381, 382

Deed dated 1820. SAMUEL SHUTE to BENJAMIN B. MOORE. S 11, T 13, R 1W. Signed SAMUEL SHUTE, SYBIL SHUTE. Witness: none. rec 1821. p 382

Deed dated 1821. DAVID BONINE to BENJAMIN HODGES. S 24, T 13, R 1W. "PRUDENCE, his wife". Signed DAVID (x) BONINE, PRUDENCE (x) BONINE. Witness: ISAAC MEEK, ISAIAH HINSHUE. rec 1821. p 383

Deed dated 1818. JOHN SMITH to JOHN McCLAIN. Richmond lot 3. Signed JOHN SMITH. Witness: none. rec 1821. pp 383, 384

Deed dated 1821. JAMES CLARK to ROBERT HILL. Richmond lot 13. Signed JAMES CLARK. Witness: JOHN SUFFRINS. rec 1821. p 384

Deed dated 1820. JOHN HALE & POLLY, his wife, to SAWYER McFADDEN. Richmond lot 57. Signed JOHN HALE, POLLY HALE. Witness: BENJ. CUSHMAN. rec 1821. pp 384, 385

WAYNE COUNTY DEEDS: Book B

Deed dated 1820. JOHN MARTINDALE to JAMES MARTINDALE S 29, T 17, R 13E. Signed JOHN MARTINDALE. Witness: HENRY GARRETT. rec 1821. p 385

Deed dated 1820. JOSHUA SHELBY to WILLIAM NICKLES. Bethlehem lot 82. Signed JOSHUA SHELBY, SUSANNA (x) SHELBY. Witness: JOHN SHELBY, JOSIAH (x) EASTWOOD. rec 1821. pp 385, 386

Deed dated 1818. JOHN SMITH to RICHARD HENDERSON. Richmond lot 69. Signed JOHN SMITH. Witness: ELI OVERMAN, WILLIAM NIXON. rec 1821. pp 386, 387

Deed dated 1821. JOHN SMITH to WILLIAM STANTON of Franklin Co. Richmond lot 44. Signed JOHN SMITH. Witness: none. rec 1821. p 387

Deed dated 1820. WILLIAM SUMNER to GEROGE MOSS of Warren Co, OH. Cntrv lots 41, 42, 43. Signed WM. SUMNER, NANCY SUMNER. Witness: none. rec 1821. p 387

Deed dated 1821. NANCY RAMBO, relick of JACKSON RAMBO, dec, ADONIJAH RAMBO & ISAAC RAMBO to JAMES SULSER S 31, T 13, R 1W. Signed ANN RAMBO, ADONIJAH RAMBO, ISAAC RAMBO. Witness: JOHN NILSON, WILLIAM HENDRICKS rec 1821. p 388

Deed dated 1820. PHILIP LYBROOK to EDMUND MOSS. S 25, T 12, R 1W. Signed PHILIP LYBROOK, ANN (x) LYBROOK. Witness: JOB L. BURGESS, ISAAC ESTELE. rec 1821. pp 388, 389

Deed dated 1821. WILLIAM DUNMAN to ROBT. MITCHEL. Cntrv lot 99. "SUSANNA, his wife". Signed WILLIAM DUNMAN, SUSANNA (x) DUNMAN. Witness: WILLIAM HOOVER ELIZABETH HOOVER. rec 1821. p 389

Deed dated 1821. JOSEPH PRATHER of Harrison Twp to JONATHAN PROTHER & HENRY PROTHER. S 32, T 13, R 1W. Signed JOSEPH PRATHER. Witness: none. rec 1821. pp 389, 390

Deed dated 1821. THOMAS CRANER to WILLIAM JACKSON. S 6, T 17, R 14. "ELIZABETH, his wife". Signed THOMAS CRANER, no wife's signature. Witness: JOHN MAXWELL. rec 1821. p 390

Deed dated 1820. BENJAMIN HODGES to JONATHAN TOWNSEND. S 27, T 13, R 1W. "JANE, his wife". Signed BENJAMIN HODGES, JANE HODGES. Witness: JOHN McCOMBS DAVID (x) BONINE. rec 1821. pp 390, 391

WAYNE COUNTY DEEDS: Book B

Deed dated 1820. SAMUEL G. MITCHELL of Bourbon Co, KY to SAMUEL HENRY SR of the same. S 36, T 15, R 1W. "NANCY, his wife". Signed SAMUEL G. MITCHELL, NANCY MITCHELL. Witness: SAM'L HENDERSON JR, CATHARINE GRANT, I. ELIZABETH GILPEN. rec 1821. pp 391, 392

Deed dated 1820. AARON COOK & TEMPERANCE, his wife, to JAMES CUPPY. S 32, T 13, R 1W. Signed AARON COOK TEMPERANCE (x) COOK. Witness: THOMAS CUPPY, JESSE STARR. rec 1821. p 392

Deed dated 1820. JOHN HALE to CHARLES CARTER. Richmond lot, no #; bounds given. Signed JOHN (x) HALE. Witness: JOHN McCLAIN JR, ISAAC JACKSON. rec 1821. rec 1821. p 393

Bill of sale dated 1820. JOHN HALE to CHARLES CARTER. Household goods, shop tools & cow. Signed JOHN (x) HALE. Witness: JOHN McCLAIN JR, ISAAC JACKSON. rec 1821. rec 1821. pp 393, 394

Deed dated 1820. JOB SPRINGER & MARY, his wife, to JOHN HALE. Richmond lot 57. Signed JOB SPRINGER, MARY SPRINGER. Witness: none. rec 1821. p 394

Deed dated 1820. DAVID HOOVER, GEORGE HUNT & AARON MARTIN, apptd Commissioners by Wayne Circuit Court to JAMES DILL of Dearborn Co. JAMES KNIGHT of Franklin Co, now dec, made bond to JAMES DILL in 1816 to convey title to S 36, T 16, R 12E. Comm'rs now grant title. Signed DAVID HOOVER, G. HUNT, AARON MARTIN. Witness: JOHN C. KIBBEY. pp 394, 395

Deed dated 1821. JAMES HUFF to WILLIAM JUSTICE. Richmond lot 11. "SIDNEY, his wife". Signed JAMES HUFF, SIDNEY HUFF. Witness: none. rec 1821. pp 395, 396

Deed dated 1821. DAVID OSBORN to JOHN COREY, dec, or his heirs or assignees. S 31, T 18, R 13E. Signed DAVID OSBORN, ELIZABETH (x) OSBORN. Witness: OWEN McMANUS. rec 1821. pp 396, 397

Deed dated 1820. MORRIS NIXON of Pasquatank Co, NC to JOSHUA MORRIS. S 19, T 16, R 13E. Signed MORRIS NIXON. Witness: CALEB MORRIS, SAMUEL NIXON (in NC). rec 1821. p 397

Deed dated 1821. LEVI JONES to OBED BARNARD. S 6, T 16, R 14E. "MARY, his wife". Signed LEVI JONES, MARY (x) JONES. Witness: none. rec 1821. pp 397, 398

WAYNE COUNTY DEEDS: Book B

Deed, no date. LEVI JONES to JOHN BRUMFIELD. S 6, T 16, R 14E. Signed LEVI JONES, MARY (x) JONES. Witness: none. rec 1821. p 398

Deed dated 1819. LAURENCE H. BRANNON to ELIAS WILLITS. Cntrv lots 5, 15. Signed LAURENCE H. BRANNON, CINTHY BRANNON. Witness: LEWIS THOMAS. rec 1821. pp 398, 399

Deed dated 1821. LAURENCE H. BRANNON to JESSE NEEL. Cntrv lot 81. Signed LAURENCE H. BRANNON, CINTHY BRANNON. Witness: KEZIAH JORDAN. rec 1821. p 399

Deed dated 1821. LAURENCE H. BRANNON to JOHN ALDERSON of Greenbrier Co, VA. Cntrv lot 65. Signed LAURENCE H. BRANNON, CINTHY BRANNON. Witness: KEZIAH JORDAN. rec 1821. pp 399, 400

Deed dated 1821. LAURENCE H. BRANNON to JOSEPH ALDERSON of Greenbrier Co, VA. Cntrv lots 118, 119. Signed LAURENCE H. BRANNON, CINTHY BRANNON. Witness: KEZIAH JORDAN. rec 1821. p 400

Deed dated 1820. THOMAS D. CARNELL & SALLY his wife and WILLIAM IRWIN & MARY his wife to NICHOLAS LONGWORTH, all of Hamilton Co, OH. S 14 & 15, T 16, R 14E; Salisbury lots 10, 19, 24, 20, 23, 22, 35; S 19, T 14, R 16E; Cntrv lots 4, 8, 14, 15, 16, 22, 33, 36, 37, 38, 55 through 64 inclusive. Signed THOS. D. CARNELL, SALLY CARNELL, WILLIAM IRWIN, MARY IRWIN. Witness: MARY R. HOWELL, GEO. P. TORRENCE (in OH). rec 1821. p 401

Deed dated 1821. MILBORN JACOBS to JOHN SUTHERLAND JR. Salisbury lot, no #; bounds given. Signed MILBURN JACOBS, CATHARINE (x) JACOBS. Witness: none. rec 1821. p 402

Deed dated 1820. JOHN SMITH to BENJAMIN FOSDICK of Franklin Co. Richmond lot 98. Signed JOHN SMITH. Witness: STEPHEN HOLLOWAY. rec 1821. p 402

Deed dated 1821. ROBERT MORRISON, JOHN McCLAIN & PETER JOHNSON to PHILIP HARTER. Richmond lot 11. Signed ROBERT MORRISON, JOHN McCLAIN, PETER JOHNSON. Witness MATHIUS SIDDALL, JESSE PEGG. rec 1821. pp 402, 403

Deed dated 1821. JAMES HUFF to WILLIAM SUTHERLAND. Richmond lot 11. Signed JAMES HUFF, SIDNEY HUFF. Witness: JESSE PEGG. rec 1821. pp 403, 404

Deed dated 1821. DAVID HARMAN & REBECCA his wife to

WAYNE COUNTY DEEDS: Book B

WILLIAM W. PHARES of OH. Salisbury lot 89. Signed DAVID HARMAN, REBECCA (x) HARMAN. Witness: none. rec 1821. p 404

Mortgage dated 1821. ROBERT MORRISON to WILLIAM NORRIS, merchant of Baltimore, MD. Richmond lot 6, now a tanyard & other buildings. Collateral security on debt by MORRISON & HILL to NORRIS. Signed ROBERT MORRISON. Witness: JOHN C. KIBBEY, EDWARD DAY. rec 1821. pp 405, 406

Deed dated 1820. WILLIAM BOYD to SAMUEL K. BOYD. S 31, T 17, R 13E. Signed WILLIAM BOYD. Witness: JOSIAH BRADBURY, JAMES BOYD, W.G. STINSON. rec 1821 p 406

Deed dated 1820. ANDREW ENDSLEY to STEPHEN G. HUNT. S 25, T 13, R 2W. Signed ANDREW ENDSLEY, SARAH ENDSLEY. Witness: none. rec 1821. pp 406, 407

Deed dated 1820. WM. SUMNER to ELIAS WILLITS. Cntrv lot 49. Signed WM. SUMNER, NANCY SUMNER. Witness: LAURENCE H. BRANNON. rec 1821. p 407

Deed dated 1820. GEORGE FARLOW & NANCY, his wife, to JAMES HANNAH. S 17, R 13, T 15. Signed GEORGE FARLOW NANCY (x) FARLOW. Witness: SAM'L. HANNAH, SIMEON FARLOW. rec 1821. p 408

Deed dated 1812. USA to BENJAMIN MORGAN & BENJAMIN MAUDLIN. S 34, T 14, R 1W. rec 1821. pp 408, 409

Deed dated 1820. BENJAMIN MORGAN & ELIZABETH his wife & BENJAMIN MAUDLIN & LEAH his wife to SAMUEL POTTS. S 34, T 14, R 1W. Signed BENJAMIN MORGAN, ELIZABETH MORGAN, BENJAMIN MAUDLIN, LEAH (x) MAUDLIN. Witness: THOMAS HILL SR, ROBERT HILL. rec 1821. pp 409, 410

Deed dated 1821. SAMUEL POTTS & MARY, his wife, to JACOB SMITH of Belmont Co, OH. S 34, T 14, R 1W. Signed SAMUEL POTTS, MARY POTTS. Witness: JOHN C. KIBBEY, JOHN HAYS. rec 1821. pp 410, 411

Deed dated 1812. USA to BENJAMIN HARRIS of Green Co (state not given) S 4, T 14, R 1W. rec 1821. p 411

Deed dated 1818. JOHN SMITH to ISAAC BEESON. Richmond lot 13. Signed JOHN SMITH. Witness: STEPHEN THOMAS, SAMUEL SMITH. rec 1821. p 411

Deed dated 1820. JOHN McKEE & MALINDA, his wife, to EZEKIEL LEAVELL. Jacksonburg lot 23. Signed JOHN McKEE, MALINDA McKEE. Witness: JOSIAH BRADBURY,

WAYNE COUNTY DEEDS: Book B

TABOR McKEE. rec 1821. pp 411, 412

Deed dated 1821. JOHN NIXON & JANE, his wife, to HENRY PALEN. S 23, T 16, R 12: "JOSIAH NIXON's line" Signed JOHN NIXON, JANE (x) NIXON. Witness: GEO. BUNDY, JONATHAN (x) PEARSON. rec 1821. pp 412, 413

Deed dated 1821. JOHN COPELAND to DAVID P. WOOD. S 5, T 16, R 14E. "SUSANNA, his wife". Signed JOHN COPELAND, SUSANNAH COPELAND. Witness: none. rec 1821. p 413

Deed dated 1821. WILLIAM WILLITS & POLLY, his wife, to LEVI WILLITS. S 5, T 15, R 13E. Signed WILLIAM WILLITS, POLLY (x) WILLITS. Witness: SAMUEL WILLITS WILLIAM SWAFFORD. rec 1821. pp 413, 414

Deed dated 1818. ARTHUR HENRIE & GRACE his wife, LOT PUGH & RACHEL, his wife, MICAJAH WILLIAMS to JOSEPH EVANS. Cntrv lot, no #: bounds given. Signed ARTHUR HENRIE, RACHEL A. PUGH, GRACE M. HENRIE, MICAJAH T. WILLIAMS, L. PUGH, HANNAH WILLIAMS. Witness: J. EMBREE, A.J. WHEELER (in OH). rec 1821. pp 414, 415

Deed dated 1821. JOSEPH COX to WILLIAM W. HULINGS. Abington lots 83, 86. Signed JOSEPH COX, MARY COX. Witness: none. rec 1821. p 415

Deed dated 1820. HENRY GARRETT to JAMES ODELL. Cntrv lot 58. Signed HENRY GARRETT, MARY GARRETT. Witness RICHARD WARNOCK. rec 1821. p 416

Sheriff's sale dated 1821. ABRAHAM ELLIOTT, Sheriff of Wayne Co to BARNABUS McMANUS. Suits by CHARLES MOFFET, JOHN SUTHERLAND & NATHAN SMITH against SAMUEL JONES. Property in S 2, T 17, R 13E ordered sold to satisfy debt; McMANUS the high bidder. Signed ABRAHAM ELLIOTT, Sheriff. Witness: none. rec 1821. pp 416, 417

Deed dated 1820. ISAAC CONLEY to JOHN McKINNON. S 2, T 12, R 1W. "his wife MARY". Signed ISAAC (x) CONLEY, MARY (x) CONLEY. Witness: none. rec 1821. p 418

Deed dated 1820. STEPHAN THOMAS to JOHN JEFFREY of Dover Twp, Monmouth CO, NJ. S 36, T 18, R 14: "at THOMAS WILLCUT's corner...to ELIJAH THOMAS' corner". Signed STEPHAN THOMAS, HANNAH THOMAS. Witness: JOHN THOMAS, ELLICK BEAUCHAMP. rec 1821. p 418

Deed dated 1820. JOHN BURGESS & SARAH, his wife, to NATHAN HOCKET. Richmond lot, no number given. Signed

WAYNE COUNTY DEEDS: Book B

JOHN (x) BURGESS, SARAH (x) BURGESS. Witness: none. rec 1821. p 419

Deed dated 1821. JOHN MILLER & CHRISTENER, his wife, to WILLIAM HOLEMAN. S 34, T 13, R 11. Signed JOHN MILLER, CHRISTENER (x) MILLER. Witness: none. rec 1821. pp 419, 420

Deed dated 1821. WILLIAM HOLEMAN & RUEA, his wife, to WILLIAM MEEK. S 24, T 13, R 11. Signed WILLIAM HOLEMAN, RUEA HOLEMAN. Witness: none. rec 1821. p 420

Deed dated 1821. WILLIAM THORN & RACHEL of Green Co, OH to JOSEPH STUMP. S 21, T 16, R 13. Signed WILLIAM THORN, RACHEL THORN. Witness: WM. ALEXANDER, JOSEPH HAMILL. rec 1821. pp 420, 421

Deed dated 1818. JOHN SMITH to CALEB WILLIAMS. Richmond lot 95. Signed JOHN SMITH. Witness: JOHN WILLIAMS, WILLIAM CAMMACK. rec 1821. pp 421, 422

Deed dated 1820. MOSES MARTINDALE & wife (HANNAH) to JAMES ODELL & RICHARD WARNOCK. S 24, T 17, R 13E. Signed MOSES MARTINDALE, HANNAH (x) MARTINDALE. Witness: JESSE MARTINDALE. rec 1821. p 422

Deed dated 1820. JOHN CLARK to ISAAC JACKSON. Richmond lot 97. (Text refers to ANNA CLARK). Signed JOHN CLARK. Witness: GEORGE BROWN. rec 1821. pp 422, 423

Deed dated 1820. ABIJAH CAIN to DRURY WALLS. S 30, T 14, R 1W. "his wife MARTHA". Signed ABIJAH CAIN, MARTHA (x) CAIN. Witness: none. rec 1821. p 423

Deed dated 1821. JOHN COX SR & JOSEPH COX to THOMAS MOFFET & JAMES WADDLE of Union Co. S3, T 12, R 2W "in town of Abington". Signed JOHN COX SR, CATHERINE (x) COX, no signature by JOSEPH. Witness: none. rec 1821. p 424

Deed dated 1821. JOSEPH COX to WILLIAM HULINGS. Abington lots 73, 74, 84, 85. Signed JOSEPH COX, MARY (x) COX. Witness: none. rec 1821. pp 424, 425

Deed dated 1821. JOHN COX to GABRIEL FENDER. Abington lots 27, 34. Signed JOHN COX SR, CATHARINE (x) COX. Witness: none. rec 1821. p 425

Deed dated 1821. JOSEPH COX to THOMAS MANNING. Abington lots 96, 97, 98. Signed JOSEPH COX, MARY (x) COX. Witness: none. rec 1821. pp 425, 426

WAYNE COUNTY DEEDS: Book B

Deed dated 1821. JOSEPH COX to THOMAS MOFFET of Union Co. Abington lot 71. Signed JOSEPH COX, MARY (x) COX. Witness: none. rec 1821. pp 426

Deed dated 1821. JOSEPH COX to DANIEL CLEAVENGER. Abington lot 87. Signed JOSEPH COX, MARY (x) COX. Witness: none. rec 1821. pp 426, 427

Deed dated 1821. JOSEPH COX to JOHN CHRYST. Abington lot 81. Signed JOSEPH COX, MARY (x) COX. Witness: none. rec 1821. p 427

Deed dated 1821. JOHN COX SR to JOEL HILL. Abington lots 35, 44. Signed JOHN COX SR, CATHARINE (x) COX. Witness: none. rec 1821. pp 427, 428

Deed dated 1821. JOHN COX SR to JOHN WHITINGER of Union Co. Abington lot 39. Signed JOHN COX SR, CATHARINE (x) COX. Witness: none. rec 1821. pp 427, 428

Deed dated 1821. JOSEPH COX to JOHN W. COX. Abington lot 63. Signed JOSEPH COX, MARY (x) COX. Witness: WILLIAM HENDRICKS, RICHARD COX. rec 1821. p 428, 429

Deed dated 1821. JOHN COX SR to ISRAEL COX. Abington lot 1 through 18, 20, 24, 29, 32, 38, 53. Signed JOHN COX SR, CATHARINE (x) COX. Witness: none. rec 1821. p 429

Deed dated 1821. JOHN COX SR to JAMES WADDLE of Union Co. Abington lot 47. Signed JOHN COX SR, CATHARINE (x) COX. Witness: JOSEPH COX. rec 1821. pp 429, 430

Deed dated 1821. JOHN COX to SAMUEL BLOOMFIELD of Preble Co, OH. Abington lots 22, 46. Signed JOHN COX SR, CATHARINE (x) COX. Witness: JOSEPH COX, ISAAC SHELBY. rec 1821. p 430

Deed dated 1821. JOHN SMITH & JANE his wife, to JOB W. SWAIN. Richmond lot 27. Signed JOHN SMITH, JANE SMITH. Witness: JOHN C. KIBBEY. rec 1821. pp 430, 431

Deed dated 1821. JOB W. SWAIN to RICHARD HENDERSON. Richmond lot 27. Signed JOB W. SWAIN. Witness: JOHN McCLAIN JR, SYLVANUS FISHER. rec 1821. p 431

End of Book B

INDEX: names in text may have variant spelling
NIFLS = not indexed for land sales

Using the index. When constructing an index, one of the most difficult tasks is to direct the reader to the people in whom he is interested. Lawyers, court clerks and muster sergeants were creative spellers -- changing vowels or adding consonants was legitimate if the sound remained the same. The "variant spelling" method of indexing seems to work best: the most common form is the standard under which names are listed, although the actual entry spelling may vary.

To reduce the sheer number of page entries, many land sales of the town proprietors were eliminated. Significant entries -- the first entry naming a wife or noting the later absence of the wife, or sale to a seemingly related person -- remain in the index. It is hoped this will simplify the task of locating meaningful information. Nothing could be done about the massive page entries of the town lawyer or Justice of the Peace. In addition, long "Christian" names may have been given common abbreviations to condense the index, making it easier to use.

Abbott, Dennis 194 Jeremiah 35 Jonathan 215 Joseph 133 144 Mary 133 144 William 23 215
Abraham(s), Israel 292 Joseph 321
Abrander, William 135
Abercrombie, Alex'r 18 35 117 Hugh 114 117 James 114 130 John 177 Rosanna 114 117
Abernathy, Benj 99 100 Hugh (NIFLS) 41 71 78 92 95 99 100 103 James 92 Mary 92 100 103 Robt 10 94 95 98 129 Thomas 160 William 12 227
Abrams/Abrahams, Benj 34 37 85 112
Abshire, James 176
Acres, Abner 234
Adair, George 3 James 3 20 161 John 3 8 38 75 79 114 151 161 309 Joseph 3 Margt 73 Polly 161 Robt 73 Sarah 309
Adams, Edmund 31 Eli 123 Elizabeth 171 G./George 10 32 John 11 Joseph

Adams, continued: 9 27 87 131 147 Lydia 131 Sabbina 147 148 167 170 171 Thomas 145 William 32 129 Wilson 147 148 167 170 171
Adamson, John 174
Adcock, Faris 13 Frana 175
Addington, John 235 Joseph 234 247 Thomas 235
Addleman, William 236
Adkins, Elizabeth 207 Martin 199 210 217 221
Adkinson, Robert 11 141 152
Agnew, David 71 84 104 Josinah 84 104
Agins, James 32 William 10
Aiken, David 7 Joseph 242
Albert, James 82
Albertson, Jesse 243
Albred, Thomas 305
Alcott, Thomas 25 William 23
Aldeman, Matthew 237

349

INDEX: names in text may have variant spelling
NIFLS = not indexed for land sales

Alderson, John 344 Joseph 344
Aldvid, George 120
Alexander, Daniel 239
 James 236 313 John 7 13 235 Sam'l 14 Thomas 317 322 326 336 William 13 25 235 347
Alger, Skilmon 136
Alison, John 82
Allaire, Andrew 27 Sam'l 25 29
Allen, Adam 14 Ann 80 Claibourn 4 18 22 25 28 D. 159 David 161 Eli 12 31 133 134 Eliphalal 114 116 117 124 131 Elizabeth 97 124 Hugh 243 Ira 22 Isaac 25 James 4 23 Jeremiah 239 John (NIFLS) 11 21 33 34 35 39 40 42 43 44 45 46 48 51 55 67 68 92 97 105 109 120 132 143 149 159 161 225 Jonathan 33 Joseph 46 48 50 78 80 81 84 87 90 92 124 242 Josiah 12 33 114 143 Peter 23 33 Rebeckah 45 Sarah 44 143 Solomon 38 78 80 86 88 90 95 103 104 105 113 114 120 121 131 136 146 149 150 156 170 171 Willm 34 97 124
Allenville (town) 191 192
Allensworth, Willm 3 20
Alley, Catharine 107 109 Cyrus 33   David 33 Dodridge 96 97 107 109 James 12 33   Jane 107 109 Jonathan 6 12 107 109 Peter 10 Samuel 33 82
Allhands, George 143
Allison, Elizabeth 286 Joshua 243
Alloway, Thomas 26
Almond, Matthew 340
Alvord, Hannah 113 Selah 113
Ambrose, Peter 39
Ames, Austin 183

An, Arthur 55
Anare, Malcolm 159
Anderson, Catharine 209 Henry 23 James 28 Martha 140 Robt 115 Silas 229 Thomas 29 Willm 184
Andrew(s), Arthur 187 J. 29 227 James 38 281 John 38 182 238 Mary 307 Robert 187 307
Angenine/Angerine, Jas 25
Annis, Thomas 6
Anthony, Catherine 130 36 157 George 40 130 136 153 157 Henry 9 157 Jacob 153 Nicholas 12 Philip 130 Willm 12
Archart, Andrew 174
Archer, David 227
Archibald, Robert 39
Ardery, William 36 79
Armstrong,-- 203 Abel 169 Eliza 161 James 158 212 228 278 John 59 124 145 186 251 278 Lutesha 278 Margt 205 Michael 169 Richard 209 Thomas 194 196 197 198 201 203 205 206 208 209 211 212 213 219 Walter 20 201 218 William 36
Arnett, Sam'l 40 49 146 233 Sarah 96 97 Thomas 11 William 32 38 49 73 96 97 124
Arnold, Drusilla 156 George 188 John 12 24 32 156 Richard 224 William 32 156
Aryres, John 39
Ashbrook, Aaron 230
Ashby, Abr'm 14 Bayliss 3 6 21 Bladen 235 271 334 339 Catharine 334 339 William 7
Asher, Sally 340 Thos 340
Ashly, William 26
Ashton, Joseph 285
Askrem, William 14
Aston, Samuel 27
Athenson, Robert 174
Athern, Prince 22

INDEX: names in text may have variant spelling
NIFLS = not indexed for land sales

Atherton, Amos 37 David 47 49 55 68 Elijah 36 Rachel 49 68
Atkins, Harriet 149 Jesse 132 149
Atkinson, R. 141
Austin, Dan'l 273 Sam'l 24 Thomas 276
Averill, P. 197 Philo 187 192 195 220
Avery, John 101
Avey, Joseph 8
Ayres, Benajah 99 Michael 117 Samuel 37 117

Babbett, A. 146 Andrew 119 156
Babbs, Noah 18 Willm 23
Babcock, James 29
Backhouse, James 90 91 94 108
Backles, James 295
Backus/Bacchus, Isaac 187 Marvin 184 186
Badollet, John 199
Bagent (see Bogart), Ratliff 25
Bailey, A. 31 238 Andrew 35 39 188 235 Chesley 124 D. 245 David 233 Dilman 14 H. 4 Henry 8 174 241 Hugh 5 12 13 14 J. 3 James 10 32 60 293 John 13 67 68 242 245 Patience 60 Richard 18 Stanton 173
Bain, James 283 Mary 282
Baird, Jonathan 198
Baire, Jonathan 188
Bake(s), Catherine 55 79 85 86 Jacob 9 79 86 90 92 97 105 138 143 224 John 79 Peter 143 Robt 187 William 79 85 97
Baker, Christopher 177 John 134 237 Mark 28 Mary 88 Moses 88
Baldridge, Sam'l 243 245
Baldwin, Amos 40 Charles 237 Dan'l 244 246 Elias 39 Jesse 245 326 John 244 246 260 Jonas 188

Baldwin, cont - 205 207 Thomas 39 244
Bales, Clark 227 Dilwin 242 Seth 284
Baley, Hiram 179
Balings, Abraham 27
Ball, Sarah 211
Ballanger, Jesse 174 John 174 179 Jorge 3
Ballard, James 335 Nathan 341
Ballinger, Jonathan 268 Joshua 242 William 242
Baltimore, Phillip 242
Ban, William 40
Bancroft, Samuel 124
Banks, Adam 13 150 237 274 277 278 282 Elizabeth 319 John 334 Thos 150 282 308 319 332
Banta (see Bonta), Albert 174 175 178 Joseph 8 Levi 8 Peter 238
Barber, Eliphalet 31 James 113 123 136 149 John 20 31 Margaret 123 Simeon 31 Thomas 132
Barclay, Stephen 100
Barkaloo (see Barricklow) John 19 20
Barker, Isaac 174 322 Mary 322
Barkman, Jacob 39 72 107
Barkshire, Jeremiah 8
Barley, Thomas 14
Bar(t)low, John 11 101 110
Barnar, Hannah 302
Barnard, Obed 343 Robert 72 101 152
Barnes, Almira 143 153 Blacksley 39 72 143 153 Francis 197 208 216 219 Henrietta 208 219 Isaac 173 John 246 Robert 7 William 173 245
Barnet, Isaac 93 James 79
Barnum, Barna 191 201 Polly 201
Barr, Mary 147 William 19 27 147 185 187 189
Barrett, Caleb 242

INDEX: names in text may have variant spelling
NIFLS = not indexed for land sales

Barricklow, Edw 94 Farrington 18 John 17 18 23
Barshman, Jacob 139
Barton, Valentine 17 William 26
Barwell, William 14
Bascom, Nathan 62 Silas 188
Basey/Basyne, Elizabeth 50 103 109 Lismund 39 43 50 57 69 103 109 110 297 300 308 311 312 328
Bassett, Benj 112 330 David 143 Jonathan 41 128 159 161 166 Nath'l 128 129
Baster, James 37
Bates, Clark 227 H. 80 Harriet 90 Hervey 87 95 96 102 105 106 107 108 110 113 116 120 121 123 124 133 140 150 159 161 170 Isaac 184 James 185 195 John 64 90 Patience 102 Seth 227 Sidney 150 159 161 Willis 17
Bath, town of 68
Baum, Ezra 35 Martin 93 98 183 228
Baxter, John 176
Bayne, John 182
Beach, Bery 29 Solomon 225 228
Beadwell, Hester 296 James 296
Beall(s), Arch'd 241 242 243 245 Isaac 12 Jonathan 341 Josiah 36 William 241
Beamer, Charles 8 Henry 26
Beard, -- 272 Jesse 239 John 226 274 281 282 286 287 291 292 320 324 Melinda 320 324 329 Patrick 274 287 Paul 175 Polly 282 Thomas 237 238 274 280 281 285 287 291 292 312 320 324 329 William 225 287 292

Beasley, William 12
Beason, Richard 180
Beat(t)y, Charles 185 Elizabeth 62 65 Hugh 17 John 33 49 62 65 72 Robert 327
Beauchamp, Elizabeth 119 Ellick 340 346 Noah 119 130
Beck, Henry 227 229 John 240 283 Sam'l 327 Sarah 283 Solomon 229 264
Beckford, Moses 24
Beckley, Henry 89
Beckworth, Samuel 21
Bedwell (see Beadwell), James 226 318 Jonathan 318
Beebe, David 195 203 204 205 211
Beekley, Ann 101 Henry 101
Beeler, Benj 310 Esther 313 George 310 Jacob 298 313 321 Sam'l 238 240 241 270 310 313 Thomas 310
Beeson, Benj 237 323 Henry 266 283 Igal 339 Isaac 14 234 251 261 289 345 Rebecca 283 William 238
Belding, John 125 L. 129 Ludovicus 128 142 143 150 151 153 159 Lydia 142 153
Belk, Jane 110 140 Joel 41 110 140
Bell, Arch'd 284 285 296 315 316 317 David 39 44 49 83 116 Hugh 230 Jacob 37 138 163 James 207 John 237 240 241 286 Jonas 316 Joseph 186 Lancelot 286 Milly 284 285 Thomas 11 Sam'l 103 155 225 Sarah 138 163 207 William 186 188 285
Benbo(w), Barclay 287 Edw 245 277 302 Mary 277
Benefield, John 238

INDEX: names in text may have variant spelling
NIFLS = not indexed for land sales

Benefield, cont- Robt 238
Bennet, James 20 John 25
 Jonathan 26 Joseph 165
 Obadiah 123 144 Robert
 12 226
Benninger, Martin 26
Benoit, Anthony 24
Benson, G. 135
Bentley, Joseph 185 192
 200
Benton, Oliver 111
Berkley, Luther 143
Berkshire, Dickey 23
Bernard, George 184
Berry, Henry 108 130
 James 37 John 242
 Joseph 13 14
Bettens, Philipe 206 207
 Rose 206
Beverlin, John 244
 William 298
Billings, Edmund 62 125
Bills, William 18
Binney, Joshua 243 Josiah
 315
Birgland, Joseph 118
Bisbee, Isaiah 41
Bishop, Lewis 40 64 89
 137 148 163 Mary 137
 Thomas 186
Black, Alex'r 239 323
 Barbary 321 David 40
 223 Elizabeth 311 Gwyn
 311 J. 275 James 241
 242 286 294 301 311
 324 325 John 152 311
 321 Robert 241 286 325
 Sam'l 238 William 238
 278
Blackburn, Edward 39
Blacker, Robert 184
Blackford, Isaac 50 52 53
Blackhouse, James 20
Blacklan, Bryson 36
Blacklidge, Jacob 33 34
 52 78 144
Blackman, Lois 116 Remember 11 116 Truman 49
Blackmore, Dawson 9
Blades, John 53
Blair, John 279 Robt 37
 240 Thomas 13 14

Blaisdell, Capt 6 Jacob
 20 Jonathan 4 7
Blake, Francis 134
Blakely, James 83
Blanc, Fanny 204 207 210
 220
Blane, David 24
Blaney, John 184 187 198
Blazedell, Enoch 4 7
Bledsoe, Abr'm 34 91 99
 183 Elizabeth 190
 Isaac 190 193
Blodget, Nathan 27
Bloomfield, Samuel 348
Blos, Henry 105
Bl(o)unt, Andrew 13 Eli
 177 Henry 199 Mary 251
 310 Willm 173 245 249
 251 310
Bloyd, Hannah 302 Jacob
 100 103 170 227 237 302
Blue, Benj 36 David 23
 John 75 152 153 154
 Margrt 153 William 23
Board, James 132
Boardman, Amos 24 D. 24
 David 24 29
Boaz, Peter 183
Bock, Samuel 238
Bocock (see Pocock), Edw
 184 Lewis 184
Bogart (see Bagent),
 Ruliff 19 25
Boggs, Anson 76
Boiles, John 13
Bolens, James 220
Boling, Enoch 227
Bolton, James 230
Bond, Anne 268 334 Charlotte 267 334 Edw 244
 248 259 265 268 331 334
 Jesse 236 244 249 253
 258 264 267 315 317 329
 Joseph 244 267 334
 Joshua 268 278 Lewis 36
 Phebe 258 329 Ruth 278
 Sam'l 18 19 244 Willm
 235 267 274 334
Bonham, Aaron 7 19 21
 Israel 6 21 78 Zedekiah
 21
Bonine, Dan'l 334 David

INDEX: names in text may have variant spelling
NIFLS = not indexed for land sales

Bonine, cont- 334 341 342
  Prudence 341
Bonner, David 12 85 225
  Francis 205 Margaret 85
  Robert 211 Sam'l 225
Bonta, John 185
Bonte, Jane 25 Peter 25
Booker, Jacob 327 Sam'l
  330 333 Theresa 302
Boon, Benj 249 Ovid 277
  295 304
Boots, Martin 177
Boret, John 25
Bork, Elisha 189
Borrally, Peter 214 222
Borron, Th. 286
Bosow/Boisseau, John 184
  185
Bosson, C. 158
Boswell, Ezra 319 337
  Isaac 234 Marion 235
Botkin, Hugh 173 William
  228
Bovard, Robert 22 184 185
Bowers, David 23
Bowen, Ephraim 173 174
  180
Bowles, David 19 180 244
  George 256
Bowlsby, Abi 115 Enos 115
  228
Bowman, Thomas 26
Bowne, Benjamin 229
Boyd, Adam 283 293 305
  310 324 James 6 185 309
  345 John 309 Peggy
  309 Samuel 14 240 345
  William 345
Boyers, John 233
Boyland, Nicholas 184
Boyson, James 228
Box, Edward 3
Bracken, Levi 19 Thos 19
Brackenridge, George 3 J.
  6 Joseph 106 120 134
  145 147 150 Lt. 6 Mary
  145 R. 168 Robert 91
  108 134 145 147 150 156
  Thomas 21
Brackney, Nimrod 11 151
  159 Reuben 135 154
Bradburn, John 44 49 113

Bradberry, Caty 273 Dan'l
  243 322 326 336 339
  David 304 Gibbons 254
  Giles 26 James 335 Josiah 243 314 318 321 322
  325 328 335 336 339 340
  345 Susanna 304 Thomas
  13 226 249 273
Bradford, David 40 Joel
  183 Robert 86 112 169
Bradley, Ann 214 Rebeccah
  59 107 160 Thomas 69 80
  111 121 124 160 214 216
  218 219 William 32 59
  90 107 131 160 206 214
  217 218 219
Bradway, John 319 Josiah
  319 Joseph 226
Brady, Joseph 163 William
  163
Brahain, Joseph 329
Bramwell, William 9
Brandenburg, Henry 132
  153 159 169 170 225
  Polly 211 William 196
  197 208 211
Brandt, Felix 27 187
Brannon, Kesiah 327 James
  67 68 96 Laurence
  (NIFLS) 239 280 282 283
  284 289 291 293 294 297
  298 299 301 310 321 335
  345 Mary 96 Sinthy 299
Brashier, Charles 53 56
  132 Jacob 18 53 56
Brattain, Anna 334 Jane
  275 Jonathan 270 274
  334 Reubin 14 274 275
  Robt 329 William 325
Bray, John 189
Breaks, Jeane 324
Breckenridge, A. 93 Joseph 97 328 Robert 7 97
  113 328 Thomas 7
Brenson, Jacob 314
Brewen, John 110 Matilda
  109 William 109
Brewer, Asa 329 Charles
  187 Christeny 305 Jesse
  175 139 305 337
Breyfogel, Jacob 196 197
Brian, Hugh 20

INDEX: names in text may have variant spelling
NIFLS = not indexed for land sales

Brice, William 13
Bridged (see Burged),
  George 224
Bridges, Charlotte 132
  James 4   John 90 132
  227   Samuel 8
Briggs, Thomas 87
Brindle, William 22 186
Bringen, Zebulon 189
Brisbin, Robert 37
Brison, Cornelius 10 12
  Hugh 3 10 32 112 113
  James 3 10 131 165 John
  12 32 82 87 170   Mary
  165   Ruth 113   Willm
  3 12
Britton, Henry 23
Brock, Betsey 194 215
  Elijah 12 246 Evan 192
  194 215   Richard 230
Broderick, Anthony 25
Bronaugh, Wm 282
Brooks,-- 176 188 Eli 39
  Daniel 33 Hannah 62 151
  Idel 224   Joab 62 151
  John 9   M. 31 175 186
  Moses 22 189   Moss 175
Brookville, town of 45 46
  56 67 80 104 108 109
  132 140 149
Broway, Robert 163
Brown, -- 33 226 228
  Alex'r 261 281   Amos 8
  183 191 215 218 219 222
  Ann 44   Benj 9 26 107
  136 234 292 Betsey 216
  David 28 29 41 97 100
  112 226 243 E. 237 Eli
  240 284 340 Ephraim 224
  Ethan 22 187 189 Eve
  149 161   Fanny 292
  George 240 347 Gurnsey
  147 155 Harvey 32 81
  Henry 81 130 131 239
  Isaac 10 J./James 5 98
  188 237 261 281 325
  Jane 97 100 102 131 337
  Jeremiah 138 Jesse 175
  John 11 20 21 32 33 40
  131 133
  208 216 220 225 228 301
  302 324 326   Johnston

Brown, cont- 212 Joseph
  187 237 337 Joshua 201
  209 Matthew 97 100 102
  131 152 227 228 Mercer
  265 Paul 25 Peggy 261
  268 281   Phebe   136
  Rachel 67 Robt (NIFLS)
  67 87 97 98 105 Sally/
  Sarah 93 103 118 145
  Samuel 35 104 145 194
  215 238 337 Stephen 26
  Thomas 49 55 58 132 137
  225 228 Timothy 94 111
  118 Willis 117   Willm
  8 149 155 161 225 228
  235 239 273 302 310 313
  322 323 324 326
Brownlee, Hugh 50   James
  113
Brownson, John 3 23
  Reuben 237
Broyles, Aaron 104
Bruce, Ames 19 24 28 Amos
  4 24 Aymos 4 Henry 4
  7 24   James 4 8 24
Brum(b)ley, John   28
  Thomas 230
Brumfield, John 344
Brush, Edward 32
Bryan, Henry 241 284 336
  Jane 284
Bryant, Joseph 188
Buck, Conrad 183   Samuel
  184 Thos 37 Willm 183
Buckanon, John 182 206
  209   Rachel 206
Buckingham, Enoch   36 39
  40
Buckles, Abraham 228
Buckley/Bulkly, Isaac 41
  147 164
Buchanon, James 3 18 John
  191 206 209 Rachel 191
Buffin, J. 21
Buffington, James 22
  Johiel 4 7 19 22   John
  19 22   Jonathan 4
Bulla, Thomas 233 William
  243 300 44 93 103 115
Bullock, Stephen 32
Bunch, Richard 236
Bundy, George 278 279 346

355

INDEX: names in text may have variant spelling
NIFLS = not indexed for land sales

Bundy, cont - John 276
 Josiah 240 275 276 Thos
 337   William 284 311
Bunn, Ezekiel 276
Bunton, John 14
Bunyard, William 163
Burb(r)age, E. 227 Elisha
 12 R. 227 Robert 10
Burch, Henry 187
Burcham, Daniel 194
Burchfield, Robert 202
Buress, Thomas 266
Burged/Buget, Charlotte
 122 George 122 Henry
 36 122
Burges(s), C. 50 Job 342
 John 323 346 347 Sarah
 323 347   Walter 226
Burham, Absalom 113
Burk(e), Jesse 295 James
 18 184   John 6 19 148
 Lewis 318 Thomas 4 148
 184 226 232 Warran 34
 William 14 34 334
Burkdoll, Abraham 185
Burkhalter, Abel 228
 Abr'm 130 158   Eliza-
 beth 158
Burkit, Sally 340 Solomon
 340
Burnet, Isaac 161 J. 188
 Jacob 31 186 237 242
 William 124
Burns, James 173 273 315
 John 228   Stephen 28
 Thomas 18   William 80
Burnsides, Andrew 140 170
 Anna 79 80 140   E. 165
 Edgehill 140 167   Jane
 140 170 Pamela 79
 Permela 140 167 T. 79
 Thomas 80
Burrell, Edward 166
Burroughs, Aaron 20 Bar-
 tlemey 335   Lotty 329
 T. 6 Thos 329 Wilm 245
Burrows, Cornelius 116
 Stephen 189 216
Burt, Zephaniah 224
Burtch, Arnold 28
Burton, Allen 188 James
 224

Bush, Charles 35 Jane 125
 T. 133   Thomas 125
Buster, Batie 76 Sarah 55
 76 Wilm 34 49 55 59 76
Butcher, George 188
Butler, Capt. 4   Amos
 (NIFLS) 33 40 42 45 46
 54 64 80 108 134 136
 149 Beale 226 234 239
 252 255 256 257 280 307
 Eli 242 250 256 258 281
 Enos 5 12 13 242 249
 250 253   George 78 91
 Hiram 239 242 253 James
 184 Jane 256 259 Joshua
 41 78   Levi 13 14 281
 283 Mary 42 91 Noble 19
 Susanna 234 235 251 268
 269 281 Willm 40 45 239
Busan, Jesse 12 14 250
 269   Isaac 249
Butterworth, Samuel 333
Byram, Benjamin 275
Byrhill, Solomon 237
Byrn, see Burns

Cadbury, Denny 17
Cadwalader, B. 312 Byron
 307 308
Caffee (see Calfee) Henry
 144 Nancy 144
Cain, Abijah 14 235 262
 347 Hardy 235 John 14
 243   Joseph 12 235
 Martha 347
Calahan, James 7
Caldwell, James 8 34 John
 8 34 68 158 Wilm 3 8 18
Calfee (see Caffee),
 Henry 33 109
Callaway, Jesse 6
Call, Montgomery 292
Cammack, James 174 Sam'l
 288 305 317   Willm 347
Camp, -- 31
Campbell, Charles 7 8 190
 Horrell 242 Howell 242
 Jennet 208   John 31 82
 190 227 228 229 277
 Polly 192 208 218 221
 Thomas 239 Wilm 182 183
 184 185 190 191 192 194

INDEX: names in text may have variant spelling
NIFLS = not indexed for land sales

Campbell, cont - 199 207 208 209 217 218 219 221 222 241
Campion, Hiram 37 Kerian 144 Mary 144
Canaday, Bowater 292 Chas 283 David 5 14 229 John 245 Robert 245
Canby, Joseph 156 245
Cane/Cain, James 7 Samuel 177
Canfield, Noyes 6
Cannon, Charles 4
Cantwell, James 10
Capp, Henry 169 Jacob 101 145 169 Margaret 169
Capper, Thomas 79
Carberry, Peter 4
Care, Jacob 228
Carel, David 99 Sarah 99 Stephen 99
Carley, Justsy 186
Carlow, Jacob 220
Carlton, Isaac 23 J. 33
Carnell, Sally 344 Thomas 239 307 344
Carney, D. 288 Edward 39
Carpenter, Joseph 14
Carr, Arthur 136 Francis 276 Robt 85 Sam'l 253 255 272 325 Sarah 253
Carrell, Benjamin 281 Thomas 317
Carroll, Bartholomew 7 John 7
Carsmore, Henry 262
Carson, -- 40 Adam 36 David 14 234 Enoch 115 Hugh 3 J. 57 John 36 76 87 92 102 Joseph 37 Polly 102 W. 115 Wilm 56
Carter, Cader 299 Chas 343 John 184 Mordecai 235 Nancy 274 Nicholas 10 Thomas 11 273 274 William 4 139 227
Cartmell, Eliza 212
Cartwright, John 227 William 224
Carver, Christian 183 William 183
Carwel, Thomas 330

Carwile, James 10 105
Carybaugh, Abr'm 7 19 22 Jacob 8
Case, David 85 Henry 38 70 97 155 Isaiah 246 Jacob 228 James 11 John 12 53 132 Nathan 175 Samuel 38 132
Cason, Jesse 135 Mary 320 Thomas 130 135 146 245 289 301 320 Wm 130 227
Cass, Sam'l 250 Sarah 250
Cassady, Joel 177 John 138
Caswell, Daniel 156
Casterline, John 229
Cater, Juel 158
Catey, Henry 244
Cathcart, James 237
Catlin, R. 33 K. 33
Caton, Abnor 339
Cenk, Thomas 5
Chaffen, Elias 4 6
Chalfont, Evan 333
Chamberlain, Willm 25 26
Chambers, B. 3 Benj 17 Enoch 13 James 9 238 Manuel 35 Minor 188 William 129
Chamberlain, Aaron 184
Chamness, Anthony 244 269 270 Martha 270 Micajah 339
Chance, John 28 Sam'l 46 Zacariah 12
Chapman, John 39 Jonathan 34 Joshua 189
Charles, Elvy 326 Gulielmi 275 John 275 304 326 337 340 Joseph 261 264 268 Samuel 176 235 246 255 264 266 275 276
Charlott, William 41
Chase, Leonard 18
Cheek/Check, Francis 19 Jas 4 8 Page 19 Wm 3
Cheeseman, Richard 245 288 309
Chenault, Abner 229 285 331 Mary 331
Chenoweth, Abraham 173 James 191 William 173

INDEX: names in text may have variant spelling
NIFLS = not indexed for land sales

Chesney, Hannah 155
Thomas 155
Childers, Benj 79 166
Chilton, William 87 101
Chism, James 4
Chirington, John 37
Chittenden, Lucius 133
Chittendon & Pearpont 114
Chmier, Frederick 190
Chunn, Thos 229 318 323
Churchill, Ashel 42 Dan'l 68 Joseph 28 Mary 147
Cilley, Joseph 36
Cilwell, James 12
Clancy, George 221 222 James 217 221 222 Nancy 217 221 222
Clanton, Edward 296 297 Rachel 297
Clar, Thomas 329
Clark, Anna 347 Austin 189 Barzilla 185 211 217 Bennett 114 122 125 136 Carlton 20 Daniel 233 243 248 270 274 Dennis 21 Ephraim 243 300 Francis 293 George 114 122 125 136 Hannah 114 122 125 136 Isaac 163 Israel 281 Jacob 4 7 James 322 341 Jane 270 274 Jesse 235 Joel 186 John 114 122 125 174 242 249 313 347 Johnson 68 85 Joshua 114 122 125 136 Martin 142 Masterson 114 122 125 136 Nancy 86 114 122 125 136 Rebecca 114 122 125 136 Richard 114 122 125 136 Susannah 211 217 Thomas 13 35 38 53 81 86 87 239 270 274 William 36 146 318
Clarkson, Abner 197 199 202 205
Clary, Nancy 135 Vachel 135 William 229
Clawson, Abner 235 293 Edw 232 Ezra 28 Josiah 235 311 Rebeckah 311 William 235

Claypool, Nathaniel 9 Solomon 108
Clayton, James 334
Clearwater, David 40 Jacob 39 Reuben 39
Clehard, H. 153
Clements, Caleb 33 82 Chas 6 Edw 6 John 23 Joseph 11 100 129 133 149 151 152 170 Mary 151 152 170 Richard 33
Cleming, Curtis 175
Clendennin, Anne 98 James 12 John 37 49 98
Clenny, Curtis 13
Clevenger, Dan'l 239 348
Clifford, Thomas 277 296
Clifton, Benj 20 John 20
Cline, Hannah 76 John 76 Michael 76 Peter 150
Clinton, John 10
Close, David 17 18 184
Cloud, Bayliss 7 21 Henry 22 23 Ira 6 James 3 6 21 John 34 Jonathan 240 William 7 21 27 37
Coates, Thomas 26
Cobb, Esther 300 Lemer 300
Coburn, Joseph 23
Cochran, John 188
Cockey, Richard 36 39 65
Coddington, William 242
Coe, William 223
Coen (see Cone), Edw 188 201 212 Hugh 201 212 Margt 201 212
Coffett, Henry 296
Coffin/Coffend, A. 184 Arthur 155
Coffman, Leonard 163
Coggeshell, G. 201 220 Tristram 244
Coldwell, Francis 14 James 14 John 68
Cole(s), Adam 188 James 21 John 27 Joseph 188 Ralph 209 Sam'l 27 Thomas 23
Coleman, Levi 251 Rowland 225 Zophar 12 100 139 153

358

INDEX: names in text may have variant spelling
NIFLS = not indexed for land sales

Colescott, James 113 120 162 Lucretia 120 Thos 92 120 139 161
Colete, Sumer 248
Coliver, Mary 139 Richard 36 139
Collett, Benj 119 Chas 34 58 89 102 Williamson 12
Collier, Eliza 266 James 194 Michael 247 Moses 266 279
Collings, Joseph 169
Collins, Jane 272 John 8 10 13 40 233 272
Colmery, Robert 55
Colvin, Michael 226
Colwell, James 27 John 25
Combs (see Cooms), Benj 9
Comer, John 322 Stephen 244
Comley, John 238
Commons, Ezekial 240 Isaac 234 322 Martha 331 Nathan 240 290 331 Robt 295 Ruth 295 Thomas 331 339 William 245
Compton, Henry 37 Jacob 19 James 236
Comstock, Joab 112
Cone/Coen, Charles 36
Congar, Dan'l 57 David 29 Enoch 29 Moses 38 57 Zacariah 29
Conklin, Freeman 304
Conley, Isaac 13 232 255 270 346 John 238 Mary 270 346
Conn(e), James 19 John 74 Jonathan 137 Willm 33
Connell, John 19
Conner, Abner 3 35 Dan'l 17 David 177 Elizabeth 58 137 169 Isaac 17 James 20 John 7 12 18 38 48 49 50 51 101 102 113 125 139 240 Lavina 50 51 101 125 Nelly 135 Richd 58 137 169 Robt 236 Stephen 244 Willm 12 135 176 179
Connersville, town of 51 52 101 123 126
Conley, James 21
Con(na)way, Betsey 179 Chas 176 177 178 179 Dan'l 22 23 James 4 8 23 230 Robert 4 23
Connover, James 237 292 301 John 237 241 282
Constant, Thomas 303
Conwell, James 163
Cook, Aaron 333 335 343 Andrew 24 Charity 235 330 Isaac 154 175 180 228 235 265 Jacob 183 246 263 266 John 182 277 278 Joseph 263 264 268 270 Joshua 185 Kezia 68 Larkin 201 Lydia 264 268 Mary 180 235 330 N. 240 Ruth 180 Seth 175 180 Temperance 333 335 343 Thomas 78 228 268 Willm 235 245 302 331 Wright 228 Zimri 249 314
Cooksey, James 11 Thomas 8 11 Zacariah 11 38 79
Coolly, Thaddeus 20
Coom(b)s, John 188 William 227
Coon, Isaac 224
Cooper, Ann 71 Christian 183 217 221 222 James 119 Moses 237 318 Rebecca 140 152 Thos 119 184 Vincent 87 90 140 152
Cope, Caleb 332
Copeland, John 241 266 346 Jonathan 37 Susanna 346
Copelin, Mary 151
Corey/Corry, Jeremiah (NIFLS) 11 53 54 56 57 62 63 66 67 75 76 124 125 139 154 John 343 Juzal 154 Rebecca 62 76 96 133 William 192 193
Cornelison, Andrew 38 73
Cornelius, Abr'm 21 Absolom 307 308 George 304 Greenberry 240 316 James 6 307 332

INDEX: names in text may have variant spelling
NIFLS = not indexed for land sales

Cornell, Rebecah 268
Corwin, Mathias 170 Thos 82 116
Cossart, Albert 183
Costin, Hanna 109 121 139 Henry 92 109 121 139
Cotton, Henry 201 205 220 Nath'l 186 Ralph 9 186 188 196 Robert 188 196 Willm 2 186 188 191 203 Zacariah 187
Cottrell, Bradbury 39
Coulson, William 169
Coulter, John 37
Courtney, Jn. 186
Covington, Thomas 6
Cowan, David 198 212
Cowgill, Caleb 331
Cox, Benj 176 235 Catharine 249 308 347 Dan'l 4 David 13 14 260 322 Dinah 336 E. 9 Elizabeth 50 56 251 272 Harry 236 Israel 348 James 13 26 Jarred 8 Jeremiah (NIFLS) 177 233 235 236 243 249 254 255 271 283 Jesse 173 John (NIFLS) 8 173 176 232 234 307 308 347 348 Jonathan 173 Joseph (NIFLS) 13 14 110 132 229 232 240 246 251 252 264 275 296 307 308 316 318 327 336 347 Joshua 176 Julian 236 Mary/ Polly 251 307 316 347 Moses 294 Peter 308 Rebecca 303 Richard 348 Stephen 285 Thomas 14 Wilm 14 32 49 50 56 251 272 277 286 293
Coy, Ariel 14 Levi 142 Matthew 9
Cozad, Jacob 296
Cozine, Martin 19
Craft, Caleb 186 201
Craig, Benj 193 Elizabeth 194 George 186 187 194 219 Jacob 39 James 70 Jane 219 Joseph 210 Lewis 210

Craig cont- Mary 70 Nancy 193 Stephen 36 Stuman 190 193 194
Crain, see Crane & Crein
Cram(n)er, John 84 166
Crane, James 21 23 Jonas 21 Joshua 9 Jonathan 224 Ruth 224
Craner, Elizabeth 342 Joshua 14 244 Thos 13 244 342
Cranon, Joshua 244 Thomas 244
Cravens/Crasen, Joseph 177 333 Thomas 12 35
Crawford, J. 65 James 279 280 Martha 279 Samuel 284 Thos 14 235 Willm 224 279 284 286 291
Crawl (see Krall), Joseph 185
Creek, John 12 225 228 230
Crein, Jeremiah 131
Crew, Joseph 174
Crisler, Allen 87
Crissey, William 120
Crist, Abr'm 146 Barbara 67 86 95 114 Cynthia 146 Dan'l 8 George 18 32 114 165 224 228 John 12 32 348 Margaret 146 Michael 86 Moses 146 Nicholas 12 86 95 110 114 William 8
Crocker, Benj 35 John 26
Croford, George 80 Thomas 173
Crogen/Cragan, Caleb 33 Elisha 33
Croggeshall, Tristram 244
Croll (see Crawl), Jacob 339
Cromwell, John 62 229 Vincent 224
Crone, Benjamin 143
Crook(s), James 37 Rich'd 110 136 William 39
Crookshank, Nathan 229
Cross, Aquilla 6 21 Demand 24 William 11
Crossan, Agnes 140 Martha

360

INDEX: names in text may have variant spelling
NIFLS = not indexed for land sales

Crossan, cont - 140 170
Crouch, Andrew 238 273
  276 Elenor 273 276
Crowell (see Croll), John
  37 77 Margaret 77 115
  Martin 185
Crozier, Decker 4 5 6
Crume, Daniel 23 185
Crump, Rhoda 33
Crumvin, Peter 173
Culbertson, Anna 310
  Francis 241 310 Robert
  242 245 Thomas 284 317
Cull, Hugh 234 300
Cullum, William 186 189
Cully, Elizabeth 135 146
  Joseph 135 Thomas 135
  146 158 227
Culp, Cornelius 22 Joseph
  211 Richard 11
Culver, Aaron 187 John
  299 Michael 226 229 299
Cumbey, James 10
Cummin(g)s, Alex'r 40 D.
  188 David 26 186 Wilm
  238 230 273
Cunningham, -- 203 Cath-
  arine 211 James 185
  John 26 182 Robt 184
  Richd 211 Sam'l 26 229
  Willm 74 83 99 108 228
Cuppy, Henry 297 James
  343 Thomas 333 343
Curry, Dan'l 36 J. 33
  James 21 183 201 223
  341 Jeremiah 43 John 32
  116 Sally 201 Thomas 32
  William 341
Cushman, Benj 330 341
Cussant, Peter 243
Cutter, Cyrus 22 Wilm 87

Dale, Lydnor 126 Saml 126
Dalhoun, William 275
Dalmazzo, James 188 192
  194 195 200 204 211 215
  216 217 219
Daily, Chas 48 53 59 89
  139 147 Sarah 89
Dains, Nancy 28
Danby, Thomas 27 238
Daniel, Joseph 8 Moses 22

Danson, Charles 18
Darby, Henry 279
Dare, Abel 10 37 100 Robt
  103 160 166
Darling, Thomas 20 26
Darlington, town of 90
Darst, Abr'm 224 Jacob
  223
Dart, Christ'r 93 Enoch
  326 James 7 Thomas
  4 7 8 William 7
Dashiell/Darkiell, Chas
  28 John 24 28
Davenport, Jesse 233 248
  258 259 277 Rebeckah
  248
Davidson, John 233 258
  261 265 268 Joseph 263
  Polly/Mary 258 261 265
Davi(e)s, Adam 325 Benj
  186 David 241 Dunham 22
  Eli 11 12 Elias 11
  George 83 Israel 35 J.
  240 James 184 223 226
  John 11 22 23 39 135
  156 245 Joseph 8 Lewis
  17 Margt 83 Nathan 55
  Nicholas 186 188 Paul 8
  83 Peter 57 223 Robt 93
  Saml 220 327 Spencer 28
  Stephen 37 113 159 Thos
  7 187 188 Timothy 18
  Travis 10 Vincent 41
  Ward 162 William 11 39
  241 Zacariah 38
Davi(d)son, Isaiah 301
  John 25 Joseph 271
  Joshua 259 267 Robt 26
Dawson, Chas 20 25 Eli
  10 12 Elijah 4 5 James
  4 8 Jesse 10 John 4 7
  8 19 20 26 Mathias 14
  Samuel 327. Thomas 4 7
  William 25
Day, David 238 Edw 345
  Jeffery 191 Rawleigh
  192 201 204 205 211
  214 218 Sally 201
Deacons, James 227
Dearmand, Alex'r 20 116
  167 Elizabeth 167
Decauney, Joel 165

INDEX: names in text may have variant spelling
NIFLS = not indexed for land sales

Decker, Abijah 6   Joel 27
Deford, John 8
DeHart, Acklin 183
Delaney, John 33
Delap, James 274
Delorac, Alex'r 119
Delorae, Alex 299
Deloy, George 175
Demaree, -- 186   Peter 186 191 192 234
Demarris, Jacob 21
Demas, John 19
Demee Trustee 158
Deming, Deborah 206   John 196 204 206
Demmitt, Miles 243   Thos 243   William 243
Demoss, John 213
Dence Trustee 20
Denman, John 224
Dennis, Elisha 14 238   Jacob 22
Denniston, Rachel 87 97 98 Willm 74 87 97 98 138 223 224
Denny, Joseph 153 Mary 36 Richard 228
Dentraz, Jeanne 205 John 187 205
Deserens, Francis 187 205 217
Despouys, Jean 200
Deterow, Henry 236   Peter 237
Devee, Jannet 71   Zacariah 10 71
Devor, John 214
Deweese, Lewis 20 38 42 135 147 150   167   Nancy 83 150
Dewey/Duey, Catherine 274   Elizabeth 273 308 311   Henry 274 281   John 273 308 311 Joseph 294 318 323 Nancy 281 Polly 273 Richard 274
Dewitt, John 22
Dexter, Isaac 18
Dick/Dike, Elizabeth 79 George 79 224
Dickard, Elizabeth 324   Jacob 14 301 324

Dicken, Joel 3 21
Dickerson, John 55 56 66   Daniel 184 Robt 31 239   Ruth 56 66   Solomon 8
Dickeson, Griffy 186   Jn. 187   John 41 67 Robt 52   William 184 187
Dickett, -- 156
Dickey, Alex'r 259 284   Benj 54   Betsy 284
Dickinson, Caleb 142   Charlotte 142 John 187 189 Walter 76 Zebulon 24
Dicks, Zacariah 239
Dickson/Dixon, Arthur 49 50 53 59 61 66 86 101 104 118 John 17 184 227 Sarah 61 66 86 101 Wilm 12 103 123 149
Diffendeffer, E. 182   Henry 21
Diggs, Armsbe 139   George 4   William 174
Dill/Dile, George 270 Jas 4 6 107 137 255 343
Dillon, Charity 276 Jesse 242   Luke 242 276
Dils, Henry 24
Direr, Patrick 25
Doan, Nathan 323
Docker, Joel 27
Doddridge, Avis 292 313   John 238 292 313 Philip 238
Dodson, Amy 328   Elijah 328 John 176 238 Major 226 232 328 47 79 83 85
Doherty, James 240
Dollarhide, Jesse 14
Donner, Amos 21
Donnsy, James 21
Donohoe, Patrick 182 183 206
Doron, Matthew 321
Dorsey, J. 310   James 87 300 John 10 Martha 87 310   Owen 93
Dorton, Anna 152 Ephraim 131 152   Joseph 77
Dotson, -- 186
Doty, Ephraim 142   James

INDEX: names in text may have variant spelling
NIFLS = not indexed for land sales

Doty, cont - 157 John 29
Dougan, John 233
Dougherty, Ann 33 Arin 33
  James 8 203 240 281
  John 8 28 Zadock 315
  321 335
Douglas, Robt 39 Thos 211
Doutoit, Eugene 187 Lydia
  212
Dow, Joseph 213 215 218
  William 213
Dowden, Samuel 19
Downey, John 22 Richd 22
Drake, Benj (NIFLS) 183
  191 196 199 Dillard 17
  Elizabeth 87 Hannah 199
  James 13 80 87 Jesse 21
  John 8 John 13 235
  Nath'l 13 Robt 17 184
Draper, Josiah 283 287
Dreeman, David 226
Drew, Mary 147 161 Willm
  33 40 41 101 107 108
  110 116 118 128 134 136
  137 138 143 144 147 154
  155 156 158 159 161 174
Driffee, James 3
Droyer, Edward 25
Droz, Zelim 192 193
Druck, John 317
Druley, Ann 335 Nicholas
  297 306 320 335 337 339
  Sally 306 335 339 Sam'l
  226 335
Drummond, David 298
Drury, Arnet 12 Edw 12
  241 312 Isaiah 12 286
  309 325 339 Jane 312
  John 309 310 Priscilla
  339 Sam'l 12 240 312
  Violet 312 Wilm 312 339
Dubois, Abr'm 18 Alex'r
  227 Benj 22 186 Corne-
  lius 143 Hannah 62
  Isaac 227 Jacob 12 163
  227 Willm 38 39 62 84
  227
Duce, Robert 18
Ducret, James 17
Duer, John 12
Duflon, Simeon 200
Dufour, Ame' 202 205 211

Dufour, cont - 214 Dan'l
  (NIFLS) 196 197 200 201
  204 206 219 Jn. David
  193 202 203 208 214
  Fanny 204 J. Francis
  (NIFLS) 184 185 187 190
  191 192 193 194 195 196
  197 202 204 206 207 210
  211 214 215 216 J.
  James (NIFLS) 184 187
  195 196 197 202 203 204
  206 207 214 215 Polly
  197 212 215
Dugan, James 206 Rebecca
  68 Samuel 37 62 68
  Thomas 182
Duit, Peter 94
Dumont, A. 187 188 197
  215 221 Abr'm 196 205
  210 216 217 John 196
  200 203 207 213 215 220
  221 222 Julia 213 215
  221 Peter 12 Rich'd 218
Dunbar, Gideon 153 Seth
  26 William 226
Dungan, James 230
Dunham, David 79 80 226
  229 John 177
Dunkin, Peter 33 145
  Richard 33 William 227
Dunlap, Elizabeth 95 282
  James 282 John (NIFLS)
  69 72 95
Dunlapsville town 95 223
Dunman, Susanna 342 Willm
  14 250 308 342
Dunn, James 37 John 162
  Michael 19 Silas 238
  Robert 141 William 13
Dunsroth, John 220
Durham, Jeremiah 9 Jesse
  325 John 6 8 Willm 13
Dutton, David 19
Dusky, Dennis 37 56 Lemon
  185 Rachel 56
Dwiggins, James 236
  Joseph 13
Dwire, Edward 91
Dye(r), Willm 14 239 335

Eads, Ann 127 Elijah 6
  Henry 70 James 6 Jane

INDEX: names in text may have variant spelling
NIFLS = not indexed for land sales

Eads, cont- 47 92 John 90 Jonathan 70 78 Rebeckah 45 54 70 Thos 105 112 118 127 143 144 145 163 Wilm 43 44 45 54 70 Wm. H.(NIFLS) 38 39 47 49 57 59 66 69 70 72 75 88 100 103 104 105 107 109 110 113 118 119 126 127 144 148 154 162 164 166 214 215 227
Easterling, Caleb 295 Martha 295
Easton, John 8 Mary 233 Samuel 237
Eastwood, Josiah 333 342
Eaton, Matthew 224 Thos 224 William 224
Eaves, Henry 188
Edgerton, M. 146 Urban 118 119 160
Edwards, Amos 12 Benj 321 331 H. 174 Jonathan 176 335 340 Peter 286 William 178 179 297 339
Edwell, James 27
Egans, Daniel 12 James 102 119 156 160
Eggers, Daniel 227 James 224
Egleston, M. 144
Ehler, Michael 29 Thos 6
Elder, Dele 18 Rebeckah 295 William 227
Eldred, J. 150
Eliasson, Joshua 241
Elkin, Garret 303
Ellerman, William 233
Ellerly, John 230
Elliot, Abner 243 Abr'm 243 245 248 249 253 255 258 262 263 267 313 316 321 322 324 325 328 336 339 346 Ann 277 301 Asa 226 Benj 334 336 Betsey 166 Daniel 165 166 224 Exum 241 Isaac 173 234 303 Israel 242 278 280 282 294 Jacob 258 277 296 301 Jane 328 Jeremiah 243 316 Job 236

Elliot, cont- John 12 116 Jonathan 139 Matthew 319 Nath'l 236 Peggy 166 Rachel 303 Riley 26 Robt 18 21 165 166 224 Samuel 3 Washington 234 273 Wellmet 278 280 282 294 William 243 320 332
Ellis, E. 184 Enos 210 John 234 239 Otis 23 Shubal 176
Elmore, A. 242 Archilaus 245 Byard 3 7 Elijah 155 John 3
Elsted, Isaac 232
Elston, Jesse 262 Josiah 248 292 Rebeckah 292
Elwell, Abr'm 107 Amasiah 227 Eli 340 Elizabeth 160 Isaac 158 Samuel 92 144 158 160 162
Ely, Adam 98 128 129 130 132 229 Elizabeth 105 128 130 132 John 230 Sam'l 10 105 130 Simon 105 130
Elzroth, Elizabeth 178 179 John 175 176 178 179 Nicholas 178
Embier, Davis 240
Embree, Esther 292 J. 29 288 289 290 291 346 Jesse 27 143 161 184 189 John 22 Thos 277 292 339
Emerson, Edward 329 Jesse 100 111 112 127 144 153 154 156 157
Emmett, John 229
Emmil, Henry 333
Emmond, Peter 229
Endsley, Abr'm 281 Andrew (NIFLS) 10 234 252 253 267 281 299 Hugh 12 234 John 234 Peter 14 Sam'l 11 Sarah 299 Thos 13 238
Engle, John 27
English, Chas 18 John 18 William 183
Ennis, John 107
Ent, Samuel 22
Erb, David 41 145

INDEX: names in text may have variant spelling
NIFLS = not indexed for land sales

Erie, town of, 191
Erving, Daniel 228
  William 228
Erwin, see Irwin
Espy, Hugh 17 23 John 23
  Robert 17 18
Este, D.K. 186 David 35
  K. 189
Estele, Betsey 247 Isaac
  247 248 251 297 320 334
  342 Nancy 296 Ruth 334
Estep/Esteb, A. 295 Jacob
  226 John 335
Estes, Fanny 83 129 146
  Obadiah 41 83 116 124
  129 146 166   Philemon
  116
Eubank(s), John 19
Evans, Jared 25 Joseph 63
  119 162 Rachel 162 208
  Robt 9 162 Saml 20 208
  Thos 218 Willm 32 149
Evelete, A. 184
Everett(s), Isaac 176
  Sylvanus 170
E(a)ves, Henry 3 188
Evans, Benj 244 245 247
  David 247 James 324 Job
  279 Joseph 239 240 244
  245 265 279 297 309 346
  Lydia 265 279 297 Saml
  243 279   Thomas 247
  William 265
Evins, (E)leanor 220
  Thomas 202 203 220
Ewan, Samuel 6
Ewart, Thomas 29
Ewing, Cassy 84 Dan'l 228
  David 10 33 84   George
  92 100 140 John 94 105
  108 110 112 117 131 140
  144 145 147 152 154 155
  156 157 159 163 227
  Rebecca 155 Robert 243
  William 97 100 140 228
Ezzell, Randolph 8

Fagely, Sophia 29
Fairfield, David 174
Fairfield, town of 71 85
  95 117 118
Falkington, Stephen 20

Fall/Fohl, George 14 226
  Tetrick 8 23   210
  William 229
Fallis, Saml 208 210 212
  214 215
Fannan, Michael 53
Farand/Ferrand see Farrar
  -- 21 Matthew 8
  Michael 3 7 8
Farlow, -- 238 George 238
  345 John 5 12 14 Nancy
  345 Reuben 13   Simeon
  292 345 William 14 226
  280 292 299
Farmer, George 19
Farner, Benj 216 218 Mary
  216
Farral, James 188
Farrar/Farraw, see Farand
  Mary 289   Matthew 33
  Michael 3
Fasset, Robert 37
Faulkridge, Mary 28
Faussett, Catherine   135
  Jacob 37 135
Fellman, Charles 219
Fellows, B. 97
Felter, Jacob 34   133
  Sally 146
Fender, Elizabeth 335
  Gabriel 239   248   347
  Henry 13 239   335
Fenter, Stacy 39
Fenton, John 3 185 Sam'l
  184 185 203 220
Ferguson, Alex'r 38 Arthur 228   Joel 5 255 260
  329 John 331 Joseph 229
  Lidia 260 329   Micajah
  282 Nimrod 237 255 275
  William 35 285 331
  Zacariah 227 230
Ferrill, Anna 122 143
  James 122 143 242
Ferri(e)s, Andrew 101
  Fredrk 70 73 89 George
  12 Gideon 101 Isaac 26
  Isaiah 26 James 29 John
  18 24 32   Joseph 101
  Susanna 89
Fielder, Reynold 4 5 12
Fielding, Jacob 6

365

INDEX: names in text may have variant spelling
NIFLS = not indexed for land sales

Fields, John 8 9
Fife, William 245
Finbrook, Abr'm 153
Finch, Chas 62 102 155 Isaac 40 Isabella 102 155 John 29 113 Jonathan 29 Moses 40 74
Fincher, John 240 Susanna 262 William 240 262
Findly, James 18 183 Nathan 19
Finley, David 100 122 James 35 Nancy 122
Fishe, John 145
Fisher, Benj 12 David 232 234 280 300 328 Elijah 300 320 Elizabeth 328 Isabel 82 92 143 James 105 334 John 33 40 82 92 139 143 225 229 246 276 Martin 238 308 Nathan 236 Rachel 308 Sarah 334 Sylvanus 348 Thomas 237
Fisk, William 22
Fislar, James 209
Fithian, Mason 243
Fitter & Hughes 212
Fitzhugh, D. 144
Fitzpatrick, Barthol'w 31
Flack/Flake, Adam 25 28 Michael 3 4 18 25 Robt 83 223 Willm 4 7 18 25
Flanagan, Matthew 243
Fleming, Alex'r 169 David 256 262 Elizabeth 284 James 260 277 John 27 314 Peter (NIFLS) 233 234 247 254 261 262 284 313 Saml 5 13 260 261 267 284 Violinda 277
Fletcher, David 10
Flint, - 37 Charlotte 154 Elizabeth 292 J. 282 308 326 John 37 41 54 57 154 160 162 Joseph 12 237 238 273 279 282 285 321 330 Thomas 162
Flood, Bj 160 Wm 11 32 53
Flornor, John 9
Flugel, John 190 192 194 195 200 201 210 214

Flum, -- 214
Fogelsong, George 50
Foland, John 244 262 Valentine 262
Folsom, Richard 27 184
Foote, Aaron 89
Forbes, William 24 37 143
Ford, Obadiah 20
Fordice, Ann 93 Francis 45 93 James 223 John 33
Foreman, John 12
Fortner, Sion 39
Fosdick, Benj 344 Chas 118 160
Fosher, Daniel 300 Mathias 317 332
Foster, Chilton 121 125 James 26 John 20 173 Thomas 147
Foulon, Mical 199
Foutch, John 35 104
Fouts, Andrew 226 256 257 Daniel 257 267 Elenor 248 Jacob 227 233 238 259 264 317 Levi 341 Michael 243 Noah 267 320 Phebe 320 Sarah/Sally 248 256 259 341 William 232 233 235 248 259 263 264 334 341
Fowler, John 175 Skelton 220
Fox, Elijah 257 298 John 12 174 238 239 Philip 238 Susanna 257 298 William 226 243 308
Foye, Lovise 327 332
Frakes/Freakes, Aaron 10 41 66 70 David 4 Joseph 8 23 Nathan 4 Phebe 70 92 Phillip 11 70 92
Fraser/ Frazier, Absolom 335 Ann 179 David 176 180 Eli 244 Elizabeth 108 122 180 Francis 180 George 108 122 175 Gideon 179 James 10 11 175 180 John 20 180 246 286 Rachel 320 Samuel 6 23 Susanna 180 Thos 175 William 240

INDEX: names in text may have variant spelling
NIFLS = not indexed for land sales

Fread/Fred, Jacb 204 John 11 65 70 82 Wilm 39 129
Free, Amy 334 Spencer 242 252 283 334
Freel, John 10 11 Wilm 11
Freeland, John 26 29
Freeman, Richard 41
French, George 8 Hannah 99 Jacob 242 244 Jeremiah 99 139 N. 109 118 120 125 Nath'l 74 76 99 109 136 139 Samuel 99
Frey, Dars 26
Froman, Jacob 20 28 Paul 185 188
Frost, Burnet 175 Edward 312 317 338
Fruhearty, Valentine 12
Fruit, Catharine 56 David 56 George 56 John 56 Jonathan 56 Martin 10
Fry, Henry 128 129 138 Phillip 197
Fryar, John 335 340 Peggy 335 340
Fuget/Fugate, John 38 73 81 96 97 James 139 170 Jesse 9
Fullen, Elizabeth 88 105 Samuel 88 105
Fuller, Isaac 41 James 19 Jhn 19 Sarah 19 Thos 19
Fulsom, James 7
Fulton, Alex'r 11 69 87 David 185 Samuel 3 4 Sarah 87 Thomas 3
Furnas, John 225

Gaines, Frncs 3 Richd 215
Galbreath, -- 241 Daniel 242 David 233 John 242 294 Robt 5 240 241 282 283 William 12 14
Gallion, Hannah 65 102 123 N. 102 141 149 150 152 Nathan (NIFLS) 60 62 65 73 86 109 124 133 156 162 166
Galyan/Galyeau, Jacob 13 14 243 291 299 308 327 328 Peggy 299 308 Polly 328 Thomas 243 299 308

Galyan, cont- Wm 299 308
Gambull, James 104
Gamble, John 10 11 92 99 110
Gano, Aaron 33 Daniel 33
Gant, Britton 38
Gapen, Eli 245
Gard/Guard, Aaron 226 Benjamin 224 David 20 Ephraim 18 Ezra 9 Josephus 227 Lot 226 William 184 216
Garden, William 68
Gardner, A. 129 160 Alx'r 77 84 99 106 118 121 144 155 167 171 Archb'd 112 David 295 Eliab 225 228 Elijah 112 Eliza 144 Elizabeth 211 214 Isaac 224 225 246 295 James 23 John 112 Joseph 112 Paul 295 Rhodes 11 Russel 11 112 Stephen 36 41
Garkill, Eli 276
Garman/German, Davd 44 92
Garner, Hnry 35 Leban 337 Nancy 138 Stephen 138
Garr, Abr'm 233 234 299 Fielding 14 Jonas 13
Garrett, -- 37 241 Cassey 162 298 Henry 236 243 262 274 293 313 318 319 326 327 328 342 346 John 13 240 Mary/Polly 274 293 327 328 346 Nathan 162 241 298 William 238
Garrison, Abr'm 5 20 93 95 Elijah 19 21 Enoch 83 Joel 93 103 John 19 71 73 81 95 101 110 123 Levi 6 Saml 32 Silas 19 Sina 73 81 95
Garton, Polly 210 Zacariah 210
Gass, Joseph 175
Gasset, William 51
Gassin, Eli 277 292 310 332 Harriet 326 Stephen 316 321 326

INDEX: names in text may have variant spelling
NIFLS = not indexed for land sales

Gaston, Robert 182 210
  Samuel 34
Gates, Jacob 70 71 125
  Noah 185
Gather, Basil 26
Gavin, John 10 11
Gavison, John 73 Sina 73
Gavit, John 204
Gay, John 275
Gayman, David 38 88 92
  Mary 88 93
Gazlay, James 81
Geisser, John 27
Gelligan, Chamnick 37
Gelso, John 27
Gentry, William 291
George, Benj 10 35 Wilm
  10 31 33
Gerard, Peter 39 Wilm 194
Gex, Elizabeth 219 222 L.
  193 210 Lewis 192 214
  Lucien 191 192 198 200
  219 222 Marianne 192
Gibbens, John 183
Gibbs, John 22 Wilm 11
Gibson, James 18 John 21
  222 325 Wilm 23 58
Giger, Jacob 115 129
  James 225
Gilbert, Amos 186 187 203
  212 217 Jonathan 12 14
  238 Josiah 258 Lyman
  212 Sally 203 212
Gilean, Jonathan 65
Gilecos, Justice 3
Gill(s), David 4 Ede 82
  Jacob 82 John 41
  Simon 82
Gillian, Thomas 237
Gillespie, James 151
  Joseph 238 Martin 188
  Robert 22
Gilliland, John 183 186
  188 191 192 193 194 195
  199 201 204 206 208 209
  210 217 220 221 222
  Joseph 207 Thos 188 193
Gillum/Gillian, David 10
  John 11 Jonathan 10 122
  Mary 122 Rachel 70
  Thomas 174 William 10
Gilmore, George 189 James

Gilmore, cont - 322 324
  325 326 328 336 340
Gilpen, Elizabeth 343
Ginn, David 51 James 142
  Job 254 267 318 John
  275 276 281 282 Laurnce
  282 292 Sarah 267
  Thomas 315 318 321 335
Girton, Christian 37
Gittner, George 127 144
Gittro/Githro, Peter 238
Givan/Given, Gilbert 28
  James 169
Glandon, James 98
Glass/Glaze, Elizabeth
  262 268 George 240 262
  268 James 117 138 John
  23 86 Robt 28 Sophia
  138 William 138
Gleantt, Tyre 155
Gleen, Joseph 33
Glenn, Hugh 84 107 187
  189 215 James 215
  Mary 107
Glidewell, Gnash 10 112
  Joana 80 Martin 229
  Robt 39 41 80 108 112
  126 127 155 158 168
  Sarah 126 155 Wilm 108
Glisson/Glisten, Thos 142
Glover, Zacariah 12
Gloyd, Asa 28
Goble, Abner 224 Alesey
  111 Alice 47 Benoni 224
  David 42 47 101 111
  Ebenezer 70 267 Robt
  225 Stephen 38 Wilm 130
Godard, R. 213
Goe, William 123 127
Goetz, John Jacob 220
Goff, William 38
Golay, David 194 207
  Elisha 184 185 193 195
  196 197 198 205 206 <u>212</u>
  214 218 222 Lewis 189
Gold, James 35 59
Golden/Golding, Thos 58
  102
Goldtrap, Ann 152 John
  152 William 152
Goldtross, John 36
Gooding, David 227

INDEX: names in text may have variant spelling
NIFLS = not indexed for land sales

Goodner, Jacob 17 186
Goodrich, Abijah 18 Jeremiah 151
Goodwin, Eleanor 127 146 James 20 Jehu 5 Jeremiah 112 Joseph 199 Saml 104 127 131 138 146
Gooshorn, William 104
Gordon, Anderson 13 Chas 12 226 229 338 Hnry 332 James 14 41 270 274 John 3 285 286 Luis 221 Mary 274 Rufus 17 Willm 12 32 275 327
Gordwine, Seth 38
Gosney, James 10
Goslin, Thurston 218
Gosnel, Adam 7
Gosset, John 10
Gotstein, Joseph 27
Goudie, James 36 40
Gough, John 12
Gount, Daniel 237
Grace, William 11
Graham, Abner 19 David 40 George 274 Margrt 274
Grandise, Philip 145
Grandon, Philip 124
Grant, Catharine 343
Graumlick, Jacob 152 154
Graves (see Grove), Betty 293 Enos 293 307 Jacob 293 322 334 Jonathan 283 293 322 334 Lydia 293 Nathan 293 William 135 Zachariah 86
Gray, Alex'r 238 David 38 James 227 John 189 227 Mary 108 Moses 11 207 Peter 108 Robt 36 Sam'l 132 William 58 76
Greaves, Benjamin 169
Green, Anna 45 105 Charity 330 Eli 17 19 Fred 188 Jesse 174 330 Mary 105 Moses 105 167 Peter 45 105 Robt 11 41 44 45 Stephen 6 Thos 110 111 115 126 142 158 161 William 8 228
Greener, Augusta 203 John 27 184 192 193 194 203

Greener cont- 213
Greenfield, John 6
Greensburgh, town 81 90
Greenstreet, J. 245
Greenwell, Asa 239
Greer, George 6
Gregg, Delilah 142 George 11 142 Harman 265 John 76 265 Mahalah 142 Rhoda 265 Sarah 94 Silas 265 Stephen 36 Thomas 36 142 271
Gregory, Isaac 302
Gresham, S. 56
Grewell, Jane 303 Laurence 303 Samuel 303
Griffin, Jacob 241 256 258 298 Mary 256 298
Griffith, John 12 Stephen 12 237 238 298 Wilm 188
Grimes, Abijah 220 Alex'r 13 14 308 332 Armstrong 13 14 315 332 Elijah 218 220 221 George 12 332 J. 234 James 329 Jane 220 221 Robt 332 William 12 234 300
Groober, Henry 150
Grooms, Joseph 136
Grose, Joseph 183
Gross, William 12
Grove (see Graves), Enos 234 237 George 7 17 22 Henry 17 Jacob 176 Jonathan 237
Grover, Edmund 284
Grubbs, William 8
Gruwell, Asa 337
Guibert, Antoine 200
Guider, James 225
Guile, Joshua 34
Guilford, -- 23
Guiltner, George 32 68 Sarah 68
Guinn, -- 245
Guisnor, Philip 73
Gulick, Joseph 22 57 105
Gullet, Robert 6
Gullifer, Stephen 243
Gullion, John 185 Robt 185
Gully(s), Adolphus 100

369

INDEX: names in text may have variant spelling
NIFLS = not indexed for land sales

Gully, cont - 110 116 157
  B. 157 Benjamin 72 117
  Harriet 157 Simon 35 72
  77 Smith 130 Wilm 117
  130 157
Gunn, William 311
Gunslade, Josiah 338
Gunwell, Samuel 14
Guthrey, Arch'd 10 32 45
  46 69 104 137 Rachel
  104 Richard 9
Guy, John 275
Gwin, Charity 287 John
  287

Hackett, Philip 277
Hackleman, Abr'm 12 41 42
  43 44 48 Isaac 3 Jacob
  3 12 38 42 64 153 John
  9 20 38 64 Michael 3 7
  64 Peggy 42 Thos 3 7
Hadley, Joshua 95
Hadlock, James 185
Hageman, Hanna 77 John 77
Haggerman, Christian 51
  John 50 51 53 80
Hague, John 307
Hains, John 276
Halberstadt, Antny 38 40
  53 55 79 83 116 126
  128 John 83 118 Mary
  118 Sarah 53 55 79 83
  116 Thomas 11
Hale, John 323 331 341
  343 Polly 331 341
Hall, Amy 173 Edward 218
  Freeburn 8 Hugh 260
  John 6 26 38 49 57 60
  153 177 Joseph 19 Richd
  17 265 Sam'l 279 Susan-
  na 265 Thos 25 Wilm 3
Hallack, Jacoby 116
Hallgath, John 189
Halstead, R. 33 Thos 102
Ham, Hezekiah 314
Hamarch, Peter 28
Hamble, John 111
Hamblin, Levi 183
Hames, George 28
Hamill, Joseph 279 347
Hamilton, -- 23 Adam 11
  Asa 18 Israel 78 James

Hamilton cont - (NIFLS) 3
  42 43 54 55 60 107 182
  183 184 Jane 150 161
  163 164 166 John 22 107
  132 184 Nancy 161 163
  164 166 Robt 182 Saml
  36 Wilm 29 Zell 8
Hammer, David 175
Hammon (see Harmon),
  Abr'm 79 86 John 10
Hammond, Abr'm 224
  Lewis 184
Hampton, Abr'm 244
  Andrew 235 Isaac 235
  Jacob 79 235 244
Preston 199
Hancock, Elisha 28 Joseph
  242 William 28
Haney, William 9
Hanley, James 85
Hanlin, Alex 194
Hann, Peter 35 171 Sarah
  171
Hannah, David 92 145 Ele-
  nor 140 169 Elizabeth
  165 167 James 81 97 100
  140 169 345 John 64 70
  80 81 87 92 100 101 103
  104 107 111 123 127 128
  129 132 138 142 145 155
  156 157 161 165 167 228
  229 Joseph 10 64 87 227
  Mary 123 127 165 Phebe
  169 Robt 41 52 53 54 60
  61 63 66 67 69 72 73 77
  92 95 119 123 128 131
  133 135 144 147 148 149
  150 153 156 159 161 162
  164 167 168 Sam'l 12 81
  169 308 345 Sally/Sarah
  128 147 148 149 150 153
  165 167 Wilm 117 121
  122 140 169
Hannis, Hannah 207 211
  Henry 188 189 207 211
  Peter 191
Hannor, William 9
Hansel, Christopher 37 38
  85 86 David 158 Dan'l
  37 Elizabeth 86 George
  9 Thomas 26
Hanson, Benjamin 119

INDEX: names in text may have variant spelling
NIFLS = not indexed for land sales

Hardcastle, William 94
Harcourt, John 205
Hardin(g), Aaron 234 Ann 315 326 Ede. 304 Eliachim 12 H. 18 Hy 20 326 Thos 12 237 319
Hardman, Benj 284 John 291
Hardy, Charles 83
Hargeredes, Benj 38
Harkersmith, Isaac 221
Harlan(d), Cathrine 56 94 Elisha 236 242 George 56 79 94 227 230 Jacob 82 John 226 230 Joshua 49 86 101 123 125 228 230 236 Sally 125 Valentine 236
Harley, John 32 82
Har(t)low, Jonas 161 Mary 161 Wilm 110 111 115 143 158 161
Harlut, William 25
Harmon (see Hammon) Abr'm 85 Andrew 233 251 253 262 266 Dan'l 233 David 13 233 251 266 268 274 336 344 345 Henry 261 263 John 8 Polly 263 Rebeckah 274 345 Wilm 8
Harper, Asa 74 104 Deward 104 Elizabeth 165 166 Ezekiel 26 Jas 10 John 19 37 153 157 213 Joseph 19 Mary 215 Peter 206 215 Thomas 84 223 Wilm 34 114 117 153 165 166 216
Harrell, Abigail 70 89 E. 208 Elijah 9 Gabriel 236 334 336 Jesse 186 John 70 89 229 Wilm 10
Harrington, Nathaniel 192
Harri(e)s, Amos 151 Benj 234 270 345 Caleb 183 Clark 107 Cornelius 183 George 102 151 Israel 124 James 12 125 236 244 John 93 99 124 143 159 336 Joshua 37 158 Miriam 263 266 Obadiah

Harris, cont- 13 175 244 262 263 266 Peter 196 197 199 Pleasant 5 12 Rachel 158 Robert 182 Martha 125 John 233 315
Harrison, Alfrd 141 Davis 213 Edmund 84 86 88 89 93 94 163 Job 39 Lewis 145 William 238
Harry, James 33 Wilm 33
Harshly, Christian 24
Hart, Daniel 234 339 John 5 13 253 281
Harter, John 303 Josph 55 223 Philip 343 Saml 228
Hartman, Fredk 99 160 166 Jacob 132 154 Ruth 154
Hartpence, James 3 20 53 153 171
Hartup, James 233 258 Mary 258
Harty, Daniel 302
Harvey, Abslm 5 12 14 277 Benj 245 254 257 Caleb 234 253 Charles 33 111 Elizabeth 298 Francis 14 226 229 298 H. 240 Hannah 112 125 170 Henderson 12 298 299 Isaac 14 243 326 Isom 323 Jane/Jean 56 253 260 315 Jhn (NIFLS) 5 12 49 56 233 236 240 241 243 253 260 264 279 315 Mary 253 Michael 12 245 Philemon 83 92 145 Sara 145 Rebecka 326 Robt 14 226 241 298 Samuel 315 Thomas 112 125 139 170 William 10 41 91 240 245 260 280
Harwood, Philip 34 137
Haskins, Jonathan 175
Hasson, Charles 154
Hastings, Isaac 134 163 Martha 163 Wilm 241 256 258 270 296 298 338
Hasty, Absolom 11 Danl 39
Hatch, Ralph 24
Hatfield, John 10 37 70 224 Jonas 311 Joseph 243 Sarah 300 Thomas

INDEX: names in text may have variant spelling
NIFLS = not indexed for land sales

Hatfield cont-(NIFLS) 243 267 296 297 300 315
Hathaway, Abiather 113 Daniel 29 Jonathan 196
Hathclaw, William 237
Hatton, Alex'r 220 Thomas 293
Haunth, William 176
Havens, Jonas 267 270
Hawes, John 8
Hawkins, Amos 236 302 313 314 H. 244 Henry 245 Isaac 302 John 31 209 236 239 257 302 313 Lydia 313 Nathan 244 William 258
Hayden, Stephen 224
Haymond, Calder 63 Catharine 63 Danl 39 Edwd 76 88 159 John 63 159
Haynes, John 188 Joshua 186 Matths 186 Thos 121
Hayward, Ebenezer 227 Paul 306
Ha(y)worth, Aaron 260 George 174 Jas 260 Joel 225 John 159 174 242 245 William 174
Hay(e)s, Abiah 77 Abijah 20 35 Caleb 3 4 185 210 Davd 40 James 20 28 303 Job 6 John 35 39 345 Joseph 3 18 20 101 193 203 209 Joshua 8 Josiah 8 Saml 242 Wilm 136
Hazlerigg, Fielding 160 162
Heady, - 186 Benj 186 220 Elias 4
Heasley, Elijah 115
Heath, James 37 Saml 186
Heaton, Abr'm 137 Catherine 137 Dan'l 70 74 96 267 282 Ebenezer 70 88 89 267 Eli 88 296 330 James 97 160 Joanna 70 88 89 267 Jonah 174 Mary 74 96
Heaston, Davd 178 179 180
Heavenridge, John 78 84 114 225 Mary 111 Sam'l 319 William 111

Hedger, Catherine 22
Hedley, Elizabeth 167 John 40 108 167 Jeremiah 167 Mary 127 167 Thos 167 William 167
Hedrich/Hetrick, Abr'm 36 93 Jacob 40 64 104 139 Margt 104 Wlm 36 93 166
Hees, Francis 182
Helder, Martin 214
Helm, Elizabeth 145 Wilm 9 38 74 81 82 87 88 93 96 98 99 102 113 127 140 145
Henarthy, David 175
Henderson, -- 102 Chas 73 84 211 Corbly 34 Eli 126 228 Ethan 98 Isaac 19 John 9 12 98 127 Martha 57 Mary 34 Nathl 102 126 228 Rachel 98 Rebecca 154 Richd 342 348 Saml 233 234 343 Sarah 84 Shadrack 234 300 Thos 38 40 48 54 102 124 131 155 Wilm 31 38 39 42 43 51 54 57 59 79 111 131 160 Zilpha 79 111 160
Hendricks, Abr'm 326 Hnry 238 Wilm 195 342 348
Hendry, Richard 238 279
Henley, Jesse 226 309 Polly 309 M. 246 Micajah 250 302
Hennegin, Peter 24
Henny, John 189
Henrie, Arthur (NIFLS) 37 40 140 141 286 288 289 Grace 140 288
Henry --, 323
Henry, Sam'l 343 Thom 41
Henshaw, Joseph 177
Hensley, Abr'm 13 Gabriel 110
Hepburn, Edward 22 27 29 182 184 187 189
He(a)rshey, Christian 24
Herbert, Ebenezer 23
Herndon, Arch'd 58 Elizabeth 56 73 Elliott 11 38 53 58 69 62 149

INDEX: names in text may have variant spelling
NIFLS = not indexed for land sales

Herndon, cont - Nathan 38
  Nathl 11 38 53 56 57 66
  73 Thos 62 Wesley 10
  William 71
Herrald, Abigail 65 70
  John 65 70
Hesler, Jacob 188
Hester, Thomas 175
Heustis, Oliver 24
Heward, Isaac 34
Hewitt, Robert 183
He(y)wood, Daniel 120
  John 238
Hiatt, Christ'r 176 Eleazar 310 314 325 336
  Isaac 234 Jonathan 176
  Moses 176 Solomon 179
  180 Wilm 234 Zacariah
  176 234 237 240 244 281
Hiatta, George 23
Hickle, Debolt 237
Hicks, Isaac 241
Hidargs, Jacob 37
Hidey, Sarah 56
Higgs, William 10
Higgins, Alex'r 10 Amos
  233 263 297 Betsey 263
  297 Jonathan 239 278
  295 296 Margaret 296
  Martin 11 Thomas 139
Higdon, Peter 19
Higgenbotham, Thomas 175
Hight, George 179
Hildebrand, Michael 188
Hill(s), -- 345 Benj 235
  236 263 287 Benoni 177
  Elaron 233 Eli 29 Elizabeth 250 286 297 Henry
  177 Isaac 19 Jas 22 243
  Jesse 250 288 303 Joel
  14 230 348 John 293
  Jonathan 277 322 Mabel
  250 Mary 103 Nathan 240
  243 250 256 258 262 264
  286 295 297 P. 25
  Penninah 262 Phineas 29
  Robert (NIFLS) 236 240
  247 249 256 262 263 284
  289 305 341 345 Samuel
  103 Susannah 247 Thos
  233 337 345
Hillis, Matthew 9 Sims

Hillis, cont- 179 180
Hinde, James 18
Hindle, Christian 325
  George 285
Hindman, Thomas 31
Hinds, Benj 37 Henry 34
  Jacobs 150
Hindsley, Hazard 60
  Patience 60
Hines, Andrew 122 Caldwell 220 George 175
Hinkson, John 20 Thos
  101 123
Hinshue, Isaiah 341
Hiser, Danl 222 David 183
  Henry 177 Mary 222
Hobbs, -- 21 Emry 21 Jas
  33 Robt 166 Wilm 10
Hobson, Joseph 241
Hockenberry, Peter 136
Hockett, Elizabeth 325
  Hezekiah 175 180 Isaac
  175 179 Joseph 175
  Nathan 325 346 Stephen
  175 William 175 176
Hodge(s), Amanuel 13 Benj
  234 255 339 341 342
  Jane 339 342 Jesse 14
  272 John 173 Mary 286
Hod(g)son, Amos 176 Danl
  176 George 245 Hav 175
  Henry 312 Solomon 242
Hoffman, Isaac 236
Hofford, John 38
Hogan, Davd 18 24 Jhn 214
Hogsheare, James 28
Holb, Harrell 136
Holcum, Matthew 13
Holder, Jesse 10 Martin
  183
Holderfield, James 141
Holdman (see Holman),
  Elizabeth 255 George
  255 334
Hole, James 213 219
Holland, Elijah 13 Henry
  279 Jane 279
Hollett, George 233 Mark
  233 273 Thomas 233
Holliday, Jas 243 John 37
Hollingsworth, Abr'm 10
  64 225 Carter 126 150

373

INDEX: names in text may have variant spelling
NIFLS = not indexed for land sales

Hollinsworth cont- Charity 126 150 David 79 126 131 224 228 230 E. 80 Edgehill 225 Ezekiel 170 George 64 227 Hanna 159 Henry 224 Isaac 78 147 228 Jacob 154 228 James 122 123 154 225 228 John 228 Jonathan 131 228 Joseph 159 173 174 228 330 Levi 126 150 Lin 228 Martha 154 Mary 330 Richard 228 Sarah 122 123 Susannah 64 Wilm 147 230 330
Hollister, Ephraim 6
Holloway, Stephen 275 287 311 312 333 344
Hollowell, Saml 21 Wlm 21
Hol(e)man, Elizabeth 247 255 George 233 234 247 255 308 Jas 14 Jesse 17 Joseph 13 226 234 241 258 270 276 279 280 281 284 301 303 323 Lydia 270 284 303 Ruea 347 Wilm 5 13 226 234 347
Holmes, James 6 247 Saml 233 261
Holsclaw, James 237 Joseph 340 William 12
Holsey, Silvanus 133
Holson, Andrew 337 Joseph 241
Holton, Alexr 192 195 Elijah 79
Homan, Martha 297
Homer (see Horner), Jacob 227 Michael 22
Honet, Joseph 239
Honeywell, Pelead 102
Hook, -- 241
Hooman, Tarleton 174
Hoover, Andrw 235 243 249 263 265 311 Catharine 329 D. 258 280 317 Davd 243 251 258 280 281 284 293 300 311 336 343 Elizabeth 257 265 288 292 319 342 Fredrk 249 Henry 226 240 255 257 262 288 292 319 Jacob

Hoover, cont- 229 243 258 319 324 325 333 John 239 288 Job 246 Peter 240 Saml 246 Wm 329 342
Hopkins, Benj 24 Thomas 182 183 184 William 81
Hopson, George 13 Wilm 12
Hornaday, John 41
Hornby, Solomon 174
Horner (see Homer), Jacob 3 Levi 246
Horney, Elizabeth 259 Jas 339 Jhn 29 258 263 Orin 3 Solomon 259 Wilm 21
Hosbrook, Daniel 38
Hosier, Lewis 240 Wilm 240 241
Hough, - 241 Benj 113 Isa 244 Israel 324 John 314 Jonathan 244 277 Joseph 223 225 241 Martha 324
Houghman, Lewis 208
How(e), Conrad 25 Ebenezer 63 80 81 82 83 111 129 140 157 226 Robt 25 Silas 17 Thomas 133
Howard, - 244 Elizabeth 151 Jhn 8 13 18 233 256 303 315 326 Saml 13 14
Howell, Chatfield 35 38 100 104 105 Chester 37 Ebenezer 225 James 100 Jason 245 Joab 36 John 10 38 100 104 229 Mary 344 Nancy 100 Samuel 105 151 153 224
Howlett, William 17
Howman, Eber 101
Howse, Jacob 226
Hubbard, Chas 279 James 8 22 John 8 22
Hubble, Richard 35
Huckleberry, Henry 222
Huddleston, Job 173 238 276 280 Jonathan 225
Hudson, Corbly 39 69 73 90 93 146 151 Edw 148 171 Mary 69 73 81 101 151 Prudy 102 115 Wilm 35 81 115 146 151
Huff, James 343 344 John 229 290 291 Sidney 343

INDEX: names in text may have variant spelling
NIFLS = not indexed for land sales

Huff, cont - 344 William 10 49 50 188
Huffman, Benj 24 Conrad 19 Dan'l 22 Jonas 239
Hughell, Joseph 34
Hughes, Thomas 229
Hugholl, Jacob 243
Hughs, Susanna 247
Huith, Anna 306
Hulick, Barnet 18 Barrent 3
Hulings, William 346 347
Hull, H. 212 213 Hezekiah 195 200
Humes, John 8
Humphrey, Ebenezer 183 John 105
Hunley, Samuel 10
Hunt, A. 176 Abner 116 139 144 170 Asa 256 Chas 229 232 249 254 273 E. 176 Edwd 238 Eliza 137 Elizabeth 268 G./George 5 12 232 247 248 249 253 261 266 267 268 270 271 274 307 343 J. 199 244 330 Jacob 77 94 Jas 254 264 Jeremiah 24 25 Jesse 17 18 28 36 137 184 186 225 John 18 197 224 232 234 252 254 255 257 260 261 268 273 298 307 327 Jonas 135 224 Jonathan 35 50 122 248 249 254 Joseph 12 Lewis 322 Libni 235 N. 199 Nathl 116 139 144 170 Patsy 268 272 Polly 255 257 267 268 Ralph 139 Robt 19 25 26 S. 5 33 40 Saml 36 41 137 253 Smith 5 229 256 261 267 268 272 Stephen 299 324 345 Thos 20 Timothy 232 254 268 Wilm 5 226 236 254 258 273 325 336
Hunter, Henry 78 114 140 225 Isabella 114 John 114 186 Joseph 26
Huntington, Jonthn 18 188
Hurlbut, Enos 336
Hurst, Dickson 304

Hurst cont- Elizabeth 330 Henry 9 J. 244 John 299 304 330
Huston, -- 228 Genet 27 Jacob 136 137 149 James 136 137 John 136 137 Joseph 6 M. 166 Paul 29 Priscilla 24 Robt 27 Saml 38 155 Sarah 136 137
Hutchins, Benj 246 314 328 Hannah 314 Isaac 175 246 Martha 328 Thomas 328
Hutchinson, Samuel 19
Hutchison, George 221 Sarah 185 William 337
Huston, William 13 14
Hyatt (see Hiatt), Nathl 137 145

Ichelberry, Henry 137
Iddings, Benjamin 268
Imel, George 13 Peter 252
Ince, James 24
Ingels, John 282
Inman, John 28 Stephen 24
Ireland, Andrew 277 313 Betsey 313 Davd 275 327 331 Elom 277 331 James 260 John 5 236 247 260 275 Mary/Polly 247 260 Nancy 327 331 Wilm 275 318
Irvin, Betsy 300 321 George 239 Henry 321 John 179 180 300 321 Thos 320 324 Wilm 240
Irwin, Andrw 273 Mary 303 344 Wlm 241 303 330 344
Isgrig, Maston 6
Ishe, George 12 14 239 241 292 315 322 Marium 292 315 322
Israel, John 165
Ivy, John 203

Jack(s), Adam 237 287 289 Hannah 287 289 John 10 11 196 Samuel 182 196 Rosannah 196
Jackman, Atwell 31 32 Edw

INDEX: names in text may have variant spelling
NIFLS = not indexed for land sales

Jackman cont- 170 Richd 12 Willm 10 38
Jackson, Andrew 149 Ebenezer 14 Elliot 4 7 Enoch 4 19 Ezekiel 4 20 21 Isaac 258 343 347 James 12 237 John 3 5 14 174 253 Joseph 333 335 Mordecai 185 193 R. 25 Wilm 177 335 342
Jacksonville town 191 194
Jacob(s), Catherine 344 Elizabeth 111 128 James 177 233 248 256 260 264 268 John (NIFLS) 62 63 73 74 89 111 124 128 136 138 160 164 177 Polly 256 260 264 268 Milburn 262 268 344
James, B. 165 Eli 56 142 151 153 154 159 167 169 Enoch 18 19 John 17 23 44 54 55 62 74 98 107 164 165 246 Julius 22 Levi 183 184 Martha 98 165 Pinckney 182
Jamison, Barbara 69 71 76 86 Martin 69 71 76 86 Thomas 9
Janney, Abel 14 243 258 306 311 Peggy 311
Jarred, Thos 175 176 179
Jarrett, Eli 302 George 239 Jesse 302 Levi 239 Nancy 302 Wilm 239 302
Jarvis, Benj. 271 329 335
Jasmon, David 130
Jason, John 111 142 Lucy 111 142
Jay, John 244 Reuben 14 Sam'l 245
Jeffery, Job 246 Joel 246 John 246 346
Jeffries, Abraham 334
Jellard, George 158
Jelly, Andrew 185 Saml 18 201
Jenkins, David 238 James 242 John 9 Prince 34 William 239
Jenks, Stephen 125
Jennings, Davd 238 Marion

Jennings, cont - 190 191 William 190 191
Jessup, Elias 310 Elizabeth 288 338 Isaac 186 235 244 Jacob 235 244 Jonathan 240 247 262 288 338 Nathan 244 Timothy 245 William 235
Jeter, Fielding 134 Lemuel 41
Jewitt, Moses 23 24
(J)Inkinson, Henry 46 53 137 140 168
Job, Levi 7 Rachel 248 249 270 271 329 Samuel 232 249 270 271 329 Thomas 226
John, Asenath 126 161 E. 140 Elizabeth 119 Eloise 88 Enoch (NIFLS) 36 59 63 65 73 76 88 94 96 107 126 131 146 148 150 156 160 163 167 171 215 Isaac 125 128 135 138 155 Jehu 94 107 119 123 127 168 John 99 Robt 36 76 86 92 94 97 99 102 103 104 106 107 109 110 111 114 115 117 119 120 121 123 125 126 127 128 136 140 143 144 146 147 150 152 155 156 159 161 164 166 167
Johnson, -- 244 Abel 27 283 294 301 Abr'm 22 Andrew 220 Ann 51 76 Bailey 131 Benj 28 224 Caleb 6 Casper 6 21 Cave 20 Chas 329 339 Chitester 55 64 71 Davd 49 Edw 3 Ezekiel 169 Gabriel 203 212 George (NIFLS) 71 95 100 101 117 328 Gideon 91 98 I. 148 Isaac 51 54 76 324 J. 135 140 James 31 53 63 233 237 314 329 339 Jremiah 6 Jerry 6 Jesse 175 179 142 John 87 185 227 Josiah 339 Kinchen 293 Lewis 3 113 Miriam 64 329 339 Nathan 280

INDEX: names in text may have variant spelling
NIFLS = not indexed for land sales

Johnson cont- 282 288 290 293 294 Peter 304 305 314 318 326 333 337 344 Prudence 339 Saml 6 Sarah 63 100 Stephen 14 244 323 Thos 6 William 278 323 Willis 10
Johnston, Caleb 27 Chas 189 Davd 24 Edw 26 Gabriel 187 George 40 Gideon 108 Henry 138 Isaac 28 James 8 112 Jeremiah 3 7 John 24 175 Lewis 11 Polly 108 Robert 8 Saml 8 Wilm 8 183 189
Jonas, Joseph 122 167
Jones, - 23 35 Abijah 244 Abr'm 38 Andrew 13 226 Christ'r 182 David 38 258 Edmund 239 Eliahim 28 Eliakim 201 Eliza 168 Garret 34 George 233 234 Henry 182 Hubbard 21 Jacob 174 James 12 20 21 22 35 39 45 51 59 81 156 168 263 274 294 300 Jesse 11 John 25 173 238 239 278 280 284 286 287 313 320 Jonas 79 271 Jones 25 Joshua 190 Lewis 183 Levi 284 289 294 304 327 343 344 Mary 43 72 304 343 344 Micajah 256 Michael (NIFLS) 42 43 46 48 60 72 Nancy 333 Phebe 274 Philip 36 Rebeccah 59 81 316 Robertson 39 93 129 168 Ruth 278 Samuel 14 155 173 243 254 255 295 316 346 Sarah 33 82 278 Simpson 32 Thos 282 283 284 294 Thompson 316 317 339 W. 151 Wilm 33 156 179 232 233 234 239 282 302 333
Jordan, Keziah 344 John 173 213 226 234 245 252 255 287 308 310 324 325 334 Rachel 310 325 334 William 310

Judd, Finley 6 Job 6 Joseph 6 Orren 20 Phineas 20
Julian, George 13 14 Isaac (NIFLS) 12 134 240 242 266 280 295 Jacob 14 244 319 Jesse 13 14 John 10 Rebeckah 280 Renny 13 176 295 339 Shubal 56 59 251 295 William 10
Junkins, Jas 276 280 297
Jurdin, William 14
Justice, Elizabeth 286 Hannah 323 Jonathan 278 286 329 Katherine 330 333 Patrick 275 301 330 333 William 288 305 323 331 343
Justus, Martin 28

Kain, Samuel 38
Kalb, George 36 Richd 36
Kamp, Danl 271 Jacob 271
Karn, see Kern
Kautze, David 78 147 Mary 147
Kayger, John 34
Keen(e), John 137 Joshua 190 191 Nancy 94 Richd 37 94 Wilm 195 196 197 198 199 200 201 202 204 205 206 207 208 209 210 211 212 213 217 219 221
Keenly, Joseph 230
Keeny, John 58 85 Jonathan 85 94 Nancy 85 Thomas 85
Keffer, Eve 83 91 163 George 83 91 116 163 225
Keightly, R.F. 25
Keith, - 186 Cathrine 213 John 195 Nicholas 183 209 214 William 213 219
Kell, John 223
Keller, Christian 45 93 Mary 93
Kellogg -- 32 Hollis 220
Kelly, Henry 11 Moses 235 William 183 Willis 228
Kelsey, Daniel 27 John 40 Lydia 166 Thomas 62 166

INDEX: names in text may have variant spelling
NIFLS = not indexed for land sales

Kely, Joseph 99
Kemp, John 22
Kemper, Eli 18 Nathan 18
Kendall, Elizabeth 269
 274 328 Euele 242 252
 253 262 268 269 274 318
 328 Francis 263 Hiram
 328 Thomas 235 Uzziah
 39 Wilm 263 300 301
Kendry, Richard 238
Kennady (see Canaday),
 Edw 305 James 117 Joel
 229 John 40 226
 William 175
Kenny, Joseph 225
Kenworthy, John 246
Kern(s), Jacob 189 203
 220 Jehu 259 Josiah 259
 Levi 250 259
Kerr, David 24 Matthew 97
 William 66 186
Kersey, John 279 Rebecca
 279 Thomas 243 279
Kesler (see Hesler),
 Caleb 35
Kessling, Jacob 233 234
 318 333 334 John 318
 Phebe 318 334
Ketcham, Andrew 217
 David 25
Keybourn, Adam 123
Kiaerley, David 276
Kibbey, John 249 264 275
 279 281 295 321 327 329
 334 343 345 348 Joseph
 242 Mary 327 334
Kibley, John 263
Kidwell, Jonathan 300
Kiger, C. 41 J. 41
Kilby, Joseph 242
Killoner, John 238
Kimble, G. 109 George 107
 113 123 137 139 145 150
 151 161 Mary 150 151
 161 Timothy 6
Kimmy, Margaret 139
King, Danl 241 Elisha 242
 Jas 6 John 241 245 298
 Joseph 241 Levinus 28
 Phineas 25 Saml 242
 William 6
Kingery, Christian 12 225

Kingery, cont - Eva 137
 George 83 Katy 83 Jacob 83 136 137 225 226
 295 John 83 Joseph 37
 91 137 224 225 Martin
 225 Michl 33 Saml 149
 164 225 Sarah 164
Kingsbury, Charles 134
 John 134
Kinsely, John 26
Kinnsy, Henry 27 Isaac 40
Kinsley, Calvin 34
Kinton, John 157 158
Kirk, Jesse 183
Kirkpatrick, William 229
Kitchell, Percy 96 156
 Samuel 226
Kite, Daniel 176
Klein, Addam 217
Knapp, Hezekiah 112
 Hiram 25 John 25
Kneeland, Ephraim 20
Knight, Jas (NIFLS) 28 40
 45 50 52 53 55 60 61 63
 73 75 77 96 115 164 166
 343 Mary 53 95 98 115
 164 166 336 Thos 44 246
Knipe (see Nype), John 13
 237 238
Knott, James 301 Wilm 229
Knowles, (see Nolls) W.
 168 William 39 109 129
Knox, George 214
Knutt, William 317
Koonse, Jasper 233
Krall, Samuel 185
Krutz, Chas 184 192 193
 194 196 198 203 206 209
 213 217 Elizabeth 198
Kyle, Thomas 6 24

L--ne, Wm 182
Labanon, town of 150
Laboyteause, Peter 97
Laboyton, Peter 118
Lackel, David 250
Lacy, Elijah 334 Ephraim
 334 Fielding 10 John
 241 246 William 246
Ladd, Jacob 327 Joseph
 246 298 Wilm 328

INDEX: names in text may have variant spelling
NIFLS = not indexed for land sales

Lafuze, Samuel 224
Lagow, William 9
Laird, Jesse 18
Lake, William 6 26
Lamb, David 238 James 253 256 267 272 299 John 331 Joseph 328 Josiah 244 266 Sarah 331 Thos 235 241 251 331
Lamberson, Samuel 186
Lambert, Josias 239 243 Nathan 29
Lambertson, Thomas 28
Lambdon, John 21 Matthew 6 21 47 Saml 21 Wilm 104 188 199
Lambkin, Ezra 22
Lamm, Daniel 275
Lampson, Amos 298 Jehill 298
Lancaster, Wright 238
Landers/Landy, Kimbraw 188
Landes, Danl 293 300 327 332 Fanny 300 327 Henry 327 Samuel 281 300
Landis, David 224
Lane, A. 132 Amos 115 Smith 238 W. 240
Langerly, Joshua 173
Langley, David 7 John 7 191
Langston, Bennett 228
Lanham, Henry 189
Lanier, James 108
Lanner, Thomas 24
Lanning, Christ'r 49 50 David 51 Margaretta 50
Lanpher, Eleoner 148
Laray, Biflyalus 306
Larch, Phlp 174 Wilm 174
Larerty, John 177
Larimore, Morgan 93
Larison, Ann 67 72 George 20 35 John 35 67 72
Larew, Benj 22 Garret 22
Larowe, David 159
Lasley, Peter 179
Latham, Davd 187 John 197
Lathrop, David 21
Latourette, John 113 138 160
Latt, William 173

Laugh, John 242
Laughlin, William 33
Lauman, Alfred 333 Daniel 318 328 333 H. 279 Hnry 294 333 Jhn 274 283 310
Laurence, Dan'l 26 Isaac 26 27 Valentine 6 26 27
Laurier, James 216
Lavison, Ann 67 72 John 67 72
Lawson, Ezra 28
Lazieres, Lauren 26
League, Green 133 135 141 147 Nancy 135
Leary. Bryan 271
Leason, Richard 240 332
Leatherburg, Charles 188
Leavell, Ezekiel 292 310 316 320 321 324 325 339 345 Nancy 316 Robert (NIFLS) 14 256 272 320 321 Sally 272 321
Lebece, U. 115
Ledgerwood, Samuel 9
Lee, Abr'm 38 138 Chas 117 David 187 Eli 106 129 Gersham 3 Jacob 234 Jhn 234 Joseph 28 37 74 105 Nancy 74 105 Phebe 71 138 Robert 287 289 Sam'l 9 10 11 71 138
Leek, Conrad 203 Elizabeth 203 209 Harmon 186 203 209 Herman 209
Le(e)per, Grizzle 130 John 8 Wilm 78 130 223
Leepes, William 27
Leeson, James 24
Leforge, John 38 55 111 130 Mary 130
Legg, William 183
Legget, John 28
Lemaster(s), Isaac 18 20 Prichard 4 Richard 8
Lemman/Lemon, Adam 26 Lemuel 36 38 77 124 Martha 27 Peter 224 225 Saml 225 Sarah 77 Wm 34
Lennon, Barbara 295 Peter 115 295 Samuel 115
Lentz, -- 187 Michael 198 Nicholas 187 188 195

INDEX: names in text may have variant spelling
NIFLS = not indexed for land sales

Leonard, Abner 37 86 112 121 142 169 Luther 165 Mehetable 86 112 142 169 Nancy 169 Nathan 243 Samuel 240
Leslie, Hugh 166
Levent, William 5
Leviston, George 58 J. 132 James 81 94 119 230 316 Joseph 47
Levy, Isaac 35 185
Lewellen, Benj 176 Marshack 174 176 Michael 234 Zacariah 14
Lewis, Abr'm 226 232 272 Alexr 9 Asahel 113 Benj 35 157 163 164 Caleb 282 286 289 298 301 304 309 310 Charity 333 David 31 333 Ebenezer 34 Elizabeth 333 George 6 10 26 Hannah 247 248 251 Isaac 278 279 297 333 James 168 Jn. 186 John 6 11 22 113 159 244 270 278 294 300 301 311 Jonathan 6 21 27 Joseph 5 12 14 244 270 276 297 306 335 Keturah 333 Major 6 Margt 335 Martha 333 Nathan 6 11 31 47 Noah 113 Patsy 279 297 Paul 265 Peggy 297 Polly 159 Reuben 21 Richd 5 14 244 270 278 293 Saml 7 136 160 186 Sarah 270 278 296 333 Thomas 228 265 267 272 295 296 333 336 William 24 35 58 175 229 230 247 251 275 333 Zimri 175 333
Lewiston, James 95
Liester, -- 187
Life, William 173
Light, Jacob 22
Likely, Henry 25
Lilley, Benj 56 John 6 Thomas 242
Linbrooke, Abraham 83
Linch/Linck, Abraham 132 Caty 57 Phillip 10 57

Linard, Thomas 176
Lindley, Abr'm 185 188 212 James 4 5 244 Vincent 22
Lin(d)sey, George 22 Jas 8 22 25 Jeremiah 177 John 183 188 Nicholas 3 Ross 8 Thos 8 Vachel 8 Vinson 8
Lineback, Frederick 214 Sally 214 Samuel 209
Linger, George 209
Linn/Lynn, Daniel 3 4 23
Litterel, Samuel 230
Little, Abr'm 13 Anna 271 318 Betsy/Elizabeth 248 255 307 Hannah 247 248 Jacob 232 238 247 248 Jas 255 306 307 Jasper 247 248 271 318 John 297 308 Lewis 232 248 255 257 307 Susanna 306
Livingston, Adam 7 28 James 303 John 4 22 228
Lock, Nancy 196 Peter 186 188 189 195 Rhoday 195 William 195 196 245
Locker/Looker, Allison 57 70 113 Rachel 113 Samuel 20
Lockwood, H. 32
Logan, Aquilla 73 130 James 39 47 84 126 299 John 10 39 Saml 12 94 315 333 338 Sarah 84 Thos 315 323 Wilm 41 228 Zenolia 338
Loller, Isaac 12 Thos 11
Lomax, Abel 246 293
Long, Fredrk 274 281 309 Henry 239 Rachel 274 Robert 138
Longfellow, John 236 Thomas 68
Longhead, David 282 John 146
Longwell, Matthew 280
Longworth, - 176 Nicholas 22 31 39 175 184 186 187 188 189 194 330 344
Loper, James 161
Lord, Abel 339

INDEX: names in text may have variant spelling
NIFLS = not indexed for land sales

Lotter, Abr'm 136 Rachel 136
Lousteller, Peter 18
Lord, Jesse 28
Lo(w)ring, Davd 46 65 127 195 Fanny 65 127
Loughman, Henry 185
Loustutter, Peter 183 222
Louthain, Absolom 316 318 Samuel 288 297 299 316
Love, Hanson 87 102 Polly 102
Lovejoy, Samuel 80
Lovelace, S. 184
Low, -- 40
Lowards, John 212
Lowderback, Abr'm 169 229 Phillip 97
Lowe(s), James 35 159 171 John 171 Josiah 35 William 35 325
Lower, Joseph 285 299
Lowrey, Saml 222 Wilm 328
Loy, Reuben 298
Loyd, Joseph 21
Lucas, William 238
Luce/Luse, James 25 John 109 112 125 Mary 138 Nathan 287 289 Robt 36 71 112 113 121 125 135 138 142 143 148 153 163
Ludlow, Jane 63 Stephen 20 43 51 63 191
Ludwig, John 262 268
Lunken, William 291 299
Luttrel, Samuel 230
Lybrook, Ann 287 342 Baltzar 287 Hannah 295 Henry 226 295 Jacob 12 287 John 287 Philip 14 226 227 287 342
Lykins, Andrew 174 175 James 175
Lympus, Elijah 32 98 Enoch 63 Isaac 65 Jonathan 63 Ledia 98 Levy 98 Sarah 63
Lynes/Lines, Hannah 79 Sarah 58 Wlm 38 79 153
Lyon(s)/Lions, -- 38 Aaron 11 Ethel 183 Greenberry 11 Henry 11 155
Lyons cont- J. 162 Jacob 112 James 222 Mos. 220 Moses 8 95 97 136 Robt 21 Timothy 222 Wilm 83
Lytle, Robert 97

Mabbett, Anthony 270 302 314 John 314 Susanna 314 Wilm 270
Maccanon, Elenor 164 John 163 164
Mac(k)lin, John 80 225
Macy, Reuben 300 302 Stephen 296 Wilm 224
Madden, Lydia 129 Thos 47 63 80 119 129 140 162 225 230 Ruth 63 80 119 129 162 Solomon 242
Madison, Joab 218
Magner, Edward 10 11
Maguire, -- 188 James 176
Mahard, John 44 50 76 84 107 137 138 143 162 194 203 213 289 298 307
Major(s), Edward 7 John 6 Robt 7 Wilm 3 6 20 21
Malat, John 4
Malbitt, Anthony 226
Malcolm, James 173
Mallin, John 47 Joseph 198 200 206 211 213 220 Nancy 200 213
Malson, Jacob 68
Manan, Jacob 32 170 Michael 32 Sarah 170
Mangorum, H.L. 27
Manley, Edw 10 Wilm 153
Manlow/Manlove, George 277 278 Mary 277 278 Wilm 278
Mann, Aaron 241 Saml 174
Mannering, Richard 20
Manning, Hezekiah 242 Thomas 316 317 347
Mansell (see Morsell). James 222
Mansur, Jane 336 Jeremiah 257 328 336 337 Jeremy 264 318
Mantle, G. 25 George 24
Manville, Martha 207 P. 220

INDEX: names in text may have variant spelling
NIFLS = not indexed for land sales

Manwarring, Elizabeth 71 72 Jane 73 84 Richd 34 46 71 72 84 S. 45 Solomon 34 43 46 63 72 73 84 85 114 168 309 Thos 35 46 57 109 115 129 130 135 146 168 169
Mapes, Henry 10 James 187
Maple, Benj 102 Stephen 10 Wilm 32
Mardock, James 228
Marine, Charles 246 Jonathan 244
Marks, John 13
Marlin(g), Elijah 211 Jhn 187 197 205 211 213 Margt 211 213 Wilm 31
Marmon, Joseph 35 152
Marsh, Webster 188 William 185 229
Marshall, John 101 Saml 28 Thos 245 Wilm 20
Marshill, John 297 298 Miles 287 Thomas 328
Martin, -- 33 Aaron 234 257 258 265 343 Abner 234 252 266 Annas 133 149 George 144 Hnry 229 264 Isaac 235 330 J. 240 James 225 Jane 144 John 14 Joseph 254 Lewis 248 Mary 266 Saml 6 13 249 251 Stephen 133 144 149 152 Thos 91 229 Wilm 24 117
Martindale, Davd 291 Elizabeth 267 287 Hannah 347 James (NIFLS) 13 243 244 267 296 342 Jesse 347 John 243 264 278 342 Martin 245 286 287 290 Moses 173 225 242 243 286 347 Wm 243
Marts, Peter 237
Masco, Peter 11
Maserve, William 6
Mason, Danl 6 26 143 171 David 260 Deborah 171 George 6 27 Horatio 32 John 6 Joseph 169 Nicholas 6 Philip 6 26 89 Thomas 236

Massey, -- 179 James 177 Tence 177 Teuce 235
Matherel, Jane 186
Mathews, George 38 Thos 110 153 William 199
Matile, David 200
Matlock, George 124 John 98 124 Sarah 124
Mattocks/Mattix, Jacob 118 119 John 229 Katherine 118 119
Maudlin, B. 236 Benj 241 256 258 276 301 345 Leah 256 276 345 Wright 276
Maxwell, Anna 275 Edw 9 Hugh 134 225 Jacob 224 John 241 276 278 280 296 310 320 338 342 Mary Anne 250 Moses 11 37 105 Richd 250 275 Robt 236 Wilm 9 228
May, H. 89 135 Hugh 63 80 101 137 159 169
Mayers, Abr'm 12 John 13
Mayor, William 53
Maze, David 128 132 229 Samuel 128 132 229
McAdams, Thomas 304
McBoon, William 232
McBride, William 8
McBroom, Betsy 286 John 320 William 271 286
McCafferty, Joseph 39
McCahan, Thomas 8
McCaisley, Thomas 233
McCallister, Alex 241
McCallum, Duncan 185 187 Niel 187
McCan(d)less, Agnes 282 William 282
McCarthy, Job 238
McCartney, Thomas 260 265 267 269 273 280 310 336
McCarty, Abner 161 164 Benj (NIFLS) 12 35 39 40 41 42 44 45 46 49 55 76 84 168 230 Desdemona 148 Elizabeth 51 Enoch (NIFLS) 8 40 42 47 49 50 51 52 53 54 55 56 57 59 64 70 71 78 79 83 84

INDEX: names in text may have variant spelling
NIFLS = not indexed for land sales

McCarty cont - 87 96 101 107 108 112 115 118 125 134 136 137 156 167 168 171 James 10 45 50 Jonathan 40 92 147 148 Patrick 65 Sarah 55
McCash, William 267
McCaw, James 11 36 Nancy 122 William 112 122
McCay, Abisha 187 Robert 187
McClain/McClane (see McLain), Catherine 284 337 341 James 153 238 John 245 278 280 284 304 306 314 317 318 337 341 343 344 348 Margt 317 Wm 3 68 245 270 277
McClanhan, Joseph 322
McClary, Bartholomew 131
McClean, A. 113
McCleary, Robert 203
McClellan(d), Ann 163 Francis 130 163 Jean/Jane 282 Margt 282 Thos 223 Wilm 282
McClerkin, James 78 130 224 John 223 Mary 116 Matthew 116 223 225 Susanna 78
McClester, James 20
McClure, David 183 196 Francis 196 Jas 21 196 198 222 Jane 261/262 John 27 201 Nath'l 14 233 238 260 261 Wilm 27
McClury/McCleary, Eleanor 115 164 165 166 Wilm 115 130 164 165 166
McClutche, John 202
McCombs, Alexr 13 Ellet 14 John 13 339 342 William 109 162
McConnell, John 8 Robt 19
McContosh, Jacob 13
McCoole, James 178 179
McCord, -- 38 James 37 John 224
McCorkle/McCorkhill, Peg 218 Robert 192 199 202 206 214 215 219 221 222 William 190 191 218

McCormick, David 185 218 Mark 26 Ralph 203 Robt 26 Saml 203 Sarah 26
McCown, Alex'r 229
McCoy (see McKoy), James 21 32 38 42 125 Margt/Peggy 233 249 256 303 317 Nancy 42 125 Robt 65 Thos 12 238 241 249 256 267 303 317 Wilm 40
McCracken, Robert 24 29
McCrary, William 183
McCrea/Cray, Elizabeth 75 Martin 96 Mary 137 Phineas 67 238 282 Sam'l 36 75 137 262 Sarah 282
McCreary, -- 186 John 185
McCullough, Hugh 162 John 18 Saml 243 Wilm 185
McCutchen, John 48 228 Susanna 48
McDade, James 14
McDaniel, William 59
McDill, Saml 164 224 225
McDonald, William 34 36
McDoughty, William 244
McDowell, John 182
McEurn, John 226
McEwen, John 226 277
McFadden, Sawyer 251 341
McFall, Joseph 185 217 219 220 Polly 220 William 8
McFarland, William 9
McGarvey, William 185
McGary, Benj 8 Saml 8
McGaughey, David 37
McGee, Eliza 212 Joseph 199 220
McGeorge, Saml 14 237 266 288 299
McGill, Robert 59
McGilliard, John 155
McGinnis, James (NIFLS) 12 40 59 65 66 72 127 156 Jane 65 Wilm 183
McGlothlin, Chas 230 285 301 303 Jane 285 301 303
McGreer, Sarah 169 Wilm 98 129 132 169 228
McGrew/McGrue, Alex'r 82

INDEX: names in text may have variant spelling
NIFLS = not indexed for land sales

McGrew/McGrue, cont - 100 112 147 Aurelia 100 112 147 James 238 Robt 82 Wilm 136 149
McGuffy, Edward 8
McGuire, Capt 6 Elizabeth 217 James 4 7 John 36 141 Jonathan 197 217 Robert 44 72
McHendry, Joseph 186
McHenry, Saml 19 33 188 233
McIlroy, Enos 185
McIntire, Edw 189 190 191 212 James 182 John 240 Roleson 174 Thomas 24
McIntosh, see McContosh
McKagg, Robert 26
McKane, David 9 John 22
McKay (see McKoy), James 189 190 Polly 193 Robt 34 190 193 194 219 Zacariah 210
McKee, John 240 248 293 295 310 332 345 Millinda 310 345 Tabor 345
McKim, Robert 185
McKinley, Elizabeth 249 Samuel 233 249
McKinney, Andrew 10 Edith 48 James 47 48 50 51 65 68 71 73 88 98 230 276 Joseph 8 24 Lambkin 8 24
McKinnon, John 346
McKinstrey, Wilm 186 219
McKinzey, Mordecai 228
McKittrick, David 4 22 Robert 22 23
McKnight, Jas 123 Josh 28
McKoy, Robert 34
McLain, Catherine 324 John 290 324
McLasky, Daniel 21
McLean, John 104 146 233 William 245
McLinn, John 84
McLucas, Mary 306 Wilm 265 306
McMahan, John 21 230 Morgan 285 307 William 228 230

McManaman, James 187
McMannis, Cthrine 101 131 John 93 99 101 119 131
McManus, Barnabus 346 Barney 313 323 Owen 319 323 335 343
McMath, Samuel 25
McMillan, Richard 138 150 Rowley 150
McMullen, Hugh 24 Richard 105
McNeal, Daniel 10
McNulty, Hugh 209 210
McNutt, Chas 186 Colin 182 James 36 63 Rebecca 63 William 182
McPhail, Cornelius 184
McQuamy, Morgan 175
McQueen, Benj 11 Thos 34
McQuin, John 12
McWorten, Tyler 33
Mead(e), Cynthia 124 Hugh 32 Ira 124 Levi 122 165 Luther 21 Mary Ann 165
Means, W. 184
Medcalf, Isaac 269 273
Medsker, David 24 George 185
Meek(s), Alex'r 194 216 Basil 234 Elenor 272 Isaac 4 233 264 341 Jacob 272 334 Jeremiah 176 233 249 272 276 280 314 John 211 214 218 219 233 235 236 253 262 264 Joseph 135 Joshua 233 Martha 216 Patsy 314 Peggy 253 262 Rebecca 314 Wilm 14 235 252 272 314 334 347
Meeker, -- 81 Moses 216
Megrue, Andrew 80
Mell, John 243
Mellander, Peter 13 274
Melendey, John 305
Melendose, Peter 232
Melton, Stephen 175
Mendel, Jacob 29
Mendenhall, Elender 313 Griffith 235 Isaac 240 306 323 James 246 316 John 210 271 307 331

INDEX: names in text may have variant spelling
NIFLS = not indexed for land sales

Mendenhall cont- Mary 306
  Mordacai 175 313 Richd
  176 Robt 176 Stephen
  237 306
Mennet, Sally 194 198 212
  Saml 187 192 193 198 212
Merchant, Samuel 10 45
Mercer, John 39
Meriam, Jhn 149 Josph 170
Merit, Archibald 184 202
Merrill, S. 221 Saml 196
  197 213 217
Messick, E 151 Isaac 323
Metcalfe (see Medcalf),--
  226 Isaac 226 Wilm 162
Metin, Thomas 116
Michael, Bennet 124 155
  Casper 25 Jared 29
  Phillip 25
Michoud, Lewis 188
Milburn, Joseph 22 Robt
  24 25
Milchim, Allen 26 Matthew
  26
Mile(s), -- 245 Benj 23
  Henry 134
Miley, Abr'm 131 George
  131
Milholland, James 34 59
  John 38 51 59 115 Mary
  59 May 40 Thomas 11
  34 38 Wilm 59 68
Millar, Henry 94 Jane 94
  Silas 130
Miller, Aaron 284 Abr'm 9
  37 90 238 285 313 Adam
  27 Alexr 32 234 250 269
  Benj 18 Caty 222 Chris-
  tena 84 285 347 Cornel-
  ius 18 Danl 4 25 37 226
  Davd 185 Elizabeth 112
  154 234 332 Esther 260
  264 341 George 33 238
  285 Henry 6 17 21 229
  260 264 341 Isaac 84
  112 238 285 Jacob 12 14
  23 176 298 Jas 25 Jane
  220 Job 20 John 18 31
  55 79 84 86 108 112 152
  154 185 190 222 223 224
  230 238 270 285 333 347
  Jonathan 235 Joseph 18

Miller, cont - Levi 4 20
  Lydia 285 Martha 285
  Mary 269 Michael 13 29
  332 Nancy 79 Nathan 8
  Peter 12 14 260 264
  Phebe 55 86 Robt 224
  Silas 91 Thomas 10 19
  20 224 Tobias 82 223
  William 18 223 224
Millikin, -- 241 Eli 243
  Samuel 241
Millis, George 7 84 145
Mills, Charity 287 Cyrus
  29 Elizabeth 321 Hannah
  321 Henry 9 245 321
  Isaac 245 287 Jacob 96
  97 Jas 24 336 John 187
  190 191 222 245 Mary 97
  Moses 245 321 Peter 175
  Richd 245 335 Seth 287
  Thos 246 Wilm 246
Millspaugh, Martinas 134
  Peter 34
Milner, John 36 William
  175 233
Mineral Springs, town 68
Ming, Peter 190 192 193
  196 209 213
Minola, John 196 197 200
Minor/Miner, Aaron 8
  Benson 239 322 Mary 226
  259 275 295 Rachel 55
  Rchd 10 55 224 Sara 295
Mintz, William 39
Mira, Peter 184
Misner, Jacb 184 John 189
  Marquis 159 Milly 159
Mitchell, Nancy 343 Robt
  342 Samuel 237 343
  William 187 189
Mix, Nathaniel 220
Mixter, Ebenezer 184
Mizer/Misor, - 241 Daniel
  222 George 238 267
  Philip 320 322
Moffit, Chas 246 258 313
  346 Jeremiah 176 177
  298 Joseph 127 159 176
  298 Mary 313 316 323
  Thos 14 230 278 312 313
  316 323 347 348
Monday, Larkin 8

INDEX: names in text may have variant spelling
NIFLS = not indexed for land sales

Monfore, Henry 175
Monroe, Felix 9 Reuben 65
Montayne, Zacariah 185
Montgomery, James 13 24 John 13 14 24 Margt 337 Peggy 279 Platt 13 239 Robt 13 239 Wilm 13 238 315 337
Montooth, Henry 209 216
Moon, Alexr 235 Joel 226 John 243 Malachi 276 Mary 276 Patrick 241
Moore, Adam 120 Alexr 167 235 Benj 258 335 340 341 C. 184 C. Gray 3 Cyrus 209 211 David 63 73 77 173 322 E. 182 Ezra 83 Hnry 88 Hugh 17 18 20 21 81 186 187 239 J. 155 Jacob 22 James 7 40 68 70 77 182 242 Joel 14 272 296 John 8 57 62 176 208 209 216 243 Joseph 11 97 Josiah 317 Malachi 236 Margt 56 Patrk 241 Polly 296 Rodrk 182 Saml 34 151 245 Sarah 216 Thos 264
Moor(e)man, Archilaus 236 James 174 246 John 246 329 Thomas 246
Moredock, James 182
Morehart, Samuel 46
Morehouse, Nemiah 27
Morgan, B. 236 Benj 236 240 258 345 Elizabeth 101 109 110 345 Enoch 21 Evan 118 303 James 24 Joseph 6 Michl 24 Mordica 292 Thomas 29 36 100 101 109 110 William 9 11
Morley, Daniel 115
Morman, Jesse 174 176 Leartton 174 Thos 246
Morris, Achillis 173 Amos 29 B. 87 89 94 99 101 102 103 104 107 110 111 113 116 118 119 124 135 138 147 156 162 Bethel 123 C. 111 148 Caleb 243 296 343 David 147

Morris cont-157 300 Elizabeth 110 147 Isaac 126 127 148 240 James 234 Jehosaphat 239 250 256 276 279 296 Jesse 250 John 37 73 124 Jonathan 256 Joseph 110 Joshua 277 343 Mary 124 Nathan 236 243 Reuben 315 317 Sarah 278 279 Sylvan 121 293 Thos 100 W. 165 William 39 95 146
Morrison, Ephraim 4 Hugh 99 103 104 106 107 108 109 112 117 124 125 126 135 140 142 145 148 161 165 170 309 J. 124 Jas 11 142 235 246 Jane/Jenny 256 Joseph 11 78 90 99 171 Maryann 99 Robt 234 256 259 283 289 296 305 334 340 344 345
Morrood/Morerod, Antoinette 206 John 185 206 207 213
Morrow, Andrew 318 Archbd 41 James 124 135 John 235 311 322 Mary 322 Sarah 124 Thomas 145
Morsell (see Mansell) Jas 199
Morton, -- 38 Elias 246 John 8
Mose, Adam 36
Mosley, James 185
Moss, Demas 188 Edmnd 341 342 Edwn 295 George 342 Isaac 158 Janet 201 John 37 Lemuel 28 29 Wilm 226 341 Zeally 183 191 201
Mosteller, Christopher 90 124 163
Mounts/Mounce, Caleb 182 215 David 32 34 51 Hezekiah 10 34 Jane 215 John 17 242 Providence 8 Thomas 183
Mous, Thomas 334
Mowe, Roderick 26
Mowery, Susanna 130 Vollentine 130 Wilm 130

INDEX: names in text may have variant spelling
NIFLS = not indexed for land sales

Mt. Sterling, town of 192
Muir, Thomas 7
Mulford, Caleb 22 Job 91
Mulhollan(d), John 25
  William 11 77
Mullikin, D 80 R 80
Mullins, John 280
Munden, Elijah 305 Jesse 310 Mary 310
Murdock, Anna 74 94 97 118 G. 148 George 31 58 73 74 94 96 97 118 134 135 167 168 170 171 James 182 John 332
Muret, Chas 190 195 196 203 206 209
Murphy, -- 244 Albert 10 11 318 Jeremiah 57 Jerry 19 Joseph 12 Miles 243 Moses 57 Robt 298
Murray, Elam 41 James 22 Joshua 65 Wilm 87 242
Musgrave, John 24 Moses 24 28
Musselman, David 88 120 Margaret 120
Myer(s)/Mires, Abr'm 12 225 Gideon 312 Henry 4 Jacob 22 Jn. 186 John 13 225 229 230 Jonathan 186 Robert 21 Simon 186 William 186

Nairin (see Vairin), John 192 Margaret 192
Nattier, Charles
Nave, Abraham 228
Naylor, John 81 90
Neal, Anna 305 334 David 184 Elizabeth 81 Jesse 344 John 32 81 144 184 Louisa 76 Rachel 322 Thomas 10 76 144 237 William 305 334
Neeley, Elizabeth 258 Isaac 229 293 Thos 236 253
Neighbors, Abraham 10
Nelson, Adam 38 92 Barbara 75 Chas 185 David 31 Francis 216 Ibberella 209 James 183 John 183 188 194 209 Joseph 196

Nelson cont - 209 224 226 Joshua 118 Levina 209 Nancy 209 Nathan 185 Sacker 21 Wlm 36 75 259
Newcomer, Peter 28
Newell, William 216
Newhouse, Jas 11 Saml 11
Newkirk, Abram 107 139 Barnabus 213 Henry 102 Jacob 227
Newland, Harrod 86 Harrold 229 James 62
Newman, William 227
Newton, Chas 197 George 22 Henry 236 James 236
New Trenton, town of 85
New Washington, town 47
New York, town of 196
Nicholas, William 69
Nichols/Nickels, Benj 141 Elizabeth 70 72 George 8 23 Henry 229 James 10 48 165 228 Josph 12 133 227 Thos 228 Wilm 70 72 94 106 107 117 121 122 125 165 228 230 342
Nicholson, Ann 212 Esther 334 John 237 334 339 Robert 212
Nihill, Laurence 220
Nikell, Lawrence 200
Nilson, John 265 267 268 274 300 308 342
Niswonger, John 190 191 193 Solomon 185 188
Nixon, Andrew 225 Caleb 288 Jane 346 John 23 239 256 277 302 310 324 346 Josiah 346 Mariam 302 Mirion 245 Morris 276 343 Saml 236 343 Thos 241 245 Wm 236 342
Noble, Dal. 115 David 4 229 Elizabeth 132 J. 197 James (NIFLS) 9 10 40 48 49 51 53 54 58 59 62 63 65 66 68 71 83 90 115 117 132 146 149 215 230 258 Joseph 187 188 196 Kitty 167 168 Mary 63 N. 102 Noah 88 94 102 108 110 111 115 126

INDEX: names in text may have variant spelling
NIFLS = not indexed for land sales

Noble cont- 150 163 167 168 171 Thos 167 Wilm 137 165
No(w)land, Daniel 238 239 329
Nolls, Emery 41
Norcross, John 299 Reuben 173 William 133 134
Norris, George 74 98 108 130 228 Jane 81 John 12 40 81 90 126 131 229 230 316 Joseph 74 Martha 94 98 108 Rebecca 90 126 Richard 8 17 19 Robert 98 157 169 Wilm 12 94 98 108 131 157 228 345
North, Danl 278 Lot 17 Thomas 183
Northrup, Asa 55 71 73 Hannah 71 73
Northup, Perin 26
Norton, B. 197 Benj 196 200 David 234 Jacob 25 James 175 William 7
Norwell, Benjamin 33
Noyes, Israel 25
Nugent, Benj 41 Elizabeth 123 165 167 John 41 100 123 127 128 165 167 Robert 128
Null, Henry 235
Nunnam, James 87
Nutt, William 257
Nutter, Benj 227 255 296 Elizabeth 255
Nye, Joshua 149
Nype (see Knipe), John 13
Nyerl, Ack 102

O'Brien, Thom 3
Obussier, L. 193 210 Lewis 192 214 Luke 191 200
Odell, Daniel 24 Gabriel 174 Isaac 230 James 243 244 280 281 313 346 347 John 24 William 236
Odom, Davd 13 239 310 323 Elizabeth 310
Odle, Isaac 10 Simon 10
Offield, James 6 Lewis 9
Ogden, -- 81 James 216

Ogden, cont - Nevi 123
Ogle, Hiram 187 188 Wilm 223 225
Ogleive, Joseph 23
Ohio County 2 181
Ohler, Henry 243
Oldaker, Jacob 241
Oldham, James 179 180 229 Rebecca 103 Stephen 103
Olensdoff, Frederick 67
Oliver, D. 39 David 143 159 161 Elial 303 Elijah 303 314 Elum 303 John 13 Joseph 303 Nixon 5 37 98
Olmstead, Ebenzer 28
O'Neal, David 184 James 200 John 184
Orange, Thomas 71 86
Orem, Levi 188
Ormsby, O. 17 Oliver 182
Orr, Andrew 37 S. 174 Joseph 186 187 Washington 10 William 108
Osborn, Abarella 98 129 Ambroy 174 Bennet 74 Chas 321 Danl 41 175 234 Davd 24 79 235 335 343 Elizabeth 335 343 James 124 170 227 John 7 175 Jonathan 33 Joseph 138 Mary 128 Saml 136 Thos (NIFLS) 36 40 41 64 71 101 108 117 128 William 338
Osgood, Charles 20
Ousley, Dianna 74 Elizabeth 89 Thos 34 74 95 Zacariah 74 89
Overman, Abner 293 Eli 174 180 250 256 276 301 305 342 Ephraim 173 180 233 Huldah 293 Joseph 293 305 Nathan 173 180 233 242 264 301 305 Reuben 245 Tamer 264 305 Thamer 180
Owen(s), Aaron 118 Danl 141 152 Eli 241 Wilm 12

Paddock, Benjamin 162
Page, John 39

INDEX: names in text may have variant spelling
NIFLS = not indexed for land sales

Palmer, Daniel 225   David 25   John 26   Joshua 228   William 12 83
Palmerton, Ichabod 23
Paris, George 230   James 20   Joshua 21   Richd 14
Park(s), Isaac 9   Jacob 19   Jonathan 18   Joseph 7 53 68   Micajah 20   Moses 246   W. 225
Parker, Abr'm 186   Archbd 11   Axseln 38   Benj 236   Henry 106 140   Isaac 235   John 247   Jeremiah 233   Micajah 40   Thomas 174   Timothy 38
Parkinson, Harriet 320   Sally 204   Willis 275 320 32
Parrish, Barrat 10
Parsmore, Henry 272 339
Parson(s), Benj 278   Davd 234   Jhn 13   Matthias 239
Parvis, Joshua 3   Wilm 84
Passwater, Zael 9
Pate, Adam 19   Danl 24   G. 27   Henry 7   Jeremiah 9
Patt, Henry 7
Patterson, Christian 280   Jhn 5 13 82 163 238 278 280 292   Saml 13 82 92 280 292   Thos 292   Wm 241
Patton, Isaac 98   John 183
Patty, James 11
Pawner, John 77
Paxson, John 338
Paxton, John 123
Paylin, Henry 237 256 285 346   Sarah 285
Payne/Pain, Aaron 7 25   John 4 7 17   Saml 4   Stephen 29
Peabody, Stephen 187 188
Peacock, Abr'm 173   Amos 173   David 243   Wilm 173
Peak, Nathan 202
Peale, John 246
Pearcy, Frances 323
Pearson, Abigail 319   Barton 301   Benj 235 260   Elliott 237   Esther 260   Henry 226 319   Isaac 176

Pearson, cont - John 236   Jonathan 346   Mathias 243   Nancy 301 324   Nathan 233   Peter 175   Thos 276 301 324
Peck, Ann 158   James 134 158   Rebecca 158
Peers, Val 284
Pegg, Hannah 140 154 156   James 264 311   Jesse 284 299 302 305 314 326 333 344   John 116 140 145 150 154 156 159 169 170 175 246   Mary 314   Valentine 249 258 314
Peggy --, 199
Peirce, John 158   Thos 63
Pelkey, Michael 10
Pemberton, Joseph 235
Pendleton, Thomas 336
Pennwell, David 34 40 182   Eli 34 182 183   Esther 62 96 105   John 40 58 62 77 78 96 105 109 147   Reubin 11 96 155   Sally 155
Pennywit, Philip 280 292
Pentecost, John 166 224
Percival, Jabez 3
Perkins, James 337
Pernet, John 203   Sophia 210
Perret, Robert 19
Perrin(e), Danl 20   David 25   John 4 126
Perry, Samuel 6 19
Personett, J. 240
Perval, James 330
Peters, Barbara 194   Henry 22 187 194   Jacob 11 47 49 51 86   Mary 51   Simon 8   Stephen 22
Petersby, Jacob 50
Peterson, John 20
Petey, Peter 187
Petro, Michael 96
Pettifish, Christian 235
Pettigrew, David 29   Nathan 26
Petty, Ezekiel 7   Joshua 182 202 215   L. 176
Pettycrew, Robert 38

INDEX: names in text may have variant spelling
NIFLS = not indexed for land sales

Phares/Pharris, Wilm 235 265 269 279 345
Phillip(s), Charles 185 Gabriel 187 John 14 25 Mary 209 Robt 212 Saml 8 Thos 173 182 Wilm 14 185 206 209 288
Piatt, J. 126 James 74 76 79 83 89 104 153 163 Jemima 104 163 John 25 124 145 147 Robt 20 William 189
Pickett, -- 186 Benj 185 Jn. 188 Joseph 323 338 Priscilla 323 338
Piele, John 246
Pierce, Nathaniel 330
Pierpont, Ezra 133 134
Pierson, Ebenezer 28 Harry 199 209 210 217 John 245 246 Wilm 184 190 201 Wyllys 297
Piggot, Joshua 235
Pike, Rachel 337 Wilm 240 337 Zebulon 18
Pile, Elijah 9
Pilkey, -- 90
Pilsher, Enoch 1375
Pinkerton, John 166
Piper, James 50 58 135 227 William 135
Pipes, Windsor 314
Pippin, Richard 6
Pitman, Jonathan 152 155 Rebecca 155
Pitts, Elijah 23
Platt, Gilbert 25 Nathan 184 186 203 204 205 209 211 Polly 209
Pleurdoff, Frederick 67
Plicard, John 141 149
Plummer, Isabella 259 Jas 26 John 226 259 298 Joseph 6 26 Luther 6 Philemon 259 287
Pocock (see Bocock), Danl 205 Edw 184 Jas 184 185 222 Salem 204 Solmn 204
Pollock, George 73 Jas 26
Pooher, Samuel 102
Pool, Elizabeth 258 J 246 John 236 239 250 256

Pool cont - 258 263 264 Thomas 236
Pope, William 76
Popens, William 156 227
Port, John 14
Porter, David 9 James 242 243 291 320 Joshua 11 Margt 63 291 320 Nathan 35 50 53 63 Nath'l 208 Sephios 153 Thomas 6 24
Posduck, Richard 81
Post, Aaron 25 James 36 John 238
Poteet, Squire 17
Potter, John 183 Thos 244
Pottinger, Sarah 97
Potts, Mary 345 Saml 345
Pound, John 159
Poundsford, W. 141
Pouner, John 77
Powell, Benj 24 Jacob 184 Jas 6 7 Simon 239 Wiley 11 Wilm 182 Witie 227
Powers, Abigail 139 B. 174 Danl 41 107 139 David 41 160 Ezekiel 39 George 160 Joseph 248 278 John 38 78 Jonathan 224 Joseph 226 Mary 78 114 165 Salome 278 Sara 160 Thos 41 65 92 114 146 165 Wilm 39
Pownes, John 115 141
Prather, Betsey 261 John 209 Joseph 252 261 292 342
Pratt, Danl 188 Robt 20
Preble, Samuel 178
Prevo,Asa 240 241 261 330
Prevost, William 166
Prewit, Samuel 153
Price, Catherine 233 Cristen 299 David 170 171 Henry 34 J. 39 Jas 58 John 10 33 Nancy 58 299 Saml 39 Thos 19 246 Wilm 5 235
Pricen, Rice 177
Priest, Obadiah 6
Priestly, David 225
Pri(t)chard, Aaron 3 Ezekiel 23 James 22

INDEX: names in text may have variant spelling
NIFLS = not indexed for land sales

Prince, J. 93
Prine, John 9
Probus, Peter 9   Wilm 9
Prother, Henry 342   Jonathan 342
Protsman, John   188   203   212   220
Pryor, Joseph 239
Puckett/Packet, Danl   174   340   Douglas 196   Joseph 174   Thomas 174   Zacariah 174
Pugh, Caleb 18   Enoch 9   18   20   J. 184   Jesse 245   Joseph 186 203 211 216   Lot (NIFLS) 286 288 289   Rachel 288   W. 304 305   323 Wlm 305 328 331 333
Pulasky, Cypriana 196 197
Pumphrey, Nicholas 39 88   95 105 127
Purcell, Benj 4 8   27   28   John 4 8 20 Laurence 28   Saml 8   Thos 4 8 23   William 3 21
Pursley, John 4
Purviance, David 250   John 250   Levi 275
Puterbaugh, Daniel 337
Putnam, James 11

Quackenbush, Petr 244 249
Quick, John 3 38 59 64 85   115   Polly 64
Quigley, Dennis 206   John 182 206 210   Mary 206

Rail/Rayl, William 37 185
Railsback, David   232 234   239   248   254   272   316   Sally 248   272
Rainey, John 117
Ralb, George 36
Ralston, Jas 243 John 294
Ralter, Samuel 224
Rambo, Absolom 13 234   Adonijah 342   Ann 342   Isaac 328 342   Jackson 234 342
Ramey (see Remey), John 9   37 40 135 Wlm 20 35 135
Ramsbaugh, Joseph 19

Ramsey, Allen   38   50   80   109 Aquilla 10 11 James 28 Thos 185   Tobias 10   William 39 225
Ramsiere, Jacob 187
Ranck, John 230   295   312   316 327 332
Randall, Isaac 6   Jonas 233 235 Thos 235   Wlm 6
Ranney, William 93
Raper, John 14 233 259   William 13 14
Rash, Joseph 11   Wilm 11
Ratliff, Cornelius   243   244 249 260 264
Rauchscraft, Samuel 222
Ravenscroft, Samuel 215
Ray, Andrew 165   Edw 189   Jas 117 146 147 165 223   Martin 117   146   147 165   Mary 146 165 Nancy 146   Robt 27 202   Saml 69   Thomas 14
Raymond, Francis 190   201   222   Louis 217
Razor, Simon 9
Reardon/Rarden, James   74   95 320 Moses 36 79 143
Reccord, Saml 21   Wilm 24
Redd, Mordecai 196 203
Reeds/Read/Reid,   Adam 36   Andrew 40 64 65 Ann 157   Archbold 104 Chas 327 332   Daniel   36   64   65   123   George 104 H. 120 Harden 74 104 Hugh 132 225   228   Jacob 74 104 240   James   4 24 132 157 177   224   Jo. 104   Joel 241   316 John 32 51 52 64 68   123 177 196 197 234 305   326   Margt 64 65 132   Robt 7 144   Sally/Sarah 104 144 Susan 240   Thos 144   William 64   234
Reeder, J. 185   Jacob 108   James 242   Jeremiah 227   Jonathan   202 212 219   Nathan 227   Sally 219   Stephen 108   Thomas 37   William 241
Rees, Davd 18 19 James 36

INDEX: names in text may have variant spelling
NIFLS = not indexed for land sales

Rees, cont - John 37
  Solomon 315
Reese, Caleb 176 Wilm 175
Reily, Benj 21   John 41
  226 227   Nathan 245
Reison, Richard 177
Remer, David 17   John 186
Remey (see Ramey), Elizabeth 114 Henry 34 91 99
  James 20   35 91   99 135
  John 91   Jonathan 99
  Marthe 91   Mary 114
  Patsy 91   Rebecca 135
  Sally 114 Wlm 35 99 114
Renberger, Ana 333 George 243   Isaac 335   Philip 297 332 333
Rench, Eli 332   Otho 332
Reno, Ben 122 Presley 187
Reyan, Nathaniel 293
Reynolds (see Runnels), Caleb   282 291   294 304 313 333   Charity 333 Charles 315 318 325 332 Isaac 19 Justus 186 L/ Larkin 281 282   298 309 318 325 327 332   Polly 332 Sarah 332 339   Wilm 13 233 237   241 277 292 318 329 339
Rhoads, see Roads, Jacb 9
Rhode, William 253
Rice, Benajah 134 160
  Joshua 31 32
Rich, Elijah 26
Richard(s), Isaac 188 189 Truman 197 198   199 200 201 202 205 206 207 208 210 216 220   Wilm 187
Richardson,- 177 Aaron 60 Anna 114 309   Danl 177 David 52 56 69 71 73 75 Hannah 198 203 Isaac 10 James   188 198   203 285 John 11 40 81 83 91 226 Joseph 21   Maria 126 Moses 3 12   Nathan 35 114 240 309   Polly 81 William 33 137 168
Richey, Adam 116 118   225 Joseph 40 68
Richmond, Sylvester 24

Ricke, Philip 34
Ricketts, Abr'm 8 Charles 199   Nathan 8 17   Robt 17 22   Wilm 215 222
Riddle, John 216 Wilm 229
Ridenour, Joseph   90   225 Samuel 163
Rider, William 241
Ridgely, William 182
Rife, John 279 296
Riferner, Peter 46
Riggs, John 33   Romulus 23 24
Riley, Benj 21   John 187
Rinard, Jeremiah 174
Rinerson, Cornelius 20
Ring, Richd 229   Wilm 228
Ringo, Peter 278   327
Rinker, George 296
Rippey, Joseph   13   14 59   92 253
Risk, Prudence 116   Thos 81 William 116
Risley, Eli 192
Ritch, Joseph 215
Ritchie, Thomas 133
Ritter/Retter, Isaac   224 Jacob 85   John 85 224 Sally 85
Roads, Jacb 178 Stphn 154
Robbins, Moses 239
Roberds, Phineas   281 283
Roberts, Basil 3 Benj 239 281   Conrad 235   David 26   Emey 284   James 11 Jesse 281 284   John 93 Jonathan 236 Minor 186 187 Moses 287 Phineas 235 281 Saml 6 220 Susanna 93   Thos 233 235 Wilson 284
Robertson, James 9 202 John 246   Landon 47 Matthew 88 107
Robins, Daniel 9
Robi(n)son, Chas   130 160 Elisha 170 H. 80 Harrison 79 94 114 121 123 157 James 19   John 213 Joshua 104   Landon 44 M. 295 Matthew 107 Sarah 170 Sidney 28 Wm 196

INDEX: names in text may have variant spelling
NIFLS = not indexed for land sales

Rockefellar, Elinor 107 Henry 330 John (NIFLS) 11 35 44 45 46 58 72 81 109 135 168 Mary 45 57 107 Pattery 57 Saml (NIFLS) 45 57 63 68 80 81 85 107 169
Roddy, Catherine 257 Christ'r 242 250 253 255 261 268 271 279 280 283 295 Isabella 255 271 279
Rodebaugh, Seth 173
Roe, Chas 278 Daniel 158 298
Rogers, Ebenezer 19 Henry 188 Isaiah 173 James 237 John 160 233 Joseph 173 Stephen 188
Ro(w)land, Dowdle 10 George 10 John 7 Wlm 21
Roll, Abrm 91 101 Henry 107 Mary 101
Rolsten, John 312 327 330 Sarah 327
Romerie/Romeril, Chas 189 Phillip 187 189
Roney, Charles 10
Rooks, Joseph 180
Roonan, Charles 11
Roop/Rupe, Jacob 14 John 159 Morgan 169
Roper, Hardy 186
Rose, Abram 41 56 227 Edgehill 227 Ezekiel 227 Rebecca 156 Uriah 131 157 Wilm 93 95 108 112 116 129 145 156 170
Roseberry, Alexr 6 Caleb 6 Thomas 8
Rosebrough, R. 188
Ross, Jacob 122 James 11 John 4 8 37 Joseph 22 Moses 298 Robert 4 8 Wilm 11 17 103 201 202 237 298
Rote, George 198 209
Roths, Jacob 178 179 Polly 178
Round, John 29
Rous, James 187 207
Row, Conrad 25 Robert 25

Rowend, Nathaniel 13
Rowsh, Jacob 226
Royster, Chas 70 266 267 Stanhope 36 49 57
Ruble, Samuel 179
Rucher, Benj 274
Rudisill, George 6 35 80 165 Jacob 6 Michl 6 35
Rue, Elizabeth/Betsy 249 327 Henry 328 Richd 233 234 249 251 327
Ruff(l)in, Elizabeth 147 John 147 Mary 147 William 38 40 147
Ruffner, -- 280
Ruick, Daniel 119
Rumbley, James 17
Rundle, William 32
Runnels, Eli 13
Runyan, Bonham 243 Hannah 133 144 Peter 242 Thos 133 144
Rusing, Agnes 78 111 John 111 140 Robt 111 159 Wilm (NIFLS) 41 78 100 103 111
Russell, Calvin 109 Elizabeth 265 Enoch 12 32 George 329 James 32 265 283 299 306 Jesse 97 John 10 12 283 299 300 303 306 Luther 81 102 156 Rhoda 97 Robt 32 265 299 306 Sarah 299 Wian 299
Ruter, A. 184
Rutherford, John 194 197 250 Robert 189
Ruthope, John 27
Ryan, Henry 238
Rybourn, John 47
Ryder, John 186

Sackett, D./David 280 282 283 288 294 301 313 314 321 322 Jesse 6 Margery 163 Martha 275 288 294 301 307 Thos 163 227
Sage, Morgan 8
Saighman, William 21
Saint, William 277 292
Salisbury, town of 247

INDEX: names in text may have variant spelling
NIFLS = not indexed for land sales

Salmon, Daniel 6   James 6
Salyer, Elizabeth 75
   John 75
Sambdon, Matthew   47
Sam(p)son, Amos 298
   George 220   Jehill 298
   Seth 182
Sample, John 174   227
   Uriah 152
Sanders, Jacob 174   Saml
   237 299
Sandoz, Erneste 200
   Phillipe 200 201
Sankey, Hannah 91   Thomas
   91 116   223
Sartwell, Justus 7 8 9
Sater, Henry 35   James 34
Savill, Philip 339
Sawman, Danl 232 John 232
Sayers, Aaron 243
Saylor, Benj 33 119 Catherine 42 47 48   Conrad
   42 43 44   45   47 48   54
   111 115 Elizabeth 66 71
   Hezekiah 112   Jacob 42
   43 48 54 83 115 John 35
   49 55 66 71 Leonard 155
   Michl 10 49 66 71 Nancy
   83 Polly 66   Thomas 71
Sayre, Benj 170   L. 35
Scan(t)land, John 262
   Robert 37 91
Sc(e)arce, Wilm 5 233 317
Scarlock, Reuben   12   225
Schenk, James 187 Jn.   187
   Philip 187
Schmidt, Fredrk   206   207
Schoonover, Benj   (NIFLS)
   118 Jeremiah 156 Joseph
   78 118 162   Lydia 118
Schroeder, Peter 3   9
Scofield, James 137 Lidia
   308   Orr 308
Scott, Alexr 182   Archibd
   214 220   Chas 38 46 47
   Elizabeth 46 47   J.   157
   158 162   James 106 107
   149 161 164 165   Jane
   132 156 Joel 75 John 88
   120   156   243   244   331
   Joseph 132   Moses 179
   Powell 10 52 230 Thos 9

Scott cont - Robt 92 135
   Saml 8 17 38 46 47
   Sarah 47   Wilm 183 184
Scranton, Joshua 21 Martin 22   Wilm 23
Scroggy, John 244
Scudder, Abner 185   Henry
   77   115   185
Seal(s), James 37 143 Joseph 70 122   Wlm 37 141
Sealy/Seely, John 35
   Morris 35   Robert 35
Seaney, Bryan 232 306
   John 14   Sally 306
Seanger, Dorothea 193
   George   190 192 193 194
Searcy, Berry 219   Elizabeth 219   Moses 219
Searles, Daniel 9
Seariger, Chs. 184
Seary, Lemuel 182
Seatten (see Sotter),
   Emery 133 153   Eli 153
Sebasten, Alexr 218 219
Sedam/Suydam, C. 184 Cornelius 184   Jacob 186
Sedgwick, -- 226   Richard
   226   273
Seldridge, Thomas 36
Sellers, Isaac 41
Seney, John 229   Owen 232
Senour, John 32
Sering, Elizabeth   75   135
   152   Saml 44 75 85 116
   135 152
Seward, John 10
Shaf(f)er, Cattarin   148
   Danl 77 148 326   Henry
   227 John 91 123 148 201
   Mary 148   Peter 148
   Rebecca 148
Shaff/Shuff, Fredrk 189
   Jonathan 185
Shane, Arthur 7 Cornelius
   173 William 7 8 24
Shaner, Daniel 259
Shank(s), George 7 J. 240
   Jacob 132   John 5 11 38
   64 89 95   Michael 19 20
   Susan 95   Thomas 12 132
Shannon, Chas 11 Saml 223
   William 10

INDEX: names in text may have variant spelling
NIFLS = not indexed for land sales

Sharp, Anna 203 James 82
    John 236   Wilm 25 203
Sharpless, Thomas 141
Shatter, Major 6
Shaver, Daniel 10   259
Shaw, Jas 14 237 266 286
    329 John 14 86 143 187
    188 257 Jonathan 14 243
    Knowles 62 74   Mary 266
    286 Phebe 86   Robt 81
    Sarah 134 Thomas 36 121
    134 142 168   Wilm 14
    239 278 308 311
Shay, David 237
Sheared, John 19
Shearin, William 26
Sheets, Ann 211 214   218
    219   John 204 211 214
    216 218 219   Peter 184
Shelby, Elizabeth 331
    Isaac 14 323 327 333
    John 311 342 Joseph 331
    Joshua 311 331 333 342
    Susanna 311 333 342
Shell(e)y, John 229 Jos-
    eph 230   Daniel 13
Shellhouse, George 95
Shepherd, Solomon   33 38
    114   William 25
Sherard, Saml   91 96 105
    106
Sherer, John 184 186
    Johni 161   Pars 25
Sherlock, John 27
Sherrill, James 136
Sherwood, Charlotte 120
    151 David 196 James 33
    81 90   Saml 82   Thos
    33 120 127 151
Shetterly, John 238
Shields, Abijah 117   230
    Robert 11
Shill, Christian 176
Shinkle, George 17
Shirer, Charles 155
Shirk, Andrew 10 36 57 62
    63 64 88 92 Davd 11 138
    Elizabeth 138 Jacob 182
    183 202   Martha 57 92
    Mary 92 202   Michl 151
    Samuel 11 119 138 149
Shively, John 26

Shoe, Thomas 250
Shoemaker, Blackly   25 29
    Ennis 235 242   Evan 249
    250   Eve 250   S. 175
Shock, David 112
Shook, David 5   John 9
Sholts, Fredrk 11   35 51
Short, Eve 116 Jacob 206
    John 116 225 Peyton 18
Shortridge, Elisha   291
    339 Esther 339   George
    241 277   John 239 291
    339   Margt 291 Saml
    241 308 318
Shugart, George 244 263
    277 288   Mary 277
Shute, Saml 341 Sybil 341
Sibbet, Eli 322
Siddall, Mathius 344
Siebenthal, Jeane 206 215
    John 9 194 195 196 197
    206 211 213 214 215 216
Siers/Sires, Alex'r 10
    Joseph 9 34 45 49 50 55
    59   Wilm 12 34 76
Silvey, Thomas 99
Simmon(s), -- 238   John 9
    13 239 Lemuel 124 Mica-
    jah 12 244   Rebecca 160
    Ryale 160 162   Wilm 12
Simonson, Abr'm 121 C. 36
    Cornelius 163 Jacob 135
Simonton, George 185
    Theo 216
Simpson, Allen 32
    Collier 173
Sim(e)s, Elizabeth   121
    157 Larkin 32   Stephen
    10 Thos 69 Wilm 32 41
    121 129 149 151 152 157
Similton, W. 50
Simons/Symons, Abr'm 324
    Hannah 286 330 Jane 324
    Lydia 239   Matthew 302
    324   Nathan 330   Thos
    239 240 286 302 319 324
    330 Saml 239 Sarah 239
Simpson, J. 303
Singer (see Seanger),
    George 209
Singhouse, George 38 Wm 9
Sinks, Jacob 241 295

INDEX: names in text may have variant spelling
NIFLS = not indexed for land sales

Sirman, Elizabth 54 58 76
  Isaac 54 58 76   Louisa
  54 58
Skaats, James 25
Skillman, Jacob 224 226
Skinner, Ann(a) 72 87 139
  147 Danl 11 139 Jo. 236
  Rebecca 137   Sarah 153
  Thomas 3 21 39 71 72 87
  116 139 147 153   Wilm
  33 72 137
Slaughter, Martha 142
  Thomas 34 142
Slater, John 294 314
  Sally   303 314
Sloe/Sloo, F. 241 H. 330
  Rebecca 330   Thomas
  303 330
Small, Benj 233 235 Eleazar   John 173 235 336
  Mary 336   Nath'l 233
  Obediah 173
Smilie/Smiley, James 223
  Ross 106   Thomas 223
Smith, Adison 280   Ann 82
  91 96 105 106 126 Archd
  11 B. 55 Benj 33 49 52
  53 55 56 57 61 65 68 69
  70 72 73 76   88 110 116
  128 131 235 307   C. 183
  Christ'r 37 82   91   96
  105 106 223   David 39
  Dudley 311 313   Eleazer
  175 246   Enoch 3 4 9 20
  104 Ed 99 Firman 40 133
  George 251   Henry 20 27
  Isabella 93 95 Jacob 18
  345   James 32 90 92 125
  126 210 224   Jane 312
  329   John (NIFLS) 9 14
  19 21 36 41   51 106 128
  132 142 147 176 201 226
  233 235 242 250 251 257
  258 274 312 313 315 317
  329 332 335 341 345
  Jonathan 103 Joseph 105
  174   Latychy 250 Leah
  257 258 Lishe 250 Liddy
  98   Mary 285 315 321
  Matthew 35   Nathan 13
  253 257 266 267 269 285
  306 307 312 315 321 346

Smith cont -   Noah 8 182
  P. 141 Patrick 134 141
  Peter 183 232   Ralph 22
  Rebecca 51 68   70 76 88
  335 Richd 23   Robt 251
  258 259   Saml 125 175
  243   275   312   314   345
  Sarah 142 251 Silas 188
  Simon 138   Tamer 307
  Thos 3   12 25 34   51 52
  93 95 114 187 Tishe 259
  Tobias 50   Willard 160
  Wilm 3 9 20 32 33 35 82
  98 142 173 184 204   211
  296 Zadock 282
Smithson, Joshua   210 213
Snell, Michl 75 Sophia 62
Snider/Snyder, James   28
  John 28 Michael 14 226
  229 230
Snodgrass, -- 85 James 10
  224 Thos 12 Wm 37 84 88
Snook, John 187
Snow, Godfrey 29   Lemuel
  35 130 149 Lorinda 130
  Lydia 149   Mary 149
  Salome 149
Snowden, Jacob 133   James
  133 227 228   P. 33
Somerset, town of 87
Somwell, William 123
Soring, Isaac 18
Sotten/Sotter, Eli 3
Southard, Benjamin 25
Southworth, Benjamin 179
Spahr, John 238
Spangler, Hnry 27 Jacb 27
Sparks, Elijah 52 54   J.
  39 Leonard 88   Levi 91
  99 Mary 130 167 Matthew
  34   55   59   88   97   143
  Prudence 143   Wilm 130
  167 228
Spear/Spiers, Alex'r 31
  Allen 34 Jacob 73 James
  223   Thomas 305
Spencer, -- 32   Anna 270
  Dianna 269 270 272
  Elijah 239 252   255 263
  James 269 270   Jane 272
  Josph 5 227 237 257 259
  269 272 296   Michael 14

INDEX: names in text may have variant spelling
NIFLS = not indexed for land sales

Spencer, cont - Rozzel 269 Thos 4 Wilm 3 23 269 341
Sperry, William 23
Spray, Hnry 340 James 243
Spriggs, Ebenezer 11 108
Spring, James 174
Springer, Barnabas 303 314 Dennis 236 Job 317 331 343 Mary 343
Springfield, town 84 85
Stafford, -- 266 Annanias 285 Elizabeth 266 276 331 James 263 John 33 38 90 Thos 235 240 266 276 326 331 Wilm 236
Stamp, Leonard 245
Stan, Jacob 39
Standiford, Israel 3
Stanford, Thomas 310
Stanley, Aaron 299 Chas 322 Jeremiah 335 John 226 Wilm 186 Zacariah 226
Stanon, James 82
Stansbury, Henry 10 John 35 William 11
Stanton, Fredrk 301 333 William 342
Staples, Joshua 6
Stapleton, Andrew 188 195 205 221 Barbara 205 211 Elizabeth 221 John 197 205 Polly 205
Starbuck, Edw 236 302 306 312 Paul 235 Phebe 306 Tristram 246 Sarah 302 312 Uriah 225 Wilm 234 237 306
Stark, Archbd 20 John 308 Wilm 308
Starlin, Ebenezer 196 199
Starr, Abner 198 Barnet 273 274 307 309 Charles 245 Jaspr 309 Jesse 343 John 226 230 337 Margt 307 309 Rachel 337
Starret, James 13
Stateler, Joseph 29
Staunton/Stanton, Aaron 82 83 224 225 Davd 227 James 83 85 225 Latham

Staunton cont- 83 129 224 Lydia 82 Mary 83
St. Clair, Henry 9
Steddon, Hnry 242 264 279
Stedham, Henry 242 John 244
Steel, Samuel 18 33 William 243
Stegall, Jeremiah 246
Stelle, Isaac 101
Step, Isaac 31
Stephens/Stevens, Aligah 111 Benj 184 Chas 4 6 Elias 11 Ezekiel 12 Jas 9 38 39 111 Jane 51 214 John 10 41 111 134 Joseph 10 111 Mary 134 Obadiah 4 8 Ranna 28 Robt 10 175 Rus 64 S. 79 203 219 Samuel 12 Sidney 218 Solomon 28 Spencer 239 Steven (NIFLS) 43 45 46 47 54 75 76 84 88 113 115 120 132 199 200 201 202 205 206 207 208 214 216 William 13 37 224
Stephenson, David 238 George 24 29 John 24 29 Susanna 271 318 Vincent 233 261 271 272 318 Wilm 39 Zadock 230
Stercet, Samuel 238
Stetler, Jacob 29
Stewart/Stuart, Abr'm 321 Absalom 335 340 James 18 34 195 224 Jehu 258 321 339 John 8 249 268 Martin 17 S. 22 Saml 37 Sarah 321 339 Stephn 17 186 Susannah 205 Thos 18 44 182 184 192 Wilm 183 189 199 205 214 219
Stickler, John 198
Stiles, Byrd 227 Stephn 3
Stillman, Thomas 28
Stillwell, -- 186
Stinson, Elizabeth 106 John 102 106 121 160 W. 345
Stipp(s), David 82 133 John 152 Mary 133

INDEX: names in text may have variant spelling
NIFLS = not indexed for land sales

Stith, Thomas 210
St. John, Samuel 100 103
Stockdale, John 40
Stocker, Nathan 245
Stockton, John 45 Wilm 45
Stodder, Seth 184 186 188 192 210
Stoddard, Owen 103
Stone, Abigail 276 289 C. 147 Daniel 241 289 E. 100 120 134 147 286 Ethan 56 201 241 243 276 289 James 189 Jesse 29 Samuel 189
Stoop(s), Abigail 86 97 110 David 34 86 95 97 110 John 70
Stout, Davd 176 Hnry 199 Jesse 100 Job 39 Jonathan 36 86 Wilm 206
Stove, Charles 299
Stover, Joseph 311 Saml 14 230
Strader, Henry 336
Straine, James 177
Strange, John 75
Straw, Jacob 226
Stringer, Eli 32 33 40 48 166 Peggy 166
Strong, Barbary 296 Reuben 296 Wilm 25
Stroube, Christopher 36 John 36
Stroud, John 301 Joseph 19 Joshua 20
Struckland, Daniel 50
Stucky, James 11
Studdan, John 244
Study, Jacob 245
Stump, Joseph 347
Sturdevant, Azor 90 117 156 Fear 117 Roswell 117
Sturgis, James 242
Suffrins, John 318 324 331 341
Sulser, James 226
Sum(m)ers, Abigail 323 John 239 323 Joseph 7 35 Robt 323 Simeon 238
Summy/Sumney, Fredrk 14 259 John 230 P.295

Summy cont - Rachel 259
Sumner, Fredrk 295 Nancy 286 Wilm (NIFLS) 276 279 280 281 282 284 286 287 297 298 301
Sumwalt, Godfry 174
Sullivan, Daniel 9
Sunderland, John 37
Sutherland, David 296 300 301 309 327 Jane 277 John (NIFLS) 28 235 241 253 255 257 267 268 269 271 272 277 279 280 281 301 303 315 318 326 344 346 Julian 304 309 321 Lydia 309 William 255 281 296 304 309 318 321 334 344
Sutton, Absalom 94 Anchor 94 Davd 94 Humphrey 322 325 John 243 Ruben 19
Swafford, Isaac 224 Nancy 134 329 Wilm 134 224 329 346
Swain, Davd 224 Elias 245 Elihu 321 Frederick 29 Job 314 348 Sylvanus 225
Swallow, Garret 6 22 23
Swann, Nancy 128 151 Robt 95 98 108 117 118 121 122 128 129 131 132 140 147 149 150 151 152 162 169 227 228
Swanson, Edward 13 229
Swearingen, Charles 97 Isaac 35
Sweet, Benjamin 87
Swett, William 36
Swift, Christian 109 Christ'r 33 Frances 109 Malachi 33 Minerva 26
Sylvester, Job 26 Joseph 26
Symmes, Daniel 206 P.S./ (Peyton) 17 18 21 36 40 242 288

Tahle, Ala 182
Talbert, Lot 225
Talbot, Arch'd 37 40 Jacb 334 Theodore 185

INDEX: names in text may have variant spelling
NIFLS = not indexed for land sales

Tanner, James 10 130 158 227 John 6 Nancy 130 William 11
Tapley, Philip 22
Tapp, Newton 185 211
Tappin, Samuel 224
Taylor, -- 176 Agners 39 Benj 119 David 11 12 G. 31 176 George 135 Griffin 120 Isaac 6 James 39 183 185 227 R. 18 Robt 176 188 Thos 14
Teagarden, Danl 33 67 114 Elizabeth 33 67 Henry 32 34 114 150 Valeriah 150
Teagle, John 320 Joseph 244 320 Ruth 320 Thomas 244
Teague/Tague, George 183 191 John 186 188
Teas, Charles 322 334
Tebbs/Tibbs, Moses 3 Warran 3 7 Willo'by 3 7 21
Teitford, Abraham 68
Telford, Alex'r 35 36
Templeton, Danl 40 David 161 James 161 John 87 90 227 Mary 103 104 161 Robt 39 41 103 104 150 161 228 Wlm 103 104 161
Tenus, George 85
Terence, G. 17 George 21
Terrell/Terielt, John 244
Terrill, Electa 148 James 36 Thomas 101 148 154
Terry, Robert 27
Test, Chas 102 John 59 60 62 72 74 75 76 88 90 95 96 158 Lydie 59 Saml 129 Sarah 129
Tevis, Cyrus 31
Tharp, Andrw 12 298 Boaz 240 Chas 303 306 John 10 14 39 57 Leah 57 Rebeca 298 Thos 244 266
Thatcher, Elijah 22 23 27
Thiebaud, Frederick 187
Thomas, Absolom 174 278 Antipas 176 227 Benj 227 236 260 Catharine 117 David 229 Edw 154
Thomas cont- 278 Elias 9 Elijah 340 346 Elizabth 322 Ephraim 229 Frncis 236 244 259 260 263 Hanna 340 346 Hazel 117 Isaac 236 263 J. 199 Jas 31 32 322 Jess 3 40 242 Jhn 117 174 234 260 263 322 346 Lewis 238 242 280 321 325 327 336 344 Lydia 260 Mary 154 Selathiel 219 T. 196 Solomon 236 340 Stephen 237 246 288 305 328 331 340 345 346 Thos 10 227 237 282 Wilm 10 239
Thom(p)son, Closs 223 Enoch 40 Jas 86 142 242 John 22 50 64 226 232 Lettice 64 Margt 154 Saml 236 Theodore 25 28 Thos 189 Wilm 3 125
Thorne, Rachel 266 Stephn 6 Wilm (NIFLS) 239 240 241 244 265 266
Thornborough, Jacob 244 Walter 245 Wilm 235 245
Thornburgh, Edw 175 James 173 Joseph 175 M. 173 Nathan 176
Thornbury, Alick 286
Thornton, Henry 127 194 Samuel 6
Thorpe (see Tharp), Boaz 240 Thomas 244 246
Thrall, Friend 188
Thruston, E. 108 143
Tibbet(s), Abner 26 Benj 24 David 24 Eli 322 John 24 Wilm 26
Tibbs, John 13
Tillotson, John 148
Timberman, Abraham 36
Tipton, John 9
Tipswords, Griffin 4
Titus, John 118
Todd, -- 23 George 36 63 165 Henry 41 James 217 Jane 218 Jhn 222 Joseph 198 207 211 Martha 63 202 Owen 218 Paxton 191 202 213 S. 33 Saml 24

INDEX: names in text may have variant spelling
NIFLS = not indexed for land sales

Todd cont- William 157
Toler (see Tahle) Asa 224
Tompkins, Jesse 320
Toms, James 102
Toner, Edw 32 87 118 119 126 Jas 87 102 119 160 Jane 160 Susan 118 119
Toppin, Samuel 80
Torrence, George 29 187 307 344 John 7 8 Mary 307 William 3 7 19
Towel, John 323
Townsend, Elvira 247 253 Jas 9 241 296 Joel 189 Jhn 233 234 247 253 258 Jonathan 247 253 342 Rosanna 296 Sarah 295 Wilm 247 262 272 295
Trail, William 83
Treadway, Griffin 308
Trifogle, Peter 38
Trimble, Daniel 233
Trindle, Daniel 233
Triplett, Daniel 277
Trotter, Robt 190 191 192
True, Abel 26
Truelock, John 7 Thos 9
Truesdell, James 182 191 201 Job 190 194 Nancy 201 Saml 182 Wilm 194
Truitt, Riley 24 28 185
Trusler, Jas 11 57 59 84 Thomas 3 10
Trustee, Demee 158
Trustee, Dence 20
Tucker, Benj 37 139 Enoch 139 Ephraim 38 Jas 241 Nancy 75 Nath'l 6 19 Saml 155 Waltr 36 75 87
Tunis, Caleb 56 63 J. 101
Turner, Ferdnd 6 George 185 Jesse 11 Jhn 5 9 13 233 237 242 252 269 280 292 308 318 336 Sarah 269 308 Smith 215 Tabitha 215 Wilm 28 215
Tydings, Edward 183
Tyler, Harmon 10 James 104 139 Viley 139
Tyner/Tiner, Haris 11 Jas 11 Jemima 139 John 11 R. 144 149 154 167

Tyner cont - Richard 145 Solomon 11 40 49 62 139 William 40 111
Uhrgart, George 263
Ulmer, Charles 200
Underhill, Danl 339 John 321 William 243
Union, town of 81
Unthank, John 336
Updike, Elijah 36 Petr 36

Vail, Jonathan 24 28
Vairin (see Nairin), Augustus 210 John 210 Justus 210 Sophia 210
Vanblaricum, -- 35 David 167 John 35 43 45 80 113 157 168 Mary 80 167 Michael 12 Peter 185
Van Bor--l, John 182
Van Briggle, John 187 Peter 187 199 209
Van Buskirk, George 239 Joseph 308
Vancamp, Charles 9 40 80
Vance, Jane 111 Joseph 111 Saml 6 18 20 23 24 25 27 28 29 38 183 238 241 Stephen 41 Wilm 179
Vancel, Mary 148 Saml 57 148
Vandeman, Mary/Polly 93 95 97 Wilm 93 95 97
Van Derveer, Petr 321 334
Vanderyne, Jacob 102
Vandolar, Jesse 23
Vandyke, Ady 119 151 166 Isaac 75 Peter 75 84 119 150 151 166
Vaneaton, Abr'm 136 Joseph 136
Vanhisel, William 184
Vanhorn, Cornelius 25
Vanhouten, H--lands 25 Hallarnies 27
Vanmeter, Aaron 97 Abr'm 237 Cornelia 114 Isaac 259 273 Joseph 224 237 Mary 97 Phebe 332 Saml 114 William 32 35 287 289 332

INDEX: names in text may have variant spelling
NIFLS = not indexed for land sales

Van Middlesworth, Henry 22 226
Vanness, Joseph 110
Vantruse, Isaac 157
Vanvect, Abram 76
Vardaman, John 10
Vatz, Charles 214
Vaughn, James 24 26
Vawter, John 9
Veal, Enos 242 243 326
Vennard, John 237
Verbryck, Richard 214
Vernon, Joseph 162
Verona, town of 116
Vevay, town of 194 204
Vigery, Jabez 127
Vi(c)ley, Cornelus 36 151
Vincent, John 40
Violet, Edward 198
Virgil, Jacob 242
Voorhees, Elizabeth 121 Garret 99 John 121 134 163 168
Vore, Isaac 235 326 Jacob 312 Ruth 326
Voshell, Obediah 6

Wadams, Louisa 119 Wilson 119 152 Wilm 126 142
Waddell, Chas 55 Elijah 296 Jas 14 275 347 348 Levina 319 Robt 226 319
Wade, David 38 40 93 Elijah 259 Elisha 182 202 Mary 259 Nancy 202 Robt 319 321 Thos 214 233 Wilm 13 95 106 109 124 138 182
Wadham, William 127
Wag(g)oner, Coonrod 217 David 217 Reuben 241
Wakefield, John 11
Walbrick, Henry 183
Waldo(w), Fredrk 18 211 220 221 222 L./Loring 291 316 332 Miriam 220 221 Otis 222
Waldon, Elijah 20 John 9 Silvanus 194
Walker, Albt 10 Grge 123 126 Isaac 329 Jas 13 22 23 337 338 John 5 13 22

Walker cont - 23 251 266 273 328 Oliver 174 Saml 230 233 242 251 325 328 337 338 Thos 325 Wilm 13 14 230
Wallace, Andrw 158 George 37 James 39 John 237 238 308 Mary 308 Nath'l 72 Thomas 14 308
Wall(s), -- 244 Drury 347 Mathew 14 Thomas 21
Walsh, Esther 26 John 17 Patrick 26
Walter, William 238
Walton, James 21
Waltz, George 186
Wamsly, Isaac 37 86 153
Wanderlick, John 36
Ward, Calvin 111 G. 127 Jane 167 John 38 69 70 72 125 162 229 Josph 12 Linus 120 Mary 120 Saml 11 Sylvnus 151 167 Thos 248 270 274 Usual 111
Warden, Barnard 215 218
Warland, John 50
Warman, Enoch 332 Henry 277 Sally/Sarah 275 T. 272 Thomas 266 275 276 279 280 291 307
Warner, Ithamar 272 316 Thomas 292 William 202
Warnock, James 18 Richard 319 346 347
Warrall, Atterill 239
Warram, Edith 267 Harmon 13 241 253 267 James 5 John 14
Warren, Benj 185 James 13 245
Washburn, John 220
Washer, Solomon 217 218
Wasson, Davd 284 John 235 Joseph 234
Wat(t)ers, Elizabeth 109 111 123 Isaac 238 Jas 40 111 123 Jubal 265 Richd 62 Thomas 109
Watkins, J. 35 Jeremiah 26 John 13 14 21 Watkin 24 Wilm 35
Watson, William 13

401

INDEX: names in text may have variant spelling
NIFLS = not indexed for land sales

Watts Jemima 299 304 John 3 27 41 233 Johnson 6 Joseph 239 299 304 Richd 258 Thos 27
Way, Alice 298 Amos 8 18 Hnry 174 244 Hulday 246 James 9 John 176 Joseph 298 323 P./Paul 174 178 179 180 246 278 Sarah 278 Seth 14 242 244 278 298 303 William 174
Wayne, Esther 272 299 Nath'l 260 266 272 299
Wayson, Joseph 235
Weathers, Jesse 8 John 4 William 4 23
Weamer, John 127
Weaver, Anny 112 Henry 58 67 68 82 91 96 105 106 George 19 Jacob 177 James 6 9 John 6 Martha 336 Petr 13 233 272 318 335 336 R. 19 Richd 185
Webb, Abel 11 Davd 11 137 Edw 87 Ezra 22 Forrest 3 7 Jesse 7 Jonathan 32 Lewis 7 Wilm 7 21 122
Weber, Barbra 56 Nichls 11
Webster, Hnry 120 151 160 James 97 99 Martha 99 Rebecca 160
Weedner, Jacob 58
Weist, Henry 182 183
Welch, George 217 J. 217 John 11 34
Welcher, Josiah 130
Weler, Samuel 35
Welkins, Michael 57
Well(s), Deborah 133 134 James 33 John 33 39 133 134
Weller, L. 22 Locovick 146 William 34
West, Samuel 182
Westcott, Ebenezer 29
Westerfield, Carey 311
Westfall, Simeon 43
Weston, Joseph 170 William 133
West Union, town 119 123
Weymire, Elizabth 274 292 Jacb 13 238 274 291 292

Whar(l)ton, Richd 241 329
Wheat, William 58
Wheeler, A. 289 290 291 346 Clark 154 J. 288 John 22 235 Saml 22
Whelan, Sarah 89 Thaddius 75 79 89
Wherrit, William 90
Whidenger, John 10
Whitaker, Danl 8 James 186 187 189 Johnson 145 Thos 12
White, A 21 Aaron 286 337 Abel 40 Alexr 3 213 145 Asa 337 Beniah 304 Benj 232 Caleb 26 188 Charity 150 Edw 11 36 46 186 Hartshon 244 Ithamer 36 70 125 153 J. 113 Jacob 184 James 14 19 236 248 248 252 271 273 300 Jhn 6 19 128 129 138 151 153 234 236 281 333 337 Joseph 19 Margry 70 125 153 Mary 68 85 128 129 138 304 337 Nancy 145 Petr 17 Robt 41 128 129 158 Tabitha 235 236 271 283 293 Wilm 3 4 20 68 68 85 145 185
Whitehead, I. 217 218 Israel 216 217 220 J. 207 273 John 234 252 262 271 335 Lazarus 234 271 Michael 157 Wilm 5 13 252 253 271 282
Whiteman, Hnry 13 John 13 L. 187 Levi 18 Lewis 18
Whitemire, Michael 154
Whitesides, William 9
Whitford, John 74 104 113 114 117 Patsy 114
Whiting, Thomas 262
Whitinger, Elizabeth 318 327 Henry 230 282 John 230 318 327 348
Whitlock, Joseph 33
Whitman, Jacob 14
Whitmore, Nathan 197 219 William 187 214
Whitney, Moses 167
Whitson, Willis 244

INDEX: names in text may have variant spelling
NIFLS = not indexed for land sales

Whitworth, John 58 62 70 72 76 78 93 100 105 125 227 Margaret 58
Wickersham, Caleb 78 167 176 228 James 237 302 336 Rachel 336
Wicoff, Allen 94 Robt 44
Wier, Samuel 71 84 117
Wigal, Jacob 206 210
Wiggins, Daniel 338
Wilcot, Clark 174 Isaac 18
Wilcox, James 243
Wilcutt, Clark 246
Wild/Wiles, Luke 185 Thos 274 Tubal 10 134
Wildridge, Chas 11 Elizabeth 80 89 146 168 Ralph 35 44 80 85 89 146 168
Wiley, -- 32 Alex'r 169 Allen 56 60 62 66 188 193 Cornelius 223 Elizabeth 56 60 62 66 Isaac James 10 56 60 62 68 John 12 34 78 224 Margt 56 62 Moses 20 34 66 68 Spencer 7 8 56 60 62 68 Thomas 236
Wilkins, Amos 320 Chas 19 John 253 Michael 10 109 Philip 36
Wilkinson, Gideon 36 John 29 265 280 337 Joseph 17 Mary 337
Willcut, Thomas 346
Willents, Thomas 340
Willete, John 247
Willetts, Brady 339 Elias 293 301 302 330 339 344 345 Elisha 238 Isaac 237 240 241 Jesse 238 245 282 298 307 Levi 13 238 239 282 313 321 332 346 Polly 346 Rachl 339 Sally 308 Saml 313 321 346 Wlm 238 239 313 346
William(s), Absolom 240 Achilles 310 Alex'r 10 Allen 278 329 336 Anthony 42 224 Azariah 338 Caleb 25 347 Charity 336 Deborah 102 125 E.

Williams cont - 173 Elmore 35 Enos 50 George 11 140 224 Hannah 288 Hezkiah 245 328 330 338 Isaac 239 329 Jacob 319 Jane 329 Jeremiah 3 Jesse 294 300 301 327 336 Joel 50 227 John 66 163 167 226 281 327 330 331 347 Josph 12 34 167 237 Joshua 223 M. 336 Mary 330 Micajh (NIFLS) 286 288 289 Nathan 242 Patsy 78 Peter 86 Ralph 33 41 78 Rebeca 281 319 330 338 Richd 10 33 34 236 237 245 Saml 42 236 Sarah 163 Stephen 246 Thos 32 40 102 125 Wilm 10 13 34 233 242 325
Williamson, David 27
Williford, Rutha 249 William 247 249 229
Willis, Jesse 245 John 12 186 Joseph 175
Willison, Daniel 141
Williver, Obediah 57
Wilmer, H. 27 Henry 27
Wilson, Benj 4 10 23 40 77 78 100 123 128 161 Cella 80 Danl 141 227 Davd 183 Elizbeth 66 78 91 128 Frankey 89 125 George 32 82 131 246 Grimes 13 Griner 319 Hannah 77 78 103 149 Hugh 188 Isaac 13 32 40 89 96 237 240 319 J. 95 Jacb 13 308 Jas (NIFLS) 8 10 43 53 54 66 69 71 77 78 86 87 90 91 117 123 125 128 177 202 Jane 133 John 10 73 77 80 285 319 329 Joshua 13 Mary 131 Morgan 265 Nancy 90 Robt 13 183 Saml 8 Sarah 319 Seth 329 W. 3 William 9 31 32 33 34 38 77 78 89 103 133 149 152 156 159 230 237
Wilyard, George 7

INDEX: names in text may have variant spelling
NIFLS = not indexed for land sales

Winchell, Abigl 64 87 Amy 58 Anna 59 Barbara 127 J. 62 64 67 69 70 72 73 74 76 77 78 95 98 James 11 45 58 65 72 79 90 96 120 136 John 5 9 11 44 51 55 58 59 104 120 Martha 69 99 125 128 143 Nath'l 99 127 Ruggles 11 40 69 99 125 128 143 144 Sarah 88 Stephen 69 88 125
Winder, James 33
Wines, Martin 115
Winfield, Henry 233
Wingfield, John 252 334
Wingley, John 313
Winkley, Joseph 17
Winn, Jonathan 34
Winchiss, Jabez 130
Winscott, Thomas 99
Winship, Jabez 43 47 48 53 57 78 Joseph 53 155
Winston, Pleasant 173
Wiseheart, Thomas 5
Witham, Morris 125 223 Rebecca 125
Withrow, James 6
Witter, Christ'r 224 225 John 225 Stophel 155
Witts, Enoch 304 339 Hezekiah 236
Wolcott, Clark 246
Wolf, Jacob 134
Wood(s), Alexr 230 Andrew 241 253 260 261 268 281 Archb'd 235 Artemas 5 Benj 37 David 346 Elizabeth 132 Isaac 36 132 James 22 36 75 Jane 260 261 268 Jerem'h 229 Jhn 34 137 Josph 23 Phillip 226 Polly/Mary 247 Richd 201 Saml (NIFLS) 24 28 235 247 253 268 271 275 296 Sarah 75 Stephn 6 21 25 26 28 29 Uzal 224 Winslow 24 28
Woodard, John 241 326 Rachel 326
Woodcock, Joseph 233
Woodkirk, John 14

Woodman, Susanna 175
Woodnut, Allen 200
Woodruff, Josiah 209 Polly 209
Woodward, Bartlett 242 Davis 26
Woodworth, Artemus 32 131 Ryleigh 38 62 83 Samuel 167
Woody, Joseph 340
Woolfington, J. 116
Wool(le)y, George 184 Joseph 21 Wilm 27
Worl, Josph 278 309 Nancy 278 Phebe 336 Robert 309 336
Worley, Francis 283 Jacob 283 John 34 Silas 34
Worman, Thomas 41 240
Worthington, William 282
Wright, Bunnel 240 Caleb 7 Chas 182 255 David 11 176 177 178 179 Eli 14 287 292 Elijah 246 Elizabeth 292 Isaac 176 178 Iry 22 J. 176 James 176 178 179 235 237 Joel 237 304 323 John 174 176 177 178 179 188 224 Jonathan 143 235 Joseph 174 Joshua 173 Nath'l 27 R. 251 Ralph 235 239 Sally 323 Saml 26 Solomon 176 178 179 Thos 105 187 225 Whitely 229 230 Wilm 178 179 276 Willis 10 252
Wyatt, Bartn 314 Davd 226 278 320 Joseph 13 304 306 335 Mary 306 Nancy 314 Thomas 232 314 William 226 306
Wyeth, Elisha 57 64 117 Hannah 102 142 Joshua 102 111 142
Wynn, Ann 151
Wysong, David 179 Henry 175 Valentine 176

Yances, Simon 322
Yands, Simon 33

INDEX: names in text may have variant spelling
NIFLS = not indexed for land sales

Yerkes, Joshua 6
Yong, David 328 Wilm 327
Youell, Cornelius 187
Young(s), David 295
　Ephraim 32 Jonathan 27
　Nathan 33   Ovid 116
　Sarah 295   William 208
　243 262 316
Youngblood, Peter 10 11
Yount, Daniel 240

Zanes, George 8
Zeek, Adam 233
Zimmerman, John 237
Zinn, George 28
Zumwald, see Sumwalt

*****

LOCAL COURTHOUSE AND LIBRARY INFORMATION CA 1994

Dearborn County Courthouse, Lawrenceburg
　8:30 a.m. to 4:30 p.m. - closed Saturday
　in summer - on Daylight Saving Time
　good library directly east of courthouse

Franklin County Courthouse, Brookville
　8:30 to 4 p.m. - closed Saturday
　year round Eastern Standard Time
　library approx 6 blocks north; does not open
　until noon, closed Saturday in summer

Ohio County Courthouse, Rising Sun
　in summer - on Daylight Saving Time
　library nearby

Randolph County Courthouse, Winchester
　worth the trip to see the murals
　open at 8:30 - closed Saturday
　year round Eastern Standard Time
　library nearby - ask directions

Switzerland County Courthouse, Vevay
　year round Eastern Standard Time
　8 a.m. to 3:30 weekdays - closed Thursday
　8 a.m. to noon Saturday
　good library - ask directions

Union County Courthouse, Liberty
　year round Eastern Standard Time
　Closed for lunch at noon and on Saturday
　good library for Indiana general research
　　southeast corner across from courthouse

Wayne County Courthouse Annex, Richmond
　8 a.m. to 4:30 weekdays - closed Saturday
　year round Eastern Standard Time
　excellent library (Morrison-Reeves) within
　walking distance north - very strong in
　local records and Quaker genealogy

www.ingramcontent.com/pod-product-compliance
Lightning Source LLC
Chambersburg PA
CBHW050832230426
43667CB00012B/1971